Michael Chiorazzi, JD, MLL
Marguerite Most, JD, MLL
Editors

Prestatehood Legal Materials
A Fifty-State Research Guide,
Including New York City
and the District of Columbia
Volume 1, A-M

Pre-publication
REVIEWS,
COMMENTARIES,
EVALUATIONS . . .

"This book's usefulness extends far beyond academic legal research. Researchers of all stripes, including legal historians, political historians, historians of the American West, specialists in Native American or environmental studies, and the bench and bar, will find useful research leads.

The development of statutes, case law, and legal institutions in the fifty states has been marked by incessant borrowing and refitting. This creative readaptation of legal materials provides a rich field for legal historians and a minefield for litigators. *Prestatehood Legal Materials* is an invaluable tool for navigating this web of relationships.

Given that laws were quite often the very first printed materials to be produced in any given jurisdiction, this book is also a useful tool for the study of the spread of printing and research into the history of the book in the United States.

While this is a focused reference tool, it is far from being a narrow one. The authors of each state section describe not only materials that are strictly legal in nature (session laws, court reports, treaties, etc.) but also studies by legal historians, general histories of the states, biographical reference works, and a host of other useful sources. The editors, Michael Chiorazzi and Marguerite Most, gave their authors leeway to choose their own styles. The results are as diverse as the fifty states themselves, and just as rewarding."

Michael Widener, BJ, MLIS
Head of Special Collections
and Joseph D. Jamail Fellow
in Law Librarianship,
Tarlton Law Library, School of Law,
The University of Texas at Austin

More pre-publication
REVIEWS, COMMENTARIES, EVALUATIONS . . .

"This two-volume work provides a fascinating glimpse into a largely overlooked aspect of the U.S. legal history and legal bibliography. Most of us in the legal profession are at best dimly aware of the prestatehood legal regime and sources of law for our own state, to say nothing of those of the other forty-nine. This work brings together for the first time a wide variety of information about the legal systems and legal materials that applied in the territory of each state's becoming a state in the federal union.

The primary use for this work will be as a one-stop source of information about the primary sources of law during the colonial and territorial periods of the states. However, the narrative histories accompanying most of the entries make interesting reading on their own. How many of us know, for instance, that Congress actually contemplated creating a Native American state of Sequoyah, or that the state of Franklin briefly held sway in part of what is now Tennessee, as did the state of Deseret in the Utah Territory? This is an essential work for law libraries, academic libraries, and large public libraries, but it shold be of interest to anyone who cares about American history."

Timothy Kearley, JD, MLL
Director of the Law Library
and Professor of Law,
George W. Hopper Law Library,
University of Wyoming
College of Law

"This publication offers legal researchers, legal educators, and legal historians an important and well-organized research tool which is long overdue. To have this kind of detailed information in one source with a method to continue its contribution via a Web site for additions/corrections/updates may mark a new beginning in legal research publishing. Even though there are multiple authors, styles, and forms, the publication maintains a sense of organization that is readable, useful, and relevant. Bravo."

Billie Jo Kaufman, JD
Professor of Law, Director
of the Law Library
and Office of Technology,
American University,
Washington College of Law

"Research in prestatehood legal materials has been a great gap in the literature; this area is either omitted by legal research guides or scattered among many guides to the materials of individual states. Yet this is an area of great interest to legal researchers, historians, and genealogists. *Prestatehood Legal Materials* superbly fills this gap.

A high standard of excellence is maintained throughout. Coverage is exhaustive, including legislative, constitutional, executive, judicial, and secondary sources, plus manuscript materials and online resources. The discussion is thoroughly footnoted, and a Web site will update the information.

Besides the obvious value to legal librarians, scholars, and students, there is considerable help for historians and genealogists here. Almost every chapter is rich in fascinating historical background."

Fred R. Shapiro, SB, JD, MSLS
Associate Librarian for Collections
and Access and Lecturer
in Legal Research,
Yale Law School; Editor,
Yale Dictionary of Quotations

Prestatehood Legal Materials
A Fifty-State Research Guide, Including New York City and the District of Columbia

Volume 1, A-M

THE HAWORTH INFORMATION PRESS®
Law Librarianship
Michael Chiorazzi, JD, MLL
Editor

Prestatehood Legal Materials: A Fifty-State Research Guide, Including New York City and the District of Columbia edited by Michael Chiorazzi and Marguerite Most

Other titles of related interest

Basics of Law Librarianship by Deborah S. Panella

Law Library Collection Development in the Digital Age edited by Michael Chiorazzi and Gordon Russell

Prestatehood Legal Materials
A Fifty-State Research Guide, Including New York City and the District of Columbia

Volume 1, A-M

Michael Chiorazzi, JD, MLL
Marguerite Most, JD, MLL
Editors

The Haworth Information Press®
An Imprint of The Haworth Press, Inc.
New York • London • Oxford

For more information on this book or to order, visit
http://www.haworthpress.com/store/product.asp?sku=5382

or call 1-800-HAWORTH (800-429-6784) in the United States and Canada
or (607) 722-5857 outside the United States and Canada

or contact orders@HaworthPress.com

Published by

The Haworth Information Press®, an imprint of The Haworth Press, Inc., 10 Alice Street,
Binghamton, NY 13904-1580.

PUBLISHER'S NOTE
The development, preparation, and publication of this work has been undertaken with great care.
However, the Publisher, employees, editors, and agents of The Haworth Press are not responsible
for any errors contained herein or for consequences that may ensue from use of materials or
information contained in this work. The Haworth Press is committed to the dissemination of ideas
and information according to the highest standards of intellectual freedom and the free exchange of
ideas. Statements made and opinions expressed in this publication do not necessarily reflect the
views of the Publisher, Directors, management, or staff of The Haworth Press, Inc., or an
endorsement by them.

Cover design by Kerry E. Mack.

Library of Congress Cataloging-in-Publication Data

Prestatehood legal materials : a fifty-state research guide, including New York City and the District
of Columbia / Michael Chiorazzi, Marguerite Most, editors.
     p. cm.
    Includes bibliographical references and index.
    ISBN 0-7890-2056-4 (hard : set : alk. paper)—ISBN 0-7890-2082-3 (hard: v. 1)—ISBN 0-
7890-2083-1 (hard : v. 2)
    1. Legal research—United States—States. 2. Law—United States—States—Sources. I.
Chiorazzi, Michael G. II. Most, Marguerite.

KF240.P688 2005
340'.072'073—dc22

                                             2005001664

CONTENTS

VOLUME I

ABOUT THE EDITORS

Michael Chiorazzi, JD, MLL, is Director of the Law Library and Professor of Law at the James E. Rogers College of Law at the University of Arizona. He holds a joint appointment as a professor in the School of Information Resources and Library Science of the College of Social and Behavioral Sciences. His scholarship interests include legal history and law library administration. He is the editor of *Legal Reference Services Quarterly* and is active in AALL, AALS, and the ABA Section on Legal Education and Admission to the Bar. Prior to his appointment at the University of Arizona, he worked at the Boston College and Duke University Law Libraries. In the summer of 2002, he was a visiting professor at the University of Washington Information School.

Marguerite Most, JD, MLL, is Collection Development and Legal Information Librarian and Lecturer in Law at Boston College Law Library. Prior to her appointment at Boston College, she worked in the law libraries at the University of North Carolina, Duke University, and the University of San Diego. She has taught courses in legal research, and Introduction to American Law at the University of North Carolina School of Law, and Law Libraries and Legal Research at the School of Information and Library Science, UNC; she recently co-taught a law library administration course at the University of Washington Information School. She is scheduled to co-teach a Law Practice Technology course at Boston College in the spring of 2005. Her interests include international legal research, and law and literature.

CONTRIBUTORS

Volume One

Luis M. Acosta is Legal Reference Librarian, Law Library of Congress, Washington, DC.

Glen-Peter Ahlers Sr. is Associate Dean for Information Services, Barry University Dwayne O. Andreas School of Law, Orlando, Florida. Before joining Barry University, Ahlers served as the library director at the University of Arkansas School of Law for a decade.

Carol D. Billings is Director of the Law Library, Law Library of Louisiana, Supreme Court Building, New Orleans, Louisiana.

Barbara Bintliff is Nicholas Rosenbaum Professor of Law and Director of the Law Library, University of Colorado at Boulder.

Robert J. Brink, Esq., is Executive Director, Social Law Library, Boston, Massachusetts.

Anna M. Cherry is Reference and Publications Librarian, Minnesota State Law Library, St. Paul, Minnesota.

Eileen B. Cooper is Director of the Law Library and Professor, Legal Information Center, Widener University School of Law, Wilmington, Delaware.

Joseph A. Custer is Associate Director and Collection Development Librarian, Wheat Law Library, University of Kansas School of Law, Lawrence, Kansas.

David I. Durham is Archivist, Bounds Law Library, University of Alabama School of Law, Tuscaloosa, Alabama.

Kristin M. Ford has served as Legislative Librarian for the Idaho State Legislature in Boise since 1999. She obtained her JD from the University of Idaho in 1994 and an MLIS with a specialty in law librarianship from the University of Washington in 1999. She is admitted to the Idaho and Alaska state bars.

Janis Fusaris is Reference Librarian, University of Connecticut School of Law Library, Hartford, Connecticut.

Judith Gaskell is Librarian of the Court, Supreme Court of the United States Library, Washington, DC.

Kris Gilliland is Director of the Library and Assistant Professor of Law, University of Mississippi School of Law, University, Mississippi.

David Hanson is Information Technology/Reference Librarian, Drake University Law Library, Des Moines, Iowa.

Ruth A. Hodgson is Research Librarian, Maryland State Law Library, Annapolis, Maryland.

Lisa Mecklenberg Jackson has been Legislative Librarian of Montana in Helena since 2001. She obtained her JD from the University of North Dakota in 1996 and an MLIS with a specialty in law librarianship from the University of Washington in 1997. She is admitted to practice in Montana, North Dakota, and Minnesota.

Jacquelyn Gayle Kasper is Reference and Government Documents Librarian and Adjunct Assistant Professor of Legal Research, James E. Rogers College of Law Library, University of Arizona, Tucson, Arizona.

David King is Reference/Computer Services Librarian, Legal Information Center, Widener University School of Law, Wilmington, Delaware.

Isa Lang is Head of Information Services, Chapman University Rinker Law Library, Orange, California.

Jennifer Lentz is Reference Librarian, Hugh & Hazel Darling Law Library, UCLA School of Law, Los Angeles, California.

Mon Yin Lung is Associate Director, O'Quinn Law Library, University of Houston Law Center, Houston, Texas.

Mary Jane Mallonee is Reference/Government Documents Librarian, Legal Information Center, Widener University School of Law, Wilmington, Delaware.

Margaret McDermott is Head of Reference and Faculty Services and Assistant Professor of Legal Research, St. Louis University School of Law Library, St. Louis, Missouri.

Robert A. Mead is Head of Public and Faculty Services, Wheat Law Library, University of Kansas School of Law, Lawrence, Kansas.

Kurt X. Metzmeier is Associate Director and Associate Professor of Legal Bibliography, Louis D. Brandeis School of Law Library, University of Louisville, Louisville, Kentucky.

Michael S. Miller is Director, Maryland State Law Library, Annapolis, Maryland.

Kristina L. Niedringhaus is Electronic Services Librarian, Texas Wesleyan University School of Law Library, Fort Worth, Texas. She was formerly Associate Law Librarian at the Georgia State University College of Law Library.

Stephen C. O'Neill is Former Curator, Social Law Library, Boston, Massachusetts. He is currently working toward his doctorate in the American and New England Studies program at Boston University.

Mary G. Persyn is Associate Dean for Library Services of the Law Library and Associate Professor of Law, Valparaiso University, Valparaiso, Indiana.

Paul M. Pruitt Jr. is Collection Development and Special Collections Librarian, Bounds Law Library, University of Alabama School of Law, Tuscaloosa, Alabama.

Maureen Quinlan is Reference/Government Documents Librarian, Garbrecht Law Library, University of Maine School of Law, Portland, Maine.

Myra K. Saunders is Law Librarian, Associate Dean, and Professor of Law in Residence, UCLA School of Law, Los Angeles California.

Leina'ala Robinson Seeger is Law Librarian and Associate Professor of Law, William S. Richardson School of Law Library, University of Hawaii at Manoa, Honolulu, Hawaii.

Janice Selberg is Head of Public Services, Ave Maria School of Law Library, Ann Arbor, Michigan.

Christopher A. Vallandingham is Faculty Services Librarian, Lawton Chiles Legal Information Center, University of Florida Levin College of Law, Gainesville, Florida.

Jessica Van Buren is Director, Utah State Law Library, Salt Lake City, Utah. She was previously the public services librarian at the Alaska State Court Law Library. She has a BA in journalism, a JD from the University of Oregon, and master of librarianship from the University of Washington.

Dee Van Nest is Research Librarian, Maryland State Law Library, Annapolis, Maryland.

Volume Two

Duncan E. Alford is Law Librarian, Princeton University, Princeton, New Jersey. He earned a BA with high distinction from the University of Virginia, Charlottesville, in 1985; a JD with honors from the University of North Carolina School of Law, Chapel Hill, in 1991; and an MLIS from the University of South Carolina, Columbia, in 2001.

John R. Barden is Head, Reference and Research Services, William Taylor Muse Law Library, University of Richmond School of Law, Richmond, Virginia.

Scott Childs is Assistant Director for Research and User Services, Kathrine R. Everett Law Library, University of North Carolina School of Law, Chapel Hill, North Carolina.

Matthew C. Cordon is Reference Librarian and Assistant Professor of Law, Baylor University School of Law, Waco, Texas.

Paul J. Donovan is Law Librarian, Vermont Department of Libraries, Montpelier, Vermont.

Melanie J. Dunshee is Deputy Director and Senior Lecturing Fellow, Duke University School of Law Library, Durham, North Carolina.

Robert A. Emery is Associate Director, Schaffer Law Library, Albany Law School, Albany, New York.

Joel Fishman, PhD, is Assistant Director for Lawyer Services, Duquesne University Center for Legal Information/Allegheny County Law Library, Pittsburgh, Pennsylvania.

Galen L. Fletcher is Government Documents/Microforms Librarian, Howard W. Hunter Law Library, Brigham Young University, Provo, Utah.

Kevin Fredette is Head of Public Services, George R. Farmer Jr. Law Library, West Virginia College of Law, Morgantown, West Virginia.

Paul Gillies is an attorney and legal historian who practices law in Montpelier, Vermont.

Thomas E. Heard is Associate Director for Library Services and Associate Professor of Law Library Services, Salmon P. Chase College of Law Library, Northern Kentucky University, Highland Heights, Kentucky.

Ann Hemmens is Reference Librarian, Gallagher Law Library, University of Washington, Seattle, Washington.

Sarah Lanier Hollingsworth is Reference Librarian, Gallagher Law Library, University of Washington, Seattle, Washington.

Ann S. Jarrell is Acting Satellite Librarian, United States Court Library, Las Vegas, Nevada.

Kyoung-Ho Jeon is a graduate student with the Franklin Pierce Law Center.

Susan Lyons is Government Documents and Reference Librarian, Rutgers University Law School at Newark, New Jersey.

William H. Manz is Senior Research Librarian, Rittenberg Law Library, St. John's University School of Law, Jamaica, New York.

Robert A. Mead is Head of Public and Faculty Services, Wheat Law Library, University of Kansas School of Law, Lawrence, Kansas.

Judith Morgan is Director, Law Library, Oklahoma City University School of Law, Oklahoma City, Oklahoma.

Lynn E. Murray is Public Services Law Librarian, University of Mississippi, Tuscaloosa, Mississippi.

Cheryl Rae Nyberg is Reference Librarian, Gallagher Law Library, University of Washington, Seattle, Washington.

Debora A. Person is Assistant Law Librarian, George William Hopper Law Library, University of Wyoming College of Law, Laramie, Wyoming.

Sandra B. Placzek is Head of Public Services and Assistant Professor of Law, Marvin and Virginia Schmid Law Library, University of Nebraska College of Law, Lincoln, Nebraska.

Brandon D. Quarles is Director of the Law Library and Associate Professor of Law, Baylor University School of Law, Waco, Texas.

Rhonda Schwartz is Assistant Director and Head of Public Services, Thormodsgard Law Library, University of North Dakota School of Law, Grand Forks, North Dakota.

Barry Shanks is Reference Librarian and Assistant Professor of Research, Franklin Pierce Law Center, Concord, New Hampshire.

Joe K. Stephens is Law Librarian, State of Oregon Law Library, Salem, Oregon.

Duane Strojny is Associate Professor and Dean for Library and Instructional Support, The Thomas M. Cooley Law School, Lansing, Michigan.

Robert Lee Warthen is Librarian, Adjunct Professor of Law, and Assistant Director and Head of Collection Building and Maintenance, S.J. Quinney College Law Library, University of Utah College of Law, Salt Lake City, Utah.

Gail I. Winson is Associate Professor of Law and Director of the Law Library, Ralph R. Papitto School of Law, Roger Williams University, Bristol, Rhode Island. She earned her BA from Moravian College, her MS from Drexel University, and her JD from the University of Florida. She is a member (inactive) of both the Florida and California bars.

Preface

This work is the end product of a chance conversation at the closing banquet of the 2001 annual meeting of the American Association of Law Libraries. Nancy McMurrer, a reference librarian at the University of Washington's Marian Gould Gallagher Law Library, approached me with an article idea. Would *Legal Reference Services Quarterly (LRSQ)* be interested in publishing a research guide to Washington's prestatehood legal materials? I was immediately intrigued, and realizing the potential, I asked if she would not only write the article but also be willing to edit a special double issue of *LRSQ* for all the western states. At this, she drew away in horror, but she said that she would consider writing the article.

But her idea had taken hold. I realized that in her article idea was the germ of a wonderful project. Why not create a fifty-state guide to prestatehood legal materials? I sent out a call for papers over the law-lib LISTSERV (law-lib@ucdavis.edu). Much to my surprise and glee, I received approximately thirty offers within two days. Other librarians offered suggestions of prospective authors who might be interested in writing such an article. In relatively short order I had authors from all fifty states. When offers came in for the District of Columbia and New York City, I realized that their unique legal histories would make for wonderful additions to the project.

I also realized this project was now much bigger than a quarterly such as *LRSQ* could handle. I also knew it was too big a project for me to handle alone. So I enlisted Marguerite Most, one of my crackerjack *LRSQ* editors, to assist in what now had become a book project. We used the Mississippi River as our dividing line. I would handle the West and Marguerite the East.

You will find that each chapter has its own style. Some authors relied on bibliographic essays while others used annotated bibliographies. Some are exhaustive, others selective. We decided to give the authors free rein; they were the experts on the individual states and would best know how to present the available subject matter.

This then is the result of that germ of an idea. It has turned out much better than I could have hoped or imagined. I think the quality of these chapters is a testament to the law librarianship profession. I am quite proud of the final product and the people who created it. There were times when we felt like we were herding cats, but we always viewed them as very cool cats! We are sincerely grateful for their hard work.

We also realize that a project like this is organic. For that reason we have created a Web page, where updates, corrections, additions, etc., will be posted (http://law.arizona.edu/prestatehood). Comments, corrections, and additions for inclusion in the Web site can be e-mailed to <prestatehood@ law.arizona.edu>.

Chapter 1

Sources of Law in the Alabama Territory and the State of Alabama, 1798-1832: A Narrative Bibliography

Paul M. Pruitt Jr.
David I. Durham

THE FUTURE ALABAMA
IN THE MISSISSIPPI TERRITORY, 1798-1817

Historical Overview

Prior to its creation in 1817, the Alabama Territory had been the eastern half of the Mississippi Territory. Congress created the latter in 1798 from lands disputed by the United States, the state of Georgia, and several Native American nations. Over two decades of Mississippi territorial history, the federal government would employ legislation, negotiation, and military activity to expand the borders of the new territory.[1]

Like the rest of the Mississippi Territory, the future Alabama was governed under a version of the Northwest Ordinance of 1787.[2] For most of the period, a series of appointed governors[3] presided over legislative arrangements consisting of an appointed council and an elected house. Appointed judges rounded out a government that, as historian Malcolm C. McMillan has pointed out, was modeled on the British system of colonial administration.[4] The Mississippi Territory was huge,[5] and residents certainly lived under primitive conditions. Yet there was little frontier democracy, as the voting and governing class was made up of white adult male property holders.[6] Slavery was legal from the first, as the antislavery article of the Northwest Ordinance was specifically excluded from Mississippi's territorial act.[7]

The authors thank James Leonard and Kris Gilliland for advice and encouragement, and for her excellent archival assistance, Mary Evelyn Tomlin of NARA's Atlanta repository. Thanks also to the staffs of the Mississippi and Alabama Departments of Archives and History.

Citizens of eastern Mississippi were isolated from the territorial government located at Natchez. Underrepresented in the legislature, they were forced to deal with unmanageable administrative units. From 1800 to 1808, most of the future state of Alabama consisted of one county.[8] Understandably, residents developed their own networks of communication and trade as new arrivals fanned out within the Tombigbee, the Black Warrior, the Alabama-Cahaba, and the Tennessee river systems.[9] At the same time, settlers shared common dangers and preserved collective memories. Some of these accounts, such as that of the 1807 capture of the fugitive Aaron Burr, have survived as little more than fireside tales, while others—versions of the settlers' long-running conflicts with the Spanish and the Creek Nation—helped establish white Alabamians' self-image as a hardy and righteous people.[10]

In the turbulent Mississippi Territory, population growth was both a cause and an effect of change. During this period the federal government facilitated settlement through successful negotiations with Native Americans and the establishment of land offices,[11] as well as the construction of a road from Georgia.[12] For some years it had been obvious that the eastern districts of the territory could support a rich cotton culture. Following the establishment of peace in 1814-1815, the people of the old southern seaboard states caught "Alabama fever"[13] in impressive numbers. In all, the influx of settlers raised the non–Native American population of the soon-to-be-created Alabama Territory to nearly 30,000 by 1816.[14] Over the next four years another 100,000 souls would join these pioneers.[15]

Boundaries

The initial southern boundary of the Mississippi Territory had been secured with the 1795 signing of the Treaty of San Lorenzo, or Pinckney's Treaty, between the United States and Spain. Following the American Revolution, Spain had been confirmed in its possession of the Floridas, subsequently claiming territory as far north as thirty-two degrees, twenty-eight minutes north latitude.[16] Pinckney's negotiations established the United States–Florida boundary at the thirty-first parallel and provided for joint supervision of a survey.[17] The latter, carried out under the supervision of Andrew Ellicott, was not finished until 1800.[18]

Congress created the Mississippi Territory in 1798 as a means of administering the lands north of Spanish Florida, east of the Mississippi River, and west of the Chattahoochee River. The new territory's northern boundary was a line drawn from the mouth of the Yazoo River (a tributary of the Mississippi) to the Chattahoochee.[19] This was approximately the line formerly claimed by the Spaniards.[20] The act also provided for appointment of three federal commissioners to meet with commissioners of the state of Georgia, which claimed all lands between thirty-one and thirty-five degrees north latitude and as early as 1785 had established "Bourbon County" on the Mississippi River.[21]

The persistence of the Georgians prolonged negotiations,[22] and hanging over the whole process was the fate of more than 30 million acres in the future states of Alabama and Mississippi—the "Yazoo" lands already sold by Georgia to speculators.[23] Finally, in April 1802, the two sides agreed to "Articles of Agreement and Cession," by which Georgia abandoned its claims in return for benefits, including the payment of 1.25 million dollars, in addition to promises that the federal government would honor legitimate land claims and "extinguish" certain Indian land titles.[24] Over the next two years Congress set in motion the machinery for establishing land offices, validating titles, and surveying the newly purchased lands south of the thirty-fifth parallel.[25] In March 1804 these lands were made part of the Mississippi Territory.[26]

In the meantime, agents of the federal government had gone about the work of obtaining full control over the broad expanses of territory still owned by Native American nations. Within the future state of Alabama, the Choctaws (1802, 1805)[27] ceded lands along the Tombigbee and Mobile rivers, while Chickasaw (1805)[28] and Cherokee (1806)[29] cessions opened the Tennessee River district for white settlement. A treaty of 1805 with the Creeks gave the government the right to build a federal road through Creek lands in what would become southeastern Alabama.[30] Officials of the territorial government responded by creating Baldwin County along the Florida border and Madison County in the Tennessee Valley.[31]

By the fall of 1810, long-standing economic and military tensions led to a popular movement to seize West Florida from the Spanish. In September, filibusterers captured Baton Rouge and established a governing "convention" there, whose leaders dispatched military forces eastward.[32] Federal officials in Baldwin County worked to prevent an expedition against Mobile,[33] and in the meantime President James Madison issued a proclamation on October 27, 1810, asserting a claim to West Florida as the rightful possession of the United States (under the terms of the Louisiana Purchase) and assigning Florida west of the Perdido River to Orleans Territory.[34]

Federal policy toward the Spanish of Mobile was pacific, and in fact the Spanish garrison there was not dislodged until 1813.[35] Most of the lands included in Madison's proclamation, however, were soon under American control and were afterward divided between the new state of Louisiana[36] and the Mississippi Territory. The latter, by a congressional act of May 14, 1812, acquired those portions of the Gulf Coast west of the Perdido River and east of the Pearl, in effect rounding out the borders of the future states of Mississippi and Alabama.[37] Several factors—secure possession of the port of Mobile, Indian cessions negotiated after the conclusion of the Creek War,[38] Congress's belated settlement of the Yazoo land claims in 1814,[39] and the revival of trade following the War of 1812—now helped to open the valleys of Alabama to a flood of immigration.[40]

Postwar efforts to achieve statehood were played out in light of long-standing west-versus-east hostilities. The act of 1798 had allowed for the possible division of the territory,[41] and on several occasions prior to the Creek War, citizens of the future Alabama petitioned for Congress to give them a separate territorial government. The territorial legislature, looking to the eventual admission of a single large state, opposed these requests.[42] These positions were reversed after the War of 1812, as leaders of the east began to believe that their growing numbers would dominate in any state government, while Natchez interests sought safety in separation. The east-erners sent longtime territorial judge Harry Toulmin to Washington where, in the winter of 1816-1817, he lobbied in favor of the single-state idea,[43] but to no avail—since the issue of Mississippi statehood had become part of the congressional contest between slave and free states.[44] The southern leadership of the U.S. Senate, encouraged by Georgia Senator Charles Tait and other Georgians, passed an act approved on March 1, 1817, allowing the western districts of Mississippi to hold a constitutional convention.[45]

This act was followed by an act approved on March 3, providing for the organization of the former eastern districts as the Alabama Territory. The northern, southern, and eastern boundaries of the new territory were un-changed, while its western boundary was a line from the mouth of Bear Creek (on the Tennessee River) to the northwestern corner of Washington County, then south to the Gulf of Mexico. With a minor adjustment made when Alabama was granted permission to hold its own constitutional con-vention, these lines completed the borders of the state of Alabama.[46]

Structure of Government, Sources of Laws, 1798-1817

Executive Power

The Mississippi Territorial Act of 1798 established a governmental re-gime similar to others set up under the Northwest Ordinance as modified in 1789.[47] Under this system[48] the executive branch consisted of an appointed governor and a governor's secretary. The governor's administrative and lawmaking powers were wide-ranging—especially prior to the organiza-tion of the general assembly, an event that required a population of 5,000 free adult white males.[49] Even when confronted with a legislature, governors had significant authority to issue proclamations and to command the militia, as well as the power to call the general assembly into session, prorogue or dissolve it, and exercise a veto over its acts.[50] The governors' secretaries were responsible for keeping the records of the executive and legislative branches of the territory.[51] In a governor's absence his secretary served as interim governor.[52]

The two Mississippi volumes of Clarence Carter's remarkable *Territorial Papers of the United States* provide the most comprehensive collection of the proclamations, appointments, orders, and correspondence of the territorial governors. Chronologically arranged and cross-referenced, these volumes are indispensable to any student of the administrative law, legislative history, or political development of the territory. Because the *Territorial Papers* are indexed, it is simple to extract from them information concerning Washington County, Madison County, or other areas of the future Alabama.[53]

The prolific Mississippi historian Dunbar Rowland published several documentary collections of interest, in particular his 1905 edition of the *Executive Journals of Governor Winthrop Sargent and Governor William Charles Cole Claiborne*.[54] There are also scatterings of gubernatorial proclamations in the statutory digests issued in 1816 by Edward Turner[55] and in 1823 by Harry Toulmin.[56] The Mississippi Department of Archives and History maintains collections of gubernatorial papers, organized under its Record Group 27.[57]

Legislative Bodies and Statutory Law

After two years in which the governor and three territorial judges exercised almost exclusive power,[58] Congress allowed voting citizens to elect representatives for two-year terms to the lower house of a general assembly.[59] Initially, settlers in the eastern district were granted one of nine seats in the territorial house.[60] By 1816, with almost forty percent of the overall population, counties east of the Pearl River were allowed eight of twenty-four seats.[61]

Members of the legislative council, the upper chamber of the legislature, were appointed to five-year terms by the president of the United States after nomination by the territorial house. Originally five in number,[62] the membership of the council was expanded to nine in 1814.[63] During the territorial period the House took pains to nominate residents of Washington and other eastern counties,[64] and it is true that these counties furnished four of nine council members in 1816.[65] Still, when Alabama's first territorial legislature convened in January 1818, its ranks drawn[66] from Alabama-dwelling members of the last Mississippi territorial legislature, only three former councilors were eligible to attend.[67]

Individual volumes of Mississippi territorial acts are scarce, but they are available in microfiche as the Mississippi segment (1799-present) of William S. Hein and Company's *State Session Laws* set.[68] More useful, however, are two authorized compilations—a digest published by Judge Harry Toulmin in 1807[69] and the collection of statutes assembled in 1816 by Edward Turner.[70]

The Judicial Branch and Its Records

For the first several years of territorial history, none of the territory's three judges lived in the future Alabama; occasionally, one would visit.[71] Bad as it was, this situation was worsened in 1802 when Governor Claiborne signed a law creating "superior" courts for each of the territory's three districts/counties. These courts required two or more territorial judges sitting en banc, thereby making it even less likely that Tombigbee settlers would have routine access to courts of record.[72] By way of remedy, Congress in 1804 created a fourth judgeship specifically for the eastern district, specifying that the new court would sit for two sessions per year and that appeals from it would run to the Superior Court of Adams County (i.e., Natchez).[73]

From 1805 through the remainder of the territorial period, the Washington/Tombigbee judge was Harry Toulmin of Kentucky.[74] Toulmin exercised a broad jurisdiction, augmented by a congressional act of 1805 that gave territorial courts the power to hear most federal cases.[75] In 1810 Congress created a separate court for Madison County in the Tennessee Valley, giving its occupant the same powers as those of the Washington district judge and likewise subjecting his rulings to the appellate review of the Superior Court of Adams County.[76] Obadiah Jones of Georgia, formerly an Illinois territorial judge, occupied the Madison County judgeship from 1810 to 1819.[77]

Congress set forth the outlines of territorial justice, but detailed regulation was up to the general assembly, and that body was constant in its willingness to slight the interests of eastern settlers. An act of 1807, for example, changed the name of the superior courts to "circuit courts" and stated that the latter were to be held by "one or more" of the territorial judges. The act also required the judges of circuit courts to hold a supreme court at the seat of territorial government but added that "it shall not be the duty of the judge of the Washington district to attend either [type] of the said courts."[78]

Two years later the lawmakers abolished the supreme court and renamed the circuit courts, calling them the "Superior Court[s] of Law and Equity." This act applied to several western counties and to Madison County.[79] Washington, Baldwin, and other eastern counties were initially left out, though they were later granted the right to hold superior courts.[80] In 1814 the general assembly revived the supreme court (now called the "Supreme Court of Errors and Appeals"), declaring that it should consist of two or more superior court judges and that it should meet twice yearly at Adams County. Yet, predictably, that statute noted that "it shall not be the duty" of the Washington or Madison judges to attend.[81]

It would have been very difficult for Harry Toulmin or Obadiah Jones to take part in a Natchez-based appellate court, not least because Toulmin was forced after 1812 to ride circuit among new counties, including Mobile.[82] Still, the plain fact was that eastern Mississippians were faced with under-manned trial courts and a regime of appellate justice that was, to use the kindest term, inconvenient. As early as 1814 there was discussion of a solution involving a judicial division of the territory into eastern and western halves, a separate appellate court, and the appointment of an additional judge for the east.[83]

The Alabama Territorial Act of March 1817 embraced this plan, creating an additional judgeship and authorizing twice-yearly meetings at St. Stephens of a new tribunal, a "general court" at which the proto-Alabama judges, sitting en banc, were to exercise appellate jurisdiction.[84] The start-up of Alabama's territorial government had been made contingent upon admission of the state of Mississippi. However, the new judicial provisions went into effect at once—meaning that for a time the territory of Mississippi had two appellate courts of approximately equal dignity.[85]

Carter's *Territorial Papers* contains much information on the operation of courts in Washington and Madison counties. The Mississippi Department of Archives and History holds certain territorial court records (see its Record Group 6).[86] At its Georgia branch, the National Archives and Records Administration (NARA) holds territorial case files in its Record Group 21, "Records of District Courts of the United States." These files include matters brought before the short-lived General Court of (eastern) Mississippi Territory and its successor, the General Court of the Alabama Territory.[87] Few of these records have been subjected to any form of analysis.[88]

THE ALABAMA TERRITORY, 1817-1819

Historical Overview

In 1817, the Alabama Territory was created from what had been the eastern half of the Mississippi Territory prior to Mississippi statehood.[89] For nearly twenty years, animosity had escalated within the vast Mississippi Territory between the more populated Mississippi Valley region and the sparsely populated and more inaccessible Tombigbee settlements to the east and Madison County residents to the north. The minority eastern region complained of inadequate representation and experienced difficulty in voicing their concerns to Congress. Petitions and memorials were an effective way for inhabitants in remote areas to make their wishes known to Congress, and several pleas were made as early as 1803 to separate the two regions.[90] In language similar in tone to revolutionary era complaints against British rule, the future Alabama Territory inhabitants wrote that the two districts were "composed of people different in their manners and customs, different in their interests, and nature appears never to have designed the two countries to be under the same government." Later, in a petition to divide the territory, they wrote in even more assertive language, "Representatives of the American People! We have petitioned for a Government.—At Present we have only the name of one. We know nothing of our Executive Officers:—we know nothing of our Delegates in Congress."[91] Western settlements continued to dominate the territorial government and hostility increased until the creation of Mississippi statehood and the formation of the Alabama Territory in 1817.

Following Andrew Jackson's defeat of the Creek Indian Confederation at Horseshoe Bend in 1814 and the subsequent cession of lower Creek lands, it was clear that not only did the future Alabama Territory have a large enough area to become a separate state, but the territory also had a substantial population.[92] "Alabama feaver" was the term used to describe the tremendous rush of settlers to the region, who were seeking cheap land and dreamed of large profits stimulated by the emerging cotton industry.[93] Numerous Mississippi territorial officials and residents had supported the admission of the entire territory as one state, and in 1816, the counties east of the Pearl River held a convention that voted against division of the territory; however, with the increase in available land in Alabama as the result of Indian cessions, the large migration of settlers, and the regional desire to protect southern interests in Congress through the voting power of two southern states, the proponents of separate Alabama statehood prevailed.[94] Although the suggestion of an east-west line dividing the territory into northern and southern halves was discussed as a way to avoid internal conflict between northern and southern interests, the east-west division found little support in Congress and the north-south division of the territory was adopted.[95]

Mississippi Statehood and the Establishment of the Alabama Territory

The Alabama Territory was formed concomitantly with the creation of Mississippi statehood from the western portion of the Mississippi Territory. The bill to establish the territory of Alabama was introduced in the Senate by Georgian Charles Tait and reported on February 5, 1817.[96] The only substantive issue before Congress was whether it should let Mississippi enter the Union as one large state or whether it should be divided. The question of Mississippi statehood had to be settled before the Alabama territorial proposals could go forward. The House of Representatives had before it on February 24, 1817, a bill to enable the western part of the Mississippi Territory to form a state, and a bill to allow the people of the whole Mississippi Territory to form a state government.[97] After a motion offered by Israel Pickens of North Carolina to admit the territory as whole was defeated, and subsequent motions and amendments were likewise defeated, the bill to admit the western part of the Mississippi Territory advanced to a third reading and passed.[98] The bill to establish Alabama as a territory was quickly passed within two days of the Mississippi bill.

The March 3, 1817, act that established a separate territorial government for the eastern portion of the Mississippi Territory declared, "this act shall commence and be in force so soon as the convention . . . shall have formed a constitution and State government for that part of the Mississippi Territory lying west of the Territory herein described."[99] The act enabling Mississippi to form a constitution and state government was passed on March 1, 1817; however, Mississippi statehood was not approved until December 10, 1817.[100] During this interim period, the language of the Alabama Territorial Act provided that all executive and legislative functions of the Mississippi Territory should continue as before until the provisions of the act were enabled by the establishment of Mississippi statehood, and thereafter until changed by the Alabama territorial legislature.[101]

In addition to the establishment of executive, legislative, and judicial structures for the new territory, the act that established the Alabama Territory provided for its precise boundaries. The boundaries were defined by the existing Georgia and Tennessee lines, the Mississippi border established by that state's enabling act, and a southern border that followed the previous Mississippi boundary at the thirty-first parallel established by Pinckney's Treaty; and further, from a line at the mouth of Bear Creek on the Tennessee River, directly to the northwest corner of Washington County, then "due south to the Gulf of Mexico, thence eastwardly, including all the islands within six leagues of the shore, to the Perdido river, and thence up the same to the beginning."[102] Alabamians were, however, reluctant to accept the West Florida boundary as permanent. As late as February 1821, Alabama's Constitutional Convention, led by the president of the convention and future Alabama Senator John W. Walker, unsuccessfully petitioned Congress in a memorial which argued that Alabama's natural boundary should include all of West Florida.[103] This petition was in response to Spain's recent cession of the Florida territory to the United States, and the Alabama attempt to persuade Congress of the importance of the land being annexed to Alabama anticipated the subsequent U.S. possession of West Florida in 1821 and the removal of Spanish troops.[104]

Alabama Territorial Government

Alabama's short territorial experience (1817-1819) did not allow time for, or focus on, defining the role of the territory much beyond the Mississippi territorial model.[105] With the exception of minor structural changes in the judiciary, as provided for in section three of the Alabama Territorial Act, the Alabama Territory was organized according to its previous Mississippi experience, which was taken from the language contained in the Northwest Ordinance.[106] Rather than establishing a unique territorial government, Alabama almost immediately began to prepare for its petition for statehood. Alabamians were aware that their rapidly increasing numbers would satisfy the population requirement of the Northwest Ordinance in a very short time.

Executive

The role of the executive in the new Alabama Territory was defined in the creating act, which was based on the Mississippi Territorial Act of 1798 and on the requirements of the Northwest Ordinance.[107] The governor and the almost equally important governor's secretary (who would act as governor in his absence) were appointed by the president of the United States and enjoyed broad governing powers. The position of the executive was so great that he was not excluded from certain powers over the legislative and judicial branches of government.[108] President James Monroe appointed ex-Senator William Wyatt Bibb of Georgia as territorial governor; Bibb, Charles Tait, and John W. Walker comprised the core of what would be known as the

"Georgia Faction," which represented a primarily northern Alabama agenda until the time of the Constitutional Convention.[109] Among the governor's duties upon entering into office at the seat of the new territorial government at St. Stephens was to convene "such members of the legislative council and house of representatives, of the Mississippi territory, as may then be the representatives from the several counties" of the new Alabama Territory. The members of the legislative council and house of representatives who were transferred to Alabama Territory were allowed to serve their full terms under the new act.[110]

Clarence Carter's *Territorial Papers of the United States* provides an excellent source for correspondence, proclamations, and appointments from and to Governor Bibb. The executive materials are organized according to year.[111] The Library of Congress microfilm compilation *Records of the States of the United States of America* offers a selection of executive correspondence, proclamations, and appointments, including militia appointments.[112] Another source of primary executive documents for the territorial period is the Alabama Department of Archives and History's executive manuscript collection. The collection includes speeches, proclamations, appointments, and commissions and is organized generally as "Correspondence of Governor William Wyatt Bibb."

Legislative

The population of the new territory increased at a pace that allowed time for only two sessions of the new territorial legislature. Both sessions were held in 1818, and the first was primarily comprised of transplanted members of the former Mississippi territorial legislature. The first session was held on January 19, 1818, and divided the territory into three judicial circuits; in addition, it created thirteen new counties. Also, the first session of the legislature authorized the taking of a census in anticipation of Alabama's population reaching the required 60,000 inhabitants for statehood under the Northwest Ordinance.[113] The second session of the territorial legislature, which met in November 1818, addressed the issue of apportionment, which would be a significant focus of sectional tensions between the northern and southern sections of the territory and state throughout much of its history.[114] The territory adopted a standard of one representative for each 1,000 free inhabitants, which favored the northern section over the southern counties with larger slave populations.[115] A compromise was reached with the southern section of the state through the establishment of a capital at Cahaba—located in the southern part of the territory; however, it was agreed that a temporary capital would be placed in the north at Huntsville until arrangements could be made for the Cahaba site.[116] The second session of the legislature also passed a petition for statehood in November 1818.[117]

Primary legislative sources from the Alabama Territory include *Journal of the House of Representatives of the Alabama Territory at the First Session of the General Assembly in the Forty-Second Year of American Independence* (St. Stephens: Thomas Eastin, 1818); *Journal of the House of Representatives of the Alabama Territory at the Second Session of the First General Assembly in the Forty-Third Year of American Independence* (St. Stephens: Thomas Eastin, 1818); *Journal of the Legislative Council of the Alabama Territory at the First Session of the First General Assembly in the Forty-Third Year of American Independence* (St. Stephens: Thomas Eastin, 1818); *Acts Passed at the First Session of the First General Assembly of the Alabama Territory in the Forty-Second Year of American Independence* (St. Stephens: Thomas Eastin, 1818); and *Acts Passed at the Second Session of the First General Assembly of the Alabama Territory in the Forty-Third Year of American Independence* (St. Stephens: Thomas Eastin, 1818). In addition to the legislative publications at St. Stephens, territorial Judge Harry Toulmin's *1823 Digest* is an excellent source.

In addition to the primary territorial legislative sources previously listed, the Alabama Department of Archives and History holds a set of the gubernatorial nominations of members to the territorial council and numerous other legislative materials, including petitions, oaths, speeches, recommendations, and collections of records concerning a financial controversy between Mississippi and Alabama over settlement of the funds of the Mississippi territorial treasury.[118] The origin of the problem can be found in section nine of the Alabama Territorial Act, which reads:

> whatever balance may remain in the treasury of the Mississippi territory, at the time when the convention authorized to form a constitution and state government, for the western part of said territory, may have formed a constitution and state government for the same, shall be divided between the new state and territory, according to the amount which may have been paid into said treasury, from the counties lying within the limits of such state and territory respectively.[119]

Judicial

The judicial system of the Alabama Territory was, for the most part, inherited from the former Mississippi Territory. The specific courts were created by Congress; however, regulation of the courts was established by the territorial general assembly. The Alabama Territorial Act essentially adapted the Mississippi system to the new territory, although it established an additional judgeship for the new territory and, as discussed earlier, created a system of two appellate courts from March through December 10, 1817.[120] Information concerning operation of the courts can be found in Volume 18 of Carter's *Territorial Papers of the United States*.[121] Actual cases are few; however, some of these can be found within the National Archives and Records Administration's East Point, Georgia, branch in Record Group 21, "Records of District Courts of the United States."[122] Reports of cases from this period are also extremely scarce; however, a few can be found in the early Alabama nominative reporters.[123] The best description of the territorial judicial system can be found in Harry Toulmin's *1823 Digest,* which offers offers a detailed look into the executive, legislative, and judicial workings of territorial Mississippi and Alabama.[124]

Indian Treaties

Indian treaties during the Alabama territorial period were primarily concerned with land cessions. The U.S. government engaged in treaty activity with three of the four remaining Indian tribes in the Alabama Territory between 1817 and 1819. Treaties were made with the Cherokees in 1817 and 1819; the Choctaws had already ceded land prior to 1816 and would cede their remaining lands in 1820, 1825, and 1830; the Chickasaws would do the same in 1818; and the largest cessions were from the Creeks in 1814 in the aftermath of their crushing defeat by General Andrew Jackson, but again in 1818 and continuing through 1838. For treaties with, and land cessions by, Indian tribes in the Alabama Territory, see *United States Statutes at Large,* Volume VII, Indian Treaties; and *American State Papers, Documents Legislative and Executive of the Congress of the United States,* Class II, *Indian Affairs,* Volume 2. Both sources contain very usable indexes that are organized by tribe.[125]

The Move Toward Statehood

Anticipating statehood, Alabama's legislature passed a petition for statehood in November 1818.[126] Written by Clement Comer Clay and John W. Walker, copies were immediately sent to the president of the United States, the Speaker of the House of Representatives, and to Charles Tait of Georgia, who had previously introduced Alabama's territorial bid in the Senate.[127] Tait not only wrote the Alabama Enabling Act, but referred it to committee (of which he was the sitting chairman) and steered it through the Senate.[128] On Monday December 7, 1818, the Speaker of the House referred the petition and a census of the inhabitants of the territory to a select committee.[129] The Alabama Enabling Act was approved on March 2, 1819 and authorized a convention to form a constitution for a new state.[130]

An earlier boundary dispute with Mississippi carried over to the debate concerning the Alabama Enabling Act, wherein Senator Tait successfully defended Alabama borders against an attempt by Mississippi senators to change the 1817 boundary to make the Tombigbee River the new boundary, giving the port of Mobile to the state of Mississippi. Section three of the Alabama Enabling Act clearly addressed this problem and called for the line to be surveyed to a new "point on the Gulf of Mexico, ten miles east of the mouth of the river Pascagola." This settled problems caused by the previous line, which had encroached on several Mississippi counties.[131]

The Alabama Enabling Act called for a forty-four-member convention to be called on the first Monday in July at Huntsville for the purpose of creating a state constitution.[132] The Alabama Territory had been in existence only fifteen months when the enabling act was passed and the territory moved forward to satisfy the requirements of statehood.

ALABAMA'S 1819 CONSTITUTION
AND THE TRANSITION TO STATEHOOD

The Alabama Enabling Act, which was approved by Congress on March 2, 1819, provided for an election on the first Monday and Tuesday in May of forty-four representatives to form a state constitution.[133] Section four of the Alabama Enabling Act listed the individual counties, stating "all white male citizens of the United States, who shall have arrived at the age of twenty-one years, and have resided in said territory three months previous to the day of election" are authorized to choose representatives.[134] Section five directed the elected convention members to meet at Huntsville in July to create the new constitution "Provided, That the same when formed, shall be republican, and not repugnant to the principles of the [Northwest] ordinance."[135] Although the document that was created was structurally republican, it was one of the most democratically inspired constitutions of the period.

On July 5, 1819, forty-four delegates arrived in Huntsville to begin the business of forming the constitution. Among the group were "at least eighteen lawyers, four physicians, two ministers, one surveyor, one merchant, and four planters."[136] John W. Walker of Huntsville was elected president of the convention and conducted the proceedings in a notably informal manner.[137] It is not surprising that under the frontier conditions of north Alabama in 1819, the convention may have suspended certain formalities. It is clear, however, that the competence of the convention was not in question. From the convention delegates, Alabama would subsequently obtain six governors, six members of the state supreme court, and six U.S. senators.[138]

The Convention

The convention appointed the most experienced of its members to a committee charged with creating the original draft of the constitution.[139] The Committee of Fifteen not only included most of the convention's talent but also was heavily representative of the planter regions of the Tennessee Valley and the Alabama and Tombigbee River Valleys. The constitution consisted of a preamble and the following articles: a declaration of rights, the distribution of powers, the legislative department, the executive department, the judicial department, and general provisions.[140] Although much of the Alabama Constitution was naturally modeled after the U.S. Constitution, as well as other southern state constitutions, its authors created a remarkable document in many respects.[141] The most notable feature of Alabama's document was that it created a legislature that was manifestly superior to the other branches of state government.

Institutional Structure

The legislative article was unique in the proportion of power that had been given to it, in its suffrage requirements, and on the issue of apportionment. The governor maintained veto power over legislation, but his veto could be overridden by a simple majority of those who were elected to each house of the legislature. Several western states had weakened the power of the governor, and likewise Alabama's governor could serve no more than two, two-year terms. A unique clause required him to be a native citizen of the United States. Executive department heads, such as secretary of state, attorney general, and treasurer, were elected by the general assembly. State judges, who were elected by a joint vote of the legislature and could be removed with a two-thirds vote of the legislative body, were also subject to the superior position of the legislature.[142]

The section that specified suffrage requirements was another remarkable and democratically inspired feature of the Alabama Constitution. The document guaranteed that "every white male person above the age of twenty-one years, who shall be a citizen of the United States, and a resident in this State at the time of the adoption of this Constitution, shall be deemed a qualified elector."[143] The article called for no property, militia, or tax-paying restrictions on the right to vote, making Alabama and Kentucky the only southern states that claimed universal white manhood suffrage as of 1819.[144]

One of the most rancorous issues that the convention faced was over apportionment. The southern section of the state would yield to a white-only basis for representation, rather than the federal three-fifths ratio, if the state's northern faction would agree to an assignment of one senate seat per county. North Alabama demanded a standard that based representation in both houses on a proportion of the white population. The northern section prevailed, willing to concede the location of the capital in an attempt to mitigate the southern section's hostility.[145]

The judiciary article established a supreme court, circuit courts organized by county, and inferior courts of law and equity. In addition, the article gave the general assembly the power to create a probate court in each county that would serve the function of the orphans' court. Life tenure for judges was recommended by the Committee of Fifteen, but an amendment was offered to limit terms to six years. Although the amendment had some support, it was defeated by a vote of twenty-five to eighteen.[146]

Historian Malcolm Cook McMillan best characterizes the Alabama Constitution when he describes it as both a liberal and conservative document. Liberal features of the constitution included no property, militia membership, or tax-paying restrictions on voting or candidacy; the election of the governor, sheriffs, and clerks of court by the people, rather than the legislature or by executive appointment; and very liberal clauses concerning the treatment and rights of slaves.[147] McMillan sees it as conservative because within ten years it would represent the mainstream of state constitutional construction as the result of Jacksonian democratic influences. Its position on suffrage and the move from a republican to a more democratic document foreshadow the frontier influence and the emergence of Jacksonian ideology.[148]

Statehood

On August 2, 1819, the forty-four members of the convention signed the document and sent the Alabama Constitution of 1819 and its accompanying ordinance to the president and Congress of the United States.[149] On December 6, 1819, the president of the United States delivered these documents to the Senate.[150] The Alabama Constitution passed both the Senate and House of Representatives and was signed by President James Monroe on December 14, 1819.[151] The resolution declaring Alabama "admitted into the Union on an equal footing with the original states" was approved the same day.[152]

Alabama experienced an interim period between the organization of a state government and the formal admission to the Union. Alabama had submitted a constitution to Washington, elected executive and legislative representatives, inaugurated William Wyatt Bibb as governor, and convened the first state assembly by late October 1819. In practice, Alabama, like other territories, retained the territorial institutions until formal statehood, yet its leaders proceeded with the formation and implementation of a state government, which was necessary at the moment of formal entry into the Union on December 14, 1819.[153]

THE STATE OF ALABAMA, 1819-1832

Historical Overview

In the first decade of statehood, Alabama's population increased from 125,000 to more than 300,000. The proportion of African Americans rose over the same period from 31 to 38 percent. These black Alabamians, the vast majority of whom were slaves, were concentrated in plantation districts along the river systems. However, planters and small-scale cultivators coexisted throughout the state. It was common, also, for white and African-American settlers to live in close proximity to one of the remaining enclaves of the Creek, Cherokee, Choctaw, or Chickasaw nations. Aside from Mobile, Huntsville, Tuscaloosa, and St. Stephens, there were no substantial towns, much less urban centers.[154]

Some public issues of the time were shaped by local circumstances. Several historians have pointed out the persistent tensions between northern and southern regions of Alabama. Other battles were of types common among frontier communities—between debtors and creditors, proponents and opponents of state-sponsored banking, or friends and critics of Andrew Jackson.[155] During the 1820s, politicians began to employ states'-rights arguments. Some of these attacks targeted federal protection of Native American lands, a major political issue of the following decade.[156]

Executive and Legislative Branches: Sources of Law

The basic structure of the executive and legislative branches remained unchanged into the 1830s. The printed *Journals* of the senate and house contain messages of the governors and skeletal remains of legislative debates.[157] Yearly volumes of the *Acts of Alabama* contain statutes,[158] which are more easily found in Toulmin's *1823 Digest* and subsequent compilations.[159]

Toulmin's 1823 work proved to be the masterpiece of his final years. Working confidently, Toulmin subdivided statutes, added historical notes based on his unique understanding of territorial law, and omitted obsolete sections.[160] The legislature had given him authority, jointly with the supreme court, to report "defects" in the state's laws.[161] The result was the foundation of state law and a standard for future compilers.[162]

Judiciary: Structure and Sources of Law

The structure of Alabama's judiciary changed little for more than a decade after statehood. The period was marked by a series of confrontations between the legislature and the supreme court, which was composed of the judges of the circuit courts. Initially these conflicts were minor skirmishes, as in 1819 when the lawmakers attempted to make the judges responsible for compiling a digest of laws. The judges modestly responded that they could not accomplish such a task "whilst they perform their own duties."[163] In 1821 a legislative committee investigated complaints that judges were not filing written opinions with the clerk of the supreme court. Again the judges pleaded the pressures of work, but this time promised to mend their ways.[164]

In truth the judges of the supreme court were overworked and the court itself was weak, subject to restructuring at the hands of the legislature.[165] As an elite body in a frontier state, its judges were easy targets for leaders of the "popular" political faction. During the 1827-1828 legislature, Chief Justice Abner S. Lipscomb had to defend himself against accusations of tyrannical behavior.[166] In the next legislature (1828-1829), the senate held a full-scale "trial" of three judges accused of ruling against the interests of debtors.[167] All were exonerated, but the episodes further threatened judicial independence. They also hastened passage of the state's first constitutional amendment, which in 1830 limited judicial terms to six years.[168]

By 1832 prevailing political winds moved lawmakers to create a separate supreme court, composed of three judges elected by the legislature for six-year terms.[169] For the first time since 1798, full-time appellate judges were able to practice their craft. The quality of supreme court reporting had already improved with the work of George N. Stewart, reporter of cases heard from 1827 to 1834.[170] Now Alabama could begin to generate its own common law.[171]

NOTES

1. For surveys of early Alabama history, see William Warren Rogers, Robert David Ward, Leah Rawls Atkins, and Wayne Flynt, *Alabama: The History of a Deep South State* 36-66 (Tuscaloosa: University of Alabama Press, 1994) [hereinafter Rogers et al.]; Malcolm Cook McMillan, *Constitutional Development in Alabama, 1798-1901: A Study in Politics, the Negro, and Sectionalism* 3-29 (Spartanburg, SC: Reprint Company, 1978) (1955); William Brantley, *Three Capitals: A Book About the First Three Capitals of Alabama* 1-42 (Tuscaloosa: University of Alabama Press, 1976) (1947); and Thomas Perkins Abernethy, *The Formative Period in Alabama, 1815-1828* 17-43 (Tuscaloosa: University of Alabama Press, 1990) (1922). For cites to primary sources see infra.

2. See An Act to Provide for the Government of the Territory Northwest of the River Ohio [hereinafter Act to Provide for Government], 1 *Stat.* 50-53 (1789); and see ibid. at 1 *Stat.* 51, note (a), reprinting An Ordinance for the Government of the Territory of the United States North-West of the River Ohio [hereinafter Northwest Ordinance].

3. The governors were Winthrop Sargeant (1798-1801), William C.C. Claiborne (1801-1804), Cato West (acting governor, 1804-1805), Robert Williams (1805-1808), David Holmes (1809-1817), and William Wyatt Bibb (Alabama territorial governor, 1817-1819); see McMillan, supra note 1, at 4-5, 24.

4. Ibid. at 3.

5. See 12 *Annals of Congress* 1343 (1803) for a description of the Mississippi Territory as 235 miles from south to north (i.e., from the thirty-first to the thirty-fifth parallels) and 380 miles from east to west.

6. See McMillan, supra note 1, at 13-14. McMillan cites many petitions for expanded suffrage.

7. See An Act for an Amicable Settlement of Limits with the State of Georgia, and Authorizing the Establishment of a Government in the Mississippi Territory [hereinafter Mississippi Territorial Act], sec. 3, at 1 *Stat.* 549, 549-550 (1798). Slaves had been imported into the district before the creation of territorial government. At least one family, circa 1792, was possessed of a "large Negro property"; see Albert James Pickett, *History of Alabama and Incidentally of Georgia and Mississippi from the Earliest Period* 416-417 (Birmingham, AL: Birmingham Book and Magazine Co., 1962) (1851).

8. See *A Digest of the Laws of the State of Alabama, Containing the Statutes and Resolutions in Force at the End of the General Assembly in January, 1823* 79-80 (Harry Toulmin comp.; Cahawba, AL: Ginn and Curtis, 1823) [hereinafter Toulmin's *1823 Digest*].

9. Rogers et al., supra note 1, at 55-61; Abernethy, supra note 1, at 28-33; and Harvey H. Jackson, *Rivers of History: Life on the Coosa, Tallapoosa, Cahaba, and Alabama* 19-30 (Tuscaloosa: University of Alabama Press, 1995).

10. Pickett, supra note 7, at 488-502, 511-598; Jackson, supra note 9, at 30-41; Rogers et al., supra note 1, at 44-53.

11. Rogers et al., supra note 1, at 44; the land offices were at St. Stephens on the Tombigbee (1803) and Huntsville on the Tennessee (1811). For negotiations with Native Americans, see infra notes 27, 28, 29, and 38.

12. Rogers et al., supra note 1, at 44-45; see generally Henry DeLeon Sutherland and Jerry Elijah Brown, *The Federal Road Through Georgia, the Creek Nation and Alabama, 1806-1836* (Tuscaloosa: University of Alabama Press, 1988).

13. Rogers et al., supra note 1, at 54. For a glimpse of the postwar optimism and speculation, see Samuel Haines, [Letter to Editor], 1817 *The Port Folio* 326-329.

14. The overall population of the territory was 75,000. See Brantley, supra note 1, at 21, and Pickett, supra note 7, at 614; see also Jackson, supra note 9, at 42-58.

15. Rogers et al., supra note 1, at 54.

16. Ibid. at 36-39; McMillan, supra note 1, at 3.

17. Treaty of Friendship, Limits, and Navigation, October 27, 1795, U.S.-Sp., arts. 2-3, at 1 *Stat.* 138, 138-140; see also Charles I. Bevans, 11 *Treaties and Other International Agreements of the United States of America, 1776-1949* 517-518 (Washington, DC: U.S. Department of State, 1969-1976).

18. Pickett, supra note 7, at 451-459.

19. See Mississippi Territorial Act, supra note 7, sec. 3, at 1 *Stat.* 549, 549-550.

20. McMillan, supra note 1, at 3.

21. Mississippi Territorial Act, supra note 7, sec. 1, at 1 *Stat.* 549; Pickett, supra note 7, at 408.

22. See Act of May 10, 1800, sec. 10, at 2 *Stat.* 69-70, prodding the parties to settle by March 1, 1803.

23. Rogers et al., supra note 1, at 43-44; see also infra note 39.

24. See Articles of Agreement and Cession (submitted by President Thomas Jefferson to Congress on April 26, 1802), in 1 *American State Papers: Documents, Legislative and Executive, of the Congress of the United States, in Relation to the Public Lands* 113-114 (Walter Lowrie, ed.; Washington, DC: Duff Green, 1834). The United States commissioners were James Madison, Albert Gallatin, and Levi Lincoln; the Georgia commissioners were James Jackson, Abraham Baldwin, and John Milledge.

25. For the recommendations of the United States Commissioners, see 12 *Annals of Congress* 1342-1352 (1803). For statutory provisions see Act Regulating the Grants of Land, and Providing for the Disposal of the Lands of the United States, South of the State of Tennessee, secs. 1-3, 4, 10, 16, at 2 *Stat.* 229, 229-230, 233, 235 (1803); and Act of March 27, 1804, 2 *Stat.* 303-306. The southern boundary of the state of Tennessee, it should be noted, is the thirty-fifth parallel.

26. Act of March 27, 1804, sec. 7, at 2 *Stat.* 305.

27. See A Provisional Convention, October 17, 1802, U.S.-Choctaw Nation, arts. 1, 2, at 7 *Stat.* 73, 74; and Treaty of Limits, November 16, 1805, U.S.-Choctaw Nation, art. 1, at 7 *Stat.* 98-99.

28. See Articles of Arrangement, July 23, 1805, U.S.-Chickasaw Nation, art. 1, at 7 *Stat.* 89.

29. See A Convention, January 7, 1806, U.S.-Cherokee Nation, art. 1, at 7 *Stat.* 101, 102; and Elucidation of a Convention with the Cherokee Nation, September 11, 1807, U.S.-Cherokee Nation, 7 *Stat.* 103, 103-104.

30. See A Convention, November 14, 1805, U.S.-Creek Nation, art. 2, at 7 *Stat.* 96, 97. Generally see sources cited supra note 12; and see An Act to Regulate and Fix the Compensation of Clerks, and to Authorize the Laying Out Certain Public Roads, sec. 7, at 2 *Stat.* 396, 397 (1806).

31. Washington County had been created by gubernatorial proclamation in 1800; Madison County was similarly created in 1808; Baldwin County was created by the territorial legislature in 1809; see Toulmin's *1823 Digest* 79-82.

32. 22 *Annals of Congress* 1252-1255 (1811); see also Pickett, supra note 7, at 506-509.

33. Pickett, supra note 7, at 509.

34. For the Proclamation of October 27, 1810, see 22 *Annals of Congress* 1257-1258 (1811); for the Treaty of Paris, see Cession of Louisiana, April 30, 1803, U.S.-Fr., 7 Bevans 812-815.

35. *Annals of Congress* 1256-1257 (1811). See also McMillan, supra note 1, at 18; and Frank Lawrence Owsley Jr. and Gene A. Smith, *Filibusters and Expansionists: Jeffersonian Manifest Destiny, 1800-1821* 63-66, 89-92 (Tuscaloosa: University of Alabama Press, 1997).

36. See An Act for the Admission of the State of Louisiana into the Union, 2 *Stat.* 701 (1812); An Act of April 14, 1812, at 2 *Stat.* 708; and An Act of April 14, 1812, at 2 *Stat.* 709.

37. See An Act to Enlarge the Boundaries of the Mississippi Territory, 2 *Stat.* 734 (1812); see also McMillan, supra note 1, at 18.

38. Andrew Jackson forced the Creeks to cede all of their lands west of the Coosa River; see Articles of Agreement and Capitulation, August 9, 1814, U.S.-Creek Nation, art. 1, at 7 *Stat.* 120; see also Articles of a Convention, March 22, 1816, U.S.-Cherokee Nation, art. 1, at 7 *Stat.* 139; Treaty with the Cherokees, September 14, 1816, U.S.-Cherokee Nation, arts. 2, 3, at 7 *Stat.* 148; Treaty with the Chickasaws, September 20, 1816, U.S.-Chickasaw Nation, art. 2, at 7 *Stat.* 150; and Treaty of Cession, October 24, 1816, U.S.-Choctaw Nation, art. 1, at 7 *Stat.* 152.

39. See An Act Providing for the Indemnification of Certain Claimants of Public Lands in the Mississippi Territory, 3 *Stat.* 116-120 (1814); and Act of January 23, 1815, at 3 *Stat.* 192-193; see also McMillan, supra note 1, at 20-21.

40. For population figures see sources cited supra notes 14 and 15.

41. Mississippi Territorial Act, supra note 7, sec. 4, at 1 *Stat.* 550.

42. For a summary of petitions for and against division, see McMillan, supra note 1, at 16-17, 19, 20. For the Georgia legislature's consent to division, see Brantley, supra note 1, at 17 (text and footnote 2).

43. See McMillan, supra note 1, at 22-23, and Brantley supra note 1, at 18-23.

44. See Brantley, supra note 1, at 22; Rogers et al., supra note 1, at 62-63; see also Abernethy, supra note 1, at 48-50.

45. See An Act to Enable the People of the Western Part of the Mississippi Territory to Form a Constitution and State Government, 3 *Stat.* 348 (1817).

46. See An Act to Establish a Territorial Government for the Eastern Part of the Mississippi Territory [hereinafter Alabama Territorial Act], sec. 1, at 3 *Stat.* 371-372 (1817). For the adjustment, enacted to preserve intact three Mississippi counties, see An Act to Enable the people of the Alabama Territory to Form a Constitu-

tion and State Government [hereinafter Alabama Enabling Act], sec. 3, at 3 *Stat.* 489, 490 (1819).

47. Mississippi Territorial Act, supra note 7, secs. 3, 6, at 1 *Stat.* 549-550.

48. See especially Northwest Ordinance, supra note 2, at 1 *Stat.* 51-53.

49. Ibid., at 1 *Stat.* 51.

50. Ibid., at 1 *Stat.* 52. See also McMillan, supra note 1, at 5-6.

51. See Northwest Ordinance, supra note 48, at 1 *Stat.* 51.

52. See Act to Provide for Government, supra note 2, sec. 2, at 1 *Stat.* 53; see also McMillan, supra note 1, at 7-8.

53. 5 *Territorial Papers of the United States* (Clarence Edwin Carter, ed., Washington, DC: Government Printing Office, 1937), covering Mississippi from 1798-1809, and 6 *Territorial Papers of the United States* (Clarence Edwin Carter, ed., Washington, DC: Government Printing Office, 1939), covering Mississippi from 1809-1817 [hereinafter 5 *Territorial Papers* and 6 *Territorial Papers;* the Alabama volume will be cited as 18 *Territorial Papers*].

54. *Executive Journals of Governor Winthrop Sargent and Governor William Charles Cole Claiborne* (Dunbar Rowland, ed.; Nashiville, TN: Brandon Printing Company, 1905); see also *Official Letter Books of W.C.C. Claiborne, 1801-1816,* in 6 vols. (Dunbar Rowland, ed.; Jackson, MS: State Department of Archives and History, 1917).

55. See *Statutes of the Mississippi Territory; The Constitution of the United States, with the Several Amendments Thereto; The Ordinance for the Government of the Territory of the United States, Northwest of the River Ohio; The Articles of Government and Cession Between the United States and the State of Georgia; and Such Acts of Congress as Relate to the Mississippi Territory* [hereinafter Turner's *Statutes*] 87-88 (Edward Turner, comp.; Natchez, MS: Peter Isler, 1816).

56. Toulmin's *1823 Digest* 79-80.

57. For inquiries e-mail <refdesk@mdah.state.ms.us>. See supra note 3 for names of the governors.

58. Northwest Ordinance, supra note 2, at 1 *Stat.* 51.

59. See Act of May 10, 1800, secs. 1-5, at 2 *Stat.* 69. It seems clear that the territory's population had not yet reached 5,000. For a survey of territorial legislatures, see 2 Dunbar Rowland, *Mississippi: Comprising Sketches of Counties, Towns, Events, Institutions, and Persons Arranged in Cyclopedic Form* (Atlanta, GA: Southern Historical Publishing Association, 1907) 76-82 [hereinafter Rowland's *Mississippi*].

60. Act of May 10, 1800, sec. 5, at 2 *Stat.* 69.

61. Petition to Congress by Members of the Territorial Legislature [c. February 1816], in 6 *Territorial Papers* 655-656; and see McMillan, supra note 1, at 22. Lands east of the Pearl River include several counties of the state of Mississippi.

62. Northwest Ordinance, supra note 2, at 1 *Stat.* 52; and Act to Provide for Government, supra note 2, at 1 *Stat.* 52-53. The five members were chosen from a list of ten names.

63. An Act Further to Extend the Right of Suffrage, and to Increase the Number of Members of the Legislative Council in the Mississippi Territory, sec. 2, at 3 *Stat.* 143 (1814).

64. See documents at 5 *Territorial Papers* 387-388, 640-644, and 6 *Territorial Papers* 413-414, 477-479.

65. See Petition, supra note 61, at 6 *Territorial Papers* 656.

66. Alabama Territorial Act, supra note 46, sec. 4, at 3 *Stat.* 372-373. The act also allowed the Alabama Territorial House to nominate candidates for three additional counselors.

67. See Brantley, supra note 1, at 25; and Pickett, supra note 7, at 615. In fact, only one former Mississippi counselor, James Titus of Madison County, attended the first Alabama legislature.

68. The earliest pamphlet acts bore little bibliographical or title-page information. For the style of later volumes, see *Acts Passed at the Second Session of the Ninth General Assembly of the Mississippi Territory, Begun and Held at the Town of Washington, on Monday, the Fourth Day of November, One Thousand Eight Hundred and Sixteen, and of American Independence the Forty-First* (Natchez, MS: Peter Isler, 1816).

69. *Statutes of the Mississippi Territory, Revised and Digested by the Authority of the General Assembly* (Harry Toulmin, comp.; Natchez, MS: Samuel Terrill, 1807); see also 2 Rowland's *Mississippi* 793-795. Toulmin, with prior experience as statutory compiler in Kentucky, would be Alabama's first digester of statutes; see Toulmin's *1823 Digest,* supra note 8; see also infra.

70. See Turner's *Statutes,* supra note 55.

71. Northwest Ordinance, supra note 2, at 1 *Stat.* 51; see 1 Rowland's *Mississippi* 980-981. Judge Daniel Tilton, for example, traveled eastward in the spring of 1800.

72. An Act to Provide for the More Convenient Organization of the Courts of This Territory, sec. 1, at 1801 *Mississippi Laws* 21-24 [in Acts of 1st Assembly, First and Second Sessions].

73. Act for the Appointment of an Additional Judge for the Mississippi Territory, secs. 1-2, 5, at 2 *Stat.* 301, 302 (1804).

74. The first judge appointed to the Washington County post was Ephriam Kirby of Connecticut; upon his death in fall 1804, President Jefferson appointed Harry Toulmin, thereafter a notable character in early Alabama. See 1 Rowland's *Mississippi* 984 and 2 Rowland's *Mississippi* 793-794; see also supra note 69.

75. See Act to Extend Jurisdiction in Certain Cases, to the Territorial Courts, 2 *Stat.* 338-339 (1805).

76. Act for the Appointment of an Additional Judge, and Extending the Right of Suffrage to the Citizens of Madison County, in the Mississippi Territory, secs. 2-3, at 2 *Stat.* 564 (1810).

77. 18 *Territorial Papers* 54, note 41; see also 1 Rowland's *Mississippi* 976-977.

78. Act Establishing Superior Courts, and Declaring the Powers of the Territorial Judges (1807), sec. 8, in Toulmin's *1823 Digest* 155-156.

79. Act to Abolish the Supreme Court of the Mississippi Territory (1809), sec. 1, in Toulmin's *1823 Digest* 160-161. Note that appeals from the decisions of either of the eastern territorial judges still ran to the Superior Court (by whatever name) of Adams County; see supra, at notes 72 and 73.

80. See Act of December 18, 1811, secs. 1-2, in Turner's *Statutes* 188-189; and Toulmin's *1823 Digest* 160 (unnumbered footnote).

81. Act to Regulate the Several Courts in This Territory, and to Create a Supreme Court of Errors and Appeals, sec. 1, in Toulmin's *1823 Digest* 161.

82. See Memorial to Congress, December 10, 1814, in 6 *Territorial Papers* 475-476.

83. See Memoranda for a Bill, in 6 *Territorial Papers* 487-489.

84. See Alabama Territorial Act, supra note 46, sec. 3, at 3 *Stat.* 372. The eastern judges were given jurisdiction over the future Alabama and parts of the future Mississippi (Wayne County, for example).

85. Ibid. at sec. 5, at 3 *Stat.* 373. Mississippi's statehood was delayed until December 1817; see McMillan, supra note 1, at 24. The third judge was Stevenson Archer of Maryland, who resigned in December 1817; Henry Y. Webb of North Carolina replaced him. See 6 *Territorial Papers* 781, 816, 18 *Territorial Papers* 54 (note 39), 238-239, and infra.

86. See e-mail address, supra note 57. The subgroups held by the MDAH include Case Files, 1798-1817 (series 531); Chancery Court Minutes, 1805-1816 (series 529); Chancery Court Rule Docket, 1809-1815 (series 528); and Superior Court of Law and Equity Minute Books, 1810-1815 (series 530).

87. See <http://www.archives.gov/facilities/ga/atlanta.html> for NARA at East Point. The files are under "U.S. Territorial Court" within the subgroup "U.S. District and Other Courts in Alabama."

88. One exception is William Baskerville Hamilton's edition of the case notes of Thomas Rodney (territorial judge, western counties, 1803-1811), containing a number of references to Harry Toulmin and the Washington district. See William Baskerville Hamilton, *Anglo-American Law on the Frontier: Thomas Rodney and His Territorial Cases* (Duke University Press, 1953).

89. For secondary sources of Alabama territorial and constitutional history, see supra note 1.

90. McMillan, supra note 1, at 12-13.

91. Ibid. at 16-17.

92. Northwest Ordinance population requirements were 60,000; see Northwest Ordinance supra note 2, art. 5 at 53. Lands from the Creek cession became available and were first auctioned on August 4, 1817; see Rogers et al., supra note 1, at 62. Indian holdings that remained until the 1830s included the Upper Creek and Cherokee Indians in the eastern territory, and a portion of Chickasaw and Choctaw lands in the northwest and southwest portions of the territory; see Abernethy, supra note 1, at 64-71.

93. Rogers et al., supra note 1, at 54-55. In the decade between 1810 and 1820, Alabama's population increased more than 1000 percent to approximately 127,000, with the majority of the increase between 1815 and 1820. For the land rush of 1817-1818 and cotton profits, see Abernethy, supra note 1, at 66-71.

94. See Rogers et al., supra note 1, at 62; and McMillan, supra note 1, at 21-23.

95. See McMillan, supra note 1, at 19-20; Rogers et al., supra note 1, at 63; Brantley, supra note 1, at n 2; and 6 *Territorial Papers* 358-359. Either division would have created strong regional tensions. Indeed, the creation of the Alabama

Territory initiated a north-south sectional rivalry for political control between the Tennessee Valley region and the Tombigbee Valley-south Alabama region that plagued the territory and state throughout much of its history.

96. See 18 *Territorial Papers* 36-39.

97. Ibid. According to Carter there are no extant copies of the bill to admit the whole territory.

98. Ibid.

99. See Alabama Territorial Act, supra note 46, at 3 *Stat.* 371-373; 30 *Annals of Congress* 1310-1311 (1817). For an April 20, 1818 amendment to the March 3 act concerning the judiciary, see An Act to Alter and Amend an Act, Approved the Third Day of March, One Thousand Eight Hundred and Seventeen, Entitled "An Act to Establish a Separate Territorial Government for the Eastern Part of the Mississippi Territory," 3 *Stat.* 468 (1818).

100. See Mississippi Territorial Act, supra note 7, at 3 *Stat.* 348-349; and Mississippi Enabling Act, supra note 45, at 472-473.

101. See sections three and five of the Alabama Territorial Act, supra note 46, at 3 *Stat.* 371-373. Also, see supra note 85. It is significant to note, however, that section five of the act, which rendered the provisions of the act null and void if Mississippi's convention failed to form a constitution and state government, allowed the judicial provisions in section three to remain in force from the date of the passage of the act. This created both structurally and practically two equivalent appellate courts within the Mississippi Territory from March through December 1817. A practical application of this court system is seen within the "Records of District Courts of the United States," Record Group 21 at the National Archives and Records Administration's East Point, Georgia, repository. See supra note 87.

102. Alabama Territorial Act, supra note 46, sec. 1, at 3 *Stat.* 372. For Pinckney's Treaty, see Treaty of Friendship, Limits, and Navigation, supra note 17.

103. See Memorial of the Convention of the People of the State of Alabama assembled to Form a Constitution and State Government, Praying that a Part of West Florida May be Annexed to Said State (Washington, DC: Gales and Seaton, 1821). This memorial is also reproduced in 18 *Territorial Papers* 664-665.

104. See An Act to Authorize the President of the United States to Take Possession of East and West Florida, and Establish a Temporary Government Therein, 3 *Stat.* 523-524 (1819); and An Act for Carrying into Execution the Treaty Between the United States and Spain, Concluded at Washington on the Twenty-Second Day of February, One Thousand Eight Hundred and Nineteen, 3 *Stat.* 637-639 (1821).

105. For a broad look at Alabama's brief territorial status, see McMillan, supra note 1, at 23-29; and Abernethy, supra note 1, at 52-54.

106. Alabama Territorial Act, supra note 46, at 3 *Stat.* 371-373; generally see Northwest Ordinance, supra note 2.

107. See Mississippi Territorial Act, supra note 7, at 1 *Stat.* 549-550; and the Northwest Ordinance, supra note 2, at 1 *Stat.* 51-53.

108. See Mississippi Territorial Act, supra note 7, at 1 *Stat.* 549-550; and the Northwest Ordinance, supra note 2, at 1 *Stat.* 51-53. Also, for a good discussion of executive function and powers see McMillan, supra note 1, at 6-8. Secretary of the Territory Henry Hitchcock, who would later serve as Attorney General for the State

of Alabama and who authored the first book both written and published in the state, titled *The Alabama Justice of the Peace, Containing All the Duties, Powers and Authorities of that Office, as Regulated by the Laws Now in Force in this State* (Cahawba, AL: William B. Allen, 1822), served as acting governor of the territory during Bibb's absence from St. Stephens during the summer of 1818. See Alabama Department of Archives and History, Correspondence of Henry Hitchcock, 1818-1819. Hitchcock's *Justice* offers, among other things, the sources of common law as they appeared in Alabama law during this period. Hitchcock's sources for the Common Law included William Blackstone's *Commentaries on the Laws of England* (Chicago: University of Chicago Press, 1979) (1765), Mathew Hale's *The History of the Common Law of England* (E. and R. Nutt, and R. Gosling, 1739), and Richard Burn's *The Justice of the Peace, and Parish Officer,* in four volumes (London: A. Strahan, 1797).

109. McMillan, supra note 1, at 22-23.

110. Alabama Territorial Act, supra note 46, at 3 *Stat.* 372; and for the capital at St. Stephens, see Brantley, supra note 1, at 1-42.

111. 18 *Territorial Papers.*

112. Records of the States of the United States, Ala. E, reel 1, 1818-1863.

113. For a good secondary treatment of the territorial legislature, see McMillan, supra note 1, at 24-26. Toulmin was Alabama's first digester of statutes, see Toulmin's *1823 Digest,* supra note 8. For the Northwest Ordinance and the population requirements therein, see Northwest Ordinance, supra note 2, at 1 *Stat.* 50-53.

114. *Journal of the Territorial House of Representatives, of the Alabama Territory, at the Second Session of the General Assembly in the Forty-Third year of American Independence* (St. Stephens: Thomas Eastin, 1818) 14. By the second session, elected representatives began to take seats in the House of Representatives. The federal property-owning requirement for holding office would be eliminated during the creation of Alabama's state constitution. For the territorial property requirement, see An Act Concerning the Territory of Alabama, at 3 *Stat.* 417-418 (1818).

115. McMillan, supra note 1, at 25.

116. Ibid. at 26-27.

117. *Journal of the Territorial House of Representatives,* supra note 114, at 44.

118. See the Alabama Department of Archives and History's Alabama Territorial materials in general and for the controversy between Alabama and Mississippi, see Collection of Records Concerning the Financial Controversy between Mississippi and Alabama Territories and States, 1816-1830, Alabama Department of Archives and History.

119. See Alabama Territorial Act, supra note 46, at 3 *Stat.* 373. The dispute originated with disagreements over the boundaries of certain counties and the methods that were used to survey the public lands.

120. See ibid. at 3 *Stat.* 372.

121. See 18 *Territorial Papers.*

122. See Records of District Courts of the United States, supra note 87.

123. See *Reports of Cases Argued and Determined in the Supreme Court of Alabama* (Henry Minor), vol. 1 (New York: Collins and Hannay, 1829); and *Reports of*

Cases Argued and Determined in the Supreme Court of Alabama (Tuscaloosa, AL: George N. Stewart, 1830).

124. See Toulmin's *1823 Digest*, supra note 8.

125. See Indian Treaties at 7 *Stat.;* and 2 *American State Papers: Indian Affairs,* supra note 24. All of the four major Alabama tribes made significant land cessions prior to territorial status and would cede their remaining lands shortly after statehood. Particularly relevant to issues concerning lands is the act that regulated the survey and sale of public lands; see An Act Respecting the Surveying and Sale of Public Lands in the Alabama Territory, at 3 *Stat.* 466-467 (1818).

126. *Journal of the Territorial House of Representatives,* supra note 114, at 44.

127. McMillan, supra note 1, at 26-27.

128. Ibid., and 33 *Annals of Congress* 66.

129. 33 *Annals of Congress* 343.

130. See Alabama Enabling Act, supra note 46, at 3 *Stat.* 489-492.

131. See ibid. at 490; 18 *Territorial Papers* 192-195, 235; and McMillan, supra note 1, at 27.

132. Alabama Enabling Act, supra note 46, at 3 *Stat.* 491.

133. The Constitution of the State of Alabama, adopted August 2nd, 1819. Also, see Toulmin's *Digest* on the constitution and the judicial article; Toulmin's *1823 Digest,* supra note 8, at 914-934.

134. Alabama Enabling Act, supra note 46, sec. 4 at 3 *Stat.* 490-491. Twenty-two counties were allowed forty-four representatives, with Madison receiving the majority of eight representatives.

135. Ibid. at 491.

136. See McMillan, supra note 1, at 31.

137. Ibid. at 33.

138. Malcolm Cook McMillan, "The Alabama Constitution of 1819: A Study of Constitution-Making on the Frontier," 3 *Alabama Review* 266 (1950).

139. An important and useful document is the *Journal of the Convention of the Alabama Territory Begun July 5, 1819* (Huntsville, AL: John Boardman, 1819). The *Journal of the Convention* is a record of the business of the convention from its beginning on July 5 through its adjournment on August 2, 1819. It covers the votes, attendance, debates, motions, resolutions, and amendments to the final version of the Alabama Constitution of 1819.

140. Ala. Const. of 1819, supra, note 133.

141. See Abernethy, supra note 1, at 54. Abernethy argues that the Alabama Constitution was largely modeled after the Mississippi document; however, most of the southern constitutions contained similar language.

142. Ibid. at 54-57; and McMillan, supra note 1, at 34-39.

143. See Ala. Const. of 1819, supra note 133, schedule, sect. 7.

144. McMillan, supra note 1, at 35; Abernethy, supra note 1, at 54-55.

145. McMillan, supra note 1, at 37.

146. Ibid. at 40-41; Ala. Const. of 1819, supra note 133, art. V; and infra note 168.

147. The language concerning slaves in Alabama's constitution directed owners to treat slaves with humanity and provide the necessary food and clothing. It re-

quired owners to abstain from injuring or neglecting slaves, and extended to slaves the right of trial by an impartial jury. Any person who maliciously killed or dismembered a slave was subject to the same punishment as if the crime had been committed on a free white person according to the language in section 3. See Ala. Const. of 1819, supra note 133. See also Slaves, secs. 1-3, in Toulmin's *1823 Digest* 931.

148. McMillan, supra note 1, at 45-46. Also, for early Jacksonian influence, see Lawrence F. Kohl's, *Politics of Individualism: Parties and the American Character in the Jacksonian Era* (New York: Oxford University Press, 1989).

149. See Resolution Declaring the Admission of the State of Alabama into the Union, 3 *Stat.* 608 (1819) [hereinafter Alabama Admission Resolution]; for Ala. Const. of 1819, Ordinance, see Toulmin's *1823 Digest* 934.

150. 18 *Territorial Papers* 753. According to Carter, the covering correspondence is missing, so there is no record of when the documents were received by the President.

151. Ibid. at 754.

152. Alabama Admission Resolution, supra note 149, at 3 *Stat.* 608.

153. 18 *Territorial Papers* 755.

154. Generally see Abernethy, supra note 1, at 67, 72-76, 80-90, 95-98; and Rogers et al., supra note 1, at 67-68, 93-112.

155. Abernethy, supra note 1, at 103-145, 172-173; Rogers et al., supra note 1, at 67-87. Some of Alabama's earliest public conflicts were caused by resentment of the "Georgia" faction, a powerful coalition of planter-politicians loyal to Georgia's William H. Crawford. These leaders included Alabama's first two governors, William W. Bibb and Thomas Bibb, former Georgia Senator Charles Tait, who was Alabama's first federal judge, and John W. Walker, president of the Alabama constitutional convention and one of Alabama's first senators.

156. Abernethy, supra note 1, at 145-151; Rogers et al., supra note 1, at 85-92, 136-138.

157. For the style of such documents, see *Journal of the Senate at the First Session of the First General Assembly of the State of Alabama, Begun and Held in the Town of Huntsville, on the Fourth Monday in October, in the Year of Our Lord One Thousand Eight Hundred and Nineteen: And Forty Fourth Year of American Independence* (Cahawba, AL: Cahawba Press-Office, 1820). Generally, the Alabama State Department of Archives and History maintains gubernatorial, legislative, and judicial records. Contact the ADAH at <http://www.archives.state.al.us>.

158. See, for instance, *Acts of the General Assembly of the State of Alabama, Passed at Its First Session* (Hunstville, AL: John Boardman, 1820).

159. Toulmin's *1823 Digest,* supra note 8.

160. For Toulmin's explanation of his methods, see quoted passage in Brantley, supra note 1, at 118-119.

161. Ibid. at 100 (citing to text and to note 2). The legislature had attempted to assign the task of digesting statutes to the Supreme Court and Attorney General; see infra.

162. After Toulmin's work, Alabama law was digested at ten-year intervals. See *A Digest of the Laws of the State of Alabama: Containing all the Statutes of a Public and General Nature, in Force at the Close of the Session of the General Assembly, in*

January 1833 (John G. Aiken, comp.; Philadelphia, PA: Alexander Towar, 1833); and *A Digest of the Laws of the State of Alabama: Containing all the Statutes of a Public and General Nature, in Force at the Close of the Session of the General Assembly, in February 1843* (C.C. Clay, comp.; Tuscaloosa, AL: Marmaduke J. Slade, 1843) [Hereinafter Clay's *Digest*]. The state's first true code was published in 1852; see *The Code of Alabama* (John J. Ormond, Arthur P. Bagby, George Goldthwaite, comps., Henry C. Semple, ed.; Montgomery, AL: Brittan and De Wolf, 1852).

163. Brantley, supra note 1, at 77-79. The digest was to have been compiled by the judges and the Attorney General.

164. Ibid., at 100-101. The opinions were not available in printed form until the publication of Henry Minor's reports in 1829. These reports are notable for their brevity; apparently Minor was forced to work with faulty notes.

165. Ala. Const. of 1819, art. V, sec. 3, in Toulmin's *1823 Digest* 925.

166. See McMillan supra note 1, at 48 note 12; and William H. Brantley, "Law and Courts in Pioneer Alabama," 6 *Alabama Lawyer* 393-395 (1945).

167. McMillan supra note 1, at 47-48, and Abernethy supra note 1, at 137, 139. This "trial" was orchestrated by the prominent attorney William Kelly, who had represented many debtors during a series of usury trials that followed the Panic of 1819.

168. Ala. Const. of 1819, amend. I, in Clay's *Digest* xliii-xliv. The amendment also clarified the procedure for removal of judges for offenses not ordinarily subject to impeachment.

169. Clay's *Digest* 286, sec. 8.

170. Stewart produced three volumes of reports by himself and five in collaboration with his successor, Benjamin F. Porter.

171. In the meantime, Congress had created a federal district court system for Alabama. See An Act to Establish a District Court in the State of Alabama, 3 *Stat.* 564 (1820). For the subsequent legislation pertaining to the Alabama federal courts, see Act of November 27, 1820, 3 *Stat.* 610; Act of April 17, 1822, 3 *Stat.* 662; Act of March 10, 1824, 4 *Stat.* 9-10, dividing Alabama into Northern and Southern districts; and Act of May 22, 1826, 4 *Stat.* 192.

Chapter 2

Alaska Prestatehood
Legal Research Resources

Jessica Van Buren

A BRIEF HISTORY

During the ninety-two years between its purchase from Russia and statehood, Alaska suffered from congressional neglect. This was manifested in myriad ways: Alaska had no court of its own, its statutes were borrowed from Oregon, its legislature's acts were subject to congressional veto, its governors were appointed by the president, and its citizens could not vote in federal elections. The memory of this ill treatment influenced the language of Alaska's constitution,[1] and evidence of Alaska's strong independence is reflected in the decisions of its courts.[2]

When Alaska was bought from Russia in 1867,[3] the purchase was viewed with scorn by many. The press called the new acquisition "Seward's Folly," "Seward's Icebox," "Uncle Sam's White Elephant," "Icebergia," and "Walrussia," among other derisive names. Some members of Congress were also skeptical. In a congressional debate about the purchase, Representative John Peters called Alaska "intrinsically and virtually valueless,"[4] while others voiced concerns that Alaska would be nothing but a financial burden to the United States. Representative Benjamin Loan stated, "this inhospitable and barren waste would never add one dollar to the wealth of our country or furnish any homes to our people"[5] and went on to add, "To suppose that any one would willingly leave the mild climate and fruitful soil of the United States . . . to seek a home . . . in the regions of perpetual snow, is simply to suppose such person to be insane."[6] Given this congressional attitude it is small wonder that there was little inclination to pay much attention to the new purchase.

Alaska was initially designated as a military and customs district under the jurisdiction of the War Department.[7] For the first seventeen years after the purchase, the U.S. Army, U.S. Navy, and the Revenue Cutter Service were the governmental agencies responsible for administering law and justice. The only civil officers were the collector of customs and his deputies. There were no courts, and very few laws applied. Military courts were expected to handle minor offenses; those charged with more serious offenses were taken to California, Oregon, or the territory of Washington to be tried in U.S. District Courts there.

Miners developed their own system of laws, having understood an 1872 mining law[8] to authorize them to make rules and regulations for their own government, organize prosecuting bodies, and settle controversies.[9] The miners' system of justice was swift and inexpensive.[10] Punishment fell into one of three categories: hanging for murder, banishment for assault and stealing, and fines for everything else.[11]

The District Organic Act of 1884[12] provided a partial government for Alaska, designating Alaska a "district"—rather than a "territory"—with only civil and judicial government. The act created a temporary seat of government at Sitka as well as provided for a governor, a district court, a clerk of court, four U.S. commissioners, a U.S. marshal, and four deputies. The act also provided that the laws of Oregon would be the laws for Alaska.[13] Oregon's laws were selected because it was the closest state to Alaska at the time, since Washington was still a territory in 1884.

This new legislation was less than ideal on several counts. The act specifically stated that there would be no legislature, nor would Alaskans be permitted to send a delegate to Congress.[14] This was eventually remedied with the 1906 passage of the Alaska Delegate Act,[15] which allowed Alaskans to elect their first (voteless) representative to Congress, and the passage in 1912 of the Territorial Organic Act,[16] which created a territorial legislature.[17]

As described by former Territorial Governor Ernest Gruening, uncertainty reigned in the newly created judicial system:

> Congress had so confused its [judicial district's] mandate that no judge could be certain what the law was, and the marshal and his deputies often lacked the wherewithal to enforce a court order or sentence when there was one.[18]

There was also some question about the legality of juries in Alaska:

> Actually juries were not legal in Alaska and the lawyers knew it. . . . The Oregon code required that to be a member of grand or petit jury in a civil or criminal case one had to be a taxpayer, and Congress had not seen fit to levy any taxes in Alaska.[19]

U.S. commissioners were given powers equivalent to justices of the peace in Oregon, which included probate, misdemeanors, felony arraignments, civil jurisdiction under $1,000, coroner duties, vital statistics, sanity hearings, adoptions, elections, recorder, marriages, and hunting and fishing licenses. The commissioners did not receive a salary; they were expected to subsist on any commissions they collected.[20]

Alaska's first appointed judge was Ward McAllister, and he had his work cut out for him. The newly formed government had few facilities and no jail. Judge McAllister tried to persuade the Navy to continue to keep criminal offenders in the "brig," but Naval Commander Nichols declined to do so.[21] McAllister lasted less than a year in Alaska. Local missionary Reverend Sheldon Jackson was outraged at several of McAllister's rulings and embarked on a letter-writing campaign to President Grover Cleveland, Cleveland's brother, and others, accusing McAllister of a wide range of wrong-doings and demanding his removal.[22] Jackson's efforts succeeded, and President Cleveland fired McAllister.

On June 6, 1900, Congress passed a law that moved the seat of government to Juneau and added two more judicial districts to Alaska, bringing the total to three.[23] The first district seat was Juneau, the second district seat was St. Michael's (later Nome), and the third district seat was Eagle City (later Fairbanks).

Alaska's most famous territorial judge was James Wickersham, appointed to the newly created third judicial district in 1900. Upon his arrival in the interior city of Eagle he had to build a house for himself and his family and supervise the construction of the courthouse and jail.[24] His jurisdiction covered 300,000 square miles, extending from the Arctic Ocean to Mt. McKinley, from the Bering Sea to the Canadian border.[25] His vast jurisdiction demanded that he travel to dispense justice, and during the seven years he was on the bench he did—by snowshoe, dog team, and ship, often under extremely inhospitable circumstances.[26]

The Oregon codes were replaced with laws drafted specifically for Alaska with the congressional passage of the Alaska Penal Code[27] in 1899, and the Alaska Civil Code[28] in 1900. In 1912 Congress passed the Territorial Organic Act,[29] which afforded territorial status to Alaska and granted residents a form of self-government. The act created a territorial legislature but provided that all acts of the legislature were subject to congressional approval.[30] The first act of the new territorial legislature was the unanimous passage of a law giving women the right to vote.[31] This was seven years before the Nineteenth Amendment gave women the right to vote nationwide.

Alaskans had been agitating for statehood as early as 1916, when Alaska's Congressional Delegate James Wickersham—the former federal judge—submitted the first statehood bill to Congress,[32] but efforts stalled until 1934 Congressional Delegate Anthony J. Dimond introduced another statehood bill.[33] Efforts stalled again until the statehood movement gained momentum in the 1940s and 1950s, as more people moved to Alaska. The new residents discovered that, even though they were U.S. citizens and paid federal taxes, they were not allowed to vote in presidential elections, they were required to go through U.S. Customs when traveling to the lower forty-eight states, and their congressional delegate had no vote in the House of Representatives.[34]

Alaskans held a constitutional convention in Fairbanks during the winter of 1955-1956, in the hopes that a well-written constitution would promote the call for statehood.[35] One commentator noted:

> The Alaska Constitution is the product of a rugged, frontier community; yet its content fits a modern day, complex, industrial society. It combines the experience of other states with contemporary ideas on constitution-making, tradition with innovation, and the classical with the modern. . . . Perhaps the Alaska Constitution has most nearly approximated the ideal.[36]

The efforts of the constitutional convention delegates succeeded, and after years of struggle Alaska attained statehood on January 3, 1959.[37]

CREATION OF A NEW JUDICIARY

Congress gave the new state court system three years to transition from the territorial federal judicial system.[38] When the Ninth Circuit Court of Appeals decided in June 1959 in *Parker v. McCarrey*[39] that it did not have jurisdiction to hear appeals from territorial courts on judgments rendered after January 3, 1959, Alaska's first Chief Justice Buell Nesbett was forced to establish the Alaska court system as quickly as possible, and he managed to do so in about six months. His impressive accomplishments include securing space for the courts throughout the state, assembling a staff, purchasing furniture and supplies needed statewide, creating law libraries, drafting court rules, and devising a court reporting system.[40]

The first three supreme court justices and eight superior court judges of the new state were appointed in late 1959 and assumed their seats on the bench on February 20, 1960, when President Eisenhower signed the executive order [41] officially ending the jurisdiction of the territorial federal court.

CONCLUSION

Alaska Constitutional Convention Delegate Mildred R. Hermann noted in an article published shortly after Alaska achieved statehood:

> The fact that Alaska has been able to build a judiciary widely heralded as the best among the fifty states perhaps stems from its chaotic youth. With no territorial judiciary it had nothing to undo, and there was no necessity to compromise. It could build its judiciary without reconciling practices of an already existing judiciary.[42]

Hermann's optimism about the judiciary suggests that some good has come out of the years of congressional neglect.

The delegates to the Alaska Constitutional Convention knew that the system they had labored under as a territory did not work, and they were driven to create a document that would meet the unique needs of Alaska's citizens. The document they produced has been noted for its flexibility and orientation toward the future.[43] Alaska's courts have been noted for their support of citizens' rights, especially freedom of expression and the right of privacy.[44] In 1868 Representative Benjamin Loan may have thought the people who "seek a home . . . in the regions of perpetual snow" were insane,[45] but those "insane" Alaskans created a constitution and judicial system praised throughout the country.

PRIMARY SOURCES OF LAW

Statutory Law and Finding Aids

Alaska Civil Code. Ch. 786, 31 *Stat.* 321 at 333 (June 6, 1900).
Code of civil procedure drafted by Congress specifically for Alaska.

Alaska Compiled Laws Annotated, cumulative supplement [ACLA] (1958).

Alaska Penal Code. Ch. 429, 30 *Stat.* 1253 (March 3, 1899).
Criminal code drafted by Congress specifically for Alaska.

Alaska Statehood Act. Public Law 85-508, 72 *Stat.* 339 (July 7, 1958).

Frederick F. Barker. *Compilation of the acts of Congress and treaties relating to Alaska from March 30, 1867, to March 3, 1905, with indices and references to decisions of the Supreme Court and opinions of the Attorney-General* [Charlton Code]. Washington, DC: GPO, 1906.

Charles T. Boone. *Alaska Codes, Political, Civil and Civil Procedure: Approved June 6, 1900* [Boone Code]. San Francisco: Bancroft-Whitney Co., 1900.

Thomas H. Carter. *The Laws of Alaska; embracing the Penal code, the Code of criminal procedure, the Political code, the Code of civil procedure, and the Civil code, with the treaty of cession, and all acts and parts of acts relating to the district, annotated with references to decisions by the courts of the United States and the Supreme court of Oregon* [Carter Code]. Chicago: Callaghan, 1900.

Compilation of the civil and criminal codes drafted by Congress specifically for Alaska.

Compiled Laws of Alaska, 1933: Containing the general laws of the territory of Alaska, annotated with decisions of the courts of the territory of Alaska and the United States [CLA]. Juneau: Daily Alaska Empire, 1933.

Contains laws in force on December 21, 1933, annotated with decisions of the courts of the territory of Alaska and the United States.

Compiled Laws of Alaska, 1949: Containing the general laws of the Territory of Alaska [ACLA]. San Francisco: Bancroft-Whitney Co., 1949.

Compiled Laws of the Territory of Alaska, 1913: Compiled, codified, arranged, and annotated, and published under authority of the Act of Congress of August 24, 1912. Washington, DC: GPO, 1913.

District Organic Act. Ch. 53, 23 *Stat.* 24 (May 17, 1884), also referred to as the First Organic Act, and An Act Providing a Civil Government for Alaska.

Contains the general laws that governed the district of Alaska.

Territorial Organic Act. Ch. 387, 37 *Stat.* 512 (August 24, 1912), also referred to as the Second Organic Act.

Legislative History and Intent

Each legislature convenes for two sessions, January-May, in successive years. Session laws are produced annually for each legislative session.

Bills

National Archives and Records Service. *Records of the Alaskan Territorial Legislature, 1913-1953.*

Bills 1941-1953 are available at Alaska State Archives, 907-465-2270.

Session Laws

Session Laws, Resolutions and Memorials. Juneau: Alaska Territorial Legislature, Daily Empire Print, 1913-1957.

1st through 23rd territorial legislatures. Biennial.

Finding Tools

Summary of Alaska legislation. Juneau: Alaska Legislative Council, 1955- .

Provides chapter summary and list of Alaska Statutes sections affected.

House and Senate Journals

House and Senate journals provide daily legislative records of floor actions for the House and Senate. The journals sometimes include letters of intent, governor's transmittal letters, governor's return letters, and governor's veto messages. Journal supplements may also include sectional analyses and commentary on bills, long committee reports, and fiscal notes.

The Journal of the House of Representatives of the . . . Legislative Assembly of the Territory of Alaska. Juneau: Alaska Daily Empire Press, 1913-1957.

Senate Journal of the . . . Legislature. Juneau: Alaska Legislature, 1913-1957.

LLIB Collection

The Legislative Reference Library's LLIB collection includes materials written by the legislature, such as reports, memoranda, and transcripts contracted by the legislature or requested by the legislature from a state agency. Prestatehood files are available 1953-1959. Contact them at 907-465-3808.

Office of the Governor Files

The governor's legislative or subject files (1909-1958) are available from the Alaska State Archives, 907-465-2270.

Executive Branch Files

Some state agencies keep legislative or subject files about bills that may affect them. These files may include the agency's testimony or position papers, and letters from citizens, groups, and federal agencies. Some files are available from the early 1900s. Contact the Alaska State Archives, 907-465-2270.

Legislators' Files

Some legislators have donated their legislative files to the Alaska State Archives, the University of Alaska–Anchorage, and the University of Alaska–Fairbanks. The Alaska State Archives accepts only those materials related to a legislator's public office; the universities accept all categories of materials. Contact the Alaska State Archives, 907-465-2270; the University of Alaska–Anchorage, 907-786-1849; and the University of Alaska–Fairbanks, 907-474-7261.

Court Reports and Finding Aids

Alaska federal reports; cases argued and determined in the United States Circuit and District courts of California and Oregon, District courts of California and Oregon, District courts of Washington, District courts of Alaska, Circuit courts of appeals, as well as decisions of the Supreme court of the United States in cases arising in Alaska. St. Paul, MN: West Publishing Co., 1869-1937.

Alaska Reports. St. Paul, MN: West Publishing Co., 1903-1959.

Digests

Alaska Digest, 1869 to Date; covering all cases decided in the Alaska District courts, the District courts of Washington as well as decisions of the

United States Circuit and District courts in California and Oregon. St. Paul, MN: West Publishing Co., 1938.

Updated with supplement volumes and pocket parts. Superseded by 1988 edition.

West's Alaska Digest. 2nd ed. St. Paul, MN: West Publishing Co., 1988.

Includes all Alaska cases reported since 1869.

Citators

Shepard's Alaska Citations. 4th ed. Colorado Springs, CO: Shepard's, 1997.

Includes citations for Alaskan prestatehood materials, including cases in Alaska Reports and Alaska Federal Reports, prestatehood session laws, and prestatehood statutes.

State Constitution

Alaska Constitutional Convention, November 8, 1955 to February 5, 1956: Guide to the files. Juneau: Legislative Reference Library, 1981.

Alaska Constitutional Convention, part 7, index: Supplementing parts 1-6 of the Minutes of the proceedings of the Alaska Constitutional Convention, 1955-56, published in 1965. Juneau: Legislative Affairs Agency, 1978.

Alaska constitutional convention: Report of Committee on Judiciary Branch (1955).

Constitution of the State of Alaska (1959).

The constitution became operative with the Formal Proclamation of Statehood, January 3, 1959. An annotated constitution is set forth in volume one of the Alaska Statutes. The constitution is also available on Alaska Legislature's Web site at <http://www.legis.state.ak.us>.

Constitutional studies, prepared on behalf of the Alaska Statehood Committee for the Alaska Constitutional Convention convened November 8, 1955. Juneau (?): Public Information Service, 1955.

Reports prepared on behalf of the Alaska Statehood Committee by the Public Administration Service for use by the Alaska Constitutional Convention.

Handbook for delegates to the Alaska Constitutional Convention, convened at College, Alaska, November 8, 1955. College: Alaska Statehood Committee, 1955.

Index and subject index to the proceedings of the Alaska Constitutional Convention on article VIII, Natural Resources, and related provisions of the constitution of the state of Alaska. Juneau: Legal Services Division, Legislative Affairs Agency, 1989.

Minutes of the daily proceedings, Alaska Constitutional Convention. Juneau: Alaska Legislative Council, 1965.

Convention debate and history of proposed provisions, organized by day. Also available at the Department of Law Web site at <http://www.law.state.ak.us/doclibrary/cc_minutes.html>.

Papers of the Alaska Constitutional Convention, 1955-1956.

Includes source reports relied upon by delegates, committee reports that include draft constitutional provisions, and committee commentary. Papers are indexed by committee and source.

Subject index and index to the proceedings of the Alaska Constitutional Convention on article VIII, natural resources, and related provisions of the Constitution of the State of Alaska (November 8, 1955-February 6, 1956). Juneau: Legal Services Division, Legislative Affairs Agency, 1990.

Attorney General Opinions

Report of the Attorney General, Territory of Alaska. Juneau: Alaska Attorney General's Office, 1917-1955.

The biennial report includes selected attorney general opinions.

ARCHIVAL COLLECTIONS

Alaska State Archives
141 Willoughby Avenue
Juneau, AK 99801-1720
907-465-2270
Fax: 907-465-2465

Alaska State Court Law Library
303 K Street
Anchorage, AK 99501
907-264-0585
Fax: 907-264-0733

Legislative Reference Library
907-465-3808
Fax: 907-465-4844

National Archives—Anchorage
654 W. 3rd Avenue
Anchorage, AK 99501
907-271-2441
Fax: 907-271-2442

University of Alaska–Anchorage—Archives
3211 Providence Drive
Anchorage, AK 99508
907-786-1849

University of Alaska–Fairbanks—Archives
Alaska and Polar Regions Department
Elmer E. Rasmuson Library
University of Alaska Fairbanks
P.O. Box 756808
Fairbanks, AK 99775-6808
907-474-7261

SECONDARY SOURCES

Books, Manuscripts, Papers, Speeches, and Theses

Alaska Bar Association and Sketch of Judiciary. San Francisco: Sanborn, Vail and Co., 1901.

Sections include *Government in Alaska,* which sets forth a history of Alaska from the time of its purchase; *The District Court of the United States in and for the District of Alaska,* which includes an address delivered by Judge Arthur K. Delaney to the Alaska Bar upon his retirement from the bench September 1, 1897; *Alaska Bar Association,* which provides the constitution and bylaws of the bar, and a roll of attorneys; and *In Memoriam,* a section of tributes to several deceased attorneys and judges.

Evangeline Atwood. *Frontier Politics: Alaska's James Wickersham.* Portland, OR: Binford and Mort, 1979.

Biography of James Wickersham, who served as a U.S. district judge in Alaska for eight years and as Alaska's congressional delegate for fourteen years.

Gerald E. Bowkett. *Reaching for a Star: The Final Campaign for Alaska Statehood.* Fairbanks: Epicenter Press, 1989

Examines the political struggle to acquire statehood for Alaska.

David S. Case. *Alaska Natives and American Laws.* Fairbanks: University of Alaska Press, 1984.

Chapter Eight, "Traditional Alaska Native Societies" by Anne D. Shinkwin, discusses the traditional law systems of five native groups before nonnative systems were imposed.

David S. Case and David A. Voluck. *Alaska Natives and American Laws.* 2nd ed. Fairbanks: University of Alaska Press, 2002.

Pamela Cravez. *Seizing the Frontier: Alaska's Territorial Lawyers.* Anchorage (?): Author, 1984.

Based largely on interviews with prestatehood bar members. Contents include "Gilt-Edged Legends: The Gold Rush Years"; "A Gentleman's Profession: Norman Banfield and the Juneau Elite"; "John Hellenthal: Breaking Out of the Fold"; "Tales of the Silver Fox" (Wendell Kay); "Getting Caught Up in the Alaskan Spirit: The United States Attorneys Office"; "Buell Nesbett: Finding a New Command in Anchorage"; "A Revolt in the Ranks: The Court/Bar Fight"; "Schaible, Taley, Delisio & Cook: Two Worlds of Practice in Fairbanks."

Victor Fischer. *Alaska's Constitutional Convention.* Fairbanks: University of Alaska Press, 1975.

A narrative account of the constitutional convention by one of the participants.

David C. Frederick. *Rugged Justice: The Ninth Circuit Court of Appeals and the American West, 1891-1941.* Berkeley: University of California Press, 1994.

Chapter Four, "Intrigue at Anvil Creek," discusses territorial Alaska and the impact gold mining had on the Ninth Circuit Court of Appeals in the early 1900s.

Ernest Gruening. *The Battle for Alaska Statehood.* College: University of Alaska Press, 1967.

An account of Alaska's struggle for statehood by Ernest Gruening, territorial governor 1939-1953 and U.S. Senator 1958-1968.

Ernest Gruening. "Let Us End American Colonialism: Alaska, the United States Colony." Keynote Address, Alaska Constitutional Convention (1955), also published in 103 *Cong. Rec.* 470-474 (1957).

Gruening's impassioned speech delivered at the opening of the Alaska Constitutional Convention decries the treatment of Alaska at the hands of the federal government.

Ernest Gruening. *The State of Alaska.* New York: Random House, 1968.

An excellent history by Gruening. The section titles indicate his strong views: *The Era of Total Neglect, The Era of Flagrant Neglect, The Era of Mild but Unenlightened Interest, The Era of Indifference and Unconcern, The Era of Growing Awareness.*

Gordon S. Harrison. *Alaska's Constitution: A Citizen's Guide.* 3rd ed. Juneau: Alaska Legislative Research Agency, 1992.

Examines origins and evolution of Alaska's constitution and is intended to be a primer for Alaska citizens. Examines the constitution section by section and includes references to supreme court interpretations.

Stephen Haycox. *The Law of the Land: A History of the Office of the Attorney General and the Department of Law in Alaska.* Juneau: Alaska Department of Law, 1998.

The first chapter, "Before Statehood: Law in the Territory of Alaska," provides an overview of prestatehood law. The chapters about prestatehood attorney generals also provide helpful insight into law practice during those years.

Stephen Haycox, Claus-M. Naske, and Pamela Cravez. *History of the Bench and Bar.* Anchorage: Alaska Bar Association, 1996.

A series of presentations to the Alaska Bar Association: "A Didactic Enterprise: Bringing Law to the State of Alaska," by Stephen Haycox; "The U.S. Commissioners in Alaska: Relentless Problems in the Federal Territorial Judicial System," by Claus-M. Naske; "The Legacy of Alaska's Lawyers: Practice on the Last Frontier," by Pamela Cravez.

Arthur E. Hippler and Stephen Conn. *Northern Eskimo Law Ways and Their Relationship to Contemporary Problems of "Bush Justice"; Some Preliminary Observations on Structure and Function* (ISEGR Occasional Papers, No. 10, July. Fairbanks: Institute of Social, Economic and Government Research, University of Alaska, 1973.

An examination of Eskimo conflict-resolution methods and how American conflict-resolution techniques differ from those methods.

Arthur E. Hippler and Stephen Conn. *Traditional Athabascan Law Ways and Their Relationship to Contemporary Problems of "Bush Justice"; Some Preliminary Observations on Structure and Function* (ISEGR Occasional Papers, No. 7, August. Fairbanks: Institute of Social, Economic and Government Research, University of Alaska, 1972.

An examination of the differences between the American legal system and traditional Athabascan law ways, and how those differences create conflicts for Athabascans.

William R. Hunt. *Distant Justice: Policing the Alaska Frontier.* Norman: University of Oklahoma Press, 1987.

The focus of this book is law enforcement in prestatehood Alaska, but there is also much relevant discussion of the prestatehood justice system.

K.S. (Kermit Syppli) Kynell. *A Different Frontier: Alaska Criminal Justice, 1935-1965.* Lanham, MD: University Press of America, 1991.

Traces the evolution of criminal justice in Alaska. Emphasis is on statistics about crimes themselves but includes useful narrative portions.

Gerald A. McBeath. *The Alaska State Constitution: A Reference Guide.* Westport, CT: Greenwood Press, 1997.

Provides the history and development of Alaska's constitution and commentary for each provision, including its origins and court interpretations.

Claus-M. Naske. *A History of Alaska Statehood.* Lanham, MD: University Press of America, 1985.

A thorough history of Alaska's efforts to obtain statehood.

Claus-M. Naske. *A History of the Alaska Federal District Court System, 1884-1959, and the Creation of the State Court System.* Anchorage: Alaska Court System, 1985.

Chapters include "The First Organic Act of 1884 Creates a Judicial System"; "The First U.S. District Court, Sitka"; "Judge James Wickersham"; "Judge Arthur H. Noyes and the Nome Scandals"; "The Case of Vuco Perovich"; "The Short and Unhappy Judgeship of Silas Hinkle Reid"; "Pelagic Sealing in the Bering Sea"; "Taking Care of Alaska's Insane"; "Insanity Is in the Eye of the Beholder"; "Judge Charles E. Bunnell"; "Moving the District Court from Valdez to Anchorage"; "The Floating Court"; "The Post World War II Period Strains Alaska's Judicial System"; and "The Creation of the Alaska State Court System."

Jeannette Paddock Nichols. *Alaska, a History of its Administration, Exploitation, and Industrial Development During its First Half Century Under the Rule of the United States.* Cleveland: The Arthur H. Clark Company, 1924.

An excellent history covering the time period from Alaska's purchase in 1867 through the creation of the territorial legislature in 1912.

Sister Mary Margaret (Carolyn O'Connell). "Alaska from District to Territory." MA thesis, University of Washington, 1935.

Thesis covers the time period from Alaska's purchase in 1867 through the passage of the 1912 Territorial Organic Act.

James Wickersham. *Old Yukon: Tales, Trails, and Trials.* Washington, DC: Washington Law Book Company, 1938.

Judge James Wickersham's memoir about his life as a territorial judge in Alaska.

Gerald O. Williams. "When the Navy Ruled Alaska" (1970-1979?) (unpublished manuscript, on file at the Alaska State Library).

Covers the time period when Alaska was governed by the military—1867-1884.

Articles

Russ Arnett. "Alaska's Floating Court Found Unusual Cases." *Alaska Bar Rag* 13 (Nov.-Dec. 1989): 11.

Arnett describes Alaska's "Floating Court" and discusses some of the cases it handled.

Russ Arnett. "Formation of the Alaska Court System." *Alaska Bar Rag* 2 (Aug. 1979): 5.

Discussion of the structure of Alaska's prestatehood judicial system and some behind-the-scenes stories of how Alaska's first state judges were selected.

Russ Arnett. "The Mudsill of the Judiciary." *Alaska Bar Rag* 20 (May-June 1996): 14.

Arnett reminisces about his experiences as a U.S. commissioner in territorial Alaska in the 1950s.

Russ Arnett. "Origins of the Alaska Bar Association." *Alaska Bar Rag* 18 (Mar.-Apr. 1994): 7.

Arnett remembers some of the lawyers involved in the creation of the Alaska Bar Association in 1955.

R.E. Baumgartner. "Organization and Administration of Justice in Alaska." *A.B.A.J.* 20 (1934): 23.

Petersburg attorney Baumgartner outlines the history and organization of Alaska's prestatehood judicial system, discusses the challenges presented to U.S. commissioners, and praises the high professional standards of territorial lawyers.

Frederic E. Brown. "The Sources of the Alaska and Oregon Codes, Part I." *UCLA-Alaska L. Rev.* 2 (1972): 15. "The Sources of the Alaska and Oregon Codes, Part II." *UCLA-Alaska L. Rev.* 2 (1973): 87.

An examination of the sources of Alaska's laws. Part I focuses on the New York and Oregon codes; Part II focuses on Alaska's code development.

Robert W. Campbell. "Brigandage by Judicial Process; An Incident in Alaskan Judicial History." *Ill. L.. Rev.* 17 (1923): 345.

A detailed examination of a 1900 dispute over mining claims in Nome, based on court records and opinions, statements from some of the participants, and observations of the author, who was himself a participant in the events that led to the removal of U.S. District Court Judge Arthur H. Noyes.

James H. Chenoweth. "The Last Voyage of the Floating Court." *Alaska Bar Rag* 22 (Jan.-Feb. 1998): 22. "The Last Voyage of the Floating Court: Stebbins to Nome." *Alaska Bar Rag* 22 (Mar.-Apr. 1998): 8. "Home from the Final Voyage of Alaska's Floating Court." *Alaska Bar Rag* 22 (May-June 1998): 8.

A three-part article excerpted from a book Chenoweth was writing about his career as a police officer and U.S. marshal in territorial Alaska. These articles center on his experiences on the last voyage of the floating court. The book, *Down Darkness Wide,* was apparently never published.

Pamela Cravez. "A Revolt in the Ranks: The Great Alaska Court-Bar Fight." *Alaska L. Rev.* 13 (1996): 1.

This article describes a fascinating episode in the history of the Alaska bench and bar, in which the Alaska Bar Association and the newly formed Alaska Supreme Court battled to determine whether the bar would be placed under the control of the judiciary.

P. Allan Dionisopoulos. "Indiana, 1851, Alaska, 1956: A Century of Difference in State Constitutions." *Ind. L. J.* 34 (1958): 34.

A comparison of the newly written Alaska Constitution and the Indiana Constitution, with many favorable comments about the Alaska Constitution.

H.S. Farris. "Alaska's Inferior Court." *Case & Com.* 22 (1915): 16.

Explanation of the duties of U.S. commissioners in territorial Alaska and a few anecdotes about nontraditional legal process in some remote parts of Alaska.

Stephen Haycox and Claus-M. Naske. "'A New Face': Implementing Law in the New State of Alaska, 1958-1960." *W. Legal Hist.* 11 (1998): 1.

Discusses the transition from the territorial to state judicial system, the cases that tested the new court, and the role of the Alaska Judicial Council and the Department of Law.

Mildred R. Hermann. "Building a State Judiciary." *Neb. L. Rev.* 39 (1960): 265.

Written by one of the delegates to the Alaska Constitutional Convention.

Arthur Hippler and Stephen Conn. "The Village Council and Its Offspring: A Reform for Bush Justice." *UCLA-Alaska L. Rev.* 5 (1975): 22.

Includes discussion of native law ways.

E. Adamson Hoebel. "Law-Ways of the Primitive Eskimos." *J. Am. Inst. Crim. L. & Criminology* 31 (1941): 663.

An examination of traditional native legal concepts.

Lewis Hopkins. "Alaska's Lawless Era." *L. Notes* 49 (May-July 1945): 27.

A description of Alaska's miners' meetings.

Raymond J. Kelly. "The Lore and Law of Alaska." *Mich. St. B. J.* 37 (May 1958): 8.

Kelly, a U.S. district court judge for the district of Alaska in Juneau, describes some of his experiences and debunks common myths about the territory. He also provides some explanation about the structure of the courts and the practice of law in Alaska.

William W. Morrow. "The Spoilers." *Cal. L. Rev.* 4 (1916): 89.

An address delivered to the Law Association of the School of Jurisprudence, at the University of California, November 19, 1915. Morrow's topic is a 1900 dispute over mining claims in Nome. The events were later fictionalized by Rex Beach in his novel *The Spoilers.*

C.D. Murane. "My Legal Experience in Alaska." *Case & Com.* 32 (1926): 39.

A former U.S. attorney in Valdez and U.S. district judge in Nome shares tales of his unique experiences, including his time presiding over a miners' court.

Claus-M. Naske. "Alaska's Floating Court." *W. Legal Hist.* 11 (1998): 163.

The origins and evolution of Alaska's "floating court," an innovation developed to cope with Alaska's vast judicial territories.

Claus-M. Naske. "The Shaky Beginnings of Alaska's Judicial System." *W. Legal Hist.* 1 (1988): 163.

The first courts and judges of Alaska, and the challenges they faced with limited resources and federal support.

Fred A. Seaton. "Alaska's Struggle for Statehood." *Neb. L. Rev.* 39 (1960): 253.

Seaton chronicles Alaska's efforts to achieve statehood.

NOTES

1. Gordon S. Harrison, *Alaska's Constitution: A Citizen's Guide,* 3rd Ed. 5 (Juneau: Alaska Legislative Research Agency, 1992).

2. Susan Orlansky and Jeffrey M. Feldman, "Justice Rabinowitz and Personal Freedom: Evolving a Constitutional Framework," 15 *Alaska L. Rev.* 1 (1998).

3. Treaty of Cession, 15 *Stat.* 539 (March 30, 1867).

4. *Cong. Globe*, 40th Cong., 2d Sess. 3668 (July 1, 1868).

5. *Cong. Globe*, 40th Cong., 2d Sess. 3808 (July 7, 1868).

6. Ibid.

7. Customs Act, ch. 273, 15 *Stat.* 240 (July 27, 1868).

8. Mining Resources Act, ch. 152, 17 *Stat.* 91 (May 10, 1872).

9. James Wickersham, "Judicial System and Courts of the Territory of Alaska," 1 *Alaska Digest* v, vii (1938); Jeannette Paddock Nichols, *Alaska, a History of its Administration, Exploitation, and Industrial Development During its First Half Century Under the Rule of the United States* 119-120 (Cleveland, OH: The Arthur H. Clark Company, 1924); K.S. Kynell, *A Different Frontier: Alaska Criminal Justice 1935-1965* 35-38 (Lanham, MD: University Press of America, 1991).

10. Nichols, supra note 9.

11. Ibid.

12. District Organic Act, ch. 53, 23 *Stat.* 24 (May 17, 1884).

13. Ibid. at §7.

14. Ibid. at §9.

15. Alaska Delegate Act, ch. 2083, 34 *Stat.* 169 (May 7, 1906).

16. Territorial Organic Act, ch. 387, 37 *Stat.* 512 (August 24, 1912).

17. Ibid. at §4.

18. Ernest Gruening, *The State of Alaska* 58 (New York: Random House, 1968).

19. Ibid. at 53, citing the testimony of Senator Carter in his arguments for civil and criminal codes specific to Alaska, 32 *Cong. Rec.* 1937-38 (1899).

20. Gerald E. Bowkett, *Reaching for a Star* 10-11 (Fairbanks, AK: Epicenter Press, 1989).

21. Gruening, supra note 18, at 43; Claus-M. Naske, "The Shaky Beginnings of Alaska's Judicial System," 1 *W. Legal Hist.* 163, 171-72 (1988).

22. Naske, supra note 21, at 174-181.

23. Alaska Government Act, ch. 786, 31 *Stat.* 321 (June 6, 1900).

24. William R. Hunt, *Distant Justice: Policing the Alaska Frontier* 97 (Norman: University of Oklahoma Press, 1987).

25. Evangeline Atwood, *Frontier Politics: Alaska's James Wickersham* 65 (Portland, OR: Binford and Mort, 1979).

26. Ibid. at 72-78.

27. Alaska Penal Code, ch. 429, 30 *Stat.* 1253 (March 3, 1899).

28. Alaska Civil Code, ch. 786, 31 *Stat.* 321 at 333 (June 6, 1900).

29. Territorial Organic Act, supra note 16.

30. Ibid. at §20.

31. Session Laws of Alaska, ch. 1 (1913).

32. H.R. 13978 (1916).

33. H.R. 3768 (1943).

34. Gerald E. Bowkett, supra note 20, at 9.

35. Gordon S. Harrison, *Alaska's Constitution: A Citizen's Guide,* 3rd Ed. (Juneau: Alaska Legislative Research Agency, 1992).

36. P. Allan Dionisopoulos, "Indiana, 1851, Alaska, 1956: A Century of Difference in Sate Constitutions," 34 *Ind. L. J.* 34 (1958).

37. Alaska Statehood Act, Pub. L. No. 85-508, 72 *Stat.* 339 (July 7, 1958).

38. Ibid. at §18.

39. *Parker v. McCarrey,* 268 F.2d 907 (9th Cir. 1959).

40. Remarks of E. Everett Harris at the memorial service for Buell Nesbett, October 28, 1993. Published in 884-890 *Alaska Rep.* XXXIV (1995).

41. Exec. Order No. 10,867, 3 C.F.R. 401 (1959-1963).

42. Mildred R. Hermann, "Building a State Judiciary," 39 *Neb. L. Rev.* 265 (1960).

43. Gordon S. Harrison, supra note 35.

44. See Susan Orlansky and Jeffrey M. Feldman, supra note 2, and Ronald L. Nelson, "Welcome to the 'Last Frontier,' Professor Gardner: Alaska's Independent Approach to State Constitutional Interpretation," 12 *Alaska L. Rev.* 1 (1995).

45. *Cong. Globe,* 40th Cong., 2d Sess. 3808 (July 7, 1868).

Chapter 3

Arizona Prestatehood Documents: Bibliography and Research Guide

Jacquelyn Gayle Kasper

Arizona is a young state . . . in a deeply wrinkled old land of intermi-
nable mountains, river valleys, and desert plains. The sight of running
water is rare.

Lawrence Clark Powell

This chapter intends to provide a research guide to documents key to the
history and development of territorial Arizona and its entry into statehood.
The time period covered is 1863 to 1912 when Arizona was its own territory, and the thirteen years preceding, 1850 to 1862, when Arizona was part
of the territory of New Mexico.

INTRODUCTION

Carved from a treaty and purchased land from Mexico, Arizona struggled to become a western territory and endured an even more arduous path
to gain admittance into the Union. Lawrence Clark Powell, eminent dean of
Southwest literature, characterized this period as the "long night of the territory."[1] Arizona was a politically beleaguered land, and the struggle for
statehood from 1891 to 1912 became the longest sustained admission fight
in U.S. history.

When Spaniards arrived in the middle 1500s, Arizona had been long possessed by the Anasazi, Hohokam, and Mogollon Indian cultures, the "ancient ones" of today's Southwest tribes. Colonized and settled by early
Spanish explorers and missionaries, the land came under the rule of Mexico
in its victory of independence from Spain in 1821. It became American soil
after the U.S.-Mexican War of 1846 with the Treaty of Guadalupe Hidalgo
(1848) and the Gadsden Purchase (1854).[2] In 1850, the U.S. government

created the great territory of New Mexico, encompassing what is now the states of Arizona and New Mexico.

Congressional bills, eighteen in all, to create a separate territory for Arizona were introduced as early as 1856. In numerous petitions and memorials, settlers "prayed" for the organization of a new territory and for its recognition on an equal footing with the other territories. Protesting that local needs were being ignored, and suffering from no representation, no vote, and no courts in the distant Santa Fe capital of New Mexico Territory, citizens held a convention in 1860 in presidio Tucson. A constitution was drafted, a delegate selected, and a memorial sent to Congress advocating territorial status—all of which Congress ignored. Not until 1863, in the middle of the Civil War, with Confederate troops marching into southwestern New Mexico (i.e., southern Arizona) and threatening federal access to valuable mineral resources, was the territory of Arizona established by President Abraham Lincoln.

During the territorial period, little was known or appreciated about Arizona outside its borders and, thus, the territory's political influence was limited.[3] Despite this neglect, officials in the federal government attempted to micromanage Arizona's government,[4] while at the same time delaying assistance or ignoring issues vital to settlement and development.[5]

Not surprising, Indian troubles were the greatest barrier to mining, ranching, and farming endeavors. Military protection provided by the federal government was often inadequate in numbers and lacked a defined mission. From 1864 to 1909, Arizona officials persistently, and insistently, appealed to Congress, the president, and the Bureau of Indian Affairs to subjugate the raiding tribes that roamed desert lands destroying human life, livestock, and property. In addition, they petitioned for the settlement of claims for these depredations and sought to establish reserves and confine Indians to reservation lands.[6] The era of conflict and hostilities did not come to an end until 1886 with the capture of Geronimo and his Apache warrior band.[7]

Not all of Arizona was constantly at war with Indian tribes during its territorial period. The study of Southwest Indian cultures and excavations of ancient Indian ruins, primarily sponsored by the Smithsonian Institution, began during Arizona's territorial years.[8]

Development of transportation was key to progress in the territory. In the early years it was limited to goods barged up the Colorado River[9] and overland freighting, and these were often subject to attack by hostiles. Following explorations and surveys of feasible railroad routes, the 1880s finally saw the creation of a northern route by the Santa Fe Railroad and a southern one by the Southern Pacific Railroad. From both routes, critical feeder lines sprang up quickly for Arizona's growing boomtowns and mining camps to connect to the West Coast. The boom in silver and copper mining—Arizona would soon lead the nation in copper production—and the coming of railroads brought an increase in population and emergence of political leadership anxious for statehood.

Attempts at statehood began as early as 1872,[10] but it was not until 1891 that the first constitutional convention was held, and a constitution was drafted and overwhelmingly approved by the residents of the territory. Congress ignored Arizona's request to join the Union, citing its low population compared with other territories at the time of the granting of their statehood. Arizona's advocacy of free silver coinage, a politically unpopular issue with eastern politicians, no doubt influenced Congress's decision.

From 1902 to 1911, numerous congressional hearings and one Senate committee's whirlwind tour of the Southwest generated several House and Senate reports on the issue of Arizona's statehood. Many barriers were noted: a comparatively sparse population; a racial profile consisting of one-fourth foreign born, many of them non–English speaking; arid lands with limited agricultural potential; and a Democratic politic at a time when the federal government was controlled by Republicans. In 1904 Congress proposed joining the lands of the Arizona and New Mexico territories into one great state, to be called New Mexico, with its capital in Santa Fe. President Theodore Roosevelt endorsed it as a reasonable and practical solution, but in Arizona it was strongly opposed. An antijointure convention in Phoenix garnered thousands of petition signatures, including 3,200 names collected in thirty minutes at the Territorial Fair. In referendums, New Mexico approved the proposal, but Arizonans soundly rejected joined statehood. Better to remain a territory "for the balance of time" was the popular sentiment.[11]

Finally, in 1908, Congress and the president relented and endorsed separate admission for Arizona and New Mexico, and in 1910, an enabling act was passed to admit Arizona into the Union. A second constitutional convention created a state constitution that reflected progressive ideas with provisions for anti-child labor, employer liability, voter initiative and referendum, and the recall of government officials, including judges on the bench. When President Taft opposed the provision for recall of judges, a resolution without the section was ratified and accepted by voters. On February 14, 1912, after sixty-two years as a territory, Arizona became the forty-eighth state in the union. At the following fall election, voters ignored President Taft's opposition and reinstated the recall provision into the Arizona Constitution.

Arizona's territorial culture was a mix of Anglo-American, Mexican-American, Mormon, and Indian peoples. Its economic institutions were the large mining corporations, small mining ventures, railroads, big ranches, the lumber industry, and U.S. military installations. Arizona's territorial publications and documents reflect the issues, concerns, and, of course, progress derived from the interaction and interblending of these many parts.

Seventy-seven percent of today's Arizona is public land—27 percent Indian reservations, 15 percent national forests, 27 percent Bureau of Land Management lands, 8 percent other—and most of it was created during the territorial period. Congress and presidents set aside reserves for more than fifteen tribes and bands of indigenous peoples. Fourteen national forest preserves were created, the earliest being the Grand Canyon Forest Reserve in 1893, which evolved into Grand Canyon National Park in 1919.

BIBLIOGRAPHIC ESSAY ON ARIZONA HISTORY

One of the best histories of Arizona's territorial period is Jay J. Wagoner's *Arizona Territory, 1863-1912: A Political History* (Tucson: University of Arizona Press, 1970), which explores in depth the federal-territorial administrations and has useful notes on location and content of archival collections and an excellent bibliography. The other critical source for history and perspective of Arizona's territorial period is Howard R. Lamar's *The Far Southwest, 1846-1912: A Territorial History,* Revised Edition (Albuquerque: University of New Mexico Press, 2000). This impressive work covers the formative period of the Four Corners states of Arizona, New Mexico, Colorado, and Utah and provides a "must see" bibliography of scholarly books and articles for the serious researcher.[12]

Labor politics played a pivotal role during territorial days and was a force and influence at the constitutional convention, all of which James Byrkitt examines in *Forging the Copper Collar: Arizona's Labor-Management War of 1901-1921* (Tucson: University of Arizona Press, 1982). James M. Murphy, in *Laws, Courts, and Lawyers Through the Years in Arizona* (Tucson: University of Arizona Press, 1970), covers development of the judicial system and laws during territorial days, and his slender volume *The Spanish Legal Heritage in Arizona* (Tucson: Arizona Pioneers Historical Society, 1966) offers insight into the roots of the state's legal system which encompasses both American and Spanish traditions. A series of books by John Goff on territorial officials provides biographical and historical information about the individuals in policymaking positions.[13] George H. Kelley's *Legislative History of Arizona: 1864-1912* (Phoenix: Manufacturing Stationer's, Inc., 1926) reviews the concerns and enactments of each legislative session and includes messages from the governors, but is otherwise not helpful.

For constitutional history of Arizona, the most comprehensive works are by John Leshy: the book *The Arizona State Constitution: A Reference Guide* (Westport, CT: Greenwood Press, 1993) and a law review article that recounts the historical information in fuller detail and with more references, "The Making of the Arizona Constitution," *Arizona State Law Journal* 20 (1988): 1-113. Gordon Bakken has a shorter analysis of the issues and forces at play at the convention in "The Arizona Constitution Convention of 1910," *Arizona State Law Journal* (1978): 1-30, and his *Rocky Mountain Constitution Making, 1850-1912* (New York: Greenwood Press, 1987) compares fundamental issues in the original constitutions of eight states, including Arizona. *Constitutional Government in Arizona* by Toni McClory (Tucson: University of Arizona Press, 2001) is a new source that provides an overview of territorial government and constitution making, then covers more recent history and the constitutional amendments. John Goff edited *The Records of the Arizona Constitutional Convention of 1910* (Phoenix: The Supreme Court of Arizona, 1991), providing the most complete compilation in one volume of minutes of floor deliberations, text of propositions, the 1910 constitution, and brief biographies of the convention delegates. *Sources and Documents of United States Constitutions,* edited and annotated by William Swindler (Dobbs Ferry, NY: Oceana Publications, 1973), reprints key Arizona constitutional materials from the preterritorial and prestatehood periods.[14]

Arizona has a rich and colorful history, so numerous scholarly texts, articles, and popular accounts abound that cover a wide historical period and still do justice to the territorial period. Of the recent publications, highly recommended is Tom Sheridan's *Arizona: A History* (Tucson: University of Arizona Press, 1995), a narrative of political, economic, social, and cultural interplay of peoples with an emphasis on the crucial role of the federal government in Arizona's development. The work includes a very comprehensive bibliographic essay from one of Arizona's foremost historical scholars. Smaller but eminently readable and engaging is Lawrence Clark Powell's *Arizona: A Bicentennial History* (New York: Norton, 1976; reissued by Albuquerque: University of New Mexico Press, 1990), which was one of a series from all states written to celebrate the nation's bicentennial. History comes alive in the pages of this book, and Powell's suggested readings are selective and insightful.[15]

Recent historical studies provide special value with bibliographies, notes, and corrections of information in older treatises, but researchers should consult classic historical studies, such as Hubert H. Bancroft's *History of Arizona and New Mexico, 1539-1888* (San Francisco: History Co., 1889) and Richard Sloan's comprehensive, four-volume *History of Arizona* (Phoenix: Record Publishing Co., 1930), two volumes of which contain biographical sketches of prominent early Arizonans. Other classic works are *Historical and Biographical Record of the Territory of Arizona* (Chicago: McFarland and Poole, 1896); James McClintock's *Arizona: Prehistoric, Aboriginal, Pioneer, Modern: The Nation's Youngest Commonwealth Within a Land of Ancient Culture* (Chicago: Clarke Publishing Co., 1916); Sidney DeLong's *The History of Arizona from the Earliest Times Known to the People of Europe to 1903* (San Francisco: Whitaker and Ray Co., 1905); Thomas E. Farish's multivolume *History of Arizona* (San Francisco: Filmer Brothers Electrotype Co., 1915) <http://southwest.library.arizona.edu/hav1>; *Arizona: The History of a Frontier State* by Rufus Wyllys (Phoenix: Hobson and Herr, 1950); and *Pioneer Days in Arizona from the Spanish Occupation to Statehood* (New York: Macmillan, 1932) by Francis Lockwood.[16]

Be It Enacted: The Creation of the Territory of Arizona by B. Sacks (Phoenix: Arizona Historical Foundation, 1964) is a detailed account of the years 1856 to 1863 and a unique and unparalleled resource of primary preterritorial documents, such as handwritten letters, petitions, and publications, many hitherto unavailable. Wagoner's *Early Arizona: Prehistory to Civil War* (Tucson: University of Arizona Press, 1975) is a narrative about New Spain, land grants, the Mexican War, and U.S.-Mexico boundary problems, all of which influenced and helped form the character of Arizona's borderlands. Robert Larson's *New Mexico's Quest for Statehood, 1846-1912* (Albuquerque: University of New Mexico Press, 1968) reviews the years prior to 1863 when Arizona and New Mexico were one territory, before they were separated into distinct entities. The negotiation, ratification, and significance of the U.S.-Mexico treaties are thoroughly discussed in Paul Garber's *The Gadsden Treaty* (Philadelphia: University of Pennsylvania, 1923) and Richard Griswold del Castillo's *The Treaty of Guadalupe Hidalgo: A Legacy of Conflict* (Norman: University of Oklahoma Press, 1990). For an excellently researched history of the Hispanic roots of southern Arizona and northern Sonora from the Spanish and Mexican points of view, including analysis of Mexican-Indian interrelationships and hostilities, consult *Hispanic Arizona, 1536-1856* by James Officer (Tucson: University of Arizona Press, 1987).

RESEARCH GUIDES

Archival collections of Arizona documents and public records are scattered throughout the state in historical society and museum libraries, university special collections, and the Arizona State Library and Archives, none of which are complete within themselves for territorial publications and documents. A good researcher must be prepared to search several locations in and outside of Arizona.[17] The best information on locations of archival collections is thoughtfully provided by Howard Lamar in *Far Southwest* and by James Murphy in *Laws, Courts and Lawyers.*

Two guides serve as primary sources to identify territorial documents.[18] *Arizona Legal Research Guide* (Buffalo, NY: Hein, 1992), by law librarians Kathy Shimpock-Vieweg and Marianne Alcorn, is a comprehensive guide to Arizona territorial and state publications, although the focus is primarily on legal and statehood materials. The second, published by the state archives, is a descriptive list of its archival collection of territorial and state public records: *A Guide to Public Records in the Arizona State Archives,* Second Edition (Phoenix: Arizona Department of Library, Archives and Public Records, 1994). Researchers should note that a 1936 inventory of documents and public records at the capitol reported the unfortunate loss and destruction of many important territorial materials due to the lack of facilities to care for documents, the shifting locations of government offices, and the variable diligence of officials in retention of papers.[19]

Richard N. Ellis collected and reprinted *New Mexico Historic Documents* (Albuquerque: University of New Mexico Press, 1975), covering 1821 to 1974, half of them territorial New Mexico-Arizona and each prefaced with helpful background notes. A unique and thorough research guide is *Spanish & Mexican Records of the American Southwest* (Tucson: University of Arizona Press, 1979) by Henry Putney Beers, which identifies and locates American publications of original Spanish and Mexican public records, such as land grant records, from the mid-1600s to the mid-1800s.

One of the best collections of Arizona documents and historical accounts is located at the Arizona Historical Society in Tucson, which has been in existence and collecting materials since early territorial times. An in-house catalog[20] of books, journal articles, manuscripts, and photographs opens up one of the largest primary and secondary archival and historical collections on Arizona, the Southwest, and northern Mexico. *Documents of Southwestern History: A Guide to the Manuscript Collections of the Arizona Historical Society* (Tucson: Arizona Historical Society, 1972) compiled by Charles C. Colley, indexes primary materials found within the manuscript papers in the library. Significant collections also are located at the Sharlot Hall Museum Library in Prescott (site of the first capital), in Special Collections at the University of Arizona in Tucson, at the Arizona Historical Foundation and Special Collections Library at Arizona State University in Tempe, and in Special Collections at the Cline Library at Northern Arizona University in Flagstaff.

Federal archival collections are well indexed and available to researchers. Donald M. Powell compiled and annotated *New Mexico and Arizona in the Serial Set, 1846-1861* (Los Angeles: Dawson's Book Shop, 1970), a very complete guide to congressional publications of that era. Territorial Arizona papers in the National Archives and Records Administration (NARA) are in several record groups: Territorial Papers of the United States (RG 46), State Department Territorial Papers (RG59), and Interior Department Territorial Papers (RG 48), which have Office of Indian Affairs letters. An additional source is *Territorial Papers of the United States Senate, 1789-1873: Dakota, March 31, 1858-February 5, 1873 and Arizona, December 17, 1857-February 27, 1865.* Records for Arizona's Territorial District Court, 1864-1912, are found in NARA's Records of the District Courts for the United States (RG 21). The Survey of Federal Archives of the Works Progress Administration (WPA) produced an *Inventory of Federal Archives in the States: Local Courts for the Territory Arizona* (1938) and *Inventory of . . . Local Executive Offices for the Territory of Arizona* (1939). The Arizona Historical Records Survey of the WPA compiled an *Inventory of the County Archives of Arizona* (Maricopa, Pima County–Tucson, Santa Cruz County–Nogales) (1938), *Inventory of Tucson City Archives* (1936), and *Inventory of Phoenix City Archives* (1936).

BIBLIOGRAPHY

Becoming a Territory

The Constitution and Schedule of the Provisional Government of the Territory of Arizona and the Proceedings of the Convention Held at Tucson. Tucson: J. Howard Wells, 1860.

Provision for government officials for a federal territory of Arizona. Includes proceedings of the 1860 constitutional convention, inaugural address of Governor Lewis S. Owings, and provisional constitution. Reprinted in B. Sacks, *Be It Enacted: The Creation of the Territory of Arizona,* app. B at 130-154 (Tucson: Arizona Historical Foundation, 1964).

Leyes Del Territorio De Nuevo Mejico, Santa Fe, a 7 de Octobre 1846/Laws of the Territory of New Mexico, Santa Fe, October 7, 1846 [Kearny Code].

First legal code issued by General Stephen Kearny of the territory under American jurisdiction. Also H. Exec. Doc. 19, 29th Cong., 2d Sess. (1846). Prepared by Colonel Alexander William Doniphan and Willard P. Hall in English and Spanish, the volume contains the "Organic Law of the Territory of New Mexico," a "Bill of Rights," and "Laws" regarding government officials, courts and judicial powers, civil matters, crimes and punishment, elections, and records and registration of titles.

[Memorial Praying for a Separate Territorial Organization Under the Name of Arizona] [Spanish], 1856. Drafted by W.C. Jones and signed by residents of Rio Grande Valley, 1856. English translation by Sylvester Mowry. Spanish and English versions reprinted in Sacks, *Be It Enacted,* app. A(1) at 113-117.

Earliest known document petitioning for separate territorial status for Arizona. Memorialists were citizens of La Mesilla and Rio Grande Valley with estimated population of nearly 21,000. Names of fifty-seven petitioners were recorded.

[Memorial Praying for the Organization of a New Territory to be Called the Territory of Arizona], August 29, 1856. From the Convention in Tucson to the Senate and House of Representatives of the United States in Congress Assembled, reprinted in Sacks, *Be It Enacted,* app. A(2) at 118-119.

Memorial from Tucson citizens with more than 260 signatures.

New Mexico. Legislative Assembly. *Revised Statutes of the Territory of New Mexico/Estatutos Corregidos Del Territorio De Nuevo Mejico.* Revised by James J. Davenport. Santa Fe: Santa Fe Weekly Gazette Office, 1856.

Contains laws affecting Arizona until adoption of Howell Code in 1864 by Arizona Legislative Assembly. In English and Spanish.

Petition for a Separate Territory Under the Name of Arizona, 1857, reprinted in Sacks, *Be It Enacted,* app. A(3) at 120-121.

Known as the "Kippen Memorial" for first signer George Kippen, the petition was signed by 500 individuals primarily from the western Gadsden Purchase area. Also reprinted in Sylvester Mowry, *Memoir of the Proposed Territory of Arizona,* 1857, without signatures <http://www.yale.edu/law web/avalon/treatise/arizona/arizona.htm>.

Petition for a Separation from New Mexico and the Organization of a New Territory to Be Called "The Territory of Arizona," 1857, reprinted in Sacks, *Be It Enacted,* app. A(4) at 122-124.

Containing over 1,000 signatures, mostly from individuals from Mesilla and along the Rio Grande, the petition is known as the "Bradley Memorial" for M.E. Bradley whose name heads the list.

Statutes at Large of the Provisional Government of the Confederate States of America, Sess. V (1862): 242-247. (An Act to Organize the Territory of Arizona.)

Act of January 18, 1862, established territorial boundaries, government structure, powers, duties and salaries of officials, provided for delegate to Confederate Congress, preserved recognized rights of Indian tribes, and protected slavery. Capital located at La Mesilla.

U.S. Congress. *[Bills for a Separate Territory],* 34th-37th Cong., 1856-1862.

Eighteen bills were introduced in Congress from 1856 to 1862 for separate territorial status for Arizona. A list of the bills appears in Sacks, *Be It Enacted* at 48 n60, with some reprinted in whole or in part in app. C at 155-165. Included is a bill approved by Jefferson Davis, January 18, 1862, for a Confederate territory of Arizona [app. C (5) at 161], and HR 357, 37th Cong., 2d Sess., 1862, which was amended and signed into law on February 24, 1863, creating a temporary government for the territory of Arizona [app. C(6) at 162-165].

U.S. Senate. *Memorial of People of Southwestern Part of Territory of New Mexico Praying for Organization of a New Territory,* 34th Cong., 3d Sess., 1856-1857. H. Rept. 2. Serial 912 [Dup. of H. Rept. 117].

Memorial citing grievances such as distance from judicial center and the need to settle land claims. People want speedy settlement of land titles, survey of public lands, establishment of postal route, protection of mining interests, and subjugation of hostile Indians.

————. *Resolutions of the Legislature of New Mexico Relative to the Organization of the Territory of Arizona and the Removal of the Wild Indians from the Territory of New Mexico,* 35th Cong., 1st Sess., 1858. S. Misc. Doc. 208. Serial 936.

Describes boundary lines for separate territory. Indians to be relocated to northern part of Arizona.

U.S. Statutes at Large 12 (1850): 446. An Act of Sept. 9, 1850 (proposing to the state of Texas the establishment of her northern and western boundaries, the relinquishment by the said state of all territory claimed by her exterior to said boundaries and of all her claims upon the United States, and to establish a territorial government for New Mexico).

Establishment of the territory of New Mexico, which included the northern half of Arizona, and provision for a government.

U.S. Statutes at Large 12 (1863): 664. Organic Act. Territory of Arizona. Feb. 24, 1863.

Establishment of territory of Arizona and provision for government.

U.S. Statutes at Large 9 (1848): 922. Treaty of Peace, Friendship, Limits, and Settlement with the Republic of Mexico. Feb. 2, 1848 [Treaty of Guadalupe Hidalgo]. United States-Mexico.

TS 207. Treaty to end war with Mexico, establish boundary between the two republics, and for United States to acquire lands for $15 million. Arizona (northern half of the state) was part of this conquered area. English and Spanish versions reprinted in Richard N. Ellis, ed., *New Mexico Historic Documents* at 10-31 (Albuquerque: University of New Mexico Press, 1975). See also <http://www.yale.edu/lawweb/avalon/diplomacy/mexico/guadhida.htm>.

U.S. Statutes at Large 10 (1853): 1031. [Gadsden Treaty]. Treaty with Mexico. Dec. 30, 1853. United States-Mexico.

Presidential proclamation announcing agreement with Mexico for United States to purchase the area south of the Gila River (Southern Arizona) for $10 million. <http://www.yale.edu/lawweb/avalon/diplomacy/mexico/mx1853.htm>.

Achieving Statehood

Arizona (Terr.). Constitutional Convention, 1891. *Constitution for the State of Arizona, As Adopted by the Constitutional Convention, Friday, October 2, 1891, and Address to the People of the Territory.* Phoenix: Herald Book and Job Print, 1891.

Draft constitution prepared within a month from 1891 convention contains "Bill of Rights" and establishes a state government. Has controversial sections on water rights and irrigation that allowed owners at time of statehood to be excluded from state regulation, and the acceptance of both silver and gold as legal tender in Arizona, which was viewed as trespassing on federal jurisdiction.

————. Constitutional Convention, 1910. *Complete Verbatim Report, Arizona Constitutional Convention,* 1910. S.L.: s.n., 1910.

Contains extended remarks not included in the *Journals.* Typescript manuscript by Convention President and later Governor G.W.P. Hunt is on file at University of Arizona Special Collections; other copy at Arizona State Library; microfilm copy at Arizona Foundation, Arizona State University, Tempe.

————. Election Ordinance No. 2, Constitutional Convention, Filed December 12, 1910. Reprinted in *Arizona Revised Statutes Annotated,* v. 1, 63. Eagan, MN: West Group, 2001.

Procedure for holding election of officials for new state government as authorized in enabling act.

————. *Journal of the Constitutional Convention of Arizona As Provided by the Enabling Act of Congress Approved June 20, 1910.* Held in the Hall of the House of Representatives in the Capitol of the Territory of Arizona, at Phoenix, October 10 to December 9, 1910. Compiled by Con P. Cronin, State Librarian of Arizona. Phoenix: s.n., 1925.

Contain remarks of the delegates on the floor. Reprinted in John Goff's *The Records of the Arizona Constitutional Convention of 1910* at 1-1012 (Phoenix: Supreme Court of Arizona, 1991). See note for *Complete Verbatim Report,* ante.

————. *Journals of the Constitutional Convention for the State of Arizona.* Convention Convened September 7, 1891, and Adjourned October 3, 1891. Phoenix: Herald Book and Job Print, 1891.

Daily proceedings of convention with list of members and officers, rules, order of business, committees and their membership and reports, discussions, and votes.

————. *Minutes of the Constitutional Convention, Territory of Arizona.* Session Began on the Tenth Day of October, A.D. 1910, Phoenix, Arizona. Phoenix: Phoenix Printing Company, 1910.

Record of days/times, attendance, and votes on motions and propositions.

————. *Proposed Constitution for the State of Arizona.* Adopted by the Constitutional Convention, Convention Held at Phoenix, Arizona, from October 10 to December 9, 1910. Phoenix: s.n., 1910.

Accepted by Congress but vetoed by President Taft because it contained a provision for recall of judges. Reprinted in Goff, *Records . . . Arizona Constitutional Convention* at 1399-1443.

————. *Propositions.* Phoenix: s.n., 1910.

Propositions (numbering 153, of sentence or article length) on subjects introduced for consideration for constitution. Western, progressive issues dominated, such as initiative, referendum, and recall; rights of workers and labor unions; home rule; prohibition; and female suffrage (debated at 1891 convention), in addition to the mechanics of government (legislative process, taxing, spending), natural resources issues, and water rights. Reprinted in Goff, *Records . . . Arizona Constitutional Convention* at 1016-1356.

————. *Standing Rules, Arizona Constitutional Convention.* Phoenix: Arizona State Press, 1910.

Rules and order of procedure for conducting business at the convention.

President. *Special Message of the President of the United States Returning Without Approval House Joint Resolution No. 14, August 15, 1911* [Veto, "To Admit the Territories of Arizona and New Mexico As States into the Union upon an Equal Footing with the Original States"]. 62d Cong., 1st Sess., 1911. H. Doc. 106. Serial 6117. Reprinted in McClory, *Constitutional Government* app. at 167-173.

President Taft vetoed the resolution because Arizona's constitution contained a provision for recall of judicial officers, which he opposed, viewing it as destructive of the independence of the judiciary.

U.S. House. *Admission of Arizona, Idaho, and Wyoming into the Union.* 50th Cong., 2d Sess., 1889. H. Rept. 4053.

Early promotion for Arizona statehood. Includes argument of Marcus A. Smith, delegate from Arizona, and statement by John Wesley Powell on reclamation of arid lands by irrigation.

————. *Admission of Arizona into the Union (to Accompany HR 7204).* 52nd Cong., 1st Sess., 1892. H. Rept. 737.

Report of Marcus Smith, delegate to Congress, on resources of Arizona to support bid for statehood.

————. *Admission of Arizona into the Union [with Constitution for the State of Arizona Adopted by the Constitutional Convention October 2, 1891].* 53rd Cong., 1st Sess., 1893. H. Rept. 168.

Report from Marcus Smith, delegate from Arizona, on resources of Arizona in support of statehood, accompanied by first constitution drafted (hastily) for statehood (to accompany HR 4393).

————. *Admission of New Mexico and Arizona.* 62nd Cong., 1st Sess., 1911. H. Rept. 162. Serial 6078.

Senate recommends passage of House Joint Resolution 156 (same as H. Jt. Res. 14 except excludes Arizona's recall provision in its constitution in order to facilitate presidential support and subsequent enactment).

————. *Arizona's Vote on Joint Statehood.* 59th Cong., 2d Sess., 1906. H. Doc. 140. Serial 5151.

Letter from the secretary of the interior transmitting certificate of the governor and secretary of Arizona showing election result of November 6, 1906, on question of joint statehood with New Mexico: 3,141 for and 16,265 against. Majority against: 13,124.

————. *Certificate of the Governor and Secretary of New Mexico As to the Election Upon Joint Statehood.* 59th Cong., 2d Sess., 1906. H. Doc. 194. Serial 5151.

Letter from the secretary of the interior transmitting the net majority from New Mexico in favor of joint statehood: 11,460. Election result: 26,195 yes; 14,735 no.

————. *Certificate of the Governor, Chief Justice, and Secretary of Arizona Transmitting a Copy of the Constitution of Arizona and the Ascertainment of the Vote Adopting the Same, March 3, 1911.* 61st Cong., 3d Sess., 1911. H. Doc. 1423.

Territorial Governor Richard Sloan submitted 1910 constitution accepted by popular vote February 9, 1911: 12,187 for; 3,822 against. Includes signatures of constitutional delegates.

————. Committee on Territories. *Further Hearing on Statehood Bill: Hearing, December 18, 1903, January 7, 14, 15, 1904.* 58th Cong., 2d Sess., 1904.

Arizona statehood authorization and review of socioeconomic conditions.

———. *Hearings . . . on House Joint Resolution No. 14 Approving the Constitutions Formed by the Constitutional Conventions of the Territories of New Mexico and Arizona, April 13-29, 1911.* 62nd Cong., 1st Sess, 1911.

Discussed presidential objection to recall provision in Arizona constitution approved by 80 percent of territory's electorate; noted that if state removed recall in order to be admitted there was nothing preventing adoption of the provision after admittance. Majority of information on New Mexico.

———. *Statehood for Arizona and New Mexico: Hearing, January 16, 17, 18, 19, and 20, 1906.* 59th Cong., 1st Sess., 1906.

On joint statehood. Arizona businessmen report on economic development, effects of joint admission, and legal conditions.

———. *Statehood for New Mexico and Arizona: Hearing, January 26, February 1, 1909.* 60th Cong., 2d Sess., 1909.

Regarding HB 27428 admitting Arizona and New Mexico as separate states. Covers school lands, federal aid, railroads.

———. *Statehood for the Territories.* 58th Cong., 2d Sess., 1904. H. Rept. 2335. Serial 4583.

Regarding HB 14749 on Oklahoma and Indian Territory as one state, and Arizona and New Mexico as one state called Arizona with capital at Santa Fe. Minority opinion reviews qualifications and resources and notes failure to consider wishes of people who want statehood. Appears as effort to minimize influence of the West and Southwest in federal system by combining states. Better to be territories indefinitely than be admitted in this fashion.

———. *Statehood for the Territories.* 59th Cong., 1st Sess., 1906. H. Rept. 496. Serial 4906.

Recommends passing HR 12707 for Oklahoma and Indian Territory as one state, and Arizona and New Mexico as one state. Minority views say Arizona and New Mexico would be too large, are separated by the Continental Divide, and each territory has its own public buildings in duplication. Arizona does not want to hand over control to New Mexico with whom it has "nothing in common," and should have right to accept bill or not. Appendix 1 is "Protest to Congress Against the Passage of the Joint State Bill for New Mexico and Arizona," including remarks from the Anti-Joint Statehood Convention, Phoenix, May 27, 1905, containing resolutions of the convention of legislators, representatives from cities, counties, and associations, and citizens. Appendix 2 lists resources of Arizona and New Mexico.

————. *Statehood for the Territories.* 60th Cong., 2d Sess., 1909. H. Rept. 2079. Serial 5384.

Recommends passing HR 27891 for Arizona and New Mexico as separate states. Brief review of qualifications. Capital of Arizona to be at Phoenix. Notes that New Mexico and Arizona repeatedly applied for admission; bills as separate states passed House, sometimes passed both Houses but failed in conference. Both 1908 Democratic and Republican national platforms supported separate states and immediate admission.

————. *Statehood for the Territories.* 61st Cong., 2d Sess., 1910. H. Rept. 152. Serial 5591.

Regarding HR 18166 for New Mexico and Arizona to form two states. Brief review of qualifications of Arizona and New Mexico for admission, concluding that both territories repeatedly tried for statehood and congressional committees have devoted much time to the issue.

U.S. Senate. *An Act Enabling the People of New Mexico and Arizona to Form a Constitution and State Government, etc.* 61st Cong., 2d Sess., 1910. S. Rept. 454. Serial 5583.

Re HR 18166 and Senate "amendment" in form of a substitute bill recommended to pass. Many changes were noted: Constitutions approved by voters of proposed states should be ratified by Congress and president as a "safety measure" to prevent "harmful provisions"; voter qualifications requiring "educational test" eliminated; and Senate bill provision for English-only taught in classroom. Includes veto message by Governor Kibbey on an Arizona law enacted over his veto requiring voters to be able to read constitution in English (because it would disenfranchise large numbers of citizens).

————. *Admission of Territories of New Mexico and Arizona* (Pt. 1)/*Admission of Arizona and New Mexico* (Pt. 2). 62nd Cong., 1st Sess., 1911. S. Rept. 100. Serial 6077.

Part 1 covers technical corrections and amendments. Part 2 is a protest by Senator Owen, Committee on Territories, of the removal of the recall provision in Arizona's constitution, a violation of the "right of self-government." Notes that fixed terms of judges amount to "automatically recalled." Exhibit A is "Manner of Election or Appointment of Judges in the Respective

State and Territories Offices," and Exhibit B is "Provision in the Respective State Constitutions Relating to the Recall of Judges."

————. *Joint Statehood for New Mexico and Arizona.* 59th Cong., 1st Sess., 1906. S. Doc. 254. Serial 4914.

Subtitle: "Answer Favoring Joint Statehood for New Mexico and Arizona to the Memorial of Its Opponents" (see S. Doc. 216, *Protest Against Union Of Arizona . . .* , supra). Declares Arizona not against joint statehood and protests submission of issues to voters because "cannot get fair expression" (farmers haying, many people out of the territory). Includes forty-seven signatures of residents from Nogales, Tucson, and Phoenix.

————. *Protest Against Union of Arizona with New Mexico. Memorial from Delegates from Arizona in Opposition to Joint Statehood of Arizona with New Mexico.* 59th Cong., 1st Sess., 1906. S. Doc. 216. Serial 4913.

Notes joint statehood opposed by 95 percent of Arizonans; state would be an "unwieldy size." Cites differences (racial, economics, laws, customs) between two territories. After forty years as independent territory, Arizona now confronted with prospect of destruction of autonomy and loss of identity by being forced into joint statehood. Citizens prefer to remain citizens of a territory. Lists thirty-four petitions, protests, and resolutions of Arizona in opposition, including one of 3,200 names obtained at the Territorial Fair in thirty minutes. Recommends amending bill by striking out "Arizona."

————. Committee on Territories. *New Statehood Bill: Hearing, November 17, 18, 19, 1902* [Arizona]. 57th Cong., 2d Sess., 1902. S. Doc. 36.

On HB 12543 regarding admission of Oklahoma, Arizona, and New Mexico. Arizona hearings held in Prescott, Phoenix, Tucson, and Bisbee. Reporting census, occupations, industry, water, immigration, university information. Includes USGS maps of Navajo reservation, Grand Canyon area, land grants, railroads, and military reserves.

————. *New Statehood Bill. Statehood for Oklahoma, Indian Territory, Arizona and New Mexico, with Views and Minority Report.* 3 pts. 57th Cong., 2d Sess., 1902. S. Rept. 2206. Serial 4410.

Regarding HB 12543. Reviews qualifications of each territory to be admitted: population, education, extent, character and development of natural resources, and value to country. Arizona fails for too few people but Committee Chairman Beveridge says do not need statehood for development. Views of dissent from majority presented by Senator Quay: the territories have more than served their time of "probation": "Many of the greatest states of the union have been admitted with much less population and half the resources that Arizona possesses." Minority views recommend passage of bill.

————. *Providing for the Admission of the Territories of Arizona, New Mexico and Oklahoma to Statehood: Hearings . . . June 28 and 30, 1902.* 57th Cong., 1st Sess., 1902. S. Doc. 36. Serial 4420.

On HR 12543. Delegate Marcus Smith presents facts concerning resources that justify Arizona statehood: "Those two territories [Arizona and New Mexico] have been made the mere whim and caprice of politicians and have been thrown as a shuttlecock through the political atmosphere until the people have become wearied with the burden from which they are everlastingly suffering—a government of carpetbag rule." Beveridge chaired the Senate Committee on Territories at this time. For congressional opposition to statehood for Arizona, see f11.

————. *Statehood Bill.* 57th Cong., 1st Sess., 1906. S. Rept. 427. Serial 4904.

Textual amendments to HR 12707 regarding Oklahoma and Indian Territory as one state, and Arizona and New Mexico as one state.

————. *Statehood for New Mexico and Arizona.* 61st Cong., 2d Sess., 1910. S. Rept. 454. Serial 5583.

Reviews House and Senate differences on HR 18166. President and Congress to approve Arizona's constitution. Arizona has education test for voters; includes veto message by Governor Kibbey that requirement to read Constitution in English would disenfranchise large numbers of citizens and put control of election in hands of registration officers and election boards.

————. *Statehood for Oklahoma and Indian Territory [and New Mexico and Arizona].* 58th Cong., 2d Sess, 1904. H. Rept. 2602. Serial 4583.

Textual amendments to HR 14749; recommends passage.

U.S. Statutes at Large 34 (1906): 267, 278-285. An Act to Enable the People of Oklahoma of the Indian Territory . . . to be Admitted into the Union . . . and to Enable the People of New Mexico and Arizona to Form a Constitution and State Government and Be Admitted into the Union on an Equal Footing with the Original States. June 16, 1906.

Sections 23ff (pp. 278-285) deal with statehood for Arizona and New Mexico as one state upon approval by both territorial electorates. Arizona voters overwhelmingly rejected joint statehood, defeating the measure, though New Mexico voters approved it.

U.S. Statutes at Large 36 (1910): 557, 568-579. Enabled People of Arizona to Form Constitution and State Government [Enabling Act]. June 20, 1910. Reprinted in *Arizona Revised Statutes, Annotated,* vol. 1, 35. Eagan, MN: West Group, 2001. <http://www.azleg.state.az.us/const/enabling.pdf>.

Sets forth conditions to attain statehood, such as electing members to a convention that would draft a constitution and plans for state government.

U.S. Statutes at Large 37 (1911): 39. Joint Resolution to Admit the Territories of New Mexico and Arizona As States into the Union upon Equal Footing with the Original States, No. 8, August 21, 1911. Edited version reprinted in *Arizona Revised States, Annotated,* vol. 1, 69. Eagan, MN: West Group, 2001.

Resolution included amendment to Arizona's constitution eliminating recall of judiciary that was ratified by Arizona electorate December 12, 1911. After Arizona was admitted as a state on February 14, 1912, the provision was restored to the constitution on November 5, 1912, by voter initiative. See *Constitutional Amendments Submitted to the People by the Legislature and Those Proposed by Initiative Petition of the People, and Acts Passed at the Regular and First Special Sessions of the First State Legislature, 1912, Against Which Referendums Were Filed, All of Which Were Approved by the Qualified Electors of the State at the Election Held on November Fifth, 1912, and Became Laws on the Proclamation of the Governor, Issued on December the Fifth, 1912.* Phoenix: [Secretary of State(?)], 1912. Also in *Session Laws of Arizona, Second and Third Special Session, First State Legislature, 1913.* Phoenix: Secretary of State, 1913.

U.S. Statutes at Large 37 (1912): 1728. "Proclamation of Admission [of Arizona As a State], February 14, 1912." Reprinted in *Arizona Revised Statutes, Annotated,* vol. 1, 71. Eagan, MN: West Group 2001.

Proclamation issued by President William Howard Taft announcing statehood.

Territorial Arizona Documents[21]

Arizona Pioneers' Historical Society. *Constitution and By-Laws, Adopted April 16, 1897; Inc. March 3, 1884.* Tucson: Author, 1897.

Foundation documents of a nonprofit state agency later renamed as the Arizona Historical Society. The original "Arizonal Historical Society," though organized, never actually functioned. See *Charter, Constitution, and By-Laws, Incorporated and Organized November 1864* (Prescott: Office of the Arizona Miner, 1864).

Arizona Railway Commission. *Annual Report.* 1909- .

Commission investigated operations, including shipping rates and passenger fares, of common carriers doing business in the territory, referred issues and complaints to Interstate Commerce Commission. Some commission reports include annual reports of railroad companies.

Arizona Rangers. 1901-1909. *Constitution, By-Laws* (n.d.).

A paramilitary organization created in 1902 originally to patrol the border, control cattle rustling, and assist in keeping the peace at miners' strikes.

————. *Report of Arizona Rangers, Arrests Made . . .* 1902-1908.

Secretary of the Territory. *Blue Book of the Territory of Arizona, 1894.* Phoenix: Secretary of Arizona, 1894.

Directory identifying congressional delegate, territorial and county government officials, notaries public, and commissioners of deeds. Cover title: *Official Register of the Territory of Arizona.* Continued as *Territorial and County Officials of Arizona* [19??] (Phoenix: Phoenix Printing Company, 1909-1911).

————. *Manner of Conducting Elections As Approved by the General Election Laws of the Territory, Revised Statutes of 1887.* Tucson: Citizen Printing and Publishing Co., 1892.

————. *Registration and Election Laws, Territory of Arizona.* Phoenix: H.H. McNeil. Co., 1900.

Reprint of statutes.

Territorial Adjutant General. *Report.* 1890-1896.

Reports on operations of the National Guard and military supplies acquired from federal government.

Territorial Attorney General. *Report/Opinions.* 1883-1911.

Reports only for most territorial years on cases to which territory was a party.

Territorial Auditor. *Report/Biennial Report.* 1879-1904.

Reports on expenditures of territory funds, appropriations and dispersals, salaries and expenses of government officials, with recommendations of measures for expenditures, such as business taxes. Appears with *Reports of the Territorial Auditor, Territorial Treasurer, and Bank Comptroller.* Tucson: State Consolidated Printing, 1902-1911.

Territorial Board of Control. *Annual Report/Biennial Report.* 1895-1912.

Reports on status and records and financial accounts of Territorial Asylum for the Insane, Yuma Prison, and Industrial School.

Territorial Board of Education. *Biennial Report/Report of Normal Schools of Arizona.* 1891- .

A "state of the school" report on Tempe Normal School (Arizona State University) and expenditures. Beginning in 1900, includes Northern Arizona Normal School at Flagstaff.

————. *Course of Study for the Common Schools of Arizona.* 1881- .

Detailed description of subjects to be taught each week per grade, with teaching suggestions. Includes book lists for reading.

————. *Public Schools of Tucson, Arizona, 1909-1910.*

Photos and report on new high school and common schools, school officers and teachers, salaries, textbooks, and excerpts from "Rules and regulations governing the certification of teachers."

Territorial Board of Equalization. *Proceedings.* 1905-1911.

Reports statistics on property tax and tax assessment for individual counties.

————. *Proceedings of the Conference of the Members of the Several County Boards of Equalization with Members of the Territorial Board of Equalization, June 29, 1906*. Phoenix: Territorial Board of Equalization, 1906.

Significant report issued for territorial assessors following decisions issued in the Arizona Supreme Court's "mine tax cases" on the territory's varying assessments of claims and producing and nonproducing mines.

Territorial Board of Health. *Public Health Laws of Arizona* [and] *Regulations of the Territorial Board of Health*. 1911.

Contains rules and regulations to prevent the spread of infectious diseases among people and domestic animals, duties of county and city boards of health, physicians, and hotel keepers, offenses against public health and safety, and vital statistics laws.

Territorial Board of Regents. *Report*. 1888-1912.

Reports to governor, consisting of territorial university president's reports and the board of regent's endorsements. See Territorial University *President's Reports*.

Territorial Capitol Site Commissioners. *Report*. Florence: Enterprise Job Rooms, 1891.

Report on site selection, grounds improvements, construction of street railway to site.

Territorial Commissioner of Immigration. *Report*. 1889.

Commission responsible for publicity and information about the territory for "home seekers and investors." Published circulars for eastern railroads, and brochures on agricultural resources, citrus, and irrigation. See f3 for specific titles of publications.

Territorial Geologist. *Report*.

Included substantial reports such as "Distribution of Metallic Wealth in Arizona" (1898) and "Minerals of Arizona: Their Occurrence and Association" (1909; 64 pages) by geologist W.P. Blake. Included in governor's reports from 1890-1910.

Territorial Governor. *Condition of the Laws of Arizona and Reasons for Congressional Legislation, by Lewis Wolfley, Governor, to Hon. O. H.*

Platt, Chairman of the Committee on Territories, U.S. Senate. Phoenix: s.n., 1889.

Governor Wolfley found status of territorial government confused and laws uncertain upon arrival to take post April 1889: laws enacted after calendar-specified legislative sessions were "no law" according to the attorney general; former governor issued invalid commissions that legislature rejected; with new regime, some commissioners absent, others refused to yield to Wolfley's appointees. Wolfley requested federal assistance to settle controversy within territorial government.

————. *Messages to the Legislative Assembly.* Phoenix: Office of the Governor, 1865-1911.

Includes annual and biennial opening messages, veto and special messages, inaugural addresses, speeches, etc. *Special Message of Joseph H. Kibbey, Governor of Arizona to the 24th Legislative Assembly on the Assessment and Taxation of Mines, March 1, 1907* addressed an important issue, specifically, that large, successful mines owned by eastern investors were not paying their fair share of the tax burden. Copies of early messages appear in the *Legislative Journals.*

————. *Proclamations.* 1864- .

Generally regarding legislative power, announcing elections, holding district court. *Proclamation to the People of Arizona . . . to Establish a Territorial Government for Arizona,* John N. Goodwin, Governor, Navajo Springs, Arizona, December 29, 1863, was the first one issued upon arrival of the governor's party in Arizona.

————. *Report of the Governor of Arizona Made to the Secretary of the Interior for the Year . . .* (1877-1911). Washington, DC: GPO.

Reports for 1880 and 1882 not published. A "state of the territory" report covering territorial affairs, progress and development, identifying areas of difficulty, with suggestions for Congress (more capital, assistance with Indian problem, need for transportation).

Territorial Historian. *Report, 1909-1911.* Phoenix: H.H. McNeill.

Report by Sharlot Hall, who is credited with preserving many of Arizona's territorial materials. First report on cataloging books and magazines in historian's office, developing card system for photos, and her travels throughout the territory to record accounts of Arizona's first pioneers before their deaths. Her materials are located at the Sharlot Hall Museum Library in Prescott.

Territoral Insane Asylum/State Hospital. *Report.* 1889-1892. Phoenix: Gazette Pub.

Reports on patients, medical conditions and treatment, diet, industry, institution's financial accounts, needed building repairs. Includes statistics.

Territorial Legislative Assembly. *Acts, Resolutions, Memorials* [Session laws]. 1st-25th, 1864-1909.

Compilations of laws from each legislative session with resolutions. Memorials directed to Congress requesting specific action, such as making the Colorado River more navigable, controlling Indian tribes, establishing a mail route, and construction of railroads across the territory.

————. *Compendio de las Leyes de Arizona, Colocadas y Traducidas.* J. Claude Jones, traductor. Tuscon: Imprenta del "Arazonian," 1865.

Selected collection of laws from Howell Code translated into Spanish.

————. *Compiled Laws of the Territory of Arizona: Including the Howell Code and the Session Laws from 1864 to 1871 Inclusive.* Coles Bashford, comp. Albany, NY: Weed, Parson and Co., Printers, 1871.

Code of legislative enactments authorized by legislature but ultimately not officially adopted. Contains civil and penal laws, U.S. Constitution, 1863 Organic Act of Arizona, 1850 Organic Act of New Mexico, U.S. Mining Law from the federal statutes, and Arizona Bill of Rights. Bashford provided an index and retained the order and titles of chapters in the Howell Code, inserting subsequent laws without resolving conflicts.

————. *Compiled Laws of the Territory of Arizona, 1864-1877.* J. Hoyt, comp. Detroit, MI: Richmond, Backus and Co., 1877.

Compilation of laws officially adopted by the legislature. Divorce actions were transferred from the legislature to the district court. Duties of country government expanded, and territorial prison and university established.

————. *Howell Code.* Adopted by the First Legislative Assembly of Arizona. Session Begun on the Twenty-Sixth Day of September and Ended on the Tenth Day of November 1964 at Prescott. Prescott: Office of the Arizona Miner, 1865.

First territorial Arizona code of laws prepared by Supreme Court Justice William T. Howell. Based on California and New York codes and incorporated many Mexican and Spanish laws already in use (community property, mining, and water law). Provided for organization of counties, government departments, and five levels of court (supreme court, district court, and courts' judicial departments).

————. *Journals.* 1st-25th, 1864-1909. Prescott: Office of the Arizona Miner.

Daily record of legislative activity with lists of members and committees.

————. *Leyes Relativas a los Jueces de Paz y Jueces de Pruebas Para el Territorio de Arizona.* C. Tulley, traductor. Tucson: Compania publicista de Arizona Imprenta a vapor, 1881.

Jurisdiction, civil and criminal procedure for justice of the peace courts, and procedure for probate courts.

————. *Memorial and Affidavits Showing Outrages Perpetrated by the Apache Indians in the Territory of Arizona During the Years 1869 and 1870.* Published by Authority of the Legislature of the Territory of Arizona. San Francisco: Francis and Valentine, 1871.

Affidavits of ninety-seven farmers, ranchers, merchants, and station masters reporting depredations and amount of property captured or destroyed, mostly in southern Arizona, which was the result of a federal order withdrawing U.S. troops from the region.

————. *Mining Laws of the Territory of Arizona.* Prescott: Office of the Arizona Miner, 1864.

Also published 39th Cong., 2d sess., 1865. House Misc. Doc. 14. Serial 1232. Committee on Public Lands considered adoption of mining code of Arizona. Covers registry of mines, rights and conveyances, abandonment, and proceedings in litigation mining cases. Later edition appeared as *Mining Laws of the Territory of Arizona and the United States, Revised to Date.* Prescott: Daily Journal-Miner, 1908.

————. *Revised Statutes of Arizona. Civil [and] Penal.* Prescott: Prescott Courier Print, 1887.

Compilation of civil and criminal laws, separate for the first time, and indexed. Additions reflected growth of municipal and expansion of territorial governments, presented new tax laws for corporations, established livestock commission, enlarged sections on wills, and added more criminal offenses.

————. *Revised Statutes of Arizona Territory.* Columbia, MO: E.W. Stephens, 1901.

Code includes the Declaration of Independence, Articles of Confederation, U.S. Constitution with case law references, Treaty of Guadalupe Hidalgo, Gadsden Treaty, and copies of federal statutes applicable to Arizona (the "Organic Law of Arizona"). Included in the two parts, civil and penal, are courts and procedure. Appendix A gives personal and special laws and Appendix B has legislative memorials and resolutions.

————. *Rules and Orders and Joint Rules of the Council and House of Representatives of the Territory of Arizona.* Prescott: Office of the Arizona Miner, 1866.

Sets forth order of business, procedures for memorials, resolutions, and amendments, and designation of standing committees with members. Later editions in 15th, 17-19th, and 23rd Assemblies known as *Standing and Joint Rules of the Council and House.*

Territorial Library. *Catalogue of the Territorial Library of Arizona.* Prepared Under the Direction of the Board of Curators by the Assistant in the Law Department. Phoenix: H.H. McNeil, 1905.

List of general and law books in library.

Territorial Live Stock Sanitary Board. *Live Stock Laws of Arizona.* Phoenix: Southwestern Stockmen Print, 1897; 1901.

Rules and regulations for livestock inspectors and detectives regarding violations of laws and quarantines. Outlines duties of livestock commissioners, ranchers for branding, ear marks, cattle transport, handling contagious diseases, trespass, conversion of brands, and criminal code on dead animals.

————. *Territorial Book of Brands and Marks . . . Cattle, Horses, Sheep and Hogs.* Phoenix: Press Arizona Republican, 1898.

Alphabetical classification of diagrams of brands, and where branded on cattle and horses (pp. 15-185), sheep (pp. 187-194), and hogs (p. 195), including registrant and location (ranch, town).

Territorial Prison (Yuma). *Report/Biennial Report.* [Phoenix(?)]: s.n., [1875-1908(?)].

Reports on state of prison and prisoners, parole laws, industry, attempts to escape, deaths, insanity, and list of prisoners with offenses and sentences. Some reports appear in governor's report.

————. *Rules and Regulations for the Government and Discipline of the Arizona Territorial Prison at Yuma.* Tucson: Star Print, 1895.

Duties of superintendent and other officials, including physician and guards, regarding discipline and cleanliness.

Territorial Public Examiner. *Annual Report.* Tucson: State Consolidated Printing Co., 1908.

Reports of an office created about 1905 to uncover and eliminate embezzlement from government funds. Also reported on conduct in government offices, such as absence from duties and public drunkenness, hiring of unlicensed teachers, purchase of unauthorized textbooks, and illegal payment of county funds. Published delinquent tax roll for counties and provided charts of tax receipts and disbursement of funds.

Territorial Superintendent of Public Instruction. *Arizona School Laws.* Phoenix: McNeill, 1897-1907.

Rules and regulations for students, teachers' duties, list of approved textbooks, course of studies per grade per topic, funds, taxing, election of school trustees, school libraries, examiners, and governance of public schools.

————. *Report/Biennial Report.* Phoenix: Superintendant of Public Instruction, [1875-1908(?)].

Report on schools, number of teachers and students. Article: "Establishment of Arizona School System" by S.P. McCrea in 1908 edition.

Territorial Supreme Court. *Amended Rules of the Supreme Court of the Territory of Arizona, Rules 1-11, Approved March 20, 1903,* in *Arizona Reports* 8(1907): iv-xiii.

Cover abstracts of records, bills of exceptions and statements of facts, motions, brief and arguments service, assignment of errors, costs, fees, and mandate from the U.S. Supreme Court.

————. *Opinions of the Supreme Court of Arizona Rendered in the Decisions of the "Mine Tax Cases," Jan. 20, 1906. Comp. for Information of the Assessors, County Boards of Equalization and Other Officials.* Phoenix: Territorial Board of Equalization, 1906.

Court's decisions regarding assessments of mines in *Copper Queen Consolidated Mining Company v. Territorial Board of Equalization,* 84 P. 511

(1906), 202 US 474 (1907) and *Territory of Arizona v. Board of Supervisors of Yavapai County, Arizona,* 84 P. 519 (1906), two highly significant cases in mining law.

————. *Order, in the Matter of the Division of the Territory of Arizona into Five Judicial Districts and the Designation of Terms and Justices to Preside Therein* [Dated March 22, 1905]; *With Supplemental Orders in Force March 1, 1908, in Ariz.* 9 (1908): iv-vii.

Frederick Nave presiding in fifth judicial district; court held at courthouse in Globe. See also An Act to Provide for an Additional Associate Justice of the Supreme Court of the Territory of Arizona and for Other Purposes, *U.S. Statutes at Large* 33 (1905): 998.

————. *[Records and Briefs, Civil and Criminal Cases].* Phoenix: Arizona Supreme Court, [1871(?)-1912].

Case files of civil and criminal cases.

————. *Report of Cases Argued and Determined in the Supreme Court of the Territory of Arizona [Arizona Reports].* v. 1-13, 1866-1911. San Francisco: Bancroft, 1884-1911.

Official reports of Arizona Supreme Court cases beginning in 1866. Volume 1 contains a list of judges appointed for the territory since its organization, the marshals, and a list of attorneys practicing before the supreme court from its organization up to 1883. Several volumes contain memorandum decisions (2, 3, 4, 6, 7, 10). Beginning with Volume 2, each volume includes a table of cases, and tables of cases and statutes cited. Some volumes contain rules and amended rules of the supreme court (vol. 1, 2, 4, 7, 8) and some contain orders (vol. 9, 13). Justices and officers of the court are listed in each volume after Volume 1. Headnotes precede each case and are compiled into an "index" at the end of the volume. Volume 10, pp. 1-139 (separate pagination), has a digest of all cases reported in Volume 1 to 10. Volume 14 purports to cover cases from 1911 to 1913, covering the last of the territorial period, but the first case reported, March 30, 1912, is after statehood. Parallel citations to the *Pacific Reporter* are provided in all volumes. A digest of all cases reported in Volumes 1 to 10 of the *Arizona Reports* appears in *Arizona Reports* 10 (1909): 1-139 (separate pagination).

————. *Revised Rules of the Supreme Court of the Territory of Arizona* [Rules 1-37] *Adopted,* in *Arizona Reports* 1 (1884): 11-23.

Rules I-XXXVII cover admission of attorneys to practice, civil procedure, writs, appeals, transcripts, formats, and calendaring.

————. *Revised Rules of the Supreme Court of the Territory of Arizona, Adopted January 7, 1887,* in *Arizona Reports* 2 (1887): xxxi-xlv.

Rules I-XXXVII cover attorney admission, appeals, transcripts, rehearings, proof of service, and writs.

————. *Revised Rules of the Supreme Court of the Territory of Arizona, As Amended by Order of the Supreme Court, October 1, 1886.* Prescott: Courier Book and Job Printing Establishment, 1886.

Covers attorney qualifications to practice law, civil procedure, appeals, form for briefs, transcripts, service of process, writs, calendaring, and court fees.

————. *Roll of Attorneys, Arizona Supreme Court.*

Ledger of signatures, dates, and ages of lawyers admitted to practice before the Arizona Supreme Court. First signed in 1882 but signatures of earlier admitted lawyers from 1860s added later. Original book in state archives.

————. *Rules of Court, Supreme Court of the Territory of Arizona,* in *Arizona Reports* 4 (1904): v-xiv.

Covers oral arguments, assignment of errors, motions, briefs, costs, fees, and files as adopted 1894.

————. *Rules of the District Court of Pima County, Adopted Nov. 2, 1883.*

Contains standards and guidelines (forty-six) for the approximately thirty-seven Tucson attorneys practicing before the district court.

————. *Rules of the District Court of the First Judicial District of the Territory of Arizona in and for the County of Pima, Adopted October 5, 1874.* Tucson: Arizona Citizen Print, 1874.

Rules of one of the three original judicial districts on pleadings, service of process, motions, trials, costs, and miscellaneous actions, such as mortgage foreclosure, judgment sales, and writs of attachment.

————. *Rules of the Supreme Court of the Territory of Arizona, Adopted Dec. 27, 1865.* S.L.: s.n., 1865.

First rules of appellate procedure.

————. *Rules of the Supreme Court of the Territory of Arizona, Adopted March 20, 1903.* S.L.: s.n., 1903.

Also as *Amended Rules of the Supreme Court of the Territory of Arizona, Rules 1-11, Approved March 20, 1903,* in *Arizona Reports* 8 (1907): iv-xiii. Covers abstracts of records, bills of exceptions and statements of facts, motions, brief and arguments service, assignment of errors, costs, fees, and mandate from the U.S. Supreme Court.

————. *Rules of the Supreme Court of the Territory of Arizona, Rule X,* in *Arizona Reports* 7 (1906): v.

Adopted 1900, on abstracts of record.

Territorial Treasurer. *Report.* 1883-1908.

Reports on territorial funds and expenditures.

Territorial University. *President's Report to the Board of Regents.* 1888- .

Reports on facilities, faculty, and students at the Territorial University in Tucson. Includes activities of School of Mines and congressionally funded Agricultural Experiment Stations headquartered at the university and located also in Florence, Phoenix, Tempe, and Blaisdell. Includes appropriations requests for residences, dorms, repairs, etc.

————. *Regulations for the Government of Students of the University of Arizona.* Tucson: University of Arizona, 1896.

General regulations adopted by board of regents, including military conduct and drill (required of all male students), rules for "young lady students," and regulations on use of the library.

————. Agricultural Experiment Station. *Annual Report.* Tucson: University of Arizona, 1889/90-1911.

Informational reports on irrigation, cattle feeding, soils, weather, crops, pests, and desert plants. Some published as *Bulletin.*

————. School of Mines. *Report.* 1896. Phoenix: Wood and Irvine Press, 1896.

Report of activities. The School of Mines published territorial geologist William P. Blake's *Sketch of the Mineral Wealth of the Region Adjacent to the Santa Cruz Valley, Arizona: With Reference to the Ore Supply and Ton-*

nage Possible for the Projected Railway from Tucson to Calabasas and Beyond in 1901.

Territorial County Documents

Documents exist for Apache, Cochise, Coconino, Gila, Graham, Greenlee, Maricopa, Mohave, Navajo, Pima, Pinal, Santa Cruz, Yavapai, and Yuma counties. (Pah-Ute County, created in 1865, was given to Nevada in 1866.) These include great registers, town site registers, assessment rolls, mortgage records, deeds, notary records, Mexican land grants (beginning 1851), articles of incorporation, tax records, and board of supervisors minutes. Judicial and vital records include judgment books, jury records, dockets, civil and criminal cases, inquest files, tax suits, probate records, insanity and guardianship cases, marriage and divorce records, naturalization petitions and records, attorney rosters, records of prisoners, and sheriff's records.

Territorial Town and City Documents

Bisbee. *Compiled ordinances of the city of Bisbee: 1902-1909.* 1909.

Contains 1902 incorporation, ordinances, and resolutions.

Douglas. *Charter and Ordinances of the City of Douglas.* Compiled and indexed by A.C. Lockwood. 1907.

Charter contains sections of *1901 Revised Statutes of Arizona.* Ordinances begin in 1905 with establishment of city government.

Jerome. *Ordinances of the Town of Jerome.* Arranged and indexed by Charles H. Rutherford, City Attorney. Jerome News, 1906.

Early laws of mining town.

Phoenix. *Charter and Compiled Ordinances and Resolutions of the City of Phoenix.* Compiled and indexed by Paul R. Inglas. Phoenix: Phoenix Printing Co., 1910.

Charter establishing city government (incorporation in 1875) and early laws.

Prescott. *Synopsis of Prescott City Charter and Special and General Laws Relating Thereto.* City of Prescott, 191?.

Charter and laws of town that was the first capital of Arizona.

Tucson. *Carta Revisada Ordenanzas De Law Ciudad Del Tucson A.T.* Tipografia del Arizona Citizen, 1883.

Spanish edition of 1871 code of ordinances.

————. *Charter and Ordinances of the City of Tucson.* 1871.

Charter establishing city government, and laws. Followed by *Proposed New Charter for the City of Tucson* (1882); *Revised Charter and Ordinances of the City of Tucson, A.T.* (1883); *Charter and Compiled Ordinances of the City of Tucson* (1897); *Charter and Compiled Ordinances of the City of Tucson* (1900); *Charter and Ordinances of the City of Tucson* (1910).

Federal Documents[22]

Colorado River

Adams, Capt. Samuel. *Communication from Captain Samuel Adams Relative to the Exploration of the Colorado River and Its Tributaries.* 42nd Cong., 1st Sess., 1871. H. Misc. Doc. 37.

Report to War Department by Captains Adams and Trueworthy on the navigability of the Colorado River for commercial purposes. Exploration demonstrated that Colorado River capable of being ascended with steamers over 620 miles from its mouth. Includes description of mineral and agricultural resources of country along river. Commercial navigation of river endorsed by Arizona legislature but opposed in California as against railroad interests.

Dutton, Clarence. *Tertiary History of the Grand Canyon District, with Atlas.* Washington, DC: GPO, 1882; reprint, Tucson: University of Arizona Press, 2001.

Presentation of the geography and geologic history of the area by one of John Wesley Powell's assistants.

Ives, Lt. Joseph C. *Report upon the Colorado River of the West Explored in 1857 and 1858.* 30th Cong., 1st Sess., 1861. H. Exec. Doc. 90.

Includes hydrographic, geologic, botanical, and zoological reports. <http://hdl.loc.gov/umich.dli.moa/ADU2374>.

Powell, John Wesley. *Explorations of the Colorado of the West and its Tributaries; Explored in 1869, 1870, 1871, and 1872 Under the Direction of the Secretary of the Smithsonian Institution.* Washington, DC: GPO, 1875.

Contains lengthy descriptions of the region's geography, geology, and hydrology, and Powell's diary of his boat trip "down the Great Unknown." <http://hdl.loc.gov/umich.dli.moa/AFK4571>.

————. *Report of Explorations in 1873 of the Colorado of the West and Its Tributaries.* Washington, DC: GPO, 1874.

Summary of Powell's explorations from the beginning to 1873 of the Colorado River, covering topography, geology, ethnology (Indian tribes), and natural history. <http://hdl.loc.gov/umich.dli.moa/AJA3599>.

Sitgreaves, Lorenzo. *Report of an Expedition Down the Zuni and Colorado Rivers.* 32nd Cong., 2d Sess., 1853. Sen. Exec. Doc. 59.

Report of 1852 land expedition that followed the courses of the rivers. Covers topography, natural history, and Indian tribes, with many illustrative plates. Includes tables of geographical positions and meteorological observations. <http://hdl.loc.gov/umich.dli.moa/AFM1949>.

Indian Tribes: Military Campaigns/Peacekeeping[23]

Colyer, Vincent. *Peace with the Apaches of New Mexico and Arizona.* Washington, DC: GPO, 1872.

Indian commissioner and Quaker humanitarian acting under "President Grant's Peace Policy," Colyer established San Carlos, Fort Apache, and Camp Verde reservations for Apache Indians to promote peace and civilization. Because he failed to include Cochise and his band, hostilities between whites and Indians began again, resulting in new military campaigns to forcibly subdue and contain all Apaches.

Crook, George. *Report of Operations Against Apache Indians, May, 1885, to April, 1886.* S.L.: s.n., 1886?

Includes letter of military instruction from General Sheridan to General Crook, and twelve reports from General Crook, Lieutenant Maus, Captain Davis, Lieutenant Davis, Captain Crawford, Sargent Mott. See also 51st Cong., 1st Sess., 1890, S. Exec. Doc. 88, Serial 2686, for additional correspondence between Crook and Sheridan regarding subjugation of hostile Apaches, and S. Exec. Doc. 83 (Serial 2686) on treatment of certain Apache Indians.

U.S. House. *Agreement with Navajo Indians.* 54th Cong., 2d Sess., 1897. H. Doc. 310. Serial 3534.

Indian Affairs commissioner review of U.S. relations with tribe from 1849 (initial treaty of peace) to 1864 (removal of tribe to Bosque Redondo Reservation in New Mexico, the historic "Long Walk" of the Navajos) to 1868 (conclusion of treaty between United States and Navajos) when remaining tribal members allowed to return to homeland. Navajos were not forced onto the reservation, however, and skirmishes between settlers—the off-reservation Indians and whites in border areas—continued, mostly over water supply. See also *Report . . . Relative to the Situation Among the Navajo Indians in New Mexico and Arizona,* 52nd Cong., 1st Sess., 1892, S. Doc. 156, Serial 2901, relating Navajo-white conflicts, and order to military officers to inspect region for indicating water supply, and survey report with contour maps at 52nd Cong., 2d Sess., 1893, S. Doc. 68, Serial 3056. For unsuitableness of Fort Sumner (Bosque Redondo), see 40th Cong., 2d Sess., 1868, H. Exec. Doc. 248, Serial 1341, and subsequent removal of tribe, H. Exec. Doc. 308, Serial 1345.

————. *Appropriations for the Navajo Indians.* 38th Cong., 1st Sess., 1864. H. Doc. 70. Serial 1193.

Ex-Superintendent of Indian Affairs James L. Collins and General Carleton on necessity to furnish Navajo Indians who were removed to Bosque Redondo Reservation with clothing, food, farm equipment, and means to become self-sufficient, supported by trained staff. "These six thousand people must be fed." See also 38th Cong., 1st Sess., 1864, S. Exec. Doc. 36, Serial 1176, on providing means of subsistence for Navajo Indians, and S. Misc. Doc. 97, Serial 1177 (same Congress), on establishing a reservation.

U.S. Senate. *Correspondence Regarding the Apache Indians.* 51st Cong., 1st Sess., 1890. Sen. Doc. 88.

General George Crook recounts his activities in the war against the Apaches.

————. *Correspondence with General Miles Relative to the Surrender of Geronimo.* 49th Cong., 2d Sess., 1887. Sen. Exec. Doc. 117. Serial 2449.

Reports of General Miles and other commanders relative to roundup of Geronimo and his band following escape from the White Mountain Reserve, their surrender, and hardship in removal of tribe to Florida.

————. *Reports upon the Condition of the Navajo Indian Country.* 52nd Cong., 2d Sess., 1893. S. Exec. Doc. 68. Serial 3056.

Indian Affairs Commissioner T.J. Morgan's report on practicality of restraining Navajo Indians within their reservation and furnishing water and irrigation for flocks. Contains many contour maps locating springs, ditches, and other sources of water on the Navajo reservation. Follow-up to earlier report by General McCook on continuing "Navajo situation" of conflicts with whites, mostly over water, from 1888, and the detailing of officers to inspect region regarding its water supply. See *Letter from the Acting Secretary of the Interior Transmitting Copy of Indian Office Report . . . Relative to the Situation Among the Navajo Indians in New Mexico and Arizona,* 52nd Cong., 1st Sess., 1892. S. Exec. Doc. 156. Serial 2901.

Indian Tribes: Treaties, Agreements, and Conventions [24]

President. *Executive Orders* [establishing the following Indian Reserves: Camp Grant, Camp Verde, Chiricahua, Colorado River, Gila Bend, Hualapai (Walapai), Moqui (Hopi), Navajo, Papago, Pima and Maricopa or Gila River, Salt River, Suppai (Havasupai), White Mountain or San Carlos Apache, and Yuma].

Executive orders reprinted in *Indian Affairs: Laws, Treaties,* Vol. 1, *Laws.* Compiled and edited by Charles Kappler. 2d ed. Washington: GPO, 1904, at 801-906. <http://digital.library.okstate.edu/kappler/Vol1/HTML_files/ARI0801.html#az>.

U.S. Statutes at Large 13 (1865): 541, 559. An Act Making Appropriations . . . and Fulfilling Treaty Stipulations . . . [Colorado River Reservation Established for Indians of Colorado River and tributaries], March 3, 1865.

Reservation boundary changes in subsequent executive orders of November 22, 1873; November 16, 1874; and May 15, 1876.

U.S. Statutes at Large 11 (1859): 388, 401. An Act Making Appropriations . . . and Fulfilling Treaty Stipulations . . . [Gila River Reservation Established for Pima and Maricopa Indians], February 28, 1859.

Treaty lands enlarged in executive order of August 31, 1876.

U.S. Statutes at Large 29 (1896): 358. Agreement with the Indians of the San Carlos Reservation in Arizona, San Carlos Agency, New Mexico Territory, February 25, 1896.

For Apache, Mohave, Yuma tribes. Reprinted in Kappler, *Indian Affairs,* vol. 1, at 609. <http://digital.library.okstate.edu/kappler/Vol1/Images/v1p 0609.jpg>.

U.S. Statutes at Large 9 (1849): 974. Treaty Between the United States of America and the Navajo Tribe of Indians, Canyon de Chelly, New Mexico Territory, September 9, 1849.

Reprinted in Kappler, *Indian Affairs,* Vol. 2, at 583. <http://digital.library. okstate.edu/kappler/Vol2/treaties/nav0583.htm>. Text of treaty in English and Navajo in Richard Ellis, ed., *New Mexico Historic Documents* at 56-71. Albuquerque: University of New Mexico Press, 1975.

U.S. Statutes at Large 15 (1868): 667. Treaty Between the United States of America and the Navajo Tribe of Indians, June 1, 1868.

Reprinted in Kappler, *Indian Affairs,* Vol. 2 at 1015. <http://digital.library. okstate.edu/kappler/Vol2/treaties/nav1015.htm>.

U.S. Statutes at Large 10 (1852): 979. Treaty with the Apache, July 1, 1852.

Reprinted in Kappler, *Indian Affairs,* vol. 2, at 598. <http://digital.library. okstate.edu/kappler/Vol2/treaties/apa0598.htm>.

International Boundary Commission

U.S. Department of the Interior. *Report on the United States and Mexican Boundary Survey* by William H. Emory. 34th Cong., 1st Sess., 1857. H. Exec. Doc. 35. Serial 861-863; reprint, Austin: Texas State Historical Society, 1987. 2 v in 3 v.

Emory charged to complete marking of U.S.-Mexico boundary, to examine the nearby country to ascertain a practical railroad route to the Pacific, and to collect information about the inhabitants and the agricultural and mineral resources. Emory's narrative and reports by surveyor, scientists, and soldiers is a scientific encyclopedia of western flora and fauna of the border country, with more than 350 lithographs and engravings, and was a major contribution to the field of geography. Map considered one of the best cartographic reports on the Trans-Mississippi West. <http://hdl.loc.gov/umich. dli.moa/AFK4546h>.

Boundary survey member John Bartlett published his *Personal Narrative of Explorations and Incidents in Texas, New Mexico, California, Sonora, and Chihuahua, Connected with the United States and Mexican Boundary Commission, During the Years 1850, 1851, 1852, and 1853* (New York:

Appleton, 1854) to provide a "useful guide to emigrants and other travelers." Though submitted as a report to the secretary of interior and introduced in a Senate resolution, the work was not published by the U.S. government.

U.S. Senate. *Report of the Boundary Commission Upon the Survey and Re-Marking of the Boundary Between the United States and Mexico West of the Rio Grande, 1891-1896.* Parts I and II. Part I: *Report of the International Commission.* Part II: *Report of the United States Section.* 55th Cong., 2d Sess., 1898. S. Doc. 247.

Colonel of Engineers J.W. Barlow reports a general description of the boundary country between the United States and Mexico, covering topography, geology, plants, wildlife, climate, water, and peoples inhabiting the area. Precise locations of old and new boundary monuments are given (latitude and longitude). Numerous plates of buildings, monuments, and country features are included. Reprints Article V of Treaty of Guadalupe Hidalgo and reviews the four conventions.

U.S. Statutes at Large 22 (1883): 986. Proclamation. Convention [I] Between the United States of America and the United States of Mexico providing for an International Boundary Survey to Relocate the Existing Frontier Line Between the Two Countries West of the Rio Grande, July 29, 1882.

Provided for reconnaissance party of members from both countries to survey conditions of markers and advise as to new markers and locations. Each country to appoint a surveying party that together forms an International Boundary Commission. The commission to establish scientific process and standards for erection of new markers has the power and authority to set markers along the proper boundary line. Commission to continue in force until work completed, but for not more than four years and four months from date of ratification. Text in English and Spanish.

U.S. Statutes at Large 24 (1888): 1011. Proclamation. Convention [II] Between the United States of America and the United States of Mexico Touching the International Boundary Line Where It Follows the Bed of the Rio Grande and the Rio Colorado, November 12, 1884.

Reestablished boundary between countries to follow original dividing line in center of rivers despite erosion and new channels. In Spanish and English.

U.S. Statutes at Large 26 (1889): 1493. Proclamation. Convention [III] Between the United States of America and the United States of Mexico To Revive the Provisions of the Convention of July 29, 1882 to Survey and Relocate the Boundary Line West of the Rio Grande and to Extend the Time Fixed in Article VIII of the Said Convention.

Articles in original convention of 1882 are revived, providing for Boundary Commission members and time period to carry out the work that lapsed because government parties did not appointment commission members. A period of five years is allowed from ratification for completion of the work. In Spanish and English.

U.S. Statutes at Large 26 (1890): 1512. Proclamation. Convention [IV] Between the United States of America and the United States of Mexico to Facilitate the Carrying Out of the Principles Contained in the Treaty of November 12, 1884, and to Avoid the Difficulties Occasioned by Reason of the Changes Which Take Place in the Bed of the Rio Grande and That of the Colorado River.

Established commission members and set forth survey changes in rivers and boundary line. In Spanish and English.

Public Lands

President. *Proclamations* [Establishing Game Reserve]: Grand Canyon Game Reserve (*U.S. Statutes at Large* 34 [1906]: 3263).

Designation of area north and west of Colorado River in Grand Canyon Forest for protection of game.

————. [Establishing National Forest Reserves]: Baboquivari (*U.S. Statutes at Large* 34 [1906]: 3251); Black Mesa (*U.S. Statutes at Large* 30 [1898]: 1782); Chiricahua (*U.S. Statutes at Large* 32: [1902]: 2019) (enlargement at *U.S. Statutes at Large* 34 [1906]: 3244); Grand Canyon (*U.S. Statutes at Large* 27 [1893]: 1064) (additions at *U.S. Statutes at Large* 34 [1905]: 3009 and *U.S. Statutes at Large* 34 [1906]: 3223); Huachuca (*U.S. Statutes at Large* 34 [1906]: 3255); Mount Graham (*U.S. Statutes at Large* 32 [1902]: 2017); Pinal Mountains (*U.S. Statutes at Large* 34 [1906]: 2991); Prescott (*U.S. Statutes at Large* 30 [1898]: 1771) (enlargement at *U.S. Statutes at Large* 31 [1899]); San Francisco Mountains (*U.S. Statutes at Large* 30 [1898]: 1780) (enlargement at *U.S. Statutes at Large* 32 [1902]: 1991); Santa Catalina (*U.S. Statutes at*

Large 32 [1902]: 2012); Tonto (*U.S. Statutes at Large* 34 [1906]: 3166); Tumacacori (*U.S. Statutes at Large* 34 [1906]: 3263).

————. [Establishing National Monuments]: Grand Canyon (*U.S. Statutes at Large* 35 [1908]: 2175) (designated in 1919 as Grand Canyon National Park); Montezuma (*U.S. Statutes at Large* 34 [1906]: 3265); Petrified Forest (*U.S. Statutes at Large* 34 [1906]: 3266).

U.S. Statutes at Large 28 (1894): 30. An Act Granting Certain Lands to the Territory of Arizona, January 27, 1894.

Adding 2,115 acres at the junction of the Gila and Colorado Rivers to Arizona Territory.

Reports, Studies, Surveys

Emory, William H. *Notes of a Military Reconnaissance, from Fort Leavenworth, in Missouri, to San Diego, in California, Including Part of the Arkansas, Del Norte, and Gila Rivers.* 30th Cong., 1st Sess., 1848. H. Exec. Doc. 41.

Report on the topography, vegetation, history, and Indian tribes in the lower half of Arizona. Includes additional reports by Abert on New Mexico, Bailey on minerals and fossils, and St. George Cooke on his march from Santa Fe to San Diego. Companion Sen. Exec. Doc. 7 includes only Emory's report.

Johnson, Royal A. *Adverse Report of the Surveyor General of Arizona, Royal A. Johnson, Upon the Alleged Peralta Grant: A Complete Expose of its Fraudulent Character.* Phoenix: Arizona Gazette Book and Job Print, 1890.

Meticulously researched and documented report on a claim made by James Addison Reavis, supposed heir to an alleged land grant by the King of Spain in 1758, the "Peralta Grant." The property, 79 miles by 236 miles in the middle of Arizona, included the rich Silver King mine, a large portion of five counties and eight cities, including Phoenix, and more than half of the forested White Mountain Indian Reservation. Report details the forgeries of letters, church records, deeds, and affidavits. Decision of U.S. Court of Land Claims in 1895 was significant for the development of settlement. For history, see Donald M. Powell's *The Peralta Grant.* Norman: University of Oklahoma Press, 1960.

Parke, Lt. John G. *Report of Explorations for that Portion of a Railroad Route, Near the Thirty-Second Parallel of North Latitude, Lying Between Dona Ana, on the Rio Grande, and Pimas Villages, on the Gila.* Washington, DC: GPO, 1855.

Survey of terrain for railroad routes to the Pacific beginning at the junction of the Gila and Colorado Rivers, up the Gila to Pimas Villages, south to Tucson, then east to the San Pedro River and to Mesilla (Dona Ana). Includes report by Captain Phillip St. George Cooke, commander of "Mormon Battalion," on marking way for wagon road. Published by 33rd Cong., 2d Sess., 1855, as S. Exec. Doc. 78, Serial 759, and H. Exec. Doc. 91, Serial 791. Also in Volume 2 of Ariel Whipple's *Explorations and Surveys, to Ascertain the Most Practicable and Economic Route for a Railroad from the Mississippi River to the Pacific Ocean, Made Under the Direction of the Secretary of War, 1855-1859* (11 volumes). 33rd Cong., 2d Sess., 1855-1859. S. Exec. Doc. 78.

Powell, John Wesley. *Report on the Lands of the Arid Region of the U.S., with a More Detailed Account of the Lands of Utah.* 2nd ed. Washington, DC: GPO, 1879.

Report to secretary of the interior on arid regions of the West, including Arizona, giving a survey of conditions of land available for agriculture and grazing purposes, and the rainfall. The impetus behind the exploration was to survey the land for homesteading. Powell's conclusion is that, because of the arid conditions, a homestead of 160 acres was incapable of supporting either a farming or ranching family. He proposed that a farm be reduced to eighty acres and be irrigated. Sufficient grazing land of 2,560 acres, not 160 nor 640 of the Desert Land Act, was required to feed cattle to support a family. Includes drafts of two bills on pasturage districts and organization of irrigation districts. Revised edition eliminates errors of first edition. <http://memory.loc.gov/cgi-bin/query/r?ammem/consrv:@field(DOCID+@lit(amrvgvg06))>.

A facsimile of the first edition was issued in 1983 by Harvard Commons Press. T.H. Watkins writes in his introduction that the 1879 report is "quite possibly the most revolutionary document ever to tumble off the presses of the Government Printing Office. That the document's intent was subverted or ignored from the very beginning, that it was distorted in the passage of the only legislation produced, and that in 1982 even that distortion was laid in the coffin of history does not make this document any less revolutionary."

U.S. Census. *Eighth Decennial Census, County of Arizona, New Mexico Territory.* 1860.

Reported population: 6,482. Provides names, age, sex, occupation, value of property, and place of birth for civilians and military personnel in towns, villages, mail stations, garrisons, and forts. Census before Arizona became its own territory.

————. *Excerpts from the Decennial Federal Census 1860 for Arizona County in the Territory of New Mexico, the Special Territorial Census of 1864 Taken in Arizona and Decennial Federal Census 1870 for the Territory of Arizona.* Reprinted in Sen. Doc. 13, 89th Cong., 1st Sess., 1965. Washington, DC: GPO, 1965.

See previous entry for 1860 information and see following entry for 1870 data. Population in 1864 was 4,573.

————. *Ninth Decennial Census, Arizona Territory.* 1870.

Reported population: 9,658. Same level of detail as in 1860 census but also with totals of states and counties represented and total valuation of property by county.

————. *Special Arizona Enumeration.* 1866.

Information from Graham, Mohave, Pah-Ute, Pima, Yavapai, and Yuma counties.

————. *Special Arizona Enumeration.* 1869.

Information from Mohave, Pima, Yavapai and Yuma counties.

U.S. Senate. *Message from the President of the United States Communicating Information in Relation to the Condition of the Records and Documents of Mexico Relating to the Land Within the Territories of Arizona and New Mexico.* 43rd Cong., 2d Sess., 1874. Sen. Exec. Doc. 3. Serial 1629.

Ulysses S. Grant on registers of land grants made by Mexican government in Arizona and New Mexico, problems with archives in Guadalajara, and proving the authenticity of transcripts and documents.

————. Select Committee on Irrigation and Reclamation of Arid Lands. *Report of the Special Committee . . . and Views of the Minority.* 2 vols. 51st Cong., 1st Sess., 1890. Sen. Rept. 928.

Survey covering many states and territories, but extensively California, Nevada, Utah, Arizona, the Dakotas, Colorado, and Montana, with testimony of farmers, ranchers, and experts. Arizona section is on crops (mostly fruits), water supply (rainfall, irrigation, canals, rivers, reservoirs, groundwater), topography and soils (vol. 2, pp. 400-494, plus maps), and "Irrigation Laws of Arizona" (pp. 495-497) for Yuma, Colorado River area, Phoenix-Maricopa County, Gila Valley, Apache County, and southern Arizona.

Wasson, John. *Compilation of Laws, Regulations, Usages and Conditions of Spain and Mexico Under Which Lands Were Granted and Held, and Missions, Presidios and Pueblos Established and Governed.* Tucson: [n.p.], 1880.

U.S. Surveyor General's report to Congress on the ordinances and procedures by which land grants were established in Sonora (Arizona) first under Spanish rule (1700s-1821) and then under the Mexican government (1821-1846). The United States succeeded to all rights, titles, privileges, and obligations associated with the land grants when the region became a U.S. territory. Covers rights to work mines.

Wheeler, George. *Annual Report upon the Geographical Explorations and Surveys West of the One-Hundredth Meridian in California, Oregon, Nevada, Texas, Arizona, Colorado, Idaho, Montana, New Mexico, Utah and Wyoming.* Washington, DC: GPO.

Reports for 1871, 1872, 1873, 1875, and 1876 contain information on Arizona. The 1875 edition on Colorado River has botanical report by Joseph T. Rothrock with remarks on the topography of Arizona, climatology, plants, timber, and irrigation. The 1876 report is on mines and diversion of Colorado River for irrigation.

————. *Preliminary Report Concerning Explorations and Surveys Principally in Nevada and Arizona.* Washington, DC: GPO, 1872.

Preliminary report of *Geographical Explorations and Surveys . . .* with description of country, climate, geologic formations, and vegetation in light of value for settlers. Examines Colorado River area. <http://southwest.library.arizona.edu/expl>; <http://hdl.loc.gov/umich.dli.moa/AJA3663>.

Whipple, Amiel. *[Report of Exploration for a Railway Route] Near the Thirty-Fifth Parallel,* vols. 3 and 4 of *Report of Explorations and Surveys, to Ascertain the Most Practicable and Economical Route for a Railroad from the Mississippi River to the Pacific Ocean, Made Under the Direction of the Secretary of War.* 33rd Cong., 2nd Sess., 1854-1855. S. Exec. Doc. 78. Serial 760-761. Also H. Exec Doc. 91. Serial 793-794.

Report of Whipple's exploration in 1849 of a northern Arizona route near modern Flagstaff to the Colorado River. Comprehensive description of region, including terrain, geology, botany, wildlife, and Indian inhabitants.

NOTES

1. Lawrence Clark Powell, *Arizona: A History* 39 (Albuquerque: University of New Mexico Press, 1976) (New Edition 1990).

2. The Treaty of Guadalupe Hidalgo established the boundary line, later modified by the Gadsden Treaty, between the United States and Mexico and appointed commissioners and surveyors from the two countries to mark the boundary. With later settlement and discovery of mines in the vicinity, some of the original markers were destroyed or removed, requiring resurveying and placement of new monuments (markers). For history of the early phase of the boundary problems, see Jay J. Wagoner, *Early Arizona: Prehistory To Civil War* 280-297 (Tucson: University of Arizona Press, 1975). For publications regarding the International Boundary Commission and its work, see Bibliography.

3. To promote immigration and knowledge about the territory, Arizona's legislative assembly authorized Patrick Hamilton to compile *The Resources of Arizona: Its Mineral, Farming, and Grazing Lands, Towns, and Mining Camps; Its Rivers, Mountains, Plains, and Mesas; with a Brief Summary of its Indian Tribes, Early History, Ancient Ruins, Climate, etc. A Manual of Reliable Information Concerning the Territory* (Prescott: n.p., 1881), <http://southwest.library.arizona.edu/reaz>. Also authorized was A. P. K. Safford's *The Territory of Arizona: A Brief History and Summary of the Territory's Acquisition, Organization, and Mineral, Agricultural, and Grazing Resources, Embracing a Review of its Indian Tribes* (Tucson: Citizen Office, 1874). Independent promotions of mineral resources were Sylvester Mowry's *Arizona and Sonora: The Geography, History, and Resources of the Silver Region of North America* (New York: Harper and Bros., 1864); and *History of Arizona Territory Showing Its Resources and Advantages* (San Francisco: W.W. Elliott, 1884) (reprinted, Flagstaff, AZ: Northland Press, 1964), <http://www.hti.umich.edu/m/moa.new>.

County Immigration Offices and Boards of Trade issued promotional booklets, such as *Resources of Yuma County* (1888), *Yavapai County, Arizona, the Treasure Vault of the Southwest* (1907), and *What the Salt River Valley Offers to the Immigrant, Capitalist, and Invalid* (1887). Pima County requested territorial geologist William P. Blake to prepare *Sketch of Pima County, Arizona: Its Mining Districts, Minerals, Climate, Agriculture, and Other Resources* (Tucson: Citizen Print, 1910).

4. Examples of legislative memorials that illustrate the degree of federal government micromanagement of the territory are a request for an increase in salaries of territorial officials because ordinary provisions cost ten times more in the remote Southwest as elsewhere in the United States (1864); a request that appointments to

territorial posts be from "bona fide residents of the territory" rather than eastern outsiders (1885); and pleas for new mail routes (1866, 1875).

5. Legislative memorials petitioned Congress for protection from roving outlaw bands stealing cattle then crossing the Mexican border to avoid capture (1885); to protest the removal of federal troops needed to contain Indians on the San Carlos Apache Reservation and the loss of livelihood of the Apaches through selling goods to the cavalry (1895); to resolve boundary issues (1864, 1865, 1866, 1895, 1903, 1905, 1909); and to improve navigation of the Colorado River, the only navigable river in the territory and channel for nearly all imports and exports for the northern half of the territory (1864, 1865, 1885, 1905, 1909).

6. A memorial from the Second Legislative Assembly, 1883, requesting removal of warring Apaches from the territory and noting Arizona's frustration in dealing with the federal government, colorfully referred to as the "whang-doodle-ism of our Indian Dept."

7. Tom Sheridan, *Arizona: A History* 77-99 (Tucson: University of Arizona Press, 1995). The best source on Apache-U.S. warfare is Dan Thrapp, *The Conquest of Apacheria* (Norman: University of Oklahoma Press, 1967).

8. Noted anthropologists and archaeologists, such as Franz Boas, Frank Cushing, Jesse Fewkes, Charles Lummis, and John Burke, wrote on Arizona's Indian culture and ancient ruins in such publications as Smithsonian reports, Bureau of American Ethnology papers, National Museum reports, Archaeological Institute of America papers, and *American Anthropology.*

9. For interesting background on Colorado River freighting and travel, consult Richard Lingenfelter, *Steamboats on the Colorado River, 1852-1916* (Tucson: University of Arizona Press, 1978). The river became well-known to scientists, government officials, and tourists with the publication of John Wesley Powell's report *Explorations of the Colorado of the West and Its Tributaries,* which contained Powell's diary of his boat trip "down the Great Unknown," the Grand Canyon.

10. John Leshy, *The Arizona State Consitution: A Reference Guide 2* (Westport, CT: Greenwood Press, 1993).

11. Delegate Marcus Smith said, "We had rather be a Territory for the balance of time than to be joined to that Republican gang," as reported in Howard R. Lamar, *The Far Southwest, 1846-1912: A Territorial History* 423, (rev. ed., Albuquerque: University of New Mexico Press, 2000). Arizona's nemesis in Congress was Albert Beveridge, Chairman of the Senate Committee on Territories from the 57th through 61st Congresses, who for years strongly opposed the territory's admission into the Union as a backward region of low population and Spanish-speaking residents controlled by large mining companies and railroad interests. He relented as far as to assent to the proposed merger of Arizona and New Mexico into one state. See John J. Wagoner, *Arizona Territory, 1863-1912* 408-412 (Tucson: University of Arizona Press, 1970); Lamar's *Far Southwest* 426-432; and John Braemar's "Albert Beveridge and Statehood For the Southwest, 1902-1912," *Arizona & the West* 10(Winter 1968): 313-342.

12. For local territorial history, consult the following texts: Lynn R. Bailey, *Bisbee: Queen of the Copper Camps* (Rev. and enl. ed., Tucson: Westernlore Press, 2002); Platt Cline, *Mountain Town: Flagstaff's First Century* (Flagstaff, AZ: North-

land Pub., 1994); Pauline Henson, *Founding a Wilderness Capital, Prescott, A. T. 1864* (Flagstaff, AZ: Northland Press, 1975); Bradford Luckingham, *Phoenix: The History of a Southwestern Metropolis* (Tucson: University of Arizona Press, 1989); C.L. Sonnichsen, *Tucson: The Life and Times of an American City* (Norman: University of Oklahoma Press, 1982); and Douglas Martin, *Yuma Crossing* (Albuquerque: University of New Mexico Press, 1954). The "helldorado" years of Tombstone have given rise to many books and articles, some little more than sensational accounts, so recommended titles for reliable information are William B. Schillingberg's *Tombstone A.T.: A History of Early Mining, Milling, and Mayhem* (Spokane, WA: Arthur H. Clarke Co., 1999) and Douglas Martin's *Tombstone's Epitaph* (rev. and enl. ed., Norman: University of Oklahoma Press, 1997) (Albuquerque: University of New Mexico Press, 1951), a history from pages of the famed newspaper.

13. *The Supreme Court Justices, 1863-1912* (vol. 1. Cave Creek, AZ: Black Mountain Press, 1975); *The Governors, 1863-1912* (vol. 2, 1978); *The Delegates to Congress, 1863-1912* (vol. 3, 1985); *The Secretaries, United States Attorneys, Marshals, Surveyors General, and Superintendents of Indian Affairs, 1863-1912* (vol. 4, 1988); *The Adjutants General, Attorneys General, Auditors, Superintendents of Public Instruction, and Treasurers* (vol. 5, 1991); *Members of the Legislature* (vols. 6-7, 1996). John Goff wrote biographies of individual territorial officials: governors George W. P. Hunt (1987), Thomas E. Campbell (1985), and Richard Mccormick (1983); Supreme Court Justice Joseph H. Kibbey (1991), and longtime legislator and delegate to Congress Marcus Smith (1989), all published by Black Mountain Press.

14. Included are Provisional Constitution of 1860; Proclamation of 1861; Confederate Territorial Act of 1862; Federal Proclamation of 1862; Federal Territorial Act of 1863; Draft Constitution of 1891; Enabling Act of June 20, 1910; Constitution of 1910 (abstract); Veto Message, August 14, 1911; Resolution of August 19, 1911; and Proclamation, February 14, 1912 (vol. 1, pp. 233-316).

15. Another reliable history is Odie Faulk's *Arizona: A Short History* (Norman: University of Oklahoma Press, 1970). Two chronologies provide researchers an overview of important events and publications in Arizona: Douglas Martin's *An Arizona Chronology: The Territorial Years 1846-1912* (Tucson: University of Arizona Press, 1963) and *Chronology and Documentary Handbook of the State of Arizona* (Ellen Lloyd Trover, ed.; Dobbs Ferry, NY: Oceana Pub., 1972).

16. Accounts by individuals with their perspective from the territorial time period include "Father of Arizona" Charles Poston's *Building a State in Apacheland* (John M. Meyers, ed.; Tempe, AZ: Aztec Press, 1963); Sylvester Mowry's *Memoir of the Proposed Territory of Arizona* (Washington, DC: Henry Polkinhorn Printer, 1857); and Martha Summerhayes's *Vanished Arizona; Recollection of My Army Life* (Philadelphia, PA: J.B. Lippincott Co., 1908), <http://southwest.library.arizona.edu/vaaz>. For additional personal accounts, see the University of Arizona's Southwest Electronic Text Center at <http://dizzy.library.arizona.edu/swetc/projects.html>.

17. Significant collections of Arizona materials are found at the Bancroft Library, University of California, Berkeley; the Huntington Library, San Marino, California; the Southwest Museum, Los Angeles; and Harvard and Yale University

Libraries. The "American Memory" Digital Project of the Library of Congress has territorial Arizona documents on its Web site: <http://memory.loc.gov>.

18. Other interesting but less useful sources include Estelle Lutrell's *A Bibliographical List of Books, Pamphlets and Articles on Arizona in the University of Arizona Library* (Tucson: University of Arizona, 1913), topically arranged and good for obscure items in government and popular accounts; *Arizona Odyssey: Bibliographic Ventures in Nineteeenth-Century Magazines* by David Goodman (Tempe: Arizona Historical Foundation, 1969), a topical, abstracted list of articles about territorial times in Arizona; and Goodman's *Empire in Print: The Printed Public Documents of Arizona Territory, 1863-1912* (Rye, N.H., 1995; typescript on file at the Arizona Historical Society Library).

19. Ida Reid Leonard, *A Preliminary Survey of the More Important Archives of the Territory and State of Arizona* (privately printed, 1936). Many office holders, says Leonard, regarded records as personal, to be removed or destroyed upon leaving office. Up until 1921 records were stored in basement rooms of the capitol, but that year the building was flooded on the lower level. "The most valuable records were washed off and dried by laundry mangles. Those placed to dry in the open were unfortunately hopelessly scattered by a heavy wind. The confused mass was burned." Then the attic was used for storage of department and commission papers, including those of the governor and auditor general, which were placed on open wooden shelves without further protection and often in no particular arrangement. "The material presents a confusion of large and small cartons heaped over with bundles of papers, many of which have been loosened, allowing the contents to scatter. Practically nothing remains of the Territorial period" (writing of governor's papers). Sacks of attorney general records were stored under the eaves. Some records were stored in vaults that were neither fire- nor waterproof, if located in the basement. Very few records of the superintendent of public instruction existed as office files and were cleared with the change of personnel. Lack of funds to bind documents of the secretary of territory records was "a serious menace to their proper preservation."

20. Most book materials are in the library online catalog at <http://lista.azhist.arizona.edu>.

21. Territorial government departments contracted with commercial printers that were usually associated with newspapers to publish their reports and documents, often changing printers each year. Because of this, some publishing information is not included in the bibliographic entries for serials and dates of coverage are approximate. See f19 for history of why some territorial records are incomplete and unavailable for complete bibliographic information.

22. No individual map documents are included in the bibliography.

23. No attempt has been made to compile a complete bibliography of documents about Native American tribes in Arizona during the territorial period. The few documents that are listed provide insight into the history and events of Indian-Arizona-U.S. relations during a formative time period. For a comprehensive listing, consult the electronic database LexisNexis, "Congressional Historical Indexes 1789-1969 and Unpublished Hearings," and *Guide to American Indian Documents in the Serial Set: 1817-1899* by Stephen L. Johnson (New York: Clearwater Pub., 1977).

24. For unratified treaties and agreements with Indian tribes, see Vine Deloria Jr. and Raymond DeMallie, *Documents of American Indian Diplomacy: Treaties, Agreements, and Conventions, 1775-1972,* vol. 2, 1237-1241 (Norman: University of Oklahoma Press, 1999).

Chapter 4

Arkansas Law Before Statehood

Glen-Peter Ahlers Sr.

Two things are striking about the colonial laws of Arkansas. The first is how quickly the common law caught on after centuries of warring cultural infusions, including the melding of civil and common law influences upon the lawless frontier. The second is that the territorial period lasted only seventeen years.

THE SPANISH AND FRENCH INFLUENCES

The indigenous people were first interrupted by the Spanish. Explorer Hernando De Soto arrived in search of gold in 1541, after he had already explored, conquered, and colonized Nicaragua and Honduras with Francisco Fernández de Córdoba, and after he had already helped topple the Incas of Peru.[1] De Soto "crossed the Mississippi and continued to the northwest until he reached the province of Autiamque in the northwestern corner of Arkansas, where he passed the winter of 1541-42 on the [Washita] River." [2] In the spring of 1542, after marching three days

> through an unpeopled region and a land so low and with so many swamps and such hard going that one day he marched all day through water that in some places reached to the knees and others to the stirrups, [De Soto] came to a deserted village, without corn called Tutelpinco [Arkansas Post, destined to become the first European settlement in Arkansas 141 years later][3]

On June 17, 1542, just weeks after he died, the remnants of De Soto's army left Arkansas heading west.[4] They returned, raided Little Rock, and wintered near there before heading south for good.

The author acknowledges the help of his reference staff at Barry, particularly Ann Pascoe and Warren McEwen, and the help of his former Arkansas colleagues Jim Jackson in the law library and Mort Gitelman on the law school faculty.

The Quapaw Indians lived in Arkansas at the time of early French exploration. The Quapaws, or Oo-gaq-pa, were also known as the downstream people, or Ugakhopag. The Algonkian-speaking Indians of the Ohio Valley called them the Arkansas, or "south wind." The name of the area has been spelled several ways throughout history. In Marquette and Joliet's 1673 journal, the Indian name is spelled Akansea. In La Salle's map a few years later it is spelled Acansa. A map based on the journey of La Harpe in 1718-1722 refers to the river as the Arkansas and to the Indians as *Les Arkansas*. Around 1811, Captain Zebulon Pike spelled it Arkansaw. In 1881, the general assembly declared that the state's name be spelled Arkansas but pronounced Arkansaw. The pronunciation preserves the memory of the original Indian inhabitants, while the spelling clearly dictates the nationality of the French adventurers who first explored the area.[5]

France's René Robert Chevelier,[6] Sieur de La Salle, floated down the Illinois River to the Mississippi and down the Mississippi to the Gulf of Mexico. On April 9, 1682, the Sieur took possession, in the name of Louis XIV, of that portion of the continent that was drained by the Mississippi and its tributaries. He named the region Louisiane in honor of the king.[7] "This was Arkansas's first exposure to civilian legal processes. It would be almost 150 years before the influence of the civil law ceased to make itself felt there."[8]

Louisiane was ceded to Spain in 1762 by the Treaty of Fontainebleau and was ceded back to France in 1800 by the Treaty of St. Ildefonso. President Thomas Jefferson stopped the French-Spanish Ping-Pong game with the Louisiana Purchase.[9] Yet when the vast semi-wilderness which stretched from the Mississippi River to the Mexican border was separated from Missouri and organized into the Arkansas Territory, the claims of the Caddos, Quapaws, and Osages had not yet been adjusted "in such a manner as to give the United States a fair and unequivocal title."[10] Other than the muddy title claims that persisted for years because of conflicting Indian-Spanish-French land claims, the Spanish and Indian influence north of the state of Louisiana is limited.

French citizens and their laws, based upon the Custom of Paris,[11] prevailed for a period as well:

> As received in Louisiana in 1712, the Custom of Paris was a written code, covering remedies and rights, so much akin to existing provisions of the Civil Code and Code of Practice of Louisiana, that we would recognize the similarity even though we did not know that the Custom was absorbed into the Napoleonic legislation, from which our Civil Code derives so much of its vitality. This local law of French Colonial Louisiana is a model of brevity, comprised within three hundred and sixty-two numbered articles of an average length of less than

fifty words to the article. This matter is distributed under sixteen titles and aside from the first two, which treat of the relations of lord and vassal, there is no part of this book that did not have application to the affairs of the colonists of Louisiana, and some of its principals are still the law there today.[12]

The *Coutume* was first reduced to writing in 1510 and treated both substantive and adjective law.[13] "Commentary on it by the time of its adoption in Louisiana was voluminous."[14] Even the French legal system that predominated, especially in the southernmost portion of the territory, dissipated. While

> faint traces of a remote European past survive, absolutely nothing remains of the laws and customs which the ancient residents of Arkansas observed. This is no accident. It was a favorite object of Jefferson to introduce the common law of England into the vast Louisiana Territory as quickly as he could. In the lower territory he waited too late.[15]

AMERICAN SOIL

As previously described, the land of present-day Arkansas was included in a portion of the Louisiana Purchase from France and ceded by the treaty of 1803.[16] An act of Congress, dated March 26, 1804,[17] named a portion of the territory the district of Louisiana. The portion included Arkansas and was governed by the governor of the Indiana Territory. Another act, dated March 3, 1805,[18] changed the name to the territory of Louisiana and established a territorial government. The name changed to Missouri by an act dated June 4, 1812.[19] The Arkansaw[20] Territory was created by the act of March 2, 1819.[21] Arkansas became a state seventeen years later in 1836.[22] Although the law of Arkansas was first French, then Spanish, then French again, "[e]xcept for the silence of its final letter, there is nowadays nothing very French about Arkansas."[23]

Native Americans, both the indigenous people and those forced to and through the territory, helped shape the law also:

> [W]hat sets Arkansas apart from the remainder of the nation, was the migration of the Eastern Indians. For white men were not the only new comers to pour across the Mississippi and lay claim to lands below the Ozarks. . . . Pushed ahead of, along with, and behind them were the Cherokees, the Choctaws, the Creeks, the Chickasaws, and a dozen other tribes and nations, piling alien culture upon alien culture

in an unprecedented array of rival titles, racial mistrust, conflicting interests, and explosive animosities, which the white man's law was challenged to keep in check.[24]

Natives directly influenced the shape of the territory. Indian land holdings complicated matters and influenced the shape of the territory. Three tribes were indigenous to Arkansas in 1804—Osages, Caddos, and Quapaws—"but additional treaty rights to Arkansas land were given by the U.S. government to such tribes as the Choctaws, Chickasaws, and Cherokees, before they were ultimately displaced and moved to the Indian Territory."[25] Although three boundaries of the territory were set in 1819, the western boundary was not established until nine years later, when the Cherokees ceded land that established the western boundaries.[26]

Some Spanish laws were considered still in effect when Louisiana became American territory, "but not the law of property and obligations, tort and contract."[27] The French and Spanish were eventually replaced by settlers from the original American colonies. Spanish legal practices and the civil law in general rapidly gave way to the common law. According to Professor Robert Wright, the switch was largely completed by 1810; Wright points out that the territory of Missouri legislature adopted the English common law and acts of Parliament in 1816:[28]

> Arkansas was influenced heavily, particularly in the uplands, by the hill people of the Southern highlands who came from the western portions of Virginia and North Carolina and from Tennessee and Kentucky.[29] The laws, customs and practices of those people were brought with them to Arkansas just as they had been brought to those places earlier by their ancestors from the north of England, from the lowlands of Scotland, and from Northern Ireland through the Scots-Irish. The low country of Arkansas—the delta in particular—was the product in part of the people who had come to the coastal and Piedmont regions of Virginia and the Carolinas and had eventually made their way westward through the deep South. South Arkansas was also settled in large measure by people of similar origins but with greater influence from the hill people in the outer reaches of that area.[30]

For example, of "the fourteen men who served on the Superior Court bench during the territorial period six were from Virginia, three from Kentucky, three from Tennessee, and two from North Carolina."[31] Wright notes that "the Americanization of Arkansas under the English common law created hostility among the French settlers of the Territory, which also seems to have been aggravated by the exclusion of the French from juries."[32]

The first statute of the new state of Arkansas adopted the common law of England and all applicable statutes of the British Parliament consistent with the state and federal constitutions. The statute is now number two, since the state renumbered its statutes in 1987. Wright[33] laments the renumbering. He feels that the statute should have remained "the first statute because, second only to the federal and state Constitutions, it is the basis of Arkansas law."[34] Professor Wright goes on to point out that by "adopting the common law of England as it existed before the fourth year of the reign of King James I," Arkansas incorporated into its legal system a body of law familiar to most of the people who settled the United States and Arkansas after the Louisiana Purchase.[35]

The actual text of the adoption statute reads as follows:

> The common law of England, so far as it is applicable and of a general nature, and all statutes of the British Parliament in aid of or to supply the defects of the common law made prior to March 24, 1606, which are applicable to our own form of government, of a general nature and not local to that kingdom, and not inconsistent with the Constitution and laws of the United States or the Constitution and laws of this state, shall be the rule of decision in this state unless altered or repealed by the General Assembly of this state.[36]

TERRITORIAL LAW

Arkansas Territory existed for only seventeen years, from 1819 to 1836.[37] The area quickly went from wilderness to statehood; "the frontier outpost, the pioneer colony, and the permanent settlement"[38] were developed during that brief span before the territory separated from Missouri.

The government of territorial Arkansas was modeled after the government set out by the Northwest Ordinance.[39] The territories were to progress through two stages of government:

> In the first stage, President Monroe appointed five officials: Governor William Miller, a brigadier general and hero of the war of 1812 and a resident of New Hampshire; the governor's assistant, Secretary Robert Crittenden, a native Kentuckian and brother of John Jordan Crittenden . . . and the three judges of the Territorial Superior Court, who were in addition to function as a legislature, until a general assembly

could be formed. The territorial government was to begin July 4, 1819,[40]

but the general assembly was elected before Governor Miller arrived.[41] The new government adopted all laws of the Missouri Territory not repugnant to the organic act establishing the Arkansas Territory and created two judicial courts and circuits.[42] In August,[43] Crittenden appointed circuit judges, attorneys, and other government officials.

While Arkansas was still a part of the Missouri Territory, its colonial laws appeared in Henry S. Geyer's *Digest of the Laws of the Territory of Missouri,* published in 1818. *Geyer's Digest* gathered the Missouri territorial laws put into force upon creation of the Arkansas Territory.[44] The sections of *Geyer's Digest* pertaining to Arkansas are included in J. Steele and J. M'Cambell's *Laws of Arkansas Territory* (1845).

The Arkansas Territorial Superior Court was the court of last resort until 1828. It was slow to commence operations. Its first judicial session took place in January 1820 at the Arkansas Post. Judge Scott presided alone.[45] Territorial superior court decisions were not systematically reported. The Honorable Morris Arnold[46] believes the oldest surviving opinion of an Arkansas trial judge[47] shows that "only five years after Arkansas had become a territory even a middling judge could be concientious, well-educated, and workman like."[48] Arnold calls Judge Thomas P. Eskridge "a thoughtful craftsman, well-trained, and more than competent."[49] The 1824 opinion, says Arnold, "reveals an acquaintance with many of the best authorities, and . . . shows the judge's appreciation at least of a well-turned phrase."[50]

Some of the territorial superior court opinions were published twenty years after statehood, in 1856, by Samuel H. Hempstead.[51] *Hempstead's Reports* also contained early state cases, as its full title makes clear.[52] In the territories, one court system handled both territorial and federal matters. "In effect, the Territorial superior court served as a combined state and federal appellate court. It was also the court of last resort, there being no appeal upward"[53] until the Judiciary Act of 1827 divided the territory into four circuits. "By this time, the Superior court had become largely an appellate body similar to what the Supreme Court of Arkansas would become."[54]

NOTES

1. *New Advent Catholic Encyclopedia,* <http://www.newadvent.org/cathen/04753a.htm>.
2. For a more thorough discussion of De Soto's adventures, visit Donald E. Sheppard and Cheryl Lucente, *De Soto's Arkansas Trails—Part I: Arkansas Conquest Trails—Northern Arkansas,* <http://www.floridahistory.com/arkansas.html>.

The fact that Arkansas history is discussed within a larger discussion of Florida reflects the fact that "Florida was originally applied to [the] territory extending northward to Virginia and westward indefinitely from the Atlantic." See *New Advent Catholic Encyclopedia,* <http://www.newadvent.org/cathen/06115b.htm>.

3. *De Soto's Arkansas Trails*—Part I, <http://www.floridahistory.com/arkansas. html>, quoting one of De Soto's officers.

4. *De Soto Conquest Trails: Louisiana and Texas,* <http://www.floridahistory. com/texas.html>.

5. Vickie Dement, <http://www.jps.k12.ar.us/junior/mac/faculty/Dement/arkh .htm>.

6. Also spelled *Cavelier.* See "René-Robert-Cavelier, Sieur de La Salle," in *New Advent Catholic Encyclopedia,* <http://www.newadvent.org/cathen/09009b. htm>.

7. "Louisiana," in *New Advent Catholic Encyclopedia,* <http://www.newadvent .org/cathen/09378a.htm>.

8. Morris S. Arnold, "The Arkansas Colonial System, 1686-1766," *UALR Law Journal* 6(1983): 391, 393.

9. Robert Ross Wright, *Old Seeds in the New Land: History and Reminiscences of the Bar of Arkansas,* at 4 (Fayetteville, AR: M&M Press, 2002), citing C. Bolton, C. Ledbetter, and G. Hanson, *Arkansas Becomes a State,* 4-5 (Little Rock: Center for Arkansas Studies, University of Arkansas at Little Rock, 1985).

10. John Reid at 2, quoting a letter from Major S. H. Long to General Thomas A. Smith, dated January 30, 1818, printed in *The Territorial Papers of the United States,* Vol. 19, 4 (Carter ed.; Washington, DC: U.S. Government Printing Office, 1953).

11. *"[N]os Edits, Ordonnances Et Coutumes Et les usages de la Prevosté Et Victomté de Paris*—our edicts, ordinances, and customs, and the usages of the Provostry and Viscounty of Paris." Morris S. Arnold, "The Arkansas Colonial System, 1686-1766."

12. Henry Plauche Dart, "The Colonial Legal Systems of Arkansas, Louisiana and Texas," *A.B.A. J.* 12(1926): 481.

13. For a précis of its provisions, title by title, see Scmidt, "History of the Jurisprudence of Louisiana," *La. L.J.* 1 (1841): 1, cited in Morris S. Arnold, "The Arkansas Colonial System, 1686-1766," n. 33.

14. The most useful eighteenth-century commentary is C. Ferriere, *Commentaire Sur La Coutume De La Prevote et Victomté De Paris,* cited in Morris S. Arnold, "The Arkansas Colonial System, 1686-1766," n. 34.

15. Morris S. Arnold, "The Arkansas Colonial System, 1686-1766."

16. 8 *Stat.* 200. A census of the "province de la Louisiane," made in 1788, states the population of Arkansas to be 119. See "Arkansas" in *New Advent Catholic Encyclopedia,* <http://www.newadvent.org/cathen/01724a.htm>.

17. An Act Erecting Louisiana into two territories, and providing for the temporary government thereof, Act of March 26, 1804, ch. 38, 2 *Stat.* 283.

18. An Act Further Providing for the Government of the District of Louisiana, Act of March 3, 1805, ch. 31, 2 *Stat.* 331 (District of Louisiana renamed Territory of Louisiana).

19. An Act providing for the government of the territory of Missouri, Act of June 4, 1812, ch. 95, 2 *Stat.* 743 (remaining territory renamed Missouri after Louisiana statehood).

20. That is the correct spelling. An Act establishing a separate territorial government in the southern part of the territory of Missouri, Act of March 2, 1819, ch. 49, 3 *Stat.* 493, 494.

21. An Act establishing a separate territorial government in the southern part of the territory of Missouri, Act of March 2, 1819, ch. 49, 3 *Stat.* 493. See "Arkansas" in the *New Advent Catholic Encyclopedia,* <http://www.newadvent.org/cathen/01724a.htm>.

22. Act of June 15, 1836, ch. 100, 5 *Stat.* 50.

23. Morris S. Arnold, "The Arkansas Colonial System, 1686-1766."

24. John Reid, "Law and the Indians on the Arkansas Frontier: 'Stand Stripped, but Strongly Nerved,'"*Ark. L. Rev. & B. Assn J.* 18(1964): 1.

25. Lynn Foster, "Their Pride and Ornament: Judge Benjamin Johnson and the Federal Courts in Early Arkansas," *U.A.L.R. L. Rev.* 22(1999): 21, 25.

26. Act of May 24, 1828. Sec. 8, 4 *Stat.* 305. See generally Charles S. Bolton, *Arkansas, 1800-1860: Remote and Restless,* 67-87 (Fayetteville: Univeristy of Arkansas, 1998), cited in Lynn Foster, "Their Pride and Ornament: Judge Benjamin Johnson and the Federal Courts in Early Arkansas." *U.A.L.R. L. Rev.* 22(1999): 21-48.

27. Robert Ross Wright, *Old Seeds in the New Land,* at 6.

28. Robert Ross Wright, *Old Seeds in the New Land,* at 9, citing Morris S. Arnold, *Unequal Laws Unto a Savage Race: European Legal Traditions in Arkansas, 1686-1836,* at 180-181 (Fayetteville: University of Arkansas Press, 1985).

29. Two law review articles touch upon this geography lesson and offer further insights. See Morris S. Arnold, "An Early Opinion of an Arkansas Trial Court," *UALR Law Journal* 5(1982): 397, 399; and Lynn Foster, "Their Pride and Ornament: Judge Benjamin Johnson and the Federal Courts in Early Arkansas." See also David Hackett Fischer, *Albion's Seed* (New York: Oxford University Press, 1989), cited in Wright, chapter 1, footnotes 1-5. See also *Albion's Seed Grows in the Cumberland Gap,* <http://xroads.virginia.edu/~UG97/albion/albion3.html>.

30. Robert Ross Wright, *Old Seeds in the New Land,* at 2.

31. Steven Smith, "Arkansas Advocacy: The Territorial Period," *Ark. L. Rev.* 3 (1977): 449.

32. Robert Ross Wright, *Old Seeds in the New Land: History and Reminiscences of the Bar of Arkansas,* at 9 (Fayetteville, AR: M&M Press, 2002, citing Morris S. Arnold, *Unequal Laws Unto a Savage Race: European Legal Traditions in Arkansas, 1686-1836,* at 181-182 [Fayetteville: University of Arkansas Press, 1985]).

33. Donaghey Distinguished Professor of Law Emeritus, University of Arkansas at Little Rock.

34. Robert Ross Wright, *Old Seeds in the New Land: History and Reminiscences of the Bar of Arkansas,* at 1 (Fayetteville, AK: M&M Press, 2002).

35. Ibid.

36. *Arkansas Code Annotated* 1-2-119 (1987). *Rev. Stat.,* ch. 28, § 1; C. & M. Dig., § 1432; Pope's Dig., § 1679; A.S.A. 1947, § 1-101.

37. See Act of March 2, 1819, 3 *Stat*. 494 and Act of June 15, 1836, ch. 100, 5 *Stat* 50.

38. John Reid, "Law and the Indians on the Arkansas Frontier: 'Stand Stripped, but Strongly Nerved.'"*Ark. L. Rev. & B. Assn J.* 18(1964): 1.

39. See <http://www.yale.edu/lawweb/avalon/nworder.htm> regarding the NW Ordinance.

40. Act of Aug. 3, 1819, *Laws of the Territory of Arkansas* 70-82 (1821).

41. Lynn Foster, "Their Pride and Ornament: Judge Benjamin Johnson and the Federal Courts in Early Arkansas," *U.A.L.R. L. Rev.* 22 (1999): 21, 22.

42. See Act of Aug. 3, 1819, *Laws of the Territory of Arkansas* 70-82 (1821).

43. Arkansas had only five counties: Arkansas and Lawrence comprised the first circuit; Clark, Hempstead, and Pulaski counties, the second. See ibid. at 73.

44. Steven Smith, "Arkansas Advocacy: The Territorial Period," *Ark. L. Rev.* 31 (1977): 449.

45. See Petition to the President by the Territorial Assembly (Feb. 11, 1820), in 19 *Territorial Papers,* supra note 10, at 143, 144-145.

46. United States Court of Appeals for the Eighth Circuit.

47. Circuit Court Records of Arkansas County, 1824-1829 (January term, 1824) (on Microfilm at Arkansas History Commission, Little Rock. Roll 59. P. 186); (reprinted in Morris S. Arnold, "An Early Opinion of an Arkansas Trial Court," *UALR Law Journal* 5(1982): 397, 400.

48. Morris S. Arnold, "An Early Opinion of an Arkansas Trial Court," *UALR Law Journal* 5(1982): 397, 399.

49. Ibid.

50. Ibid.

51. Lynn Foster, "Their Pride and Ornament: Judge Benjamin Johnson and the Federal Courts in Early Arkansas," *U.A.L.R. L. Rev.* 22(1999): 21, 24.

52. *Reports of Cases Argued and Determined in the United States Superior Court for the Territory of Arkansas, from 1836 to 1849; and in the United States District Court for the State of Arkansas, In the Ninth circuit, from 1839 to 1856.*

53. Lynn Foster, "Their Pride and Ornament: Judge Benjamin Johnson and the Federal Courts in Early Arkansas," *U.A.L.R. L. Rev.* 22(1999): 21, 24.

54. Robert Ross Wright, *Old Seeds in the New Land: History and Reminiscences of the Bar of Arkansas,* at 2 (Fayetteville, AR: M&M Press, 2002).

Chapter 5

California Legal History Revisited: Researching the Spanish, Mexican, and Early American Periods

Myra K. Saunders
Jennifer Lentz

HISTORICAL BACKGROUND

Although California[1] was first explored by the Spanish in about 1540, it was not colonized by Spain until the late eighteenth century,[2] toward the end of Spain's colonization of the New World and well after the English colonized the eastern coast of the United States. The establishment of the California missions, led principally by Franciscan Father Junipero Serra, took place from about 1769 to 1800, although the missions continued to operate until the 1830s.[3] California remained a Spanish colony until the Mexican Revolution in 1821, when it became a Mexican territory. California was occupied by U.S. forces at the beginning of the war with Mexico in the spring of 1846, but California technically remained a part of Mexico until it was ceded to the United States by the Treaty of Guadalupe Hidalgo in February 1848.[4] Congress never conferred territorial status upon California. Instead, a constitutional convention was held in the fall of 1849, and the constitution

This piece is an updated (through October 2003) and revised version of information first published in three articles by Myra Saunders in the *Law Library Journal*; "California Legal History: A Review of California's Spanish and Mexican Legal Institutions," 87 *Law Libr. J.* 487-514 (1995); "California Legal History: The Legal System Under the United States Military Government, 1846-1849," 88 *Law Libr. J.* 488-522 (1996); "California Legal History: The California Constitution of 1849," 90 *Law Libr. J.* 447-480 (1998).

Many thanks are owed to Gabriel Juarez and Brett Roller of the UCLA Hugh and Hazel Darling Law Library who obtained many of these materials for us and to John Wilson, Reference Librarian at the UCLA Law Library, for his assistance with the bibliographic verification of materials.

developed at that convention was ratified by the voters later that fall. The government was turned over to civil authorities on December 12, 1849. California became a state on September 9, 1850.[5]

The Spanish colonial system imported the Moorish office of the alcalde[6] as the head governmental official of the pueblos, or towns, and this office was extended to California in 1781.[7] The alcaldes were laymen, as were the judicial officers of the early English colonies of North America,[8] possessing a combination of powers parallel to those of mayor, arbitrator, justice of the peace, trial judge, and, in some instances, legislator. This combination of powers was destined to confuse, trouble, and offend the later settlers— and eventual conquerors—who had been reared in the common law tradition and venerated the concept of separation of powers.[9]

Under the Spanish-Mexican system, the alcalde courts were not courts of law but were informal arbitration hearings where equity and local custom controlled the proceedings, and conciliation was the primary goal. In that respect, the alcalde courts were not very different from the courts of the Puritan colonies, where "the magistrates administered a rude system of popular law and equity, on the basis of the Scriptures and their own ideas of right, generally to the satisfaction of the homogeneous Puritan communities."[10] As the California population grew and included more Anglo-Americans and non-Spanish Europeans, enforcing commonly held community values became increasingly difficult. By the end of the Mexican period, dissatisfaction with the Spanish-Mexican legal system was widespread among the non-Latino residents.[11]

California was seized by U.S. military forces shortly after the outbreak of the Mexican-American War in 1846. From spring 1846 to December 1849, California was governed by a succession of military leaders.[12] The difficulty that Anglo-Americans had in understanding the Spanish and Mexican colonial legal system can be partly attributed to the fact that the immigrants coming to California after 1846 never experienced it. Many immigrants confused the Spanish-Mexican system with that of the military regime. Despite articulated intentions to the contrary, the military governors of California and their civil officers substantially altered the Spanish-Mexican legal system. The military government responded to the changing demographics of California brought on by the gold rush and the concomitant pressure to instate an "American" form of government by developing a hybrid legal system that clung to Spanish colonial nomenclature but engrafted upon it Anglo-American legal values and traditions.[13] In addition, the military government's failure to publish and distribute the text of those Mexican laws that were to be enforced fueled Anglo-American objections to the system.[14] Beyond this, the new immigrants' desire for land conflicted sharply with the military government's intention to respect Mexican land laws and to discourage the acquisition of property outside of pueblo limits.[15] The validity of claims to lands acquired during the Spanish, Mexican, and military periods was an important legal issue for the latter half of the nineteenth century.

Moreover, in 1849, after news of the discovery of gold reached the eastern United States, California was inundated with Anglo-Americans seeking their fortunes. The mining camps were located in areas not colonized by either the Spanish or Mexicans, hundreds of miles from the military (and colonial) capitol at Monterey. Servicemen were not immune to gold fever, and soldiers began to desert the service in order to pan for gold themselves, leaving the military government with little enforcement power anywhere in California.[16] In the absence of any central governmental presence, the miners developed their own legal systems, with the individual mining camps serving as independent townships functioning entirely under self-created rules, but which, confusingly, often used Spanish-Mexican terminology.[17] The local laws developed for protecting gold mine claims in the California mining camps became the foundation of U.S. mining law.

After the war with Mexico ended in early 1848, the U.S. Congress, which was bogged down by the debate over slavery in the territories, did not move quickly to create a territorial government for California.[18] Congress adjourned in March 1849 without having made provisions for the establishment of a territorial government in California. Settlers' groups, impatient with the federal government and unhappy with the military regime, met throughout northern California and began to organize a civil government on their own.[19] By June 1849, civilian unhappiness with the governmental system had culminated with the inhabitants of San Francisco establishing an independent legislative assembly that began passing laws. To quash the activities of these ad hoc groups, General Bennett Riley, then military governor of California, issued a call for a general constitutional convention to meet in the fall of 1849 to create a civil government in California.[20]

The constitutional convention met in Monterey, California, from September 1 through October 13, 1849.[21] On October 12, 1849, military Governor Riley issued the new constitution with a proclamation calling for an election to ratify the document. The constitution was adopted by the voters on November 13, 1849. Governor Riley proclaimed the constitution ratified on December 12, 1849, and turned the government over to civil authorities. The state government operated on a de facto basis until California was admitted into the Union on September 9, 1850.[22]

GENERAL RESEARCH OVERVIEW

This overview provides an introduction to the English-language sources that can be used to research the legal institutions of Spanish and Mexican California as well as the U.S. military regime that was in force from 1846 to 1849.

A fair amount of material is helpful to research California's early legal systems, but many sources will not be found in law libraries. Comprehensive research into California history of this period cannot be done without consulting the archival collections of the Spanish and Mexican periods and the personal papers of government officials and prominent individuals of this era. Earlier historians had access to material that current researchers do not: most of the Spanish and Mexican government documents that had been located by U.S. government officials were destroyed in the fire that resulted from the 1906 San Francisco earthquake.[23] Fortunately, copies and notes of many documents in the original archive had been made by historian Hubert Bancroft[24] and his staff of researchers, and this collection is what is currently regarded as the California Archives.[25] Many mission, municipal, and other local records also exist.

The online catalogs listed in the bibliography contain the holdings of several of California's largest libraries and archival institutions. These catalogs currently serve as the best means of identifying prestatehood legal materials. Although few full-text sources exist in digital format,[26] the Online Archive of California provides full-text access to selected finding aids from over fifty archival institutions in the state. In addition, many individual cities and counties in California maintain local historical societies and museums with libraries or archival centers. Although their holdings are not online, contact information, as well as descriptions of their collections, is available on their Web sites.[27] In addition, *A Guide to the History of California*[28] includes (now somewhat dated) essays describing the major special collections of California historical materials, including government archives. Libraries with special or rare book collections may also produce their own guides to these collections.[29]

The records of the U.S. military government are key sources in understanding the period between 1846 and 1850. Of these, the most comprehensive is *California and New Mexico,*[30] which covers the period from February 1847 through October 1849. Although a number of secondary sources cite individual items in these collections, they rarely reproduce complete documents. Those who seek a more thorough and unfiltered understanding of the military regime would do well to read through the numerous individual documents available in the military records.

The first U.S. government examination of the Spanish and Mexican archives apparently occurred in 1849.[31] The Treaty of Guadalupe Hildago required that Spanish and Mexican property rights be respected, but later immigrants were determined to acquire land in California. Thus, the area of Spanish and Mexican law that most concerned these settlers and the U.S. government was land law. In March 1849, California Secretary of State Halleck produced a report on Spanish and Mexican land grants.[32] Later that year, William Carey Jones was appointed by the U.S. government as a special agent to examine land titles in California.[33] Also of value is the brief submitted on behalf of the city of San Francisco to the district court for the northern district of California in support of the city's claim for four square leagues of land under Spanish and Mexican law.[34] English translations of various Spanish and Mexican laws from this period can be found in a variety of materials that are listed in the bibliography.

Insight into the concerns of the Anglo-American community can be gleaned from the editorials and letters published in the local Anglo-American newspapers of the time. References to many articles and editorials can be located through secondary sources, but, again, since only excerpts of documents are normally reproduced in secondary tools, it is helpful to read through the papers themselves (most issues are quite brief) to gain a fuller understanding of the American perspective. Most of these newspapers are available on microfilm.

General California histories are helpful in developing a broader understanding of the period, for locating information relating to specific issues or events, and for providing references to source materials. At the same time, researchers need to keep in mind the clear Anglo-American biases of many of these works, particularly older texts. An excellent guide to secondary sources, as well as archival collections, is *A Guide to the History of California*.[35] This text contains introductory bibliographic essays on various eras in California history, including two essays that cover the period of military rule: "Hispanic California, 1542-1848" and "Early American California, 1848-1880." Both are quite thorough and can be used to direct researchers to most of the significant literature for this period. Consulting this text early in the research process will streamline the process considerably.

Quite detailed and thorough studies of the legal institutions of the Spanish and Mexican periods can be found in Langum's *Law and Community of the Mexican California Frontier; Anglo-American Expatriates and the Clash of Legal Traditions, 1821-1846*,[36] and Robertson's *From Alcalde to Mayor: A History of the Change from the Mexican to the American Local Institutions in California*.[37] Both authors conducted in-depth studies of the official records and documents of California during these eras. Perhaps as important, these texts present a more balanced picture of the period than do many other studies. Langum uses case studies revealed through the examination of the judicial records of Mexican California to demonstrate how the legal system actually functioned on a day-to-day basis. Robertson studied archival records to trace the evolution of the office of alcalde in California.

A number of works focus on the transition from Mexican to U.S. government in California. The most useful for studying legal issues are *Military Governments in California 1846-1850;*[38] "The Legal Status of California 1846-49"[39]; and "The Hobbesian Constitution: Governing Without Authority."[40] Also useful is Harlow's *California Conquered.*[41] Harlow was a special collections librarian, and this background is reflected in the thoroughness of research and the completeness of his documentation. All of these works are invaluable for the access they provide to primary materials and secondary authorities.

Land grant and mining claims remained concerns well after California entered the Union. Several sources concentrate on the special issues relating to land ownership and mining rights, and the major sources on these topics are included in the bibliography.

SELECTED BIBLIOGRAPHY

Bibliographic Aids and Finding Tools

Online Catalogs

California State Library: http://www.lib.state.ca.us/

The California State Library's formation coincided with California's entrance into the Union in 1850. The library's original mission was to serve as a research institution to support the state's new legislature. While continuing to fulfill this purpose, the library also seeks to collect and preserve historical materials on California and the West.

Melvyl Catalog: http://melvyl.cdlib.org/

The Melvyl catalog contains the combined holdings of all the University of California campuses as well as the California State Library. The Melvyl catalog also includes special collections and archives for individual UC campuses.

Online Archive of California: http://www.oac.cdlib.org/

The Online Archive of California is a searchable database of finding aids from the archives of over fifty California universities, libraries, museums, and historical institutions. An ongoing project of the California Digital Library, the online archive currently provides full-text access to selected finding aids from these institutions. The database is searchable by subject, keyword, and institution.

Web Sites

California Historical Society: http://www.californiahistoricalsociety.org

First formed in 1871, the California Historical Society was disbanded several times before becoming a permanent institution in 1921. The Historical Society offers over 35,000 books and pamphlets pertaining to early California settlements. An index to *California History Quarterly,* the Historical Society's quarterly publication, is provided on their Web site.

California State Archives: http://www.ss.ca.gov/archives/archives.htm

Located in Sacramento, the California State Archives serves as a repository for California's state and local government institutions. The archives collection includes records of the Spanish and Mexican land grants and original documents pertaining to the California constitutional conventions.

Library of Congress, American Memory Project: http://memory.loc. gov/ammem/cbhtml/cbhome.html

This digital manuscript collection, titled "California As I Saw It: First-Person Narratives of California's Early Years, 1849-1900," contains a searchable database of nearly 200 full-text accounts of early Californians' experiences. The database is searchable by keyword, subject, and author.

Society of California Pioneers: http://www.californiapioneers.org

The Society of California Pioneers, formed in 1850, maintains a permanent collection of over 10,000 volumes of diaries, manuscripts, newspapers, and maps for the time period immediately prior to and following the gold rush. Approximately one-third of the manuscripts predate statehood. Selected holdings appear in WorldCat.

Print Sources

Bowman, J. N. "History of the Provincial Archives of California." *Southern California Quarterly* 64(1982): iv-97; and Grenier, Judson A. "Addenda to J.N. Bowman's 'History of the Provincial Archives of California'," *Southern California Quarterly* 66(1984): 257-261.

This is a very thorough and interesting study of the collection of materials that constituted the California Archives and is essential reading for anyone hoping to examine any original documents. Includes some discussion of municipal archives as well.

California Local History: A Bibliography and Union List of Library Holdings, 2nd ed. Edited by Margaret Miller Rocq for the California Library Association. Stanford, CA: Stanford University Press, 1970 (Supplement, 1976).

This work, which contains more than 20,000 items contributed by more than 100 California libraries, attempts to identify, among other categories, "histories of counties, cities, and other geographical and governmental areas." The supplement brings this work up to date through 1970. Arranged by county, with separate sections for regional and statewide works. Includes an index and "Bibliographical References" that list additional major published bibliographic tools. An earlier edition, *California Local History: A Centennial Bibliography,* was published in 1950.

Clagett, Helen L. and David M. Valderrama. *A Revised Guide to the Law and Legal Literature of Mexico.* Washington, DC: Library of Congress, 1973.

Very helpful in developing an overall understanding of Mexican legal bibliography; also offers more detailed information on specific sources.

Cowan, Robert. *A Bibliography of the History of California, 1510-1930.* 4 vol. San Francisco: J.H. Nash, 1933-1964; reprint, Mansfield Centre, CT: Martino Fine Books, [1977?].

This work is comprehensive in scope for the period it covers, but the arrangement of this bibliography (alphabetical order by author, with title and date indexes) makes it extremely difficult to use, minimizing its usefulness for locating materials, although it can be useful to assist in verifying incomplete citations.

Fritz, Christian G. and Gorden M. Bakken. "California Legal History: A Bibliographic Essay." *Southern California Quarterly* 70(1988): 203.

Not focused on Spanish and Mexican California but does contain good references to materials dealing with land grants and other land issues.

Guide to the History of California, edited by Doyce Nunis Jr. and Gloria Ricci Lothrop. New York: Greenwood Press, 1989.

Although not totally comprehensive for legal materials, these bibliographic essays are so thorough that they are the logical starting point for research into this period. Of particular usefulness is Iris Engstrand and Daniel Tyler's "Hispanic California, 1542-1848" (at 3-19), as well as the descriptions of archives and other special collections located throughout the state. An essential tool.

Hall, Kermit L. *A Comprehensive Bibliography of American Constitutional and Legal History.* 5 vol. Milwood, NY: Kraus International Publications, 1984.

This five-volume set is organized by subject across jurisdictions. Volume 4 includes what Hall terms "geographical" bibliographies. As the title implies, the California bibliography available in Volume 4 (pp. 2540-2560) is quite comprehensive and is a good starting point for research. Unfortunately, the single alphabetical listing of articles is a bit cumbersome and the bibliography is unannotated, but the author does provide information on the chronological periods covered in each work that is listed.

Harper, Lawrence A. *Guide to Materials on the History of Law in California.* Berkeley: University of California, [1956].

This typewritten combination outline and annotated bibliography is available at the UC Berkeley Law Library (Boalt Hall) and at the Bancroft Library (under the title *Introduction and Guide to the Legal History of California*). Harper attempts to guide historians who need to do legal research. Though dated now, it does provide helpful references to legal and local governmental records, as well as a legal chronology (pp. 97-122) that highlights the dates of important political and legal events through 1955. Includes a bibliography.

Kemble, Edward C. *A History of California Newspapers 1846-1858.* Edited by Helen Harding Bretnor. Los Gatos: The Talisman Press, 1962.

Useful for identifying relevant publications and their dates of publication.

————. "Libraries in Provincial California." *Historical Society of Southern California Quarterly* 43(1961): 426.

As the title implies, this piece reviews the holdings of libraries in Spanish and Mexican California. Interesting from a number of perspectives, it does document the presence of legal materials in colonial and provincial California.

Kurutz, Gary F. *The California Gold Rush: A Descriptive Bibliography of Books and Pamphlets Covering the Years 1848-1853.* San Francisco: The Book Club of California, 1997.

According to the preface, this annotated bibliography "covers eyewitness and contemporary accounts of the years 1848 through 1853 published in books and pamphlets."[42] Arranged alphabetically by author, with an index and bibliography. A better tool for bibliographic verification than for research.

Nash, Gerald D. "California and Its Historians: An Appraisal of the State." *Pacific Historical Review* 50(1981): 387-413.

Part I of this piece reviews the histories that cover what Nash terms the Pioneer Era (1850-1890) and alerts researchers to the strengths and weakness of the various approaches taken by the authors of the major California histories.

Nunis, Doyce B. "Legal History in Southern California, a Review Essay." *Western Legal History* 3(1990): 67-77.

Useful for leads to southern California archival sources for research.

Palmer, Thomas W. *Guide to the Law and Legal Literature of Spain.* Washington, DC: Government Printing Office, 1915.

It is not as in-depth as Claggett's work on Mexican law, but this text provides helpful information on Spanish legal bibliography.

Reynolds, Thomas H. and Arturo Flores. *Foreign Law: Current Sources of Codes and Basic Legislation in Jurisdictions of the World.* Littleton, CO: Rothman, 1991- .

Researchers might be surprised to discover that this essential reference tool for locating current materials is equally helpful for gaining background on the historical development of other countries' legal systems, including, in this case, Spain and Mexico.

Santos, Robert L. *A Bibliography of Early California and Neighboring Territory Through 1846: An Era of Exploration, Missions, Presidios, Ranchos, and Indians.* Turlock, CA: privately published, 1992 (Supplement, 1990-2002. Turlock, CA: Alley-Cass Publications, 2002. Supplement available at <http://www.library.csustan.edu/bsantos/California biblio.htm>).

This bibliography, held by a few California libraries, is divided into eleven subject categories. Section H covers government and is most helpful for locating materials relating to Spanish and Mexican laws governing California. Includes author and subject indexes.

Primary Source Materials

Reports and Records

Browne, J. Ross. *Report on the Mineral Resources of the State and Territories West of the Rocky Mountains,* 226-264. 39th Cong., 2nd Sess., House Ex. Doc. No. 29, Serial No. 1289. Washington, DC: U.S. Government Printing Office, 1867.

This 678-page report provides details on many of the individual mines in California, Nevada, Arizona, Utah, Montana, Idaho, Washington, Oregon, and Alaska. Pages 226-264 provide information on mining laws, as well as some of the regulations of specific mining communities. This "preliminary" report was followed up by a second, expanded study: J. Ross Browne. *Resources of the Pacific Slope,* 40th Cong., 2nd Sess., House Ex. Doc. No. 202 (1868), Serial No. 1342. Washington, DC: 1868. Reprinted as J. Ross Browne. *Resources of the Pacific Slope.* New York: D. Appleton and Company, 1887, which contains less information on mining codes.

Dwinelle, John W. *The Colonial History of the City of San Francisco.* San Francisco: Towne and Bacon, 1863; reprinted under the direction of the City Attorney of San Diego, San Diego: Frye and Smith, 1924.

Less easy to read than the following Halleck report, Dwinelle's successful brief filed in support of San Francisco's claim for pueblo status (and therefore four square leagues of municipal land) nonetheless contains valuable information.

Halleck, H. W. "Report on the Laws and Regulations Relative to Grants or Sales of Public Lands in California," in U.S. Congress. House. *Presidential Message Transmitting Information on California and New Mexico,* at 118-180. 31st Cong., 1st Sess., House Ex. Doc, No. 17, 31-2, Serial No. 573. Washington, DC: 1850. Also in U.S. Congress. Senate. *Message from the President of the United States Communicating Information Called for by a Resolution of the Senate of the 17th Instant, in relation to California and New Mexico,* 120-183. 31st Cong., 1st Sess., Senate Ex. Doc. No. 18, Serial No. 557. Washington, DC: s.n., 1850.

Straightforward and easy to read, this document is critical to understanding the early U.S. interpretation of Spanish and Mexican California land law. There are four major parts of the report: a section on public lands, a section on mission property, a section on lands of importance for strategic or governmental purposes, and appendixes containing translations of relevant Spanish and Mexican documents.

[Jones, William Carey]. *Report on the Subject of Land Titles in California,* in U.S. Congress. Senate. 31st Cong., 2nd Sess., Senate Ex. Doc. No. 18, Serial No. 589. Washington, DC: Gideon, 1850.

Not to be confused with Senate Executive Document 18 from the *first* session of the 31st Congress (listed in the following). In addition to examining the archives in Monterey, Jones went to Mexico to research this report. Less critical of the condition of land titles than the Halleck report, it was not as well received in Congress.[43] Includes English versions of thirty-three documents (as appendixes) relating to the distribution of land in California.

U. S. Congress. House. *Occupation of Mexican Territory,* 29th Cong., 2nd Sess., House Ex. Doc. No. 19, Serial No. 499 [1846, 1847].

The second compilation of the records of the occupation of New Mexico and California includes correspondence and proclamations of Stockton, as well as Kearny's reports on the occupation of New Mexico.

U.S. Congress. House. *Presidential Message Transmitting Information on California and New Mexico,* 31st Cong., 1st Sess., House Ex. Doc. No. 17, Serial No. 573. Washington, DC: 1850.

The major compilation of official government papers for the military government of California. This compilation covers the period from approximately February 1847 through October 1849 and includes the Kearny and Mason governorships. Although lengthy, unindexed, and poorly paginated, this is a critical document to understanding the U.S. perspective relating to the acquisition of California and the U.S. government's understanding of Spanish and California law. Includes the Halleck report on Spanish and Mexican land laws and the constitution developed at the 1849 Constitutional Convention in Monterey.

U.S. Congress. Senate. *Documents from State Department on Relations with Mexico,* 29th Cong., 2nd Sess., Senate Ex. Doc. 1/2, Serial No. 493. Washington, DC: s.n., 1847.

The first compilation of the military government records, this document contains the earliest records of the occupation of New Mexico and California from 1846.

U.S. Congress. Senate. *Message from the President of the United States Communicating Information Called for by a Resolution of the Senate of the 17th Instant, in Relation to California and New Mexico,* 31st Cong., 1st Sess., Senate Ex. Doc. No. 18, Serial No. 557. Washington, DC: s.n., 1850.

Not as comprehensive a collection of documents as House Executive Document 17, this volume is not as rare (and therefore more available) and contains many important documents, such as the Halleck report on Spanish and Mexican land laws.

U.S. Congress. Senate. *Presidential Message Communicating Further Information on Formation of State Government in California, and Also on Civil Affairs in Oregon,* 31st Cong., 1st Sess., Senate Ex. Doc. No. 52, Serial No. 561. Washington, DC: s.n., 1850.

The document contains the later records of the military government. Includes General Riley's civil correspondence from the end of October 1849 through mid-December, when the government was turned over to civil authorities.

U.S. Public Land Commission. *Report of the Public Lands Commission Created by the Act of March 3, 1879, relating to Public Lands in the Western Portion of the United States and to the Operation of Existing Land Laws,* 46th Cong., 1st Sess., House Ex. Doc. No. 46, Serial No. 1923. Washington, DC: U.S. Government Printing Office, 1880. Published separately as U.S. Public Lands Commission. *Report of the Public Lands Commission Created by the Act of March 3, 1879, Relating to Public Lands in the Western Portion of the United States and to the Operation of Existing Land Laws.* Washington, DC: Government Printing Office, 1880. Reprinted as U.S. Public Lands Commission. *Report of the Public Lands Commission Created by the Act of March 3, 1879, Relating to Public Lands in the Western Portion of the United States and to the Operation of Existing Land Laws.* New York: Arno Press, 1972.

As the title indicates, this report examines public land and its distribution to individuals. Includes letters and transcripts of testimony of numerous individuals. Indexed.

Laws and Codes

Laws of the Town of San Francisco 1847. Introduction by William Clary. San Marino, CA: Friends of the Huntington Library, 1947.

Copies of the original pamphlet of laws passed by the San Francisco ayuntamiento, or town council, in 1847 are held by the Huntington and Bancroft Libraries. In 1947, the Huntington issued 1,000 copies of this edition. It is interesting to see the issues that concerned the early residents of San Francisco sufficiently to prompt them to enact legislation to deal with them.

Local Mining Laws and Regulations, appendix to Clarence King, *The United States Mining Laws,* 14 *Final Report on the Tenth Census, 1880,* 247-345, in U.S. Congress. House. 47th Cong., 2nd Sess., House Misc. Doc. No. 42, Part 14, Serial No. 2144. Washington, DC: U.S. Government Printing Office, 1885.

Includes a county-by-county listing of the rules of the local mining districts gathered as part of the 1885 census.

Mason, R. B. *Laws for the Better Government of California, "the Preservation of Order, and the Protection of the Rights of the Inhabitants," During the Military Occupation of the Country by the Forces of the United States.* San Francisco: Brannan, 1848.

The code of laws developed for General Mason that was intended for publication in the summer of 1848 but was never released. The original is held by the Huntington Library, and copies are available at various libraries. The Bancroft Library at the University of California at Berkeley has a copy of an edition that contains both the English and Spanish versions of this proposed code.

Translation and Digest of Such Portions of the Mexican Law of March 20 and May 23, 1837 As Are Supposed to Be Still in Force As Adapted to Present Conditions. Introduction and notes by J[abez] Halleck and W[illiam] E. P. Hartnell (government translator). San Francisco: Office of the *Alta Californian,* 1849; reprinted in the appendix of *Report of Debates in the Convention of California on the Formation of the State Constitution in September and October, 1849,* XXIV XL, J. Ross Browne, reporter. Washington, DC: John T. Towers, 1850.

The translation of the Mexican Laws of 1837 which was published by General Bennett Riley in July 1849 and which stands as the only compilation of Spanish or Mexican laws actually issued by the military government.

Memoirs and Correspondence

Bryant, Edwin. *What I Saw in California.* New York: D. Appleton and Co., 1848.

Bryant, briefly an alcalde in San Francisco, provides insight into the information and materials available to U.S. officials on the function of the alcalde and the laws of Spain and Mexico.

Burnett, Peter H. *Recollections and Opinions of an Old Pioneer.* New York: D. Appleton and Co., 1880; reprint, New York: Da Capo Press, 1969.

Burnett was the first civil governor after the U.S. acquisition of California. Burnett was also very active in the provisional government movement that pushed for a civil government during the military regime, and he gives a good, firsthand account of the movement and its goals.

Colton, Walter. *Three Years in California.* New York: A.S. Barnes and Co., 1850; reprint, Stanford, CA: Stanford University Press, 1949.

The Reverend Colton, the first alcalde in Monterey appointed by U.S. officials, provides a readable description of life in California just after U.S. conquest. While most useful for his firsthand descriptions of Spanish and Mexican legal materials and the role of alcalde, his description of searching for gold early in the gold rush is even more fascinating. The original edition includes several chapters (XXVII-XXXIII) dealing with events that took place after Colton's departure from California, which were eliminated from the 1949 edition (presumably because they described events that Colton did not personally witness).

Davis, William H., Jr. *Sixty Years in California.* San Francisco: A. J. Leary, 1889; reprinted as *Seventy-Five Years in California.* San Francisco: John Howell, 1929.

William Davis came to California in the early 1830s, married the daughter of Estiduillo (a large landowner in Alameda County), and earned and lost several fortunes. More integrated than most Anglo-Americans into the local culture, he wrote an interesting, firsthand account of life in Mexican California.

Larkin, Thomas O. *The Larkin Papers; Personal, Business, and Official Correspondence of Thomas Oliver Larkin, Businessman and United States Counsel in California.* Edited by George P. Hammond. Berkeley, CA: Published for the Bancroft Library by the University of California Press, 1951-1968.

According to the description of the archival collection upon which the print set was based (available through the Online Archive of California at <http://www.oac.cdlib.org>), this eleven-volume set includes Larkin's correspondence concerning business, politics, consular affairs, and issues relating to the U.S. conquest of California. Also included are government and business documents. Well indexed.

M'Collum, William M. D. *California As I Saw It: Its New Cities and Villages, Its Rapid Accession of Population, Its Soil, Climate and Productions: Pencilling by Way of Its Gold Diggers! and Incidents of Travel by Land and Water.* Buffalo, NY: G. H. Derby, 1850; reprint, Los Gatos, CA: The Talisman Press, 1960.

Useful for the author's firsthand account of mining camp laws and other gold rush recollections.

Sherman, William Tecumseh. *Recollections of California 1846-1861.* Oakland, CA: Biobooks, 1945.

This volume was excerpted verbatim from the first four chapters of Volume 1 of Sherman's two-volume autobiography, *Memoirs of General William T. Sherman* (New York: D. Appleton and Co., 1875). Sherman wrote well, and his assignment to the governor's office provided him with a unique perspective on the military government's activities.

Willey, Samuel. *Thirty Years in California; A Contribution to the History of the State.* San Francisco: A. L. Bancroft and Co., 1879.

To mark his thirtieth anniversary in California, the Reverend Willey, a Presbyterian minister who came to California in early 1849 and served as the Protestant chaplin to the 1849 Constitutional Convention, relied upon "memoranda" that he collected over the years, including documents provided to him by other prominent Californians, to assist him in compiling his recollections of early American California.

————. *The Transition Period in California from a Province of Mexico in 1846 to a State of the American Union in 1850.* San Francisco: Whitaker and Ray Company, 1901.

Twenty-two years after publishing *Thirty Years in California,* previously listed, the Reverend Willey produced this longer memoir, which is largely focused on the 1849 Constitutional Convention. It is annotated with references to a number of other works.

Newspapers

Alta Californian (weekly edition). San Francisco: January 4–December 29, 1849. Continued by *Alta Californian* (triweekly edition), December 10, 1949–January 18, 1850; followed by the *Daily Alta Californian.* Available in microfilm.

California Star. San Francisco: January 9, 1847–December 23, 1848; suspended June 10–November 18, 1848. United with *The Californian* to form *The California Star and Californian*; followed by the *Alta Californian.* Available in microfilm.

A facsimile version of the first volume was published by Howell-North Books of Berkeley, California, in 1965.

The Californian. Monterey, CA: August 15, 1846–May 6, 1847. Continued by the *San Francisco Californian;* united with *California Star* to form *California Star and Californian;* followed by the *Alta Californian.*

The rarest of the three newspapers. A facsimile version of the first volume was published by J. Howell Books in 1971. A microfilm copy is available at the Bancroft Library, University of California, Berkeley.

Translations of Primary Materials

A Compilation of Spanish and Mexican Law in Relation to Mines, and Titles to Real Estate in Force in California, Texas and New Mexico. John A. Rockwell, compiler. New York: J.S. Voorhies, 1851; (reprinted as no. 25715-25722, *19th Century Legal Treatises,* Woodbridge, CT: Research Publications, 1984-1994.

The preface of this work (pp. 7-24) reviews the key sources of relevant Spanish and Mexican law and provides information on the editions and translations of the laws that Rockwell used as source material. Includes translations of the mining ordinances of New Spain, laws relating to gold, silver, and quicksilver in the *Novisima Recopilación* [New Recompilation] and the *Recopilación de las Indias* [Laws of the Indies], and in the decrees of the Cortes of Spain and of Ferdinand VII. In addition, it includes the laws and decrees of Mexico on the subject of mines, colonization, and the right of foreigners to hold real estate. Also included are extracts from public documents and from the laws of California regarding mines and mineral lands, as well as a digest of the common law on the subject of mines and mining.

A New Collection of Laws, Charters and Local Ordinances of the Governments of Great Britain, France and Spain Relating to the Concessions of Land in Their Respective Colonies together with the Laws of Mexico and Texas on the Same Subject. 2 vol. J[oseph] A. White, compiler. Philadelphia: T. and J. W. Johnson, 1839.

Very confusingly organized; although the book is indexed, one still needs to hunt around to find material. Includes Institutes of the Civil Law of Spain, the Laws of the Indies, Decrees and Orders of the Cortes of Spain, the Constitution of Mexico, and other materials.

The Coming of Justice to California: Three Documents. John Galvin, editor, and Adelaide Smithers, translator. San Francisco: John Howell Books, 1963.

Includes Rules and Regulations for the Presidios on the Frontier Line of New Spain, Ordered by King Carlos III in a Decree of September 10, 1772; Speech of Carlos Antonio Carrillo in the Mexican Chamber of Deputies, Requesting Adequate Courts for the Administration of Justice in Alta California, 1831; Decree of President Santa Anna of Mexico, May 22, 1834, Establishing Circuit Tribunals and District Courts; Select Articles of a Decree of the Spanish Cortes, of October 9, 1812, Concerning the Constitutional Magistrates of the Towns; Articles of the Mexican Law of May 20, 1826, Concerning Circuit Courts and District Judges.

Crouch, Dora P., Daniel J. Garr, and Axel I. Mundigo. *Spanish City Planning in North America.* Cambridge, MA: The MIT Press, 1982.

A translation of the Laws of the Indies ordinances relating to new towns can be found on pages 6-19.

Dwinelle, John W. *The Colonial History of the City of San Francisco.* San Francisco: Towne and Bacon, 1863; reprint, under the direction of the City Attorney of San Diego, San Diego: Frye and Smith, 1924.

Includes translations of portions of the Laws of the Indies relating to pueblos (Addenda I and II), the DeNeve Regulations (Addendum IV), Decrees of the Cortes applied to Mexico (Addenda X and XI), and the Colonization Act (Addendum XII), as well as many documents relating to secularization and the recognition of San Francisco as a pueblo by the Mexican government.

Halleck, H. W. "Report on the Laws and Regulations Relative to Grants or Sales of Public Lands in California," in U.S. Congress. House. *Presidential Message Transmitting Information on California and New Mexico,* 31st Cong., 1st Sess., House Ex. Doc. No. 17, 31-2 at 118-180 (1849), Serial No. 573. Washington, DC: s.n., 1850.

The translations contained in the appendixes to the report include the DeNeve Regulations (Appendix 2), the Colonization Act, and implementing regulations (Appendixes 4 and 5). In addition to the texts of official documents contained in the archives, translations made from the 1844 edition of the *Ordenanzas de Tieras y Aguas,* edited by Mariano Galvan (Appendix 9), are included.

[Jones, William Carey]. *Report on the Subject of Land Titles in California,* in U.S. Congress. Senate. 31st Cong., 2nd Sess., Senate Ex. Doc. No. 18 (1850), Serial No. 589. Washington, DC: Gideon, 1850.

Includes the Colonization Act and implementing regulations (Appendixes 1 and 2); Titles XIV and XV of the DeNeve Regulations (Appendix 4); a variety of secularization laws (Appendixes 6-16); and a list of land grants (Appendix 33).

Powell, Richard B. *Compromises of Conflicting Claims: A Century of California Law, 1760-1860.* Dobbs Ferry, NY: Oceana, 1977.

Includes Gov. Felipe DeNeve, "Regulations for Governing the Province of the Californias Approved by His Majesty by Royal Order, Dated October 24, 1781." Translated by John Everett Johnson. First published by Grabhorn Press in 1929, reprinted in Powell at 239-250, which contains Titles Fourteen (dealing with Political Governments and Instructions for Settlements) and Fifteen (dealing with Missions).

Translation and Digest of Such Portions of the Mexican Law of March 20 and May 23, 1837 As Are Supposed to Be Still in Force As Adapted to Present Conditions, with introduction and notes by J[abez] Halleck and W[illiam] E. P. Hartnell (government translator). San Francisco: Office of the *Alta Californian,* 1849; reprinted in the appendix of *Report of the Debates in the Convention of California on the Formation of the State Constitution in September and October, 1849,* XXIV-XL. J. Ross Browne, reporter. Washington, DC: John T. Towers, 1850.

The translation of the Mexican Laws of 1837 that was published by General Bennett Riley in July 1849.

Wilson, R. A. "The Alcalde System of California." *California Reports* 1(1850): 559, 560-566.

Includes excerpts of the laws of March 20, 1837, and May 23, 1837. Professor Langum advises against relying too much on the accuracy of this translation: "The problems with the translation are that the sections have been renumbered, not all sections of the statute are translated, and those sections that are translated are not all complete."[44]

Secondary Materials

August, Ray. "*Gringos v. Mineros:* the Hispanic Origins of American Mining Law." *Western Legal History* 9(1996): 147-175.

The author reexamines the evolution of mining camp laws to argue that the mining laws developed in the camps during the gold rush merely "plagiarized" traditional Spanish mining practices.

Avalos, Francisco. "The Legal Personality of the Colonial Period of Mexico," *Law Library Journal* 83(1991): 393-400.

Although this article does not deal specifically with any California materials, it is helpful for providing general background on Spanish colonial law.

Bancroft, Hubert Howe. *History of California.* 7 vols. San Francisco: The History Company, 1884-1890; facsimile edition of the first American edition, Santa Barbara: W. Hebberd, Santa Barbara, 1963- .

The classic California history. Bancroft's highly judgmental prose can be irritating; nonetheless, this comprehensive history is an essential tool for California historical research: "The most valuable contribution of the series is the extensive footnoting to primary sources, including Spanish and Mexican government documents, letters and diaries of early residents, interviews of first generation pioneers, maps, and other memorabilia, most of which form the core of the Bancroft Library collections."[45]

Berwanger, Eugene H. *The Frontier Against Slavery: Western Anti-Negro Prejudice and the Slavery Extension Controversy.* Urbana: University of Illinois Press, 1971.

In Chapter 3, "In Eldorado," the author presents an interesting discussion of the slavery and racial bias issues during the gold rush. The work is well documented and includes a bibliography.

Bynum, Lindley. "Laws for the Better Government of California, 1848." *Pacific Historical Review* 2(1933): 279-291.

Includes a fairly in-depth review of the events leading to the suppression of the Mason Code and briefly reviews the arrangement and content of the code.

Cate, Chester March. "The First California Laws Printed in English." In *Bibliographic Essays: Tribute to Wilberforce Eames* 330-336. Cambridge, MA: Harvard University Press, 1924.

Cate, then the assistant librarian at the Huntington Library, provides a good summary of the newspaper reports and official correspondence referring to the development and ultimate suppression of the Mason Code.

Chapman, Charles. *Colonial Hispanic America: A History.* New York: Macmillan, 1933.

Although not concerned with California, this text is useful for developing a broader understanding of the Spanish colonial system. Few in-text notes but includes an informative, annotated bibliographic "Essay on Authorities."

————. *A History of California: The Spanish Period.* New York: Macmillan, 1921.

Although the book is not focused on legal history, one may still stumble upon fragments of helpful information, but there are no notes citing source documents. This work, however, does contain a useful appendix titled "The Literature of California History," which provides an annotated, evaluative bibliography of materials.

Clay, Karen. *Trade, Institutions and Law: The Experience of Mexican California.* [Pasadena: All-UC Group in Economic History, 1993.]

This work uses game-theory to explore the institutions in Mexican California that permitted trade to develop despite the relative lack of legal institutions. Includes an unannotated bibliography.

Cleland, Robert Glass. *The Cattle on a Thousand Hills.* San Marino, CA: The Huntington Library, 1941 (Second Edition, 1951).

A much-cited history, this is a vividly written account of the development of southern California. The first two chapters focus on the Spanish-Mexican land grant system, with helpful references to the laws contributing to its development, as well as biographical information on some of the leading ranchers. Includes extensive chapter notes and an unannotated bibliography.

Cushing, Charles S. "The Acquisition of California, Its Influence and Development Under American Rule." *California Law Review* 8(1920): 67-85.

Despite its title, this transcript of a California Bar Association speech deals largely with the development of law after statehood. This piece does, however, briefly summarize gold rush mining law issues.

Davis, John F. "The History of the Mining Laws of California." In *History of the Bench and Bar of California* 279-331, edited by Oscar T. Shuck. Los Angeles: The Commercial Printing House, 1901.

Reviews the development of mining law in California from the gold rush through the end of the nineteenth century. Includes, on pages 292-296, a list of the major gold rush mining districts and the dates upon which those districts adopted codes or regulations.[46]

Ellison, Joseph. "The Struggle for Civil Government in California, 1846-1850." *California Historical Society Quarterly* 10(1931): 4-26; 129-164; 226-244.

While highly sympathetic to the Anglo-American settlers' complaints, this multiple-part article is heavily noted and provides access to numerous primary materials. The first three chapters deal with issues that arose prior to the 1849 Constitutional Convention. Includes a bibliography on pages 243-244. An important tool.

Ellison, William Henry. *A Self-Governing Dominion; California, 1849-1860*. Berkeley: University of California Press, 1950.

The author devotes the first chapter, titled "Steps Toward Self Government," to the period from 1846 to the calling of the constitutional convention in 1849. Better sources are available, as this chapter provides a traditional Anglo-American overview of the transition period. Includes an annotated bibliography.

Engstrand, Iris H. W. "The Legal Heritage of Spanish California." *Southern California Quarterly* 75(1993): 205-236.

This article focuses more on how the Laws of the Indies and the regulations issued by Governor DeNeve were actually enforced in various California settlements rather than on legal analysis. Nonetheless, this article demonstrates the active role that these laws played in the development of Spanish and Mexican California.

Franklin, William E. "Peter H. Burnett and the Provisional Government Movement." *California Historical Society Quarterly* 40(1961): 123-136.

A detailed look at the Provisional Government Movement and the role that Peter Burnett (California's first "American" civil governor) played in the push for civil government after the U.S. acquisition of California.

Gates, Paul W. *Land and Law in California*. Ames: Iowa State University Press, 1991.

This collection of previously published articles provides a more modern assessment of historical land issues in California law. Well written and footnoted, this is an essential tool.

Geary, Gerald J. "The Secularization of the California Missions (1810-1846)." *Studies in American Church History* 17. Washington, DC: Catholic University Press, 1934; reprint, New York: AMS Press, 1974.

While presenting a somewhat romantic view of the California missions, this piece (the author's PhD dissertation) is extensively researched and includes a lengthy bibliography.

Gilbert, Benjamin Franklin. "Mexican Alcaldes of San Francisco, 1835-1846." *Journal of the West* 2(1963): 245-256.

This piece provides information on the nine men who served as alcaldes during this period and gives a brief description of the major events that took place while each was in office. One of the very few pieces that looks at non-Anglo alcaldes.

Grivas, Theodore. *Military Governments in California* 1846-1850. Glendale, CA: Arthur H. Clark Company, 1963.

The chapter "Alcalde Rule" is essentially a reprint of an earlier article: Grivas, Theodore, "Alcalde Rule: The Nature of Local Government in Spanish and Mexican California." *California Historical Society Quarterly* 40(March 1961): 11-32. Written from a clearly Anglo-American perspective and more focused on the period after the U.S. acquisition of California, this too is an essential resource. Grivas's book includes a close study of the military records and an extensive bibliography. The bibliography is one of the few that includes serial set volume information in its citations to congressional documents, a small, but exceedingly helpful, feature.

Grossman, Lewis. "John C. Frémont, Mariposa, and the Collision of Mexican and American Law." *Western Legal History* 6(1993): 17-50.

The author uses John C. Frémont's claim in federal court for the Mariposa (Mexican) land grant as a vehicle for reviewing Spanish and Mexican land law, as well as a case study for analyzing the federal courts' treatment of Spanish and Mexican land law. No bibliography, but the notes are helpful.

Guest, Francis F. "Municipal Government in Spanish California." *California Historical Society Quarterly* 46(1967): 307-335; reprinted in *Hispanic California Revisited, Essays by Francis F. Guest, O.F.M.* Edited by Doyce B. Nunis Jr. Santa Barbara, CA: Santa Barbara Mission Archive Library, 1996.

A discussion of the day-to-day functioning of local government in Spanish California, this article is most helpful for historical background.

Gunther, Vanessa Ann. "Ambiguous Justice: Native Americans and the Legal System in Southern California, 1848-1890." PhD diss., University of California at Riverside, 2001 (UMI Number: 3017356).

This thesis reviews the mistreatment suffered by native Californians under the Spanish, Mexican, and American legal systems. Includes a bibliography.

Hansen, Woodrow. *The Search for Authority in California.* Oakland, CA: BioBooks, 1960.

The Anglo-American bias here is quite pronounced, and the author's own views come through rather too clearly (at times obscuring the impact of the original sources he cites), but the chapter notes are filled with references to a wide variety of helpful materials. The appendix includes an extensive bibliography.

Harlow, Neal. *California Conquered.* Berkeley: University of California Press, 1982.

Harlow was a special collections librarian throughout his career, and the notes are well documented. Harlow provides a more modern reading of the source material relating to the U.S. acquisition of California. Includes a detailed index and an extensive bibliography. An important tool.

Heizer, Robert F. and Alan F. Almquist. *The Other Californians: Prejudice and Discrimination Under Spain, Mexico and the United States to 1920.* Berkeley: University of California Press, 1971.

The authors explore the historic prejudice and discrimination against non-Anglo ethnic groups in California. Two chapters cover the treatment of Native Americans under Spain, Mexico, and the United States. Includes an unannotated bibliography.

Hittell, Theodore H. *History of California.* 4 vols. San Francisco: N. J. Stone and Co., 1885-1897.

Heavily noted and clearly written, this multivolume history provides access to source materials other than the Bancroft Collection[47] and remains a valuable research tool.

Holladay, Samuel W. "A Review of the Military-Civil Government, 1846-50." In *History of the Bench and Bar of California* 3-32, edited by Oscar T. Shuck. Los Angeles: The Commercial Printing House, 1901.

Provides useful background on the military government and reviews some of the proclamations and governmental activities of the military leadership.

Homan, Ann M. "Some Transitional Alcaldes in Northern California, 1846-1850." *Dogtown Territorial Quarterly* 42(2002): 50-61.

This article describes some of the judgments rendered by alcaldes appointed by the military government from various locations in California and gives the reader a vivid picture of how justice was dispensed during the military government.

Hundley, Norris, Jr. *The Great Thirst: Californians and Water, a History.* Berkeley: University of California Press, revised edition, 2001.

The second chapter provides information on Spanish and Mexican laws and polices relating to water rights. Includes a bibliography.

Hunt, Rockwell D. "Legal Status of California 1846-49." *Annals of the American Academy of Political and Social Science* 12(Nov. 1898): 63-84.

While relying perhaps too heavily on the rhetoric of the Anglo-American press, this article draws upon a wide variety of sources to survey the important issues facing the military government. An essential tool.

Hutchinson, C. Alan. "The Mexican Government and the Mission Indians of Upper California." *The Americas* 21(April 1965): 335-362.

A helpful discussion of the Mexican government's policies regarding the native inhabitants and the motivations for promoting the secularization of the missions.

Johnson, David Alan. *Founding the Far West: California, Oregon and Nevada 1840-1890.* Berkeley: University of California Press, 1992.

Chapter 1 gives a good historical overview of the period and highlights the issues relating to the transition from Mexican to American rule. Well researched but does not include a bibliography.

Langum, David J. "The Introduction of Conciliation into Modern Spanish Law and Its Practice in the Spanish-American Borderlands." In *Studies in Roman Law and Legal History in Honour of Ramon D'Abadal i de Vinyals on the Occasion of the Centenary* 325-341, edited by Manuel J. Pelaez. Barcelona: Promociones Publicaciones Universitarias, 1989.

This article traces the development of conciliation in Spanish law and discusses its limited application in Spanish California.

———. "The Legal System of Spanish California: A Preliminary Study." *Western Legal History* 7(1994): 1-23.

While lacking the in-depth study of archival material that characterizes Langum's earlier work on the Mexican-California system, this brief but helpful essay sets forth the major issues, with illustrative examples gleaned largely from Bancroft's work.

———. *Law and Community of the Mexican California Frontier; Anglo-American Expatriates and the Clash of Legal Traditions, 1821-1846.* Norman: University of Oklahoma Press, 1987.

The most accessible and clearly written secondary source discussing the Mexican legal system, this text is essential reading for students of this period. The chapters titled "The Mexican California Legal System," "Civil Litigation," and "Legal Values in Collision" are particularly valuable for general research, but the book also includes chapters on criminal law, contracts, commercial law practices, and family law, which are helpful to more focused research. The footnotes are also very informative. A thorough bibliography that includes both Spanish and English language sources is included.

Lawson, Gary and Guy Seidman. "The Hobbesian Constitution: Governing Without Authority." *Northwestern Law Review* 95(2001): 581-628.

This piece makes careful use of a wide range of primary materials, both legal and historical, as well as secondary sources to examine the constitutionality of California postwar military government.

Lothrop, Gloria Ricci. "Rancheras and the Land: Women and Property Rights in Hispanic California." *Southern California Quarterly* 76(1) (1994): 59.

This piece reviews Spanish and Mexican laws concerning women's property rights (which enabled women to hold 13 percent of all Spanish-Mexican land grants in California) and explores the implications of those laws on the role of women in Spanish-Mexican California.

McDowell, Andrea G. "From Commons to Claims: Property Rights in the California Gold Rush." *Yale Journal of Law & Humanities* 14(2002): 1-72.

This article examines the development of property rights by the miners in California from 1848 to 1850 and the impact of those unique conditions on that development. The author made extensive use of both primary and secondary materials that are cited in the notes. Includes a brief appendix outlining the research sources used.

McKnight, Joseph W. "Law Books on the Hispanic Frontier." *Journal of the West* 27(1988): 74-84.

While largely focused outside of California, this piece gives a good overview of the types of legal sources available during the Spanish and Mexican periods.

Morrow, William W. *Spanish and Mexican Private Land Grants*. San Francisco: Bancroft Whitney, 1923; reprinted as *Spanish and Mexican Land Grants,* New York: Arno Press, 1974.

A frequently cited source, but not as well written or organized as other materials on the same subject.

Palmer, William J. and Paul P. Selvin, "The Development of Law in California," in *California Constitution,* Art. 1-4-1. St. Paul, MN: West Publishing Company, 1954; reprint, St. Paul, MN: West Publishing Company, 1983.

This often-cited source tremendously oversimplifies and undervalues the Spanish and Mexican systems but is helpful for the early U.S. period.

Paul, Rodman W. *California Gold: The Beginning of Mining in the Far West*. Lincoln, NE: University of Nebraska Press, 1947.

A very helpful and easy-to-read source covering the gold rush period. While not a legal text, the author has read the legal texts, highlighted the legal issues, and provided appropriate references. Appendix C includes a thorough, annotated bibliography of sources.

————. *Mining Frontiers of the Far West 1848-1880*. New York: Holt, Rinehart and Wilson, 1963.

This text examines the impact of mining activities on the westward migration in frontier America, but is not as helpful as Paul's *California Gold*. Includes some useful maps indicating the locations of major deposits of gold and silver in the west.

Pisani, Donald J. " 'I Am Resolved Not to Interfere, but Permit All to Work Freely': The Gold Rush and American Resource Law." *California History* 77(4)(1998/99): 123-148.

This essay reviews the influence of the gold rush on the development of U.S. mining and natural resources law.

Pitt, Leonard. *The Decline of the Californios*. Berkeley: University of California Press, 1968.

The author of this study of Latinos in California used a wider variety of materials (including the personal papers of prominent Californios and other Spanish language documents) to offer a different perspective from traditional Anglo-American histories. Includes an unannotated bibliography of both Spanish and English language sources.

Powell, Richard R. *Compromises of Conflicting Claims: A Century of California Law, 1760-1860*. Dobbs Ferry, NY: Oceana, 1977.

One of the last works by eminent law professor Richard Powell. While dismissive of the alcalde system, it is (as one might expect from the author of *Powell on Real Property*) particularly useful for information on Spanish and Mexican land law and for legal issues during early statehood. In addition, this work offers a treasure trove of information in its notes and appendixes. The documents included are reprints or translations of the text of many significant documents, including the DeNeve regulations.

Richman, Irving B. *California Under Spain and Mexico, 1535-1847.* Boston and New York: Houghton Mifflin Co., 1911.

The author studied both the Spanish Archives in Madrid and Seville and the Mexican Archives in Mexico City as well as other major collections to produce this general history of the period. Includes extensive chapter notes that are preceded by a brief summary which highlights "new" (in 1911) sources identified by the author beyond those contained in the (original) Bancroft Collection.

Robertson, James R. "From Alcalde to Mayor: A History of the Change from the Mexican to the American Local Institutions in California." PhD diss., University of California at Berkeley, 1909.

While very frustrating to use because it is poorly typed, edited, and organized, the research in this dissertation is extensive and the perspective unbiased; if one perseveres, ultimately this study is enormously helpful. It includes a confusing, but lengthy, bibliography of archival materials. An unpublished dissertation, it is available at both the Main and the Bancroft Libraries of the University of California at Berkeley.

Robinson, W.W. *Land in California.* Berkeley: University of California Press, 1948.

Considered a classic. One of the few sources that discusses the Land Commission activities with clarity, this text also includes an engagingly written and thorough commentary of sources, which unfortunately is scanty on bibliographic information, but it does include a helpful evaluative bibliographic essay.

Royce, Josiah. *California from the Conquest in 1846 to the Second Vigilance Committee in San Francisco, Study of the American Character.* Boston and New York: Houghton Mifflin and Co., 1886; other editions published by Knopf in 1948 and Peregine Publishers in 1970.

This helpful one-volume history provides a less Anglo-American, more critical perspective than the other early histories.

Saunders, Myra K. "California Legal History: A Review of California's Spanish and Mexican Legal Institutions." *Law Library Journal* 87(1995): 487-514.

This bibliographic essay reviews the Spanish colonial and Mexican legal systems, particularly the alcalde system, in frontier California and explores the various sources available to research this era. Includes an annotated bibliography.

————. "California Legal History: The Legal System Under the United States Military Government, 1846-1849." *Law Library Journal* 88(1996): 488-522.

This article explores the legal institutions operating in California from 1846-1849 and reviews the materials available to researchers investigating this period. Includes an annotated bibliography.

Schmidt, Gustavus. *The Civil Law of Spain and Mexico*. New Orleans: Thomas Rea, 1851.

Remarkably readable, this text provides a more contemporaneous view of the Spanish and Mexican legal systems.

Shinn, Charles Howard. *Mining Camps; A Study in American Frontier Government*. Baltimore, MD: Johns Hopkins University, 1884; reprint Glouscester, MA: Peter Smith, 1970.

One of the seminal studies of California mining camp law, Shinn's study includes helpful information on Spanish and Mexican law as well. Includes a bibliography of sources consulted.

Stevenson, Noel C. "The Glorious Uncertainty of the Law 1846-1851." *Journal of the State Bar of California* 28(1953): 374-380.

A discussion of the scarcity of both Spanish language and Anglo-American legal materials in California after U.S. occupation.

Taming the Elephant: Politics, Government, and Law in Pioneer California. Edited by John F. Burns and Richard J. Orsi. Berkeley: University of California Press, 2003.

Simultaneously published as a special edition of *California History* (81 [3/4] *California History* [2003]), this compilation of essays is the fourth and last volume of the California Historical Society's California History Sesquicentennial Series.[48] While largely focused on government during and after the 1849 Constitutional Convention, the nine essays[49] in this latest contribution to the series provide a good starting point for those interested in researching early American California law and government.

Umbeck, John R. *A Theory of Property Rights, with Application to the California Gold Rush*. Ames: Iowa State University Press, 1981.

In testing his theory of the development of property rights, the author studied the provisions of 180 mining camp association agreements in gold rush California in detail. Includes a bibliography of mining sources.

Vance, John T. *The Background of Hispanic-American Law.* New York: Central Book Co., 1943; originally published under the title *The Background of Hispanic-American Law: Legal Sources and Juridical Literature of Spain.* Washington, DC: Catholic University of America, 1937.

A good text to consult to understand the development of the law in the former Spanish-American colonies. Contains a particularly thorough discussion of the Laws of the Indies.

Wilson, R. A. "The Alcalde System of California." *California Reports* 1(1850): 559, 560-566 [not included in all editions].

Primarily a collection of translated excerpts of the laws of March 20, 1837, and May 23, 1837. The narrative is highly biased and unappreciative of the alcalde system under both the Mexican and military governments, but this piece does provide a survey of the important legal issues of this period.

Wright, Flora Alice. "Richard Barnes Mason, Governor of California." MA thesis, University of California at Berkeley, 1919.

This typewritten manuscript does a good job of identifying and reviewing the relevant documents in collections of primary materials. It is available at both the Doe and Bancroft Libraries of the University of California at Berkeley.

Yale, Gregory. *Legal Titles to Mining Claims and Water Rights in California.* San Francisco: A. Roman, 1867.

Difficult to read in part and not as clearly organized as one might wish, this text is the earliest and most often cited legal reference dealing with California mining law.

NOTES

1. The area that is now the State of California was known as *Alta* (upper) *California* under both Spain and Mexican rule (the eastern boundary of *Alta California* was not clearly defined, but included all of Nevada and the western portions of present-day Utah and Arizona). *Baja* (lower) *California,* of course, was and is a Mexican state. This chapter will use the term *California* to refer to the area that became the state of California.

2. Richard Powell, *Compromises of Conflicting Claims: A Century of California Law, 1760-1860* at 6 (Dobbs Ferry, NY: Oceana Publications, 1977).

3. Ibid. at 19-30. For a fascinating discussion of the romanticizing of the mission period, see Carey McWilliams, "The Growth of a Legend," in Dean Stewart and Jeannine Gendar, eds., *Fool's Paradise: A Carey McWilliams Reader* 3-16 (Santa Clara, CA: Santa Clara University; Berkeley, CA: Heyday Books, 2001).

4. Treaty of Peace, Friendship, Limits, and Settlement Between the United States of America and the United Mexican States, February 2, 1848, 18-2 *Stat.* 492 (1875).

5. 9 *Stat.* 452, ch. L (1850).

6. See Theodore Grivas, *Military Governments in California 1846-1850* at 151 (Glendale, CA: A. H. Clark Co., 1963).

7. Gov. Felipe DeNeve, *Regulamento Para el Goberno de la Provinca de Californias* (1784). For translated editions, see sources cited infra in bibliography.

8. Erwin C. Surrency, *A History of American Law Publishing* 22-26 (New York: Oceana Publications, 1990); Paul S. Reinsch, *English Common Law in the Early American Colonies* 56 (Madison, WI: s.n., 1899).

9. David J. Langum, *Law and Community of the Mexican California Frontier: Anglo-American Expatriates and the Clash of Legal Traditions* 1821-1846, at 51 (Norman: University of Oklahoma Press, 1987); Powell, supra note 2, at 30. The cultural conflict is also studied in Craig Arthur Swanson, "Vanguards of Continental Expansion: Americans in Alta California 1790-1846" (unpublished PhD dissertation, University of Maryland, College Park, 2000).

10. Reinsch, supra note 8, at 19.

11. Langum, supra note 9.

12. See Myra Saunders, "California Legal History: The Legal System Under the United States Military Government 1846-1849," *Law Libr. J.* 88(1996): 488-522 , at 491-492.

13. See ibid. at 495-498.

14. See ibid. at 498-504.

15. See ibid. at 504-506. Land within pueblo limits was actively transferred. The land grants made within the "pueblo" of San Francisco between 1836-1851, for example, are listed in Alfred Wheeler, *Land Titles in San Francisco* (San Francisco: Alta California Steam Printing Establishment, 1852).

16. Letter from R.B. Mason to Adjutant General R. Jones (Aug. 17, 1848), in U.S. Congress. House. *Presidential Message Transmitting Information on California and New Mexico,* 31st Cong., 1st Sess., H.R. Ex. Doc. No. 17 at 533, Serial No. 573 (1850); letter from R.B. Mason to Adjutant General R. Jones (Nov. 24, 1848), ibid. at 648; William Tecumseh Sherman, *Recollections of California 1846-1861* at 44-45 (Oakland, CA: Biobooks, 1945).

17. See Saunders, supra note 12, at 506-509.

18. Bills that would have provided for a territorial government for California were introduced in Congress in July and December 1848 but were not enacted. See William Henry Ellison, *A Self-Governing Dominion; California, 1849-1860,* 16-17 (Berkeley: University of California Press, 1950). For a good discussion of the impact of the slavery issue on the congressional effort to establish a territorial govern-

ment in California, see Joseph Ellison, "The Struggle for Civil Government in California, 1846-1850" (pt. 2), *Cal. Hist. Soc'y. Q.* 10(1931): 129, 132-138.

19. See Saunders, supra note 12, at 509-510.

20. See Cardinal Goodwin, *The Establishment of State Government in California 1846-1850,* at 80 (New York: MacMillan, 1914); Saunders, supra note 12, at 509-511.

21. The constitutional convention is beyond the scope of this guide. For more detail on the constitutional convention, as well as a bibliography of research sources, please see Myra Saunders, "California Legal History: The California Constitution of 1849," *Law Libr. J.* 90(1998): 447-480. See also Neal Harlow, "California Conquered" 338-353 (Berkeley: University of California Press, 1982) and "Taming the Elephant: Politics, Government, and Law in Pioneer California," (John F. Burns and Richard J. Orsi, eds.; Berkeley: University of California Press, 2003); simultaneously published as *Cal. Hist.* 81(3/4) (2003).

22. An Act for the Admission of the State of California into the Union, ch. L, 9 *Stat.* 452 (1850).

23. Fortunately, most of the documents that related to land grants were stored in a safe and survived. Those documents are now held in the National Archives; copies of documents relating to land claims filed with the U.S. government stayed with the district court and are now on deposit at the Bancroft Library. *A Guide to the History of California,* at 189 (Doyce B. Nunis Jr. and Gloria Ricci Lothrop, eds.; New York: Greenwood Press, 1989) [hereinafter Nunis].

24. Hubert Howe Bancroft, *History of California* (facsimile edition of the first American edition, Santa Barbara: W. Hebberd, 1963-1970) (1884-1890).

25. That collection is located in the Bancroft Library of the University of California at Berkeley. For a detailed description of the California Archives see J. N. Bowman, "History of the Provincial Archives of California," *S. Cal. Q.* 64(1953): iv-97 and Judson A. Grenier, "Addenda to J.N. Bowman's 'History of the Provincial Archives of California,'" *S. Cal. Q.* 66(1984): 257-261.

26. Only a very small percentage of full-text primary source documents relating to California legal history are available in digital format. Two digital collections currently available include the California State Library's exhibit on the gold rush, which contains digital facsimiles of many prestatehood materials (http://www.library.ca.gov/goldrush/), and the Library of Congress' American Memory Project (http://memory.loc.gov/ammem/cbhtml/cbhome.html), a collection of digitized manuscripts from early California settlers.

27. Selected Web sites are listed in the bibliography. For a listing of regional California historical societies and museums, see: http://www.californiahistory.com/museums.html.

28. Nunis, supra note 23.

29. One example is Henry E. Huntington Library and Art Gallery, *California Legal History Manuscripts in the Huntington Library: A Guide* (San Marino, CA: The Library, 1989).

30. H.R. Ex. Doc. No. 17, supra note 16.

31. Theodore H. Hittell, 2 *History of California* 739, 743 (San Francisco: Pacific Press Publishing House, 1885-1897).

32. H. W. Halleck, Report on the Laws and Regulations Relative to Grants or Sales of Public Lands in California in H.R. Ex. Doc. No. 17, supra note 16, at 118-180.

33. [William Carey Jones], Report on the Subject of Land Titles in California, in U.S. Congress. Senate., 31st Cong., 2nd Sess., S. Ex. Doc. No. 18, Serial No. 589 (1850).

34. John W. Dwinelle, *The Colonial History of the City of San Francisco* (San Diego, CA: Frye and Smith, 1924) (1863).

35. Nunis, supra note 23.

36. Langum, supra note 9.

37. James R. Robertson, "From Alcalde to Mayor: A History of the Change from the Mexican to the American Local Institutions in California" (unpublished PhD dissertation, University of California at Berkeley, 1909).

38. Grivas, supra note 6.

39. Rockwell D. Hunt, "Legal Status of California 1846-49," *Annals of the American Academy of Political and Social Science* 12(1898): 63-84.

40. Gary Lawson and Guy Seidman, "The Hobbesian Constitution: Governing Without Authority," *Nw. U. L. Rev.* 95(2001): 581-628.

41. Neal Harlow, *California Conquered* (Berkeley: University of California Press, 1982).

42. Andrea McDowell has found that many of the most important firsthand accounts are available online at the Library of Congress Web site, http://lcweb2. loc.gov/ammem/cbhtml/cbhome.html. Andrea G. McDowell, "From Commons to Claims: Property Rights in the California Gold Rush," *Yale J. L. & Human* 14 (2002): 68, note 243.

43. Paul W. Gates, *Land and Law in California* 8-9 (Ames: Iowa State University Press, 1991), and accompanying notes.

44. Professor Langum advises against relying too much on the accuracy of this translation: "The problems with the translation are that the sections have been renumbered, not all sections of the statute are translated, and those sections that are translated are not all complete." Langum, supra note 9, at 35-37, nn. 21-22.

45. Nunis, supra note 23, at 4.

46. This information was taken from Local Mining Laws and Regulations, appendix to Clarence King, The United State Mining Laws, 14 *Final Report on the Tenth Census, 1880,* 247-345, in U.S. Congress. House. 47th Cong., 2nd Sess., House Misc. Doc. No. 42, Part 14, Serial No. 2144 (1885), as well as sources cited in the text.

47. See Charles Chapman, *A History of California: The Spainsh Period* 500 (New York: Macmillan, 1921).

48. Earlier volumes in the series are *Contested Eden: California Before the Gold Rush* (1998); *A Golden State: Mining and Economic Development in Gold Rush California* (1999); *Rooted in Barbarous Soil: People, Culture, and Community in Gold Rush California* (2000).

49. The nine essays are John F. Burns, "Taming the Elephant: An Introduction to California's Statehood and Constitutional Era"; Roger D. McGrath, "Violent Birth: Disorder, Crime, and Law Enforcement, 1849-1890"; Gorden Morris Bakken, "The Courts, the Legal Profession, and the Development of Law in Early California";

Shirley Ann Wilson Moore, "'We Feel the Want of Protection': The Politics of Law and Race in California, 1848-1878"; Joshua Paddison, "Capturing California; Judson A. Grenier, 'Officialdom': California State Government, 1849-1879"; Donna C. Schuele, "'None Could Deny the Eloquence of this Lady': Women, Law, and Government in California, 1850-1890"; Edward Leo Lyman, "The Beginnings of Anglo-American Local Government in California"; Robert J. Chandler, "An Uncertain Influence: The Role of the Federal Government in California, 1846-1880."

Chapter 6

Colorado Prestatehood Legal Resources: Sixteenth Century to 1876

Barbara Bintliff

The Colorado region has a long history, stretching hundreds of years from the first native inhabitants, through claims of ownership by several European nations, Mexico, and the Republic of Texas, to inclusion in a number of U.S. territorial governments, before eventual statehood. In addition to formal, although sometimes only technical, governmental oversight, the region experienced a variety of unique local governments created out of a necessity for orderly dispute resolution.[1]

Although governments have been plentiful, legal materials documenting decisions and actions are sparse at best. The following essay includes not only known sources of "Colorado law," but also information on the various jurisdictions that have exercised sovereignty over the geographical region. The purpose of including this material is to assist in the identification of the appropriate jurisdiction in which to conduct legal research for a given time period. Those seeking information on preterritorial legal resources for Colorado will need to exercise creativity and determination in locating relevant materials.

THE COLORADO REGION
BEFORE THE TERRITORY OF COLORADO

The first Europeans to visit the Colorado region were Spaniards, whose first expeditions entered the area in the early sixteenth century. The Spanish-claimed territory in North America, called New Spain, covered an immense region. It included all of what is now the nation of Mexico and the entire region west of the Mississippi River in what became the United States, in addition to substantial portions of the present-day southern United States. Concurrent with Spain's claims to the region, the British colony of Virginia was granted all the lands extending 200 miles north and south of Point Comfort, Virginia, from "sea to sea," under a 1609 grant from England's King James I.[2] A significant portion of Colorado was at one time claimed within this land grant.

Spanish emissaries paid greater attention to the more southern portions of their North American claims, and there is little evidence that the English colonial powers recognized the true nature of their grant; the conflicting claims coexisted peacefully for many years (if, indeed, there was even an awareness of conflicting claims). Little, if any, lawmaking regarding the region occurred. The first serious challenge to the Spanish claims came from the French in 1682, when the explorer La Salle reached the mouth of the Mississippi River and claimed possession of the entire Mississippi River drainage basin for his country.[3] He named the region "Louisiane," or Louisiana, in honor of his king, Louis XIV.

In November 1762, France and Spain secretly negotiated a treaty in which France transferred its claims to western North America to Spain.[4] At almost the same time, in 1763, England gave up its claims to the lands west of the Mississippi in favor of Spain.[5] By means of the San Ildefonso Treaty of October 1800, Spain was forced to return the secretly transferred lands to France.[6] In 1803, a cash-starved Napoleon sold the territory to the United States,[7] which was in fear of his launching an expedition to colonize the region. The "Louisiana Purchase" put the eastern part of Colorado in U.S. ownership, with Spain still controlling the remainder of the region.

Mexico assumed ownership of most of Spain's North American claims following its 1810-1821 wars of independence with Spain.[8] The 1848 Treaty of Guadalupe Hidalgo[9] established the majority of the current boundary between the United States and Mexico, with Mexico ceding its northern territories (including most of western Colorado) to the United States. At the same time, the Republic of Texas included in its boundaries the remaining, southernmost portion of Colorado's territory. When Texas relinquished its independence in favor of joining the United States,[10] the entire geographical area of Colorado was wholly within U.S. ownership for the first time.[11] In 1850, Texas's borders were redrawn to their present configuration and its northern territory was ceded to the federal government.[12] At this point, the United States began to organize its vast western holdings into territories; Colorado as we know it eventually would become one of these new western territories.[13]

Portions of Colorado were parceled out to four territories: Utah,[14] New Mexico,[15] Nebraska, and Kansas.[16] None of the territories took much specific notice of the region in its lawmaking, as there was little population and the land itself remained largely uncharted. About the only source of official justice was the occasional territorial district judge riding circuit.[17] Kansas Territory held the most populated segment of the modern-day state's land, including Denver and Colorado Springs. In 1854, this area was organized as Arapahoe County, Kansas Territory. This included most of the early mining settlements of the eastern slopes of the Rockies, the Front Range, and the eastern plains. In large part, the first years of Colorado's modern history are defined by the activities of the Arapahoe County residents, because this is where the most people and the most industry were found.[18] Other settlements, most notably those in the southern parts of the region, were sparse and localized in the dispensation of justice.[19]

PRE–COLORADO TERRITORY
EXTRALEGAL GOVERNMENTS

The Kansas territorial government paid little attention to Arapahoe County. From its organization in 1854 through the establishment of the territory of Jefferson in 1861 (see last paragraph of this section), the region's legal system consisted primarily of extralegal governments formed to bring order to a local area: the mining districts passed rules and established courts that adjudicated mining claims and mining-related problems; claim clubs settled agricultural land claims in the days before the area was surveyed; and peoples' courts sat occasionally to settle disputes and mete out justice for especially egregious acts. All of these entities were active in dispensing justice but were characterized by a measure of vigilantism; most had written rules and procedures.[20] Many of their actions were ratified by the subsequent territorial government (see the following paragraphs).

Many mining districts had well-organized systems of government, with written constitutions, officers, councils, and courts to govern mining claims and activities in the new communities that sprang up around the more productive mines.[21] The rules created by some of these councils[22] were adopted by the Jefferson Territory[23] and became the basis of the laws of the territory and later the state of Colorado.[24] Miners' courts were devised in response to the great influx of gold seekers during the 1859 Colorado gold rush and offered an accepted, if swift and spontaneous, form of justice.[25]

Claims clubs, sometimes called neighborhood clubs, were common throughout the American West.[26] The clubs wrote a constitution and rules, chose officers that included a judge and arbitrator, and settled disputes regarding land claims and, later, water rights. The records and decisions of the claims clubs were adopted by the territory of Jefferson[27] and the territory of Colorado.[28] The surviving records of claims clubs can often be found in Colorado's county courthouses or with the Colorado State Historical Society. The *Rocky Mountain News* frequently reported on the proceedings of claims clubs and is often the best source of information on their activities.[29]

Peoples' courts were occasional entities, unlike the semipermanent mining district governments and the claims clubs. Peoples' courts were convened in the settlements to resolve disputes and hand out justice for especially egregious acts.[30] Few documents were produced by the peoples' courts, either before or after their deliberations. However, ratification of certain actions of the peoples' courts was among the first acts of the Colorado territorial legislature.[31]

In addition to the local extralegal governments, several attempts were made at organizing a territory or a state, in hopes that the U.S. Congress would recognize the area. In October 1860, the residents of Denver City established the "People's Government of the City of Denver" and elected a slate of officers.[32] The actions of the People's Government were ratified by the Colorado territorial legislature.[33] The United Mining District formed at about the same time, chose officers, and selected a delegate to Congress.[34] The Idaho Territory, based in Central City, organized in October 1860 and divided itself into three judicial districts. The courts created for each district were instructed to recognize the decisions of the miners' courts in the district and to function as a court of appeals for them.[35] The acts of all these governments regarding land titles were later ratified by the Colorado territorial legislature.[36]

The best-organized extralegal government arose in 1859, when a large group of Arapahoe County residents, frustrated by the lack of involvement by the Kansas territorial government, formed the territory of Jefferson.[37] Their goal was twofold: to provide a local government and to impress upon the U.S. Congress their desire to be a separate territory.[38] The territory of Jefferson's legislature considered and passed a great deal of legislation.[39] Among its earliest acts was the establishment of a court system consisting of a supreme court, district courts, county courts, justices of the peace, and mining courts.[40] These courts were active at first but had no real power; no known written decisions remain, although local newspapers often carried reports of the "government's" activities. The U.S. government never recognized the legality of this entity, and Kansas Territory continued to regard the region as part of its jurisdiction.[41] The territory of Jefferson abolished itself in favor of the new Colorado Territory in June 1861.[42] The several courts organized under the laws of Kansas Territory went out of existence when Colorado Territory was created. By the end of that year, even the miners' courts had begun to cease activities, leaving the way clear for the Colorado territorial government to assume control.

COLORADO TERRITORY

The U.S. Congress established the territory of Colorado in February 1861.[43] As noted in the following discussion, the government of the new territory was organized in a manner similar to the other territories in existence at a time, with a supreme court and lower courts, a legislature, and an executive branch headed by a territorial governor.

An act enabling the territory of Colorado to draft a constitution and become a state was passed by Congress in 1864.[44] A constitutional convention was convened in Golden on July 4, 1864, then immediately moved to Denver. Its members drafted a constitution that was submitted to the populace and defeated by popular vote.[45] A second draft constitution, written in 1865,[46] was approved by a vote of the populace and submitted to President Andrew Jackson according to the terms of the enabling act. President Jackson refused to proclaim Colorado a state, citing the irregularity of two draft constitutions, one of which was rejected by the residents.[47] Congress subsequently passed two bills calling for the admission of Colorado as a state,[48] but President Andrew Johnson vetoed both.[49]

In 1875, a new enabling act for a state of Colorado was passed by Congress.[50] Under the terms of the new act, Colorado was to convene a constitutional convention no later than December 1, 1875. However, the convention was not called until December 20 of that year. Despite the irregularities in assembling the drafters, the document drafted became the constitution of the new state.

The conveners of the convention decided not to keep verbatim records of the debates because of the cost involved.[51] Local newspapers, primarily the *Rocky Mountain News,* provided fairly accurate coverage of the sessions and some debates, however, and copies of the newspaper were provided to the delegates daily to keep them informed.

Rocky Mountain News. Denver, CO: Byers and Dailey.[52]

The official record of the constitutional convention is O'Connor, *Proceedings of the Constitutional Convention.* This is referred to as a "minute book" of the constitutional convention and includes records of the meetings at which the constitution was drafted.

Proceedings of the Constitutional Convention held in Denver, December 20, 1875, to frame a constitution for the state of Colorado, together with the enabling act passed by the Congress of the United States and approved March 3, 1875, the address to the people issued by the Convention, the con-

stitution as adopted and the President's proclamation. Published by authority, Timothy O'Connor, Secretary of State. Denver, CO: The Smith-Brooks Press, state printers, 1907.

The Colorado Constitution

The constitution was unanimously approved by the convention on March 14, 1876, and approved by the territory's citizenry on July 1 of that year. On August 1, 1876, President Grant proclaimed Colorado the thirty-eighth state admitted to the Union.[53] Several members of Congress protested this move, pointing out that only Congress has the power to admit new states and approve their constitutions, but Grant's actions prevailed. The constitution of 1876, as amended, is in effect today.[54]

Court Reports and Other Judicial Materials

The court system of the state of Colorado had its recognizable beginnings in 1861, when the territory of Colorado was created by an act of the U.S. Congress.[55] By the territory's organic act, judicial power was vested in a supreme court, district courts, probate courts, and justices of the peace, giving Colorado a judicial system very similar to most of the newly created states and territories. Reported cases of the supreme court of Colorado,[56] dating from territorial days, can be found in the *Colorado Reports.*

Reports of Cases at Law and in Chancery Determined in the Supreme Court of Colorado Territory to the Present Time. Volumes 1-3. Chicago: Callaghan and Company, 1891.

Cases from the territorial supreme court are included in the *American Digest,* Century Edition.

Several commercial publishers included decisions from Colorado's territorial supreme court in their selective case reporters, including the *American Decisions* and the *American Reports.* In addition, some federal district court decisions from the Colorado Territory were published in the *American Law Times Reports.*

The American decisions: Cases of general value and authority decided in the courts of the several states from the earliest issue of the state reports to the year 1869: Extra annotated. San Francisco, CA: Bancroft-Whitney Co.; Rochester, NY: Lawyers Co-operative Pub. Co., 1910-1911.

The American reports: Containing all decisions of general interest decided in the courts of last resort of the several states, with notes and references. San Francisco, CA: Bancroft-Whitney Co., 1871-1888.

The American law times reports. Washington, DC: [s.n.], 1870-1877.

The Colorado State Archives maintains a collection of territorial and state supreme court decisions and records; this frequently includes briefs. Most county and district courts also send their records to the archives, although there is no uniformity in coverage of any of these collections. Access to court records is by case numbers, which means that the number is needed to access a file. Case numbers are available from the court in which the case was heard.[57] The Colorado State Archives recommends calling ahead to determine coverage:[58]

> Colorado State Archives
> 1313 Sherman Street, Room 1B-20
> Denver, CO 80302
> (303) 866-2358

Statutes and other Legislative Materials

The Organic Act for Colorado Territory created a bicameral legislature with a council and a house of representatives.[59] When Colorado became a state in 1876, the state constitution changed the designation of the upper house from "council" to "senate."[60]

Bills

Availability of bills from the territorial period is spotty until 1867. It may be best to check local newspapers for the text of important bills prior to that date. Beginning in 1867 for senate bills and 1870 for house bills, the Colorado State Archives maintains a collection of original bills, final bills as passed, and "engrossed" bills, which includes documentation of the changes made by each house as the bills traveled through the legislative process.[61]

Session Laws

There are session laws from Colorado Territory, from the first general assembly held in 1861 through the eleventh, and last, session in 1876.

General laws, joint resolutions, memorials, and private acts: Passed at the . . . session of the Legislative Assembly of the Territory of Colorado. Denver: T. Gibson, Colorado Republican and Herald Office, 1861-1876.

Copies can be found in older public and academic libraries, law libraries, and at the state archives.

Statutory Compilations

Revised Statutes of Colorado [Territory] 1868

This was the only compilation of Colorado statutory law during the territorial period. Laws are divided into ninety subject-based chapters, arranged alphabetically. Rules of statutory construction are included in Chapter 79. The last law in the volume lists all statutes passed between 1861 and 1868 (when this revision was effected) that were subsequently repealed, either by the seventh legislative assembly or in prior years.

The revised statutes of Colorado: Passed at the seventh session of the Legislative Assembly, convened on the second day of December, A.D. 1867. Also, the acts of a public nature passed at the same session, and the prior laws still in force. Together with the Declaration of Independence, the Constitution of the United States, the Organic Act, and the amendments thereto. Central City: David C. Collier, 1868.

Court Rules

One of the first laws passed by the Colorado territorial legislative assembly in 1861 was "An Act Concerning Practice in Civil Cases."[62] This was the procedural code for Colorado's territorial district courts.[63] As with the procedures for civil cases, the procedures for criminal practice were first enacted by the territorial legislature in 1861.[64]

House and Council Journals

Proceedings of Colorado Territory's legislative assembly were reported in separate journals for the house and the council, beginning with the first session and concluding with the final territorial legislative assembly in 1876.

Council journal of the Legislative Assembly of the Territory of Colorado [S.l.: s.n.], 1862-1876. Denver: Thos. Gibson.

House journal of the Legislative Assembly of the Territory of Colorado [S.l.: s.n.], 1861-1876. Denver: Thos. Gibson.

Copies are available at older public and academic libraries, law libraries, and the state archives.

The Executive Branch Materials

The executive department of Colorado Territory was established by the organic act in 1861.[65] The governor was given executive authority, with enumerated powers.[66] The other territorial officers were a secretary,[67] U.S. attorney,[68] marshal,[69] and surveyor-general.[70] By 1868, the size of the territorial executive branch had grown to include the original five officers and a treasurer,[71] an auditor,[72] and an assayer,[73] and several boards, including a census board[74] and a military board.[75] Most officials served in more than one capacity. For example, the census board was made up of the secretary, auditor, and treasurer.[76] In addition, the treasurer was ex officio state librarian[77] and ex officio superintendent of public instruction.[78] New offices and boards were created throughout the territorial period.

The Territorial Governors Collection at the Colorado State Archives is the most complete collection of surviving executive department publications from Colorado Territory.[79] Included in the collection are copies of the executive record, which has executive orders, proclamations, legislative messages, and similar documents issued by the territorial governors. Correspondence from the several governors with the federal government, including regarding the organization of the territory and the campaign for statehood, is part of the collection. There are also reports of various territorial officials (territorial secretary, treasurer, auditor, superintendent of public instruction, commissioner of Indian affairs, etc.). Many other materials, including photographs, are included in this collection.

OTHER COLORADO PRESTATEHOOD LEGAL MATERIALS

Colorado had a small but active publishing industry in its territorial days. Predictably, many books were published on mining laws, but education law, elections, and land laws were also subjects of multiple works. The most complete record of prestatehood Colorado legal materials is found in the catalog of the Colorado Territorial Library and, more important, its supplement, kept in the Western History Collection of the Denver Public Library. Some of the items listed in the catalog are no longer extant.

Colorado. Territorial Library. *Catalogue of the territorial library of the territory of Colorado.* Denver: Byers and Dailey, printers, 1866.

Colorado. Territorial Library. *Additional catalogue of the territorial library of Colorado, comprising law, miscellany, science, United States public documents, state and territorial documents.* Golden City, CO: George West, printer, Transcript Office, 1867.

Libraries throughout Colorado have in their collections individual items published before 1876. Colorado has three main unified library catalogs. There is a great deal of overlap among the catalogs, but searching all three should result in a fairly complete listing of the available prestatehood publications.

The Marmot Library Network (http://www.millennium.marmot.org/) provides an integrated library computer system service for a consortium of academic, public, and school libraries in western Colorado.

The Colorado Virtual Library (ACLIN) (http://www.aclin.org/) is a cooperative project of the Colorado State Library and the Colorado library community to provide access to the information resources of libraries throughout the state.

Prospector (http://prospector.coalliance.org/screens/opacmenu.html) is a unified catalog of sixteen academic, public, and special libraries in Colorado and Wyoming, giving information on more than 13 million books, journals, and other materials held in these libraries.

The state archives include several collections of interest to legal researchers, in addition to those just noted. The City Directories Collection has information on mostly Denver metro area cities that includes names and addresses and, frequently, city maps and lists of city officials.[80] The Incorporation Records document the legal history of businesses, ditch and road companies, and several types of not-for-profit associations.[81]

NOTES

1. For an account of Colorado's early history, see Carl Abbott, Stephen J. Leonard, and David McComb, *Colorado: A History of the Centennial State,* ch. 2-3 (rev. ed., Boulder: Colorado Associated University Press, 1982) or Jerome C. Smiley, Frank C. Goudy, and Fred P. Johnson, *Semi-Centennial History of the State of Colorado,* Vol. 1, ch. 1-8 (Chicago: Lewis Publishing Co., 1913).

2. Second Charter of Virginia, 1609, in William Swindler, ed., 10 *Sources and Documents of United States Constitutions,* second series, 24 (Dobbs Ferry, NY: Oceana Publications, 1979); William Waller Henning, *The Statutes at Large: Being a Collection of All the Laws of Virginia from the First Session of the Legislature in the Year 1619,* Vol. 1, 80-98 (New York: Printed for the Editor, 1819-1823).

3. Robert S. Weddle, ed., *La Salle, the Mississippi, and the Gulf: Three Primary Documents* 56 (College Station: Texas A&M University Press, 1987).

4. Preliminary Act of Cession between France and Spain, signed at Fontainebleau, November 3, 1762. Clive Perry, ed., *Consolidated Treaty Series,* Vol. 42, 239 (Dobbs Ferry, NY: Oceana Publications, 1969).

5. The definitive Treaty of Peace and Friendship Between His Britannick Majesty, the Most Christian King, and the King of Spain. Concluded at Paris the 10th day of February, 1763. To which the King of Portugal acceded on the same day (Perry, *Consolidated Treaty Series,* Vol. 42, 279). It is interesting to note that, as the parties drew their boundaries down the middle of the Mississippi River, his Brittanick Majesty was given "every thing which he possesses . . . on the left side of the river." Ibid., at sec. VII. Presumably the parties were standing at the headwaters of the river, looking south.

6. Preliminary and Secret Treaty Between France and Spain, signed at San Ildefonso, October 1, 1800, Perry, *Consolidated Treaty Series,* Vol. 55, 375.

7. The Louisiana Purchase was accomplished through a series of three conventions, generally gathered under a single heading. Treaty for the Cession of Louisiana and Payments Conventions Between France and the United States, signed at Paris, April 30, 1803, 8 *Stat.* 200, 206, 208; Perry, *Consolidated Treaty Series,* Vol. 57, 27.

8. Treaty of Peace and Friendship Between Mexico and Spain, signed at Madrid, December 28, 1836, Perry, *Consolidated Treaty Series,* Vol. 86, 361. Mexicans founded the earliest permanent settlements in Colorado, in the southernmost regions of the territory. Mexico awarded huge land grants to "patrons," to encourage colonization and strengthen its ownership claims to the region. The patrons controlled most of their settlement's activities, settling disputes among the inhabitants and providing a conduit for law enforcement by Mexican authorities. See Abbott et al., *Colorado: A History of the Centennial State,* ch. 2-3.

9. Treaty of Peace, Friendship, Limits, and Settlement, signed at Guadalupe Hidalgo, February 2, 1848, Charles I. Bevans, *Treaties and Other International Agreements of the United States of America 1776-1949,* Vol. 9, 791; 9 *Stat.* 922 (1962); T.S. 207.

10. Jt. Res. No. 8 for Annexing Texas to the United States (March 1, 1845), 5 *Stat.* 797.

11. During the period in which most of Colorado's land mass was acquired by the United States in 1803 through the Louisiana Purchase, until it was included within Utah, New Mexico, Nebraska, and Kansas Territories beginning in 1850, the region was included in several U.S. territorial governments. First, it was part of the Indiana Territory of the District of Louisiana, Treaty Between the United States of America and the French Republiç, April 30, 1803, U.S.-Fr., 8 *Stat.* 200; Act of March 26, 1804, ch. 38, 2 *Stat.* 283. Then, in succession, it was part of Louisiana Territory (Act of March 3, 1805, ch. 31, 2 *Stat.* 331) and Missouri Territory (Act of June 4, 1812, ch. 51, 9 *Stat.* 453), where it remained until 1850.

12. An Act to Set Texas' Boundaries and . . . to Establish a Territorial Government for New Mexico, September 9, 1850, 9 *Stat.* 446.

13. Although the United States now asserted ownership to the region, it recognized some priority of claims by the native inhabitants. These claims to the Colorado region were not resolved until the 1890s. The United States reached treaty agreements with the plains Indians, the Cheyenne-Arapahoe, in the 1860s (February 18, 1861, 1865, 1867; Kappler II, 887-891, 984-989), and the mountain and western Indians, the Utes, in 1868, 1870-1880s (1863; Kappler v. 2, 990, 856-859; v. 1, 151-152, 180-182; ratified by Congress June 15, 1880).

14. The eastern boundary of Utah Territory was the Continental Divide. Thus, the early mining camps, including Breckenridge and Grand Lake, and Colorado's eastern slope, were part of Utah Territory. An Act to Establish a Territorial Government for Utah, September 9, 1850, 9 *Stat.* 453.

15. New Mexico Territory encompassed that part of modern day Colorado that was south of the thirty-eighth parallel between the Continental Divide and the eastern boundary of today's state of New Mexico. An Act . . . to Establish a Territorial Government for New Mexico, September 9, 1850, 9 *Stat.* 446.

16. Nebraska Territory included the area north of the fortieth parallel, bounded on the west by the Continental Divide. Kansas Territory's boundaries were defined by the thirty-eighth parallel to the south, the fortieth parallel to the north, and the Continental Divide on the west. Kansas-Nebraska Bill, ch. 59, 10 *Stat.* 277 (1854).

17. J. Harold Jameson, *A Preliminary Inventory of Certain Supreme Court Records of the State of Colorado* (1965) (manuscript at 8, on file with the Colorado Supreme Court Library). There do not appear to be any written reports of the judge's actions.

18. The Colorado State Archives maintains microfilmed copies of the federal general population census for the Colorado region beginning with 1850. In addition to a population count, the census documents a range of vital statistics. See <http://www.colorado.gov/dpa/doit/archives/census.html> for full information.

19. Abbott et al., supra n. 1 at 45; Howard Lamar, *The Far Southwest, 1846-1912: A Territorial History* 225 (New Haven, CT: Yale Univeristy Press, 1966).

20. There is no comprehensive collection of the rules or actions of these extralegal governments. A good source for individual documents is a newspaper published at or near their location. Some were eventually deposited with the clerk of the county in which they were located once the territory of Colorado was formed; many county clerks, public libraries, or local historical societies still have these materials. See also the sources in fn. 21-22, 25-26, 30, infra.

21. For general information on the miners' courts, see, e.g., George E. Lewis and D. F. Stackelbeck, eds., *Bench and Bar of Colorado* 13-15 (1917) and Calvin W. Gower, "Gold Rush Governments," *Colo. Mag.* 42(7)(1965): 114, 118.

22. The rules of the miners' districts were usually printed in pamphlets or broadsides. The Colorado State Historical Society in Denver, the Denver Public Library's Western History Collection, and the Western History Collection in the Norlin Library of the University of Colorado at Boulder have collections of these publications. Some were published in *Rocky Mountain News*, the first newspaper in the region. Selected records of nineteen mining districts are collected in Thomas Maitland Marshall, ed., *Early Records of Gilpin County, Colorado: 1859-1861* (Boulder: s.n., 1920). Some local historical societies also have a copy of local miners' districts rules.

23. *Jeff. Terr. Laws,* ch. 29, §1 (1860).

24. See, Act of November 7, 1861, §12, *1861 Colo. Terr. Sess. Laws* 166-167; Act of November 7, 1861, §8, 1861 *Colo. Terr. Sess. Laws* 380-381. Compare, for example, this rule of the Gregory District:

> When water Companies are engaged in bringing water into any portion of the mines they Shall have the right of way Secured to them and may pass over any claim road or other Ditch, but shall so guard themselves in passing as not to injure the party over whose ground they pass . . . (*Early Records of Gilpin County,* ibid. at fn. 19, at 15)

with a Colorado territorial statute:

> Whenever any person or persons are engaged in bringing water into any portion of the mines, they shall have the right of way secured to them, and may pass over any claim, road ditch, or other structure: *provided* the water be guarded so as not to interfere with prior rights. (*Colo. Terr. Rev. Stat.* Ch. 62, §2 [1868])

Almost identical language is found in *Colo. Rev. Stat.* §34-48-101 (2001):

> Whenever any persons are engaged in bringing water into any portion of a mine, they have the right-of-way secured to them, and may pass over any claim, road ditch, or other structure, if the water is guarded so as not to interfere with prior rights.

The validity of the miners' rules and the statutes adopting them were upheld by the Colorado territorial supreme court in *Sullivan v. Hense,* 2 Colo. 424 (1874).

25. *Rocky Mountain News* occasionally published proceedings of some of the miners' courts.

26. See Larry M. Boyer, *Frontier Justice* 4 (Washington, DC: Library of Congress, Law Library, 1979); Lawrence M. Friedman, *A History of American Law,* 2nd ed., 366 (New York: Simon & Schuster, 1985); George L. Anderson, "The El Paso Claim Club, 1859-1862," *Colo. Mag.* 13(1936): 41.

27. *Jeff. Terr. Laws,* ch. 18, §5 (1860).

28. Act of August 15, 1862, 1862 *Colo. Terr. Sess. Laws* 98 (second act); *Law Terr. Colo. 1861,* p. 249; *Laws Terr. Colo. 1862,* p. 69.

29. See, e.g., *Rocky Mountain News,* February 15, 1860; ibid., June 13, 1860.

30. See Francis S. Williams, "Trials and Judgments of the People's Courts of Denver," *Colo. Mag.* 27(1950): 294, which includes accounts of six Denver peoples' courts that handed down capital punishment judgments between 1858 and 1869.

31. See Act of November 7, 1861, §8, 1861 *Colo. Terr. Sess. Laws* 380, 380-382.

32. Wm. Hedges Robinson Jr., "the Growth of a Judicial System in Colorado," in Le Roy Reuben Hafen, *Colorado and Its People,* Vol. 2, 369 (New York: Lewis Publishing Company, 1948).

33. Act of November 7, 1861, art. VIII, §8, 1861 *Colo. Terr. Sess. Laws* 483, 492.

34. Le Roy Reuben Hafen, *Colorado and Its People,* Vol. 1, 218 (New York: Lewis Publishing Company, 1948).

35. Ibid. at 219.

36. Act of November 1, 1861, §5, 1861 *Colo. Terr. Sess. Laws* 249.

37. The territory of Jefferson was the successor to an attempt to create a state of Jefferson in 1859. However, voters turned down a proposed constitution for the proposed state, and no further attempts were made at statehood.

38. The constitution of Jefferson Territory was printed in *Rocky Mountain News,* October 20, 1859, and included in *The Laws of the Territory of Jefferson, Provisional Laws and Joint Resolutions Passed at the First and Called Sessions of the General Assembly of Jefferson Territory* (Omaha, N.T.: Robertson and Clark, 1860). See Rodney J. Bardwell Jr., "The Territory of Jefferson," *Dicta* 8(1931): 3.

39. *Laws of the Territory of Jefferson, Provisional Laws and Joint Resolutions passed at the First and Called Sessions of the General Assembly of Jefferson Territory* (Omaha, N.T.: Robertson and Clark, 1860).

40. *Jeff. Terr. Laws,* ch. 4, sec. 1 (1860).

41. See, e.g., William F. Swindler, ed., *Sources and Documents of United States Constitutions,* Vol. 2, 21-22 (Dobbs Ferry, NY: Oceana Publications, 1973).

42. R.W. Steele, governor of Jefferson Territory, directed all officers of the territory to surrender their commissions in favor of the officers of the new Colorado Territory on June 6, 1861. *Proclamation,* microfilmed on William S. Jenkins, ed., *Records of the United States of America,* Colo., reel 1, unit 6 (1949).

43. Act of February 28, 1861, ch. 59, 12 *Stat.* 172 (1861).

44. An Act to Enable the People of Colorado to Form a Constitution and State Government . . . 13 *Stat.* 32, ch. XXXVII, March 21, 1864.

45. The text of the proposed 1864 constitution, both as a printed pamphlet and in manuscript form, is microfilmed on William S. Jenkins, ed., *Records of the United States of America,* Colo., reel 1, unit 2 (Library of Congress Photoduplication Serv., 1949). Included in this collection is an "Address to the People," explaining the provisions of the draft constitution, and an "ordinance," essentially a resolution of the drafters, in which certain provisions of the enabling act and the U.S. Constitution are expressly incorporated into the draft state constitution. In addition, the proceedings of the 1864 constitutional convention between July 1 and July 20, 1864, were reported by the *Daily Rocky Mountain News.* The proceedings of the 1864 convention are included in the *Records of the United States of America,* ibid.

46. The text of the 1865 draft constitution is reproduced in William F. Swindler, ed., *Sources and Documents of United States Constitutions,* Vol. 2, 31(1973), and microfilmed on William S. Jenkins, ed., *Records of the United States of America,*

Colo., reel 1, unit 2 (Library of Congress Photoduplication Serv., 1949). The proceedings of the 1865 constitutional convention, as reported in the *Daily Rocky Mountain News* between July 31 and August 17, 1865, are also included in this collection.

47. Presidential Message, January 12, 1866 in James D. Richardson, ed., *A Compilation of Messages and Papers of the Presidents,* Vol. 6, 375 (New York: Bureau of National Literature and Art, 1909).

48. S. 74, 39th Cong., 1st Sess. (1866); S. 462, 40th Cong., 1st Sess. (1867). Whether there was sufficient population and the denial of suffrage to "colored people" by the draft constitution were the main questions in the debate on Colorado's admission as a state. See, e.g., the Senate's debate at XX *Cong. Globe* 2165-2180 (April 25, 1866).

49. Andrew Johnson, Veto Message, 71 *Cong. Globe* 2609, 39th Cong., 1st Sess. (1866), reprinted in James D. Richardson, ed., *A Compilation of the Messages and Papers of the Presidents,* Vol. 8, 3611 (1897); Andrew Johnson, Veto Message, 75 *Cong. Globe* 1867, 39th Cong., 2d Sess. (1866), reprinted in James D. Richardson, ed., *A Compilation of the Messages and Papers of the Presidents,* Vol. 8, 681 (1897).

50. Act of March 3, 1875, 18 *Stat.* P. III 474. The enabling act is reprinted in Volume 1 of the *Colorado Revised Statutes* at 24 (2001).

51. Harold H. Dunham, "Colorado's Constitution of 1876," *Dicta* 36(1959): 121, 126.

52. *The Rocky Mountain News* was first published in Cherry Creek, Kansas Territory, in 1859. It has been continuously published since under several names, including the *Weekly Rocky Mountain News* (1864-1865) and the *Daily Rocky Mountain News* (1860-1861), and, more recently, the *Denver Rocky Mountain News* (2001). It absorbed many of the other newspapers published in the Colorado region, including the *Cherry Creek Pioneer* (1859), the *Denver Weekly Mountaineer* (1860-1861), and the *Weekly Commonwealth* (1863-1864). Other early newspapers in the region included the *Rocky Mountain Gold Reporter and Mountain City Herald* (1859; continued by the *Western Mountaineer* [1859] and then the *Canon [City] Times* [1860-1861]), and the *Weekly Colorado Republican and Rocky Mountain Herald* (1861-1862), which became the *Weekly Commonwealth and Republican* (1862-1863; continued by the *Weekly Commonwealth*).

53. Proclamation of August 1, 1876, 19 *Stat.* 665.

54. The original Colorado Constitution is stored at the state archives. The archives also has the Jefferson Territory Constitution of 1859 and the Colorado Territorial Constitutions of 1864, 1865, and 1875. The current text of the Colorado Constitution can be found in Volume 1 of the *Colorado Revised Statutes* at 28 (2001).

55. Act of February 28, 1861, ch. 59, sec. 9, 12 *Stat.* 172, 174 (1861) (referred to as the Organic Act); see Albert T. Frantz, "Colorado Appellate Courts—The First Hundred Years," *Dicta* 36(1959): 103, 106.

56. The first Colorado Court of Appeals was authorized in 1891, well after statehood.

57. The Colorado Court homepage includes a section giving addresses, phone numbers, and locations of the district and county courts at <http://www.courts.state.co.us/district/districts/htm>.

58. That which is not available from the state archives may be accessible at the individual court.

59. The extralegal government of Jefferson Territory had a bicameral legislature, referring to the chambers as the council and the house of representatives. Colorado's territorial government adopted the name and structure of the Jefferson territorial legislature. *Jeff. Terr. Laws,* ch. 9, sec. 1-7 (1859).

60. Colo. Const., art. V, §1.

61. See <http://www.colorado.gov/dpa/doit/archives/legis.html> for full information. This collection includes resolutions and memorials.

62. 1861 *Colo. Terr. Sess. Laws* 275.

63. The code, as amended to 1868, was included in the 1868 *Colo. Terr. Rev. Stat.* ch. LXX, p. 498. It was based on the Illinois practice statutes, and the 1868 statutes include many annotations referring to Illinois interpretations of statutory provisions. Practice before the justices of the peace was governed by the Act of October 31, 1861, 1861 *Colo. Terr. Sess. Laws* 220. Probate courts used the procedures of the justices of the peace. Act of November 7, 1861, 1861 *Colo. Terr. Sess. Laws,* sec. 3, 382.

64. Act of November 5, 1861, 1861 *Colo. Terr. Sess. Laws* 318. The 1861 criminal procedures remained in effect, as amended, until 1961, when the Colorado Supreme Court issued the "Rules of Criminal Procedure for Courts of Record in Colorado."

65. Act of February 28, 1861, ch. 59, 12 *Stat.* 172 (1861).

66. Ibid. sec. 2

67. Ibid. sec. 3.

68. Ibid. sec. 10.

69. Ibid.

70. Ibid. sec. 17.

71. *Colo. Terr. Rev. Stat.* ch. IX, art. 1 (1868).

72. Ibid.

73. Ibid., ch. LXIII, sec. 3 (1868).

74. Ibid., ch. LXXV, sec. 29 (1868).

75. Ibid., ch. LXI, art. 1 (1868).

76. Ibid., ch. LXXV, art. 1 (1868).

77. Ibid., ch. LII, sec. 1 (1868).

78. Ibid., ch. LXXVII, sec. 1 (1868).

79. A complete description of the collection is found at <http://www.colorado.gov/dpa/doit/archives/offic/gov.html>.

80. <http://www.colorado.gov/dpa/doit/archives/dcd/dirhome.htm>.

81. <http://www.colorado.gov/dpa/doit/archives/busin.html>.

Chapter 7

A Guide to Connecticut Prestatehood Legal Research

Janis Fusaris

INTRODUCTION

This is a guide to locating Connecticut prestatehood legal materials. It includes both primary and secondary Connecticut legal resources for the period up to and including the year 1788, when Connecticut became a state. Included as well are selected materials relating to the New Haven Colony before it was absorbed into Connecticut in 1662.

This guide focuses primarily on materials that are readily available to the researcher. Materials that are not easily accessible, such as manuscript sources, historical society pamphlets, unpublished dissertations, and archival materials, are not included in this guide. However, resources that will assist the researcher in locating these materials are included.

HISTORICAL BACKGROUND

The colony of Connecticut originated in 1636 when the inhabitants of three Massachusetts towns left the Bay Colony and settled in Connecticut. The three towns cooperated under a simple form of government that was composed of magistrates and representatives from each town, but the towns had no formal instrument of government. In 1639, Roger Ludlow, the only attorney in the colony at the time, drafted the Fundamental Orders, which established a general government framework for the colony and stood as the basic governing document for Connecticut until 1662, when Connecticut sought and received a royal charter from Charles II. The Charter of 1662 provided for the absorption of the colony of New Haven into Connecticut and granted Connecticut the right of self-government. When Connecticut became a state in 1788, the charter continued in force.

GOVERNING DOCUMENTS

The Fundamental Orders of Connecticut, 1639.

Widely regarded as America's first written "constitution," the orders consisted of eleven short paragraphs that established a framework of government for the colony of Connecticut. The orders remained the basic governing document for the colony until the Charter of 1662. A copy of the orders can be found in numerous publications, including the Connecticut "Colonial Records," the Connecticut State Register and Manual at <http://www. sots.state.ct.us/RegisterManual/regman.htm>, and online at Yale Law School's Avalon Project, <http://www.yale.edu/lawweb/avalon/order>.

Charter of the Colony of Connecticut, 1662.

The charter essentially incorporated the principles of the Fundamental Orders and the practices that had developed since their adoption. The charter stood as Connecticut's basic governing document until 1818, when Connecticut adopted its first official constitution. A copy of the charter can be found in numerous publications, including the Connecticut "Colonial Records," the Connecticut State Register and Manual at <http://www.sots. state.ct.us/RegisterManual/regman.htm>, and online at Yale Law School's Avalon Project, <http://www.yale.edu/lawweb/avalon/states/ct03.htm>.

LEGISLATIVE SOURCES

Session Laws

Hoadly, Charles J., ed. *Records of the Colony and Plantation of New Haven, from 1638 to 1649; transcribed and edited in accordance with a resolution of the General Assembly of Connecticut, with occasional notes and an appendix.* Hartford: Case, Tiffany and Company, 1857.

Hoadly, Charles J., ed. *Records of the Colony or Jurisdiction of New Haven, from May, 1653, to the Union; together with the New Haven Code of 1656; transcribed and edited in accordance with a resolution of the General Assembly of Connecticut.* Hartford: Case, Lockwood and Company, 1858.

These volumes contain the cumulative laws and orders of the New Haven Colony before it was absorbed into Connecticut in 1662. The original manuscripts for the years 1649 to 1652 were lost, so those years are not covered. Each set is indexed primarily by names, although a few subject entries are included. The second volume includes the New Haven Code of 1656.

The Public Records of the Colony of Connecticut, from April 1636 to October 1776 . . . transcribed and published (in accordance with a resolution of the General Assembly). Hartford: Brown and Parsons, 1850-1890. 15 volumes (Volumes 1-3 edited by J. Hammond Trumbull; Volumes 4-15 edited by Charles Jeremy Hoadly) ("Colonial Records").

The Connecticut "Colonial Records" contain all the resolutions, petitions, appointments, and other positive acts of the general assembly, or "general court," from 1636 to 1776. The Code of 1650 is also included. Volumes 1 and 2 include a name index as well as a general index; the remaining volumes include only a general index. The records are also available online at <http://www.colonialct.uconn.edu/> (see Web site section of this chapter for further details).

The Public Records of the State of Connecticut, published in accordance with a resolution of the General Assembly. Hartford: Case, Lockwood and Brainard Company, 1894. 12 volumes.

This set, which continues the Connecticut "Colonial Records," includes the acts and proceedings of the Connecticut legislature beginning in 1776. Laws from the prestatehood period appear in the following volumes: Vol. 1: 1776-1778; Vol. 2: 1778-1780; Vol. 3: 1780-1781; Vol. 4: 1782; Vol. 5: 1783-1784; Vol. 6: 1785-1789.

Codes

The first codification of Connecticut laws was the Code of 1650, drafted by Roger Ludlow. The code was completely revised a number of times during Connecticut's prestatehood period: in 1673, 1702, 1750, and 1784. The codes can be found in various compilations and have been reprinted a number of times, but they were each originally published as follows.

Code of 1650 ("Ludlow's Code").

The Code of 1650 was distributed in manuscript form to the various towns in Connecticut and was never officially printed. The transcribed manuscripts of the code were first published in the Connecticut "Colonial Records" (as described previously).

The Book of the General Laws for the People Within the Jurisdiction of Connecticut. Cambridge, MA: Samuel Green, 1673.

Acts and Laws of His Majesty's Colony of Connecticut in New England. Boston, MA: Bartholomew Green and John Allen, 1702 (compiled by Allen, Fitch, and Kimberly).

Acts and Laws of His Majesty's English Colony of Connecticut in New England in America. New London: Timothy Green, 1750 (compiled by Wolcott, Fitch, Trumbull, and Bulkley).

Acts and Laws of the State of Connecticut, in America. New London: Timothy Green, 1784 (compiled by Sherman and Law).

Compilations

Cushing, John D., ed. *The Earliest Laws of the New Haven and Connecticut Colonies, 1639-1673.* The Colony Laws of North America Series. Wilmington, DE: M. Glazier, 1977.

This volume is a compilation of the earliest printed laws of what eventually became the colony of Connecticut. Included are facsimile reproductions of laws from the New Haven Code of 1656 and the Connecticut Code of 1673.

Trumbull, J. Hammond, ed. *The True-Blue Laws of Connecticut and New Haven and the False Blue-Laws Invented by the Rev. Samuel Peters: to which are added specimens of the laws and judicial proceedings of other colonies and some blue-laws of England in the reign of James I.* Hartford: American Publishing Company, 1876 (reprinted, Littleton, CO: F.B. Rothman, 1987).

This volume reproduces selected laws from a number of early legislative sources, including the Capital Laws of Connecticut, 1642; the Code of 1650; the Laws and Orders of the Connecticut Court, 1636-1662; the New Haven Code of 1656; and the Laws and Judgments of the New Haven General Court, before 1655. Also included is the full text of the blue law "forgeries" written by Reverend Samuel Peters.

Bates, Albert Carlos. *Connecticut Statute Laws: A bibliographical list of editions of Connecticut laws from the earliest issues to 1836.* Hartford: Hartford Press, the Case, Lockwood and Brainard Co., 1900.

This bibliography lists and describes the various original issues of the laws of Connecticut through the year 1836, with bibliographic descriptions for 494 different issues. Also included are references to Connecticut libraries where the issues described can be found, with a particular emphasis on the Connecticut State Library, the Connecticut Historical Society, and Yale University's Sterling Memorial Library. It is a valuable guide for researchers working with original manuscript sources.

JUDICIAL SOURCES

During the colony's first years, the general assembly, or "general court," performed the judicial as well as the legislative functions of the colony. In 1638, the general court ordered that "particular courts," to be conducted by magistrates, be convened. Until the Charter of 1662, the particular courts remained the principal adjudicatory body in the colony, while the general court functioned as the court of last resort. In 1665, the particular court was abolished and two new levels of courts were established: the court of assistants in 1665 and the county courts in 1666. In 1711, the superior court was created and assumed the powers of original and appellate jurisdiction from the court of assistants, which was abolished. Finally, in 1784, the supreme court of errors was created, assuming the general court's role as the highest appellate tribunal in Connecticut. Records and decisions of these courts, as well as those of the courts of the colony of New Haven, have been published as follows.

Court Records and Case Reporters

Hoadly, Charles J., ed. *Records of the Colony and Plantation of New Haven, from 1638 to 1649; transcribed and edited in accordance with a resolution of the General Assembly of Connecticut, with occasional notes and an appendix*. Hartford: Case, Tiffany and Company, 1857.

Hoadly, Charles J., ed. *Records of the Colony or Jurisdiction of New Haven, from May, 1653, to the Union; together with the New Haven Code of 1656; transcribed and edited in accordance with a resolution of the General Assembly of Connecticut*. Hartford: Case, Lockwood and Company, 1858.

These volumes contain the records and decisions of the courts of the New Haven Colony before it was absorbed into Connecticut in 1662. The original manuscripts for the years 1649 to 1652 were lost, so those years are not covered. Each set is indexed primarily by names, although a few subject entries are included.

The Public Records of the Colony of Connecticut, from April 1636 to October 1776 . . . transcribed and published, (in accordance with a resolution of the General Assembly). Hartford: Brown and Parsons, 1850-1890. 15 volumes (Volumes 1-3 edited by J. Hammond Trumbull; Volumes 4-15 edited by Charles Jeremy Hoadly).

The Connecticut "Colonial Records" contain the records and decisions of the general court, as well as the records and decisions of the particular court from 1639 to 1663. Volumes 1 and 2 include a name index as well as a general index; the remaining volumes include only a general index. The records are also available online at <http://www.colonialct.uconn.edu/> (see Web site section of this chapter for further details).

Farrell, John T., ed. *The Superior Court Diary of William Samuel Johnson, 1772-1773, with appropriate records and file papers of the Superior Court of the Colony of Connecticut for the terms December 1772 through March 1773.* American Legal Records, Vol. 4. Washington, DC: The American Historical Association, 1942.

Not an official reporter but a collection of 228 cases based on the private notes and direct observations of a judge of the Connecticut Superior Court during the winter of 1772-1773. A table of cases and a subject index are included. A lengthy introduction includes a brief history of the court system in Connecticut, a review of the forms of civil actions filed during this period, and a description of the criminal process.

Kirby, Ephraim. *Reports of Cases Adjudged in the Superior Court of the State of Connecticut. From the Year 1785, to May 1788; with some determinations in the Supreme Court of Errors.* Litchfield: Collier and Adam, 1789.

The first American case reporter, the one-volume "Kirby's Reports" covers approximately 200 cases decided by the Connecticut Superior Court and Connecticut Supreme Court of Errors from 1785 to 1788. A table of cases and a subject index are included.

Kirby, Ephraim. *Reports of Cases Adjudged in the Superior Court, Taken by Ephraim Kirby After the Time of His Reports.* Acorn Club of Connecticut, Publication No. 16. Hartford: Lockwood and Brainard, 1933 (reprinted, Philadelphia: Joseph M. Mitchell, 1949).

Known as "Kirby's Reports," Volume 2, this quasi-official volume of cases consists of thirty cases decided by the Connecticut Superior Court from 1785 to 1789. The decisions were found in Kirby's library after his death and were later organized and published. The volume does not contain a table of cases or an index.

Root, Jesse. *Reports of Cases Adjudged in the Superior Court and Supreme Court of Errors, from July A.D. 1789 to June A.D. 1793; with a variety of cases anterior to that period.* Hartford: Hudson and Goodwin, 1798-1802.

Volume 1 of "Root's Reports" includes a number of reported decisions of the Connecticut Superior Court and the Connecticut Supreme Court of Errors for the period 1764 to 1788. A table of cases and subject index are included. The preface to this volume includes the author's commentary on the government and laws of Connecticut, including a discussion of slavery, marriage, real property, wills and estates, and the nature of the common law.

Digests

The following digests all include cases from both volumes of Kirby and from Volume 1 of Root's Reports:

Baldwin, Simeon Eben. *A Digest of All the Reported Cases Decided in the Supreme Court of Errors and the Superior Court of the State of Connecticut, and in the United States Courts for the District of Connecticut, down to those contained in Volume XLVII. Connecticut Reports, and Volume XVII. Blatchford's Circuit Court Reports, inclusive.* Boston, MA: Little, Brown, 1871-1872 ("Baldwin's Digest").

Gray, Joseph Alexander. *A Digest of All the Reported Cases Decided by the Supreme Court of Errors and the Superior Court of the State of Connecticut as well as the United States Courts in the District of Connecticut, from Kirby to Volume 99 Connecticut Reports inclusive.* New York: Baker, Voorhis, 1925-1926 ("Gray's Digest").

Phillips, Richard Henry. *Connecticut Digest, 1785 to Date. Kirby to Volume 129 inclusive with current cumulative pocket parts.* Hartford: State of Connecticut, 1945 ("Phillips' Digest").

West's Connecticut Digest, 1764 to Date, covering cases from state and federal courts. St. Paul, MN: West Publishing Company.

Citators and Other Finding Aids

Sharswood, George. *A Table of Cases in the Reports of the State of Connecticut [1785-1876], Which Have Been Cited, Explained, Limited, Doubted, or Overruled in Subsequent Decisions.* Philadelphia: T. and J.W. Johnson, 1878.

Unlike *Shepard's Citations,* this volume, known as "Sharswood's Tables," lists cases alphabetically rather than by case citation.

Shepard's Connecticut Citations. New York: Shepard's, 2001.

Includes citations to cases reported in both volumes of Kirby and in Volume 1 of Root's Reports.

Coffin, Helen and Frances Davenport. "Index to Material Printed in the Connecticut Reports (Through Volume 199), Other Than Reports of Decisions and Biographical Memorials." *Connecticut Bar Journal* 10 (1936): 139-144.

This index to the miscellaneous materials published in early Connecticut case reporters includes materials from Volume 1 of Root's Reports.

EXECUTIVE SOURCES

The Public Records of the Colony of Connecticut and *The Public Records of the State of Connecticut* (more fully described in previous sections of this chapter) contain the messages of the governor as well as the "Council Journal," a record of the meetings that took place between the governor and the council.

SECONDARY SOURCES

Articles

Cohn, Henry S. "Connecticut Constitutional History 1636-1776." *Connecticut Bar Journal* 64 (1990): 330-354.

This survey of Connecticut's constitutional history includes a discussion of the Fundamental Orders, the Ludlow Code of 1650, the Connecticut Charter, and the development of the Connecticut courts. It also examines three eighteenth-century cases that the author believes "tested the limits of the Constitution": *Winthrop v. Lechmere; The Spanish Ship Case;* and *The*

Sesquehannah Dispute. This article is also available online at <http://www.cslib.org/cts4cc.htm>.

Cohn, Henry S. "Connecticut's Divorce Mechanism: 1636-1969." *American Journal of Legal History* 14(1) (1970): 35-54.

This article traces the development of Connecticut's divorce procedures, with an emphasis on the means employed by parties to obtain a divorce and the new developments that arose during each era. Sources include court proceedings and legislative records. Nine pages are devoted to the 1636-1790 period.

Collier, Christopher. "The Connecticut Declaration of Rights Before the Constitution of 1818: A Victim of Revolutionary Redefinition." *Connecticut Law Review* 15 (1982): 87-98.

This brief article explains what the Connecticut Declaration of Rights was, how it evolved, and why it eventually became part of the constitution. The author traces the declaration's development from its initial passage and incorporation into the Code of 1650, to its subsequent inclusion in the Connecticut Constitution of 1818.

Gaskins, Richard. "Changes in the Criminal Law in Eighteenth-Century Connecticut." *American Journal of Legal History* 25 (1981): 309-342.

This article traces the evolution of criminal law in Connecticut during the eighteenth century. Through a detailed survey of court records, the author analyzes the categories of crimes that existed and the frequency with which they were prosecuted. He concludes that there was a distinct movement away from Puritan conceptions of crime (as represented by such "moral" offenses as swearing, drunkenness, and sabbath breaking) toward a more modern, economic viewpoint at the end of the century. The general eighteenth-century statutory framework and the changes in severity of punishment that occurred during this period are also discussed.

Gibson, Lawrence H. "The Criminal Codes of Connecticut." *Journal of the American Institute of Criminal Law and Criminology* 6(2) (July 1915): 177-189.

This is a brief look at the differences among the Code of 1650, the New Haven Code of 1656, and the Code of 1784. Includes a description of the criminal offenses provided for in each code, as well as a discussion of the penalties imposed and the way the codes were applied.

Horton, Wesley W. "Day, Root and Kirby." *Connecticut Bar Journal* 70 (1996): 407-421.

This article provides a brief survey and description of some of the interesting cases from Connecticut's three historical case reporters, covering cases from 1786 to 1818.

Lyman, Dean B., Jr. "Notes on the New Haven Colonial Courts." *Connecticut Bar Journal* 20 (1946): 178-189.

A survey of the proceedings of the courts of the early colony of New Haven, this article includes a discussion of the founding of the courts, court procedures and policies, and an examination of selected cases.

Maltbie, William M. "Judicial Administration in the Connecticut Colony Before the Charter of 1662." *Connecticut Bar Journal* 23 (1949): 147-159, 228-247.

This detailed study of early Connecticut laws pertaining to both civil and criminal procedure includes a discussion of how the laws were applied. Laws relating to the organization of the judicial system are also examined.

Santos, Hubert J. "The Birth of a Liberal State: Connecticut's Fundamental Orders." *Connecticut Law Review* 1 (1968): 386-400.

This provides a detailed discussion of the historical background of the constitutional principles and practices embodied in the Fundamental Orders, from their roots in English law to their formulation into America's first written "constitution."

Schwartz, Pamela. "Liberty and Autonomy versus Confinement and Commitment: The History of Legal Intervention in Colonial Connecticut." *Journal of Psychiatry and Law* 11 (1983): 461-501.

This article studies the legal mechanisms used to manage and control mentally ill persons living in colonial Connecticut. The author describes in detail the pertinent legislation of the era and weaves together the stories of individual cases throughout. The interplay among judicial, quasi-judicial, and legislative bodies in formulating policies to alleviate the problems posed by the presence of insane individuals within the community is also explored.

Wrinn, David H. "Manslaughter and Mosaicism in Early Connecticut." *Valparaiso U. Law Review* 21 (1987): 271-319.

This article evaluates the influence of scripture on Connecticut's early criminal laws. With a specific focus on the introduction of the manslaughter doctrine, the author reconstructs the early homicide laws and traces their evolution away from the mosaical law of scripture toward principles based primarily on the common law. The differences between the force and intent of the printed laws and their application in actual proceedings before Connecticut tribunals are highlighted throughout.

Books

Capen, Edward Warren. *The Historical Development of the Poor Law of Connecticut*. New York: Columbia University Press, 1905 (reprinted, New York: AMS Press, 1968).

This book traces the development of Connecticut's poor law, from 1634 to 1903, with two chapters devoted to the colonial period. Each chapter provides a detailed description of the system of laws in place for the public relief and support of the poor, including a discussion of the methods of relief prescribed, legislation affecting special groups (such as minors and the insane), and laws designed to prevent pauperism. Sources include court proceedings, town records, journals and correspondence, and the relevant laws and statutes. It is a study of what the author calls "one of the most interesting of American poor laws."

Dayton, Cornelia Hughes. *Women Before the Bar: Gender, Law, and Society in Connecticut, 1639-1789.* Chapel Hill: University of North Carolina Press, 1995.

This study analyzes the changing patterns of women's participation in early Connecticut courts, with an emphasis on the five major types of legal actions that brought women into court: debt, divorce, rape, slander, and illicit consensual sex. Drawing on colonywide criminal cases and the extensive court records of the New Haven jurisdiction, the author examines what the everyday practice of early Connecticut law courts meant for women, i.e., how they used available legal procedures and how they were treated by the legal system. She concludes that women's relation to the legal system shifted from one of integration in the mid-seventeenth century to one of marginality by the eve of the revolution.

Loomis, Dwight and J. Gilbert Calhoun, eds. *The Judicial and Civil History of Connecticut*. Boston: The Boston History Co., 1895.

This survey of Connecticut judicial and civil history includes a discussion of the settlement of the colony; the charter; the growth of the common and statutory law; obsolete laws and punishments; the judiciary; court reports and reporters; and the general assembly. Over 1,000 biographical sketches of judges and attorneys are also provided.

Mann, Bruce H. *Neighbors and Strangers: Law and Community in Early Connecticut.* Chapel Hill: University of North Carolina Press, 1987.

This book is a study of the changes in legal culture and community in Connecticut from the middle of the seventeenth century to the eve of the Revolution. Through an analysis of civil litigation patterns, the author explores the shift away from "neighborly" or communal forms of disputing, which treated disputes individually within a community context, toward a formalistic, rationalized legal system that "treated neighbors and strangers alike." The changes in how people used the law—the legal forms and procedures they chose, and how they pleaded their cases and had them decided—are explained in the context of the economic and social conditions of the time.

Swift, Zephaniah. *A Digest of the Laws of the State of Connecticut: In Two Volumes.* New Haven: S. Converse, 1822-1823.

This treatiselike work attempted to organize the common law principles of Connecticut and England into a systematic presentation. The volumes are broken down into five main topics, which are arranged in essay form with footnoted references to cases and statutes. A general index is included in each volume.

Swift, Zephaniah. *A System of the Laws of the State of Connecticut.* Windham: Printed by John Byrne, for the author, 1795-1796 (reprinted, New York: Arno Press, 1972).

The first American legal treatise, this work is both a compilation of Connecticut case law and a detailed commentary on the philosophy of government, political theory, and the differences between American and English common law.

Tomlinson, R.G. *Witchcraft Trials of Connecticut: The First Comprehensive, Documented History of Witchcraft Trials in Colonial Connecticut.* Hartford: Bond Press, 1978.

This work provides a complete history of the relatively small number of witchcraft trials that took place in Connecticut from 1633 to 1692. Sources include court papers, depositions, diaries, letters, and genealogies.

WEB SITES

Colonial Connecticut Records 1636-1776
<http://www.colonialct.uconn.edu>

The complete digitized volumes of the public records of the colony of Connecticut, which contain documents from the legislative, judicial, and executive branches of government. Scanned images of all fifteen volumes can be accessed by browsing an A-Z subject index, searching by date, or searching by volume and page number. Full-text and keyword searching are not yet available but are planned for future phases of the digitization project. Users can also retrieve certain groups or classes of documents (such as charters, laws, letters, and court proceedings) by using the Colonial Pathways feature.

Connecticut History Reference Shelf
<http://www.ctheritage.org/biography/bibliography.htm>

A series of short bibliographic essays on topics in Connecticut's history, compiled by state historian Christopher Collier. Many of the essays pertain to the colonial period and/or Connecticut's legal history. The essays are arranged by time period, topic, subject, and name and can be searched by keyword as well. Citations to manuscript sources and historical society publications are included in many of the essays.

Connecticut State Library
<http://www.cslib.org>

The primary repository for Connecticut historical materials, the library's Web page provides a number of online bibliographies and research guides pertaining to Connecticut history, several of which include information about the prestatehood period. The state archives page also includes an online guide to the records of the Connecticut Judicial Department, from 1636 to the present day.

Doses of Connecticut Legal History
<http://www.jud.state.ct.us/lawlib/History/default.htm>

This site includes a series of brief narratives about various milestones in Connecticut legal history, compiled by the Connecticut Judicial Branch

Law Libraries. Each narrative includes citations to primary and/or second-ary legal sources, and new entries are added periodically. Topics pertaining to the colonial period include Ludlow's Code; Tapping Reeve and the Litch-field Law School; America's First Court Reporter Ephraim Kirby; and Zephaniah Swift's First Legal Texts in America.

Chapter 8

Colonial Delaware Legal Bibliography

Eileen B. Cooper
David King
Mary Jane Mallonee

HISTORICAL BACKGROUND

This work is a comprehensive, albeit not all-inclusive, bibliography of the primary sources of law for the Delaware Colony, along with selected historical and biographical materials to aid the researcher. Colonial New York and Pennsylvania materials will be incorporated to the extent that they relate to Delaware; however, we will leave an in-depth analysis to our colleagues compiling bibliographies for those jurisdictions. The following provides a brief historical context, and it is recommended that the researcher consult the comprehensive historical works listed herein.

Delaware's 145-year colonial period, from the first settlement in lower Delaware to the signing of the Declaration of Independence in 1776 (see Figure 8.1), was predominantly under English rule. However, the colony was influenced by a heterogeneous population mix of European nationalities, including Swedes, Dutch, Finns, English, and Scotch-Irish, resulting from successive colonizing efforts on the part of the Netherlands, Sweden, and England. Throughout this period, the small colony was often characterized as an outpost or satellite and was annexed to Pennsylvania for more than ninety years as the "three lower counties," "territories," or "three counties on the Delaware."

The authors wish to thank members of the staff of the Legal Information Center, Widener University School of Law; Delaware Public Archives; Historical Society of Delaware; University of Delaware Morris Library; and the Library Company of Philadelphia for their assistance.

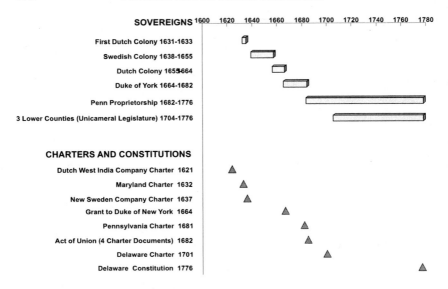

FIGURE 8.1. Delaware Colonial Legal History: A Timeline.

Dutch and Swedish Period (1631-1664)

Early exploration of the Delaware Bay by Henry Hudson in 1609 established the Dutch claim to the region.[1] In 1631, Swanendael, near Lewes, Delaware, became the home of the first small settlement set up by the Dutch West India Company under the "Charter of Freedoms and Exemptions."[2] Two years later, the settlers were killed by Indians.[3] However, because the colonies' short existence occurred prior to the issuance of the Maryland Charter in 1632, it served as the legal foundation for defeating Maryland's claim to the lands of lower Delaware during the eighteenth century.[4]

The colony of New Sweden, the first permanent settlement along the Delaware River, was established in 1638 at Fort Christina in what is now Wilmington. It was founded at the behest of former West India Company officials after gaining the backing of Swedish King Gustavous Adolphus and his successor.[5] Johan Printz was governor of the colony for ten years (1643-1653), retaining both administrative and judicial authority as an agent of the New Sweden Company, as well as the Swedish government.[6] He governed under a set of broad "instructions" that provided him with almost unlimited authority, although Swedish law was to be followed to the extent possible.[7]

Regular courts were established, and special courts were held whenever circumstances required.[8] There was little support for the small colony, and, in 1655, the Dutch governor of New Amsterdam, Peter Stuyvesant, defeated the Swedes but allowed them to remain upon taking an oath of allegiance.[9]

During the Dutch period (1655-1664), a highly centralized government was headquartered in New Amsterdam (Manhattan), and the center for trade and government was shifted to New Amstel (now New Castle) for the South River (the Dutch name for the Delaware) region.[10] New Amstel was governed by a vice director, who also sat on judicial tribunals of limited jurisdiction, with appellate review to the governor and council in New Amsterdam for serious matters.[11] Available legal records for this period include translations of laws and writs of appeal from the court at New Amstel as well as council minutes and correspondence with the vice directors. It is not a complete collection since some records were lost or destroyed.[12]

Duke of York Period (1664-1682)

English hegemony on the eastern coast of America came to fruition when King Charles II granted a patent conveying proprietary rights to his brother James, Duke of York, to most of the lands held by the Dutch. Although the initial grant did not include New Amstel and the lands located on the western side of the Delaware River, they were captured by force.[13] The Dutch were offered liberal terms of surrender and became citizens of the English colony, renamed New Castle, which, for a time, continued to retain its existing local government.[14] Gradually, the Duke of York's laws were introduced, and courts of limited jurisdiction were held on a regular basis in New Castle, Upland (now Chester, Pennsylvania), and Whorekill (now Sussex, Delaware).[15] In 1680 the St. Jones (now Kent County, Delaware) court was established in the newly formed county of that name.[16] The colony continued to be governed from New York (formerly New Amsterdam) by a governor, his council, and the court of assizes.[17] Many of the court records for this period are extant.

Penn Proprietorship (1682-1776)

In 1681 Charles II gave the province of Pennsylvania to William Penn in satisfaction of a sizeable debt owed to Penn's father, allowing him to proceed with his "holy experiment."[18] One year later Penn was successful in obtaining title to the "three lower counties" (current-day Delaware) providing him with strategic access to the sea.[19] The Act of Union with Pennsylvania was completed with the conveyance of four documents in 1682: the charter; the transfer document; and two 10,000-year leases, making Delaware a part of Pennsylvania until statehood.[20] Despite the Act of Union, the colony continued to retain its separate identity from Pennsylvania. One of the reasons for persistent discord with Pennsylvania throughout the colonial period related to the legitimacy of Penn's title.[21]

The Penn proprietary period heralded profound political change with the implementation of an elected legislature, an extension of privileges enjoyed by the inhabitants of the province,[22] as well as the development of a comprehensive judicial system. However, several conflicts arose between Pennsylvania and its territories, and Penn was forced to grant the counties the ability to have a unicameral legislature in 1701 by his famous codicil.[23] From 1704 to 1776, Delaware enjoyed a great deal of autonomy under its independently elected general assembly and separate court structure, although it continued to remain under the governor of Pennsylvania.[24] Its first general assembly, held in 1704,[25] was a milestone toward creating Delaware as a distinct governmental entity. The three county courts were already in effect upon Penn's arrival; however, major improvements in the judicial system occurred during the proprietary period, especially upon the enactment of the Gordon statute. The statute, passed between 1726-1736, was modified in 1760 and remained in operation until the Revolution. It provided for county courts of common pleas, general quarter sessions, and, most important, a supreme court.[26]

Although Delaware's unique court of chancery was not established until 1792, mention should be made of its colonial antecedents. There is evidence that equity jurisdiction was exercised throughout the colonial period, and the Gordon statute expressly mandated that the courts of common pleas were to hold courts of equity.[27] According to former Chancellor Quillen, the Gordon statute was the single most important enactment in the development of equity jurisdiction in Delaware.[28] Extant court records for the Penn period from the latter part of the seventeenth century to the early eighteenth century have been compiled and published for each of the "lower counties." Subsequent surviving colonial court records are preserved in the Delaware State Public Archives microfilm collection.[29]

Toward the end of the colonial period, the fifth Lord Baltimore revived his claim that Maryland was entitled to the lower portion of Delaware. The resulting litigation continued in chancery court from 1735 to 1750, resulting in a disposition in favor of Penn's heirs,[30] with the boundaries established by the Mason-Dixon line completed in 1768, and final acceptance by Penn and the general assembly in 1775.[31]

Delaware was one of the original thirteen colonies to declare independence from England. Finally, this unique colony received its name, The Delaware State, pursuant to a resolution of the Continental Congress, marking its official separation from Pennsylvania in 1776.[32] The words "December 7, 1787" are proudly flown on the Delaware state flag, indicating that Delaware was the first state to ratify the Constitution of the United States of America.

LEGAL BIBLIOGRAPHY

Executive

Articles, Wills and Deeds Creating the Entail of Pennsylvania and Three Lower Counties upon Delaware in the Penn Family. Philadelphia: [n.p.], 1870.

Includes Articles of Agreement Between John, Thomas, and Richard Penn, 8th May 1732, Regarding the Entail; Will of John Penn; Articles of Agreement Between Thomas and Richard Penn; 31st January 1750, Regarding the Entail; Will and Codicil of Richard Penn; etc. Provides documentation for the hereditary division of Pennsylvania and the three lower counties.

Baltimore, Charles Calvert. *Articles of Agreement Made and Concluded upon Between the Right Honourable the Lord Proprietary of Maryland, and the Proprietarys of Pensilvania, &c. Touching the Limits and Boundaries of the Two Provinces with the Commission, Constituting Certain Persons to Execute the Same.* Philadelphia: printed by B. Franklin at the New Printing-Office near the Market, 1733. 19 pp. (Miller 63, Evans 3710)

Copy at the Historical Society of Delaware belonged to George Read and bears his signature on p. 3. Read's name is signed in what appears to be another hand on the title page, and notes are made in a third hand on p. 14. Bound with *A Collection of Charters and Other Publick Acts* (Philadelphia: B. Franklin, 1740). (Miller 203, Evans 4583)

―――. *Articles of Agreement, &c,* [Docket-title] *True Copies of I. The Agreement Between Lord Baltimore and Messieurs Penn, Dated 10 May 1732. II. The Commissions Given to the Commissioners to Mark Out the Lines Between Maryland, and Pensilvania and the Three Lower Counties of Delaware. III. The Return or Report of the Commissioners on Both Sides, Made 24 Nov. 1733. Shewing for What Reasons the Lines Were Not Marked Out Within the Time Appointed for That Purpose.* [Philadelphia: B. Franklin, 1737?]. 8 pp. (Miller 130, Evans 4182)

Ascribed by Miller to Franklin's press on the evidence of the type, this second Philadelphia printing of the Penn-Baltimore *Articles of Agreement* was a resetting of the London edition of 1734-1735 and was ordered by the Penn family solicitor.

Baltimore, Frederick Calvert. *Indenture of Agreement 4th July, 1760, Between Lord Baltimore and Thomas and Richard Penn, Esquires, Settling the Limits and Boundaries of Maryland, Pennsylvania, and the Three Lower Counties of Newcastle, Kent and Sussex, on Delaware.* Philadelphia: Kite and Walton, 1851. 31 pp.

One hundred copies were printed by Edward D. Ingraham for private distribution.

Charter to William Penn, and Laws of the Province of Pennsylvania, Passed Between the Years 1682 and 1700, Preceded by Duke of York's Laws in Force from the Year 1676 to the Year 1682, with an Appendix Containing Laws Relating to the Organization of the Provincial Courts and Historical Matter. Published Under the Direction of John Blair Linn, Secretary of the Commonwealth. Edited and compiled by Staughton George, Benjamin M. Nead, and Thomas McCamant. Harrisburg: L.S. Hart, 1879.

The appendix consists of two parts: a compilation of the laws and ordinances establishing the several courts of judicature covering the period from 1682 to 1722, and historical notes on the early government and legislative councils and assemblies, covering a period extending from the first European settlement on the Delaware in 1623 to 1700. Facsimiles of documents are tipped in.

A Collection of Charters and Other Publick Acts Relating to the Province of Pennsylvania, viz. I. The Royal Charter to William Penn, Esq.; II. The First Frame of Government, Granted in England, in 1682; III. Laws Agreed upon in England; IV. Certain Conditions or Concessions; V. The Second Frame of Government, Granted 1683; VII. The Charter of the City of Philadelphia, Granted October 25, 1701; VIII. The New Charter of Privileges to the Province, Granted October 28, 1701. Philadelphia: printed and sold by B. Franklin in Market Street, 1740. 46 pp. (Miller 203, Evans 4583)

According to Miller, there is evidence for only three charters having been printed previously: the *First Frame* printed in London in 1682, the *Second Frame* printed in Philadelphia by William Bradford in 1689, and the *Charter of Privileges* printed by Samuel Keimer in Philadelphia in 1725. The copy examined at the Historical Society of Delaware belonged to George Read and bears his signature on the title page and is bound with *Articles of Agreement*. Philadelphia: B. Franklin, 1733. (Miller 63, Evans 3710)

Delaware Papers (Dutch Period): A Collection of Documents Pertaining to the Regulation of Affairs on the South River of New Netherland, 1648-1664. Edited and translated by Charles T. Gehring. New York Historical Manuscripts: Dutch 18-19. Baltimore: Genealogical Publishing, 1981.

Delaware Papers (English Period): A Collection of Documents Pertaining to the Regulation of Affairs on the Delaware, 1664-1682. Edited by Charles T. Gehring. New York Historical Manuscripts: Dutch 20-21. Baltimore: Genealogical Publishing, 1977.

Provides the complete texts of all documents in the New York Colonial Secretary's file of Delaware papers from the English period.

Documents Relative to the Colonial History of the State of New-York; Procured in Holland, England, and France, by John Romeyn Bordhead, Esq., Agent . . . Edited by E. B. O'Callaghan. Albany: Weed, Parsons and Company, 1853-1857. 15 vols.

Vols. 1 (1856) and 2 (1858) include the Holland documents; Vol. 12 (*New Series,* also labeled Vol. 1) includes documents relating to the history of the Dutch and Swedish settlements on the Delaware River.

The Federal and State Constitutions, Colonial Charters, and Other Organic Laws of the States, Territories, and Colonies Now or Heretofore Forming the United States of America. Edited and compiled by Francis Newton Thorpe. Washington, DC: Government Printing Office, 1909 7 vols.

Index. Volumes are paged consecutively. The entries for Delaware are in Vol. 1, pp. 557-636, and include the charter (1701) on pp. 557-562 and the constitution of Delaware (1776) on pp. 562-568. For other organic acts relating to the land now included within Delaware, see other volumes of this work: Virginia Charter of 1606 (Virginia, p. 3783); Dutch West India Company, 1621 (p. 59); Maryland Charter, 1632 (Maryland, p. 1669); Grant to the Duke of York, 1664 (Maine, p. 1637); Grant to the Duke of York, 1674 (Maine, p. 1641); Grant to Penn, 1681 (Pennsylvania, p. 3035); Concessions to Pennsylvania, 1681 (Pennsylvania, p. 3044); Frames of the Government of Pennsylvania, 1682, 1683, 1696 (Pennsylvania, pp. 3052, 3064,

3070). All of these documents are available through the Avalon Project at Yale Law School at <www.yale.edu/lawweb/avalon>.

Governor's Register, State of Delaware, Appointments and Other Transactions by Executives of the State from 1674 to 1851. Wilmington: Public Archives Commission of Delaware, Star Publishing, 1926.

The appointments under the colonial government prior to the organization of the state are given on pp. 3-23. The volume is complete in itself. Index.

Johnson, Amandus. *The Instruction for Johan Printz, Governor of New Sweden, "The First Constitution or Supreme Law of the States of Pennsylvania and Delaware." Translated from the Swedish with Introduction, Notes and Appendices, Including Letters from Governor John Winthrop, of Massachusetts, and Minutes of Courts, Sitting in New Sweden.* Philadelphia: Swedish Colonial Society, 1930.

Includes a biography of Printz, instructions in both Swedish and English translations, Printz's reports of 1644 and 1647, court records, and letters.

Keith, William. "The First Report of Lieutenant-Governor Sir William Keith, of Pennsylvania, to the Lords Commissioners for Trade and Plantations, 1717." Transcribed by Helen Jordan. *Pennsylvania Magazine of History and Biography* 23(1899): 488-497.

The report was "copied from a duplicate in the collection of the Historical Society of Pennsylvania."

Laws & Writs of Appeal, 1647-1663. Edited and translated by Charles T. Gehring. New Netherland Documents Series 16, part one, [N.p.]: Holland Society of New York, Syracuse University Press, 1991.

Narratives of Early Pennsylvania, West New Jersey, and Delaware, 1630-1707. Edited by Albert Cook Myers. New York: Charles Scribner's Sons, 1912.

Narratives include Johan Printz's reports of 1644 and 1647, Johan Rising's reports of 1654 and 1655, Penn's accounts of the province of Pennsylvania, etc. Index.

Original Land Titles in Delaware Commonly Known as the Duke of York Record/Being an Authorized Transcript from the Official Archives of the

State of Delaware, and Comprising the Letters Patent, Permits, Commissions, Surveys, Plats and Confirmations by the Duke of York and Other High Officials, from 1646 to 1679, Printed by Order of the General Assembly of the State of Delaware. Wilmington: Sunday Star Print, 1903.

Index. Published in an edition of 1,000 copies in paper wraps.

[Penn, William]. *The Excellent Priviledge of Liberty & Property Being the Birth-Right of the Free-Born Subjects of England. Containing I. Magna Charta, with a Learned Comment upon It; II. The Confirmation of the Charters of the Liberties of England and of the Forrest, Made in the 35th Year of Edward the First; III. A Statute Made the 34 Edw. I. Commonly Called De Tallageo non Concedendo; Wherein All Fundamental Laws, Liberties and Customs Are Confirmed. With a Comment upon It; IV. An Abstract of the Pattent Granted by the King to William Penn and His Heirs and Assigns for the Province of Pennsilvania; V. And Lastly, The Charter of Liberties Granted by the Said William Penn to the Free-Men and Inhabitants of the Province of Pennsilvania and Territories Thereunto Annexed, in America. Major Haereditas Venit Unicunq; Nostrum a Jure & Legibus, Quam a Parentibus.* Philadelphia: printed by William Bradford, 1687. [8] 63 pp. (Evans 433)

Formerly in the library of the Meeting for Sufferings in Philadelphia, the copy is now available in Special Collections, Magill Library of Haverford College. A facsimile was printed in an edition of 155 copies by the Philobiblon Club of Philadelphia in 1897.

Thomas, George. *The Speech of the Honorable George Thomas, Esq; Lieutenant Governor of the Province of Pennsylvania, and Counties of New-Castle, Kent and Sussex on Delaware. To the Representatives of the Freemen of the Said Province, in General Assembly Met.* Philadelphia: printed and sold by B. Franklin at the New Printing-Office, near the Market, 1738. 3 pp. (Miller 158, Evans 4298)

According to Miller, this, the maiden address of the governor to the assembly, was delayed over a year after his appointment in 1737 because Lord Baltimore insisted that the Penns had no right to name a governor for the lower counties while the Pennsylvania-Maryland boundary was in dispute. Includes the text of the assembly's reply and that of the governor's reply. Reprinted in the *Pennsylvania Gazette* (August 17, 1738).

Legislative (Arranged Chronologically)

New York (Colony)

New Netherland Council, Council Minutes, 1655-1656. Edited and translated by Charles T. Gehring. New Netherland Document Series 6. Syracuse, NY: Syracuse University Press, 1995.

Includes early references to Fort New Amstel (New Castle).

Calendar of Council Minutes, 1668-1783. Compiled by Berthold Fernow. New York State Library Bulletin 58. Albany: University of the State of New York, 1902.

A facsimile was reprinted by Harbor Hill Books (Harrison, New York, 1987). Some of the earliest actions by council pertain to New Castle, Delaware.

Pennsylvania (Colony)

The Laws of the Province of Pennsilvania Collected into One Volumn, by Order of the Governour and Assembly of the Said Province. Philadelphia: printed and sold by Andr[ew] Bradford, 1714. [4] 184 pp. [i.e., 174] pp. (Evans 1712)

The Pennsylvania Assembly approved a contract with Andrew Bradford to print fifty copies of this title, the first compilation of Pennsylvania laws, and purported to contain the text of all laws then in force. No sooner was it published than the queen disallowed sixteen of the acts. The province purchased the entire run for distribution within the government. *The Laws* begin, "At a General Assembly begun at New-Castle the fourteenth Day of October [. . .] and in the year of our Lord 1700." A slightly reduced facsimile edition was printed from a copy at the Historical Society of Pennsylvania and published in *The Earliest Printed Laws of Pennsylvania, 1681-1713.* The Colony Laws of North America Series. Editorial note by John D. Cushing. Wilmington: Michael Glazier, 1978.

Minutes of the Provincial Council of Pennsylvania, from the Organization to the Termination of the Proprietary Government [First Series]. Harrisburg: published by the state, printed by Theophilus Fenn, 1838-1840. 3 vols.

Vol. 1 covers March 10, 1683, to November 27, 1700; Vol. 2 covers December 18, 1700, to May 16, 1717; Vol. 3 covers May 31, 1717, to January 23, 1735-1736.

Delaware (Colony)

Note: Delaware Colony received its charter in 1701 but did not have a general assembly separate from that of the Pennsylvania Colony until 1704. For the early Pennsylvania laws that held dominion over the three lower counties, please consult Joel Fishman's bibliography of colonial Pennsylvania laws in this series.

Anno Regni Georgii II. Regis Magnae Britanniae, Franciae, & Hiberniae. Septimo. At a General Assembly of the Counties of New-Castle, Kent and Sussex upon Delaware, Begun and Holden at New-Castle, the Twentieth Day of October, Anno Dom. 1733. In the seventh year of the reign of our Sovereign Lord George II, by the grace of God, of Great Britain, France and Ireland, King, Defender of the faith, &c. And from thence continued by adjournment to the twentieth of March, 1733. Philadelphia: printed and sold by B. Franklin, at the New Printing-Office near the Market, 1734. 24 pp. (Miller 82, Evans 3767)*

Delaware's colonial assembly met at New Castle, but since there were no printers in Delaware at the time, official documents were printed in Philadelphia. Benjamin Franklin served as Delaware's official printer from 1729 until 1760 when James Adams, printer, moved from Philadelphia to Wilmington.

[Delaware. General Assembly. Laws for Session of October 21, 1734. George II. 1735.] (not seen by Miller; Miller 100, Evans 3895, Hildeburn 506)

According to Miller, Hildeburn described this item as a folio of twenty pages, which tallies with Franklin's ledger charge of May 10, 1735.

Laws of the Government of New-Castle, Kent and Sussex Upon Delaware. Published by Order of the Assembly. Philadelphia: B. Franklin, 1741. 282 pp. + 3 pp. index. (Miller 232, Evans 4707)

According to Miller, bound copies are generally preceded by *The Charter of Privileges* (Philadelphia: B. Franklin, 1741). A facsimile was printed in *The Earliest Printed Laws of Delaware, 1704-1741.* The Colony Laws of North America Series. Editorial note by John D. Cushing. Wilmington: Michael Glazier, 1978. Facsimile also includes *The Charter of Privileges, Granted by William Penn, Esq. to the Inhabitants of Pensilvania and Territories.* Philadelphia: printed and sold by B. Franklin, 1741. (Miller 252, Evans 4782)

Facsimiles were made from originals in the collections of the American Philosophical Society.

[An Act for Establishing a Militia Within This Government]. Philadelphia: B. Franklin, 1741. (Miller 231, Evans-Bristol 11222; not seen by Miller)

According to Miller, Franklin appears to have charged for a separate printing of 282 copies of the Militia Act, the text of which Franklin included in his *Laws of the Government of New-Castle, Kent and Sussex upon Delaware* (1741).

Minutes of the House of Assembly of the Three Counties upon Delaware at Sessions Held at New Castle in the Years 1740-1742. Dover: Public Archives Commission of Delaware, 1929.

The incomplete original manuscript was found among the papers of the Public Archives Commission.

Laws of the Government of New-Castle, Kent and Sussex, upon Delaware. Published by Order of the Assembly. Philadelphia: printed and sold by B. Franklin and D. Hall at the New Printing-Office, in Market-Street, 1752. 364 pp. + 17 pp. index. (Miller 548, Evans 6835)

Compiled by Benjamin Chew and significant for its inclusiveness, as it contains 129 laws, or more than twice the number found in the first edition of 1741.

Anno Regni Vicesimo Septimo Georgii II. Regis, Magnae Britanniae, Franciae & Hiberniae, Vigesimo Septimo. At an Assembly held at New-Castle, the Twentieth Day of October, 1753. Philadelphia: printed and sold by B. Franklin and D. Hall at the New Printing Office, near the Market, 1754. 9 pp. (Miller 584, Evans-Bristol 11240)

Provides the text of an act concerning written and nuncupative wills.

Votes and Proceedings of the House of Representatives of the Government of the Counties of New-Castle, Kent and Sussex, upon Delaware, at a Session of Assembly Held at New-Castle the Twentieth Day of October, 1762. Published [. . .] by Order of the Assembly. Wilmington: Thomas

M'Kean and Caesar Rodney, printed by James Adams, in Market-Street, 1762. 27 pp. (Rink 5, Evans-Bristol B2271)

Reprinted by the Public Archives Commission of Delaware (Dover, 1930).

Laws of the Government of New-Castle, Kent and Sussex, upon Delaware. Vol. I[-II]. Wilmington: printed by James Adams, in Market-Street, 1763. Vol. 1, 363 pp. + 17 pp. index. (Rink 11, Evans 41337); Vol. 2, 81 pp. (Rink 12, Evans 9375)

According to Evans, Vol. 1 was printed in 1752 by Franklin and Hall in Philadelphia (Evans 6835, Miller 548). According to Rink, the only known copy of the Adams imprint of Vol. 1 is at the Peabody Institute. According to Shipton and Mooney, the "best copy available" of the Adams imprint is at the Peabody Institute, now incorporated into the collections of the Enoch Pratt Free Library. The Adams Vol. 1 was not examined for this bibliography.

Anno Quarto Georgii III. Regis. At a General Assembly begun at New-Castle, in the government of the counties of New-Castle, Kent and Sussex, upon Delaware, the twentieth day of October, in the third year of the reign of our Sovereign Lord George the Third, King of Great-Britain, &c. annoque Domini 1763, and continued by adjournments till the thirty-first day of March following, the following acts were passed. Wilmington: printed by James Adams, 1764. pp. 83-97. (Rink 17, Evans 9632)

Anno Quinto Georgii III. Regis. At a General Assembly begun at New-Castle, in the government of the counties of New-Castle, Kent and Sussex, upon Delaware, the twentieth day of October, in the fourth year of the reign of our Sovereign Lord George the Third, King of Great-Britain, &c. annoque Domini 1764, the following act was passed . . . Wilmington: printed by James Adams, 1764. pp. 99-106. (Rink 18, Evans 9633)

Votes and Proceedings of the House of Representatives of the Government of the Counties of New Castle, Kent and Sussex: upon Delaware, at a Session of Assembly Held at New Castle the Twenty-First Day of October . . . 1765. Published . . . by Order of the Assembly. Wilmington: George Read and Thomas M'Kean, printed and sold by James Adams, in Market Street, 1770. 233 pp. (Rink 47, Evans-Bristol 42081)

Includes the votes and proceedings through March 24, 1770. Reprinted by the Public Archives Commission of Delaware (Dover, 1931). Microfilmed by Delaware State Archives, Division of Historical and Cultural Affairs (Dover, 1989).

Anno Regni Sexto Georgii III. Regis. At a General Assembly begun at New-Castle, in the government of the counties of New-Castle, Kent and Sussex, upon Delaware, the twentieth day of October, in the sixth year of the reign of our Sovereign Lord George the Third, King of Great-Britain, &c. annoque Domini 1766, the following acts were passed . . . Wilmington: printed by James Adams, 1766. pp. 107-123. (Rink 32, Evans 10278)

Anno Regni Septimo Georgii III. Regis. At a General Assembly begun at New-Castle, in the government of the counties of New-Castle, Kent and Sussex, upon Delaware, the twentieth day of October, in the seventh year of the reign of our Sovereign Lord George the Third, King of Great-Britain, &c. annoque Domini 1767. The following acts were passed . . . Wilmington: printed by James Adams, 1767. pp. 125-131. (Rink 37, Evans 10600)

Anno Regni Octavo Georgii III. Regis. At a General Assembly begun at New-Castle, in the government of the counties of New-Castle, Kent and Sussex, upon Delaware, the twentieth day of October, in the eighth year of the reign of our Sovereign Lord George the Third, King of Great-Britain, &c. annoque Domini 1768, the following acts were passed . . . Wilmington: printed by James Adams, 1769. pp. 133-153. (Rink 44, Evans 11235)

Anno Regni Nono Georgii III. Regis. At a General Assembly begun at New-Castle, in the government of the counties of New-Castle, Kent and Sussex upon Delaware, the twentieth day of October, (and continued by adjournment to the Twenty-fourth day of March following) in the ninth year of the reign of our Sovereign Lord George the Third, King of Great-Britain, &c. annoque Domini 1769, the following acts were passed . . . Wilmington: printed by James Adams, 1770. pp. 155-222. (Rink 48, Evans 11628)

Anno Regni Decimo Georgii III. Regis. At a General Assembly begun at New-Castle, in the government of the counties of New-Castle, Kent and Sussex, upon Delaware, the twentieth day of October, in the tenth year of

the reign of our Sovereign Lord George the Third, King of Great-Britain,
&c. annoque Domini 1770, and continued by adjournment to the third
day of November following, the following act was passed . . . An act
obliging persons returned and appointed for constables to serve accordingly . . . Wilmington: printed by James Adams, 1770. pp. 223-227.
(Rink 49, Evans 11629)

*Anno Regni Undecimo Georgii III. Regis. At a General Assembly begun at
New-Castle, in the government of the counties of New-Castle, Kent and
Sussex, upon Delaware, the twentieth day of October, in the eleventh
year of the reign of our Sovereign Lord George the Third, King of Great-
Britain &c. annoque Domini 1771, and continued by adjournment to the
thirteenth of June following, the following acts were passed . . .* Wilmington: printed by James Adams, 1772. pp. 229-278. (Rink 64, Evans
12373)

*Anno Regni Duodecimo Georgii III, Regis. At a General Assembly begun at
New-Castle, in the government of the counties of New-Castle, Kent and
Sussex, upon Delaware, the twentieth day of October, (and continued by
adjournments to the twelfth of April following) in the twelfth year of the
reign of our Sovereign Lord George the Third, King of Great-Britain,
&c. Anoque domini 1772, the following acts were passed . . .* Wilmington: printed by James Adams, 1773. pp. 279-286. (Rink 71, Evans
12747)

[Votes of the Assembly for Session Ending April, 1773] [Wilmington:
printed by James Adams, 1773]. pp. 25-32. (Rink 70, Evans-Bristol
42433)

Lacking title page. The only known copy is at the Library Company of Philadelphia.

*Anno Regni Decimo Tertio Georgii III. Regis. At a General Assembly begun
at New-Castle, in the government of the counties of New-Castle, Kent
and Sussex, upon Delaware, the twentieth day of October, in the thirteenth year of the reign of our Sovereign Lord George the Third, King of
Great-Britain, &c. annoque Domini 1773, the following acts were
passed . . .* Wilmington: printed by James Adams, 1773. pp. 287-299.
(Rink 72, Evans 12748)

*Votes and Proceedings of the House of Representatives of the Government
of the Counties of New-Castle, Kent and Sussex, on Delaware, in Gen-*

eral Assembly Met at New-Castle, on Wednesday, October 20, 1773. Wilmington: printed and sold by James Adams, in High Street, 1774. 46 pp. (Rink 77, Evans-Bristol 42583)

Anno Regni Decimo Quarto Georgii III. Regis. At a General Assembly begun at New-Castle, in the government of the counties of New-Castle, Kent and Sussex, upon Delaware, the twentieth day of October, in the fourteenth year of the reign of our Sovereign Lord George the Third, King of Great-Britain, &c. annoque Domini 1774, (and continued by adjournments to the twenty-first of August following), the following acts were passed . . . Wilmington: printed by James Adams, 1775. pp. 301-351. (Rink 89, Evans 14005)

Anno Regni Decimo Quinto Georgii III. Regis. At a General Assembly begun at New-Castle, in the government of the counties of New-Castle, Kent and Sussex, upon Delaware, the twentieth day of October in the fifteenth year of the reign of our Sovereign Lord George the Third, King of Great-Britain, &c. annoque [!] Domini 1775, the following act was passed . . . Wilmington: printed by James Adams, 1775. pp. 353-355 and pp. 336-337 [i.e., 356-357]. (Rink 90, Evans 14006)

Votes and Proceedings of the House of Representatives of the Government of the Counties of New-Castle, Kent and Sussex, on Delaware, in General Assembly Met at New-Castle, from October Sessions 1774 'till the End of August Sessions 1775. Wilmington: printed and sold by James Adams, in High Street, 1775. 74 pp. (Rink 88, Evans-Bristol B3963)

The only known copy, examined at the Library Company of Philadelphia, lacks all pages after p. 74. A manuscript note in a contemporary hand states, "Minutes: Oct. 1775, omitted here—Also, the minutes of the Convention & forms of the new constitution."

City of Wilmington

The Ordinances of the City of Wilmington: To Which is Prefixed a Collection of Acts and Parts of Acts of Assembly, Relating to the Corporation: And the Original Charter, Granted Anno Domini 1739. Published by Authority. Wilmington: Porter and Naff, 1841.

Includes *Charter of the Borough of Wilmington . . .* Nov. 16, 1739, which granted approval for building a courthouse, and begins on p. 111. Indexes.

Delaware (State)

Anno Millesimo Septingentesimo Septuagesimo Sexto, at a General Assembly begun at New-Castle, in the Delaware state, the twenty-eighth day of October, anno Domini 1776, and continued by adjournment to the twenty-second day of February 1777, the following acts were passed . . . Wilmington: printed by James Adams, 1777. pp. 339-369 [i.e., 359-389]. (Rink 108, Evans 43241)

Laws of the State of Delaware, From the Fourteenth Day of October, One Thousand Seven Hundred, to the Eighteenth Day of August, One Thousand Seven Hundred and Ninety-Seven. In Two Volumes. Published by Authority. New Castle: printed by Samuel and John Adams, 1797. (Rink 438, Evans 32030)

Vol. 1 includes the *Constitution of the United States,* followed by the *Laws of the State of Delaware,* beginning on pp. [51]-590 with the preamble "At a General Assembly, begun at New-Castle, the Fourteenth Day of October, and continued by adjournment until the Twenty-Seventh Day of November, in the Twelfth Year of the reign of King William, and in the Year of our Lord One Thousand Seven Hundred. On which Day the following Acts were passed by William Penn, Esq; Proprietary and Governor in Chief of the Province of Pennsylvania and Territories." Vol. 1 includes the laws enacted through October 28, 1775, and is followed by an appendix containing various public papers, including *The Duke of York's Deed of Feoffment of New-Castle, and Twelve Miles Circle, to William Penn* and *The Charter of Privileges, Granted by William Penn, Esq. to the Inhabitants of Pennsylvania, and Territories.* Vol. 2 begins with the laws created after 1776, on pp. [595]-1376, and is followed by a table of acts repealed, expired, or obsolete, a table of private acts, and an index to both volumes. Copies examined at Special Collections, Widener University School of Law, bear the signature of Caesar A. Rodney on the title pages of both volumes. Reprinted in facsimile in *The First Laws of the State of Delaware.* Edited and compiled by John D. Cushing. Wilmington: Michael Glazier, *First Laws of the Original Thirteen States,* 1981. The original two-volume edition of Delaware laws was so bulky that it was necessary to divide each facsimile volume into two parts. Vol. 1, Part 1 ends at p. 348; Vol. 1, Part 2 ends at p. 590, with the appendix of 101 pages; Vol. 2, Part 1 ends at p. 1024; Vol. 2, Part 2 ends at p. 1376 and is followed by tables and an index. Vol. 1, lacking the *Constitution of the United States* and appendixes, is available in microfiche in Hein's *Colonial Session Laws—Delaware.*

Proceedings of the Assembly of the Lower Counties on Delaware 1770-1776, of the Constitutional Convention of 1776, and of the House of Assembly of the Delaware State, 1776-1781. Edited by Claudia L. Bushman, Harold B. Hancock, and Elizabeth Moyne Homsey. Newark: University of Delaware Press and Associated University Presses, 1986.

Minutes of the Council of the Delaware State from 1776 to 1796. Papers of the Historical Society of Delaware 6. Wilmington: Historical Society of Delaware, 1887.

The council of Delaware was a part of the legislative body of the state, corresponding to what is now the senate. It was organized under the constitution of 1776 and continued in existence until the constitution of 1792 went into effect.

Proceedings of the Joint Session of the Legislature of the State of Delaware in Accepting the Gift of the Royal Charter of Charles II and the Deeds to William Penn of the Land and Waters Comprising the State of Delaware. [n.p.], 1909.

In 1909 Delaware was presented the gift of the Royal Patent of Charles II to James, Duke of York, for the lands comprising the domain of the state of Delaware, together with the deeds from the Duke of York to William Penn, and the Duke's leases to Penn. This commemorative publication provides an interesting account of how these documents came to America and descended to the donor, Sarah Wistar Miller.

Judicial

Calendar of Kent County, Delaware Probate Records, 1680-1800. Compiled by Leon de Valinger Jr. Dover: Public Archives Commission, State of Delaware, 1944.

Index. Volume functions as a calendar and does not attempt to give a complete abstract of the wills and administration accounts.

Chew, Samuel. *The Speech of Samuel Chew, Esq; Chief Justice of the Government of New-Castle, Kent and Sussex upon Delaware: Delivered from the Bench to the Grand-Jury of the County of New-Castle, Nov. 21, 1741; and Now Published at Their Request.* Philadelphia: printed and sold by B. Franklin, 1741. 16 pp. (Evans 4708, Miller 229)

Chew gives expression of his belief, as a Quaker judge, in the rightness of defensive war.

————. *The Speech of Samuel Chew, Esq. Chief Judge of the Counties of Newcastle, Kent, and Sussex, on Delaware. On the Lawfulness of Defence Against an Armed Enemy. Delivered from the Bench to the Grand Jury of the County of Newcastle, Nov. 21, 1741. First Published at the Request of Said Grand Jury; and Now Re-Published by Desire of Several Gentlemen.* Philadelphia: printed and sold by R. Aitken, Front-Street, 1775. 8 pp. (Evans 13867)

Running title: *The Lawfulness of Defence Against an Armed Enemy.*

————. *The Speech of Samuel Chew, Esq; Chief Justice of the Government of New-Castle, Kent and Sussex upon Delaware; Delivered from the Bench to the Grand-Jury of the County of New-Castle, Aug. 20, 1742; and Now Published at Their Request.* Philadelphia: printed and sold by B. Franklin, 1742. 16 pp. (Miller 276, Evans 4930)

After Chew was expelled from the Duck Creek Monthly Meeting of Friends (Quakers) for his refusal to disavow the assertion he made in his grand jury speech of November 21, 1741, Chew's speech was republished as a rejoinder, restating his opposition to the meeting's interference, as a religious society, in the affairs of state.

Court Records of Kent County, Delaware, 1680-1705. Edited by Leon de Valinger Jr., with a prefatory note by John Biggs Jr. American Legal Records 8. Washington, DC: American Historical Association, 1959.

The historical introduction presents brief accounts of the Swedish, Dutch, Duke of York, and William Penn periods of Delaware history. Full index of names and a list of cases, but no subject index.

Delaware Cases, 1792-1830. Edited by Daniel J. Boorstin, editorial assistants Bennett Frankel and Irving J. Helman. St. Paul, MN: West Publishing Co., 1943. 3 vols.

Combined table of cases and full index digest in Vol. 3. Despite its title, a few reports of cases from the 1770s are included. Although the cases covered by these volumes are generally beyond the scope of this bibliography, the title is included because of the prefatory materials and because "the present volumes comprise virtually the only Delaware cases in print for the years before 1814, and the only cases at common law before 1832." Fifty chancery cases decided from 1814 to 1829 can be found in 1 *Delaware Chancery* 1-341 and two cases for the year 1788 can be found in 4 *Dallas* i-xix.

[Penn, John]. *John Penn, plaintiff. Breviate. In Chancery. John Penn, Thomas Penn, and Richard Penn, esqrs; plaintiffs. Charles Calvert esq; Lord Baltimore in the kingdom of Ireland, defendant. For the plaintiffs. Upon a bill to compell a špecifick execution of articles of agreement entered into between the partys for setling the boundarys of the province of Pensilvania, the three lower countys, and the province of Maryland, and for perpetuating testimony, &c.* . . . [London: n.p., 1742]. 116 pp. (Sabin 34416[1])

Includes two maps, one of which displays "parts of the Provinces of Pennsylvania and Maryland with the Counties of New Castle, Kent and Sussex on Delaware according to the most exact Surveys yet made drawn in the year 1740." The map shows the 1635 northern boundary of Maryland according to Lord Baltimore's map and the temporary limits of the jurisdictions of Pennsylvania and Maryland fixed in the year 1739. The *Breviate* is a summary of the legal history of the dispute to that point which was presented on behalf of the Penn family. Table of contents. A recent acquisition of Special Collections at the University of Delaware.

Pennypacker, Samuel W. *Pennsylvania Colonial Cases: The Administration of Law in Pennsylvania prior to A.D. 1700 as Shown in the Cases Decided and in the Court Proceedings.* Philadelphia: Rees Welsh and Company, 1892.

Although the cases were heard and determined in Pennsylvania, some of the cases may have been on appeal from the three lower counties, then a part of Pennsylvania. Available in microform in *Law Books Recommended for Libraries, Legal History,* No. 138.

Records of the Court of New Castle on Delaware, 1676-1681, Published by the Colonial Society of Pennsylvania. Lancaster, PA: Wickersham Printing, 1904.

Vol. 1 was published in an edition of 200 copies. Reprinted from Vols. 68 and 69 of the *Collections of the Genealogical Society of Pennsylvania* in the Library of the Historical Society of Pennsylvania, which were copied from the original manuscript in the Office of the Prothonotary of the Superior Court for New Castle County at Wilmington, Delaware. Vol. 2 (Meadville, PA: Tribune Publishing, 1935) was published in an edition of 500 copies and covers 1681-1699. It is "limited to such extracts from the original court minutes as were ordered made by the Government of the Three Lower Counties on Delaware, in the year 1770, of all items respecting land titles and probate proceedings. These extracts are the only survivals of the original records for the period named."

Records of the Courts of Sussex County, Delaware, 1677-1710. Edited by Craig W. Horle. Philadelphia: University of Pennsylvania Press, 1991. 2 vols.

Vol. 1 includes 1677-1689; Vol. 2 includes 1690-1710.

The Registrar's Book of Governor Keith's Court of Chancery of the Province of Pennsylvania, 1720-1735. Harrisburg: Pennsylvania Bar Association, 1941.

A facsimile printed with comments prepared by the Committee on Legal Biography and History of the Pennsylvania Bar Association. The organization in 1720 of a provincial version of the English High Court of Chancery held brief and questionable dominion over Pennsylvania and, arguably, the lower three counties.

Some Records of Sussex County, Delaware. Compiled by C[harles] H[enry] B[lack] Turner. Philadelphia: Allen, Lane and Scott, 1909.

Court records for Sussex County, 1681 to ca. 1700, are printed at pp. 54-133. Miscellaneous probate records for the same period are printed at pp. 133-156. Includes seventeenth- and eighteenth-century civil and court records, ecclesiastical, vestry, Bible, and miscellaneous records.

Biographical: General

Bendler, Bruce A. *Colonial Delaware Assemblymen, 1682-1776.* Westminster, MD: Family Line Publications, 1989.

Provides biographical information for all men who served in the legislature of the colony under the Penn proprietorship. Source list. Index.

Keith, Charles P. *The Provincial Councillors of Pennsylvania Who Held Office between 1733 and 1776 and Those Earlier Councillors Who Were Some Time Chief Magistrates of the Province, and Their Descendants.* Philadelphia: W. S. Sharp Printing, 1883.

Provides brief biographies and fairly extensive genealogies of members of the provincial council. It includes those members appointed when Pennsylvania was a royal province as well as those appointed when Pennsylvania was a proprietary province. Index.

Biographical: Individual

Chew, Benjamin

Konkle, Burton Alva. *Benjamin Chew, 1722-1810, Head of the Pennsylvania Judiciary System Under Colony and Commonwealth.* Philadelphia: University of Pennsylvania Press, 1932.

Chapters VI and VII are especially relevant to the legal and political situations in the lower counties during the years 1740-1758. Benjamin Chew held positions in the lower counties assembly, the executive council of Delaware and Pennsylvania, and the courts of Pennsylvania. Index.

Dickinson, John

Flower, Milton E. *John Dickinson, Conservative Revolutionary.* Charlottesville: published for the Friends of the John Dickinson Mansion by the University Press of Virginia, 1983.

John Dickinson lived and farmed in Kent County and practiced law in Philadelphia. He was a member of the Delaware assembly (1759-1761) before serving in the Pennsylvania assembly. Selected bibliography. Index.

Powell, J. H. "John Dickinson and the Constitution." *Pennsylvania Magazine of History* 60(January 1936): 1-14 .

Richards, Robert H. *The Life and Character of John Dickinson.* Papers of the Historical Society of Delaware 30. Wilmington: Historical Society of Delaware, 1901.

A paper read before the society on May 21, 1900.

McKean, Thomas

Buchanan, Roberdeau. *Life of the Hon. Thomas McKean.* Lancaster, PA: Inquirer Print, 1890.

Coleman, John M. *Thomas McKean, Forgotten Leader of the Revolution.* Rockaway, NJ: American Faculty Press, 1975.

Principally concerned with the political and social developments in Delaware and surrounding areas prior to the Revolution. Bibliography. Illustrations.

———. "Thomas McKean and the Origin of an Independent Judiciary." *Pennsylvania History* 34(April 1967): 111-130.

Rowe, Gail S. "Thomas McKean and the Coming of the Revolution." *Pennsylvania Magazine of History and Biography* 96(January 1972): 3-47.

———. *Thomas McKean: The Shaping of an American Republicanism.* Boulder, CO: Associated University Press, 1978.

———. "A Valuable Acquisition in Congress: Thomas McKean, Delegate from Delaware to the Continental Congress, 1774-1783." *Pennsylvania History* 38(July 1971): 225-264.

Penn, William

Geiter, Mary K. *William Penn.* Harlow, England, and New York: Longman, 2000.

Analyzes William Penn's motives as a member of the influential upper class and as a businessman. Stresses the importance of the three lower counties and how their part in history has been underresearched. Written by a Pennsylvanian who has researched extensively in England and has brought a British viewpoint to Penn's reputation. Index.

Penn, William. *The Papers of William Penn.* Edited by Mary Maples Dunn and Richard S. Dunn; associate editors Richard A. Ryerson, Scott M. Wilds; assistant editor Jean R. Soderlund. [Philadelphia]: University of Pennsylvania Press, 1981-1987. 5 vols.

Indexes and calendars of the microfilmed William Penn documents are included. Bibliography.

Remember William Penn, 1644-1944. Edited by William W. Comfort, Francis B. Haas, Greg L. Neel, and Stanley R. Yarnall. [n.p.]: William Penn Tercentenary Committee, Pennsylvania Historical Commission, 1944.

The numerous illustrations are of particular note. Index. Bound with William Penn's *Some Fruits of Solitude and More Fruits of Solitude,* also published by the Tercentenary Committee.

Wildes, Harry Emerson. *William Penn.* New York: Macmillan, 1974.

A well-rounded, practical, and objective biography that mentions the three lower counties many times in the context of the problems they caused and endured. Appendixes. Index.

Read, George

Read, William Thompson. *Life and Correspondence of George Read, a Signer of the Declaration of Independence, with Notices of Some of His Contemporaries.* Philadelphia: Lippincott, 1870.

A commentary by Read's grandson, interspersed with letters and biographies of other eminent colonial figures. Chapters 1-3 are concerned with events leading up to 1776.

Rodney, Caesar

Haas, John Henry. "Caesar Rodney: Delaware's Prudent Engineer of Revolution." PhD diss., Claremont Graduate School, 1994.

Unpublished, it is available at the Historical Society of Delaware. Provides an analysis of the political situation and Rodney's response to it preceding and following the Revolution. Bibliography.

Rodney, Caesar. *Letters to and from Caesar Rodney, 1756-1784; Member of the Stamp Act Congress and the First and Second Continental Congresses; Speaker of the Delaware Colonial Assembly; President of the Delaware State; Major General of the Delaware Militia; Signer of the Declaration of Independence.* Edited by George Herbert Ryden. Philadelphia: published for the Historical Society of Delaware by the University of Pennsylvania Press, 1933.

The basis of this book is the collection of letters purchased by the Historical Society of Delaware at the sale of the Rodney papers in Philadelphia in 1919, with additional letters provided by the Delaware Public Archives, Library of Congress, Genealogical Society of Pennsylvania, and New York Public Library. "Sources of material" given on pp. 449-452. Reprinted by Da Capo Press (New York, 1970).

Scott, Jane Harrington. *A Gentleman as Well as a Whig: Caesar Rodney and the American Revolution.* [n.p.]: National Society of the Colonial Dames of America in the State of Delaware, University of Delaware Press, Associated University Presses, 2000.

Describes the life of one of Delaware's most influential pre-Revolutionary citizens.

Spry, Thomas

Lewis, John Frederick. *Thomas Spry, Lawyer and Physician, The First Attorney Admitted to Practice Under English Law in the Delaware River Settlements Now Included in the States of Pennsylvania, New Jersey, and Delaware.* Philadelphia: Patterson and White, 1932.

Guides and Bibliographies

Bibliography of Delaware Through 1960. Compiled by H. Clay Reed and Marion Bjornson Reed. [n.p.]: published for the Institute of Delaware History and Culture by the University of Delaware Press, 1960.

Includes nearly 5,000 entries arranged under broad subject headings.

Bristol, Roger P. *Supplement to Charles Evans' American Bibliography.* Charlottesville, VA: Bibliographical Society of America and the Bibliographical Society of the University of Virginia, 1970. 1 vol., plus index vol.

Gehring, Charles T. *Guide to Dutch Manuscripts Relating to New Netherland in United States Repositories.* Albany: University of the State of New York, State Department of Education, New York State Library, 1978.

Provides a state-by-state list of holdings of individual manuscripts.

Eddy, Henry Howard. *Guide to the Published Archives of Pennsylvania Covering the 138 Volumes of Colonial Records and Pennsylvania Archives, Series I-IX . . . with an Alphabetized Finding List and Two Special Indexes Compiled by Martha L. Simonetti.* Harrisburg: Division of Public Records of the Pennsylvania Historical and Museum Commission, 1949.

Evans, Charles. *American Bibliography: A Chronological Dictionary of All Books, Pamphlets and Periodical Publications Printed in the United States of America from the Genesis of Printing in 1639 Down to and Including the Year 1820.* New York: Peter Smith, 1941. 13 vols., plus index vol.

Guide to the Manuscript Groups in the Pennsylvania State Archives. Edited and Compiled by Harry E. Whipkey. Harrisburg: Pennsylvania Historical and Museum Commission, 1976.

Guide to the Microfilm of the Papers of William Penn. Philadelphia: Historical Society of Pennsylvania, 1975.

Many of the papers of William Penn are at the society.

Guide to the Microfilm of the Records of the Provincial Council, 1682-1776, in the Pennsylvania State Archives . . . Edited by George Daily and George R. Beyer. [n.p.]: Pennsylvania Historical and Museum Commission, 1966.

Provides a chronological list of provincial records.

Hazard, Samuel. *General Index to the Colonial Records: In 16 Volumes: And to the Pennsylvania Archives in 12 Volumes . . . Under an Act of the General Assembly of Pennsylvania.* Philadelphia: printed by Joseph Severns, 1860.

Index to History of Delaware, 1609-1888, J. Thomas Scharf. Edited by Gladys M. Coghlan and Dale Fields. Wilmington: Historical Society of Delaware, 1976. 3 vols.

Provides a much-needed index to Scharf's *History of Delaware.*

Inventory of the County Archives of Delaware, No. 1, New Castle County. Dover: Public Archives Commission, State of Delaware, 1941.

Prepared by the Delaware Historical Records Survey Division of Community Service Programs, Works Projects Administration. Index. Bibliography. In addition to an excellent general historical sketch, the inventory includes brief histories of the clerk of the peace, prothonotary, court of general sessions, chancery court, etc. Virtually every record that existed in New Castle County up to 1941 is included. Inventories were never issued for the other counties. Facsimile reprint published by Heritage Books (Bowie, MD, 1994).

"A List of Legal Treatises Printed in the British Colonies and the American States Before 1801." Compiled by Eldon Revare James. In *Harvard Legal Essays, Written in Honor of and Presented to Joseph Henry Beale and Samuel Williston* (Cambridge: Harvard University, 1934), pp. 159-211.

Gives full bibliographic information on forty-five treatises printed between 1763 and 1789.

Miller, William C. *Benjamin Franklin's Philadelphia Printing, 1728-1766/ A Descriptive Bibliography.* Memoirs of the American Philosophical Society 102. Philadelphia: American Philosophical Society, 1974.

Provides the definitive bibliography of 800 items from broadsides to books printed by Franklin or by the partnership of Franklin and Hall.

A Preliminary Inventory of the Older Records in the Delaware Archives. Compiled by Joanne Mattern and Harbold B. Hancock. Dover: Division of Historical and Cultural Affairs, Bureau of Archives and Records, 1978.

Provides a general inventory of the agencies represented by older records in the archives. Available on microfiche: Document No. 20-06-78-02-02.

Rink, Evald. *Printing in Delaware, 1761-1800: A Checklist.* Wilmington: Eleutherian Mills Historical Library, 1969.

The lower counties retained close ties with Philadelphia, then the most significant center of printing in America, and depended upon its printers. It was not until 1761 that James Adams moved his print shop from Philadelphia to Wilmington. In 1762, he began publishing the proceedings of the general assembly of the three counties, followed by the Delaware (Colony) Laws in 1763. Provides a good bibliographic checklist and holdings for Delaware colonial laws and related works after 1761.

Shipton, Clifford K. and James E. Mooney. *National Index of American Imprints Through 1800: The Short-Title Evans.* [n.p.]: American Antiquarian Society, Barre Publishers, 1969. 2 vols.

Secondary Sources

Acrelius, Israel. *A History of New Sweden; or, The Settlements on the River Delaware.* Translated by William M. Reynolds. Memoirs of the Historical Society of Pennsylvania 11. Philadelphia: Publication Fund of the Historical Society of Pennsylvania, published under the joint auspices of the Historical Societies of Pennsylvania and Delaware, 1874.

Translation of *Beskrifning om de swenska församlingars forna och närwarande tilst ånd.* Index. Facsimile printed by University Microfilms (Ann Arbor, 1966).

Brophy, Alfred L. "For the Preservation of the King's Peace and Justice: Community and English Law in Sussex County, Pennsylvania, 1682-1696." *American Journal of Legal History* 40(1996): 167-212.

A study of court records to create an understanding of the role of the civil court and Penn's laws in settling disputes and bringing harmony and structure to society.

————. Rev. of *Records of the Courts of Sussex County Delaware, 1677-1710,* edited by Craig W. Horle. *Cumberland Law Review* 26(1995): 145-164.

Caldwell, Robert Graham. *Red Hannah: Delaware's Whipping Post.* Philadelphia: University of Pennsylvania Press; London: G. Cumberlege, Oxford University Press, 1947.

The first record of whipping was in 1656 under the Dutch. Its imposition as a punishment was common under English rule and was authorized by Act of Assembly in 1719. It remained in effect following the Revolution and it was not until 1905 that it finally was abolished.

Carson, Hampton L. "Dutch and Swedish Settlements on the Delaware." *Pennsylvania Magazine of History and Biography* 33(1909): 1-21.

Paper read before the Historical Society of Pennsylvania on November 9, 1908.

Carter, Edward Carlos and Clifford Lewis III. "Sir Edmund Plowden and the New Albion Charter, 1632-1785." *Pennsylvania Magazine of History and Biography* 83(1959): 150-179.

In 1634 Plowden received a charter from Charles I and became, in theory, the possessor of a vast tract of land that included half of what is today Delaware and Maryland, two-thirds of New Jersey, and the southern half of eastern Pennsylvania. His early attempt to establish a British settlement on the Delaware resulted in mutiny.

Chafee, Zechariah. "Rev. of *Delaware Cases, 1792-1830,* edited by Daniel J. Boorstin, assisted by Bennett Frankel and Irving J. Helman." *Harvard Law Review* 57(1943-1944): 399-419.

Provides an excellent discussion of the adoption of English common law in Delaware.

Christoph, Peter R. *Delaware Under the New York Governors, 1664-1682*. Radnor, PA: Peter Alrich Foundation, 1992.

The text of a paper presented October 13, 1990, at the Alrich Family Reunion. Bibliographical notes.

Clay, Jehu Curtis. *Annals of the Swedes on the Delaware, from Their First Settlement in 1636, to the Present Time*. Philadelphia: J. C. Pechin, 1835.

Conrad, Henry C. *Address Delivered at the Dedication of a Tablet Given by the Judiciary of Delaware and Members of the Delaware Bar in Memory of Ryves Holt, Chief Justice of the Government of the Counties of New Castle, Kent and Sussex upon Delaware*. Papers of the Historical Society of Delaware 63. Wilmington: Historical Society of Delaware, 1914.

Paper read in St. Peter's Church, Lewes, on December 14, 1913.

―――. *History of the State of Delaware . . . from the Earliest Settlements to the Year 1907*. Wilmington: published by the author, 1908. 3 vols.

Paged continuously: Vol. 2 begins at p. 397; Vol. 3 begins at p. 795. Profusely illustrated. Index.

Cooch, Edward W. *Delaware Historic Events: A Compilation of Articles and Addresses*. Cooch's Bridge, DE: Edward W. Cooch, 1946.

Especially interesting is the article "Delaware-Pennsylvania Wedge (Owned by One State—Governed by Another) Address before Hiram Lodge of Newark in 1933" on pp. 35-48. The "wedge" refers to the tract of land between the Delaware curve and the state of Maryland.

Cooper, Alexander B. *Fort Casimir: The Starting Point in the History of New Castle, in the State of Delaware, Its Location and History, 1651-1671*. Papers of the Historical Society of Delaware 43. Wilmington: Historical Society of Delaware, 1905.

Paper read before the society on February 20, 1905.

Dahlgren, Stellan and Hans Norman. *The Rise and Fall of New Sweden: Governor Johan Risingh's Journal, 1654-1655, in Its Historical Context*. Acta Universitatis Upsaliensis 27. Stockholm: Almqvist and Wiksell International, 1988.

Indexes of names and places. Bibliography.

Daughtery, M[artin] M. *Early Colonial Taxation in Delaware.* Wilmington: Delaware Tercentenary Commission, 1938.

Bound with George H. Ryden's *Delaware: The First State in the Union* and Leon de Valinger's *Colonial Military Organization in Delaware, 1638-1776.*

de Valinger, Leon, Jr. *Colonial Military Organization in Delaware 1638-1776.* Wilmington: Delaware Tercentenary Commission, 1938.

Bound with George H. Ryden's *Delaware: The First State in the Union* and M. M. Daugherty's *Early Colonial Taxation in Delaware.*

―――. "The Development of Local Government in Delaware, 1638-1682." MA thesis, University of Delaware, 1935.

Unpublished, a copy is on file at the University of Delaware. Perhaps the best-organized and most-comprehensive work describing the early Swedish and Dutch governments on the Delaware.

Dolan, Paul. "The Justice of the Peace System in Delaware." *Delaware Notes* 29(1956): 1-47.

Eastman, Frank M. *Courts and Lawyers of Pennsylvania: A History, 1623-1923.* New York: American Historical Society, 1922. 3 vols.

Includes the following relevant chapters: Administration of Law Under the Dutch; Government Under the Duke of York; Trial of the "Long Finn"; Duke of York's Laws; Courts at New Castle and Upland; Judiciary in 1685; etc. Microform available in *Law Books Recommended for Libraries, Biography* No. 105. Littleton, CO: Fred B. Rothman, 1989.

Eckman, Jeannette. *Crane Hook on the Delaware, 1667-1699, an Early Swedish Lutheran Church and Community, with the Historical Background of the Delaware River Valley . . . Drawings by Walter Stewart.* Newark: Institute of Delaware History and Culture, University of Delaware, published for the Delaware Swedish Colonial Society, 1958.

Bibliography. Index. Includes maps of Lindeström's Map B (1655) and the Crane Hook Church site and vicinity, 1680-1685 and 1787.

Essah, Patience. *A House Divided: Slavery and Emancipation in Delaware, 1638-1865.* Charlottesville and London: University Press of Virginia, 1996.

Examines the sociological causes of Delaware's prolonged emancipation stalemate.

Ferris, Benjamin. *A History of the Original Settlements on the Delaware, from Its Discovery by Hudson to the Colonization under William Penn. To Which Is Added an Account of the Ecclesiastical Affairs of the Swedish Settlers, and a History of Wilmington, from Its First Settlement to the Present Time.* Wilmington: Wilson and Heald, 1846.

Facsimile printed by Kennikat Press (Port Washington, NY, 1972). Illustrations and map.

Gould, E. R. I. "Local Self-Government in Pennsylvania." *Pennsylvania Magazine of History and Biography* 6(1882): 156-173.

Grubb, Ignatius C. *The Colonial and State Judiciary of Delaware.* Papers of the Historical Society of Delaware 17. Wilmington: Historical Society of Delaware, 1897.

Read before the society on December 21 and 22, 1896.

Hancock, Harold B. "Delaware's Captured Colonial Records." *Delaware History* 9(1960-1961): 355-364.

A recounting of Delaware records captured, lost, destroyed, and stolen.

————. "County Committees & the Growth of Independence in the Three Lower Counties on the Delaware, 1765-1776." *Delaware History* 15 (1972-1973): 269-294 .

————. "The Indenture System in Delaware, 1681-1921." *Delaware History* 16(1974-1975): 47-59.

Hayes, Manlove. *William Penn and His Province.* Papers of the Historical Society of Delaware 24. Wilmington: Historical Society of Delaware, 1899.

Address read before the Historical Society of Delaware, December 2, 1898.

Hazard, Samuel. *Annals of Pennsylvania, from the Discovery of the Delaware . . . 1609-1682.* Philadelphia: Hazard and Mitchell, 1850.

The list of authorities includes Ferris's *Early Settlements on the Delaware,* Clay's *Annals of the Swedes, Delaware Register, Breviat of Evidence in the Case of Penn and Lord Baltimore,* Thurlow's *State Papers,* Hazard's *Historical Collections,* and O'Callaghan's *History of New Netherlands.* Index.

Heite, Louise B. "New Castle Under the Duke of York: A Stable Community." MA thesis, University of Delaware, 1978.

Unpublished, a copy is available at the University of Delaware. New Castle enjoyed stability and a strong sense of self-identity, as demonstrated through the study of land use patterns in the town, relationships between the governor and the court, the careers of prominent citizens, and crime records.

History of Delaware Past and Present. Edited by Wilson Lloyd Bevan and E. Melvin Williams. New York: Lewis Historical Publishing, 1929. 4 vols.

Vols. 1 and 2 are continuously paginated. Vol. 1 covers the colonial period and ends at p. 444; Vol. 2 includes an index for both volumes; Vols. 3 and 4 are continuously paginated and contain contemporary biographical material; Vol. 4 includes a biographical index. Illustrated.

Hoffecker, Carol E. *Delaware: A Bicentennial History.* New York: W. W. Norton and Company; Nashville: American Association for State and Local History, 1977.

Providing an excellent history of the state, the author writes of the Native Americans and the deleterious impact the Europeans and their trading interests had on the Indian culture.

The Honest Man's Interest as He Claims Any Lands in the Counties of New-Castle, Kent, or Sussex, on Delaware. [Philadelphia: Andrew Bradford, 1726]. 4 pp. (Evans 2749)

Involves the disputed title to Delaware land then under the jurisdiction of Pennsylvania. Landowners are told that it is in their interest to oppose Sir William Keith, who was governor and sympathetic to the popular or anti-proprietary interests.

Houston, John W. *Address on the History of the Boundaries of the State of Delaware.* Papers of the Historical Society of Delaware 2. Wilmington: Historical Society of Delaware, 1879.

A paper read on February 21, 1878.

Johannsen, Robert W. "The Conflict Between the Three Lower Counties on the Delaware and the Province of Pennsylvania, 1682-1704." *Delaware History* 5(1952): 96-132.

Johnson, Amandus. *The Swedish Settlements on the Delaware, Their History and Relation to the Indians, Dutch and English, 1638-1664, with an Account of the South, the New Sweden, and the American Companies, and the Efforts of Sweden to Regain the Colony.* Philadelphia: University of Pennsylvania Press, D. Appleton, 1911.

Simultaneously published by the Philadelphia Swedish Colonial Society (Lancaster, PA: New Era Printing, 1911). 2 vols. Reprinted by Burt Franklin (New York, 1970). Extensive bibliography. Index.

Keith, Charles P. *Chronicles of Pennsylvania from the English Revolution to the Peace of Aix-la-Chapelle, 1688-1748.* Philadelphia: Patterson and White, 1917. 2 vols.

Index.

Kinsman, F. J. and Hon. George Gray. *Celebration of the Three Hundredth Anniversary of the Landing of DeVries Colony at Lewes, Delaware, September 22d, A. D. 1909.* Papers of the Historical Society of Delaware 54. Wilmington: Historical Society of Delaware, 1909.

Konkle, Burton Alva. "Delaware: A Grant Yet Not a Grant." *Pennsylvania Magazine of History and Biography* 54(1930): 241-254.

Reprinted in *Papers of the Historical Society of Delaware,* New Series No. 2, pp. 33-46 (Wilmington: Historical Society of Delaware, 1930). Includes a draft of King James II's proposed grant of Kent and Sussex counties to William Penn, December 10, 1688. The subject of a claim upon Delaware, the grant was never signed and became a moot issue at the time of the American Revolution.

Lewis, Lawrence, Jr. "The Courts of Pennsylvania in the Seventeenth Century . . . Read Before the Historical Society of Pennsylvania, Monday,

March 14, 1881." *Pennsylvania Magazine of History and Biography* 5 (1881): 141-190.

Reprinted (Philadelphia: Collins, 1881) under the title *The Constitution, Jurisdiction and Practice of the Courts of Pennsylvania in the Seventeenth Century.*

Lincoln, Anna T. *Wilmington, Delaware: Three Centuries Under Four Flags, 1609-1937.* Rutland, VT: Tuttle Publishing, 1937.

Index. Bibliography.

Louhi, E. A. *The Delaware Finns, or, the First Permanent Settlements in Pennsylvania, Delaware, West New Jersey and Eastern Part of Maryland.* New York: Humanity Press, 1925.

Provides an interesting anecdotal account of the early Finns but lacks an index, bibliography, or footnotes.

Loyd, William H. *The Early Courts of Pennsylvania.* University of Pennsylvania Law School, Series 2. Boston: Boston Book Company, 1910.

Facsimile printed by Fred B. Rothman and Company (Littleton, CO, 1986). Covers the earliest years of the courts of the three lower counties.

Lunt, Dudley. "The Bounds of Delaware." *Delaware History* 2(March 1947): 1-40.

A study of Delaware's boundaries based upon research conducted in England in preparation for litigation over the boundary between Delaware and New Jersey in the U.S. Supreme Court.

McIntire, Nicholas S. *William Penn and New Castle.* New Castle: William Penn Landing Commemoration Committee of New Castle, 1982.

Published in commemoration of the 300th anniversary of the landing of William Penn at New Castle.

Meade, Burford K. *Report on Surveys of Delaware-Maryland Boundaries: In Cooperation with the States of Delaware and Maryland.* Washington, DC: U.S. Department of Commerce, 1982.

Provides historical background and documents, photographs of markers, and detailed geographical locations of the stones placed at every mile of the Delaware border with Maryland between 1751 and 1765.

Micley, Joseph J. *Some Account of William Usselinx and Peter Minuit, Two Individuals Who Were Instrumental in Establishing the First Permanent Colony in Delaware.* Papers of the Historical Society of Delaware 3. Wilmington: Historical Society of Delaware, 1881.

Munroe, John A. *Colonial Delaware: A History.* History of the American Colonies. Millwood, NY: KTO Press, 1978.

————. *Federalist Delaware, 1775-1815.* New Brunswick, NJ: Rutgers University Press, 1954.

————. *History of Delaware.* Newark: University of Delaware Press, 1979.

————. "Reflections on Delaware and the American Revolution." *Delaware History* 17(1976): 1-11.

Nash, Gary B. *Quakers and Politics: Pennsylvania, 1681-1726.* Princeton, NJ: Princeton University Press, 1968.

Provides an analytical study of the sociology of politics that existed after Penn's charter was issued in 1681. Index.

Neuenschwander, John A. *The Middle Colonies and the Coming of the American Revolution.* National University Publications Series in American Studies. Port Washington, NY, and London: Kennikat Press, 1973.

New Castle Common: New Castle Delaware. Wilmington: Trustees of the New Castle Common, Hambleton Printing and Publishing, 1944.

William Penn was closely identified with the New Castle Common, and his heirs granted the original charter creating its governing body. Includes the 1701 warrant from Penn for the survey for the common, return of survey in 1704, charter from Thomas and Richard Penn incorporating the trustees in 1764, and subsequent legislative documents.

New Sweden in America. Edited by Carol E. Hoffecker, Richard Waldron, Lorraine E. Williams, and Barbara E. Benson. Newark: University of Delaware Press; London: Associated University Presses, 1995.

The proceedings of the conference titled "New Sweden in America: Scandinavian Pioneers and Their Legacy," held in honor of the 350th anniversary of the founding of the New Sweden colony. Especially of interest are Stellan Dahlgren's "The Crown of Sweden and the New Sweden Company" and Charles T. Gehring's "Hodie Mihi, Cras Tibi: Swedish-Dutch Relations in the Delaware Valley."

Offutt, William M., Jr. *Of "Good Laws" and "Good Men": Law and Society in the Delaware Valley, 1680-1710.* Urbana and Chicago: University of Illinois Press, 1995.

Examines the social and religious authority wielded by the Society of Friends (Quakers) through the mid-eighteenth century and the establishment of the rule of law in its colonies.

Peltier, David P. "Border State Democracy: A History of Voting in Delaware, 1682-1897." PhD diss., University of Delaware, 1967.

Unpublished, it is available at the Historical Society of Delaware. Chapters 1 and 2 trace voting provisions, procedures, and patterns from Penn's First Frame of Government in 1682 to the state's constitution in 1776. Bibliography.

Pennsylvania Colonial and Federal: A History, 1608-1903. Edited by Howard M. Jenkins. Philadelphia: Pennsylvania Historical Publishing, 1903. 3 vols.

Vol. 1 is concerned with the colonial period. Each volume has its own index.

Pusey, Pennock. *History of Lewes, Delaware.* Papers of the Historical Society of Delaware 38. Wilmington: Historical Society of Delaware, 1903.

Text read before the society on November 17, 1902.

Quillen, William T. "Equity Jurisdiction in Delaware Before 1792." *Delaware Lawyer* 2(Spring 1984): 18-31.

Provides an abbreviation of Judge Quillen's dissertation, which follows.

———. "Historical Sketch of the Equity Jurisdiction in Delaware." LLM diss., University of Virginia, 1982.

Unpublished, a copy is available at the Widener University School of Law Legal Information Center. Provides the premier study of chancery before its incarnation under the first Delaware Constitution.

Quillen, William T. and Michael Hanrahan. "A Short History of the Delaware Court of Chancery." In *Court of Chancery of the State of Delaware, 1792-1992* (n.p.: Bicentennial Commemoration Committee of the Historical Society for the Court of Chancery of the State of Delaware, 1992), pp. 21-64.

Reprinted in *Delaware Journal of Corporate Law* 18(1993): 819-866. Includes a study of the rather primitive equity jurisprudence practiced in the three lower counties and the impact of the enactment in 1726 or 1727 of a comprehensive act for the establishment of courts of law and equity.

Reed, H. Clay. "The Court Records of the Delaware Valley." *William and Mary Quarterly* 4(April 1947): 192-202.

————. "The Delaware Constitution of 1776." *Delaware Notes* 6(1930): 7-42.

————. *The Delaware Colony.* New York and London: Crowell-Collier Press and Crowell Macmillan, 1970.

Though brief, at slightly more than a hundred pages, and aimed at a youthful audience, it provides an informed history of Delaware's colonial period.

————. "The Early New Castle Court." *Delaware History* 4(June 1951): 227-245.

Reed, H. Clay and Joseph A. Palermo. "Justices of the Peace in Early Delaware." *Delaware History* 14(October 1971): 223-237.

Rodney, Richard S. *The Collected Essays of Richard S. Rodney on Early Delaware.* Edited by George H. Gibson. Wilmington: Society of Colonial Wars in the State of Delaware, 1975.

A posthumous collection of Judge Rodney's writings, which include *Early Delaware Judges; The Old State House or Court House, New Castle, Delaware; John Dickinson; Delaware Under Governor Keith, 1717-1814; Early Relations of Delaware and Pennsylvania; Colonial Finances in Delaware; Early Delaware Judges.*

————. *Colonial Finances in Delaware.* Wilmington: Wilmington Trust Company, 1928.

The first act authorizing the issuance of paper money in Delaware was passed on April 25, 1723, and committed the three lower counties to a policy of paper money to be in use for over a half century. Illustrates the various issues of paper money and documents the authorized signers and trustees of the county loan offices. Published in an edition of 500 copies.

————. "Delaware Under Governor Keith, 1717-1726." *Delaware History* 3(March 1948): 1-36.

Includes the known addresses of Governor Keith dealing with the lower counties and the 1724 charter of New Castle.

————. "Early Relations of Delaware and Pennsylvania." *Pennsylvania Magazine of History and Biography* 54(1930): 209-240.

Reprinted in *Papers of the Historical Society of Delaware,* New Series No. 2, pp. 1-32. Wilmington: Historical Society of Delaware, 1930. Also reprinted in *The Collected Essays of Richard S. Rodney on Early Delaware,* pp. 53-76. Delaware's status as an independent state is explained.

————. "The End of Penn's Claim to Delaware, 1789-1814: Some Forgotten Lawsuits." *Pennsylvania Magazine of History and Biography* 61 (April 1937): 182-203.

Scharf, J. Thomas. *History of Delaware, 1609-1888.* Philadelphia: L. J. Richards, 1888. 2 vols.

Paged consecutively, Vol. 2 begins at p. 611. Index.

Schwartz, Sally. "Society and Culture in the Seventeenth-Century Delaware Valley." *Delaware History* 20(1982-1983): 98-122.

Unlike the ideologically tolerant society that developed under Penn's proprietorship, the tolerance of the earlier societies in the Delaware Valley was pragmatic in nature, the result of frequent changes in government and the need to attract and keep settlers.

Shepherd, William R. *History of Proprietary Government in Pennsylvania.* New York: Columbia University, 1896.

Index. Facsimile printed by AMS Press, Studies in History, Economics and Public Law 6 (New York, 1967).

"A Signer of the Declaration of Independence Orders Books from London: Two Documents of George Read of Delaware in the Hampton L. Carson Collection of the Free Library of Philadelphia." Edited by Howell J. Heaney. *American Journal of Legal History* 2(April 1958): 172-185.

Provides a description of the ninety-three law books ordered by Read in 1762.

Thayer, Theodore. *Pennsylvania Politics and the Growth of Democracy, 1740-1776.* Harrisburg: Pennsylvania Historical and Museum Commission, 1953.

Provides a study of the power struggle waged between the legislative assembly and the proprietors and the subsequent criticism of the Quaker Party after it had broken the power of the Penns. Index. Bibliography.

350 Years of New Castle, Delaware: Chapters in a Town's History Published in Honor of the 350th Anniversary of the Founding of New Castle, Delaware. Edited by Constance J. Cooper. Wilmington: Cedar Tree Books, New Castle Historical Society, 2001.

Bibliography.

Ward, Christopher. *The Dutch & Swedes on the Delaware, 1609-64.* Philadelphia: University of Pennsylvania Press, 1930.

Covers the discovery of Delaware Bay by Henry Hudson in 1609 through 1664 when the English took from the Dutch New Amsterdam and its appanage, the Delaware River Territory.

Weslager, C. A. "The City of Amsterdam's Colony on the Delaware, 1656-1664" with "Unpublished Dutch Notarial Abstracts." *Delaware History* 20(1982-1983): 1-26, 73-97.

————. *Dutch Explorers, Traders and Settlers in the Delaware Valley, 1609-1664.* Philadelphia: University of Pennsylvania Press, 1961.

Index. Appendix A includes Swanendael (Lewes) documents.

————. *The English on the Delaware: 1610-1682.* New Brunswick, NJ: Rutgers University Press, 1967.

Intended to be used as a companion to the author's *Dutch Explorers, Traders and Settlers in the Delaware Valley.* Index, appendixes, and maps.

————. *New Sweden on the Delaware: 1638-1655.* Wilmington: Middle Atlantic Press, Kalmar Nyckel Commemorative Committee, Delaware Heritage Commission, Swedish Council of America, 1988.

Bibliography.

————. *The Swedes and Dutch at New Castle.* New York: Middle Atlantic Press, 1987.

Describes the earliest settlement of the area of Delaware by Europeans. Provides information about treaties with the local Indians, actions of Dutch and Swedish officials, and the takeover by the English.

Wharton, Walter. *Land Survey Register, 1675-1679, West Side Delaware River, from Newcastle County, Delaware, into Bucks County, Pennsylvania.* Edited by Albert Cook Myers. Wilmington: Historical Society of Delaware, 1955.

Includes the area of "Big Bend" on the Brandywine through Christiana.

Williams, William H. *Slavery and Freedom in Delaware, 1639-1865.* Wilmington: Scholarly Resources, 1996.

A description and analysis of slavery and freedom and their impact on the lives of Delaware's whites and African Americans, within the context of the state's economic, social, and political history.

Wooley, Victor B. *Practice in Civil Actions and Proceedings in the Law Courts of the State of Delaware.* Wilmington: Star Printing, 1906. 2 vols.

Gives a good summation of the history of the colonial judiciary, the judicial system under William Penn, and the establishment of a more efficient judicial system under Lieutenant-Governor Gordon's administration (1726-1736) in Vol. 1, pp. 1-5.

Wuorinen, John H. *The Finns on the Delaware, 1638-1655, An Essay in American Colonial History.* New York: Columbia University Press, 1938.

A tercentenary publication with appendixes that include contemporary state legislative actions. Index.

Directory of Libraries and Archives

Delaware Public Archives
121 Duke of York St.
Dover, DE 19901
Phone: 302-744-5000
Fax: 302-739-1732
www.state.de.us/sos/dpa

Historical Society of Delaware Library
505 Market St.
Wilmington, DE 19801
Phone: 302-655-7161
Fax: 302-655-7844
www.hsd.org

Historical Society of Pennsylvania
1300 Locust St.
Philadelphia, PA 19107-5699
Phone: 215-732-6200
Fax: 215-732-2680
www.hsp.org

Legislative Council Library
PO Box 1401
Legislative Hall
Dover, DE 19903
Phone: 302-744-4308
Fax: 302-739-7322
www.delaware.gov

Library Company of Philadelphia
1314 Locust St.
Philadelphia, PA 19107
Phone: 215-546-3181
Fax: 215-546-5167
www.librarycompany.org

Pennsylvania Historical and Museum Commission
Pennsylvania State Archives
300 North St.
Harrisburg, PA 17120-0090
Phone: 717-787-3362
Fax: 717-783-9924
www.phmc.state.pa.us

University of Delaware
Morris Library, Special Collections
181 South College Ave.
Newark, DE 19717-5267

Phone: 302-831-2229
Fax: 302-831-6003
www.lib.udel.edu

Widener University School of Law
Legal Information Center
4601 Concord Pike
P.O. Box 7475
Wilmington, DE 19803
Phone: 302-477-2114
Fax: 302-477-2240
www.law.widener.edu/Law-Library.edu

NOTES

1. John A. Monroe, *Colonial Delaware: A History of the American Colonies* 3 (Millwood, NY: KTO Press, 1978).
2. Ibid. at 8.
3. Ibid. at 11.
4. Ibid. at 13.
5. Amandus Johnson, *The Swedish Settlements on the Delaware, Their History and Relation to the Indians, Dutch and English, 1638-1664, with an account of the South, the New Sweden, and the American Companies, and the Efforts of Sweden to Regain the Colony,* Vol. 1, 81 (Philadelphia: University of Pennsylvania Press, D. Appleton, 1911).
6. Monroe, supra note 1, at 22, 24.
7. Johnson, supra note 5, at 450. See also Amandus Johnson, *The Instructions for Johann Printz Governor of New Sweden, "The First Constitution or Supreme Law of the States of Pennsylvania and Delaware"; Translated from the Swedish with Introduction, Notes and Appendices, Including Letters from Governor John Winthrop, of Massachusetts, and Minutes of Courts, Sitting in New Sweden* 62-99 (Philadelphia: Swedish Colonial Society, 1930) (containing a complete translation of the instructions for Governor Printz).
8. See ibid. at 456.
9. See Monroe, supra note 1, at 41-42.
10. Ibid.
11. Ignatius C. Grubb, "The Colonial and State Judiciary of Delaware," *Papers of the Historical Society of Delaware* 17(1897): 4.
12. See *Laws and Writs of Appeal : 1647-1663,* edited and translated by Charles T. Gehring, New Netherland Document Series 16, Part 1 (S.L.: Holland Society of New York, Syracuse University Press, 1991); see also *Delaware Papers (Dutch Period): A Collection of Documents Pertaining to the Regulation of the Affairs on the South River of New Netherland, 1648-1664,* edited and translated by Charles T.

Gehring, New York Historical Manuscripts: (Dutch) 18-19 (Baltimore, MD: Genealogical Publishing, 1981).

13. See Monroe, supra note 1, at 59-62.

14. H. Clay Reed, "The Early New Castle Court," *Delaware History* 4(1951): 236.

15. Ibid. at 239-240.

16. Ibid. at 228.

17. H. Clay Reed and Joseph A. Palermo, "Justices of the Peace in Early Delaware," *Delaware History* 14(1971): 227.

18. Jeannette Eckman, *Delaware: A guide to the First State* 36 (2nd ed., New York: Hastings House, 1955).

19. See Carol E. Hoffecker, *Delaware: A Bicentennial History* 21 (New York: Norton, 1977).

20. Monroe, supra note 1, at 83. See infra *Proceedings of the Joint Session of the Legislature of the State of Delaware in Accepting the Gift of the Royal Charter of Charles II and the Deeds To William Penn of the Land and Waters Comprising the State of Delaware* to obtain an account of how the original charter documents came into the possession of the state of Delaware in 1909.

21. Hoffecker, supra note 19, at 141.

22. Monroe, supra note 1, at 84.

23. See Richard S. Rodney, "Early Relations of Delaware and Pennsylvania," *Pennsylvania Magazine of History and Biography* 14(1930): 235, reprinted in *The Collected Essays of Richard S. Rodney on Early Delaware* 59 (George H. Gibson, ed.; Wilmington: Society of Colonial Wars in the State of Delaware, 1975).

24. Monroe, supra note 1, at 120-121.

25. Ibid.; Rodney, supra note 23, at 237.

26. Grubb, supra note 11, at 14-15.

27. See William T. Quillen and Michael Hanrahan, "A Short History of the Delaware Court of Chancery—1792-1992," in *Court of Chancery of the State of Delaware 1792-1992,* 23-24 (S.L.: Bicentennial Commemoration Committee of the Historical Society for the Court of Chancery of the State of Delaware, 1992), reprinted in *Delaware Journal of Corporate Law* 18(1993): 822-824; see also Quillen, "Equity Jurisdiction in Delaware Before 1792," *Delaware Lawyer* 2(1984): 18.

28. William T. Quillen, "Equity Jurisdiction in Delaware Before 1792," *Delaware Lawyer* 2(1984): 24.

29. See Harold Hancock, "Delaware's Captured Colonial Records," *Delaware History* 9(1960-1961): 355 (contains an account of how colonial sources were saved from complete destruction).

30. Monroe, supra note 1, at 139-140.

31. Ibid. at 143.

32. Rodney, supra note 23, at 209.

Chapter 9

The Legal History
of the District of Columbia
Prior to Home Rule:
A Bibliographic Essay

Luis M. Acosta

INTRODUCTION

As the capital of the United States since 1800, the District of Columbia
has been the setting of profound political and social transformation. The local history of the District is an important part of the national history of the
United States. Historians, political scientists, and legal scholars often have
occasion to research aspects of the legal history and governance of the seat
of the federal government.

The main focus of this book is the prestatehood history of the fifty states.
Unlike states that had colonial histories prior to the establishment of the
United States, the District of Columbia did not exist as a colony. Moreover,
in the case of the District of Columbia, the prestatehood era continues to the
present, and statehood is only one of several possible futures for the District.[1] Still, the District has many of the characteristics of a state, and often is
deemed a state for legal purposes.[2] Over the course of 200 years, the District
has developed its own distinct political culture like that of a state.

In keeping with the historical focus of this book, this chapter will cover
the legal history of the District of Columbia prior to the passage in 1973 of
the District of Columbia Home Rule Act,[3] which provided limited home
rule and set forth the current basic framework for governance in the District.

The forms of local government, degrees of relative local autonomy, and
sources of law in the District fluctuated greatly prior to home rule. The first
part of this chapter provides a chronological description of the various legal
and political structures that created local law in the District during the pre-
home rule era. The court system in the District of Columbia has its own
complex history, and the second part of this chapter describes the history of

the courts of the District. The final part describes resources for researching the pre-home rule law and legal history of the District.

HISTORY AND GOVERNANCE
OF THE DISTRICT OF COLUMBIA

The Constitutional Provision for a National Capital

During the revolutionary period, the Continental and Confederation Congresses met in several different cities.[4] For various reasons, the delegates to the Constitutional Convention determined that a single, permanent seat for the federal government would be advantageous,[5] and provided that the Congress is empowered:

> To exercise exclusive Legislation in all Cases whatsoever, over such District (not exceeding 10 miles square) as may, by Cession of Particular States, and the Acceptance of Congress, become the Seat of the Government of the United States, and to exercise like Authority over all Places purchased by the Consent of the Legislature of the State in which the Same shall be, for the Erection of Forts, Magazines, Arsenals, dock-Yards, and other needful Buildings.[6]

While the existence of a separate federal seat of government was provided for at the Constitutional Convention, controversy about the location of the seat of government (the "residency question") was avoided at the Convention and the ratification debates by leaving that matter for the first Congress.[7]

Location of the National Capital

During the first session of the first Congress, convened in New York on March 4, 1789, the residency question evoked considerable strategic maneuvering among sectional interests. Both houses of Congress voted to permanently locate the capital in Germantown, Pennsylvania, but final action was not taken before adjournment of the first session.[8] In the second session of the first Congress, convened January 1790, the unfinished business from the first session was wiped clean.[9] After further bargaining and maneuvering, the question of the capital's location became intertwined with a separate controversy, Alexander Hamilton's proposal for the federal assumption of the states' debts from the Revolutionary War (which proposal most southern states opposed). A deal was struck, and in the "Compromise of

1790," it was agreed that the federal government would assume outstanding state debts, while the permanent seat of government would reside, after a ten-year temporary placement in Philadelphia, on the Potomac River, at an exact location to be chosen by the president.[10]

The Residency Act provided that the existing state law in the land set aside for the district would not be affected until the seat of government was placed there.[11] The act also authorized the president to appoint three commissioners to survey, define, and acquire the ten-by-ten mile territory within a specified seventy-mile stretch of the Potomac.[12]

President George Washington immediately set upon the task of defining and acquiring the territory, and was ready when Congress reconvened in January 1791 to announce the location on the Potomac where he intended to place the capital. In a presidential proclamation dated January 24, 1791, President Washington defined the territory at a point along the Potomac that encompassed the existing municipalities of Georgetown, Maryland, and Alexandria, Virginia.[13]

The Residency Act was amended on March 3, 1791, to expand somewhat the area covered by the statute, in order to allow the inclusion of Alexandria, as President Washington wanted.[14]

During the period Congress met in Philadelphia, President Washington worked to transform the city of Washington into a place suitable for a national capital. Washington commissioned Pierre-Charles L'Enfant, a French engineer and architect who served in the American Revolutionary War, to develop a plan for the city (see Figure 9.1). Because Congress gave exclusive authority to the president for appointing the commissioners and did not appropriate any money for the construction of federal buildings in the new capital, President Washington had exclusive authority to control development of the District, and he worked diligently, until his death in 1799, to establish the new city so that it would be ready to serve as the seat of government.[15]

Early Governance of the Capital

The groundwork having been laid by President Washington, the federal capital moved to the city of Washington in 1800.[16] But the question of the form of government in the territory had been deferred.[17] Congress finally addressed the question of the governance of the District while it met there for the first time. In an act approved February 27, 1801, the Organic Act of 1801, Congress:

Provided that the accumulated laws of Maryland and Virginia as they existed as of 1801 would continue in force in the respective portions of the District ceded by these states (section 1);

Provided that the District would be divided into two counties: the county of Washington (on the Maryland side) and the county of Alexandria (on the Virginia side) (section 2);

Created a court for the District, the Circuit Court of the District of Columbia, which was given general trial and appellate jurisdiction over criminal matters and civil matters in law and equity arising within the District, as well as civil matters at law or equity in which the U.S. was a plaintiff, and seizures, penalties or forfeitures arising under the laws of the U.S. (sections 3-6);[18] and

Provided that the powers of the existing corporations of Georgetown and Alexandria would not be impaired (except with respect to the powers of the municipal courts, which were transferred to the new circuit court) (section 16).[19]

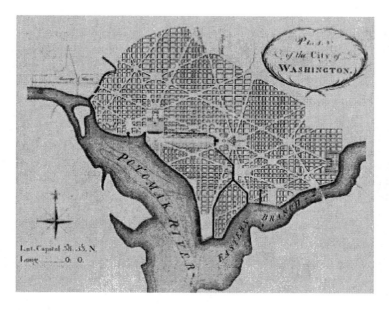

FIGURE 9.1. Pierre Charles L'Enfant's Plan of the City of Washington, as published in *The Universal Asylum and Columbian Magazine,* March 1792. *Source:* Library of Congress Geography and Map Division, <http://hdl.loc.gov/loc.gmd/g3850.ct000509>.

The following year, in May 1802, Congress passed an act formally incorporating the city of Washington.[20] This act provided for a mayor to be appointed by the president, for a twelve-member city council to be elected annually by white male taxpaying residents, and for the city government to have the power to pass ordinances, impose taxes, and regulate certain specified activities.

Thus under the Organic Act of 1801 and the 1802 act incorporating the city of Washington, there were five units of local government within the District of Columbia: the cities of Washington, Georgetown, and Alexandria, and the counties of Washington and Alexandria. On the Maryland side, the law consisted of federal law, the statutes, and common law in effect in Maryland as of 1801, except as modified by later acts of Congress, and the ordinances of Georgetown, the city of Washington, and the county of Washington. Similarly, on the Virginia side, the law consisted of federal law, the statutes, and common law of Virginia operative as of 1801, except as modified by Congress, and the ordinances of the city and county of Alexandria.

In 1804, Congress passed a law that extended the city of Washington's charter for another fifteen years, expanded the number of members in each house to nine members each, and enlarged its regulatory powers.[21] Congress amended the Charter of Alexandria at the same time.[22]

In 1812, Congress amended the charter of the city of Washington to change the structure of the city council so that it consisted of an eight-member board of aldermen elected for two-year terms and a twelve-member common council elected for one-year terms. It also provided for the election of the mayor by the two houses of the city council, and again expanded the city's powers to regulate and tax.[23]

In 1820, the former city charter expired and Congress enacted a new charter that allowed for direct election of the mayor by white male property owners. The new charter reduced the number of members of the board of aldermen and the common council, and also enlarged self-rule by enhancing various municipal regulatory powers.[24]

Retrocession of Alexandria

As early as 1802, there had been intermittent discussion of retrocession of the two parts of the District to Maryland and Virginia as a solution to the problem of lack of political rights for residents of the District.[25] In Alexandria, where no federal buildings were located, there were fewer benefits from being part of the District of Columbia. After years of maneuvering among Alexandria citizens before the federal and Virginia legislatures,[26] on July 9, 1846, legislation was signed into law by President James Polk allowing Alexandria to retrocede, contingent on approval in a referendum among eligible voters.[27] The referendum was held on September 1 and 2, 1846, and the eligible white male voters in Alexandria voted overwhelmingly in favor of retrocession.[28] On September 7, 1846, President Polk issued a proclamation transferring jurisdiction from the federal government to Virginia.[29] On March 13, 1847, the Virginia legislature passed a bill accepting the retrocession, thus turning qualified residents of Alexandria into full Virginia citizens.[30]

Antebellum and Civil War Periods

The charter of 1820 for the city of Washington remained in effect until 1848. That year, Congress approved without change a new charter that had been drafted by city residents. The 1848 charter abolished the property qualifications for voting and allowed all white males who had paid the school tax to vote. It also increased the number of offices that were subject to vote and expanded the powers of the municipal government.[31]

Because Maryland and (until 1846) Virginia law applied in the District, except as modified by congressional action, in the absence of abolition by the federal government slavery remained legal in the national capital until the Civil War period.[32] Indeed, the federal government, through the federal marshal and other offices, enforced the right to own, buy, and sell slaves in the District during the first half of the nineteenth century.[33] The federal government often held slaves for safekeeping on behalf of slaveholders, and at times even seized and sold slaves to satisfy an adjudicated claim of the United States.[34] The federal government also enforced federal, state, and municipal laws aimed at controlling free blacks.[35] Under laws inherited from Maryland and Virginia, black people apprehended in the District who could not prove they were free were assumed to be runaway slaves and would be jailed. In the event they went unclaimed as property but still could not prove they were free, the federal marshal would sell them into slavery to pay the cost of the incarceration.[36] During the early months of the Civil War prior to emancipation, runaway slaves from Maryland were still subject to capture and return to their masters by the federal marshal; in some instances Union soldiers abducted runaways from the marshal before he could return them to slavery in Maryland.[37]

Trading in slaves in the District was abolished as part of the Compromise of 1850.[38] Slavery in the District was ended when President Abraham Lincoln signed the District of Columbia Emancipation Act on April 16, 1862, nine months prior to the Emancipation Proclamation.[39] Notwithstanding emancipation in the District, the Circuit Court of the District of Columbia continued to enforce the Fugitive Slave Law on behalf of slaveholders in Maryland.[40]

The Civil War increased the significance of the District of Columbia in national affairs. Washington was the headquarters of the Army of the Potomac and was a primary target of the Confederate army. The District was protected by a surrounding ring of federal forts. Federal attention to the District grew tremendously during the war, as did Washington's population. The city was filled with wounded soldiers in hospitals and improvised wards in buildings throughout the city, some commandeered by the Army.[41]

By an act passed August 6, 1861, a metropolitan police force under federal control was established.[42]

After the Civil War, in December 1866, Congress passed a bill granting universal male suffrage in the District, which was opposed by the council of the city of Washington. President Andrew Johnson vetoed this bill, but Congress overrode the veto, and it became law on January 8, 1867.[43]

Territorial Government

On February 21, 1871, President Grant signed into law an act containing two far-reaching changes for the District.[44] First, a new municipal corporation bearing the name "District of Columbia," encompassing the entire area within the boundaries of the District, was established.[45] The District of Columbia became the successor to the cities of Washington and Georgetown and the county of Washington.[46] Second, a new government for the District of Columbia was established, with a governor and upper chamber appointed by the president, and the lower chamber popularly elected.[47] The law also provided for the first time for a nonvoting delegate to Congress, popularly elected by district voters.[48]

The territorial government lasted only three years, because of financial mismanagement by the offices and boards appointed by the president, most notably by Alexander "Boss" Shepherd, an appointed member of the Board of Public Works (and appointed as governor of the District in 1873), who undertook massive public works projects that dramatically overspent the available funds.[49]

Commissioner Form of Government

Congress replaced the territorial government with a three-member board of commissioners, appointed by the president, to administer local government, one of whom would be an officer from the Army Corps of Engineers dedicated to oversee public works in the District.[50] The board of commissioners served a dual role as the head of the executive branch in the District and as a legislature, enacting ordinances within parameters of authority set by Congress. More important legislation required congressional action.[51]

The act creating the board of commissioners intended this arrangement to be temporary; it called for the creation of a joint select committee to determine a "suitable frame of government" for the District.[52] Such a committee was created, but the committee's report called for making permanent the commissioner form of government.[53] Legislation implementing this recommendation was enacted in 1878.[54]

Despite significant recognition of its deficiencies from the standpoint of both the democratic rights of District residents and efficiency,[55] the commissioner form of government remained in effect for ninety-four years, until 1967. Its inadequacies were apparent well before then. By 1939, a study commissioned by Congress described the system of government, which by then consisted of over sixty agencies in addition to numerous boards and committees lacking effective coordination, as "unbelievably complex, confused, illogical, and cumbersome."[56]

In 1952, President Truman sent to Congress his Reorganization Plan No. 5,[57] pursuant to the Reorganization Act of 1949.[58] Because there was no congressional resolution of disapproval, the plan became effective July 1, 1952. It gave authority to the commissioners to reorganize the agencies and offices of the city. Pursuant to this authority, the commissioners consolidated ninety-four local government entities into thirteen departments, four boards, and six offices, and centralized common administrative services.[59] In 1954, Congress reasserted its authority over the District of Columbia by rescinding Reorganization Plan No. 5.[60]

Reform in district government, which was favored by a bipartisan majority in Congress and all of the post-WWII presidents, was hindered by the control of the House Committee on the District of Columbia by southern segregationists, most notably Representative John McMillan of South Carolina, who chaired the committee for most of the period from 1949 to 1972. During the 1950s, African Americans became a majority of the population in Washington; however congressmen who controlled the House committee opposed the empowerment of black people, and obstructed reform efforts that would have increased District residents' self-determination.[61]

In 1960, legislation for a constitutional amendment outlawing the poll tax was introduced in Congress.[62] In debate in the Senate, this legislation was amended to include extending federal suffrage to District of Columbia residents, including proportional representation in the House (which at the time would have given the District three seats), and in the Electoral College (which would probably have given the District five electoral votes); the legislation passed the Senate as amended.[63] The House killed the poll tax portion of the legislation but agreed to a watered-down version of the District suffrage proposal that did not include congressional representation and limited the number of the District's electoral votes to that of the least populous state; the Senate agreed to the House amendment.[64] The amendment was ratified by the states by March 1961, and it became the Twenty-Third Amendment to the U.S. Constitution.[65]

Movement Toward Home Rule

In 1967, President Lyndon Johnson sent to Congress Reorganization Plan No. 3.[66] This plan replaced the three-commissioner form of government with a single mayor/commissioner, who would handle executive functions, and a nine-member council that would perform legislative or quasi-legislative functions. Under this plan both the mayor/commissioner and the council were appointed by the president, with the advice and consent of the Senate. Efforts in the House to disapprove the plan failed, and it was adopted August 11, 1967. President Johnson appointed Walter E. Washington, an African American, as mayor/commissioner, and appointed a racially mixed city council.[67]

Several further measures toward greater district self-representation followed over the next few years. In 1968, Congress enacted legislation providing for the popular election of the board of education.[68] In 1970, Congress enacted the District of Columbia Court Reform and Criminal Procedure Act, which created a comprehensive local court system.[69]

In 1972, Congressman McMillan was defeated in the Democratic primary. In the 93rd Congress, which convened in 1973, Congressman Charles Diggs of Michigan, a home-rule supporter, became chair of the House Committee on the District. That year, after prolonged negotiation among proponents of different versions of home rule legislation, on December 24, 1973, President Nixon signed the District of Columbia Self-Government and Governmental Reorganization Act, also known as the Home Rule Act.[70] The Home Rule Act provided, inter alia, for the popular election of a mayor and a thirteen-member legislative council, which was given legislative authority over "all rightful subjects of legislation," with limited exceptions. This act established the basic form under which the District government currently operates.

HISTORY OF THE COURTS
IN THE DISTRICT OF COLUMBIA

As with the legislative and executive branches of government, the judicial branch in the District of Columbia saw numerous changes throughout the pre-home rule era.

Courts During the Development of the District

During the period from 1790 to 1800, before the federal government moved to the District, the laws of Maryland and Virginia continued to apply in the territory chosen for the seat of government. The existing courts in Alexandria and Georgetown continued in existence. While the city of Washington was being developed in preparation for becoming the seat of government, the litigation that arose was heard in the courts of Maryland, in Annapolis.[71]

The Circuit Court of the District of Columbia
and Its Successors

The Organic Act of 1801 created the Circuit Court of the District of Columbia, the predecessor to what is now called the U.S. Court of Appeals for the District of Columbia Circuit. The organic act gave the circuit court very broad jurisdiction, including jurisdiction over various federal matters, as well as civil and criminal matters arising locally. It possessed both trial and appellate jurisdiction.[72] The circuit court held sessions both in Washington County, where Maryland law applied, and in Alexandria County, where Virginia law applied.[73] While generally the powers of the municipalities of Alexandria and Georgetown were retained under the organic act, the circuit court was given the powers of the courts of these cities.[74]

The Circuit Court of the District of Columbia was the highest court of original jurisdiction in the District of Columbia, similar to that of the highest court of a state court system, and pursuant to the organic act obtained subject matter jurisdiction coextensive with that of the Maryland Court of Appeals under the laws of the State of Maryland as they existed in February 1801. This included the equitable and common law powers of English courts as they existed in 1776. Because of this, unlike other federal circuit courts throughout the country at this time, the Circuit Court of the District of Columbia possessed common law powers such as the power to issue a writ of mandamus.[75]

As the capital developed, the circuit court's broad jurisdiction made its docket a busy one.[76] Congress took several steps that altered the circuit court's jurisdiction. On March 1, 1823, the jurisdictional amount in controversy that justices of the peace could hear was increased from $20 to $50, to help relieve the circuit court's docket.[77] In 1838, Congress created a specialized court, the Criminal Court of the District of Columbia, to handle the circuit court's criminal docket. Appeals from the criminal court remained with the circuit court.[78] With the retrocession of Alexandria to Virginia in 1846, the Alexandria County division of the circuit court was abolished, freeing the circuit court from having to hear local matters arising in Alexandria.[79] Although these developments contracted the circuit court's jurisdiction in some respects, the court over time also gained jurisdiction over various matters.[80]

In 1863, the Circuit Court of the District of Columbia ran afoul of President Lincoln in a dispute involving the court's power to issue the writ of habeas corpus against the Union government. In order to remove judges he felt were unsupportive of the war effort, President Lincoln requested that Congress abolish the circuit court. Congress did so, abolishing the circuit court, district court, and criminal court, and in their place created a new court named the Supreme Court of the District of Columbia, with jurisdiction encompassing that of the former courts.[81]

In 1893, in order to rectify the circumstance of judges sitting on the appeal of cases they tried in the first instance, Congress gave the appellate jurisdiction of the Supreme Court of the District of Columbia to a new appellate court, the Court of Appeals of the District of Columbia, to hear appeals from the supreme court.[82]

In 1934, after the U.S. Supreme Court ruled that the Court of Appeals for the District of Columbia and the Supreme Court of the District of Columbia were in the nature of Article III courts,[83] Congress renamed the Court of Appeals the "United States Court of Appeals for the District of Columbia" to reflect that status.[84] Likewise, in 1936, Congress renamed the Supreme Court of the District of Columbia the "United States District Court for the District of Columbia."[85]

In 1948, Congress renamed the court of appeals the United States Court of Appeals for the District of Columbia Circuit and designated it as one of the judicial circuits of the United States.[86] In 1970, Congress relieved the court of its jurisdiction over local matters and placed that jurisdiction in the District of Columbia Court of Appeals; the latter court became the court of last resort over local matters.[87]

Lower Courts in the District

A variety of inferior courts existed throughout the District of Columbia's history prior to the 1973 Home Rule Act. The Organic Act of 1801, in addition to creating the Circuit Court of the District of Columbia, also created the office of the justices of the peace, with jurisdiction over matters up to $20.[88] The act also provided for establishment of an orphan's court and a register of wills, for probate matters.[89] Shortly thereafter, a levy court, similar to the levy courts of Maryland counties, was established to handle certain types of executive matters that arose in Washington County.[90]

A United States District Court was also established for the District of Columbia under the circuit court by the Judiciary Act of April 29, 1802, with the same limited powers other U.S. district courts had at that time.[91]

By Act of June 17, 1870, the Police Court of the District of Columbia was established to handle minor criminal offenses, generally those not punishable by imprisonment in the penitentiary.[92] A few days later, by an act dated June 21, 1870, Congress abolished the orphan's court and transferred its jurisdiction to the Supreme Court of the District of Columbia.[93]

On March 19, 1906, the juvenile court was created to take over all criminal matters handled by the police court involving juvenile delinquents.[94] In 1938, Congress passed a law overhauling the juvenile court to bring it within contemporary conceptions of juvenile justice.[95]

In 1909, the Municipal Court of the District of Columbia was created to replace the office of the justices of the peace.[96] In 1921, the municipal court's jurisdiction was expanded to increase the amount in controversy (and thereby help relieve a busy docket at the D.C. supreme court); to allow it to hear trials by jury; to make it a court of record; and to provide for direct appeals to the Court of Appeals for the District of Columbia.[97]

In 1942, the jurisdiction of the police court was merged into the municipal court, so that the municipal court heard both civil and criminal matters.[98] In the same legislation, Congress created the municipal court of appeals, to serve as an intermediate appellate court hearing appeals from the municipal court. Appeals from decisions of the municipal court of appeals could be heard as a discretionary matter by the U.S. Court of Appeals for D.C.

In 1962, Congress changed the name of the municipal court to the District of Columbia Court of General Sessions, and changed the name of the municipal court of appeals to the District of Columbia Court of Appeals.[99]

1970 Reorganization of the Court System

From 1801 until 1970, the United States Court of Appeals for the District of Columbia Circuit and the United States District Court for the District of

Columbia, and their predecessors, were possessed of both federal jurisdiction and extensive local jurisdiction over matters arising in the District of Columbia. In 1970, Congress undertook a comprehensive reorganization of the D.C. courts and created the District of Columbia Court of Appeals and the Superior Court of the District of Columbia. Congress withdrew the local jurisdiction from the D.C. Circuit and U.S. District Court for the District of Columbia and made those courts exclusively federal.[100] The District of Columbia Court of Appeals became a unitary appellate court that has the final word on matters of District of Columbia law, like that of the highest court of a state. The various lower courts of the District of Columbia were folded into various divisions of the superior court, so that the former jurisdiction of the court of general sessions was placed in the Civil Division, the former jurisdiction of the juvenile court was placed in the Family Division, and so on. The basic structure for the local courts of D.C. created by the Court Reform Act continues to the present with only minor changes.

BIBLIOGRAPHY

Legislation

Codification of D.C. Laws

For years, beginning in the earliest decades of the District of Columbia's existence, confusion about applicable law in the District resulted in calls for an official codification. The confusion rested largely from the multitude of sources of law deemed to apply in the District, which included the principles of equity, the common law, and statutes that existed in England in 1776; the laws inherited from colonial Maryland and the state of Maryland at the time of the 1801 organic act (which were applicable on the Maryland side of the District); the laws inherited from colonial Virginia and the state of Virginia in 1801 (which were applicable on the Virginia side of the District prior to retrocession); and the laws passed by the U.S. Congress relating to the District.[101]

A series of unofficial codes of the law of the District of Columbia were published, including some prepared under the direction of the U.S. Congress, but it was not until 1901 that Congress officially approved a version of the District of Columbia Code and thereby provided some clarity regarding the positive law for the District.[102]

Prior to 1901, several separate versions of the District of Columbia Code had been formally submitted to Congress for approval but were not taken up, and one version was submitted to the voting citizens of the District in 1858 but was rejected.[103] Although these pre-1901 codes did not by themselves serve as evidence of positive law in the District, they were cited by courts as authoritative and demonstrate the prevailing understanding of District law by prominent members of the District Bar. They include the following.

Code of laws for the District of Columbia: Prepared under the Authority of the Act of Congress of the 29th of April, 1816, Entitled "An act authorizing the judges of the Circuit Court, and the attorney for the District of Columbia, to prepare a code of jurisprudence for the said District." W. Cranch, ed. Washington, DC: Davis and Force, 1819.

The Revised Code of the District of Columbia, Prepared Under the Authority of the Act of Congress, entitled "An act to improve the laws of the District of Columbia, and to codify the same," Approved March 3, 1855. Robert Ould and William B.B. Cross, eds. Washington, DC: A.O.P. Nicholson, Public Printers, 1857.

Revision of the Laws of the District of Columbia, Prepared by the Commissioners Appointed under the Act of the Legislative Assembly of the District of Columbia, Approved December 18, 1871. Washington, DC: Government Printing Office, 1873.

Several other statutory compilations and unofficial versions of the D.C. Code are mentioned in the article "History of the D.C. Code" reprinted in volume 1 of the current *District of Columbia Code Annotated*.[104]

The 1901 District of Columbia Code, printed in full in volume 31 of the *United States Statutes at Large* at pages 1189 to 1436, was approved by Congress by an act of March 3, 1901, and provided that as of the effective date of January 1, 1902:

> The common law, all British statutes in force in Maryland on the twenty-seventh day of February, eighteen hundred and one, the principles of equity and admiralty, all general acts of Congress not locally inapplicable in the District of Columbia, and all acts of Congress by their terms applicable to the District of Columbia and to other placed under the jurisdiction of the United States, in force at the date of the passage of this act shall remain in force except in so far as the same are inconsistent with, or are replaced by, some provision of this code.[105]

A code covering District law as amended through March 4, 1929, was prepared under the auspices of the House Committee on Revision of the Laws.[106] A new edition followed in 1940.[107] Editions of the D.C. Code prepared under the direction of the House Judiciary Committee were prepared in 1951,[108] 1961,[109] and 1967.[110] The House Office of the Law Revision Council published another edition in 1973.[111] Since the onset of home rule, codification of District law has been under the authority of the D.C. Council.

D.C. Legislation by United States Congress

Prior to home rule, significant legislation pertaining to the District of Columbia was enacted by the U.S. Congress. Such legislation is available in sources in which federal legislation is published, such as the *United States Statutes at Large*.[112] In addition, at times federal legislation specific to the District has been compiled. For example, a publication compiling the acts of Congress relating to the District of Columbia was published in 1831.[113] A similar publication, *Acts of Congress Affecting the District of Columbia,* was compiled and published by the Commissioners of the District from approximately 1877 to 1964.

Legislative history and related legislative materials produced by the U.S. Congress regarding the District of Columbia can be researched in the same manner as other types of historical Congressional materials, through the use of finding aids such as the *CIS U.S. Serial Set Index,* the *CIS Congressional Committee Hearings Index,* and the like.[114] Numerous hearings and committee prints by the House and Senate Committees on the District have been published by the Government Printing Office.[115] The extensive holdings in the National Archives of records of the House Committee on the District of Columbia, maintained in Record Group 233, are described in Chapter 8 of the *Guide to the Records of the United States House of Representatives at the National Archives,* H.R. Doc. No. 100-245, at 113-22 (1989), which is available on the Web at <http://www.archives.gov/records_of_congress/house_guide/chapter_08.html>. The similarly extensive holdings in the National Archives of the Senate Committee on the District of Columbia, held in Record Group 46, are described in Chapter 8 of the *Guide to the Records of the United States Senate at the National Archives,* S. Doc. No. 100-42, at 87-93 (1989), which is available on the Web at <http://www.archives.gov/records_of_congress/senate_guide/chapter_08.html>.

Municipal Ordinances and Regulations

Corporation of Alexandria: Many of the records of the Corporation of Alexandria, including those from the period prior to its retrocession to Virginia, are available on microfilm at the Special Collections division of the Alexandria Library. In addition, various compilations of the laws of Alexandria were occasionally published.[116]

Corporation of Georgetown: The ordinances and resolutions of the Corporation of Georgetown for the period from 1791 to 1871, and indexes thereto, as well as other records of the Corporation of Georgetown, are available at the National Archives in Record Group 351. In addition, some published collections of historical Georgetown ordinances are available.[117]

City of Washington: As noted previously, the city of Washington was formally incorporated in 1802 and existed as an entity separate from the District of Columbia until the 1871 formation of the territorial government. Volumes entitled *Laws of the Corporation of the City of Washington* were published regularly, usually on an annual basis, from 1803 to 1870, and printed by various publishers under the direction of the council of the city. There are also some compilations of the ordinances of the city of Washington, including Andrew Rothwell, *Laws of the Corporation of Washington, to the End of the Thirtieth Council* (Washington, DC: F.W. De. Krafft, Printer, 1833); James W. Sheahan, *Corporation Laws of the City of Washington, to the End of the Fiftieth Council* (Washington, DC: R.A. Waters, 1853); and William B. Webb, *Laws of the Corporation of the City of Washington* (Washington, DC: R.A. Waters, 1868). Other records of the city of Washington are available at the National Archives in Record Group 351.

County of Washington: The county of Washington, which prior to the territorial government of 1871 consisted of that area within the Maryland side of the District of Columbia outside the corporate boundaries of Georgetown and the city of Washington, was governed by the levy court, which, in addition to the functions of justices of the peace, engaged in various administrative duties including levying taxes and financing roads and bridges. Records of the proceedings of the levy court are available at the National Archives in Record Group 351. In addition, some published ordinances by the levy court are available at the Library of Congress.[118]

Territorial Government: Acts of the Legislative Assembly of the Territorial Government, which existed from 1871 to 1874, were published in various collections.[119] Manuscript copies of the acts of the territorial government are available at the National Archives in Record Group 351.

Commissioner Government: For the period 1874 to 1952, meeting minutes and orders of the board of commissioners that governed the District of Columbia were published. These contain ordinances and administrative materials. These are available at the National Archives in Record Group 351. In addition, beginning in 1874, the commissioners published *Annual Reports,* which describe various administrative matters such as the finances of the District, public improvements, education, and the like. The *Annual Reports* are available in the National Archives, the Washingtoniana Division of the D.C. Library, and the Library of Congress.

On July 19, 1954, the Board of Commissioners began publishing the *District of Columbia Register.* The *D.C. Register* includes proposed regulations, adopted regulations, information on changes in the organization of the District government, notices of public hearings, and other matters of general public interest. Early volumes of the *D.C. Register* are available at libraries with extensive District of Columbia holdings.

Government Under Reorganization Plan No. 3: In 1967, the quasi-legislative powers previously enjoyed by the commissioners (prescribing regulations, setting local taxes, and the like) were turned over to the District of Columbia Council.[120] Notice of actions adopting, amending, or repealing regulations was required to be published in the *D.C. Register.*[121] The mayor/commissioner was required to publish an indexed version of the *D.C. Register* that would compile all rules adopted and in effect at the time of the publication.[122] These compiled versions were called "Special Editions" of the *D.C. Register,* and were published intermittently by title.

Miscellaneous Compilations of Legislation

Unofficial compilations of legislation applicable in the District of Columbia of particular historical interest include the following.

Worthington G. Snethen, *The Black Code of the District of Columbia in Force September 1st, 1848.* William Harned, 1848.

Digitally reproduced in the *History Resource Center: U.S.,* Gale Group, <http://galenet.galegroup.com/servlet/HistRC>.

Slavery Code of the District of Columbia, 1860. N.p. 1860. Available at <http://memory.loc.gov/ammem/sthtml/stpres02.html>.

The Slavery Code of the District of Columbia, Together with Notes and Judicial Decisions Explanatory of the Same, by a Member of the Washington Bar. Washington, DC: L. Towers and Co., Printers, 1862. Available at <http://memory.loc.gov/ammem/sthtml/stpres02.html> (see Figure 9.2).

THE

SLAVERY CODE

OF THE

DISTRICT OF COLUMBIA,

TOGETHER

WITH NOTES AND JUDICIAL DECISIONS EXPLANA-
TORY OF THE SAME.

BY A MEMBER OF THE WASHINGTON BAR.

WASHINGTON:
L. TOWERS & CO., PRINTERS.
1862.

FIGURE 9.2. Title Page from *The Slavery Code of the District of Columbia, Together with Notes and Judicial Decisions Explanatory of the Same, by a Member of the Washington Bar* (Washington, DC: L. Towers and Co., Printers, 1862).

Case Law

Circuit Court of the District of Columbia and Successors

As noted earlier, the court presently known as the United States Court of Appeals for the District of Columbia Circuit ("D.C. Circuit") is the successor to the court created by the Organic Act of 1801 as the Circuit Court of the District of Columbia. The majority of published decisions issued by the D.C. Circuit and its predecessors have been reprinted in the various federal reporters published by West Publishing, including the *Federal Cases* and the three *Federal Reporter* series,[123] as well as the Westlaw "District of Columbia Cases" database and the Lexis "D.C. Circuit Court" database. For certain bibliographic and research purposes, however, it is valuable to be aware of the history of the publication of the opinions of the Circuit Court of the District of Columbia and its successors.

The modern system of official court reporters in which the opinions of the D.C. Circuit are published is called the *United States Court of Appeals Reports,* abbreviated as "U.S. App. D.C." The numbering of this reporter has been sequential beginning with Volume 1 of the reporter called *Appeal Cases, District of Columbia* (abbreviated "App. D.C."), published in 1893, which reported cases issued by the Court of Appeals for the District of Columbia.

Opinions by the Circuit Court of the District of Columbia (1801 to 1863) and the Supreme Court of the District of Columbia (1863 to 1893) were published in various nominative reporters, sometimes referred to collectively as the "District of Columbia Reports."[124] The early case law of the Circuit Court of the District of Columbia was first published by William Cranch in a six-volume set covering decisions issued from 1801 to 1840. The first five volumes of the Cranch set consist of decisions by the circuit court, while the sixth volume is an index of the cases in the first five volumes. Decisions by the circuit court for the period following the Cranch period were published by John A. Hayward and George C. Hazleton, who published two volumes of decisions, the first covering the 1840 through 1850 terms and the second covering the 1851 through 1863 terms.[125]

In 1863 the Supreme Court of the District of Columbia replaced the Circuit Court of the District of Columbia. Decisions from 1863 to 1869 were subsequently published in a reporter by Franklin H. Mackey, and decisions from 1869 to 1872 were published in a second volume by Mackey. The reporter MacArthur published three volumes of opinions by the Supreme Court of the District of Columbia dating from the period from 1873 to 1879. Next, MacArthur and Mackey teamed up to publish one volume of decisions issued in 1879-1880. Thereafter, Mackey published nine additional volumes of decisions by the Supreme Court of the District of Columbia, which decisions were issued during the period 1880 to 1892. Last, one volume was published by the reporters Tucker and Clephane, consisting of decisions issued by the Supreme Court of the District of Columbia during 1892-1893.[126] With the advent of the Court of Appeals for the District of

Columbia, in 1893, Volume 1 of *Appeal Cases, District of Columbia* commenced.

Minor Courts

With limited exceptions, the decisions of the inferior courts of the District of Columbia generally were not published. In rare instances, decisions of inferior D.C. courts were published in the nominative reporters.[127] The *Daily Washington Law Reporter,* which began publishing in 1874, throughout its history has published selected opinions, as well as legal notices and stories, relating to matters in the District of Columbia courts, including the lower courts. Decisions of the Municipal Court of Appeals (1942-1962) and the District of Columbia Court of Appeals (1962-present) have been published in West's *Atlantic Reporter, Second Series.*

Supreme Court Case Law Affecting the District

In addition to the decisions of the District of Columbia courts, it should be noted that there have been a number of cases by the U.S. Supreme Court directly relating to the governance and law of the District of Columbia. Among the more significant decisions are *Loughborough v. Blake,* 18 U.S. (5 Wheat.) 317 (1820) (Congress may tax residents of the District of Columbia despite their lack of representation in Congress); *Hepburn v. Ellzey,* 6 U.S. (2 Cranch) 445 (1804) (District of Columbia is not a "state" for purposes of establishing diversity of citizenship for jurisdictional purposes); *National Mutual Ins. Co. v. Tidewater Transfer Co.,* 337 U.S. 582 (1949) (upholding constitutionality of 1940 statute that made D.C. residents diverse from nonresidents for jurisdictional purposes); *O'Donoghue v. United States,* 389 U.S. 516 (1933) (District of Columbia Court of Appeals and Supreme Court of the District of Columbia constitute Article III courts).

Resources on District of Columbia History

There are several excellent libraries and archives that researchers inquiring into the legal history of the District of Columbia should be aware of, some of which have already been mentioned in this chapter.

The Washingtoniana Division of the District of Columbia Public Library, housed at the Martin Luther King Jr. Memorial Library, has perhaps the largest collection of local history concerning the District of Columbia, including a substantial amount of historical legal materials.

The resources of the Library of Congress, including the Law Library of Congress, the Manuscript Division, and the library's general collections, include substantial holdings relating to District of Columbia legal and political history.

Many governmental records relating to the legal, political, social, and economic history of the District of Columbia are stored at the National Archives. Records of the government of the District of Columbia and its predecessors (e.g., the municipalities of Georgetown and the City of Washington) are held primarily in Record Group 351.[128] Other record groups at the National Archives relevant to District of Columbia history include, inter alia, Record Group 42 (Records of the Office of Public Buildings and Public Parks of the National Capital), Record Group 302 (Records of the National Capital Housing Authority), Record Group 328 (Records of the National Capital Planning Commission), Record Group 132 (Records of the Rent Commission of the District of Columbia), Record Group 46 (Records of the United States Senate, especially those of the Senate Committee on the District of Columbia), and Record Group 233 (Records of the United States House of Representatives, especially those of the House Committee on the District of Columbia).[129]

The Archives Division of District of Columbia Office of Public Records maintains historical government records, including land records, birth, death, and marriage certificates, and agency records. The Library of Governmental Information Division of the Office of Public Records maintains reports, monographs, and other printed material relating to the history of the government of the District of Columbia.

The Historical Society of Washington, DC, has outstanding resources on the history of the District of Columbia, including its political and legal history. The Historical Society's current publication, *Washington History,* and its predecessor's annual publication, the *Records of the Columbia Historical Society,* contain numerous articles of interest to those researching the legal history of the District. In 2003, the Historical Society moved to the renovated former Carnegie Library Building that now houses the City Museum of Washington, DC. The Historical Society's library, which was renamed the Kiplinger Research Library, obtained larger space within the new location.

The Special Collections Department of the Gelman Library at The George Washington University has an exceptionally strong collection of Washingtoniana, including substantial legal historical materials, and an impressive array of manuscripts by historians, local political leaders, and organizations.

An extensive bibliography of books on District of Columbia history can be found on the Web site of the online magazine *D.C. Watch,* at <http://www.dcwatch.com/biblio.htm>.

Last, a resource of enormous value to anyone conducting research into the history of the District of Columbia is the H-DC Discussion Network, the Web site for which is <http://www2.h-net.msu.edu/~dclist/>. H-DC, an electronic discussion list, is one of several lists on the H-Net Humanities and Social Sciences discussion networks. The Web site includes links to various discussion logs, syllabi, pathfinders, and other resources pertaining to the history of the District of Columbia.

NOTES

1. Unlike the residents of seats of government in other modern democracies, the citizens of the District of Columbia lack voting representation in the federal legislature. See Eugene P. Boyd and Michael K. Fauntroy, Congressional Research Service, *Washington, D.C. and 10 Other National Capitals: Selected Aspects of Governmental Structure* 4 (March 29, 2002), at <http://www1.worldbank.org/wbiep/decentralization/library1/boyd.pdf> (in study comparing eleven national capitals around the world, "only the District of Columbia does not have voting representation in the national legislature."). Statehood for the District is one proposed solution to this problem. In 1993 the House of Representatives rejected the New Columbia Admission Act, H.R. 51, 103rd Cong. (1993), which would have admitted the District of Columbia, renamed "New Columbia," as the fifty-first state of the Union. 139 *Cong. Rec.* 31508-25 (1993). Statehood remains a goal for many activists. See, e.g., the platform of the D.C. Statehood Green Party, at <http://dcstatehoodgreen.org/platform.htm>. Other organizations, such as DC Vote, <http://www.dcvote.org>, have focused on securing voting represenation.

2. For example, the District is treated as if it were a "state" for purposes of over 500 laws in the United States Code. Jamin B. Raskin, "Is This America? The District of Columbia and the Right to Vote," *Harv. C.R.-C.L. L. Rev.* 34 (1999): 39, 92 n. 271.

3. Pub. L. No. 93-198, 87 *Stat.* 774 (1973).

4. The Continental Congress met variously at Philadelphia, Baltimore, Lancaster, York, Princeton, Annapolis, Trenton, and New York. H.P. Caemmerer, *Washington: The National Capital* 3 (Washington, DC: U.S. Government Printing Office, 1932).

5. See Caemmerer, supra, at 3-9. One incident in Philadelphia proved especially significant. On June 21, 1783, a group of Revolutionary War soldiers, who had not been paid for their service, marched against the Continental Congress as it was meeting in Philadelphia, and threatened the members. State and municipal authorities failed to protect the Congress, forcing it to flee Philadelphia and reconvene in Princeton. Ibid.

6. U.S. Const. art. I, § 8, cl. 17.

7. Kenneth R. Bowling, *The Creation of Washington, D.C.: The Idea and Location of the American Capital* 74-76 (Fairfax, VA: George Mason University Press, 1991).

8. Ibid. at 158-60.

9. Ibid. at 168.

10. The act providing that the seat of government would be located on the Potomac, after a ten-year temporary residence in Philadelphia, was approved July 16, 1790. Act of July 16, 1790, ch. 28, 1 *Stat.* 130. For a discussion of the circumstances surrounding the Compromise of 1790, including debate on the degree to which the vote on the residency requirement in fact depended on a compromise on the assumption of debt question, see Bowling, supra, at 168-207; Joseph J. Ellis, *Founding Brothers: The Revolutionary Generation* 48-80 (New York: Alfred A. Knopf, 2000); Don E. Fehrenbacher, *The Slaveholding Republic: An Account of the United States Government's Relations to Slavery* 53-60 (Ward M. McAfee, ed., New York: Oxford University Press, 2001).

11. 1 *Stat.* 130, § 1. Because Maryland and Virginia, unlike Pennsylvania, were pro-slavery states, retaining the existing state law in the territory meant that slavery would be present in that territory at least until transfer of the capital from Philadelphia to the District. This served later as an "entering wedge" for legitimizing slavery in the federal seat of government. Fehrenbacher, supra, at 60.

12. 1 *Stat.* 130, §§ 2 and 3.

13. Bowling, supra, at 208-34. President Washington's proclamation dated January 24, 1791, is reprinted in 1 *D.C. Code Ann.* at 43-44 (West, 2001). The original manuscript has been digitized and placed on the Web at <http://memory.loc.gov/ammem/gwhtml/gwser4.html> (choose the period from January 7, 1790 to September 10, 1791 and turn to images 185 to 189). Georgetown, Maryland, had been settled in the late seventeenth century, laid out as a town in 1751 under the name of George, and incorporated as a municipality in Maryland in 1789 as the city of George Town. *Encyclopaedia Britannica Online,* Georgetown, at <http://search.eb.com/eb/article?eu=37221>. Alexandria, Virginia, had been first settled in the late seventeenth century, organized in 1749, and incorporated as a municipality in 1779. *Encyclopaedia Britannica Online,* Alexandria, at <http://search.eb.com/eb/article?eu=5703>.

14. Act of March 3, 1791, ch. 16, 1 *Stat.* 214.

15. Some northerners in Congress who voted for the Residency Act thought that the capital temporarily based in Philadelphia for ten years would in fact remain there permanently because of governmental inertia. Bowling, supra, at 193-94. Washington's efforts helped ensure that the capital would in fact move to the Potomac in 1800. Ibid. at 208-34. Washington's activities relating to the development of the District continued well beyond his retirement from the presidency in March 1797. Ibid. at 233-34; Ellis, supra, at 160-61.

16. Pursuant to an act of Congress approved April 24, 1800, President Adams moved the executive departments to Washington in June 1800. Act of April 24, 1800, ch. 37, 2 *Stat.* 55-56. (Section 5 of this act, 2 *Stat.* 56, which appropriated $5,000 "for the purchase of such books as may be necessary for the use of Congress at the said city of Washington," was the first appropriation for the Library of Con-

gress.) Congress first met in the District in November 1800, for the second session of the Sixth Congress. The Supreme Court's first session in Washington was in February 1801. William Tindall, *Origin and Government of the District of Columbia* 12-13 (Washington, DC: U.S. Government Printing Office, 1909).

17. The towns of Georgetown and Alexandria had municipal governments chartered by Maryland and Virginia, respectively, but apart from such municipal authority, under the 1790 Residency Act the governing law in the territory was that of the state governments of Maryland and Virginia.

18. The Circuit Court of the District of Columbia was like other federal circuit courts at that time in that it possessed both trial and appellate functions, but it was unlike other federal circuit courts in that it adjudicated not only federal matters but also local criminal and civil cases. Susan Low Bloch and Ruth Bader Ginsburg, "Celebrating the 200th Anniversary of the Federal Courts of the District of Columbia," *Geo. L.J.* 90(2002): 549, 552.

19. Organic Act of 1801, ch. 16, 2 *Stat.* 103, reprinted in 1 *D.C. Code Ann.* 46-49 (West, 2001).

20. Act of May 3, 1802, ch. 53, 2 *Stat.* 195.

21. Act of Feb. 24, 1804, ch. 14, 2 *Stat.* 254.

22. Act of Feb. 25, 1804, ch. 15, 2 *Stat.* 255.

23. Act of May 4, 1812, ch. 75, 2 *Stat.* 721.

24. Act of May 15, 1820, ch. 104, 3 *Stat.* 583.

25. Constance McLaughlin Green, *Washington: Village and Capital, 1800-1878* 29-30 (Princeton, NJ: Princeton University Press, 1962).

26. See Mark David Richards, *Fragmented Before a Great Storm,* paper presented before the Arlington Historical Society, May 9, 2002, available at <http://www.dcwatch.com/richards/020509.htm>.

27. Act of May 9, 1846, ch. 35, 9 *Stat.* 35.

28. Green, supra, at 174.

29. The September 7, 1846, proclamation is reprinted at 1 *D.C. Code Ann.* 75-76 (West, 2001).

30. Act of March 13, 1847, ch. 53, 1846 *Va. Acts* 41.

31. Act of May 17, 1848, ch. 42, 9 *Stat.* 223.

32. Because Maryland and Virginia were slave states, slavery became the law of the national capital sub silentio, by operation of the Organic Act of 1801. Some of the laws in effect in Maryland in 1801 that became law on the Maryland side of the District of Columbia are reprinted in Worthington G. Snethen, *The Black Code of the District of Columbia in Force September 1st, 1848* (New York: William Harned, 1848). This book is reproduced electronically in the History Resource Center: U.S., <http://galenet.galegroup.com/servlet/HistRC>.

33. Fehrenbacher, supra, at 61-66.

34. Ibid. at 65.

35. Ibid. at 64-65.

36. Ibid. at 65.

37. Green, supra, at 273-74.

38. Act of Sept. 20, 1850, ch. 63, 9 *Stat.* 467; Fehrenbacher, supra, at 83-84.

39. Act of April 16, 1862, ch. 54, 12 *Stat.* 376. Two unofficial compilations of the law of slavery in the District of Columbia dating from 1860 and March 1862 have been placed on the Web by the Library of Congress at <http://memory.loc.gov/ammem/sthtml/stpres02.html>.

40. *United States v. Copeland,* 25 F. Cas. 646 (C.C.D.C. 1862) (No. 14,865a). Even after the national Emancipation Proclamation, which freed the slaves in Confederate states but not those in Union states, the federal courts in the District continued to enforce the Fugitive Slave Act, which remained law until June 28, 1864, when it was repealed. Bloch and Ginsburg, supra, *Geo. L.J.* 90: 582-83; Act of June 28, 1864, ch. 166, 13 *Stat.* 200.

41. Green, supra, at 244-71 (civil and economic impact of Civil War in District of Columbia).

42. Act of August 6, 1861, ch. 62, 12 *Stat.* 320. The act made the mayors of Washington and Georgetown ex officio members of the commissioners of police. The act also required a loyalty oath. The mayor of Washington, James Berret, argued that as an elected representative of the people of Washington he was exempt from the loyalty oath requirement for federal employees. He was taken away by the Army and imprisoned at New York Harbor, and the city's board of aldermen elected a replacement. Green, supra, 248-50.

43. *Cong. Globe,* 39th Cong. 2d Sess. 303-06 (1867) (President Johnson's letter stating reasons for veto); ibid. at 313-314 (Senate vote overriding veto); ibid. at 344 (House vote overriding veto); ibid. at 328 (Senate certification of overriding of veto); Act of Jan. 8, 1867, ch. 6, 14 *Stat.* 375.

44. Act of Feb. 21, 1871, ch. 62, 16 *Stat.* 419.

45. Ibid. at § 1.

46. 16 *Stat.* 428, § 40.

47. Ibid.

48. 16 *Stat.* 426, § 34.

49. See U.S. Congress, House of Representatives, *Governance of the District of Columbia,* H. Rept. 647, 43rd Cong. 1st Sess., June 16, 1874 (report of the Joint Select Committee created to investigate the fiscal problems of the territorial government).

50. Act of June 20, 1874, ch. 337, 18 *Stat.* (Part 3) 116.

51. Steven J. Diner, *Democracy, Federalism, and the Governance of the Nation's Capital, 1790-1974* 24 (Washington, DC: Center for Applied Research and Urban Policy, 1987).

52. 18 *Stat.* (Part 3) 118, § 5.

53. U.S. Congress, *Report of the Joint Select Committee to Frame a Government for the District of Columbia,* H. Rept. 64, 44th Cong. 2nd Sess. (December 27, 1876).

54. Act of June 22, 1878, ch. 180, 20 *Stat.* 102.

55. See House Committee on the District of Columbia, 101st Cong., 2nd Sess., *Governance of the Nation's Capital: A Summary History of the Forms and Powers of Local Government for the District of Columbia, 1790 to 1973,* 44-46 (Comm. Print 1990) (describing numerous studies conducted from 1903 to 1939 concerning inefficiency, reorganization, or reform of the District government).

56. Ibid. at 45 (quoting transmittal letter of study by Griffenhagen and Associates on modernization of District government).

57. 66 *Stat.* 824 (1952).

58. Act of June 20, 1949, ch. 226, 63 *Stat.* 203.

59. Diner, supra, at 49.

60. D.C. Appropriations Act of 1954, § 16, 67 *Stat.* 278, 296 (1953).

61. Martha Derthick, *City Politics in Washington, D.C.* 48-57 (Cambridge, MA: Harvard/MIT Joint Center for Urban Studies, 1962); Diner, supra, 45-47 and 59-61.

62. S.J. Res. 39, 86th Cong., 106 *Cong. Rec.* 1320 (1960).

63. 106 *Cong. Rec.* 1757-65 (1960); Diner, supra, at 49-50.

64. 106 *Cong. Rec.* 12571 (1960) (House amendment); ibid. at 12580-88 (Senate concurrence in House amendment); 74 *Stat.* 1057 (1960).

65. Diner, supra; U.S. Const. amend. XXIII.

66. Reorganization Plan No. 3 of 1967, 81 *Stat.* 948 (1967).

67. See Diner, supra, at 54-55.

68. District of Columbia Elected Board of Education Act, Pub. L. 90-292, 82 *Stat.* 101 (1968).

69. District of Columbia Court Reform and Criminal Procedure Act of 1970, Pub. L. No. 91-358, 84 *Stat.* 473 (1970).

70. District of Columbia Home Rule Act, Pub. L. 93-198, 87 *Stat.* 774 (1973).

71. Edwin Melvin Williams, "The Circuit Court of the District of Columbia, 1801-63," in *Washington: Past and Present, A History,* 209-10 (John Clagett Proctor, ed., New York: Lewis Historical Publishing, 1930).

72. 2 *Stat.* 106, § 5.

73. 2 *Stat.* 106, § 4.

74. 2 *Stat.* 107, § 14.

75. *Kendall v. United States, ex rel. Stokes,* 12 Peters (37 U.S.) 524, 614, 620-21 (1838); *The Constitution of the United States of America: Analysis and Interpretation* 637-38 (Johnny H. Killian and George A. Costello, eds., Washington, DC: U.S. Government Printing Office, 1996).

76. Bloch and Ginsburg, *Geo. L.J.* 90: 552 n. 9.

77. Act of March 1, 1823, ch. 24, 3 *Stat.* 743.

78. Act of July 7, 1838, ch. 192, 5 *Stat.* 306-08.

79. Act of July 7, 1846, ch. 35, 9 *Stat.* 35.

80. Act of March 3, 1839, ch. 88, 5 *Stat.* 353 (patent appeals); Act of Aug. 19, 1841, ch. 9, 5 *Stat.* 440 (bankruptcy cases).

81. Act of March 3, 1863, ch. 91, 12 *Stat.* 762. Four "justices" replaced the three judges of the circuit court. The Supreme Court of the District of Columbia was modeled on the state courts of New York, with one judge conducting civil and criminal trials in "special terms" and the full court sitting in "general terms" to hear appeals from single-judge rulings. Bloch and Ginsburg, supra, at 556.

82. Act of Feb. 9, 1893, ch. 74, 27 *Stat.* 434.

83. *O'Donoghue v. United States,* 389 U.S. 516 (1933).

84. Act of June 7, 1934, ch. 426, 48 *Stat.* 926.

85. Act of June 25, 1936, ch. 804, 49 *Stat.* 1921.

86. Act of June 25, 1948, ch. 646, 62 *Stat.* 869, 870 § 41.

87. District of Columbia Court Reform and Criminal Procedure Act of 1970, Pub. L. No. 91-358, 84 *Stat.* 473 (1970).

88. 2 *Stat.* 107, § 11. The presidential power to appoint the District's justices of the peace was the underlying issue in *Marbury v. Madison,* 5 U.S. (1 Cranch) 137 (1803). President Adams, in the waning hours of his presidency, appointed a large number of justices of the peace for the District of Columbia. Four appointees whose commissions were not "delivered," including William Marbury, sued James Madison, secretary of state in the Jefferson administration, in an original action filed in the U.S. Supreme Court sounding in mandamus. Chief Justice Marshall ruled against the appointees but took the opportunity to enunciate the doctrine of judicial supremacy in constitutional interpretation. Bloch and Ginsburg, supra, at 564-65. The rest is legal, political, and cultural history. See Paul W. Kahn, *The Reign of Law:* Marbury v. Madison *and the Construction of America* 11 (New Haven, CT: Yale University Press, 1997) ("the rule of law as a particular construction of American political meaning—one within which we continue to operate—traces its origins to a conception of the courts and of the conflict between law and political action that first appears with clarity in *Marbury.*").

89. 2 *Stat.* 107, § 12.

90. Act of March 3, 1801, ch. 24, 2 *Stat.* 115, § 4.

91. Judiciary Act of April 29, 1802, ch. 31, 2 *Stat.* 156, 166, § 24. For about one year there was a U.S. District Court for the District of Potomac, which encompassed Fairfax and Loudoun counties in Virginia, and Montgomery and Prince George's counties in Maryland. Judiciary Act of 1801, ch. 32, 2 *Stat.* 123. The Judiciary Act of March 8, 1802, ch. 9, 2 *Stat.* 132, repealed the 1801 act and thereby abolished the U.S. District Court for the District of Potomac.

92. Act of June 17, 1870, ch. 132, 16 *Stat.* 153.

93. Act of June 21, 1870, ch. 141, 16 *Stat.* 160.

94. Act of March 19, 1906, ch. 960, 34 *Stat.* 73.

95. Act of June 1, 1938, ch. 309, 52 *Stat.* 596; Edgar Silverman, "The Juvenile Court for the District of Columbia: An Historical View of Its Development from 1937 to 1957" (DSW dissertation, Catholic University of America, 1971).

96. Act of Feb. 17, 1909, ch. 134, 35 *Stat.* 623.

97. Act of March 3, 1921, ch. 125, 41 *Stat.* 1310.

98. Act of April 1, 1942, ch. 207, 56 *Stat.* 190.

99. Act of Oct. 23, 1962, Pub. L. No. 87-873, 76 *Stat.* 1171.

100. District of Columbia Court Reform and Criminal Procedure Act of 1970, Pub. L. No. 91-358, 84 *Stat.* 473 (1970).

101. See "History of the D.C. Code," first published as an introduction to the 1929 edition of the *District of Columbia Code,* reprinted at 1 *D.C. Code Ann.* 1-15 (West, 2001). Portions of this history are excerpts from a December 5, 1898 address to the Columbia Historical Society by Justice Walter S. Cox of the Supreme Court of the District of Columbia. Ibid. at 4-13.

102. Ibid. at 3.

103. Ibid. at 13.

104. Ibid. at 2-4. For a comprehensive listing of District of Columbia codes and statutory compilations throughout its history, see the listing for D.C. in *Singal*

Zubrow, Pimsleur's Checklist of Basic American Legal Publications (Littleton, CO: Fred B. Rothman Pubs., 2001).

105. 31 *Stat.* 1189, § 1 (1901).

106. *Code of the District of Columbia* (to March 4, 1929) (Washington, DC: U.S. Government Printing Office, 1930).

107. *District of Columbia Code* (1940 ed., Washington, DC: U.S. Government Printing Office, 1941).

108. *District of Columbia Code* (3rd ed., Washington, DC: U.S. Government Printing Office, 1952).

109. *District of Columbia Code, Annotated* (1961 ed., Washington, DC: U.S. Government Printing Office, 1961).

110. *District of Columbia Code, Annotated* (1967 ed., Washington, DC: U.S. Government Printing Office, 1967).

111. *District of Columbia Code, Annotated* (1973 ed., Washington, DC: U.S. Government Printing Office, 1973). Pursuant to the 1973 home rule legislation, the House Office of Law Revision Council delegated authority for the publication of the D.C. Code to the D.C. Council, effective December 31, 1977. The "Seventh Edition" of the D.C. Code was published under the authority of the D.C. Council in 1981; the current edition, published in 2001, is the "Eighth Edition."

112. The first seventeen volumes of the *United States Statutes at Large,* which include statutes enacted in the U.S. through March 1873, as well as various published proceedings and journals of the Continental Congress, the Constitutional Convention, and the U.S. Congress, can be viewed at the Web page by the Library of Congress titled "A Century of Lawmaking For a New Nation: U.S. Congressional Documents and Databases 1774-1873," at <http://memory.loc.gov/ammem/amlaw>. The complete set of the *United States Statutes at Large* from 1789 to the present is available electronically on Lexis and Westlaw to subscribers of those services.

113. *The Acts of Congress, in Relation to the District of Columbia, From July 16th, 1790, to March 4th, 1831, Inclusive* (Washington, DC: Wm. A. Davis, 1831).

114. The CIS Legislative Historical Index database on Lexis aggregates these indexes into one database, and thus researchers with access to Lexis can conduct research on these indexes electronically. With respect to the content of the *United States Serial Set,* in which House and Senate reports and documents are reprinted, as this series goes to press two electronic publishing concerns, Lexis and Readex, are in the process of digitizing the entirety of the *Serial Set* and making it available electronically to subscribers. On researching Congressional materials generally, see Morris L. Cohen, Robert C. Berring, and Kent C. Olson, *How to Find the Law* 217-60 (9th ed., St. Paul, MN: West, 1989); J. Myron Jacobstein, Roy M. Mersky, and Donald J. Dunn, *Fundamentals of Legal Research* 188-229 (7th ed., New York: Foundation Press, 1998).

115. These can be searched on online catalogs, such as that of the Library of Congress at <http://catalog.loc.gov/>, using the name of the committee as the author. Thus the Senate Committee reports can be researched by typing in the author field, "United States. Congress. Senate. Committee on the District of Columbia." Similarly, the House Committee reports can be found using "United States. Congress. House. Committee on the District of Columbia."

116. For example, the collections of the Library of Congress include *The Laws of the Corporation of the Town of Alexandria* (Alexandria, DC: Samuel Snowden, 1811); and *Laws of the Corporation of Alexandria, as Revised and Passed on the Twentieth of January, Eighteen Hundred and Twenty One* (Alexandria, DC: Rounsavell and Pittman, 1821).

117. The collections of the Library of Congress include *Ordinances of the Corporation of Georgetown* (Georgetown, DC: W.A. Rind, 1811); and *Ordinances of the Corporation of Georgetown* (Georgetown, DC: J.C. Dunn, 1821).

118. *Ordinances Passed by the Levy Court of the County of Washington, D.C., from May 4, 1863 to May 4, 1868* (n.p., n.d.).

119. E.g., *Laws of the District of Columbia, 1871-1872* (Washington, DC: Chronicle Pub., 1872); *Acts and Resolutions of the Regular Session of the Third Legislative Assembly of the District of Columbia* (Washington, DC: Republican Book and Job Office Printers, 1873).

120. The powers transferred to the council are set forth in § 402 of the Reorganization Plan No. 3 of 1967, 80 *Stat.* 948, 951-977 (1967).

121. See District of Columbia Administrative Procedure Act, Pub. L. 90-614 § 5, 82 *Stat.* 1203, 1206 (1968).

122. Ibid., 82 *Stat.* 1207, § 8.

123. See Cohen, Berring, and Olsen, supra, at 39-43.

124. There is significant confusion about the numbering of the *District of Columbia Reports.* Matching up the nominative volumes with the numbering of the *District of Columbia Reports* confounded even the publishers of *The Bluebook: A Uniform System of Citation* (17th ed., Cambridge, MA: Harvard Law Review Association, 2000). For example, *The Bluebook* incorrectly states that the first Hayward and Hazelton volume may be cited as "5 D.C.," when the fifth volume was published by Cranch. A correct matching of the nominative volumes with the *District of Columbia Reports* is in Miles O. Price and Harry Bitner, *Effective Legal Research: A Practical Manual of Law Books and Their Use* 390 (New York: Prentice Hall, 1953). A helpful table setting forth the proper numbering of the *District of Columbia Reports* is set forth in Helen Newman, "Memorials and Notes in District of Columbia Reports," *Law Libr. J.* 26(1933): 33, 36.

125. The first five Cranch volumes are also referred to as volumes one through five of the *District of Columbia Reports;* the sixth Cranch volume, as an index, is not included in the *District of Columbia Reports.* The first and second Hayward and Hazleton volumes are sometimes erroneously called volumes six and seven, respectively, of the *District of Columbia Reports,* but because they were published retroactively in 1892 and 1895, they should not be cited as part of the *District of Columbia Reports* to avoid confusion with the Mackey volumes published earlier and assigned volume numbers six and seven. See Price and Bitner, supra; Newman, supra.

126. The two Mackey volumes covering 1863 to 1869 and 1869 to 1872 should be cited as volumes six and seven, respectively, of the *District of Columbia Reports.* The three MacArthur volumes should be cited as volumes eight, nine, and ten of the *District of Columbia Reports.* The MacArthur and Mackey volume should be cited as volume eleven of the *District of Columbia Reports.* The nine Mackey volumes comprise volumes twelve through twenty of the *District of Columbia Reports.* The

Tucker and Clephane volume is volume twenty-one of the *District of Columbia Reports.* See Price and Bitner, supra; Newman, supra.

127. For example, a small number of opinions by the orphans' court were published in the Hayward and Hazleton volumes, and were reprinted in West's *Federal Cases.* See, e.g., *Wilson v. Taylor,* 2 Hay. and Haz. 334, 30 Fed. Cas. 230 (No. 17,840a) (D.C. Orphans' Court, 1859).

128. Dorothy S. Privine, *Preliminary Inventory of the Records of the Government of the District of Columbia, Record Group* 351 (Washington, DC: National Archives and Records Service, 1976), is a useful guide to the National Archives' holdings of D.C. government materials.

129. An overview of the various record groups at the National Archives is available on the Web at <http://www.archives.gov/research_room/federal_records_guide/>.

Chapter 10

Tracking Down Legal Sources on Prestatehood Florida

Christopher A. Vallandingham

When the Spanish left Florida in 1821, few seemed to mourn their departure. A decrepit old man, much like the Ottoman Empire would become in the latter part of the nineteenth century, the Spanish Empire was dying an ignoble death as, one by one, her colonies were breaking free from her grasp. Gone were the once-invincible armada, the fabled conquistadors, the endless caravans of riches sailing across the Atlantic to fill the royal coffers. Centuries of Spanish rule hardly left a mark on the political and legal institutions of the territory of Florida, swept away by the representative democracy and common law jurisprudence of the upstart American republic.

If we take the founding of the city of St. Augustine in 1565 as the starting point of the Spanish colonial period in Florida, or push it back further in time to 1513, the year Ponce de León landed on the east coast of Florida, then it will take the United States until 2057 or 2109 before it has had dominion over Florida for as long as Spain did. Therefore, the story of Florida prior to Florida's admission to the Union as a state in 1845 is largely the history of Spanish Florida. The purpose of this chapter is to provide a starting point for those interested in the legal history of prestatehood Florida by guiding the reader through some of the salient events in Florida's history prior to 1845.

THE FIRST SPANISH PERIOD, 1513-1763

On April 30, 1492, Christopher Columbus received a royal commission from the rulers of Aragon and Castile, King Ferdinand and Queen Isabella, to find a westward route to the Indies.[1] On August 2, 1492, Columbus, accompanied by ninety crewmen, set sail on the Niña, Pinta, and Santa Maria in search of the Indies. Early in the morning of October 12, 1492, a crew member spotted land, most probably in the Bahamas. Threatened by the news of Columbus's discovery, the king of Portugal asserted that the discovery was within the limits set forth in a series of papal bulls[2] in the fifteenth century, which gave Portugal political and spiritual hegemony over the Indies.[3] The king and queen of Castile disputed the claim of the Portuguese king and petitioned Pope Alexander VI to intervene.

Pope Alexander VI, a native of Valencia and a friend of the Castilian king, responded with a series of bulls that were highly favorable to Castile. One of these bulls, *Inter Caetera,* became one of the major foundations for Spanish claims in the western hemisphere.[4] The bull assigned to Castile the exclusive right to acquire territory, to trade in, or even to approach the lands lying west of the meridian located 100 leagues west of the Azores and Cape Verde Islands. An exception was made, however, for any lands actually possessed by any other Christian prince beyond this meridian prior to Christmas 1492. Later, on June 7, 1494, Spain and Portugal met at Tordesillas, Spain, and signed a treaty moving the line 270 leagues west, to 370 leagues west of the Cape Verde Islands.[5]

The arrival of Europeans to the islands of the Caribbean was devastating to the indigenous population, a majority of whom were wiped out by disease (such as smallpox, to which the native population had no immunity), starvation, and maltreatment.[6] With the decline of the indigenous population of the Caribbean islands, the lack of sufficient manpower for agriculture and mining operations caused the Spanish to turn to slave labor provided by Africans and indigenous people captured elsewhere. It is unclear precisely when Europeans first encountered Florida, but it is possible that slave traders had visited and antagonized the indigenous population of Florida years before Juan Ponce de León ever stepped foot on the shores of Florida.[7]

Juan Ponce de León came to the New World in 1493 during Columbus's second voyage.[8] While residing on the island of Hispaniola (Haiti), Ponce heard that there was an abundance of gold on the nearby island of Boriquien (Puerto Rico). During a visit to Puerto Rico, Ponce did, in fact, find gold, and he sent samples of his findings to the governor of Hispaniola. When the Spanish king heard of Ponce's success, the king made Ponce governor of Puerto Rico; Ponce subsequently conquered the island. However, Ponce's political career in Puerto Rico was short-lived when the king realized that Ponce's appointment violated the rights that the Spanish monarchy had guaranteed to the descendants of Christopher Columbus.[9]

Unemployed and looking for adventure, Ponce petitioned Charles V for a patent to explore an island called Bimini, which was to the north of Hispaniola.[10] Legend has it that miraculous waters, the so-called Fountain of Youth, restored people's youth. Whether in search of riches, slaves, fame, or magical waters, Ponce set out in 1513.[11] Ponce failed to find riches or the legendary fountain, but he did discover the Bahama Channel, a narrow body of water between Florida and the Bahamas. Soon after his discovery, treasure ships from Mexico and Havana began to sail past Florida through the Bahama Channel en route to Spain.

Early attempts to colonize Florida were hampered by hostile attacks from Native Americans[12] and the lack of sufficient provisions, and ultimately met with disastrous failure.[13] These early attempts were so costly that in 1561 Philip II of Spain decided to forgo further attempts to colonize Florida.[14] However, Philip reversed his hands-off policy when France tried to establish settlements in Guale (South Carolina) and later along the St. Johns River in northeast Florida.[15] Attacks by English and French pirates, losses of ships due to storms, and the growing threat of French and English colonization of the New World convinced Spain that the establishment of settlements in Florida was imperative to protect her treasure fleet sailing through the Bahama Channel. After forcibly expelling the French and massacring many of them,[16] the exploits of Pedro Menéndez de Avilés guaranteed a stronger Spanish foothold in North America by creating settlements and constructing forts from Santa Elena in Guale to Charlotte Bay on the Gulf Coast of Florida.[17] In Florida, the main Spanish settlements were located east of the St. Johns River in the northeast and, later, around Pensacola Bay in the Panhandle.

To administer the affairs of Spain's growing colonial empire, Emperor Charles V founded the *Real y Supremo Consejo de las Indias* (Council of the Indies) on August 1, 1524.[18] All laws and decrees relating to administration, taxation, and law enforcement in the Spanish colonies in the New World were prepared and dispatched by the council, with the approval of the king. The principal representatives of the council in the New World were the viceroys, captains-general, and the *audiencias*.[19] Local authority was vested in *regidores* (councilors) and *alcaldes* (magistrates). While the Council of the Indies was the highest legislative authority after the king, officials in the colonies were permitted to issue local ordinances, provided these ordinances received royal confirmation. Given the difficulties in travel and communications in colonial periods, local officials often had to act without specific authority from Spain. In the New World, the chief way to curb abuse of authority by local officials was the *residencia*.[20]

Unlike the legal traditions of Great Britain and, subsequently, the United States, the Spanish legal system was based on civil law, not common law.[21] Prior to the final expulsion of the Moors from Spain in 1492, the collections of laws that emerged periodically were usually an amalgam of Roman, Visigothic, and local laws.[22] With the ascendancy of the Castilian monarchy in the latter part of the fifteenth century, the law of Castile eventually became the law of Spain.[23]

The laws of the Council of the Indies were promulgated in the form of *cedulas, decretos, resoluciones, ordenamientos, reglamentos, autos acordados,* and *pragmaticas.*[24] No compilation of these orders and decrees had been completed prior to 1680, so determining which laws were in force in the colonies was a perplexing task.[25] On May 18, 1680, the *Recopilación de leyes de los Reynos de las Indias* was promulgated. Although this nine-volume work was not a complete set of laws for the colonies, it was a digest of the orders and decrees that applied to the colonies.[26] The *Recopilación* laid out the fundamentals of the judicial system in the New World. The *audiencias* were the highest courts of appeal in the colonies. During the colonial period, *audiencias* were located throughout the Spanish colonies; for example, audiencias were located in Santo Domingo, Lima, Buenos Aires, Mexico, Guatemala, Panama, Guadalajara, and Manila. The *audiencia* of Santo Domingo had jurisdiction for Florida.[27] The *alcaldes,* chosen by the *cabildes* (town councils), were the chief judicial officials of the lower-level criminal and civil courts. *Fiscales* (legal counsels) and *procuradors* (prosecutors) tried criminal cases. *Defensors* worked on behalf of the accused.[28]

Throughout the first Spanish period, Florida remained a backwater in New Spain, sparsely populated by Spanish subjects.[29] Early settlers found that the soil around the coastal settlements was much too sandy to sustain extensive agriculture, and many feared attacks by the indigenous population if they ventured too far from the forts. Colonists depended almost exclusively on a yearly subsidy *(situado)* of money and supplies from Spain.[30] Because the settlements in Florida were thinly populated, not self-sufficient, and beneficial to Spain primarily for strategic purposes, Spain did not invest more resources in the territory than were necessary to keep it afloat.

Candidates for governor were required to have already attained the military rank of colonel prior to application and to have been born in Spain.[31] When the candidate for governor was approved by the council and the king, he received a dispatch of title in which his duties were delineated. Regulations governing the governor's behavior were also described in the *Recopilación*. During the first Spanish period, the governor often had to fulfill many functions that were delegated to other officials in larger Spanish settlements in the New World.[32]

Spanish colonial Florida did not have the resources to support a court system, so the governor usually fulfilled the role of both judge and *procurador*. Other court functions were handled by soldiers. Unfamiliar with the civil legal procedures for handling cases proscribed by Spanish law, the governor usually resorted to familiar summary court-martial proceedings, from which there was no appeal process.[33] The lack of supervision of the governor's handling of judicial affairs encouraged favoritism, corruption, and arbitrariness. Despite frequent pleas to the king and council for trained legal personnel to be sent to Florida, little was done to improve the situation.

THE BRITISH PERIOD, 1763-1783

Prior to the founding of the city of Charleston in present-day South Carolina in 1670, England showed little interest in challenging Spain's holdings in the New World.[34] After 1670, continued English attacks on Spanish settlements in Gaule forced the Spanish to retreat to Florida, leaving the area between the Savannah and St. Johns rivers as a buffer zone between the British settlements around Charleston and Spanish Florida. Spain's position in Florida became even more tenuous when Britain founded the colony of Georgia in 1733. The Spanish-British conflict over the southeastern part of the North American continent was an extension of a larger battle for supremacy in North America among Spain, France, and England. Despite their ongoing dispute, England sought the support of Spain in the complex series of events called the Seven Years War.[35] Ultimately, England's attack on Spanish colonies and shipping alienated Charles III of Spain and the king rejected the proposal to support the English in the conflict. Opting to support the French, the king signed a pact with France, and Spain entered the war in 1762.[36]

Spain's entry into the war came too late to have much effect on the outcome. The English had already taken Canada from the French, and, in August 1762, an English fleet attacked and captured the city of Havana. Eventually the warring nations met to negotiate the end of the conflict. By the terms of the Treaty of Paris, on February 10, 1763, France ceded Canada and all of its territory east of the Mississippi River to England, and Spain yielded Florida to England in exchange for the return of Havana.[37] In 1763, King George proclaimed that Great Britain would form distinct governments for East and West Florida.[38] The proclamation laid out a framework of government consisting of a governor, courts of law, and general assemblies comprised of representatives of the people.[39] The general assembly was empowered to make laws and other regulations pertaining to the colony, provided that they did not conflict with the laws of England. The governor was granted the power to establish criminal and civil courts, as well as courts of equity. However, the general assembly in East Florida was not formed until 1781 and in West Florida until 1766.[40]

Attempts to settle the new colony were generally not successful.[41] East Florida was developed more extensively than West Florida. The borders of West Florida were less secure, and heavy forestation and sandy soil discouraged large-scale cultivation. Florida remained largely untouched by the Revolutionary War until the British began to use St. Augustine as a staging base for operations in the Southeast.[42] Due to Florida's economic dependence on Great Britain, settlers in Florida generally remained loyal to the Crown.

THE SECOND SPANISH PERIOD, 1783-1821

The Anglo-American treaty ending the Revolutionary War was signed on September 3, 1783,[43] and East and West Florida reverted back to Spanish control.[44] The treaty fixed the northern boundary of West Florida at the thirty-first parallel. However, when the Spanish ceded West Florida in 1763, the northern boundary of West Florida had extended 100 miles north of the thirty-first parallel. This difference of 100 miles led to a major dispute between Spain and the United States.[45] To undermine American authority in the disputed region and to provide a buffer zone between the American and Spanish territories, Spain supplied various tribes of Native Americans with weapons to launch raids against American settlers. In addition, in 1784, Spain attempted to deny American ships access to the Gulf of Mexico via the Mississippi River.[46] However, the U.S. government and American settlers insisted on the right of free navigation of the Mississippi River, and the Spanish relented in 1788 in exchange for payment of duties.[47]

The French Revolution and the Napoleonic Wars that followed the revolution had a profound effect on Spanish power in the New World. As Spain became embroiled in the European war, the United States noted Spain's growing weakness in the Americas. Taking advantage of Spain's desire to prevent war with the United States, the United States forced Spain to sign the Treaty of San Lorenzo in 1795.[48] Among the terms of the treaty was the fixing of the Florida boundary at the thirty-first parallel and a Spanish promise to restrain the Native Americans along the border.[49]

For centuries, the cost of maintaining the North American colonies had been substantial to the Spanish treasury. The primary value of these colonies was to protect the northern approach to its more lucrative colonies to the south. Given the open designs of the United States on Louisiana and Florida, and the increasing inability and unwillingness of Spain to shoulder the costs of the administration and defense of these territories, Spain's eagerness to get rid of Louisiana and Florida is hardly surprising. In 1802, in exchange for the kingdom of Tuscany in northern Italy, Spain ceded Louisiana to France.[50] Mistrustful of Napoleon's pledge to cede Tuscany, the Spanish monarch Charles IV demanded that France not transfer Louisiana to a third power, but this is precisely what Napoleon did. After failing in his designs to fully incorporate his New World territories into his empire, Napoleon reneged on his promise to Spain by selling Louisiana to the United States.[51] American negotiators even tried to include West Florida in the purchase, but to no avail.[52] On April 30, 1803, the treaty ceding Louisiana to the United States was signed by both parties.[53]

When the Spanish colonies in Latin America began to rise up in revolt against Spain, American settlers, also yearning to overthrow Spanish rule in West Florida,[54] seized the Spanish fort at Baton Rouge in 1810. On October 27, 1810, President Madison declared that the Louisiana Purchase granted to the United States jurisdiction all the way to the Perdido River, which presently divides Alabama and Florida.[55] To justify his claim, the president went so far as to alter documents to achieve the appearance of legitimacy.[56] On May 14, 1812, Congress annexed all of West Florida to the Perdido River.[57]

Not content with just obtaining parts of West Florida, American authorities secretly provided support to armed American insurgents attacking Spanish positions in East Florida. Spanish troop withdrawals to quell revolts in Latin America left Spain unable to restrain attacks by Native Americans, runaway slaves,[58] and others coming into the American territories, as required by the Treaty of San Lorenzo. Soon, Spain realized that withdrawing from the American territories was inevitable. In the meantime, Andrew Jackson was commissioned by President Monroe to pursue the Native Americans across the Spanish boundary, provided that Jackson leave the Spanish posts alone. However, Jackson went on a killing spree through Spanish Florida, eventually seizing virtually every important Spanish post, deposing the Spanish governor, and naming an American successor.[59] The American administration condemned Jackson's unauthorized seizure of Spanish territory.[60] Even though the captured posts were returned, Secretary of State John Quincy Adams responded to Spanish outrage by claiming that the United States had the right to defend its borders since Spain was unable or unwilling to restrain the attacks on American settlers.[61]

TERRITORY OF FLORIDA, 1821-1845

Rather than risk a costly war against the United States, Spain decided that it was in her best interest to cede Florida. On February 22, 1819, after lengthy negotiations, the United States and Spain signed the Adams-Onís Treaty, by which the United States acquired East Florida and the previous annexation of West Florida was confirmed.[62] The U.S. Senate unanimously approved the treaty on February 22, 1819, but had to reapprove the treaty on

February 19, 1821, because the Spanish government failed to meet the sixteen-month time limit for approval as stipulated by the treaty.

On March 3, 1819, Congress authorized President Monroe to take possession of East and West Florida.[63] Until Congress made permanent provisions for the governance of the newly acquired territories, Congress vested military, civil, and judicial authority in persons to be named by the president.[64] According to the act, the laws of the United States extended specifically to the collection of revenue and the "importation of persons of colour."[65] Otherwise, officials in Florida could exercise their authority as they deemed fit, provided that they permitted the residents of the territory "the free enjoyment of their liberty, property, and religion."[66] In May 1821, President Monroe appointed former Kentucky Congressman William Pope DuVal[67] (later appointed governor) as judge of East Florida, and former U.S. Senator Eligius Fromentin[68] of Louisiana as judge of West Florida.

On July 17, 1821, Governor Andrew Jackson proclaimed that the laws which were in existence when Spain relinquished possession of Florida would remain in effect until Congress organized the territorial government on a more permanent basis.[69] Governor Jackson divided Florida into two counties: Escambia in the west, and St. Johns in the east.[70] Each county would have a court composed of five justices of the peace. Civil suits were to follow either the existing laws or the laws of Spain,[71] except for the examination of witnesses, which followed the common law.[72] Common law procedures governed criminal court proceedings.[73]

Jackson's frequent quarrels with officials convinced Congress of the importance of speedily establishing a more permanent framework for the government in Florida.[74] Power that had been concentrated in the hands of the governor was now divided among three branches of government: executive, legislative, and judicial.[75] Appointed by the president, the governor held the executive power.[76] The governor controlled the militia, granted pardons and reprieves, acted ex officio as superintendent of Indian affairs, and could appoint those officials whose appointments were not provided for by Congress. A council of thirteen members, annually appointed by the president, held limited legislative power.[77] The council could not settle land claims, and legislation approved by the council was subject to veto by Congress. Two superior courts were established—one in Pensacola and one in St. Augustine.[78] Each court consisted of one judge.[79] The courts had jurisdiction over criminal cases, exclusive jurisdiction over capital cases, and original jurisdiction over all civil cases whose disputed amount was $100 or more.[80] In addition, the legislative council was authorized to create lower courts when needed. In 1826, Congress passed legislation providing for the first popular election of members of the territorial council, with one legislator from each of the thirteen electoral districts that were created.[81] Congress provided for a county system of representation in 1829.[82] Finally, in 1838, Congress created a bicameral legislation in Florida.[83]

Traditionally, Florida had been divided into East and West Florida. However, a large region east of the Apalachicola River and west of the Suwannee River, sometimes referred to as Middle Florida, began to develop in a way quite distinct from the older parts of Florida. Virtually untouched while under Spanish occupation, this region took on the flavor of much of the Old South as families from neighboring states moved into the region to take advantage of the rich soil. This influx of settlers was aided by the decision of the legislative council to locate the territorial capitol near an old Indian village called Tallahassee, which was located approximately midway between Pensacola and St. Augustine.[84]

As settlers expanded into regions occupied by Native Americans, it became obvious to the U.S. government that the successful development of Florida required a resolution to the problem of what to do with the Native Americans. Initially, the solution in Florida was to push the Native Americans further south, away from the areas the white settlers coveted.[85] Neither side respected the terms of the agreements that were signed, and white settlers soon moved into areas designated for Indians, seizing the best land, and often horses and cattle. When the complaints of the Native Americans were ignored by the territorial government, the Native Americans began launching sporadic retaliatory raids on white settlements. The prospect of widespread violence between white settlers and Native Americans provided the impetus for the decision to remove Native American peoples west of the Mississippi, as the federal government planned to do with other Native American groups in the southeast.

The Adams-Onís treaty contained a section which implied that Florida would eventually become a state.[86] To become a state, Florida had to reach the population level set for representation by Congress.[87] Even if the latest census indicated that Florida had reached this level, support for Florida becoming a state was far from unanimous. For one matter, the states of Georgia and Alabama had both proposed to annex the sections of Florida adjacent to their respective regions,[88] and there were continuing fears that Florida could not sustain the costs of supporting a state government. Up to this time, the costs of territorial government had been subsidized by the federal government. However, the advantages of statehood were many. First, Florida would have control over the power of appointing officials, currently exercised by the president of the United States. Second, Florida would have more control over the settling of land disputes, which had plagued the territory ever since the Spanish relinquished control. Third, as a state, Florida could receive grants of public lands currently owned by the federal government.

On February 12, 1837, the legislative council enacted legislation which mandated that the question of statehood be submitted to the voters at the upcoming election in May.[89] Election results indicated that a majority of the residents of Florida wanted statehood.[90] At the following session of the legislative council, the representatives voted to convene a convention where the constitutional framework of the proposed state of Florida could be discussed.[91] The convention convened on December 3, 1838, and adjourned on January 11, 1839.[92] After much debate on the section involving bank charters, the delegates were able to finish a draft constitution.[93]

Admission to statehood was ultimately linked to the admission of the territory of Iowa to statehood. Because Florida permitted the ownership of slaves and Iowa did not, it was necessary to admit both Florida and Iowa at the same time to maintain the balance of power between the North and the South.[94] On March 3, 1845, both territories were admitted into the Union.[95]

THE DISPUTES OVER LAND GRANTS

Throughout the early history of Florida, the complex problems generated by the issuance and verification of land grants filled court dockets, endangered the lives of public surveyors, prevented large tracts of land from being settled, and poisoned the otherwise relatively peaceful transfer of authority from one sovereign nation to another. Land grants were among the most important means by which the Spanish, British, and Americans could induce settlers to come to Florida, which was viewed by many as a less than desirable location. Land grants were also used to reward individuals for distinguished service to the Crown or as gifts to favorite subjects.

In theory, upon transfer of power, grants that were made by previous governments were honored provided that the grants were genuine, sufficiently documented, filed within the stipulated time period, and did not conflict with the larger designs of the incoming government. In many cases, claims were abandoned upon transfer of power, as the subjects of the Spanish and British governments often preferred to leave Florida rather than take an oath of allegiance to a foreign sovereign.[96]

In 1763, by the Treaty of Paris, Spain ceded Florida to Great Britain. Under the terms of the treaty, Great Britain promised that the British government would recognize all authentic titles to immovable property held by Spanish subjects.[97] If Spanish subjects chose to emigrate, they were granted eighteen months to sell their property. However, under the treaty, they were permitted to sell only to British subjects. In 1765, the British signed a treaty with the Native American chiefs from the Upper and Lower Creek Nations at Picolata. This treaty limited British colonization in East Florida to the areas south of the St. Marys River and east of the St. Johns River.[98] To encourage settlement, the British government offered heads of families 100 acres and each member of the family fifty acres.[99]

Under the terms of the Adams-Onís Treaty, all grants of land made before January 24, 1818, by Spain were to be confirmed,[100] and in 1822, Congress passed legislation appointing three commissioners to handle land claims in Florida.[101] Originally, Congress granted the commissioners one year to hear and settle cases.[102] Anyone "claiming title to lands under any patent, grant, concession, or order of survey" dated prior to January 4, 1818, could file a petition with the commissioners. These claims must have been valid claims under the Spanish government that were not rejected by the treaty between the United States and Spain. British land claims were not addressed in the treaty.[103]

The commissioners were required to report on their activities to the secretary of the treasury and forward all documents in their possession regarding claims.[104] For claims that did not exceed 3,500 acres, the commissioners were authorized to favor claims submitted by the actual settlers of the land, even if the settlers could not prove the chain of title dating back to the original grantee.[105] Two of the largest claims were the Arredondo grant in Alachua County,[106] comprising almost 300,000 acres, and the vast Forbes Purchase, over 1 million acres on both sides of the Apalachicola River.

When the Second Seminole War ended in 1842, the areas where the fighting had been concentrated were largely unpopulated. To encourage settlers, Congress passed legislation that granted land to heads of families and single men over eighteen, provided that they were able to bear arms.[107] A number of land claim disputes were tied up in litigation until the end of the nineteenth century.[108]

CONCLUSION

Compared to the mountains of legal materials published and indexed every year in the present-day United States, legal materials on Florida prior to 1845 seem scarce and disorganized. Materials after 1821 are generally much easier to obtain. Copies of microfilmed materials can often be obtained from the Florida Archives and other libraries. In-depth research of the Spanish period may require a trip to archives in Spain. The territorial laws of Florida and the various treaties mentioned in this research guide, as well as indexes to many of the collections in the Spanish archives, are available online.

NOTES

1. Privileges and Prerogatives Granted to Columbus, April 30, 1492. Reprinted in Henry S. Commager and Milton Cantor, *Documents of American History,* vol. 1, 1-2 (10th ed., Englewood Cliffs, NJ: Prentice Hall, 1988) (available at <http://www.yale.edu/lawweb/avalon/colum.htm>).

2. A papal bull, derived from the Latin word *bulla,* meaning seal, is an official edict or decree issued by the pope.

3. Romanus Pontifex (Nicolas V), January 8, 1455. Reprinted in *European Treaties Bearing on the History of the United States and Its Dependencies,* vol. 1, 20-26 (Francis Gardner Davenport, ed., Washington, DC: Carnegie Institution, 1917) (available at <http://www.nativeweb.org/pages/legal/indig-romanus-pontifex.html>). This bull authorized the Portuguese Crown to subdue, enslave, or conquer any pagan or Muslim peoples whom the Portuguese may encounter on their voyages of discovery between Cape Bojador (Morocco) and the Indies.

4. The papal bull *Inter Caetera* (Alexander VI), May 4, 1493. Reprinted in Commager, *Documents of American History* at 2 (available at <http://cca2000.4t.com/bull2.htm>).

5. Ibid. at 4. *Treaty of Tordesillas* (June 7, 1494) (available at <http://www.yale.edu/lawweb/avalon/modeur/mod001.htm>).

6. Clarence Henry Haring, *The Spanish Empire in America,* 38-68 (New York: Harcourt, 1947). Haring's chapter "Race and Environment" discusses the treatment of the indigenous people throughout the Spanish Empire.

7. Junius Elmore Dovell, *Florida: Historic, Dramatic, Contemporary,* vol. 1, 19 (New York: Lewis Historical Pub. Co., 1952).

8. For an account of Ponce's life in the New World prior to his exploration of Florida, see Woodbury Lowery, *The Spanish Settlements Within the Present Limits of the United States, 1513-1561,* 131-137 (New York: G.P. Putnam's Sons, 1911) (available at <http://palmm.fcla.edu/> in the Florida Heritage Collection).

9. Commager, *Documents of American History* at 1.

10. For an English translation of the patent granted by Charles V on February 23, 1512, see T. Frederick Davis, "Ponce de León's First Voyage and Discovery of Florida," *Fla. Hist. Quar.* 14(1935): 9. The *Florida Historical Quarterly* is available online through the Florida Heritage Collection at <http://palmm.fcla.edu>.

11. Ibid. at 16.

12. The Spanish encountered a number of different bands of indigenous people during the fifteenth and sixteenth centuries. The peoples that eventually became known as the Seminoles were not native to Florida and showed up in sizeable numbers only after the extinction of many of the indigenous tribes in Florida. James W. Covington, "Migration into Florida of the Seminoles, 1700-1820," *Fla. Hist. Quar.* 46(1968): 340.

13. Accounts of early Spanish explorers such as Ponce de León, Ayllón, Narváez, and De Soto can be found in Herbert E. Bolton, *The Spanish Borderlands: A Chronicle of Old Florida and The Southwest* (New Haven, CT: Yale University Press, 1921); Theodore Irving, *The Conquest of Florida* (Philadelphia, PA: Carey, Lea, and Blanchard, 1835); Michael Kenny, *The Romance of the Floridas: The Finding*

and the Founding (New York: AMS Press, 1970); Edward W. Lawson, *The Discovery of Florida and Its Discoverer Juan Ponce de León* (St. Augustine, FL: E.W. Lawson, 1946); Garcilaso de la Vega, *La Florida del ynca. Historia del adelantado Hernando de Soto, governador y capitan general del reyno de la Florida, y de otros heroicos cavalleros españoles è indios* (Lisbona: Impresso por Pedro Crasbeeck, 1605). For a chronological history of Florida from 1512-1722, see Barcia's *Chronological History of the Continent of Florida* (Anthony Kerrigan, trans., Gainesville, FL: University of Florida Press, 1951).

14. Justin Winsor, *Narrative and Critical History of America: Spanish Exploration and Settlements in America from the Fifteenth to the Seventeenth Century,* vol. II, 260 (Boston: Houghton Mifflin, 1886).

15. Dovell, *Florida: Historic, Dramatic, Contemporary* at 31-37.

16. The southern shore of Matanzas Inlet, twelve miles south of St. Augustine, was the scene of an infamous massacre of Frenchmen by Spanish forces under the command of Menéndez. Over 200 men, including Jean Ribaut, the leader of the expedition, were beheaded.

17. Bolton, *The Spanish Borderlands: A Chronicle of Old Florida and The Southwest* at 140-154; Eugene Lyon, "Pedro Menéndez's Strategic Plan for the Florida Peninsula," *Fla. Hist. Quar.* 67(1988): 1; Eugene Lyon, *The Enterprise of Florida: Pedro Menéndez de Avilés and the Spanish Conquest of 1565-1568* (Gainesville: University Presses of Florida, 1976).

18. See Haring, *The Spanish Empire in America* at 94-109 for an introduction to the Council of the Indies.

19. It is not always easy to distinguish the functions of these officials. Viceroys were the principal representatives of the Spanish monarchy in the New World and had supreme authority in political and judicial matters in their designated viceroyalties. The rank of captain-general was primarily a military rank and given to those whose training and experience merited this rank. Captains-general were sometimes the chief representatives of the Crown in areas outside of the viceroyalties. The *audiencias* were the courts of appeal for disputes arising in lower civil, criminal, and administrative courts. The *audiencias* also served as an advisory council to the viceroys and captains-general. For a discussion of this organization of the Spanish colonial government, see Haring, *The Spanish Empire in America* at 110-165.

20. A *residencia* was an official review of the outgoing official's conduct during his tenure. In the colonies, this became one of the main ways the Spanish king held officials accountable for their actions while in office. However, the *residencia* proved to be fairly ineffective in colonial Florida, and few governors during the first period of Spanish rule were subjected to it. For those who did not escape the *residencia,* the process was often long and painful. For accounts of two *residencias* of Spanish governors in Florida, see John Jay TePaske, *The Governorship of Spanish Florida: 1700-1763,* 40-56 (Durham, NC: Duke University Press, 1964).

21. The key difference between a civil law system and a common law system is that in civil law jurisdictions judges are not bound by precedent decisions. In civil law jurisdictions, judges do not make laws; they only interpret them.

22. Excellent introductions to the sources of Spanish law include John T. Vance, *The Background of Hispanic-American Law: Legal Sources and Juridical Litera-*

ture of Spain (Westport, CT: Hyperion Press, 1937); Gustavus Schmidt, *The Civil Law of Spain and Mexico,* 9-102 (New Orleans: printed for the author by Thomas Rea, 1851); Clifford Stevens Walton, *The Civil Law in Spain and Spanish America,* 1-84 (Washington, DC: W.H. Lowdermilk and Co., 1900). To find more information about the nature of the Spanish legal system during this time period, see Richard L. Kagan, *Lawsuits and Litigants in Castile, 1500-1700* (Chapel Hill: University of North Carolina Press, 1981).

23. According to the *Recopilación de Leyes de los reynos de las Indias,* if there was no provision on a particular subject found in the *Recopilación,* then the laws of Castile controlled. Schmidt, *The Civil Law of Spain and Mexico* at 95.

24. "*Autos Acordados* and *Cedulas* were orders emanating from some superior tribunal, promulgated in the name, and by the authority of the sovereign. *Decretos* were similar orders in ecclesiastical matters. *Ordenamientos* and *Pragmaticas* were also orders emanating from the king, and differing from *Cedulas* only in form, and in the mode of promulgation. *Reglamentos* were written instructions given by a competent authority without the observance of any peculiar form. *Resoluciones* were opinions formed by some superior authority on matters referred to its decision, and forwarded to the inferior authorities for their instruction and government." (Schmidt, *The Civil Law of Spain and Mexico* at 93)

25. In the *Archivo general de Indias* in Seville, Spain, a large collection of *legajos* (bundles) of documents pertaining to the American colonies exists. Included in this collection are royal decrees, legal investigations, reports of lawsuits, *residencias,* and other correspondence between officials in the colonies and Spain. Documents pertaining to Florida have been gleaned from the archives and published separately. Examples include Archivo General de Indias, *Libro de la florida de capitulaçiones y asientos de governadores y generales . . . 1517-1578* (Madrid: Author, 1922) (copy located at the P.K. Yonge Library of Florida History at the University of Florida); Archivo General de Indias, *Registros: Reales ordenes y nombratos dirigidos a autoridades y particulares de la Florida, 1570-1604* (exact publication date unknown) (copy located at the P.K. Yonge Library of Florida History at the University of Florida); *Cedulario de la Florida, 1570-1604* (microfilmed by the University of Florida from photostats copied from the originals in Seville, Spain) (copy located at the P.K. Yonge Library of Florida History at the University of Florida); Irene Aloha Wright, *Descriptive Lists of Documents Relating to the History of Louisiana and the Florida: In the Papers of the Audiencia de Santo Domingo Deposited in the Archivo General de Indias in Seville* (Los Angeles: University of California, 1939); and A.M. Brooks, *The Unwritten History of Old St. Augustine, Copied from the Spanish Archives in Seville, Spain* (Annie Averette, trans., St. Augustine, FL: The Record Co., 1909?). For further information about Spanish archival sources, see James A. Robertson, "The Archival Distribution of Florida Manuscripts," Tenth Annual Session, *Fla. Hist. Quar* 35 (1931); Charles W. Arnade, "Florida History in Spanish Archives: Reproductions at the University of Florida," *Fla. Hist. Quar.* 34(1955): 36; Charles W. Arnade, "A Guide to Spanish Source Material," *Fla. Hist. Quar.* 35(1957): 320; Bruce S. Chappell, Michael Getzler-Eaton, and D. Lorne D. McWatters, "A New Guide to Sources of Spanish Florida History," *Fla. Hist. Quar.* 56(1978): 495.

The Spanish Borderlands Collection at the P.K. Yonge Library of Florida History at the University of Florida is comprised of the following:

a. Stetson Collection

The John Batterson Stetson Collection (150,000 photostats) contains documents drawn from the Archivo General de Indias and relates to all phases of Spanish activity in the Southeast Borderlands from 1518-1819. The Stetson Collection reveals records of voyages of exploration, the attacks of English and French corsairs, the development of negro slavery in the Borderlands, the emergence of the English presence on the Atlantic seaboard, and reports on Indian customs, languages, migrations, and populations, as well as the civil, military and ecclesiastical development of posts and missions. (http://web.uflib.ufl.edu/spec/pkyonge/stetsonp.html)

b. East Florida Papers

The East Florida Papers (178 microfilm reels) contain the complete archives of the Second Spanish Administration of East Florida (1784-1821). In 1821, when the United States government assumed sovereignty in East Florida, the confusion produced by various interpretations of the Adams-Onis Treaty of 1819 caused U.S. authorities to seize the archives to prevent its shipment to Havana. The archives remained virtually intact during the turbulent nineteenth century and was finally shipped to the Library of Congress in 1906. The great quantity of diverse materials contained in these archives makes it uniquely useful for intensive research into the whole spectrum of Borderlands topics defined in a relatively short period of years. The calendar to the East Florida Papers is arranged by sections that represent broad subject areas and reflect the original organization of the archives. The calendar comprises approximately 56,000 catalog cards. (http://web.uflib.ufl.edu/spec/pkyonge/eflapap.html)

Select items of interest:

Section 57: Papers on the Delivery of East Florida to the United States, 1819-1821

Section 58: Miscellaneous Civil and Criminal Proceedings, 1784-1819

Section 64: Records of Court Materials, 1785-1821

Section 65: Records of Criminal Proceedings, 1785-1821

Section 66: Records of Criminal Proceedings: Rebellion of 1795

Section 71: Records of Testamentary and Probate Proceedings, 1756-1821

Section 77: Records of Civil Proceedings, 1785-1821

Section 90: Book of Mortgages, 1785-1821

Section 93: Proceedings of the St. Augustine Ayuntamiento, 1812-1815, 1820-1821

Section 95: Index of Royal Decrees and of Letters from the Court to Governors of Florida, 1595-1762

c. *Papeles Procedentes de Cuba*

The Papeles Procedentes de Cuba (761 microfilm reels) is a section of the *Archivo General de Indias* in Sevilla holding records of the Spanish colonies throughout the Caribbean and on the North American continent. They contain documentation from the mid-seventeenth century well into the nineteenth century and are particularly rich for the period from circa 1760 to 1821. (http://web.uflib.ufl.edu/spec/pkyonge/papdcuba.html)

26. Schmidt, *The Civil Law of Spain and Mexico* at 94. For an extensive discus- sion of the Recopilación, see Juan Manzano Manzano, *Historia de las Recopilaciones de Indias* (Mexico City: Ediciones Cultura Hispánica, 1950-).

27. However, appeals from Florida usually went directly to the Council of the Indies in Spain. TePaske, *The Governorship of Spanish Florida: 1700-1763* at 58.

28. Ibid. at 59.

29. Juan Ignacio Arnaud Rabinal, *Estructura de la población de una sociedad de frontera: la Florida Española, 1600-1763* (Madrid: Universidad Complutense, 1991).

30. William R. Gillaspie, "Survival of a Frontier Presidio: St. Augustine and the Subsidy and Private Contract Systems, 1680-1702," *Fla. Hist. Quar.* 62(1984): 273; John J. TePaske, "Economic Problems of Florida Governors, 1700-1763," *Fla. Hist. Quar.* 37(1958): 42.

31. TePaske, *The Governorship of Spanish Florida: 1700-1763* at 10.

32. "The governor had wide powers that spread into all phases of colonial life. His titles alone —governor, captain general, royal vice patron of the church—gave him more than just executive responsibility. As governor he received political power usually inherent in such a title—administrative authority and limited appointive power. As captain general he took command of all soldiers serving in the colony. As royal vice patron of the church he had at least partial control over religious activities. Since Florida was too poor and too meagerly populated to support a court system, the governor was also the chief colonial judicial officer. He arranged all civil and criminal trials and forwarded legal documents to the Council of the Indies in Spain when the offense warranted review or trial by this body." (Ibid. at 20)

33. TePaske notes that because extensive documentation of the cases was not kept, it must have been quite difficult for higher authorities to determine what evidence was presented and what procedures were followed by the governors. Ibid. at 63.

34. England did launch raids in the Caribbean and southeastern part of the American continent in an attempt to undermine Spain's power and sources of gold and silver. Sir Francis Drake's attack on St. Augustine in 1586 was a notable instance of such a raid. See James W. Covington, "Drake Destroys St. Augustine: 1586," *Fla. Hist. Quar.* 44(1965): 81; J. Leitch Wright Jr., "Sixteenth Century English-Spanish Rivalry in La Florida," *Fla. Hist. Quar.* 38(1960): 265; Charles W. Arnade, "The English Invasion of Spanish Florida, 1700-1706," *Fla. Hist. Quar.* 41(1962): 29.

35. The Seven Years' War (1756-1763) was a worldwide conflict fought in Europe, North America, and India with France, Austria, Russia, Saxony, Sweden, and Spain on the one side and Prussia, Great Britain, and Hanover on the other. The chief reasons for the conflict were the battle between France and Great Britain for colonies in North America and India, and the struggle for supremacy in Germany between Prussia and Austria.

36. Particular Convention of Offensive and Defensive Alliance between France and Spain (Feb. 4, 1762), 42 C.T.S. 133.

37. Definitive Treaty of Peace between France, Great Britain and Spain (Feb. 10, 1763), 42 C.T.S. 279 (available at <http://www.yale.edu/lawweb/avalon/paris763.htm>).

38. "The government of East Florida, bounded to the Westward by the Gulf of Mexico and the Apalachicola river; to the East and South by the Atlantic Ocean, and the Gulf of Florida, including all islands within six leagues of the sea coast . . . The government of West Florida, bounded to the Southward by the Gulf of Mexico, including all islands within six leagues of the coast from the river Apalachicola to lake Pontchartrain; the lake Maurepas, and the river Mississippi; to the Northward, by a line drawn due East from that part of the Mississippi which lies in thirty-one degrees North latitude, to the river Apalachicola, or Catahouchee; and to the Eastward by the said river." (Commager, *Documents of American History* at 47, 48; *Annual Register* vol. VI, 208 [Dec. 1763])

39. *Annual Register,* ibid. at 210. For background information on English law and political and legal institutions in the British colonies in the western hemisphere, J.H. Baker, *An Introduction to English Legal History,* 2nd ed. (London: Butterworths, 1979).

40. *The Minutes, Journals, and Acts of the General Assembly of British West Florida* (compiled by Robert R. Rea with Milo B. Howard Jr.) (University: University of Alabama Press, 1979); Earl Glynn Ingram, "A critical study of the British West Florida legislative assembly" (unpublished MA thesis, Auburn University, 1969) (copy on file at the P.K. Yonge Library of Florida History at the University of Florida); *Transcriptions of the British Colonial Office Records* (N.P.: Writer's Program, Florida, 1939?-); Charles L. Mowat, "British East Florida in the Clements Library," *Fla. Hist. Quar.* 18(1939): 46. For a brief description of the records of the Colonial Office, see M.S. Giuseppi, *A Guide to the Manuscripts Preserved in the Public Record Office* (London: His Majesty's Stationery Office, 1924).

41. Perhaps the definitive work on British East Florida is Charles Loch Mowat, *East Florida As a British Province, 1763-1784* (Gainesville: University of Florida Press, 1964); on West Florida, Cecil Johnson, *British West Florida, 1763-1783* (New Haven, CT: Yale University Press, 1943). The *Florida Historical Quarterly* is also an excellent source of articles on British Florida. See Charles L. Mowat, "St. Augustine Under the British Flag, 1763-1775," *Fla. Hist. Quar.* 20(1941): 131; Clinton N. Howard, "Early Settlers in British West Florida," *Fla. Hist. Quar.* 24(1945): 45; Linda K. Williams, "East Florida as a Loyalist Haven," *Fla. Hist. Quar.* 54(1976): 465; Clinton N. Howard, "Colonial Pensacola: The British Period. Part I," *Fla. Hist. Quar.* 19(1940): 109; Clinton N. Howard, "Colonial Pensacola: The British Period. Part II," *Fla. Hist. Quar.* 19(1941): 246; Clinton N. Howard, "Colonial Pensacola: The British Period. Part III," *Fla. Hist. Quar.* 19(1941): 368; Albert W. Haarman, "The Spanish Conquest of British West Florida, 1779-1781," *Fla. Hist. Quar.* 39 (1960): 107; Clinton N. Howard, "Governor Johnstone in West Florida," *Fla. Hist. Quar.* 17(1939): 281; Mark F. Boyd, Jose N. Latorre, "Spanish Interest in British Florida, and in the progress of the American Revolution," *Fla. Hist. Quar.* 32 (1953): 92.

42. See Edgar Legare Pennington, "East Florida in the American Revolution, 1775-1778," *Fla. Hist. Quar.* 9(1930): 24; Burton Barrs, *East Florida in the Ameri-*

can Revolution (Jacksonville, FL: Guild Press, 1932); Joseph Barton Starr, *Tories, Dons, and Rebels: The American Revolution in British West Florida* (Gainesville: University of Florida Press, 1976); James Leitch Wright, *Florida in the American Revolution* (Gainesville: University Presses of Florida, 1975).

43. Definitive Treaty of Peace between the United States of America and his Britannic Majesty (Sept. 3, 1783), 8 *Stat.* 80. (available at <http://www.yale.edu/lawweb/avalon/diplomacy/britian/paris.htm>). Helen Hornbeck Tanner, The Transition from British to Spanish Rule in East Florida, 1783-1785 (MA thesis, University of Florida, Gainesville, 1949).

44. For an account of the tenure of a Spanish governor of East Florida during the second Spanish era, see Helen Hornbeck Tanner, *Zéspedes in East Florida, 1784-1790* (Jacksonville: University of North Florida Press, 1989). Antonio Alvarez, "Governors of Spanish East Florida, 1784-1821," *Fla. Hist. Quar.* 6(1927): 117; Joseph E. Caro, "Governors of Spanish West Florida," *Fla. Hist. Quar.* 6(1927): 118; D.C. Corbitt, "The Return of Spanish Rule to the St. Marys and the St. Johns, 1813-1821," *Fla. Hist. Quar.* 20(1941): 47; see also John H. Matthews, "Law enforcement in Spanish East Florida, 1783-1821" (PhD dissertation, Catholic University of America, 1987) (microfilmed on University Microfilms International, 1988) (copy located at the P.K. Yonge Library of Florida History at the University of Florida); Robert Franklin Crider, "The Borderland Florida, 1815-1821: Spanish sovereignty under siege" (PhD dissertation, Florida State University, 1979) (microfilmed on University Microfilms International, 1980) (copy located at the P.K. Yonge Library of Florida History at the University of Florida); Ramón Romero Cabot, "La defense de Florida en el segundo periodo Español, 1783-1821" (unpublished MA thesis, Universidad de Sevilla, 1982) (copy located at the P.K. Yonge Library of Florida History at the University of Florida).

45. When Great Britain received East and West Florida from Spain in 1763, the northern boundary of West Florida was set at the thirty-first parallel. However, Britain later moved this boundary approximately 100 miles north to the thirty-second parallel to where the Yazoo River empties into the Mississippi. When Spain reconquered this land, Spain insisted that the right of conquest gave Spain dominion over the land between the thirty-first and thirty-second parallel. (Spain actually claimed dominion over lands even further north than the thirty-second parallel.) The boundary issue would not be resolved until 1795. Hubert Bruce Fuller, *The Purchase of Florida: It's History and Diplomacy* 31 (Gainesville: University of Florida Press, 1964); Thomas Andrew Bailey, *A Diplomatic History of the American People* 59 (6th ed., New York: Appleton-Century Crofts, 1958).

46. Fuller, *The Purchase of Florida* at 33-75.

47. John Jay, the American secretary of state, out of eagerness to secure a commercial treaty with Spain to help alleviate severe financial problems of the United States, suggested that the United States forsake free navigation of the Mississippi since the newly acquired territories were still sparsely populated by American settlers. *Journals of the Continental Congress, 1774-1789,* vol. 31, 480 (available online at <http://memory.loc.gov/ammem/amlaw/lwjclink.html>); *The American Secretaries of State and their Diplomacy,* vol. II, 232-250 (Samuel Flagg Bemis, ed.,

New York: Cooper Square Publishers, 1963); Gilbert C. Din, "War Clouds on the Mississippi: Spain's 1785 Crisis in West Florida," *Fla. Hist. Quar.* 60(1981): 51.

48. Treaty of Friendship, Limits and Navigation: Between the United States of America and the King of Spain (Oct. 27, 1795) 8 *Stat.* 138. The *Statutes at Large* from 1789-1873 can be found online at <http://memory.loc.gov/ammem/amlaw/ lwsl.html>. 4 *Annals of Congress* (Appendix, 2526-2567) contains documents and correspondence relating to the treaty with Spain in 1795. The *Annals of Congress* (1789-1824) can be found online at <http://memory.loc.gov/ammem/amlaw/lwac. html>.

49. ". . . both parties oblige themselves expressly to restrain by force all hostilities on the part of the Indian nations living within their boundary: so that Spain will not suffer her Indians to attack the citizens of the United States . . . nor will the United States permit these last-mentioned Indians to commence hostilities against the subjects of his Catholic Majesty." (Treaty of Friendship, Limits and Navigation: Between the United States of America and the King of Spain. art. V (Oct. 27, 1795) 8 *Stat.* 138 [available at <http://www.yale.edu/lawweb/avalon/diplomacy/spain/ sp1795.htm>])

50. Preliminary and Secret Treaty between the French Republic and Spain, signed at San Ildefonso (Oct. 1, 1800), 55 C.T.S. 377 (available at <http://www. yale.edu/lawweb/avalon/ildefens.htm>).

51. Napoleon's forces occupied Santo Domingo and crushed the slave revolt led by Toussaint L'Ouverture. However, heavy losses in manpower due to fighting and disease led to Napoleon's decision not to risk more losses by sending in reinforcements, and he gave up on his New World ambitions. In Napoleon's mind, without Santo Domingo, keeping Louisiana was pointless since he intended to use Louisiana primarily as a granary for his more-valued Caribbean possessions. Because the agreement between Spain and France was contingent on France not ceding Louisiana to a third party, there was fear in the United States that Spain would refuse to honor the treaty between the United States and France. See Fuller, *The Purchase of Florida* at 104.

52. 9 *Annals of Congress* 946 (1806) (discussion in the House of Representatives over the proposed purchase of Florida); Wanjohi Waciuma, *Intervention in Spanish Floridas, 1801-1813: A Study in Jeffersonian Foreign Policy* (Boston: Branden Press, 1976).

53. Treaty between the United States and the French Republic (Apr. 30, 1803), 8 *Stat.* 200 (available at <http://www.yale.edu/lawweb/avalon/diplomacy/france/louis1. htm>).

54. Spanish West Florida extended well past the current Florida-Alabama border into Louisiana.

55. Resolution: Relative to the occupation of the Floridas by the United States of America, 3 *Stat.* 471 (1811); An Act to enable the President of the United States, under certain contingencies, to take possession of the country lying east of the river Perdido, and south of the state of Georgia and the Mississippi territory, and for other purposes, 3 *Stat.* 471 (1811).

56. See Bailey, *A Diplomatic History of the American People* at 165; Joseph Burkholder Smith, *The Plot to Steal Florida: James Madison's Phony War* (New

York: Arbor House, 1983); James Cooper, *Secret acts, resolutions, and instructions under which East Florida was invaded by the United States troops, naval forces, and volunteers, in 1812 and 1813: together with the official correspondence of the agents and officers of the government* (Washington, DC: G.S. Gideon, 1860); T. Frederick Davis, "United States Troops in Spanish East Florida, 1812-1813," *Fla. Hist. Quar.* 9(1930): 3; T. Frederick Davis, "United States Troops in Spanish East Florida, 1812-1813," Part II, *Fla. Hist. Quar.* 9(1930): 96; T. Frederick Davis, "United States Troops in Spanish East Florida, 1812-1813," Part III, *Fla. Hist. Quar.* 9(1931): 135; T. Frederick Davis, "United States Troops in Spanish East Florida, 1812-1813," Part IV, *Fla. Hist. Quar.* 9(1931): 259; T. Frederick Davis, "United States Troops in Spanish East Florida, 1812-1813," Part V, Tenth Annual Session, *Fla. Hist. Quar.* 24(1931).

57. An act to enlarge the boundaries of the Mississippi territory, 2 *Stat.* 734 (1812).

58. Spain had long permitted runaway slaves to come to Florida, thereby creating difficulties with American and British slave owners. Jane Landers, "Spanish Sanctuary," *Fla. Hist. Quar.* 62(1984): 296; Robert L. Anderson, "The End of an Idyll," *Fla. Hist. Quar.* 42(1963): 35.

59. Jackson's invasion of Florida is often referred to as the First Seminole War. John K. Mahon, "The First Seminole War, November 21, 1817-May 24, 1818," *Fla. Hist. Quar.* 77(1998): 62.

60. 15 *Annals of Congress.* 583-922, 926-1074, 1078-1100, 1103-1138 (1819) (extensive debate on Andrew Jackson's actions during the Seminole War, and the trial and execution of British subjects Alexander Arbuthnot and Robert C. Ambrister).

61. ". . . Spain must immediately make her election, either to place a force in Florida adequate at once to the protection of her territory, and to the fulfillment of her engagements, or cede to the United States a province, of which she retains nothing but the nominal possession, but which is, in fact, a derelict, open to the occupancy of every enemy, civilized or savage, of the United States, and serving no other earthly purpose than as a post of annoyance to them." (Letter from John Quincy Adams to Erving, Am. State Papers, Foreign Relations, V, 542. Quoted in Bailey, *A Diplomatic History of the American People* at 172; Lester Harris, "The Cession of Florida and John Quincy Adams, Secretary of State," *Fla. Hist. Quar.* 36[1958]: 223)

62. Treaty of Amity, Settlement, and Limits, Between the United States of America and his Catholic Majesty (Feb. 22, 1819) 8 *Stat* 252. 16 *Annals of Congress.* 1338-1470 (discussion of the treaty with Spain); 16 *Annals of Congress* 1743-1781 (1820) (discussion of the Spanish treaty in the House of Representatives). A list of the congressional acts that relate to the territory of Florida can be found at 3 *Stat.* 654.

63. An act for carrying into execution the treaty between the United States and Spain, 3 *Stat.* 637 (1821). An earlier version of this act was passed on March 3, 1819. An Act to authorize the President of the United States to take possession of East and West Florida, and establish a temporary government therein. 3 *Stat.* 523 (1819).

64. 3 *Stat.* at 639.

65. Ibid.

66. Ibid.

67. *Territorial Papers of the United States, Florida Territory,* vol. 22, 42-43 (Clarence E. Carter, ed.; Washington, DC: Government Printing Office, 1956).

68. Ibid. at 36.

69. *Proclamation by Major General Andrew Jackson, Governor of the Provinces of the Floridas, exercising the powers of the Captain General and of the Intendant of the Island of Cuba, over the said Provinces, and of the Governors of said Provinces respectively,* Acts and resolutions of the legislative council of the Territory of Florida XIV, XV (1822). Hereinafter cited as T.A. The acts of the Legislative Council are available online at Florida Historical Legal Documents at <http://palmm.fcla.edu/law>. PALMM (Publication of Archival, Library and Museum Materials) is a cooperative initiative of the state universities of Florida. For an index of the acts of the legislative council, see William A. Wolfe and Janet B. Wolfe, *Names and Abstracts from the Acts of the Legislative Council of the Territory of Florida, 1822-1844* (Pass-A-Grille Beach, FL: W.A. and J.B. Wolfe, 1985).

70. T.A. at XX (1822).

71. For a digest of Spanish law as it existed in Louisiana at the time, see 8 *Annals of Congress* (Appendix, 1526-1570).

72. T.A. at XX (1822).

73. "The following common law practices would govern criminal proceedings: (1) No person could be charged with a capital crime (or "otherwise infamous" crime), unless indicted by a grand jury; (2) The accused shall have a right to a speedy and public trial by a jury chosen from the residents where the crime was committed; (3) The accused shall be informed of the charges against them; (4) The accused can confront the witnesses against him; (5) The accused can compel the participation of witnesses in his behalf; and (6) The accused shall have a right to legal counsel in his defense." (Ibid.)

74. Soon after his arrival, Judge Fromentin ran afoul of Andrew Jackson over judicial matters, especially over Jackson's arrest of the former Spanish governor of West Florida, José Callava, for failure to hand over documents in the case of *The Heirs of Vidal v. John Innerarity.* For the court documents and correspondence concerning this case, see 17 *Annals of Congress* (Appendix) 2328-2339.

75. An Act for the establishment of a territorial government in Florida. 3 *Stat* 654, ch. 13 (1822).

76. The papers of the territorial governors are collected in the *Territorial Papers of the United States,* vol. XXII-XXVI: *Florida Territory.*

   a. *Territorial Papers of the United States,* vol. XXII: *Florida Territory 1821-1824:*

      Part One: Papers Relating to the Transition from Spanish to American Rule

      Part Two: Papers Relating to the Administration of Governor Jackson, 1821

      Part Three: Papers Relating to the Administrations of Acting Governors Worthington (East Florida) and Walton (West Florida)

Part Four: Papers Relating to the First Administration of Governor DuVal, 1822-1825

b. *Territorial Papers of the United States,* vol. XXIII: *Florida Territory 1824-1828:*

Part Four: (Continued) Papers Relating to the First Administration of Governor DuVal, 1822-1825

Part Five: Papers Relating to the Second Administration of Governor DuVal, 1825-1828

c. *Territorial Papers of the United States,* vol. XXIV: *Florida Territory 1828-1834:*

Part Six: Papers Relating to the Third Administration of Governor DuVal, 1828-1831

Part Seven: Papers Relating to the Fourth Administration of Governor DuVal, 1831-1834

d. *Territorial Papers of the United States,* vol. XXV: *Florida Territory 1834-1839:*

Part Eight: Papers Relating to the Administration of Governor Eaton, 1834-1836

Part Nine: Papers Relating to the First Administration of Governor Call, 1836-1839

Part Ten: Papers Relating to the Second Administration of Governor Call, 1839

e. *Territorial Papers of the United States,* vol. XXVI: *Florida Territory 1839-1845:*

Part Eleven: Papers Relating to the Administration of Governor Reid, 1839-1841

Part Twelve: Papers Relating to the Third Administration of Governor Call, 1841-1844

Part Thirteen: Papers Relating to the Administration of Governor Branch, 1844-1845

77. "The First Session of the Legislative Council of Florida" *Fla. Hist. Quar.* 11(1933): 184; Frederick T. Davis. "Pioneer Florida: The First Session of the Legislative Council of Florida," *Fla. Hist. Quar.* 24(1946): 207; Herbert J. Doherty Jr., "Political Factions in Territorial Florida," *Fla. Hist. Quar.* 28(1949): 131; Allen Morris, "Florida Legislative Committees: Their Growth Since 1822," *Fla. Hist. Quar.* 61(1982): 125; William Graham Davis, "The Florida Legislative Council, 1822-1838" (MA thesis, Florida State University, 1970) (copy on file at the P.K. Yonge Library of Florida History at the University of Florida). There are no known printed journals of the proceedings of the Legislative Council prior to 1829. However, newspaper accounts of the proceedings have been gathered for all sessions beginning with the 2nd Session, May 1823, to the 8th Session, October 1829. The proceedings from the sessions of the Legislative Council after the 8th Session, October 1829 to 1845, were printed. The entire collection, *A Journal of the proceedings of the Territory of Florida at its . . . session,* can be found in the State Library of Florida. For a short description of these journals, see "Journals of Early Florida Legislative Proceedings" *Fla. Hist. Quar.* 21(1943): 365.

Items of interest in the Florida Archives include these documents:
> Confirmed Spanish land grant claims, 1763-1821 (S 990)
> Unconfirmed Spanish land grant claims, 1763-1821 (S 991)
> Minutes of and testimony taken before the Board of Land Commissioners for East Florida, 1823-1825 (S 995)
> Concessions for new settlers, 1791-1821 (S 997)
> Surveys of Spanish land grants, 1791-1836 (S 1836)
> Minutes, 1838-1839 (Florida Constitutional Convention) (S 535)
> Territorial Court of Appeals minutes, 1825-1845 (S 985)
> Territorial Legislative Council unicameral period records, 1822-1838 (S 876)
> Territorial Legislative Council bicameral period records, 1839-1845 (S 877)
> Territorial Legislative Council Journal, 1831-1836 (S 1240)
> Territorial Court of Appeals case files, 1825-1845 (S 73)
> Records of the late [Adams-Onís] Treaty with Spain and the cession of the Floridas by his Catholic Majesty Ferdinand the VII (S 976)

A description of these records located at the state archives can be found online. Reference the titles by their collection number (i.e., S 991).

78. An act for the establishment of a territorial government in Florida, 3 *Stat.* 654, ch. 13, section 6 (1822). For an overview of the establishment of courts in territorial Florida, see Charles D. Farris, "The Courts of Territorial Florida," *Fla. Hist. Quar.* 19(1941): 346; James M. Denham, "From a Territorial to a State Judiciary: Florida's Antebellum Courts and Judges," *Fla. Hist. Quar.* 73(1995): 443. An excellent resource for bibliographical information on the judges of territorial Florida is Walter W. Manley II and E. Canter Brown Jr., *The Supreme Court of Florida and Its Predecessor Courts, 1821-1917* (Gainesville: University Press of Florida, 1997).

79. 3 *Stat* 654, ch. 13, section 6 (1822).

80. Cases files for approximately 450 cases are located in the Florida State Archives. These case files include the original handwritten court documents, opinions, complaints, and correspondence.

81. An Act to amend the several acts for the establishment of a territorial government in Florida, § 10, 4 *Stat.* 164 (1826). The Territorial Council responded by passing the following act: An Act Dividing the Territory of Florida into thirteen election Districts and providing for the election of members of the Legislative Council. T.A. (1827); Allen Morris and Amelia R. Maguire, "Beginnings of Popular Government in Florida," *Fla. Hist. Quar.* 57(1978): 19.

82. An Act to authorize the citizens of the territories of Arkansas and Florida, to elect their officers, and for other purposes, § 5, 4 *Stat.* 332 (1829). More populous counties were granted two representatives; less populous counties only one representative.

83. An Act to reorganize the Legislative Council of Florida and for other purposes. 5 *Stat.* 263 (1838). This act created a bicameral legislature with a senate and house of representatives.

84. An Act to provide for the laying off the town of Tallahassee and the sale of the Lots therein. T.A. (1824).

85. For example, in the Treaty of Moultrie Creek, a number of Native American chiefs agreed to move their people south to several areas in the interior of Florida

south of present-day Alachua County. Treaty with the Florida Tribes of Indians (Sept. 18, 1823) 7 *Stat.* 224. For a discussion of this treaty, see John K. Mahon, "The Treaty of Moultrie Creek, 1823," *Fla. Hist. Quar.* 40(1962): 350. An article on subsequent treaties by the same author: John K. Mahon, "Two Seminole Treaties: Payne's Landing, 1832, Ft. Gibson, 1833," *Fla. Hist. Quar.* 41(1962): 1.

Volume 7 of the *United States Statutes at Large* contains treaties between the United States and various tribes of Native Americans. The index contains the names of the tribes and underneath each name are citations to the treaties signed between that tribe and the United States. Other treaties between the United States and the Native Americans of Florida include the following:

> Treaty with the Seminoles (May 9, 1832), 7 *Stat.* 368 (Payne's Landing) (in exchange for releasing claims to land in Florida, the Indians were to emigrate to lands west of the Mississippi)
>
> Treaty with the Appalachicola Band (Oct. 11, 1832), 7 *Stat.* 377 (removed Native Americans to areas west of the Mississippi)
>
> Treaty with the Seminole Indians (Mar. 28, 1833), 7 *Stat.* 423. (Ft. Gibson) (in exchange for releasing claims to land in Florida, the Indians were to emigrate to lands west of the Mississippi)

86. Treaty of Amity, Settlement, and Limits, Between the United States of America and his Catholic Majesty, art. 6. (Feb. 22, 1819), 8 *Stat.* 252. A very helpful resource concerning Florida's path to statehood is Dorothy Dodd, *Florida Becomes a State* (Tallahassee: Florida Centennial Commission, 1945).

87. In 1832, the number of residents needed for representation in Congress was 47,700. Dovell, *Florida: Historic, Dramatic, Contemporary* at 272.

88. Walter Martin, "The Proposed Division of the Territory of Florida," *Fla. Hist. Quar.* 20(1942): 260.

89. An Act to take the sense of the people of this Territory on the policy and propriety of becoming a state. T.A. (1837).

90. Dovell, *Florida: Historic, Dramatic, Contemporary* at 274.

91. An Act to call a Convention for the purpose of organising a State Government. T.A. (1838).

92. For an unofficial account of what took place at the St. Joseph Convention, see F. W. Hoskins, "The St. Joseph Convention: The Making of Florida's First Constitution," *Fla. Hist. Quar.* 16(1937): 33; F. W. Hoskins, "The St. Joseph Convention II: The Making of Florida's First Constitution," *Fla. Hist. Quar.* 16(1937): 97; F. W. Hoskins, "The St. Joseph Convention III: The Making of Florida's First Constitution," *Fla. Hist. Quar.* 16(1937): 242; F. W. Hoskins, "The St. Joseph Convention IV: The Making of Florida's First Constitution," *Fla. Hist. Quar.* 17(1938): 125. The official account of the proceedings is found in *Journal of the proceedings of a convention of delegates to form a constitution for the people of Florida, held at St. Joseph, December 1838* (printed at the Times Office, 1839).

93. Stephanie D. Moussalli, "Florida's Frontier Constitution: The Statehood, Banking and Slavery Controversies," *Fla. Hist. Quar.* 74(1996): 423; James B. Whitfield, "Florida's First Constitution," *Fla. Hist. Quar.* 17(1938): 73; Emily Porter, "The Reception of the St. Joseph Constitution," *Fla. Hist. Quar.* 17(1938): 103.

A copy of the Florida Constitution of 1838 can be found online at Florida Historical Legal Documents, supra.

94. The Missouri Compromise banned slavery in the territory north of thirty-six degrees and thirty minutes latitude. Maine, a free state, was admitted at the same time as Missouri, a slave state. An Act to authorize the people of the Missouri Territory to form a constitution and state government, and for the admission of such state into the Union on an equal footing with the original states, and to prohibit slavery in certain territories, sec. 8, 3 *Stat.* 545, 548 (1820); An ordinance for the government of the Territory of the United States northwest of the River Ohio (July 13, 1787). (The Northwest Ordinance) Commager, *Documents of American History* at 126 (available at <http://www.yale.edu/lawweb/avalon/nworder.htm>).

95. An Act for the admission of the States of Iowa and Florida into the Union, 5 *Stat.* 742 (1845); An Act supplemental to the act for the admission of Florida and Iowa into the Union, and for other purposes, 5 *Stat.* 788 (1845); An Act supplemental to the act for the admission of the States of Iowa and Florida into the Union, 5 *Stat.* 789 (1845).

96. Robert L. Gold, "The Settlement of the East Florida Spaniards in Cuba, 1763-1766," *Fla. Hist. Quar.* 42(1964): 216; Thelma Peters, "The Loyalist Migration from East Florida to the Bahama Islands," *Fla. Hist. Quar.* 40(1961): 123; Carole Watterson, "Loyalist Refugees and the British Evacuation of East Florida, 1783-1785," *Fla. Hist. Quar.* 60(1981): 1; Wilbur H. Siebert, "The Departure of the Spaniards from East Florida, 1763," *Fla. Hist. Quar.* 19(1940): 145; Wilbur H. Siebert, "How the Spaniards Evacuated Pensacola in 1763," *Fla. Hist. Quar.* 11 (1932): 48.

97. Definitive Treaty of Peace between France, Great Britain and Spain, art. 4 (February 10, 1763), 42 C.T.S., 279 (available at <http://www.yale.edu/lawweb/avalon/paris763.htm>). Robert L. Gold, "Politics and Property During the Transfer of Florida from Spanish to English Rule, 1763-1764," *Fla. Hist. Quar.* 42(1963): 16.

98. *Transcriptions of the British Colonial Office Records*, vol. 2., 593-596 (Writer's project, FL, 1939?-).

99. *American States Papers, Public Lands*, vol. 5, 756-757.

100. Treaty of Amity, Settlement, and Limits, Between the United States of America and his Catholic Majesty, art. 8 (Feb. 22, 1819), 8 *Stat.* 252.

101. An Act for ascertaining claims and titles to land within the territory of Florida, 3 *Stat.* 709 (1822). In the footnote to this act, there is an extensive discussion of the decisions of U.S. courts pertaining to claims to land in Florida.

102. From July 1822 to January 1823, the commissioners would handle land claims in Pensacola; from January 1823 to June 1823, the claims would be heard in St. Augustine. These dates were extended on a number of occasions:

    a. An Act amending, and supplementary to, the "Act for ascertaining claims and titles to land in the territory of Florida," and to provide for the survey and disposal of public lands in Florida, 3 *Stat.* 754 (1823)

    b. An Act to extend the time limited for the settlement of private land claims in the territory of Florida, 4 *Stat.* 6 (1824)

    c. An Act to extend the time for the settlement of private land claims in the territory of Florida, to provide for the preservation of the public archives in said territory, and for the relief of John Johnson, 4 *Stat.* 125 (1825)

    d. An Act to provide for the final settlement of land claims in Florida, 4 *Stat.* 405 (1830)

103. In their 1825 report to Congress, Commissioners Samuel Overton and Joseph White argued that any British claims to land in the territory of Florida that were not confirmed by the Spanish government or disposed by the Treaty of 1783 were void. *American State Papers, Public Lands,* vol. 4, 154-156. However, Congress did address the issue of the claims of Americans based on lawful grants in British West Florida when it passed "An Act confirming grants to lands in the Mississippi territory derived from the British government of West Florida, not subsequently regranted by the government of Spain or of the United States." 2 *Stat.* 776 (1812). *Claimants under British Grants in the Mississippi Territory, American State Papers, Public Lands,* vol. 3, 145 (1816); Frank P. Hamilton, "Spanish Land Grants in Florida," *Fla. Hist. Quar.* 20(1941): 20; Clinton N. Howard, "Alleged Spanish Grants in British West Florida," *Fla. Hist. Quar.* 22(1943): 74; George C. Whatley and Sylvia Cook, "East Florida Land Commission: A Study in Frustration," *Fla. Hist. Quar.* 50(1971): 39; *The Impact of Spanish Land Grants on the Development of Florida and the South Eastern United States* (available at <http://www.fig.net/pub/fig_2002/HS3/HS3_knetsch>). For transcriptions of Spanish land grants, see *Spanish Lands Grants in Florida: Briefed translations from the Archives of the Boards of Commissioners for Ascertaining Claims and Titles to Land in the Territory of Florida,* 5 vol. (Florida Historical Records Survey, 1940).

104. The *American State Papers* has an extensive collection of the records of the land commissioners. These include reports, surveys, copies of grants, and correspondence between the various parties. *American State Papers: Public Lands* (select entries):

    a. *American State Papers, Public Lands,* vol. 3:

        No. 257. Land Titles in Florida (letter to Congress from the Louisiana Legislature, December 19, 1817), 250

        No. 412. Land Claims in Florida (includes reports of commissioners, correspondence between Spanish officials from the early 1800s, the testimony of witnesses in the cases of *John H. McIntosh vs. the United States* and *Moses E. Levy vs. United States,* and the proceedings of the Board of Land Commissioners, 624-734

        No. 413. Commissioners of Land Titles in East Florida (official report submitted to the House of Representatives, May 26, 1824), 735-758

    b. *American State Papers, Public Lands,* vol. 4:

        No. 432. Claims to Lands in East and West Florida (communicated to the House of Representatives, February 22, 1825), 83-301

        No. 440, 442. Land Claims in West Florida (communicated to the House of Representatives, December 28, 1825, and January 5, 1826, respectively), 316-321

        No. 474. Land Claims in East Florida (communicated to the House of Representatives, February 23, 1826), 400-500

c. *American State Papers, Public Lands,* vol. 5:

    No. 599. Land Claim in Florida, Known as "Forbes' Purchase" (includes titles to lands, and Spanish ordinances, January 3, 1828), 329-341

    No. 630. Reports and Decisions upon Private Land Claims in East Florida (communicated to the U.S. Senate, January 30, 1828), 402-430

    No. 735. Spanish and French Ordinances Affecting Land Titles in Florida and Other Territories of France and Spain (communicated to the House of Representatives, February 13, 1829), 631-774

d. *American State Papers, Public Lands,* vol. 6:

    No. 784. Land Claims in East Florida (final report of commissioners submitted to the U.S. Senate January 18, 1830), 55-121

    No. 1085. Correspondence and Instructions Relative to Surveys of Private Confirmed Land Claims in Florida (submitted to Congress on January 4, 1833), 519-555

    No. 1087. Extracts from Solorzano's *Politica Indiana,* showing the powers of the Spanish Viceroys and Governors of the Indies in Reference to Land Grants, 556-558

    No. 1097. On claims to land in West Florida, Under British Patents Prior to the Treaty of 1783.

e. *American State Papers, Public Lands,* vol. 8:

    No. 1348. Number of Spanish Claims to Land Depending in the Courts of Florida (communicated to the House of Representatives, December 16, 1835), 247-296.

105. An Act amending, and supplementary to, the "Act for ascertaining claims and titles to land in the territory of Florida," and to provide for the survey and disposal of the public lands in Florida, 3 *Stat.* 754 (1823).

106. The Arredondo dispute eventually ended up in the Supreme Court, 31 U.S. 691 (1832).

107. An Act to provide for the armed occupation and settlement of the unsettled part of the peninsula of East Florida, 5 *Stat.* 502 (1842); An Act to amend an act entitled "An act to provide for the armed occupation and settlement of the unsettled part of the peninsula of Florida," 5 *Stat.* 671 (1844). James W. Covington, "The Armed Occupation Act of 1842," *Fla. Hist. Quar.* 40(1961): 41; Michael E. Walsh, "Legislating a Homestead Bill: Thomas Hart Benton and the Second Seminole War," *Fla. Hist. Quar.* 57(1978): 157.

108. Edward F. Keuchel, Joe Knetsch, "Settlers, Bureaucrats, and Private Land Claim: The 'Little Arredondo Grant,'" *Fla. Hist. Quar.* 68(1989): 201.

Chapter 11

Georgia Prestatehood Legal Research

Kristina L. Niedringhaus

The first historically noted incursion of Europeans into the territory that now comprises the state of Georgia occurred in 1540 under the leadership of Hernando de Soto. De Soto made his way up from the Florida peninsula to a point just south of Augusta and then turned west, making his way toward present-day Alabama and Mississippi. Although the expedition ultimately ended poorly for the Spaniards, this adventure was the precursor to European settlement of the area. By the time statehood was achieved, the Creek Indian term for the European settlers who followed de Soto was *E-cun-nau-nux-ulgee*—people greedily grasping after the lands of the red men.[1]

In 1564, the French formed the first settlement near what was to become Georgia on the St. Johns River. However, the Spaniards claimed this area, and in 1565, they settled St. Augustine in Florida and proceeded to destroy the French incursions into the area that would become Georgia. The first Spanish settlement in present-day Georgia was on St. Catherine's Island. Spain built a string of missions along the coast and laid claim to the area for the next century, until the English settlers began to come south from Charleston.[2]

In 1663, King Charles II granted the charter for the Carolina Territory, encompassing land that would eventually become Mississippi, Alabama, Georgia, South Carolina, and North Carolina. In 1665, the English charter for the Carolina territory was expanded, in direct conflict with the Spanish,

Ms. Niedringhaus would like to express her gratitude for the support and assistance of her colleagues at Georgia State University, particularly Nancy Johnson and Elizabeth Adelman, and the support of her colleagues at Texas Wesleyan University School of Law Library.

The importance of the works done by Leah Chanin and Suzanne Cassidy *(Guide to Georgia Legal Research and Legal History)* and Rebecca Simmons Stillwagon *(Georgia Legal Documents: An Annotated Bibliography)* cannot be emphasized enough. Both these works are excellent resources for researchers of Georgia legal materials and were relied on heavily by this author.

as far south as St. Augustine. In 1721, the first English settlement in what would become Georgia was established on the Altamaha River at Fort King George. During the early part of the eighteenth century, the Carolinians were feeling significant pressure from the Spaniards to the south and later from the French to the south and west. Several proposals, which never reached fruition, were put forth to settle colonies on Carolina's southern border (now Georgia) as a buffer zone. Seeds of these plans can be seen in the plan for the trusteeship that would govern Georgia from the Charter of 1732 until it was surrendered in 1752.[3]

THE CHARTER PERIOD

. The real beginnings of Georgia as a distinct entity are not found until the beginning of the trusteeship under charter from the English Crown. In 1730, a group of petitioners, the Bray Associates,[4] asked the Crown for a grant of land for the establishment of a charitable colony south of the Savannah River. When King George II granted the charter on June 9, 1732, for a period of twenty-one years, governance of the colony was given to the responsibility of twenty-one trustees, former Bray Associates. The number of trustees gradually increased significantly and an executive council of trustees was formed, but the true power resided in only a small number of interested trustees.

The Charter of 1732, establishing the colony of Georgia, granted the territory between the Pacific Ocean and the headwaters of the Savannah and Altamaha Rivers to the thirteenth colony.[5] The Georgia trustees were forbidden from holding office in the colony or gaining profit from the position of trustee.[6] Contrary to previous colonial charters in America, there was no requirement to form a legislative body. In fact, full responsibility, subject to Crown approval, for legislation in the Georgia Colony was in the hands of the trustees.[7] This led to an amazing dearth of legislative materials from that time period.

Only three legislative acts were passed during the trusteeship.[8] These acts were "An Act for . . . prohibiting the Importation and Use of Black Slaves or Negroes . . . ," "An Act to prevent the Importation and Use of Rum and Brandies in the Province of Georgia," and "An Act for maintaining the Peace with the Indians in the Province of Georgia."[9] These laws generated a great deal of conflict with the colonists and had little lasting influence.[10]

The judiciary under the trusteeship, although active, left no official records.[11] The court was created while the colonists were still in England. The court had unlimited power, and although appeals could be made to the trustees, accounts state that the trustees saw their role as supporting the decisions of the courts.[12] Lawyers were not allowed in the courts, and Albert Saye, in his *Constitutional History,* states that this was viewed as a selling point—its courts were "free from the pest and scourge of mankind called lawyers."[13] The only records of court proceedings from this period appear to be from the journal entries of William Stephens.[14] Stephens attended many sessions of the town court in Savannah between 1737 and 1741 while he was secretary to the trustees.

In 1752, the trustees surrendered the charter for the colony back to the Crown and the established government was asked to remain in place until the officers of the new government arrived.

ESTABLISHMENT OF A ROYAL COLONY

The first royal governor, Captain John Reynolds, arrived in Savannah, the capital, in October 1754. According to Abbot in *The Royal Governors of Georgia,* the population of the colony, "strung out as they were some three hundreds of miles, numbered hardly more than three thousand men, women, and children, black and white."[15] Captain Reynolds was governor until 1757, when Henry Ellis arrived from England to serve as governor until 1760. In 1760, Governor James Wright took the office that he would hold until the Revolution.

Under the royal colony a general assembly was established consisting of the commons (lower) house and the upper house. The commons house seated nineteen elected members, while the upper house was composed of the twelve appointees by the Crown to the governor's council.[16] All legislation originated in the upper house, except for measures dealing with revenue.[17] The assembly met continuously from its first meeting in January 1755 until 1776. Most records of legislation passed during this time can be found in Volumes 13, 18, and 19 of Candler's *Colonial Records* or in Hein's microfiche set of colonial session laws.[18]

The government plan submitted in 1754 detailed a structure of five courts with various jurisdictions. The general court admitted lawyers and held the same jurisdiction as the Court of the King's Bench, Common Pleas, and Exchequer over civil matters where the amount in controversy was over forty shillings.[19] The general court was to convene four times per year. William Grover arrived as the first chief justice in 1759 with three assistant judges.[20] The Court of Session and Oyer and Terminer and General Gaol Delivery was held twice yearly and heard criminal matters.[21] Maritime cases in the colony were heard by the four members of the Court of Admiralty.[22] The governor sat as the chancellor over equity cases in the Court of Chancery. Finally, similar to modern-day justices of the peace, there were the Justice of the Peace Courts or Courts of Conscience, who heard complaints of petty crimes or where the amount in controversy was not great enough to be heard in the other courts.[23] On April 24, 1760, the assembly passed an act that would influence the judicial system into statehood. "An Act for the More Easy and Speedy Recovery of Small Debts and Damages" gave justice courts civil jurisdiction.[24] This led to the establishment of small-debt courts with criminal jurisdiction.[25]

Reports of cases prior to 1800 in Georgia (except for Stephens's journal from the charter period noted earlier) appear to be found only incidentally in writings of the period.[26]

THE REVOLUTION

Georgia was the last of the thirteen colonies to join the American Revolution and did not send any representation to the First Continental Congress in 1774.[27] There is some scholarly disagreement about when Georgia actually declared itself a separate entity from England.[28] The Second Provincial Congress met in Savannah on July 4, 1775, where the delegates adopted resolutions advocating American rights and sent a petition to the king.[29] The final royal officers did not leave, however, until March 1776.[30] The Third Provincial Congress met in Augusta (due to rising violent conflicts in Savannah) and on April 15, 1776 issued the *Rules and Regulations of 1776,* which is considered the first, albeit temporary, state constitution for Georgia.[31] The document was short but established a one-chamber legislature and an executive branch strictly controlled by the legislature, and tampered very little with the colonial court system and laws.[32] The *Rules and Regulations of 1776* can be found in Volume 1 of Candler's *Revolutionary Records* and in McElreath's *A Treatise on the Constitution of Georgia.*[33]

BIBLIOGRAPHY

Minutes of the Bray Associates

Creating Georgia: Minutes of the Bray Associates, 1730-1732, and Supplementary Documents. Rodney M. Baine, ed. Athens: University of Georgia Press, 1995.

Charter of 1732

Georgia's Charter of 1732. Albert B. Saye, ed. Athens: University of Georgia Press, 1942.

Allen D. Candler. *Colonial Records of the State of Georgia*. Atlanta: Franklin Printing and Publishing Co., 1904-1916.

This set was originally thirty-nine volumes with a five-volume index set. The Charter of 1732 begins on page 1 of Volume 1 of the set. Many of the volumes have been reprinted (without indexes) by either AMS Press or University of Georgia Press, and a complete set on microfilm is available from the Georgia Department of Archives.

A microform index was compiled under the auspices of the Savannah Historical Research Association, the Federal Emergency Relief Administration, and the United States Work Projects Administration under the title *Index to Candler's The Colonial Records of Georgia,* vols. 1-19, 21-26; *The Revolutionary Records of Georgia,* vols. 1-3; *Index to Unpublished Volumes of Colonial Records,* vols. 20, 27-39 and issued in 1937 and 1959.

Walter McElreath. *A Treatise on the Constitution of Georgia, Giving the Origin, History and Development of the Fundamental Law of the State, with all Constitutional Documents Containing Such Law, and with the Present Constitution, as Amended to Date, with Annotations* § 225-237 Atlanta, GA: Harrison Co., 1912.

Rev. George White. *Historical Collections of Georgia*. New York: Pudney and Russell, 1854, 1855.

Reverend White's work was reprinted in 1968 by Heritage Papers of Danielsville, Georgia, and in 1969 and 1996 by the Genealogical Publishing Company of Baltimore and is available on microfiche from Library Resources.

Charter of Georgia: 1732 (The Avalon Project at Yale Law School), available at <http://www.yale.edu/lawweb/avalon/states/ga01.htm> (as of October 1, 2003).

Legislative Materials

Allen D. Candler. *Colonial Records of the State of Georgia*. Atlanta, GA: Franklin Printing and Publishing Co., 1904-1916.

See annotation under *Georgia's Charter of 1732* supra.

Allen D. Candler. *Revolutionary Records of the State of Georgia.* 3 volumes. Atlanta, GA: Franklin-Turner, 1908.

John D. Cushing. *Earliest Printed Laws of the Province of Georgia, 1755-1770.* 2 volumes. Wilmington, DE: Michael Glazier, Inc., 1978.

Georgia Colonial Session Laws. 16 microfiche pieces. Buffalo, NY: Hein, 1987.

Judicial Materials

"The Journal of William Stephens, 1737-1741." In Allen D. Candler, *Colonial Records of the State of Georgia,* IV and Supp. Atlanta, GA: Franklin Printing and Publishing Co., 1904-1916.

See annotation under *Georgia's Charter of 1732,* supra. These journal entries detail cases in the Town Court of Savannah from 1737-1741.

Journal of William Stephens. E. Merton Coulter, ed. Athens: University of Georgia Press, 1958-1959.

These journal entries detail cases in the Town Court of Savannah from 1737-1741.

Rules and Regulations of 1776

Allen D. Candler. *Revolutionary Records of the State of Georgia.* 3 volumes. Atlanta, GA: Franklin-Turner, 1908.

Walter McElreath. *A Treatise on the Constitution of Georgia, Giving the Origin, History and Development of the Fundamental Law of the State, with all Constitutional Documents Containing Such Law, and with the Present Constitution, as Amended to Date, with Annotations* § 52. Atlanta, GA: Harrison Co., 1912.

Miscellaneous Documents of Interest

Abstracts of Colonial Wills of the State of Georgia, 1733-1777. [Atlanta?]: Atlanta Town Committee of the National Society Colonial Dames of America in the State of Georgia for the Department of Archives and History in the Office of Secretary of State, State of Georgia, 1962.

Abstracts of Georgia Colonial Conveyance Book C-1, 1750-1761. Frances Howell Beckemeyer, comp. Atlanta, GA: R. J. Taylor Jr. Foundation, 1975.

This is a compilation of records from the first of a series of unpublished books recording conveyances in Georgia prior to 1777. The volumes are held by the Georgia Department of Archives and History.

Abstracts of Georgia Colonial Book J, 1755-1762. George Fuller Walker, comp. Atlanta, GA: R. J. Taylor Jr. Foundation, 1978.

This is a compilation of miscellaneous documents from a series of unpublished books held by the Georgia Department of Archives and History. The documents include bills of sale, deeds, marriage records, powers of attorney, and other documents. Slavery had been allowed in the colony since 1750, and this is reflected in the records.

Entry of Claims for Georgia Landholders, 1733-1755. Pat Bryant, comp. Atlanta, GA: State Printing Office, 1975.

A List of the Early Settlers of Georgia. E. Merton Coulter and Albert B. Saye, eds. Atlanta: University of Georgia Press, 1949.

This provides a list of Georgia settlers through 1941 along with notes, for many, as to how or why they arrived and their fate.

Constitution of Georgia; February 5, 1977 (The Avalon Project at Yale Law School), available at <http://www.yale.edu/lawweb/avalon/states/ga02.htm> (as of May 16, 2005).

Works on Georgia Legal Research

Leah F. Chanin and Suzanne L. Cassidy. *Guide to Georgia Legal Research and Legal History.* Norcross, GA: Harrison Co., 1990, and supp. 1992.

Georgia Legal Documents: An Annotated Bibliography. Rebecca Simmons Stillwagon, comp. Government Documents Special Interest Section, State Documents Bibliography Series. Chicago: American Association of Law Libraries, 1991.

Nancy P. Johnson and Nancy Adams Deel. "Researching Georgia Law (1998 Edition)." *Ga. St. U. L. Rev.* 14(1998): 545.

Works on Georgia History

George Gillman Smith. *The Story of Georgia and the Georgia People, 1732 to 1860.* Macon, GA: George G. Smith, 1900 (printed by Franklin Printing and Publishing Co. of Atlanta).

James Ross McCain. *Georgia as a Proprietary Province: The Execution of a Trust.* Boston: Richard G. Badger, 1917.

Amanda Johnson. *Georgia as Colony and State.* Atlanta, GA: Walter W. Brown Publishing Co., 1938.

James Etheridge Callaway. *The Early Settlement of Georgia.* Athens: University of Georgia Press, 1948.

W. W. Abbot. *The Royal Governors of Georgia, 1754-1775.* Chapel Hill: University of North Carolina Press, 1959.

Albert B. Saye. *A Constitutional History of Georgia, 1732-1968,* Rev. ed. Athens: University of Georgia Press, 1970.

Georgia: History Written by Those Who Lived It. Mills Lane, ed. Savannah, GA: Beehive Foundation, 1995.

Kenneth Coleman. *Colonial Georgia: A History.* New York: Charles Scribner's Sons, 1976.

The History of Georgia in the Eighteenth Century, as Recorded in the Reports of the Georgia Bar Association. Orville A. Park, comp. Macon, GA: s.n., 1921.

NOTES

1. Thomas A. Scott, ed., *Cornerstones of Georgia History* 24 fn. 5 (Athens: University of Georgia Press, 1995). Scott cites the writings of Benjamin Hawkins. Hawkins was appointed as the Indian agent for territory south of the Ohio River in 1796 and lived with the Creeks until his death in 1816.

2. For a brief, but excellent, discussion of French and Spanish interests during the sixteenth and early seventeenth centuries in what we know today as Georgia, see Kenneth Coleman, *Colonial Georgia* (New York: Charles Scribner's Sons, 1976).

3. Coleman provides an excellent discussion of this topic, Ibid., Ch. 1-2, and see James Ross McCain, *Georgia As a Proprietary Province* 17-18 (Boston: Richard G. Badger, 1917).

4. Minutes of the meetings of the Bray Associates along with supplementary materials are collected in Rodney M. Baine, *Creating Georgia* (Athens: University of Georgia Press, 1995).

5. Coleman, supra note 2, at 17.

6. Ibid.

7. Albert B. Saye, *A Constitutional History of Georgia, 1732-1968* 26, Rev. ed. (Athens: University of Georgia Press, 1970).

8. Leah F. Chanin and Suzanne L. Cassidy, *Guide to Legal Research and Legal History* § 3-1 (Norcross, GA: Harrison Co., 1990).

9. McCain, supra note 3, at 176-177, citing Allen D. Candler, *Colonial Records of the State of Georgia,* Vol. 1, 31-54 (Atlanta, GA: Franklin Printing and Publishing Co., 1904-1916).

10. See generally Saye, supra note 7, at 26-31 (discussing controversial legislation that never survived the trusteeship).

11. Rebecca Simmons Stillwagon, comp., *Georgia Legal Documents: An Annotated Bibliography* 27 (American Association of Law Libraries, 1991) (Chicago: Government Documents Special Interest Section, State Documents Bibliography Series).

12. Ibid., at 27, and Chanin and Cassidy, supra note 8, at 60.

13. Saye, supra note 7, at 25.

14. E. Merton Coulter, ed., *Journal of William Stephens* (Athens: University of Georgia Press, 1958-1959), and contained in "The Journal of William Stephens, 1737-1741," in Volumes IV and Supp. of Candler's *Colonial Records.*

15. W. W. Abbot, *The Royal Governors of Georgia, 1754-1775* 4 (Chapel Hill: University of North Carolina Press, 1959).

16. Coleman, supra note 2, at 177, and Chanin and Cassidy, supra note 8, at 26.

17. Chanin and Cassidy, supra note 8, at 26.

18. *Georgia Colonial Session Laws* (microform) (Buffalo, NY: Hein, 1987).

19. Coleman, supra note 2, at 178-179, and Chanin and Cassidy, supra note 8, at § 4-2.

20. Ibid.

21. Ibid.

22. Ibid.

23. For an excellent discussion of the courts under the Royal Colony, see Coleman, supra note 2, at 178-179, and Chanin and Cassidy, supra note 8, at § 4-2.

24. Chanin and Cassidy, supra note 8, at § 4-2.

25. Ibid.

26. Ibid. at § 4-4.

27. Melvin B. Hill Jr., *The Georgia State Constitution: A Reference Guide* 2-3 (Westport, CT: Greenwood Press, 1994), and Coleman, supra note 2, at 264.

28. Compare Hill, supra note 27, at 3-4, with Coleman, supra note 7, at 273-277.

29. Coleman, supra note 2, at 273-275.

30. Ibid. at 276.

31. Ibid. at 276-277, and Chanin and Cassidy, supra note 8, at § 2-1.

32. Coleman, supra note 2, at 276-277, and Hill, supra note 27, at 3-4.

33. Candler, supra note 9, at Volume 1, and Walter McElreath, *A Treatise on the Constitution of Georgia, Giving the Origin, History and Development of the Fundamental Law of the State, with all Constitutional Documents Containing Such Law, and with the Present Constitution, as Amended to Date, with Annotations* § 52 (Atlanta, GA: Harrison Co., 1912).

Chapter 12

Hawaii Prestatehood Legal Materials

Leina'ala Robinson Seeger

HISTORICAL SUMMARY

In 1967, the Honorable William S. Richardson, then chief justice of the Hawaii State Supreme Court,[1] observed:

> Hawaii is the only state whose government has successively evolved from feudal absolutism, through constitutional monarchy, independent Republic, territory of the United States, and finally the Fiftieth State of the Union. This remarkable evolution has taken place in the less than 200 years since Captain James Cook discovered the Islands in 1778.[2]

At the time of Cook's arrival, Hawaiians were living in a feudal system, with several small kingdoms, each ruled by a powerful chief *(ali'i)*. All legislative, executive, and judicial powers were vested in the highest chiefs. In addition, there was a substantial body of unwritten legal custom, passed on by oral tradition. Political, social, and religious systems were closely intertwined, and the largest body of law was the religious taboos *(kapu)*.

By 1795, Kamehameha I had conquered all islands, except Kaua'i and Ni'ihau. The chief of those islands acknowledged Kamehameha's sovereignty in 1810.[3] One of the earliest "public" laws proclaimed by Kamehameha is known as the "law of the splintered paddle" *(mamala hoe kanawai)*, which was translated as "Let the woman and the child, the aged and the infirm walk freely along the byways and lie down peacefully at the side of the road. No one shall molest them."[4]

As Western contact increased, Kamehameha had both Western advisors as well as an advisory council of chiefs, but his was still an absolute monarchy. After Kamehameha I's death in 1819, his son Kamehameha II abolished the *kapu* system and most of the ancient religion, setting the stage for early receptivity to the arrival of American missionaries in 1820 and Christianity.

With the missionaries came printing presses, which were used to print laws. Early lawmaking, under Ka'ahumanu, Kamehameha I's favorite consort and his high councillor *(Kuhina Nui),* and her council of chiefs, consisted primarily of sumptuary laws proclaimed from 1825-1829, which reflected their newly found commitment to Christianity.[5] These religiously influenced laws ranged from community prohibitions (e.g., prohibitions against murder and theft; replacement of capital punishment at the will of the king or high chiefs to trial by jury) to legislated changes in human behavior (e.g., prohibitions against adultery, fighting). Unfortunately, these laws also criminalized certain native cultural and artistic practices, such as *'awa* drinking and *hula.* Dr. Jon Osorio observes:

> The sumptuary laws proceeded to change the relationship between the various elements of Hawaiian society by creating kingdom wide regulations, granting to the state, for instance, the right to intrude into the kanaka family in ways that had not been allowed or ever before imagined.[6]

The continuing and growing influence of American and European advisers upon the affairs and laws of the kingdom and upon the national government ultimately led to the overthrow of Queen Liliuokalani in 1893 and annexation by the United States in 1898. Remediation of the ongoing erosion of Hawaiian nationhood, society, and spirit begun during these years is still being fought politically and legally at all levels of bodies and tribunals today. Still, the process of achieving statehood for a noncontiguous, multiracial territory would prove to take almost as long as dismantling the kingdom.

Locally, the rise of the sugar plantations was influential in several respects. For a brief period in the 1800s, there was legitimate mainland concern for annexing Hawaii as a potential new market and as a conduit to trade with Asian nations. The demand for Hawaiian sugar in the northern states skyrocketed during the Civil War, necessitating a rapid increase in production for isle sugar. The native Hawaiian population continued to decline in numbers and generally was unwilling to work for the *haole* (foreign) plantation "masters." Thus, plantation owners looked to Asia (China, Japan, Korea, the Philippines) and, to a lesser degree, Europe for their labor force. By 1900, Japanese comprised the largest single ethnic group in Hawaii's diverse population.[7]

While contributing to Hawaii's diversity, the growing mix of nonwhite ethnicities raised class, status, and racial issues. The local power structure, most of which derived from white missionary or plantation roots, had to consider the impacts statehood would bring to their rule (e.g., the possibility of extending the franchise to these mostly disenfranchised nonwhite groups). Racially and classwise, the local power players were not quite ready to accept the ethnic vote, nor were they anxious to dilute their own power. Active pursuit of statehood did not coalesce among the plantation owners until Congress eliminated the tariffs on sugar but proceeded to pay a bounty for continentally produced domestic sugar.

Nationally, states struggled to keep a balance of power among themselves in Congress. The southern states in particular wanted to protect their sugar market and were never supportive of Hawaiian statehood. Sugar interests in Hawaii wanted to ensure duty-free access to its continental market. Increasingly, the United States grew more interested in Hawaii from a security perspective rather than an economic one. It was particularly interested in establishing naval station rights at Pu'uloa (now Pearl Harbor). Ultimately, the reciprocity treaty that took effect in 1876 (and was renewed and extended in 1884 and 1887, at which time exclusive rights to Pearl Harbor were granted) essentially gave both sides what they sought.[8] Treaty terms mandated that no territorial concessions would be made to other foreign powers, which further served notice to other colonial powers of the extension of the Monroe Doctrine beyond the continental United States.[9]

Despite the outcome of the Civil War, the United States as a whole was still a fairly segregated society. Hawaii's multiracial population was unacceptable to the nation's mind-set, particularly in light of the perceived threat of Japan's imperial aims; this was later manifested in the federal Asian exclusion acts. After Hawaii's citizenry demonstrated its loyalty to the United States through sterling service in World War II and draft civil rights legislation began emerging at the national level, Hawaii's vital role in fostering national economic and military imperatives would be fully recognized. Statehood was achieved on August 21, 1959.

This annotation attempts to share some of the rich legal and law-related materials from Hawaii's monarchy through its territorial and early statehood period in 1959/1960. Only English-language versions or translations of the earlier materials are included here. Hawaiian diacritical marks are not used in the bibliographic entries, consistent with practices of those periods. Consult the Judd and Pimsleur sources under Selected Bibliography, final section of the chapter, for listings of Hawaiian language materials. Where feasible, the materials were examined directly in print or microform.

In the territorial portion, the session laws were reviewed and notations made for changes affecting the executive branch, the legislature, and the state and federal courts.

MONARCHY (1795/1796 TO JANUARY 17, 1893)

Constitutions

The First Constitution of Hawaii, Granted by Kamehameha III., October 8,
1840. 9 pp. Translation reprinted in *The Fundamental Law of Hawaii.*
Edited and indexed by Lorrin A. Thurston. Honolulu: The Hawaiian Gazette Co., Ltd., 1904. pp. [1]-9; indexed at pp. [291]-294. Prefatory notes
at pp. vii-viii.

Written by the king and his chiefs.[10] Prefaced by an amended version of the
1839 Declaration of Rights of the people and the chiefs. Provides "that the
King shall be the chief judge of the Supreme Court, and that it shall be his
duty to execute the laws of the land, also all decrees and treaties with other
countries, all however in accordance with the laws" [pp. 3-4]. Also provides
for appointment of a premier by the king, four island governors, a house of
nobles (hereditary), and a representative body. The king, premier, and four
appointees of the representative body constitute a six-person supreme court
of the kingdom.

Constitution, Granted by His Majesty Kamehameha III., King of the Ha-
waiian Islands, by and with the Advice and Consent of the Nobles and
Representatives of the People in Legislative Council Assembled, June
14th, 1852. Reprinted in *The Fundamental Law of Hawaii.* Edited and
indexed by Lorrin A. Thurston. Honolulu: The Hawaiian Gazette Co.,
Ltd., 1904. pp. [155]-168; indexed at pp. [325]-336. p

Drafted by a legislatively created, three-person commission, with one appointee each from the king, the house of nobles, and the house of representatives.[11] The Declaration of Rights is much expanded in this second constitution. Provides for appointment by the king of a "special Counsellor
[Kuhina Nui]," with powers approaching that of the king; an advisory privy
council of state, ministers, governors; a legislative body comprised of the
house of nobles (life appointment by the king) and the house of representatives; and an appointed three-member supreme court, and such inferior
courts as the legislature may establish. The privy council advised the king
and directed the affairs of the kingdom. The chief justice was the chancellor
of the kingdom. Provides for universal (male) suffrage.

Constitution. Granted by His Majesty Kamehameha V., by the Grace of
God, King of the Hawaiian Islands, on the Twentieth Day of August,
A. D. 1864. Reprinted in *The Fundamental Law of Hawaii.* Edited and

indexed by Lorrin A. Thurston. Honolulu: The Hawaiian Gazette Co., Ltd., 1904. pp. [169]-179, 180; indexed at pp. [337]-348.

Kamehameha V refused to take the oath upholding the 1852 constitution, being opposed to universal suffrage without a property qualification and to restrictions on royal power.[12] The king called a constitutional convention to enact a new constitution, but even before it was to convene on July 7, 1864, it was clear that there would be no agreement by members on these and other issues. The king abolished the Constitution of 1852, and with his advisors drafted a new third constitution, which allowed the king more power and unilateral action, and abolished universal suffrage in favor of property and literacy qualifications on voting.

Constitution. Granted by Kalakaua, July 6, 1887. Reprinted in *The Fundamental Law of Hawaii.* Edited and indexed by Lorrin A. Thurston. Honolulu: The Hawaiian Gazette Co., Ltd., 1904. pp. [181]-194; indexed at pp. [349]-362.

Referred to as the "Bayonet Constitution of 1887" because it was imposed upon the king by the white-dominated Hawaiian League under the leadership of attorney/publisher Lorrin Thurston, this fourth constitution curtailed the power of the king accorded by the 1864 constitution and effectively transferred power to his appointed cabinet and the legislature.[13]

Property qualifications were imposed for the electorate, thus disenfranchising about three-quarters of the native Hawaiian electorate. Queen Liliuokalani attempted to proclaim a new constitution in 1893 to restore monarchical powers, but that attempt ended with her overthrow.

Laws and Compilations

Laws of the Sandwich Islands, by Kauikeaouli, the King [Kamehameha III]. [Honolulu], Oahu: Mission Press, 1835. 8 pp.

January 5, 1835: Kamehameha III proclaims and signs a penal code of five chapters, relating to murder and homicide, theft, unlawful sexual intercourse and divorce, fraud and false witness, drunkenness, and offenses committed while intoxicated.

Hawaiian laws 1841-1842; translation of the constitution and laws of the Hawaiian Islands, established in the reign of Kamehameha III . . . [Lahaina, Maui]: Lahainaluna, 1842; Green Valley, NV: Ted Adameck, 1994. 120, v, 123 pp.

First compilation published 1841, republished in 1842, with additional laws enacted that year. Popularly referred to as the "Blue Book."[14]

The laws and resolutions passed at the Annual Council of the Hawaiian Council of the Hawaiian Nobles and Representatives: Convened according to the Constitution, at Lahaina, April, 1843. Lahaina, Maui: Lahainaluna, Seminary Press, 1843. 6 pp.

Statute laws of His Majesty Kamehameha III., King of the Hawaiian Islands: passed by the Houses of Nobles and Representatives, during the twenty-first[-twenty-second] year of his reign and the third and fourth [and fifth] years of his public recognition, A.D., 1845 and 1856 [and 1847]: to which are appended the acts of public recognition, and the treaties with other nations. Honolulu, Oahu: C.E. Hitchcock, printer, government press, 1846-1847. 2 vols. Vol. 1: 1845-1846; Vol. 2: 1847.

First comprehensive acts to organize government in 1845, 1846, and 1847.[15] A joint resolution authorized the attorney general to draw up laws for the organization of government: the First Act of Kamehameha III to Organize the Executive Ministries, the Second Act of Kamehameha III to Organize the Executive Departments, and the Third Act of Kamehameha III to Organize the Judiciary Department. Collectively, these acts are referred to as the Organic Acts of 1845-1846.

Also includes legislation introducing a western land tenure system through establishment of a board of land commissioners. This led to the division *(mahele)* of lands beginning in 1848.

A Supplement to the statute laws of His Majesty, Kamehameha III., king of the Hawaiian Islands: containing the acts and resolutions passed by the Houses of Nobles and Representatives, during the twenty-third year of his reign, and the sixth year of his public recognition, A.D. 1848. Honolulu, Oahu: Government Press, 1848.

Supplements 1845-1846 and 1847 acts, and includes laws of 1848.

Penal Code of the Hawaiian Islands, passed by the House of Nobles and Representatives on the 21st of June, A.D. 1850, to which are appended the other acts passed by the House of Nobles and Representatives during their general session for 1850. Honolulu, Oahu: Printed by H.M. Whitney, Government Press, 1850. xxxi, 243 pp.

Penal code, with separate chapter numbers enacted 1850, prepared by W.L. Lee.

Laws of His Majesty Kamehameha III., king of the Hawaiian Islands: passed by the Nobles and Representatives at their session, 1851. Honolulu: Printed by order of the government, 1851. 120 pp.

Constitution and laws of His Majesty Kamehameha III., king of the Hawaiian Islands: passed by the Nobles and Representatives at their session, 1852. Honolulu: Printed by order of the legislature, 1852. 88 pp.

Laws of His Majesty Kamehameha III., king of the Hawaiian Islands: passed by the Nobles and Representatives at their session, 1853. Honolulu: Printed by order of the government, 1853. 78 pp.

Laws of His Majesty Kamehameha III., king of the Hawaiian Islands: passed by the Nobles and Representatives at their session, 1854. Honolulu: Printed by order of the government, 1854. 46 pp.

Laws of His Majesty Kamehameha IV., king of the Hawaiian Islands: passed by the Nobles and Representatives at their session, 1855. Honolulu: Printed by order of the government, 1855. 71 pp.

Includes treaties between the Hawaiian Kingdom and Great Britain (1851), the Free Hanseatic Republic of Bremen (1854), and the kingdoms of Sweden and Norway (1855), pp. [53]-71, following index.

Laws of His Majesty Kamehameha IV., king of the Hawaiian Islands: passed by the Nobles and Representatives at their session, 1856. Honolulu: Printed by order of the government, 1856. 70 pp.

The Civil code of the Hawaiian islands, passed in the year of Our Lord 1859: to which is added an appendix, containing laws not expressly repealed by the Civil code; the session laws of 1858-9; and treaties with foreign nations. Published by authority. Honolulu: Printed for the government, 1859. iv, [5]-555 pp.

Written by a committee appointed by the king, with reviewers to compare the Hawaiian and English versions.

Laws of His Majesty Kamehameha IV., king of the Hawaiian Islands: passed by the Nobles and Representatives at their session, 1860. Honolulu: Printed by order of the government, 1860. 66 pp.

Includes "Constitution granted by His Majesty Kamehameha III, king of the Hawaiian Islands, by and with the advice and consent of the Nobles and

Representatives of the people, in Legislative Council assembled, June 14, 1852." Honolulu: Reprinted by order of the government, 1860 (pp. [45]-62).

"Articles of amendment of the Constitution of this kingdom proposed and agreed to, pursuant to the 105th article of the original Constitution" (pp. [63]-64), signed: 18th day of April, A.D., 1856. Kamehameha.).

Laws of His Majesty Kamehameha IV., king of the Hawaiian Islands: passed by the Nobles and Representatives at their session, 1862. Honolulu: Printed by order of the government, 1862. 45 pp.

Laws of His Majesty Kamehameha V., king of the Hawaiian Islands: passed by the Legislative Assembly, at its session, 1864-65. Honolulu: Printed by order of the government, 1865. 102 pp.

Includes 1864 constitution.

Laws of His Majesty Kamehameha V., king of the Hawaiian Islands: passed by the Legislative Assembly, at its session, 1866-67. Honolulu: Printed by order of the government, 1866. 26 pp.

Laws of His Majesty Kamehameha V., king of the Hawaiian Islands: passed by the Legislative Assembly, at its session, 1868. Honolulu: Printed by order of the government, 1868. 63+ pp.

The Penal code of the Hawaiian Kingdom, compiled from the Penal code of 1850: and the various penal enactments since made, pursuant to Act of the Legislative Assembly, June 22d, 1868. Published by authority. Honolulu, Oahu: Printed at the Government Press, 1869. xlii, 367, [1], 13, [1] pp.

"Constitution granted by His Majesty Kamehameha V . . . on the twentieth day of August, A.D. 1864" and amendment, May 13, 1868: 13, [1] pp. at end.

Laws of His Majesty Kamehameha V., king of the Hawaiian Islands: passed by the Legislative Assembly, at its session, 1870. Honolulu: Printed by order of the government, 1870. 100 pp.

Includes treaties.

Laws of His Majesty Kamehameha V., king of the Hawaiian Islands: passed by the Legislative Assembly, at its session, 1872. Honolulu: Hawaiian Government Printing Office, 1872. 51 pp.

Includes treaties.

Laws of His Majesty Kalakaua, king of the Hawaiian Islands: passed by the Legislative Assembly, at its session, 1874. Honolulu: Black and Auld, 1874. 79 pp.

Laws of His Majesty Kalakaua, king of the Hawaiian Islands: passed by the Legislative Assembly, at its session, 1876. Honolulu: Printed by H.L. Sheldon, 1876. 187 pp.

Includes treaties.

Laws of His Majesty Kalakaua, king of the Hawaiian Islands: passed by the Legislative Assembly, at its session, 1878. Honolulu: Printed by J.H. Black, 1878. 72 pp.

Laws of His Majesty Kalakaua, king of the Hawaiian Islands: passed by the Legislative Assembly, at its session, 1880. Honolulu: P.C. Advertiser Co. Steam Print, 1880. 80 pp.

Chapter 32 of these laws is an act "To provide for the codification and revision of the Laws of the Kingdom."

Laws of His Majesty Kalakaua I., king of the Hawaiian Islands: passed by the Legislative Assembly, at its session, 1882. Honolulu: Printed by order of the government, Hawaiian Gazette Book and Job Print, 1882. 133 pp.

Includes treaties.

Compiled laws of the Hawaiian Kingdom: published by authority. Honolulu: Printed at the Hawaiian Gazette Office, 1884. vi, 777 pp.

Caption title: The Civil code of the Hawaiian Islands . . . (May 17th, A.D. 1859).

The Ministers sought the advice of the Supreme Court as to what form this compilation should take. "The Justices suggested that the compilation be made so as to present in a convenient arrangement all the laws now in force, and as they stand amended, but without any changes in the words and phrases of the statutes" (compiler's Preface, at iv).

"Appendix to the Civil code": pp. [493]-701. "The matter here reproduced from the original 'Appendix to the Civil Code' extends only to page 499. The pages following contain such of the session laws from 1860 to1882 as have not been repealed or placed elsewhere in the compilation" (compiler's note, p. [492]).

Laws of His Majesty Kalakaua I., king of the Hawaiian Islands: passed by the Legislative Assembly, at its session, 1884. Honolulu: Printed by order of the government, P.C. Advertiser Steam Print, 1884. 139 pp.

Laws of His Majesty Kalakaua I., king of the Hawaiian Islands: passed by the Legislative Assembly, at its session, 1886. Honolulu: Printed by order of the government, P.C. Advertiser Steam Print, 1886. 180 pp.

Laws of His Majesty Kalakaua I., king of the Hawaiian Islands: passed by the Legislative Assembly, at its session, 1887. Honolulu: Printed by order of the government, Hawaiian Gazette Print., 1887. 88 pp.

Includes constitution of 1887.

Laws of His Majesty Kalakaua I., king of the Hawaiian Islands: passed by the Legislative Assembly, at its session, 1888. Honolulu: Printed by order of the government, Gazette Pub. Co., 1888. 248 pp.

Chapter 66 abolished the offices of the third and fourth associate justices [verso of title page, VIII *Hawaiian Reports*].

Laws of His Majesty Kalakaua I., king of the Hawaiian Islands: passed by the Legislative Assembly, at its session, 1890. Honolulu: Printed by order of the government, Gazette Pub. Co., 1890. 271 pp.

Laws of Her Majesty Liliuokalani, queen of the Hawaiian Islands: passed by the Legislative Assembly, at its session, 1892. Honolulu: Printed by order of the government, Robert Grieve, [1892]. 412 pp.

"Constitution, 1887": pp. [343]-361; "Amendments to the Constitution, passed by the Legislature of 1892": pp. 362-363. Includes an act to significantly reorganize the judiciary department as a governmental department.

Chapter 57 made the supreme court appellate only and transferred all other business to newly created circuit courts [verso of title page (p. v) VIII *Hawaiian Reports*].

Legislative Records

General Records of the Hawaii Legislature, 1840-1893. Honolulu. 49.04 linear ft. (includes 8 vols.). Forms part of *Records of the Legislature of the Hawaiian Kingdom.*

Consists of the official files of the legislative council (1840-1850); house of nobles and house of representatives (1851-1863); and legislative assembly

(1864-1893) of the Hawaiian Kingdom. Records routine proceedings of the legislature. Contains bills and laws, including constitutional amendments; communications and messages, including the king's speeches, broadside, and proclamations; correspondence; financial records; draft journals, and minutes, used to create the official journals in series 221; notices; petitions; procedural records, including house rules, records of votes, and orders of the day; reports; and resolutions.

Official Journals, 1841-1892. 5.63 linear ft. (42 vols.). Forms part of *Records of the Legislature of the Hawaiian Kingdom.*

Contains approved minutes of the daily sessions of the legislative council (1841-1850); house of nobles (1851-1862); house of representatives (1854-1859); and legislative assembly (1864-1892) of the Hawaiian Kingdom. Consists primarily of a summary record of motions; bills and resolutions introduced, referred, and read; and results of votes, sometimes including a record of individual votes cast. Occasionally includes a summary of discussion, points of order, waiver of rules, and a record of petitions and other communications received. Normally includes the monarch's speech and names of members in the journal for the first day of each legislative session. Unlike journals of later legislatures, this series does not include the full text of committee reports.

Treaties with the United States

Treaty with the Hawaiian Islands. Signed December 23, 1826; entered into force December 23, 1826.

Treaty of commerce, friendship, and navigation with Kamehameha III. Available on the Web at <http://www.pixi.com/~kingdom/hawaiis.html>.

Treaty with the Hawaiian Islands. Signed December 20, 1849; ratified August 24, 1850; proclaimed November 9, 1850. Washington, DC: GPO, 1875. T.S. No. 160, 9 *Stat.* 178; 18 (part 2) *Stat.* 406.

Treaty of commerce, friendship, and navigation with Kamehameha III. Available on the Web at <http://www.pixi.com/~kingdom/hawaiis.html>.

Postal Convention between the United States of America and the Hawaiian Islands. Signed May 4, 1870. Boston, MA: Little, Brown, 1871. 16 *Stat.* 1113. Concluded by Kamehameha V.

Convention between the United States of America and His Majesty the King of the Hawaiian Islands. Commercial Reciprocity. Concluded January 30, 1875; . . . Entered into Force September 9, 1876. Washington, DC: GPO, 1877. T.S. No. 161, 19 *Stat.* 625. Supplemented by Convention of December 6, 1884.

Concluded by Kalakaua, this treaty allowed set schedules of goods to flow between Hawaii and the United States, including "Sandwich Island Sugar" and related products. Art. 5 extended the treaty for seven years, was supplemented in 1884, and renewed in 1887 with an amendment granting the United States exclusive naval station rights at Pearl Harbor. It remained in force until June 14, 1902. Available on the Web at <http://www.pixi.com/~kingdom/hawaiis.html>.

Convention between the Post-Office Department of the Kingdom of Hawaii and the Post-Office Department of the United States of America, concerning the exchange of money-orders, September 11, 1883. Washington, DC: GPO, 1885. 23 *Stat.* 736.

Concluded by Kalakaua. Available on the Web at <http://www.pixi.com/~kingdom/hawaiis.html>.

Supplementary Convention between the United States of America and his Majesty the King of the Hawaiian Islands to limit the duration of the Convention respecting commercial reciprocity between the United States of America and the Hawaiian Kingdom, concluded January 30, 1875. Concluded December 6, 1884. Washington, DC: GPO, 1889. 24 *Stat.* 1399.

Concluded by Kalakaua, this convention renewed the 1875 convention for another seven years. Available on the Web at <http://www.pixi.com/~kingdom/hawaiis.html>.

Parcels Post Convention between the United States of America and the Hawaiian Kingdom, December 19, 1888. Washington, DC: GPO, 1889. 24 *Stat.* 1472.

Concluded by Kalakaua January 10, 1889.

Case Law

Hawaiian Reports, Vols. I-VIII, 1847-1893. 1 Haw.-8 Haw.

Vol. I: *Reports of Some of the Judgments and Decisions of the Courts of Record of the Hawaiian Islands for the Ten Years Ending with 1856,* by

George M. Robertson. Honolulu: Printed at the Government Press, 1857. Honolulu: Reprinted by Robert Grieve, Book and Job Printers, 1889.

"This book is a complete reprint of the original publication of Volume I of Hawaiian Reports, which was first printed in the year 1857. The marginal figures refer to pages of the original, it being necessary that they be preserved on account of the references to them made in the decisions reported in later volumes of the Hawaiian Reports. December, 1889" [From verso of title page].

Vol. II: *Reports of a Portion of the Decisions Rendered by the Supreme Court of the Hawaiian Islands, in Law, Equity, Admiralty, and Probate, 1857-1865,* by Robert G. Davis, Justice of the Supreme Court, and Member of His Majesty's Privy Council of State. Honolulu: Government Press—J. H. Black, Printer, 1866. Honolulu: Reprinted by Robert Grieve, Book and Job Printers, 1890.

Includes a listing of judges of the supreme court, a table of cases, and a topical index with abstracts.

Vol. III: *Reports of Decisions Rendered by the Supreme Court of the Hawaiian Islands, in Law, Equity, Admiralty and Probate, 1866-1877.* Compiled by the Associate Justices. Honolulu: H.S. Sheldon, Printer, 1877. Honolulu: Reprinted by Hawaiian Printing Co., Ltd., 1935; Buffalo, NY: Reproduced by Dennis and Co., 1966.

Includes a listing of judges of the supreme court and the attorney general, a prefatory note on court and attorney general reorganizations, a table of cases, an index with abstracts, and court rules and orders (1877).

Vol. IV: *Reports of Decisions Rendered by the Supreme Court of the Hawaiian Islands, in Law, Equity, Admiralty and Probate, 1877–1883.* Compiled by Chief Justice Judd. Honolulu: Pacific Commercial Advertiser Company, 1883. Honolulu: Reprinted by Paradise of the Pacific, 1935; Buffalo, NY: Photoreproduced by Dennis and Co., 1966.

Includes a listing of judges of the supreme court, a prefatory note on supreme court and attorneys general succession, a table of cases, memorials to judges, court rules and orders (1883), and a topical index with abstracts.

Vol. V: *Reports of Decisions Rendered by the Supreme Court of the Hawaiian Islands: Admiralty, Criminal, Divorce, Equity, Law, and Probate, July Term, 1883, to October Term, 1886, Inclusive.* Compiled by William

Foster, Clerk Supreme Court. Honolulu: Hawaiian Gazette Co. Print, 1887. Buffalo, NY: Photo-reproduced by Dennis and Co., 1969.

"The Supreme Court has original and appellate jurisdiction: cases reported in this book are only those decided by the Full Court, on appeal or exceptions. The Legislature of 1886 increased the number of the justices of the supreme court to five [Statutes 1886, Chap. 59]. The decisions in this volume are printed from slips revised by the Justice writing the opinion: head-notes and index are by the compiler" [from Prefatory Note].

Includes listing of the justices of the supreme court and the attorneys general during the term of these reports, corrections, court rules, cases reported, memorials of judges, the 1887 Hawaii constitution, and a topical index.

A new feature is introduced in Vol. V's index which carries forward. Under the index heading "Cases" is a list of cases from *Hawaiian Reports* Vols. I-IV, which were approved, cited, distinguished, or reversed in cases included in this volume. Under the index heading "Statutes" is a list of statutes, code, and constitutional sections cited in cases included in this volume.

Vol. VI: *Decisions at Chambers by Single Justices of the Supreme Court of the Hawaiian Islands: Admiralty, Criminal, Equity, Law, and Probate. Not Appealed from, and not Hitherto Reported, 1866–1889.* Compiled by William Foster. Honolulu: Printed by the Hawaiian Gazette Co., 1889. Honolulu: Reprinted by Mercantile Printing Co., Ltd., 1935.

"The present volume is made up entirely of decisions of the Single Judges, at Chambers, not appealed from, from 1866 to date, arranged chronologically. Many of these decisions have been printed in the local newspapers, revised contemporaneously by the Judges who wrote them: more than one-third of them have never appeared in print, but have been found by searching the records in the Clerk's office, and are given verbatim. Cases involving only questions of fact have generally been omitted. Cases found too late for insertion in their proper order are added in an Appendix. Head-notes and Index are by the compiler" [from Prefatory Note].

Includes listing of the justices of the supreme court, cases reported, an appendix of cases out of chronological order, and topical index with citation features.

Vol. VII: *Reports of Decisions Rendered by the Supreme Court of the Hawaiian Islands: Admiralty, Criminal, Divorce, Equity, Law, and Probate, January Term, 1887, to October Term, 1889, Inclusive.* Compiled by the Justices of the Supreme Court. Honolulu: Printed by the Hawaiian Gazette Co., 1890.

Includes listings of the justices of the supreme court and attorneys general, cases reported, an appendix of cases out of chronological order, and topical index with citation features.

Vol. VIII: *Reports of Decisions Rendered by the Supreme Court of the Hawaiian Islands: Criminal, Divorce, Equity, Law, Probate. September, 1889, to December, 1892, Inclusive.* Compiled by William Foster. Honolulu: Printed by the Hawaiian Gazette Co., 1893.

An appendix includes opinions to the government, decisions of the full court and of single judges out of chronological order, memorials, and topical index with citation features.

Case Digests and Tools

Edings, W.S. *A Digest of the Hawaiian Supreme Court Reports, Volumes 1-14, January 6, 1847-May 20, 1903.* Honolulu: Bulletin Publishing Co., 1903.

Provides topical index to supreme court opinions.

Finley, Elizabeth and Bernhard Knollenberg. *Hawaiian Citations.* New York: s.n., 1924. 63 pp. with 1931 and 1941 supps.

Includes citations of cases in the Supreme Court of Hawaii, U.S. District Court for the District of Hawaii, Hawaiian cases in the Circuit Court of Appeals for the Ninth Circuit, and Hawaiian cases in the Supreme Court of the United States.

Indexes of Court Cases, ca. 1845-1893: cases handled by the Circuit or Supreme Courts during the Hawaiian monarchy. Honolulu: Hawaii State Judiciary, 1981. 1 vol. (various pagings).

Includes indexes for civil cases, criminal cases, circuit and supreme court divorce cases and remarriage petitions, and for governor's divorce cases and remarriage petitions. Circuits included during this time period are the first, second, third, and fourth.

Manual of Citations of the Hawaiian Reports Published by the Supreme Court of the Territory of Hawaii. [Honolulu]: Printed by Tongg Publishing Co., 1947. 105 pp.

"The manual follows the principles familiar to all attorneys who have used Shepard's Citations" [Preface]. Includes citations of *Hawaiian Reports,* Vols. 1-36 and *U.S. District Court Reports,* Vols. 1-4.

Shepard's Hawai`i Case Names Citator: A Compilation of Case Names and Citations of Hawaii Cases Decided from 1847 to the Present. Colorado Springs, CO: LexisNexis (formerly published by Shepard's/McGraw-Hill), 1988- . One hardbound vol., updated semiannually with cumulative softbound pamphlets.

"A compilation of case names and citations of Hawaii cases decided from 1847 to the present" [from title page]. Cases reported are from the *Hawai`i Reports* and reports of the U.S. District Court for the District of Hawaii.

Shepard's Hawai`i Citations. 4th ed. Colorado Springs, CO: LexisNexis (formerly Shepard's Company), 1997- . 1 vol., updated bimonthly with softbound supplements and advance sheets. Also available in Shepard's Online and LexisNexis.

"A compilation of citations to Hawai`i cases reported in various series of *Hawai`i Reports,* in the Pacific Reporter, and in the United States District Court for Hawai`i, the United States Constitution and statutes, and the Hawai`i Constitution, codes, revised laws, court rules" [from title page]. Includes a popular names table for acts.

Thayer, Wade W. *A Digest of the Decisions of the Supreme Court of Hawaii. Volumes 1 to 22 Inclusive, January 6, 1847, to October 7, 1915.* Honolulu: Paradise of the Pacific Press, 1916. 907 pp.

West's Hawaii Digest. St. Paul, MN: West (formerly West Pub. Co.), 1967- . 12 numbered volumes in 20 volumes. Updated by annual pocket parts, cumulative supplements, and weekly reporter advance sheets. Also available in CD-ROM (West).

Digest of reported Hawaii state appellate and federal court opinions from 1847 to date, arranged according to the West topic-key number system. Incorporates case law digested in *A Digest of the Hawaiian Supreme Court Reports.*

Newspapers

Newspapers played a vital role in chronicling Hawaii's transformation from monarchy to statehood, including reproducing laws, proclamations, and orders. For further research, please consult the Chapin and Mo'okini titles included in the Selected Bibliography and the Ulukau Web site at <http://ulukau.org/english.php>.

PROVISIONAL GOVERNMENT
(JANUARY 17, 1893 TO JULY 3, 1894)

Constitution

The 1887 constitution continued in effect until the 1894 constitution was proclaimed.

Laws

Laws of the Provisional Government of the Hawaiian Islands, passed by the Executive and Advisory Councils. Honolulu: R. Grieve, 1893-1894. 3 vols.

1893, Acts 1-86 ([1894]); 1894 issued in separate English and Hawaiian vols. Act 69, "An Act to Provide for a Constitutional Convention," was approved March 15, 1894.

Case Reports

Hawaiian Reports, Vol. IX, 9 *Haw.,* 1893-1894

Vol. IX: *Reports of Decisions Rendered by the Supreme Court of the Hawaiian Islands: Criminal, Divorce, Equity, Law, Probate. Years 1893 and 1894.* Honolulu: Robert Grieve, 1895.

Includes opinions of the court under the provisional government and the Republic of Hawaii. Appendix C: Constitution of the Republic of Hawaii, July 3, 1894.

Case Digests and Tools

See Case Digests and Tools, under Monarchy, for applicable titles.

REPUBLIC OF HAWAII
(JULY 4, 1894 TO AUGUST 11, 1898/APRIL 29, 1900)

Constitutional Convention

Constitution of the Republic of Hawaii. Draft submitted to the constitutional convention by the executive council. [Honolulu: 1894]. vi, 111 pp.

Proceedings of the Hawaiian Constitutional Convention, Wednesday, May 30-Thursday, July 5, 1894. Compiled from the reports of the Pacific commercial advertiser, together with the full text of the constitution as it was finally adopted. Honolulu: Hawaiian Gazette Co., [1894]. 110, 55, vi pp.

"Constitution of the Republic of Hawaii": 55, vi pp.

Laws and Compilations

Constitution of the Republic of Hawaii and laws passed by the Executive and Advisory Councils of the Republic. Honolulu: R. Grieve, 1895. 130 pp.

Constitution of the Republic of Hawaii (pp. [75]-123). Includes laws for 1894 (the first year of the republic).

Laws of the Republic of Hawaii passed by the Legislature at its session. Honolulu: R. Grieve, 1895-1898. 3 vols. Annual (varies).

None published in 1897; 1895-1898. Laws for 1895 passed in special session.

The Civil laws of the Hawaiian Islands, 1897: Compiled from the Civil code of 1859 and the Session laws of 1860 to 1896 inclusive: published by authority. Honolulu: Hawaiian Gazette Print, 1897. xiii, 902 pp.

"Compiler's preface" signed: Sidney Miller Ballou. "Appendix. Rules and regulations for administering oaths and holding elections": pp. [785]-831.

The Penal laws of the Hawaiian Islands, 1897. Compiled from the Penal code of 1869 and the Session laws of 1879 to 1896 inclusive: published by authority. Honolulu: Hawaiian Gazette, 1897. viii, 601 pp.

"Compiler's preface" signed: Sidney Miller Ballou.

The Laws of Hawaii. Comprising the civil laws and the penal laws compiled by Sidney M. Ballou and published by authority in 1897, and the session laws of 1898, modified in conformity with the recommendations of the Commission appointed by the President of the United States to recommend to Congress legislation concerning the Hawaiian Islands, under the provisions of the Joint resolution of Congress approved July 7, 1898. Washington, DC: U.S. GPO, 1898. 560 pp.

Not enacted as "Civil Laws" (basis: compiled laws of 1884, with total reorganization of chapters and other changes) and "Penal Laws" (based on 1869

Penal Code, using the same scheme with new matter added at the end). This compilation made changes dictated by the 1894 constitution, added chapter notes referring to original statutes as amended, and included case notes of decisions from the first ten volumes of the *Supreme Court Reports.*

Legislative Records

General Records of the Hawaii Legislature, 1895-1898. Honolulu. 13.17 linear ft. (finding aid available). Forms part of *Records of the Legislature of the Republic of Hawaii.*

Consists of the official files of the Senate and House of Representatives of the Republic of Hawaii. Most of the records appear to have been assembled and maintained by the clerks of the respective bodies. Contains some material that may be personal papers; records routine proceedings of the legislature, such as legislative histories of bills; and provides information and opinion on specific issues. Contains bills and laws; communications; financial records; draft journals; petitions; procedural records; reports; and resolutions.

Official Journals, 1895-1898. 2.02 linear ft. (12 vols.). Finding aid available. Forms part of *Records of the Legislature of the Republic of Hawaii.*

Records the proceedings of the Legislature of the Republic of Hawaii, including a summary of daily sessions, including roll call, motions, votes, summaries of discussion, questions to ministers, rulings from the chair, committee reports, and communications; tabulated information on members of the legislature, such as their electoral district, committee assignments, and leadership positions; histories of house and senate bills; and indexes of the journals. The senate journal of 1895 contains the proceedings of the executive sessions in which the annexation issue is prominent. Records debates on the public lands bill and such matters as outlawing foot binding and regulating plumbing.

Draft Treaty

Resolution of the Senate of Hawaii Ratifying the Treaty of Annexation. Honolulu: 1897. Signed in Duplicate in Washington, D.C. June 16, 1897; Adopted by Special Session of the Senate of the Republic of Hawaii and Certified by Senate President on September 9, 1897. Reprinted in *Revised Laws of Hawaii,* 1905, at 36-39.

The treaty text is included in this resolution. The treaty was not ratified by the U.S. Senate.

Case Reports

Hawaiian Reports, Vol. IX-12, 1893/1894-1900[16]

Vol. IX: *Reports of Decisions Rendered by the Supreme Court of the Hawaiian Islands: Criminal, Divorce, Equity, Law, Probate. Years 1893 and 1894.* Honolulu: Robert Grieve, 1895.

Includes opinions of the court under the provisional government and the Republic of Hawaii. Appendix C: Constitution of the Republic of Hawaii, July 3, 1894.

Vol. 10: *Reports of Decisions Rendered by the Supreme Court of the Hawaiian Islands: Law, Civil and Criminal; Equity, Admiralty, Probate and Divorce. April 2, 1895 to March 17, 1897.* Honolulu: Hawaiian Gazette Co., 1897.

Vol. 11: *Reports of Decisions Rendered by the Supreme Court of the Hawaiian Islands: Law, Civil and Criminal; Equity, Admiralty, Probate and Divorce. March 25, 1897 to April 20, 1899.* Honolulu: Hawaiian Gazette Co., 1899.

Vol. 12: *Reports of Decisions Rendered by the Supreme Court of the Republic of Hawaii: Law, Civil and Criminal; Equity, Admiralty, Probate and Divorce. May 1, 1899 to June 20, 1900.* Honolulu: Hawaiian Gazette Co., 1900.

Case Digests and Tools

See Case Digests and Tools, under Monarchy, for applicable titles.

Newspapers

In understanding Hawaii's journey to statehood, the importance of newspapers as primary documents cannot be overlooked. Refer to sources discussed previously for more information.

TERRITORY OF HAWAII
(AUGUST 12, 1898/APRIL 30, 1900 TO AUGUST 20, 1959)

This section of federal and territorial materials focuses on laws that governed the creation of the territory.

Constitution

Constitution of the Republic of Hawaii and laws passed by the Executive and Advisory Councils of the Republic [1894]. Honolulu: R. Grieve, 1895. 130 pp.

Constitution of the Republic of Hawaii (pp. [75]-123). Continued in effect until 1900.

Selected Federal Acts Relating to the Territory of Hawaii

Joint Resolution of Annexation of July 7, 1898, 30 *Stat.* 750 (2 Supp. R.S. 895). Took effect August 12, 1898. Reprinted in *Revised Laws of Hawaii,* 1955, Vol. I, at 13-14.

Resolution No. 55, commonly known as "Newlands Resolution," transferred sovereignty of the Republic of Hawaii to the United States. The formal transfer took place on August 12, 1898, but the joint resolution provided for continuation of the republican government, subject to the application of the federal Constitution and laws to Hawaii, between annexation and establishment of the territorial government on June 14, 1900.

Organic Act: An Act to Provide a Government for the Territory of Hawaii, April 30, 1900, Ch. 339, 31 *Stat.* 141 (1899-1901). Took effect June 14, 1900. Reprinted in *Revised Laws of Hawaii,* 1905, and later.

CHAPTER I.–GENERAL PROVISIONS.

Sec. 1 defines that "the laws of Hawaii" shall mean the constitution and laws of the Republic of Hawaii in force on August 12, 1898, at the time of the transfer of the sovereignty of the Hawaiian Islands to the United States. Refers specifically to the Sidney M. Ballou two-volume compilation of "Civil Laws" and "Penal Laws" and the "Session Laws" of the legislature of 1898.

Sec. 2 notes that the islands were acquired by the United States under an act of Congress titled "Joint resolution to provide for annexing the Hawaiian Islands to the United States," approved July 7, 1898, and shall be known as the territory of Hawaii.

Sec. 3 provides for the establishment of the territorial government, with its capital at Honolulu on the island of Oahu.

Sec. 4 provides that all citizens of the Republic of Hawaii on August 12, 1898, are declared to be citizens of the United States and of the territory of Hawaii. This section further provides that all citizens of the United States resident in the islands on or since August 12, 1898 and all citizens of the United States who shall thereafter reside in the territory of Hawaii for one year shall be citizens of the territory of Hawaii.

Sec. 5 provides that the Constitution and all laws of the United States which are not locally inapplicable shall have the same force and effect within the territory as elsewhere in the United States, with the exception of enumerated provisions of the Revised Statutes of the United States.

Sec. 6 provides that the laws of Hawaii not inconsistent with the Constitution or laws of the United States shall continue in force, subject to repeal or amendment by the legislature of Hawaii or the Congress of the United States.

Secs. 7-9 enumerate specific provisions of the constitution and laws of the Republic of Hawaii for repeal, abolish certain offices, and amend official titles.

Sec. 10 provides for construction of existing statutes for existing obligations, offenses, criminal proceedings, and bars specified actions and contracts.

Revisions to the Organic Act took the form of joint resolutions passed by the territorial legislature.

CHAPTER V.–UNITED STATES OFFICERS.

Sec. 85 provides for the qualifications and election of the territorial delegate to the U.S. House of Representatives.

Secs. 87-88 created the internal revenue and customs districts and provided for officers therein.

An Act to amend an Act entitled "An Act to provide a government for the Territory of Hawaii," approved as amended, to establish an Hawaiian Homes Commission, . . . July 9, 1921, Ch. 42, 41 (pt. I) *Stat.* 108. Washington, DC: GPO, 1921.

Set aside a small portion of 1.75 million acres of government and Crown lands, ceded by the Republic of Hawaii to the United States upon annexation for native Hawaiian homesteading. The United States assumed a trust obligation to benefit and rehabilitate native Hawaiians.

Compilations of Territorial Laws

Revised Laws of Hawaii, Comprising the Statutes of the Territory, Consolidated, Revised and Annotated. Published by Authority. Honolulu: Hawaiian Gazette Co., Ltd., 1905. 1 vol. 1451 pp.

"The general basis of the present volume is the Civil Laws and the Penal Laws of 1897 and the session laws enacted since. These and a number of other earlier laws not included in the compilations of 1897 are combined in one volume . . ."[17] More than a quarter of the 1897-derived laws are omitted because of express or implicit repeal or declaration of unconstitutionality. Case references included are from the first fifteen volumes of *Hawaiian Reports,* the volume of *Estee's Reports, Opinions of the Attorney General, the United States Reports,* and the *Federal Reporter.*

Preliminary materials include Act 45, Laws of 1903, authorizing the appointment of a Code-Commission; the U.S. Constitution; Resolution of the Senate of Hawaii Ratifying the Treaty of Annexation [hereafter, Resolution; never ratified by the U.S. Senate]; the Joint Resolution to Provide for Annexing the Hawaiian Islands to the United States [hereafter, Joint Resolution]; and the Organic Act. A topical index is included (pp. [1315]-1451).

Revised Laws of Hawaii, Comprising the Statutes of the Territory, Consolidated, Revised and Annotated. Published by Authority. Honolulu: Honolulu Star-Bulletin, 1915. 1 vol. 1835 pp.

"The general plan of the work follows that adopted by the compilers of the Revised Laws of 1905. . . . The last revision, therefore, forms the basis of this, obsolete and repealed matter being omitted and new matter contained in the session laws of 1905 to 1913 being incorporated. The most important of the new legislative enactments, the county act of 1905, and the municipal act of 1907, as amended and supplemented by later legislation, have been included" [Preface].

Preliminary materials include L. 1913, c. 11, appointing compilation commission (pp. 5-6); Contents (pp. [7]-16); Joint Resolution (pp. [17]-19); Organic Act (pp. [20]-69); Index to Organic Act (pp. [70]-90). Includes Appendix (pp. [1483]-1509); Table Showing Disposition made of Statutes (pp. [1510]-1543); and Index (pp. [1545]-1835).

Revised Laws of Hawaii, Comprising the Statutes of the Territory, Consolidated, Revised and Annotated, in Two Volumes. Published by Authority.

Honolulu: Honolulu Star-Bulletin, Ltd., 1925. 2 vols. (Vol. I, pp. 1-1840; Vol. II, Appendix, pp. 1843-2249).

"The Revised Laws of Hawaii 1915 has been the basis of the work of the Commission," in addition to the session laws through 1923 [Preface]. Preliminary material in Vol. I includes L. 1923, c. 17, appointing compilation commission; detailed Tables of Contents for both volumes; the U.S. Constitution; the Joint Resolution; Organic Act and Its Index; and a Bill of Rights (L. 1923, c. 86, approved April 26, 1923). Vol. I includes the text of the session laws, a Table Showing Disposition made of Statutes, and an Index. Vol. 2 repeats the Table of Contents for Vol. 2 and continues session laws.

Revised Laws of Hawaii, Comprising the Statutes of the Territory, Consolidated, Revised and Annotated. Published by Authority. Honolulu: Honolulu Star-Bulletin, 1935. 1 vol. 1453 pp.

Preliminary material includes an act authorizing the formation of the Compilation Commission (L. 1933, c. 178; p. 5), the Hawaiian Bill of Rights (L. 1923, c. 86; pp. 6-10); the Hawaiian Declaration of Rights (L. 1925, c. 222; pp. 10-12); a detailed Table of Contents (pp. 12-20); the U.S. Constitution (pp. 21-31); the Joint Resolution (pp. 32-34); the Resolution (p. 34A); Organic Act (pp. 35-67); Hawaii National Park (pp. 67-69); and Index to Organic Act (pp. 70-72).

This rearrangement of the code is an alphabetical sequence by topic, where possible, and is arranged in four parts: Part I. General Laws; Part II. Counties; Part III. Courts; Part IV. Corporations, Business Law, and Miscellaneous Territorial Provisions. It also includes an Index (pp. 1289-1422); Tables of Disposition of Statutes from the Revised Session Laws, 1925; Session Laws 1925; Session Laws 1927; Session Laws 1929; Session Laws 1931; Session Laws 1932, 1st; Session Laws 1932, 2d; Session Laws 1933 and Session Laws 1933-4 (pp. 1423-1435); Appeals from Supreme Court of Territory, 1915-1934 (p. 1436); Table of 1925-1934 Appeals from the U.S.D.C. Hawaii (p. 1437); and a Citator from Hawaiian Decisions, 27 H.-32 H. (pp. 1438-1453).

Revised Laws of Hawaii, Comprising the Statutes of the Territory, Consolidated, Revised and Annotated, as of January 1, 1945. Published by Authority. Honolulu: Honolulu Star-Bulletin, 1945. 1 vol. 1882 pp.

Prefix section includes U. S. Constitution (pp. 5-15); Chronological Note of Acts Affecting Hawaii from February 15, 1933 to December 10, 1943 (pp. 16-17); Joint Resolution (pp. 18-20); Organic Act (pp. 21-57); Hawaiian Homes Commission Act (pp. 58-71); Chapter 10 of Title 48 of the U.S.

Code [Territorial Provisions of a General Nature] (pp. 72-74); Hawaii National Park Act (pp. 75-77); and Index to Organic Act and Other Federal Statutes (pp. 78-80).

Arrangement of statutes: Part A: General Laws and Territorial Departments; Part B: County Governments; Part C: Business Laws and Regulations; Part D: Courts and Related Matters; and Part E: Miscellany: Military and Defense.

Includes Appendix (pp. 1673-1689); Tables of Disposition (pp. 1690-1701); and General Index (pp. 1702-1882).

Star Annotation supplement includes Acts of Congress Affecting Organic Act and Territorial Laws, from August 7, 1946 through June 14, 1948.

Star Annotation Service Hawaii. Cumulative for 1945-1947-1949. By A.M. Cristy. Annotations to *Revised Laws of Hawaii,* 1945, for Amendments, Repeals, New Sections and Cross References Found in 1945, 1947, and 1949 Session Laws. 1 softcover vol., unpaged.

Star Annotation Service Hawaii. Cumulative Annotations to *Revised Laws of Hawaii,* 1945, to August 15, 1951. By Jon Wiig. Honolulu: [Honolulu Star-Bulletin, Ltd., c. 1951]. 42 pp.

"The purpose of 'Star Annotation Service of Hawaii' is to provide a ready reference to all who work with or are interested in the laws of Hawaii showing amendments of sections of Revised Laws of Hawaii 1945, new sections added to the basic law, repeals, and cross references" [Foreword].

Revised Laws of Hawaii, 1955, in Three Volumes, comprising the statutes of the Territory including the acts passed at the regular session of 1955, and special session of 1956, consolidated, revised and annotated. Published by Authority. Compiled by the Compilation Commission. San Francisco: Filmer Bros. Press, [1957]. 3 vols., with 1957, 1960, 1961, 1963, 1965 bound supplements.

Vol. 1: Preliminary material includes the Constitution of the United States (pp. 1-8); "Chronological Notes of Federal Acts Affecting Hawaii" (pp. 9-12) listing statutes, resolutions, executive orders, proclamations from December 17, 1943 to August 24, 1954; Joint Resolution (pp. 13-15); Organic Act (pp. 17-44); Hawaiian Homes Commission Act (pp. 45-60); Other Federal Acts [Provisions of Chapter 10 of Title 48 of the United States Code Applicable to Hawaii] (pp. 61-62); Hawaii National Park Act (pp. 63-64); and Index to Organic Act (pp. 65-67). Chapters 1-154.

Vol. 2: Chapters 155-361, including Title 39, Chapter 360 Statehood, and an Appendix of appropriations, franchises, and public works matters.

Vol. 3: Tables of Disposition from Revised Laws of Hawaii 1945, and Unlisted Acts, General Index to contents of Vols. 1 and 2. Includes typewritten pocket part titled "Cumulative Table Showing Sections of Revised Laws of Hawaii 1955 Affected by Subsequent Legislation Through the First Special Session 1960 of the First State Legislature, compiled by Joseph M. Gedan, Legislative Reference Bureau, University of Hawaii, September, 1960." This Cumulative Table replaces referencing the following sources: (1) 1957 Supplement to the Revised Laws of Hawaii 1955 or Session Laws of Hawaii, 1957; (2) Session Laws of Hawaii, 1959; (3) Session Laws of Hawaii, Special Sessions of 1959; (4) Acts of Budget Session of 1960, First State Legislature; and (5) Acts of the First Special Session 1960, First State Legislature [Preface].

Territorial Session Laws

Laws of the Territory of Hawaii Passed by the Legislature. Honolulu: Published by Authority Under the Direction of the Secretary of State, [1st], 1901-30th, 1959. 38 vols. Includes Regular and Special Sessions.

Selected Federal and Territorial Legislation
Related to the Legislature

Organic Act: An Act to Provide a Government for the territory of Hawaii, April 30, 1900, Ch. 339, 31 *Stat.* 141 (1899-1901). Took effect June 14, 1900. Reprinted in *Revised Laws of Hawaii,* 1905, and later.

CHAPTER II.–THE LEGISLATURE.

Secs. 1-40 provide for a two-house legislature of the territory of Hawaii, the senate and house of representatives, with members elected under and in conformity with requirements of this act.

Secs. 41-55 address legislation and legislative power.

Sec. 56 permits the legislature to create counties and town and city municipalities with the territory and to provide for the government thereof.

Secs. 57-65 address elections.

Laws of the Territory of Hawaii Passed by the Legislature. Honolulu: Published by Authority Under the Direction of the Secretary of State, [1st], 1901-30th, 1959. 38 vols. Includes Regular and Special Sessions.

1901: *Act 13* provides that the secretary of state shall promulgate every law enacted by the legislature by speedy publication in English and

Hawaiian language newspapers, followed by printing and binding in book form.

1903: *Act 45* provides for a Code Commission of three to compile, print, and distribute statutory compilations upon adjournment of each legislative session. This resulted in the publication of the *Revised Laws of Hawaii* (1905).

J.R. lobbies Congress to authorize citizens to meet in convention and adopt a state constitution.

1909: *Act 84* divides the territory into districts, including for election and taxation purposes.

1913: *Act 151* provides for elections.

1918: (Spec. Sess.) *Act 19* defines and provides penalties for disloyalty to the United States.

1919: *Act 29* increases distribution of not more than fifty copies of Hawaii statutes and Supreme Court reports to libraries and similar institutions.

Act 40 provides for publication of the 1919 session laws in English and Hawaiian.

1921: *Act 216* prohibits the publication, circulation, or distribution of articles or matter contrary to the public welfare, and provides regulations and penalties.

Act 223 creates the Hawaii Legislative Commission to assist the congressional delegate in presenting matters to Congress (as set forth in S. Con. Res. 8).

1923: *Act 17* authorizes appointment of a commission to compile the statute laws of the territory.

Act 86, referred to as the "Bill of Rights," is "an act to define and declare the claims of the Territory of Hawaii concerning its status in the American Union, and to provide for the appointment of a Commission to secure more complete recognition of such claims by the federal government" [Title from act, p. 87].

1925: *Act 222* is "An Act to define and declare the claims of the Territory of Hawaii concerning the status of its citizens and their rights and privileges and to appoint a Commission for presenting such claims and for securing complete recognition of such status by the federal government" [Title from act, p. 264].

1927: *J.R. No. 1* declares the implementation of the federal Hawaiian Homes Commission Act, 1920, a success, and requests that the

Secretary of the Interior extend and Congress approve the provision of additional lands for homesteads on all of the Hawaiian Islands.

1931: *J.R. No. 9* memorializes Congress to provide for the issuance by the Bureau of Immigration of the Department of Labor of certificates of citizenship to all residents of the territory who are citizens of the United States and who apply for such certificates with proof of citizenship.

1933: *Act 178* provides for a three-person commission to compile the statute laws of the territory, as they exist after adjournment of this session.

1935: *Act 1 (A-1)* provides for enactment and approval of the Revised Laws of Hawaii 1935.

1939: *J.R. 7* requests Congress to amend the Hawaiian Homes Commission Act of 1920.

1941: *J.R. 12* requests Congress to recognize the right of this territory to equality of treatment with the states of the Union when it enacts legislation affecting the territory [follow-up to *Act 86* (1923)].

1941: (Spec. Sess.) *Act 24 (A-1)* enacts the Hawaii Defense Act to deal with the national public emergency.

1945: *Act 1 (A-1)* enacts the Revised Laws of Hawaii 1945.

Act 148 (D-171) provides for receiving as prima facie evidence reports of missing or other status persons issued pursuant to Federal Missing Persons Act.

J.R. 3 memorializes Congress to extend the right to become a naturalized citizen to those whose child or children have served honorably in the armed forces and who themselves have not been disloyal to the United States.

1947: *Act 115* relates to statehood for Hawaii. It establishes a Statehood Commission to press for admission of the territory into the Union.

1949: *Act 61* provides for a holdover committee of 1949 in the event that Hawaii obtains statehood before the November 1950 general election. Gives the committee powers to shape the form of government and its institutions and agencies.

Act 334 provides for a constitutional convention to form a constitution and state government in preparation for admission to the Union.

1949: (Spec. Sess.) *Act 40* relates to legislative hearings, procedures, and powers.

1950: (Spec. Sess.) *J.R. 1* provides for referring to electorate for ratification of the 1950 constitution.

1953: *Act 179* provides for a Compilation Commission for the Revised Laws of Hawaii 1955.

1954: (Spec. Sess.) *J.R. 1* requests Congress to grant immediate statehood by H.R. 3575 of the 83d Congress.

1955: *Act 191* amends election laws in anticipation of statehood.

J.R. 4 requests Congress to transfer back to the territory title to remaining public lands and to enact provisions authorizing the legislature to have jurisdiction and control over such lands.

1957: *Act 2* enacts the Revised Laws of Hawaii 1955 and charges the Compilation Commission with editing the compilation.

J.R. 1 requests that Congress enact legislation providing for admission of Hawaii to statehood.

1959: *Act 127* establishes a Joint Legislative Committee to study problems of governmental organization and transition from territorial status to statehood.

Selected Federal and Territorial Legislation Related to Cities and Counties

Organic Act: An Act to Provide a Government for the Territory of Hawaii, April 30, 1900, Ch. 339, 31 *Stat.* 141 (1899-1901). Took effect June 14, 1900. Reprinted in *Revised Laws of Hawaii,* 1905, and later.

CHAPTER II.–THE LEGISLATURE.

Sec. 56 permits the legislature to create counties and town and city municipalities within the territory and to provide for the government thereof.

Laws of the Territory of Hawaii Passed by the Legislature. Honolulu: Published by Authority Under the Direction of the Secretary of State, [1st], 1901-30th, 1959. 41 vols. Includes Regular and Special Sessions.

1903: *Act 31* provides for the organization and government of counties and districts, and the management and control of public works and public institutions therein. Chapter 5 provides for the governor to fill any vacancies on the boards of supervisors.

1905:   *Act 39* provides for the creation and government of five counties. Chapter 21 provides for the county attorney, who serves as deputy to the attorney general.

1907:   *Act 67* provides counties with the power of eminent domain for certain public purposes.

1909:   *Act 24* provides for biennial reports from the counties to the territorial legislature.

  Act 84 divides the territory into districts, including for city and county purposes.

1911:   *Act 41* provides for funding of district court judges and expenses by counties.

1923:   *Act 266* provides for licensing and regulation of certain businesses, professions, and trades by the city and counties.

1927:   *Act 222* provides for direct appeal to the Supreme Court of any negative permit action from the Honolulu Sewer and Water Commission.

1935:   *Act 121 (A-4)* defines "county" to include the city and county of Honolulu, unless specifically excepted.

  Act 128 (B-70) relates to advertisement in newspapers of bills and resolutions.

1939:   *Act 242 (B-79)* substantially revises provisions for the city and county of Honolulu, including establishment of a City Planning Commission.

Selected Federal and Territorial Legislation
Related to the Executive

Organic Act: An Act to Provide a Government for the Territory of Hawaii, April 30, 1900, Ch. 339, 31 *Stat.* 141 (1899-1901). Took effect June 14, 1900. Reprinted in *Revised Laws of Hawaii,* 1905, and later.

CHAPTER III.–THE EXECUTIVE.

  Sec. 66 vests the executive power of the territorial government in a governor, appointed by the president, with the advice and consent of the U.S. Senate, who shall hold office for four years.

  Secs. 67-68 detail the enforcement and general powers of the governor.

  Secs. 69-80 provide for government officers, detail their duties, and provide for terms and conditions of appointment.

Laws of the Territory of Hawaii Passed by the Legislature. Honolulu: Published by Authority Under the Direction of the Secretary of State, [1st], 1901-30th, 1959. 41 vols. Includes Regular and Special Sessions.

1903: *Act 31* provides for the organization and government of counties and districts, and the management and control of public works and public institutions therein.

Chapter 5 provides for the governor to fill any vacancies on the boards of supervisors.

Act 60 provides against embezzlement by public officers.

Act 4, extra session, provides for compilation, translation, and printing of the *House of Representatives Journal.*

1915: *Act 111* provides for governor-appointed commissioners on three-year terms in other states and territories and abroad.

1917: *Act 128* provides that the secretary of the territory shall promulgate enacted laws by publication in English (daily) and Hawaiian (weekly) language newspapers, followed by publication in printed, bound book form.

Act 120 creates "The Historical Commission," appointed by the governor, to compile and publish a revised history of the Hawaiian people, to secure information in regard to historical places, and to secure information in regard to Hawaii's part in the Great War.

1929: *Act 57* provides for appraisal of all taxable property in the territory, economic study of the tax laws, creation of a Tax Board and advisory tax appraisal boards.

Act 104 provides for appointment by Board of Health of marriage license agents in each judicial district.

1932: (2d Spec. Sess.) *Act 10* abolishes the Historical Commission (1921) and delegated its functions and powers to the regents of the University of Hawaii.

Acts 40-42 provide for revision of the taxation scheme, including creation of a tax appeal court.

Act 71 creates a five-member Hawaii Legislative Commission, appointed by the governor who was ex officio chairman, to assist the congressional delegate in fully presenting, advancing, and protecting Hawaii's position on matters before Congress.

1933: *Act 195* amends and expands provisions for the tax appeal court.

1937: *Act 207 (A-42)* creates a nine-member Territorial Planning Board to create master plan for physical development of territory.

Act 223 (D-153) enacts Unfair Practices Act and defined duties of attorney general in regard thereto.

1939: *Act 196 (A-3)* authorizes the governor to accept federal acts that grant or allot federal aid monies for the territory.

Act 208 (A-33) provides for appeal to supreme court from decision of the tax appeal court.

1941: *Act 80 (A-12)* relates to rules and regulations having the force and effect of law.

Act 128 (A-13) enacts the Hawaii loyalty law.

1941: (Spec. Sess.) *Act 88 (A-5)* provides for a classification system for government employment.

Act 90 (D-61) substantially amends provisions of the Hawaii Equal Rights Commission, empowered to equalize standing of Hawaii citizens with those of the other states.

1943: *Act 8 (E-196)* authorizes a three-person Compilation Commission to compile all statute laws at conclusion of this session.

J.R. 10 creates a three-member Land Laws Revision Commission charged with reviewing all laws governing the public lands of the territory.

1947: *Act 246* creates a Bureau of Civil Identification in the Department of the Attorney General.

1959: *Act 127* establishes a Joint Legislative Committee to study problems of governmental organization and transition from territorial status to statehood. The attorney general was directed to compile the Constitutional Convention of 1950 and compile and analyze all territorially and federally created laws that would be affected by statehood under P.L. 86-3, March 18, 1959.

1959: (Spec. Sess. [poststatehood]) *Act 13* relates to the publication and sale of the proceedings of the Constitutional Convention of 1950, under the direction of the archivist.

Selected Federal and Territorial Legislation
Related to the Judiciary

Organic Act: An Act to Provide a Government for the Territory of Hawaii, April 30, 1900, Ch. 339, 31 *Stat.* 141 (1899-1901). Took effect June 14, 1900. Reprinted in *Revised Laws of Hawaii,* 1905, and later.

CHAPTER IV.–THE JUDICIARY.

Secs. 81-84 vest the judicial power in one supreme court, circuit courts, and other inferior courts as the legislature may establish; provide for composition and appointment of the supreme court by the president of the United States, with the advice and consent of the Senate; provide for laws continued in force, with exceptions.

Laws of the Territory of Hawaii Passed by the Legislature. Honolulu: Published by Authority Under the Direction of the Secretary of State, [1st], 1901-30th, 1959. 41 vols. Includes Regular and Special Sessions.

1901: *Act 2* provides for the criminal jurisdiction of district magistrates, removing exclusive original jurisdiction from the language of the 1892 law.

Act 10 provides for the appointment of bailiffs and defines duties, powers, and compensation.

Act 12 provides for a circuit judge from another circuit to preside at trial upon specific causes (disqualification, vacancy, etc.).

Act 22 creates an annual term for the supreme court and provides for notice before adjournment.

1903: *Act 5* provides for notice of judicial proceedings by publication in suitable newspapers.

Act 9 provides for waiver of jury trial in criminal cases less than felony.

Act 16 amends the civil code to give circuit judges jurisdiction to appoint guardians to minors and others.

Act 31 provides for the organization and government of counties and districts. Chapter 1 defines the jurisdictions of the circuit courts and circuit judges. Chapter 8 empowers the board of supervisors to build appropriate courthouses. Chapter 17 details the duties of the district attorney and his deputies.

Act 32 extensively revises the 1892 "Act to Reorganize the Judiciary Department," and establishes its independence from the executive and legislative branches.

Act 38 provides for selection and empaneling of grand and trial jurors.

Act 64 provides and appropriates monies for the compilation and publication of a *Digest of Hawaiian Supreme Court Reports,* subject to the approval of the supreme court justices.

1905: *Act 5* regulates voir dire of jurors.

1909: *Act 22* prescribes the treatment and control of dependent and delinquent children, particularly as to the court's role.

 Act 84 divides the territory into districts, including for judicial purposes.

1911: *Act 41* provides for funding of district court judges and expenses by counties.

 Act 84 relates to supreme and circuit court clerks.

1913: *Act 40* allows circuit court judges to promulgate rules for court and judges, with approval of supreme court.

 Act 68 provides that counties shall pay expenses of respective circuit courts.

 Act 101 details the judicial role in provision for support and maintenance of children out of wedlock.

1915: *Act 73* provides for challenges to jurors in trials where the offense is punishable by death or life imprisonment.

 Act 85 provides for preparation, printing, and sale of a *Digest of the Reports of the Supreme Court of the Territory of Hawaii,* with appropriation.

 Act 220 waives costs for actions for amounts under $25.00 brought in district court by indigents.

1917: *Act 67* provides for publication of summons in attachment cases where personal service upon the defendant cannot be effected.

 Act 112 provides for the display of patriotic emblems in the courthouses and courtrooms of the territory and the United States to express patriotism of the citizenry and to inspire patriotism in participants or witnesses of proceedings of such courts and magistrates.

1919: *Act 29* increases distribution to not more than fifty copies of Hawaii statutes and supreme court reports to libraries and like institutions.

 Act 31 provides for publication of applicable notices and rules of court in newspapers where judicial proceeding commenced or was held.

 Act 47 relates to reserved questions.

1921: *Act 79* prohibits grand jurors and witnesses from divulging proceedings of grand jury.

Act 81 gives the supreme court authority to regulate attorneys and the practice of law.

Act 183 establishes a division of domestic relations in the first judicial circuit (city and county of Honolulu).

Act 208 relates to land registration and the land court.

1923: *J.R. 2* creates commission to recommend changes in judicial procedure.

1925: *Act 226* provides for judicial determination of contested election situations.

1927: *Act 73* adds *lis pendens* provisions in actions involving title or possession of real property.

Act 158 provides for filing an index to probate cases and related documents with supreme court.

Act 258 significantly amends land court provisions.

Act 270 provides for intervention in district and circuit court proceedings.

1929: *Act 165* adopts the Uniform Foreign Executed Wills Act.

Act 213 amends provisions for special court proceedings.

1931: *Act 42* amends provisions relating to powers of the supreme court in cases brought before it on exceptions or writs of error.

Act 204 amends provisions relating to qualifications of attorneys practicing in district courts.

1933: (Spec. Sess.) *Act 35* directs judges presiding in divorce to modify decrees and orders upon wife's remarriage.

1935: *Act 28 (C-89)* amends provisions regarding qualifications of practitioners in district courts.

1937: *Act 104 (C-96)* substantially revises the Small Claims Act.

Act 173 (C-81) revises attorney qualifications provisions.

1939: *Act 208 (A-33)* provides for appeal to the supreme court from decisions of the tax appeal court.

1941: *Act 110 (C-135)* adopts the Uniform Notice of Foreign Law Act.

1949: *Act 88* relates to appointment of referees by judges of juvenile court.

(Spec. Sess.) *Act 67 (D-36)* removes residency requirement for attorneys but imposes voter eligibility requirement for entry into the practicing bar.

1951: *Act 35 (D-227)* authorizes jury commissioners to issue question-
naires to prospective jurors and provides for contempt charges.

1955: *Act 87* creates an Interstate Compact on Juveniles.

Act 150 prohibits the practice of law by unlicensed persons and defines offenses and penalties.

1957: *J.R. 4* requests that Congress extend the provisions of the Judicial
Code (28 U.S.C. 373) to territorial circuit court judges.

1959: *Act 259* provides for the administration of the courts, an appointed
judicial council, and rule-making powers.

Selected Federal and Territorial Legislation
Related to the Federal District Courts

Organic Act: An Act to Provide a Government for the Territory of Hawaii,
April 30, 1900, Ch. 339, 31 *Stat.* 141 (1899-1901). Took effect June 14,
1900. Reprinted in *Revised Laws of Hawaii,* 1905, and later.

CHAPTER V.–UNITED STATES OFFICERS.

Sec. 86 establishes the federal district court and provides for the appointment of the single judge, attorney, and marshal for six years.

Laws of the Territory of Hawaii Passed by the Legislature. Honolulu: Published by Authority Under the Direction of the Secretary of State, [1st],
1901-30th, 1959. 38 vols. Includes Regular and Special Sessions.

1917: *Act 111* provides for publication and sale of *Decisions of the United
States District Court of Hawaii by the Secretary of the Territory.*

Act 112 provides for the display of patriotic emblems in the courthouses and courtroom of the territory and the United States to
express patriotism of the citizenry and to inspire patriotism in
participants or witnesses of proceedings of such courts and magistrates

Territorial Legislative Journals

*The First Legislative Assembly of the Territory of Hawaii. Journal of the
Senate, 1901- .* [Honolulu: 1901-]. 40 vols. Biennial.

1901 thru 1959. Includes regular, special, and extra sessions. Special sessions: 1902, 1904, 1909, 1920, 1932, 1933, 1941, 1950, 1954, 1956, 1957.
Extra sessions: 1901, 1903, 1905. Includes lists of senators, officers of the
senate, and senate standing committees.

Journal of Proceedings of the House of Representatives of the First Legislature of the Territory of Hawaii in Regular Session. Honolulu: Bulletin Publishing Co., 1901- . 40 vols. Biennial. Includes General Index.

1901 thru 1959. Includes regular, special, and extra sessions. Special sessions: 1904, 1909, 1918, 1920, 1932, 1933, 1941 (2 vols.), 1949, 1950, 1954. Extra sessions: 1901, 1903, 1905. Includes directory of representatives and standing committee membership, rules of procedures, and index.

Territorial Case Law

Hawaiian (later, *Hawaii*) *Reports,* Vol. 13-43, 1900-1959 (31 vols.), 13 *Haw.*-43 *Haw.*

Vol. 13: *Cases Decided in the Supreme Court of the Territory of Hawaii. June 21, 1900, to January 2, 1902.* Honolulu: Hawaiian Gazette Company, 1902- .

Title in later volumes varies to "Cases Determined . . ." Vol. 43 includes opinions from August 18, 1958, to July 24, 1959. Vol. 44 contains opinions of the court under statehood and commences with November 23, 1959.

Territorial Case Law (Federal District Court)

Reports of Cases Determined in the United States District Court for the District of Hawaii, Vols. I-IV. 4 vols.

Vol. I, edited and reported by Elizabeth H. Ryan. Honolulu: Hawaiian Gazette Co., 1903. Vol. II: November 27, 1903, to April 30, 1906. Honolulu: Hawaiian Gazette Co., 1906. Vol. III: November 3, 1906, to March 30, 1911. Honolulu: Hawaiian Gazette Co., 1911. Vol. IV: April 1, 1911, to January 15, 1918. Honolulu: Printed at the New Freedom Press, 1918. Later opinions were included in West's *Federal Reporter* and the *Federal Supplement.*

Case Digests and Tools

See Case Digests and Tools, under Monarchy, for applicable titles.

Court Records and Briefs

[Hawaii Appellate Records and Briefs][18]

The Office of the Chief Clerk of the Hawaii Supreme Court is the primary source for accessing appellate records and briefs filed in cases before that court. Unless designated confidential, the materials in these files are made available to the public as soon as they are logged into the court's internal system and are retained physically in the office until the file is closed. Closed files are sent to the Judiciary Records Center for storage until microfilmed.

Records and briefs from October term, 1904, to the present are available. Microfilm archives are currently available for Case 1, January 13, 1905, through Case 10930, December 19, 1985. Records and briefs prior to 1905 may be available from the circuit from which the appeal was taken.

Administrative Rules and Regulations

Issued separately by agencies.

Selected Administrative Decisions and Opinions

Opinions of the Attorneys General of Hawaii. Honolulu: Department of the Attorney General, 1904- .

Also available on microform. No opinions were issued for 1947-1950, 1952, and 1954.

Newspapers

Also consult information regarding newspapers as given earlier, since their value in detailing the Hawaiian statehood process is immeasurable.

SELECTED FEDERAL ACTS RELATING TO STATEHOOD

An Act to Provide for the Admission of the State of Hawaii into the Union, March 18, 1959. P.L. 86-3, 73 *Stat.* 4 (1959). Reprinted in *Session Laws of Hawaii,* First State Legislature, First and Second Special Sessions of 1959, at 75-84.

The Enabling Act, which recognized a state government that was already established and set certain conditions for the admission of Hawaii into the Union, all of which were approved by territorial voters on June 27, 1959.

Sec. 4 required that the Hawaiian Homes Commission Act of 1920 be adopted as a provision of the state constitution.

Admission of the State of Hawaii Into the Union by the President of the United States of America: A Proclamation . . . August 21, 1959. 73 *Stat.* C74; Proc. No. 3309. Washington, DC: GPO, 1959.

Statehood proclaimed by President Eisenhower, August 21, 1959.

An Act to Amend Certain Laws of the United States in Light of the Admission of the State of Hawaii into the Union, and for Other Purposes. PL 86-624, 74 *Stat.* 411 (1960). Washington, DC: GPO, 1959.

Cited as the "Hawaii Omnibus Act," this act mandated revision of federal laws regarding Hawaii's status.

Hawaiian Homes Commission Act, 1920 (Act of July 9, 1921, c. 42, 42 *Stat.* 108). Reprinted in *Hawaii Revised Statutes.*

Now a part of the State Constitution, Art. XII, Section 1. Hawaiian Affairs, Hawaiian Homes Commission Act.

STATE CONSTITUTION
AND CONSTITUTIONAL CONVENTION

Constitution of the State of Hawaii. Drafted at Constitutional Convention, July 22, 1950; Ratified by People on November 7, 1950, and Amended by Primary Election on June 27, 1959. Reprinted in *Session Laws of Hawaii,* First State Legislature, First and Second Special Sessions of 1959, at 85-114.

The second amendment approved on June 27, 1959, adopted the Hawaiian Homes Commission Act of 1920 in Article XI of the Constitution.

Proceedings of the Constitutional Convention of Hawaii, 1950. Honolulu: Published under the Supervision of the Attorney General's Office and the Public Archives, 1960-1961. 2 vols.

Vol. I. Journal and Documents; Vol. II. Committee of the Whole Debates. Includes "Origin of Sections of the Constitution," and Appendixes (Act 334 of 1949, Rules of Convention, and the State Constitution, with changes made by Admission Act in 1959.

SELECTED BIBLIOGRAPHY

Anthony, J. Garner. *The Judiciary Under the Constitution of the State of Hawaii.* [Chicago]: American Judicature Society, [1959]. [13]-16 leaves. (Reprint of article from *J. Am. Judicature Soc'y.* 43[1959]: 13.)

Bell, Roger. *Last Among Equals: Hawaiian Statehood and American Politics.* Honolulu: University of Hawaii Press, 1984. 377 pp.

Blackman, William Fremont. *The Making of Hawaii: A Study in Social Evolution.* New York: Macmillan Co., 1906. 266 pp.

Budnick, Rich. *Stolen Kingdom: An American Conspiracy.* Honolulu: Aloha Press, 1992. 204 pp.

Chapin, Helen G. "Newspapers of Hawai'i, 1834 to 1903: From 'He Liona to the Pacific Cable.' " *Hawaiian Journal of History* 18(1984): 47.

Chronology and Documentary Handbook of the State of Hawaii. Helen Jennings, State Editor. Dobbs Ferry, NY: Oceana Publications, 1978. 148 pp.

Includes a chronology of historical events in Hawaii, a biographical directory, an outline of the state constitution, and selected historical documents.

Constitutional and Statutory Historical Documents Relating to Administration of the Judiciary of Hawaii. Honolulu: The Judiciary, [n.d.].

Contains excerpts of laws and two articles relating to the judiciary from the constitution of 1840 through 1975.

Daws, Gavan. *Shoal of Time: A History of the Hawaiian Islands.* Honolulu: University of Hawaii Press, 1968.

Frost & Frost, AIA. *Ali'iolani Hale: A Century of Growth and Change (1872-1977).* Honolulu: Prepared for the Department of Accounting and General Services, State of Hawai'i, 1977. 260 pp.

Includes rich historical information on the development of the judiciary in Hawaii. "Compiled and written by Frost & Frost AIA, Historical Consultants to Architects Hawaii. Prepared for the Department of Accounting and General Services, State of Hawaii" [cover].

Hawaiian Acts Excerpted from the U.S. Statutes at Large, 1845-1941. Honolulu: Supreme Court Law Library, 1995. 1 vol. (various pagings).

Johnson, Donald D. *The City and County of Honolulu: A Governmental Chronicle.* Honolulu: University of Hawaii Press and City Council of the City and County of Honolulu, 1991. 462 pp.

Judd, Bernice. *Laws of Hawaii, 1839-1939: A Checklist of the Statute Laws, Compiled Laws and Constitutions, both English and Hawaiian Issues.* Honolulu: Hawaii Library Association, Government Documents Committee, 1941. 9 pp.

Kuykendall, Ralph S. *The Hawaiian Kingdom,* Vol. 1. Honolulu: University of Hawaii Press, 1938.

————. *The Hawaiian Kingdom: 1854-1874, Twenty Critical Years,* Vol. 2. Honolulu: University of Hawaii Press, 1953.

————. *The Hawaiian Kingdom: 1874-1893, The Kalakaua Dynasty,* Vol. 3. Honolulu: University of Hawaii Press, 1967.

Lee, Ann Feder. *The Hawaii State Constitution: A Reference Guide.* Westport, CT: Greenwood Press, 1993. 247 pp. (Reference guides to the state constitutions of the United States, no. 14.)
Includes bibliographic references and index.

MacKenzie, Melody K., ed. *Native Hawaiian Rights Handbook.* Honolulu: Native Hawaiian Legal Corporation, 1991. 320 pp.
Provides a good historical overview of the monarchical period and in-depth treatment of native Hawaiian rights issues.

Melendy, H. Brett. *Hawaii: America's Sugar Territory, 1898-1959.* Studies in American History, Vol. 25. Lewiston, NY: The Edwin Mellen Press, 1999. 339 pp.

Merry, Sally Engle. *Colonizing Hawai'i: The Cultural Power of Law.* Princeton Studies in Culture/Power/History. Princeton, NJ: Princeton University Press, 2000. 371 pp.
Includes bibliographic references and index.

Moʻokini, Ester T. *The Hawaiian Newspapers.* Honolulu, HI: Topgallant Pub. Co., 1974.

Provides a historical summary and an alphabetical list of Hawaiian newspapers (1834-1948), many of which were published in English, as well as in Hawaiian.

Official Publications of the Territory of Hawaii, 1900-1959. Compiled by the Hawaiiana Section, Hawaii Library Association. Honolulu: State of Hawaii, Dept. of Accounting and General Services, Public Archives, 1962. 250 pp.

Osorio, Jonathan Kay. *Dismembering Lahui: A History of the Hawaiian Nation to 1887.* Honolulu: University of Hawaii Press, 2002. 310 pp.

Russ, William Adam, Jr. *The Hawaiian Republic (1894-98) and Its Struggle to Win Annexation.* Selinsgrove, PA: Susquehanna University Press, 1961. 398 pp.

Thurston, Lorrin A., ed. *The Fundamental Law of Hawaii.* Honolulu: Hawaiian Gazette Co., 1904. 428 pp.

Edited and indexed by Lorrin A. Thurston. "Instead of one general index, each [law, constitution and document] is indexed separately" [Preface at iv]. Documents included span 1840-1900.

Zubrow, Marcia S., ed. *Pimsleur's Checklist of Basic American Legal Publications.* Littleton, CO: Fred B. Rothman, 2001. 3 looseleaf vols.

Edited by Meira G. Pimsleur from 1962-1978, this work provides a fairly comprehensive listing of Hawaii's statutory compilations, session laws, and attorneys general reports and opinions.

SELECTED WEB SITES

These Web sites provide a variety of historic and contemporary Hawaiian, federal, and international documents, including the monarchical constitutions, annexation documents, historic and contemporary treaties, and commentary.

Aloha First, Waimanalo, HI
<http://www.alohaquest.com/>

Free Hawaii.org: The Online Voice for the Kindgom of Hawaii, Honolulu, HI
<http://www.freehawaii.org/>

Hawaiian Independence Home Page, Honolulu, HI
<http://www.hawaii-nation.org/>

The Hawaiian Kingdom Government, Honolulu, HI
<http://www.hawaiiankingdom.org>

Kingdom of Hawaii, Honolulu, HI
<http://www.pixi.com/~kingdom/hawaiis.html>

Office of Hawaiian Affairs, Honolulu, HI
<http://www.oha.org/>

Ulukau: The Hawaiian Electronic Library, Honolulu, HI
<http://ulukau.org/>

NOTES

1. Justice Richardson, after whom the School of Law at the University of Hawaii is named, served as Chief Justice of the Hawaii Supreme Court from March 25, 1966, to December 30, 1982.

2. William S. Richardson, "The Judicial System of Hawaii," in 1 *Haw. Dig.* xvii, xvii (1967).

3. Regnal years, derived from *Chronology and Documentary Handbook of the State of Hawaii* (Dobbs Ferry, NY: Oceana Publications, 1978), edited by Helen Jennings and William F. Swindler, at [1]-21, follow:

Kamehameha the Great (1795-1796 to May 8, 1819)
Kamehameha II (Liholiho; May 20, 1819 to July 14, 1824)
Kamehameha III (Kauikeaouli; June 6, 1825 to December 15, 1854)
Kamehameha IV (Alexander Liholiho; December 15, 1854 to November 30, 1863)
Kamehameha V (Lot; November 30, 1863 to December 11, 1872)
Lunalilo, William Charles (elected; January 8, 1873 to February 3, 1874)
Kalakaua, David (elected; February 13, 1874 to January 20, 1891)
Liliuokalani (January 29, 1891 to January 17, 1893)

4. Richardson, supra note 2, at xviii. Added by the Constitutional Convention of 1978 and election of November 7, 1978, this law, in amended form, is now codified at Article IX, Public Health and Welfare, Section 10, Public Safety of the Hawaii State Constitution.

5. Jonathan K.K. Osorio, *Dismembering Lahui: A History of the Hawaiian Nation to 1887,* at 13 (Honolulu: University of Hawaii Press, 2002).

6. Ibid.

7. Roger Bell, *Last Among Equals: Hawaiian Statehood and American Politics,* at 11 (Honolulu: University of Hawaii Press, 1984).

8. Ibid., at 22-23.

9. Ibid., at 23.

10. Ann Feder Lee, *The Hawaii State Constitution: A Reference Guide,* at 3 (Westport, CT: Greenwood Press, 1993).

11. Ibid., at 3.

12. Ibid., at 3-4.

13. Ralph S. Kuykendall, *The Hawaiian Kingdom: 1874-1893, The Kalakaua Dynasty,* Vol. 3, at 368-369 (Honolulu: University of Hawaii Press, 1967).

14. *Rev. L. Haw.,* Preface at [3] (1905).

15. Ibid.

16. With volume 10, volume numbering on title pages changed from Roman to Arabic numerals.

17. Ibid., at 4.

18. From interview with the Chief Clerk, Office of the Clerk, Supreme Court of Hawaii, February 12, 2002.

Chapter 13

Frontier Justice in the Territory of Idaho

Kristin M. Ford

INTRODUCTION

When President Lincoln signed the Organic Act of the Territory of Idaho in 1863, Idaho was in the midst of undergoing dramatic changes. Discovery of gold in both northern and southern Idaho led to a sudden influx of settlers, and new towns and populations boomed overnight. Justice was of the frontier variety, and crime and scoundrels existed even among the territory officials appointed to bring law and order to the region. The second governor, Caleb Lyon, embezzled over $46,000 in monies meant to fulfill Indian treaties and then fled the territory. Many of the men appointed as governors of the territory of Idaho were Easterners who spent scarcely any time in the territory, and some never came to the territory at all. They averaged less than two years in office.

Many of the judges appointed to Idaho Territory were also brand-new to the region. Early judges were faced with the daunting task of administering justice in an environment fraught with greedy disputes over gold and land claims and were under a great deal of pressure from mining interests and others. Judges found themselves immediately in the midst of controversy, and as a result of their decisions, they became controversial themselves. One such judge, Judge Joseph R. Lewis, made an enemy who forged a letter of resignation and sent it off to Washington. The unfortunate judge was surprised to find himself out of a job when his replacement arrived from Washington. His attempts to correct the situation and prove that the letter of resignation had neither been submitted on his behalf nor was desired by him took some time. In the meantime, the new judge blithely settled into his duties, and eventually Judge Lewis moved from Idaho and became a justice in Washington Territory.

Anecdotal evidence of vigilante justice abounds in the early history books of Idaho. Although sheriffs were elected, there was such a concentration of criminals and highwaymen in some areas that the election of a sher-

iff did not always promote law and order. Henry Plummer, an infamous outlaw who led the "Plummer Gang," was actually elected sheriff; such was the
abundance of criminals in one area. Thus, early attempts to impose law and
order in mining camps and small towns sometimes manifested in the formation of "vigilance committees." These committees were formed to create
constitutions and bylaws, but they also sometimes acted as judge, jury, and
executioner (the three usual punishments were exile, public horsewhipping,
or execution), often dispensing with the inconvenience of a trial. However,
they did usually succeed in persuading outlaws to move on to communities
less organized to resist crime.

Unfortunately, a recurring theme throughout accounts of this time was a
raging prejudice against Chinese immigrants and Native Americans. In addition, the bitter disputes between those favoring the Union or the Confederacy (Idaho became a territory during the Civil War and pioneers arrived
from both the North and the South) surfaced even in state government. A
Republican governor battled a legislature largely made up of southern
Democrats and required them to swear allegiance to the Union and de-
nounce the Confederacy if they wanted to receive their salaries. Finally, one
of the most divisive issues of the time arose around the Mormon settlers in
the country, with the legislature passing a "test oath" provision during the
1884-1885 session, requiring public officials to swear that they did not be-
long to a religion that advocated plural marriages, and also passing an act
disenfranchising Mormon voters. These actions were hotly debated, especially in Bear Lake County, whose population was mostly Mormon, and a
lawsuit was filed in the territorial court challenging the action. Shortly
thereafter, the issue sparked heated debate during the constitutional convention proceedings, when the constitution proposed to disenfranchise Mor-
mons. Resources for finding materials, transcripts, and arguments on this
subject are included in this bibliography.

Idaho's boundaries, like its population, underwent dramatic changes between 1848 and 1868. In 1848, Idaho was part of the Oregon Territory,
which also included what is now Washington State and parts of Montana
and Wyoming. In 1853, northern Idaho was lopped off and made a part of
the new Washington Territory, while southern Idaho remained part of the
Oregon Territory. In 1859, what is present-day Oregon became a state, and
Washington Territory was expanded to include all of Idaho and parts of
Montana and Wyoming. In 1863, Idaho became a territory in its own right
and encompassed not only all of what is today Idaho but all of Montana and
much of Wyoming as well, an area greater in size than Texas. However, this
early, unwieldy Idaho Territory proved hard to manage, and, in 1864, what
is today Montana was removed from the Idaho Territory and much of today's Wyoming became the Dakota Territory. Finally, in 1868, Wyoming

became a state and took part of eastern Idaho Territory with it. The 1868 boundaries of Idaho became the final boundaries when Idaho gained statehood in 1890.

Early official primary sources of law are not plentiful, but unofficial, secondary compilations and explanations provide a great deal of background and help to fill in the picture of early Idaho justice. This bibliography has been a very interesting research project, and I would like to thank Michael Chiorazzi for inviting me to take part in it. I hope this compilation of early legal research resources in Idaho will prove useful to researchers.

PRIMARY SOURCES

Legislative Branch Materials

Federal Acts

Organic Act of the Territory of Idaho, ch. 117, 12 *Stat.* 808 (1863). "An Act to Provide a Temporary Government for the Territory of Idaho."

Also reprinted in the first volume of the Idaho Code published by the Michie Company.

Idaho Admission Bill, ch. 656, 26 *Stat.* 215 (1890). "An Act to Provide for the Admission of the State of Idaho into the Union."

Ratifies the Idaho state constitution and admits Idaho as a state into the union. Also reprinted in the first volume of the Idaho Code published by the Michie Company.

Acts of Congress Affecting the Territory and State of Idaho, Idaho Code Containing the General Laws of Idaho Annotated, vol. 1, 517-522. Charlottesville, VA: Michie Company, 1993.

A list of selected federal acts affecting Idaho from 1818-1978.

The Idaho State Constitution

Constitution of the State of Idaho, adopted in convention at Boise City, August 6, 1889. Boise City, ID: The Statesman Printing Company, 1889.

Copy of the Idaho Constitution as originally adopted in 1889. Also reprinted in Hart, infra.

I.W. Hart, ed. *Proceedings and Debates of the Constitutional Convention of Idaho, 1889,* vols. 1 & 2. Caldwell, ID: Caxton Printers, Ltd., 1912.

Includes Proclamation by Governor E.A. Stevenson calling for a constitutional convention; Proclamation by Governor George L. Shoup on the advantages of statehood for Idaho; a transcript of the debates of the constitutional convention; the constitution as finally adopted; an "Address to the People of Idaho" from members of the convention urging adoption of the constitution; and the "Mitchell and Platt Admission Bills," which were not adopted in Congress but were often referenced during the constitutional convention.

In the Senate of the United States, Hearing Before the Committee on Territories on the Constitution of the Proposed State of Idaho, January 13, 1890. Washington, DC: Government Printing Office, 1890.

Remarks by Mr. Jeremiah M. Wilson, representing the Mormon Church, in opposition to the submitted constitution.

Anti-Mormon Test Oath, Arguments of Hon. J.M. Wilson, Hon. A.B. Carlton, and Bishop William Budge, in Opposition to the Constitution of the Proposed State of Idaho Adopted at Boise City, August 6, 1889, Made Before the Committee on the Territories of the House of Representatives January 21 and February 8, 1890. Washington, DC: Government Printing Office, 1890.

Territorial Statutes

The Compiled and Revised Laws of the Territory of Idaho of a General Nature Passed at, or Continued in Force by the Eighth Session of the Legislative Assembly, convened on the seventh day of December, A.D. 1874, at Boise City. Together with the Constitution of the United States, Declaration of Independence and Acts of Congress Concerning the Territory. Boise City, ID: Milton Kelly, Territorial Printer, 1875.

This is a collection of session laws, still in session law format, grouped roughly by subject and with a subject index, but no sequential numbering system; not quite a codification.

The Revised Statutes of Idaho Territory, Enacted at the Fourteenth Session of the Legislative Assembly, in Force June 1, 1887. Boise City, ID: Henry Gibson, Printer and Binder, 1887.

Includes the Declaration of Independence, the Constitution of the United States, 23 U.S.C. §§ 1839-1895 (federal statutes governing the territories), and the statutes for the territory of Idaho, with subject index.

Territorial Session Laws

Laws of the Territory of Idaho, First Session. Lewiston, ID: James A. Glascock, Territorial Printer, 1864.

Includes the Declaration of Independence, the Constitution of the United States, the Organic Act of the Territory of Idaho, selected federal acts regarding settlers and public lands in the Oregon and Washington Territories, the naturalization of aliens, miscellaneous acts governing the territories, and the Statutes of the Territory of Idaho, with subject index.

House and Council (Senate) Journals

Years: 1863-1889, except fifth and eighth sessions, for which I was unable to find any record of publication. Records of the reading and voting on legislative bills, and some correspondence. Some editions include copies of state agencies' biennial reports as appendixes. Some publication dates may look erroneous, but they are the publication dates as given on the publications.

Journal of the First Session of the House of Representatives, Idaho Territory. Lewiston, ID: James A. Glascock, Territorial Printer, 1864.

Journal of the First Session of the Council of Idaho Territory. Lewiston, ID: James A. Glascock, Territorial Printer, 1864.

Journal of the Second Session of the House of Representatives of Idaho Territory. Boise City, ID: Frank Kenyon, Territorial Printer, 1866.

Journal of the Second Session of the Council of Idaho Territory. Boise City, ID: Frank Kenyon, Territorial Printer, 1864.

Journal of the Third Session of the House of Representatives of Idaho Territory. Boise City, ID: Frank Kenyon, Territorial Printer, 1866.

Journal of the Third Session of the Council of Idaho Territory. Boise City, ID: Frank Kenyon, Territorial Printer, 1866.

Journals of the Council and House of Representatives of the Fourth Session of the Legislative Assembly of the Territory of Idaho. Boise City, ID: Statesman Publishing Company Printers, 1867.

An unusual year in which a combined journal was kept, with council's and house of representatives' proceedings intermixed.

Journal of the Sixth Session of the House of Representatives of Idaho Territory. Boise City, ID: James S. Reynolds, Territorial Printer, 1871.

Journal of the Sixth Session of the Council of Idaho Territory. Boise City, ID: James S. Reynolds, Territorial Printer, 1871.

House Journal of the Seventh Session of the Legislative Assembly of the Territory of Idaho. Boise City, ID: Milton Kelly, Territorial Printer, 1873.

Journal of the Seventh Session of the Council of Idaho Territory. Boise City, ID: Milton Kelly, Territorial Printer, 1874.

House Journal of the Ninth Session of the Legislative Assembly of the Territory of Idaho. Boise City, ID: Milton Kelly, Territorial Printer, 1877.

Council Journal of the Ninth Session of the Legislative Assembly of the Territory of Idaho. Boise City, ID: Milton Kelly, Territorial Printer, 1877.

House Journal of the Tenth Session of the Legislative Assembly of the Territory of Idaho. Boise City, ID: D. Bacon, Territorial Printer, 1879.

Council Journal of the Tenth Session of the Legislative Assembly of the Territory of Idaho. Boise City, ID: D. Bacon, Territorial Printer, 1879.

Journal of the House of Representatives of the Eleventh Legislative Assembly of the Territory of Idaho. Boise City, ID: A.J. Boyakin, Territorial Printer, 1881.

Journal of the Council of the Eleventh Legislative Assembly of the Territory of Idaho. Boise City, ID: A.J. Boyakin, Territorial Printer, 1881.

Journal of the House of Representatives of the Twelfth Legislative Assembly of the Territory of Idaho. Boise City, ID: Milton Kelly, Territorial Printer, 1883.

Journal of the Council of the Twelfth Legislative Assembly of the Territory of Idaho. Boise City, ID: Milton Kelly, Territorial Printer, 1883.

Journal of the House of Representatives of the Thirteenth Legislative Assembly of the Territory of Idaho. Boise City, ID: Jas. A. Pinney, Territorial Printer, 1885.

Journal of the Council of the Thirteenth Legislative Assembly of the Territory of Idaho. Boise City, ID: Jas. A. Pinney, Territorial Printer, 1885.

Journal of the House of Representatives of the Fourteenth Legislative Assembly of the Territory of Idaho. [Boise City, ID?]: Henry Gibson, Territorial Printer, 1887.

Journal of the Council of the Fourteenth Legislative Assembly of the Territory of Idaho. S.L.: Henry Gibson, Territorial Printer, 1887.

Journal of the House of Representatives of the Fifteenth Legislative Assembly of the Territory of Idaho. Boise City, ID: Jas. A. Pinney, Territorial Printer, 1889.

Journal of the Council of the Fifteenth Legislative Assembly of the Territory of Idaho. Boise City, ID: Jas. A. Pinney, Territorial Printer, 1889.

Judicial Branch Materials

Decisions of the Supreme Court of Idaho Territory

H.E. Prickett, associate justice. *Reports of Cases Argued and Determined in the Supreme Court of Idaho Territory from January Term, 1866, to September Term, 1880, Inclusive.* San Francisco, CA: Bancroft-Whitney Company, Law Publishers and Law Booksellers, 1904. (1 Idaho Reports)

Reports the decisions of the supreme court from 1866-1880, as well as providing the rules of the supreme court and a roster of the justices and attorneys admitted to practice in the territory.

Sol. Hasbrouck, ex-officio reporter, *Reports of Cases Argued and Determined in the Supreme Court of Territory of Idaho.* San Francisco, CA: Bancroft-Whitney Company, Law Publishers and Law Booksellers, 1903. (2 Idaho Reports)

Reports the decisions of the Supreme Court of the Territory of Idaho from 1881-1890.

Trial Transcripts, Briefs, and Arguments

Transcript [of the proceedings of the trial of C.F. Kimball, in the case of] *Territory v. John Williams, Edward Elwood, and C.F. Kimball* (June 1865) in the Justice Court of T.H. Callaway, Boise County.

Original book from the Boise County Clerk, Idaho City, Idaho; microfilmed in Boise by Idaho Historical Society, 1960. On file with the University of Idaho.

The Rights of Citizenship. Brief in re: H.R. bills numbered 1478 and 6153 and the petition of the Citizens of Bear Lake County, Idaho Territory (1885).

The Idaho Test Oath: argument delivered in the Supreme Court of Idaho Territory, Feb. 10, 1888: appeals from Bear Lake County by Richard Z. Johnson, in the cases of William Heyward, appellant, vs. Henry Bolton, et al., respondents, and James B. Innis, appellant, vs. same respondents. Salt Lake City, UT: Deseret News Company, 1888.

Executive Branch Materials

Gubernatorial Messages to the Territorial Legislatures

Although governors' messages to the territorial legislatures also appear in the house or council journals of the time, the following governors' messages are publications in their own right, on file with the Idaho State Law Library.

Governor's Message of Acting Governor William B. Daniels, First Session Idaho Territorial Legislature, December 9, 1863.

Eight legal-size typed pages, signed at the Executive Office, Lewiston, I.T., Dec. 9, 1863.

The Biennial Message of Thomas W. Bennett, Governor of Idaho, to the Seventh Session of the Legislature of Idaho Territory. Boise City, ID: Milton Kelly, Book, Job and Newspaper Printer, 1872.

The Biennial Message of Mason Brayman, Governor of Idaho, to the Ninth Session of the Legislature of Idaho Territory. Boise City, ID: Milton Kelly, Book, Job and Newspaper Printer, 1876.

The Biennial Message of Mason Brayman, Governor of Idaho, to the Tenth Session of the Legislature of Idaho Territory. Boise City, ID: D. Bacon, Book, Job and Newspaper Printer, 1879.

The Biennial Message of John B. Neil, Governor of Idaho, to the Eleventh Session of the Legislature of Idaho Territory. Boise City, ID: printed at the Statesman Office, 1880.

Biennial messages for 1884, 1886, and 1888 are also on file with the Idaho State Law Library.

Message of Governor Bunn Transmitting Council Bill No. 5 (Known as the Test Oath) with his approval on February 3, 1885, Thirteenth Territorial Session of the Idaho Legislature.

Congratulates legislature on passing law disenfranchising polygamists. Typewritten letter on file with the Idaho State Law Library.

The Biennial Message of Edward A. Stevenson, Governor of Idaho, to the Fifteenth Session of the Legislature of Idaho Territory, 1888-1889. Boise City, ID: Statesman Print, 1888.

In addition to the usual "state of the territory" type of address, this edition also includes the governor's letters of pardon for prisoners. The governor reminded the legislators that the act of Congress approved July 30, 1886, prohibited them from passing local or special laws and limited their ability to increase the territorial indebtedness, and he recommended that the legislature hold a convention to form a constitution and then proceed to statehood.

Reports of the Governor of Idaho Made to the Secretary of the Interior for the year 1878. Washington, DC: Government Printing Office, 1878.

"A report of the condition of affairs and of the progress and development of the Territory." Reports for the years 1878, 1879, 1880, 1884, 1885, 1886, 1888, 1889, and 1890 are on file with the Idaho State Law Library.

SECONDARY SOURCES

Books

Leonard J. Arrington. *The History of Idaho,* vol. 1 of 2. Moscow: University of Idaho Press, 1994.

Description of early Idaho includes politics, law, and justice in territorial days, including details of the controversial relocation of the capital from northern Idaho to southern Idaho.

Hubert Howe Bancroft. *The Works of Hubert Howe Bancroft, History of Washington, Idaho, and Montana, 1845-1889,* vol. XXXI, 393-588. San Francisco, CA: The History Company Publishers, 1890.

Early history of Idaho includes description of early governors, legislatures, judges, territorial limits, politics, and relations with Native Americans.

Carl Bianchi, ed. *Justice for the Times: A Centennial History of the Idaho State Courts.* Boise, ID: Idaho Law Foundation, 1990.

Contains description of the court system and photographs of courthouses in Idaho, from the earliest preterritory roots to the present day.

W.J. Brockelbank. *The Community Property Law of Idaho.* Boise, ID: Idaho State Bar Association and the Idaho State Bar Foundation, Inc., 1962.

Contains some discussion of the early roots of community property law in Idaho Territory days.

Cornelius J. Brosnan. *History of the State of Idaho.* New York: Charles Scribner's Sons, 1935.

Early history of Idaho, including "how law and order were established" and "territorial organization."

Dennis C. Colson. *Idaho's Constitution: The Tie That Binds.* Moscow: University of Idaho Press, 1991.

Discusses background of founders of the Idaho Constitution and explains debate and background of controversial issues arising in the convention proceedings.

Donald Crowley. *The Idaho State Constitution: A Reference Guide.* Westport, CT: Greenwood Press, 1994.

Contains chapter on territorial Idaho and constitutional convention proceedings, as well as section-by-section discussion of the constitution.

Byron Defenbach. *Idaho: The Place and Its People, a History of the Gem State from Prehistoric to Present Days,* vol. 1 of 3. Chicago, IL: American Historical Society, Inc., 1933.

This history of Idaho was written by a former Idaho state treasurer and state senator and includes delightful old photos.

Thomas Donaldson. *Idaho of Yesterday.* Caldwell, ID: Caxton Printers, Ltd., 1941.

Chapters on "Courts, Judges and Attorneys" and "Idaho's Territorial Governors" (pp. 185-275) may be especially helpful. Includes a full account of the colorful story of Territorial Judge Lewis who inadvertently "resigned."

Fred T. Dubois. *The Making of a State.* Rexburg, ID: Eastern Idaho Publishing Company, 1971.

Autobiographical account of politics in territorial Idaho by former congressional delegate for the territory of Idaho.

Dick d'Easum. *Fragments of Villainy.* Boise, ID: Statesman Printing Company, 1959.

Essays on frontier "justice" in Idaho.

Hiram T. French. *History of Idaho, a Narrative Account of its Historical Progress, its People and its Principal Interests,* vol. 1 of 3. Chicago: Lewis Publishing Company, 1914.

Includes two chapters on the territorial government.

John Hailey. *The History of Idaho.* Boise, ID: Press of Syms-York Company, Inc., 1910.

Pages 45-292 summarize the territorial sessions, including legislation passed, legislators, territorial officers, infamous crimes, etc.

James H. Hawley, ed. *History of Idaho, the Gem of the Mountains.* Chicago: The S.J. Clarke Publishing Company, 1920.

Volume 1 includes the political history of Idaho, beginning in the 1500s through pioneer and territory days. Discusses "lawlessness," early governors and legislatures, etc. Volumes 2 and 3 contain brief biographies of many characters and officials from pre- and poststatehood Idaho.

An Illustrated History of North Idaho, Embracing Nez Perces, Idaho, Latah, Kootenai and Shoshone Counties. Western Historical Publishing Co., 1903.

Appears to be a compilation by different authors, though no individuals are named. This book appears to be the best source for information on local governments in early Idaho, for the five counties enumerated.

Ronald H. Limbaugh. *Rocky Mountain Carpetbaggers: Idaho's Territorial Governors 1863-1890.* Moscow: University Press of Idaho, 1982.

Most of Idaho's territorial governors were sent from the East Coast, were not familiar with Idaho, and averaged less than two years in office. Information on the individuals filling this office, their background, and their deeds as governors.

A Look at Idaho's Constitution, Then and Now (1889-1962). League of Women Voters, 1962. [No other publication information available.]

Description of territorial Idaho and discussion of constitutional provisions in context of the territory.

John F. MacLane. *A Sagebrush Lawyer.* New York: Pandick Press, Inc., 1953.

A former Idaho judge and lawyer writes about his friend/mentor James H. Hawley, who was a lawyer, legislator, and governor of Idaho, and shares his recollections and personal experiences of practicing law in Idaho during the territory days and the early days of statehood.

John Rogers McBride (1832-1904). *Idaho Pioneer Reminiscences,* vols. 1 and 2. [No publication information, possibly unpublished.]

Memoirs of an attorney, with description of politics and justice in Idaho Territory. On file with the Idaho State Law Library.

W.J. McConnell. *Early History of Idaho.* Caldwell, ID: the Caxton Printers, Ltd, 1913.

This history was written by a former U.S. Senator and Idaho governor, who claims he "was present and cognizant of the events narrated" and also that the book is "published by authority of the Idaho State Legislature." Although I have doubts about the strict accuracy of these two statements, this is a very interesting history, full of anecdotal evidence of early vigilante justice and the difficulties faced by the early territorial legislators and governors.

Carey H. Nixon. *Community and Separate Property and Homesteads.* Boise: Idaho State Bar, 1947.

A "Chronological Synopsis of Idaho Laws with Effective Dates Concerning Community and Separate Property and Homesteads 1864-1946."

Mrs. V.J. O'Farrell. "Historical Review, Bench and Bar of the Pacific Northwest." In *Eminent Judges and Lawyers of the Northwest 1843-1955.* Palo Alto, CA: C.W. Taylor Jr., 1954.

Lists accomplishments of early Idaho governors, judges, legislators, and lawyers.

John E. Rees. *Idaho: Chronology, Nomenclature, Bibliography.* Chicago, IL: W.B. Conkey Company, 1918.

Contains chronology of events of Idaho Territory from 1863-1890; also explains origin of Idaho place names.

Government Documents

The Governors and Secretaries of Idaho Territory, Together with Other Matters Relating to Early Idaho History ("Compiled by and Under the Direction of George H. Curtis, Secretary of State, 1942").

Contains discussion and biographical information on the governors and secretaries of Idaho Territory, as well as the origin of the territorial seal and the name "Idaho."

The Idaho Almanac. Boise, ID: Published by the Executive Office of the Governor John V. Evans and the Idaho Division of Tourism and Industrial Development, 1977.

Provides general Idaho historical information, including helpful maps of the evolution of today's state boundaries.

The Idaho Blue Book 2001-2002. Published by the Secretary of State Pete T. Cenarrusa for the State of Idaho. Caldwell, ID: Caxton Printers, Ltd., 2001.

Provides a chronicle of early Idaho history, as well as providing information on legislators and governors from the territory days.

Journal Articles

Annie Laurie Bird. "Idaho's First Territorial Governor." *Idaho Yesterdays* 10(1966): 8-15.

Evaluates career of William Wallace.

Clyde A. Bridges. "The Counties of Idaho." *Pacific Northwest Quarterly* 31(April 1940):187-206.

Details evolution of Idaho Territory and county boundaries.

David L. Crowder. "George Laird Shoup." *Idaho Yesterdays* 33(1990): 18-23.

Discusses Idaho's last territorial and first state governor.

Ronald H. Limbaugh. "The Carpetbag Image: Idaho Governors in Myth and Reality." *Pacific Northwest Quarterly* 60(1969): 77-83.

Discusses Idaho's territorial governors.

Ronald H. Limbaugh. "Fighter on the Bench: Milton Kelly's Idaho Legal Career 1862-1870." *Idaho Yesterdays* 25(1981): 3-13.

Discusses a controversial judge in Idaho Territory, who also became the territorial printer of session laws and journals, and the publisher of the *Idaho Statesman,* after stepping down from the bench.

D. Duff McKee. " 'The People vs. Caleb Lyon and Others': The Capital Relocation Case Revisited." *Idaho Yesterdays* 36(1992): 2-18.

Discusses lawsuit filed against Idaho territorial officials after controversial relocation of the capital from Lewiston to Boise.

Earl S. Pomeroy. "Running a Territory: They Had Their Troubles." *Idaho Yesterdays* 14(1970): 9-13.

"Discusses the territorial government of the Idaho Territory, 1860's-80's."

Merle W. Wells. "Clinton Dewitt Smith: Secretary, Idaho Territory 1864-1865." *Idaho Yesterdays* 44(2001): 27-35. [Reprinted from *Oregon Historical Quarterly,* March 1951.]

Smith served as acting governor as well as territorial secretary.

Merle W. Wells. "The Creation of the Territory of Idaho." *Pacific Northwest Quarterly* 40(April 1949): 106-123.

Merle W. Wells. "Law in the Service of Politics: Anti-Mormonism in Idaho Territory." *Idaho Yesterdays* 25(1981): 33-43.

Merle W. Wells. "S.R. Howlett's War with the Idaho Legislature, 1866-1867." *Idaho Yesterdays* 20(1976): 20-27.

Idaho territorial treasurer "refused to pay legislators until they signed an oath of allegiance to the United States."

Owen Wister. "The Second Missouri Compromise." *Idaho Yesterdays* 20 (1976): 2-17. [Reprinted from *Harpers Monthly,* March 1895.]

Struggle between Idaho Territory's Democratic legislators and Republican governor after the Civil War.

Miscellany (Speeches, Personal Papers, Correspondence)

Letter from David W. Ballard, Idaho Territorial Governor (1866-1870), Boise City, Idaho Territory, to Ulysses S. Grant, President of the United States (Apr. 18, 1870).

On file with the University of Idaho's Special Collections. Comments on Grant's judicial appointments in Idaho.

Grievances of the Nez Perces. Speeches of Shadow of the Mountain, or Lawyer (head chief) and Gov. Lyon at Lewiston, Idaho Territory, Aug. 21, 1864.

On file with University of Idaho's Special Collections.

William H. Homer. "History of the Moony [i.e., Michael Mooney] and [Frank] Barns murder case, 1882."

"Account of a murder at Franklin Station near the Idaho-Utah border in October 1881 written by the sheriff of Oneida County, Idaho Territory. This typewritten copy and notes were made by Eugene W. Whitman in 1932."

On file with the University of Idaho's Special Collections.

Dwight Wm. Jensen. "Come Weal, Come Woe, a History of Idaho's First Territorial Legislature."

Undated typed manuscript, probably not published, on file with the Idaho State Historical Society.

Henry Z. Johnson. "A Pioneer Judiciary."

Probably not published. Typed legal-size papers in a folder, undated, on file with the Idaho State Law Library. Discusses territorial judges in Idaho.

"Judicial History of Idaho."

Unidentified author of letter to Clark Bell, Esq., editor of the *Medico-Legal Journal* in New York, circa 1912. Cover letter and information on justices and judges in early Idaho and their terms of office, beginning with 1863 appointments made by Abraham Lincoln. On file with the Idaho State Law Library.

Richard G. Magnuson. Proceedings, Sept. 2, 1861-Aug. 18, 1863. Notes taken by Richard Magnuson, Book A, commissioner's record of Shoshone County, Washington Territory, for that period while Shoshone County government operated as a subdivision of Washington Territory until their being taken into Idaho Territory: typescript, [1961?].

On file with the University of Idaho's Special Collections.

Letter from Robert Newell, 1807-1869, Lewiston, Idaho Territory, to Medorem Crawford, 1819-1891 (Feb. 8, 1869).

Concerning Idaho Territorial Governor David W. Ballard (1866-1870). On file with the University of Idaho's Special Collections.

Records relating to the appointment of federal judges, attorneys, and marshals for the Territory and State of Idaho, 1861-99. Washington, DC: The National Archives, National Archives and Records Service, General Services Administration, 1967.

On file with the University of Idaho.

Reports on the Aftermath of the 1863 Nez Perce Treaty by Chief Lawyer, Governor Caleb Lyon, General Benjamin Alvord and Indian Agent James O'Neill. Boise: University of Idaho, 1999.

Transcriptions of conversations and negotiations between Nez Perce tribal leaders and U.S. officials in 1864, taken from original manuscripts from the National Archives and Records Administration. On file with the Idaho State Law Library.

State Department territorial papers; Idaho, 1863-72. Washington, DC: The National Archives, National Archives and Records Service, General Services Administration, 1963.

Microform of a number of State Department territorial papers relating to the administration of affairs in Idaho Territory, on file with the University of Idaho.

"The treaty of 1855 has not been lived up to, and we have no faith that this will be lived up to": the 1867 Nez Perce Treaty Council. Transcription, editing, and introduction by Donna K. Smith. Moscow: University of Idaho Library, 2001.

Documents and correspondence of council proceedings leading up to the Treaty of 1868 with the Nez Perce and the Nez Perce War of 1877. On file with the Idaho State Law Library.

A True Copy of the Record of the Official Proceedings at the Council in the Walla Walla Valley, Held Jointly by Isaac I. Stevens Gov. & Supt. W.T. and Joel Palmer Supt. Indian Affairs O.T. on the Part of the United States with the Tribes of Indians Named in the Treaties Made at that Council (June 9 & 11, 1855).

Certified copy of the original minutes of the official proceedings at the Council in Walla Walla Valley, which culminated in the Stevens Treaty of 1855, on file with the National Archives and Records Administration. On file with the Idaho State Law Library.

Merle Wells. "The Fourth Session of the Territorial Legislature: A Study in Early Idaho Politics." 1939.

Typed manuscript, probably not published, on file with the Idaho State Historical Society. Discussion of early territorial session, including excerpts from old letters and telegrams

Theses

Fred Woodward Blase. "Political History of Idaho Territory, 1863-1890." MA thesis, University of California, Berkeley, 1925.

On file with the Idaho State Historical Society.

Madeline Kelley Buckendorf, "Building a Profession: A History of the Idaho State Bar, 1860s to 1950s," MA thesis, Boise State University, 1992.

On file with the Idaho State Historical Society.

Maude Cosho Houston. "Idaho Territory: Its Origins, Its Governors, and Its Problems." Unpublished MA thesis, University of Idaho, Moscow, 1951.

Discusses lawyers and practice of law in early Idaho. On file with the University of Idaho.

Warren Aldrich Roberts. "A History of Taxation in the Territory and State of Idaho." PhD thesis, Harvard University, Boston, 1932.

Merle William Wells. "Idaho: A Study in Statehood and Sectionalism, 1863-1890." MA thesis, University of California, 1947.

Discusses political forces behind the struggle to define Idaho's boundaries.

Chapter 14

Illinois Legal Research Before Statehood in 1818: A Bibliographical Guide

Judith Gaskell

INTRODUCTION

The legal researcher looking for pre-1818 Illinois material is fortunate because quite a few primary and secondary sources are available. Many historians,[1] several legal historians,[2] and a few intrepid law librarians[3] have illuminated the research path in Illinois. Of special note are the volumes in the series of the *Collections of the Illinois State Historical Library,* which contain reprints of a great number of primary and secondary historical sources from this period. Moreover, the Internet age has made some primary sources accessible online.[4]

The early law of the Illinois country is intertwined with its history, so I will discuss legal sources in the context of the major historical events that shaped the evolution of the rule of law. For thousands of years before the arrival of the French explorers, the area that in 1818 became the state of Illinois was under the unwritten law of the Native American tribes who lived there. The Illiniwek tribes, who lived along the Illinois River, gave their name to the area, and the French shortened the name and added a French ending.[5] Customary tribal law included the concept that land used for agriculture and for hunting was held in common by the tribe.[6] Depending on the subject matter, disputes were settled by family, clan, or tribal councils.[7]

After European settlers arrived in the area, Illinois was under a succession of different rules of law between 1682 and statehood in 1818. From 1682 until 1763, Illinois was under the control of France. From 1763 to 1778, Illinois was under the rule of Great Britain. From 1778 to 1782, Illinois was governed by the Republic of Virginia. Finally, from 1782 to 1818, Illinois was under American control, eventually becoming the territory of Illinois in 1809. This territory, however, included parts of present-day Michigan and Wisconsin. In 1818, Illinois was admitted as the twenty-first state in the Union.

THE ILLINOIS COUNTRY UNDER THE FRENCH
FROM 1673 TO 1765

In 1671, a meeting at Sault Sainte Marie between nineteen Frenchmen and representatives from fourteen Native American tribes resulted in an agreement to allow France dominance over the lands in return for protecting those tribes.[8] The first documented record of French explorers entering Illinois was in 1673. Louis Jolliet and Pere Jacques Marquette traveled down the Mississippi as far as the Arkansas River, then back up and along to the Illinois River, portaging at the Chicago River to Lake Michigan. In 1682 the explorer Rene Robert, Sieur de La Salle, traveled to the mouth of the Mississippi and claimed for France an area including the entire Mississippi basin from Lake Superior down to the Gulf of Mexico.[9] Thus, Illinois officially came under French rule.

The Native Americans should have owned the land because of their rights of possession. Indeed, some of their land was purchased by French settlers, but, for the most part, the French ignored those rights and routinely conveyed land directly to settlers.[10] In April 1683, La Salle made a grant of lands at Starved Rock, giving the grantee, Jacques Bourdon, Sieur D'Autray, the right to administer low justice *(basse justice)*. Low justice included jurisdiction over petty offenses.[11] The wording of the grant included "and further we grant to the aforesaid Sieur D'Autray and his successors rights of dovecote, of wine press, of fortifications, and of low justice."[12] Rent was to be collected from D'Autray under "the custom of fiefs in the county of provostry of Paris."[13]

Later grants and contracts also refer to this Custom of Paris (Coutume de Paris).[14] On September 14, 1712, Louis XIV proclaimed the Custom of Paris to be the law of the province of Louisiana under a fifteen-year trading charter issued to Antoine Crozat.[15] Because there was no uniform system of law in France at that time, provinces and cities followed their local "customs" of traditional law practices. The Custom of Paris was probably chosen as the law because Louisiana was a royal province.[16]

Early French settlements in Illinois had been established along the Mississippi, south of present-day East St. Louis at Cahokia in 1699 and at Kaskaskia in 1703. In 1719 Fort de Chartres was constructed between these two villages. During those times the area called the Illinois had no clearly defined borders.[17] At first the French settlements were considered to be part of the province of Quebec, but by an ordinance drawn in 1717, they were separated from Quebec and annexed to the province of Lousiana.[18] Regulations submitted to the king created nine districts in Louisiana, one of which was the Illinois district.[19]

Although a provincial council was authorized in 1718,[20] it was not established by edict until 1722, at which time it was given authority over all civil and criminal cases with the right to appeal to the Superior Council of Louisiana in New Orleans.[21] This council, which functioned throughout the district of Illinois at least until 1726, was comprised of French officers who worked for the Company of the Indies (Compagnie d'Occident). The Company of the Indies governed the province of Louisiana until 1731,[22] after which the province reverted to the rule of the king. Pierre Dugue, Sieur de Boisbriant, the commandant of the Illinois who built Fort de Chartres, was the head of the council. Next a Court of Audience of the Royal Jurisdiction of the Illinois was created in 1726 to hear minor civil cases. This court had one judge and two officers, who were the king's attorney, and a recording clerk. Sessions were held at Fort de Chartres and then at Kaskakia until the end of French rule.[23]

One of the issues taken to the superior council in 1728 was that of the inheritance rights of Native American widows of Frenchmen. Could they inherit under French law and could childless widows subsequently leave their property to their native families? The council decided that "savages" could not inherit from Frenchmen and that the property of childless widows was to be controlled by the Company of the Indies. Real estate was to be taken over or, if there were children, was to be placed in a trust with one-third interest to the widow and two-thirds to the children.[24]

French Research Sources

There are a number of official records for this French era, but they are scattered widely. Prior to the establishment of Fort de Chartres, the priests in the villages handled all routine transactions, and this practice continued thereafter. Thus, parish records give a good picture of daily life in early French Illinois.[25] Before formal courts were set up, and even thereafter, commandants of the fort and of the villages also settled disputes. Notaries, who signed all contracts and other agreements, were appointed by the provincial council, the commandant, or the judge. Copies of these notarial documents were kept in a central location.

Several bibliographies by Henry Putney Beers provide invaluable guidance to finding and accessing the major sources of these original records.[26] Beers includes a complete description of the official records in the Archives Nationale in Paris, France; the Canadian Archives; the Library of Congress; and various state archives.[27]

The surviving originals of court and notarial records from Kaskaskia can be found in the Randolph County Courthouse in Chester, Illinois; in the Illinois State Archives in Springfield, Illinois; and in the Chicago Historical Society. Those records would not be available today if not for the efforts of Clarence Walworth Alvord, who discovered them in southern Illinois while he was gathering sources for the monumental *Centennial History of Illinois,* of which he was the managing editor.[28] Later in the twentieth century, Margaret Kimball Brown supervised the indexing and microfilming of the Kaskaskia Manuscripts prior to 1766.[29] In her article describing these records, she summarizes the lives and work of the notaries active in the Illinois country. Her estimation is that 3,770 records survived out of 6,138 originals.

An excellent source for reprinted and translated documents are the three volumes in the French Series of the collections of the Illinois State Library.[30] These volumes include dispatches and notarial documents gathered from a variety of sources, such as the Canadian Archives and the Chicago Historical Society. George Fiedler's history of the Illinois courts reprinted selections from these volumes.[31] Another major historical study reprinted selected documents from the church, notarial, and court records of the village of Chartres.[32]

THE ERA OF ENGLISH RULE FROM 1763 TO 1778

From 1689 until 1763, France and England were at war over their holdings in North America. In 1762, France conveyed by secret treaty all of its territorial holdings west of the Mississippi and New Orleans to Spain. Then, on February 10, 1763, England and France signed the Treaty of Paris.[33] This was the official end of French rule in Illinois but not the end of French law.

On the following October 7, King George III issued a proclamation that reserved the entire western territory, including Illinois, for the use of Native Americans.[34] On December 30, General Thomas Gage issued another proclamation granting freedom of religion and the ability to keep all of their land and property to French subjects, who swore oaths of "fidelity and obedience" to the British king.[35] An elaborate structure was proposed for governing this new territory but was never fully implemented, for in the meantime a tribal rebellion, led by Chief Pontiac and fueled by resentment against British rule, had erupted in the territory.

In response to a letter written by General Gage about the difficulty of administering civil law in this "Indian" territory, parliament enacted the Mutiny Act, which was effective March 24, 1765, and gave anyone the power to arrest persons accused of committing crimes and turn them over to an English commanding officer, who would take them "to the civil magistrate of the next adjoining colony."[36] The next adjoining colony to the entire territory was Pennsylvania; no record has been found of anyone being taken to Fort Pitt for trial.[37]

Travel was so difficult it took the British several years to make their way to Fort de Chartres. On October 9, 1765, the fort was officially surrendered to Captain Thomas Stirling.[38] At the start of British rule, Illinois had only about 2,000 civilian residents in five villages along the Mississippi River; around 1,000 French citizens had crossed over to the Spanish side of the Mississippi.[39] In December 1765, Captain Stirling wrote that the French troops and the two remaining French judges had crossed over to the Spanish side, and, therefore, Stirling appointed Jean Baptiste LaGrange to decide disputes according to French civil law.[40] Unfortunately, no record has been found of LaGrange's decisions. The first court proceedings recorded in English in Illinois were of a court-martial in November 1766.[41]

In 1768, the commander Colonel John Wilkins set up a "Civil Court of Judicatory . . . to Hear and Try in a Summary Way all Causes of Debt and Property."[42] He might have done this to stop the still-common practice of arbitration, which was thought to favor the French settlers and merchants over the British. This court had six judges and sat alternatively at Kaskaskia and at New Chartres until June 1770, when Wilkins ordered the court to sit solely at New Chartres. The court decided to meet only at Kaskaskia, however; therefore, Wilkins abolished the court. In 1771, the French residents sent two men to ask General Gage to remove Wilkins and set up a French civil government. Late in 1771, more for economic than political reasons, General Gage was ordered to destroy both Fort De Chartres and Fort Pitt and to withdraw all troops from them.

Parliament passed the Quebec Act in 1774, attaching the northwest area, which included Illinois, to Quebec and Canada.[43] The Quebec Act gave French inhabitants the right to practice their religion and to continue using French civil law, but criminal law was to be British law. In 1775, instructions sent to Governor Guy Carlson ordered the creation of an Inferior Court of Criminal and Civil Jurisdiction in the "District of the Illinois."[44] This court was never established. In 1776, Phillipe Francois de Rastel, Chevalier de Rocheblave, was appointed as the last commander of the British troops stationed at Kaskaskia. Based on a letter he wrote in 1777, it appears that both French and English law were being applied in the Illinois area.[45]

English Research Sources

Beers's guide to French and British sources provides a road map to finding the original sources.[46] Many of the major sources for researching this chaotic period are reprinted in the three volumes of the British Series of the *Collections of the Illinois State Historical Library*.[47] The original sources of the documents in those volumes include the Kaskaskia Manuscripts; the British Museum; the Chicago Historical Society; the Pennsylvania Historical Society; the Library of Congress; the Wisconsin Historical Society; the Canadian Archives; and the Archives Nationales in Paris, France. George Fiedler's history of the Illinois courts reprints selections from the British Series volumes.[48]

THE COUNTY OF ILLINOIS IN THE REPUBLIC OF VIRGINIA FROM 1778 TO 1782 AND AWAITING U.S. RULE FROM 1782 TO 1787

The Revolutionary War had begun in 1775 and was supported in the Illinois country by a few American merchants and some of the French inhabitants. On the night of July 4, 1778, George Rogers Clark captured Kaskaskia for Virginia without firing a shot, then went on to take Cahokia and Fort de Chartres. Commander de Rochblave was sent to Williamsburg in irons.[49] Clark established a civil court at Cahokia, and a judicial election was held in October 1778. The earliest record of this court was a writ of attachment from November 24, 1778. The order itself was in English, but the return was in French.[50]

On December 9, 1778, the Virginia General Assembly passed a law to create the county of Illinois in Virginia and to establish a civil government.[51] This county included all land west of the Ohio River. John Todd, a lawyer, was appointed military commander of the new county on December 12, 1778. After Todd was installed in Kaskaskia on May 12, 1779, he organized the county into three districts—Kaskaskia, Cahokia, and Vincennes (now in Indiana)—and held judicial elections. All of the judges elected in the districts were French. These courts continued under the rule of Virginia until the law establishing the county of Illinois expired on January 5, 1782.

On December 20, 1783, Virginia passed a law authorizing the transfer of the territory northwest of the Ohio River to the United States.[52] The deed of cession conveying the area was signed on March 1, 1784.[53] Even after this, the courts at Kaskaskia and Cahokia continued to administer the same hybrid French and English system of law.[54] In 1786, the court at Cahokia put off making a final decision in one case, stating "we remit this decision to the government which we are expecting."[55]

Virginia Research Sources

Many of the court records and other historical documents, such as letters, from 1778 to 1790 are reprinted in the first two Virginia Series volumes of the collections of the Illinois State Historical Society.[56] The originals came from a variety of sources and locations, including the Kaskaskia Manuscripts; the Chicago Historical Society; the Library of Congress; and the Virginia State Library. The third and fourth volumes of the Virginia Series and other sources reprinted the papers of George Rogers Clark and other valuable documents from that era.[57] George Fiedler's study of the Illinois courts reprinted selections from the volumes in the Virginia Series.[58]

ILLINOIS IN THE NORTHWEST TERRITORY FROM 1787 TO 1809

In 1784, Thomas Jefferson chaired a committee to draft a plan for governing the new western territory, but it was not until 1787 that Congress passed the Northwest Ordinance.[59] This new Northwest Territory included all land northwest of the Ohio River and east of the Mississippi River. This land was planned to be divided eventually into three to five states.

The ordinance attempted to provide liberty for the inhabitants while also maintaining a strong central government. Inhabitants had no right to vote, but many of their rights were guaranteed in the ordinance itself. For example, Section 2 of the ordinance established the common law but allowed inhabitants who had settled and acquired title to land under French and English rule to have the laws and customs at the time of their settlement apply to their conveyances and bequests.[60] The ordinance also provided for representative government with elected representatives to take effect after the population of a district grew to 5,000 male inhabitants.

The ordinance gave newly appointed Territorial Governor Arthur St. Clair and the three appointed territorial judges the power to pass legislation. In addition, the governor held the executive powers and the judges held the judicial powers. On September 2, 1788, the first territorial court was convened at Marietta (Ohio). The legislature began to function in July 1788 and passed over 200 printed pages of laws, most of which were adapted from the laws of the eastern states.[61]

Although Governor St. Clair was appointed in February 1788, he did not make the long and difficult trip to Kaskaskia until March 5, 1790. When St. Clair arrived in Illinois, he was forced to govern by proclamation because the judges had not yet arrived.[62] He organized a county that included all of present-day Illinois and named it St. Clair County.

A court of common pleas was established in each of three judicial districts at Cahokia, Kaskaskia, and Prairie de Rocher because these settlements were so far apart and travel was so difficult. There were three appointed judges, and a court of quarter sessions was held every three months. The first three judges appointed were John de Moulin of Cahokia, John Edgar of Kaskaskia, and Jean Baptiste Barbeau of Prairie de Rocher. The clerk of the court was William St. Clair, a cousin of the governor. The recording of deeds, marriages, and other transactions was done in one record book for all of St. Clair County. Justices of the peace were appointed throughout the county. Their judgments were subject to appeal to the court of common pleas. In 1795, Governor St. Clair divided this county in two, with Cahokia as the seat of St. Clair County and Kaskaskia as the seat of Randolph County.

In 1793, the first courthouse in Cahokia was a French-style house purchased for that purpose and used for the next twenty years. The structure was dismantled in 1901, moved to St. Louis and then to Chicago, and finally rebuilt at its original location in 1931.[63]

Northwest Territory Research Sources

Now we begin to see, in addition to the historical sources noted earlier, the commonly available legal sources a modern researcher would expect to find. The Northwest Ordinance was published in the *Revised Statutes* and has been reprinted in a variety of places, including on the Internet. The ordinance and the laws passed by the government of the Northwest Territory were reprinted in the first volume in the Law Series of the *Collections of the Illinois State Historical Library*.[64] Theodore Calvin Pease's introduction to this volume examined these laws in their historical context. George Fiedler's history of the Illinois courts reprinted selections from this volume.[65] Francis S. Philbrick, in his introduction to fifth volume in the Law Series, analyzed at length the historical origins and drafting of the Northwest Ordinance and the problems in its application.[66]

The official papers from this period were reprinted in the second volume of the *Territorial Papers of the United States*.[67] The decisions of the courts were never published.

ILLINOIS IN THE INDIANA TERRITORY
FROM 1800 TO 1809

In May 1800, the Northwest Territory was divided into smaller sections.[68] The western section, including what is now Illinois, Indiana, and

Wisconsin, became the Indiana Territory. Because only 4,875 residents were in the entire new territory, it went back to having an appointed government under the Northwest Ordinance. Thus, the new governor, General William Henry Harrison, and the three new judges had the same powers as those originally appointed for the Northwest Territory. In January 1801, they met in the new capital of St. Vincennes to pass laws. Included was a law passed on January 23, 1801, to establish courts of quarter sessions in the two Illinois counties.[69] This law was adapted from an earlier Pennsylvania law.

The inhabitants of the Indiana Territory voted in 1804 to go to the second stage of representative government.[70] On July 29, 1805, the first general assembly convened at St. Vincennes. Its activities included setting up (among other things) a court of chancery "to exercise all the powers and authority usually exercised by courts of equity."[71] In 1807, a law was passed proclaiming the common law of England and the laws of the territory to be in force, without any clause continuing to allow French law to be applied.[72] This was the end of French law in Illinois.

Indiana Territory Research Sources

The laws of the Indiana Territory from 1801 to 1809 were reprinted in the second volume of the Law Series of the *Collections of the Illinois State Historical Library.*[73] Francis S. Philbrick's introduction to this volume discussed in depth how the laws were passed and how they were applied. This volume also reprinted the codified and indexed revision of the laws published in Vincennes in 1807. Fiedler's study of the Illinois courts reprinted selections from this volume.[74] The journals of the General Assembly of Indiana Territory from 1805 to 1815 were reprinted in Volume 32 of the *Indiana Historical Collections.*[75]

The official papers of the Indiana Territory from this time were reprinted in Volume 7 of the *Territorial Papers of the United States.*[76] The court decisions were never printed.

THE TERRITORY OF ILLINOIS FROM 1809 TO 1818

In 1805, 325 Illinois inhabitants petitioned Congress to split from the Indiana Territory. Eventually, in 1809, Congress divided the Indiana Territory, and the western part became the territory of Illinois.[77] The appointed governor of this new territory was Ninian Edwards; the three appointed judges were Alexander Stuart, Obadiah Jones, and Jesse Burgess Thomas.

Under the same powers granted by the Northwest Ordinance as to the previous territorial governments, these men determined that most of the laws of the former Indiana Territory were still in force in Illinois.[78] They proceeded to enact new laws, including one to reorganize and simplify the court system.[79] The first session of the new court was held in Kaskaskia in June 1809.

In March 1812, Governor Edwards issued a proclamation calling for an election. A majority of the 300 votes cast approved moving to the second stage of representative government under the Northwest Ordinance. The first general assembly was elected on November 25, 1812; began to legislate in Kaskaskia on December 13; and adopted all the laws of the previous territory. The courts were reorganized in 1814 and a supreme court was established.[80] The final session of the General Court of the Illinois Territory was held in June 1818.

The enabling act to allow Illinois to become a state was passed by Congress and approved on April 18, 1818.[81] The first constitutional convention met in Kaskaskia in August 1818. The constitution drafted for Illinois was based on those of New York, Kentucky, and Ohio.[82] On December 3, 1818, Illinois became the twenty-first state admitted to the Union.[83]

Illinois Territory Research Sources

The laws of the Illinois Territory were reprinted in the fifth volume of the Law Series of the *Collections of the Illinois State Historical Library.*[84] Philbrick's 477-page introduction to this volume analyzed in depth these laws and their historical relationship to the earlier territorial laws.

Nathaniel Pope had been appointed secretary of the territory in 1809, after having practiced law in Missouri and in Randolph County. An 1814 statute authorized Pope to revise the current laws, index them, and print them for $300.[85] When the two volumes of *Pope's Digests* were printed in 1815, they were the first encyclopedic treatment of the laws of Illinois. *Pope's Digest* was reprinted in the third and fourth volumes of the Law Series of the *Collections of the Illinois State Historical Library.*[86] The official papers from the Illinois Territory found in the National Archives were reprinted as Volumes 16 and 17 of the *Territorial Papers of the United States.*[87] The court decisions were never printed, but the dockets are in the Office of the Clerk of the Illinois Supreme Court in Springfield.[88]

NOTES

1. Most notably, Clarence Walworth Alvord, *The Illinois Country 1673-1818* (Urbana: University of Illinois Press, 1987). This volume was first published in 1920 as Volume I of the *Centennial History of Illinois* and is still one of the most comprehensive treatments of the prestatehood era. Other essential historical sources include Sidney Breese, *The Early History of Illinois* (Chicago: E.B. Myers & Company, 1884); Joseph Wallace, *The History of Illinois and Louisiana Under the French Rule* (Cincinnati, OH: Robert Clarke & Co., 1893); Natalie Maree Belting, *Kaskaskia Under the French Regime* (Urbana: University of Illinois Press, 1948; reprinted with a new foreword by Carl J. Ekberg [Carbondale: Southern Illinois University Press, 2003]); Marcel Giraud, *A History of French Louisiana,* Volume Five, *The Company of the Indies 1723-1731* (Baton Rouge: Louisiana State University Press, 1987, trans. 1991); Charles Balesi, *The Time of the French in the Heart of North America 1673-1818* (Chicago: Alliance Francaise, 1992); Carl J. Ekberg, *French Roots in the Illinois Country* (Urbana: University of Illinois Press, 1998); Clarence Edwin Carter, *Great Britain and the Illinois Country, 1763-1774* (Washington, DC: The American Historical Association, 1910); Robert Livingston Schuyler, *The Transition in Illinois from British to American Government* (New York: The Columbia University Press, 1909); Theodore Calvin Pease and Marguerite Jenison Pease, *George Rogers Clark and the Revolution in Illinois, 1763-1787: A Sesquicentennial Memorial* (Springfield: Trustees of the Illinois State Historical Library, 1929); David Curtis Skaggs, ed., *The Old Northwest in the American Revolution* (Madison: State Historical Society of Wisconsin, 1977). An example of an excellent comprehensive history of Illinois is by Robert P. Howard, *Illinois: A History of the Prairie State* (Grand Rapids: William B. Eerdmans Publishing Company, 1972). Ellen M. Whitney, comp., Janice A. Petterchak, ed., and Sandra M. Stark, assoc. ed., *Illinois History: An Annotated Bibliography* (Westport, CT: Greenwood Press, 1995) provides valuable descriptions of these and many other historical sources.

2. George Alexander Dupuy, "The Earliest Courts of the Illinois Country," *Ill. L. Rev.* 1 (1906): 1-8; Frederic Beers Crossley, *Courts and Lawyers of Illinois* (Chicago: The American Historical Society, 1916); Laurin A. Wollan Jr., ed., "Law in Illinois Under France: A Chapter in History from Roger L. Severns," *Ill. B. J.* 56 (1968): 384-391; William F. Zacharias, ed., "Illinois Courts Prior to Statehood," *Ill. B. J.* 56(1968): 556-568; and George Fiedler, *The Illinois Law Courts in Three Centuries 1673-1973: A Documentary History* (Berwyn: Physicians' Record Company, 1973).

3. Bernita J. Davies and Francis J. Rooney, *Research in Illinois Law* (New York: Oceana Publications, 1954); Roger Jacobs, Carol Boast, Edward F. Hess Jr., and James A. Sprowl, *Illinois Legal Research Sourcebook* (Springfield: Illinois Institute for Continuing Legal Education, 1977); Laurel Wendt, *Illinois Legal Research Manual* (St. Paul: Butterworth Legal Publishers, 1988); Laurel Wendt, *Illinois Legal Research Manual,* 2nd ed. (Buffalo, NY: William S. Hein & Co., 2005).

4. For example, the texts of primary sources, such as the Northwest Ordinance, are available at the Web site of the Avalon Project at Yale Law School at <http://www.yale.edu/lawweb/avalon>.

5. Howard, supra at 21.

6. Alvord, supra at 42; Fiedler, supra at xxx.

7. See Alvord at 43; Fiedler at xxx.

8. Alvord, supra at 61-62; Howard supra at 25-26.

9. Fiedler, supra at 4-5; Alvord, supra at 87. This proclamation is translated and reprinted in Wallace, supra at 142-144.

10. Fiedler, supra at 17.

11. The original is in the Otto L. Schmidt Collection of the Chicago Historical Society, translated and reprinted in Theodore Calvin Pease and Raymond C. Werner, eds., *The French Foundations, 1680-1693. Collections of the Illinois State Historical Library,* Vol. XXIII, *French Series,* Vol. I (Springfield: Trustees of the Illinois State Historical Library, 1934) at 19-27 [hereinafter *The French Foundations*]. Among other volumes in the collections, this has been digitized by the Library of Congress and is available at <http://hdl.loc.gov/loc.gdc/gcfr.0006>.

12. *The French Foundations,* supra at 22; Fiedler, supra at 9.

13. See *The French Foundations,* supra at 19; Fiedler, supra at 9.

14. First published in Paris in 1512, Balesi, supra at 231.

15. Alvord, supra at 203; Fiedler, supra at 16.

16. Crossley, supra at 22; Zacharias, supra at 387, n7.

17. Ekberg, supra, discusses the shifting boundaries in depth at 32-33. By the end of French rule, Illinois usually referred to the area settled along both sides of the Mississippi from St. Louis down to Kaskaskia.

18. Belting, supra at 16; Balesi, supra at 145. The original is in the Archives Nationale, Coloniales, Paris, France, at B39:457 [hereinafter ANC].

19. Belting, supra at 16; original in ANC, supra at B:43:28.

20. Belting, supra at 16-17; original in ANC, supra at B42bis:230-232.

21. Belting, supra at 17; original in ANC, supra at B43:103.

22. Crossley, supra at 21; Alvord, supra at 154-155; Belting, supra at 16-17; Giraud, supra at 440; Ekberg, supra at 34. The records of this council are in ANC.

23. Crossley, supra at 21.

24. Giraud, supra at 463-464.

25. See ibid. at 24.

26. Henry Putney Beers, *French and Spanish Records of Louisiana: A Bibliographic Guide to Archive and Manuscript Sources* (Baton Rouge: Louisiana State University Press, 1989); Henry Putney Beers, *The French & British in the Old Northwest: A Bibliographical Guide to Archive and Manuscript Sources* (Detroit: Wayne State University Press, 1964); Henry Putney Beers, *The French in North America: A Bibliographical Guide to the French Archives, Reproductions, and Research Missions* (Baton Rouge: Louisiana State University Press, 1957).

27. *The French in North America,* supra.

28. The entertaining story of Alvord's efforts to collect historical documents and to edit all of and write parts of the *Centennial History* can be found in Robert M. Sutton's new introduction to the 1987 edition of Illinois Country.

29. Margaret Kimball Brown, "The Kaskaskia Manuscripts," *Ill. Libraries* 62 (1980): 312-324.

30. *The French Foundations,* supra; Theodore Calvin Pease and Raymond C. Werner, eds., *Anglo-French Boundary Disputes in the West 1749-1763, Collections of the Illinois State Historical Library,* Vol. XXVII, *French Series,* Vol. II (Springfield: Trustees of the Illinois State Historical Library, 1936) available at <http://hdl. loc.gov/loc.gdc/gcfr.0007>; Theodore Calvin Pease and Ernestine Jenison, eds., *Illinois on the Eve of the Seven Years War, Collections of the Illinois State Historical Library,* Vol. XXIX, *French Series,* Vol. III (Springfield: Trustees of the Illinois State Historical Library, 1940) available at <http://hdl.loc.gov/loc.gdc/gcfr.0008>.

31. Fiedler, supra at 1-34.

32. Margaret Kimball Brown and Lawrie Cena Dean, eds., *The Village of Chartres in Colonial Illinois, 1720-1765* (New Orleans: Polyanthos, 1977).

33. 42 Consol. T.S. 279-345, available at <http://www.yale.edu/lawweb/avalon/ paris763.htm>.

34. Reprinted in Clarence Walworth Alvord and Clarence Edwin Carter, eds., *The Critical Period 1763-1765, Collections of the Illinois State Historical Library,* Vol. X, *British Series,* Vol. 1. at 39-45 (Springfield: Trustees of the Illinois State Historical Library, 1915) available at <http://hdl.loc.gov/loc.gdc/gcfr.0004> [hereinafter *The Critical Period*], reprinted in Fiedler supra at 28-29.

35. The French original was lost, but a translation is reprinted in *American State Papers; Public Lands,* 2:209; reprinted in *The Critical Period,* supra at 395-396; reprinted in Fiedler, supra at 29-30; available at <http://memory.loc.gov/cgi-bin/ ampage?collId=llsp&fileName=029.db&recNum=4> (select Image 180).

36. 26 *Statutes at Large* 305; reprinted in *The Critical Period,* supra at 484 et seq.; reprinted in Fiedler, supra at 31.

37. Fiedler, supra at 32.

38. *The Critical Period,* supra at 221, note.

39. See ibid. at 209 et seq.

40. Fiedler, supra at 36.

41. Clarence Walworth Alvord and Clarence Edwin Carter, eds., *The New Regime 1765-1767, Collections of the Illinois State Historical Library,* Vol. XXI, *British Series,* Vol. II at 433-437 (Springfield: Trustees of the Illinois State Historical Library, 1916) available at <http://hdl.loc.gov/loc.gdc/gcfr.005> [hereinafter *The New Regime*]. Fiedler, supra at 38.

42. Alvord, supra at 267.

43. 14 George III, c. 83.

44. Fiedler, supra at 44.

45. See ibid. at 45.

46. Beers, *The French & British in the Old Northwest,* supra.

47. *The Critical Period,* supra; *The New Regime,* supra; Clarence Walworth Alvord and Clarence Edwin Carter, eds., *Trade and Politics 1767-1769, Collections of the Illinois State Historical Library,* Vol. XVI, *British Series,* Vol. III (Springfield: Trustees of the Illinois State Historical Library, 1929).

48. Fiedler, supra at 35-74.

49. See ibid. at 49.

50. Reprinted in Clarence Walworth Alvord, ed., *Cahokia Records 1778-1790, Collections of the Illinois State Historical Library,* Vol. II, *Virginia Series,* Vol. I (Springfield: Trustees of the Illinois State Historical Library, 1907) at 2-3 [hereinafter *Cahokia Records*]. Originals are at the Chicago Historical Society.

51. Act for Establishing the County of Illinois (9 Hening [Va.] 552 [Oct. 1778]), reprinted in Fiedler, supra at 59.

52. 11 Hening, [Va.] 326 (1782-1784).

53. See ibid. at 571; IV Journal of Congress 379-380, reprinted in Fiedler, supra at 86-89.

54. See generally *Cahokia Records* and Clarence Walworth Alvord, ed., *Kaskaskia Records 1778-1790, Collections of the Illinois State Historical Library,* Vol. V, *Virginia Series,* Vol. II (Springfield: Trustees of the Illinois State Historical Library, 1909) [hereinafter *Kaskaskia Records*]. Cahokia kept a majority of its French population and was more stable during this period.

55. *Kaskaskia Records,* supra at 227, reprinted in Fiedler, supra at 93.

56. *Cahokia Records,* supra; *Kaskaskia Records,* supra.

57. James Alton James, ed., *George Rogers Clark Papers 1781-1784, Collections of the Illinois State Historical Library,* Vols. VIII and XIX, *Virginia Series,* Vols. III and IV (Springfield: Trustees of the Illinois State Historical Library, 1912 and 1926); Kathrine Wagner Seineke, *The George Rogers Clark Adventure in the Illinois: And Selected Documents of the American Revolution at the Frontier Posts* (New Orleans: Polyanthos, 1981).

58. Fiedler, supra at 51-96.

59. *U.S. Rev. Stat.* 2d ed. 1878, 13-16; reprinted in *Documents Illustrative of the Formation of the Union of the American States,* House Doc. 398 (Washington, DC: GPO, 1927); available at <http://www.yale.edu/lawweb/avalon/nworder.htm>.

60. *U.S. Rev. Stat.* 2d ed. 1878, 13.

61. Reprinted in Theodore Calvin Pease, ed., *The Laws of the Northwest Territory 1788-1800, Collections of the Illinois State Historical Library,* Volume XVII, *Law Series,* Vol. I (Springfield: Trustees of the Illinois State Historical Library, 1925) [hereinafter *Laws of the Northwest Territory*].

62. Fiedler, supra at 111-114, in a reprinted letter from St. Clair to the President dated May 1, 1790.

63. Fiedler, supra at 124. Photo available at <http://www.state.il.us/HPA/hs/Courthouse.htm>.

64. *Laws of the Northwest Territory,* supra.

65. Fiedler, supra at 97-130.

66. Francis S. Philbrick, ed., *The Laws of Illinois Territory, Collections of the Illinois State Historical Library,* Vol. XXV, *Law Series,* Vol. V (Springfield: Trustees of the Illinois State Historical Library, 1950) [hereinafter *Laws of Illinois Territory*].

67. Clarence Edwin Carter, ed., *The Territory Northwest of the River Ohio, 1787-1803, The Territorial Papers of the United States,* Vol. II (Washington, DC: U.S. Government Printing Office, 1934).

68. Act of May 7, 1800, 2 *Stat.* 58, reprinted in Fiedler, supra at 132-133.

69. Francis S. Philbrick, ed., *The Laws of Indiana Territory, Collections of the Illinois State Library,* Vol. XXI, *Law Series,* Vol. II, at 8-15 (Springfield: Trustees of

the Illinois State Historical Library, 1930) [hereinafter *Laws of Indiana Territory*]; reprinted in Fiedler, supra at 137-138.

70. *Laws of Indiana Territory,* supra at XXVI.

71. See ibid. at 108-112; reprinted in Fiedler, supra at 143.

72. *Laws of Indiana Territory,* supra at 323; reprinted in Fiedler, supra at 145.

73. *Laws of Indiana Territory,* supra.

74. Fiedler, supra at 131-152.

75. Gayle Thornbrough and Dorothy Riker, eds., *Journals of the General Assembly of Indiana Territory, Indiana Historical Collections,* Vol. 32 (Indianapolis: Indiana Historical Bureau, 1950).

76. Clarence Edwin Carter, ed., *The Territory of Indiana, 1800-1810, The Territorial Papers of the United States,* Vol. VII (Washington, DC: U.S. Government Printing Office, 1939).

77. An Act for Dividing the Indiana Territory into Two Separate Governments, 2 *Stat.* 514 (1809); reprinted in Fiedler, supra at 153-155.

78. *Laws of Illinois Territory,* supra at 5; reprinted in Fiedler, supra at 158.

79. *Laws of Illinois Territory,* supra at 8-10; reprinted in Fiedler, supra at 161-162.

80. *Laws of Illinois Territory,* supra at 136-141; reprinted in Fiedler, supra at 169-172.

81. An Act to Enable the People of the Illinois Territory to Form a Constitution and State Government and for the Admission of Such State into the Union on an Equal Footing, 3 *Stat.* 428 (1818); reprinted in Fiedler, supra at 182-185.

82. Fiedler, supra at 187.

83. Resolution Declaring the Admission of the State of Illinois into the Union, 3 *Stat.* 536 (1818); reprinted in Fiedler, supra at 188.

84. *Laws of Illinois Territory,* supra.

85. *Laws and Joint Resolutions Passed by the Legislative Council and House of Representatives of Illinois Territory at Their Third Session Held at Kaskaskia in 1814; First Complete Printing from the Original Records* (Boston: The Chipman Publishing Company, 1921) at 86, 99.

86. Francis S. Philbrick, ed., *Pope's Digest 1815, Collections of the Illinois State Historical Society,* Vols. XXVII and XXX, *Law Series,* Vols. III and IV (Springfield: Trustees of the Illinois State Historical Library, 1938, 1940).

87. Clarence Edwin Carter, ed., *The Territory of Illinois, 1809-1814, The Territorial Papers of the United States,* Vol. XVI (Washington, DC: U.S. Government Printing Office, 1948); Clarence Edwin Carter, ed., *The Territory of Illinois, 1814-1818, The Territorial Papers of the United States,* Vol. XVII (Washington, DC: U.S. Government Printing Office, 1950).

88. Fiedler, supra at 175.

Chapter 15

Indiana Prestatehood Legal Materials

Mary G. Persyn

A SHORT LEGAL HISTORY OF INDIANA BEFORE STATEHOOD

In the years before statehood, the land that is now Indiana fell under the control of several different countries. Besides the Native Americans who had lived in the area for thousands of years, Indiana was claimed by the French, who called the area the Illinois country; Great Britain, who called it the Ohio country; the Confederation, who referred to it as the area northwest of the Ohio River or the Northwest Territory; and the United States, which created the Indiana Territory. Each group had laws that governed the operation of the area, although it was not until the Northwest Ordinance in 1787 that a government applied a structured plan of law to the area. Prior to that time, the population was so small that a well-developed set of laws was unnecessary.

Following is a short legal history of the land that became Indiana, and a bibliography of sources to use to research law in the time before Indiana statehood in 1816.

Early History and Jurisdiction

Native Americans

The earliest residents of the land that became Indiana were the Native American tribes and their predecessors, such as the Mississippian culture. Different parts of the state were controlled by the Miami and two closely related groups, the Wea and Piankashaw, as well as the Potowatomi, Delaware, and several other eastern tribes whose land spread across what became the Northwest Territory. Some of the land was held in common.[1] Their titles to the lands were extinguished by a series of treaties starting in 1784.[2]

French

The first white men known to have set foot in Indiana were Robert Cavelier de La Salle and his group of explorers, who entered Indiana in 1679.[3] The French inhabited this land, which they called the Illinois country, during the 1700s.[4] They had a continuing presence in the land around Fort Wayne (Fort Miami, founded in 1715), Lafayette (Fort Ouiatenon, 1720), and Vincennes (Fort Vincennes, 1732 or 1733).[5] They established these forts as trading posts for the Indian trade and as a means of combating the aggression of the Iroquois and English, who were trying to exert control in the area, but they did not turn the trading posts into large settlements.[6]

During this period, the territory that was to include Indiana was controlled by military law.[7] The commandants exercised a combination of legislative, administrative, and judicial powers.[8] Vincennes was under the control of the Louisiana colony by the Charter of 1718,[9] but Ouiatenon was under the control of Quebec.[10] However, in the Treaty of Paris of 1763, which followed the French and Indian War, France gave the territory, which included Indiana, to the English.[11]

English Control, 1763-1779

Even prior to the Treaty of Paris, the English had an influence in the Indiana Territory. As early as 1607, portions of the Ohio country, which included Indiana, came under the charter and laws of the Virginia colony.[12] In fact, several of the British colonies[13] held conflicting charter claims to the same land. However, the British made little attempt to actually enforce their laws in the area north of the Ohio, even after the land officially came into their hands.

After the Treaty of Paris in 1763, the British possessed the land northwest of the Ohio River. By instructions to the governors of the royal colonies in 1761,[14] and by the Proclamation of 1763,[15] Great Britain established the principle that any purchases from the Indians or settlements beyond the mountains had to take place under the auspices of the British colonial government, and not under the individual colonies. In fact, the British expected the French settlers to abandon the territory.[16] After a decade of trying to decide how to deal with the land northwest of the Ohio, Britain finally attached it to Canada by the Quebec Act of 1774,[17] which added this territory to the province of Quebec and also provided for the French inhabitants of the area the free exercise of the Roman Catholic religion and a government based on French civil law.[18]

American Revolution and Territory of Virginia, 1779-1787

By the eve of the American Revolution, settlers from Virginia had moved over the mountains and into the Kentucky region, which included the land northwest of the Ohio River. By virtue of these actions of its citizens, Virginia had the most conspicuous claim to the land in what became the Northwest Territory.[19] Protecting this area from the British and Indians led to George Rogers Clark's raid into British territory, which, in turn, gave control of the territory northwest of the Ohio to the fledging nation.

George Rogers Clark, a Virginian with land interests in Kentucky, was chosen in 1776 to represent Kentucky in the Virginia House of Burgesses. He presented a plan to organize county government in Kentucky and to protect the people from Indian attacks. Clark received a commission as a major of the militia and developed a plan to attack the old French villages, now held by the British, on the Mississippi and Wabash Rivers. The villages of Kaskaskia and Cahokia on the Mississippi surrendered to Clark's army in June 1778. Clark then sent a group of Frenchmen to Vincennes, to ask the inhabitants to take an oath of allegiance to Virginia, which they did.[20] The British, under Lieutenant Governor Henry Hamilton, recaptured Vincennes for the British in December 1778.[21] George Rogers Clark then marched from Kaskaskia and recaptured Vincennes for Virginia on February 25, 1779.[22] For all intents and purposes, what the Virginians referred to as the Illinois Territory remained under the control of Virginia from that point on.

The state of Virginia established the county of Illinois on December 9, 1778.[23] This county included all the land north and west of the Ohio River.[24] Under the Treaty of Paris of 1783, which ended the American Revolution, the British ceded this territory to the United States, and it remained under the control of Virginia until Virginia ceded its control to the Continental Congress in 1784.[25] Virginia established courts at Vincennes and Kaskaskia, but conditions were in so much tumult that Virginia cannot be said to have extended actual control over the territory.[26] The other colonies who claimed the land northwest of the Ohio under their royal charters executed deeds of cession to the land—New York in 1780, Virginia in 1784, Massachusetts in 1785, and Connecticut in 1786.[27]

Northwest Territory

The governance of the territory northwest of the Ohio was unclear until the adoption of the Northwest Ordinance of 1787. Congress adopted an ordinance in 1784[28] for the governing of all its territories, but it was never put

into effect.[29] The ordinance of 1785[30] provided for the surveying of all territorial lands, provided that the lands were to be divided into townships and
sections, and this was done. However, it was not until 1787 that governance
of the area was determined.[31]

The Northwest Territory, which was created by congressional ordinance
in 1787,[32] provided for three stages of government. The first stage provided
for a governor and three judges, all appointed by Congress, who determined
what would be the controlling laws of the territory.[33] The first court session
was held in Marietta on September 2, 1788.[34] At this session, the governor
and judges set up county governments, organized the court system, and established a militia.[35] The second stage of governance provided for the election of a legislature as soon as there were "five thousand free male inhabitants of full age." The ordinance provided that the Northwest Territory was
to be divided into no less than three and nor more than five states from the
territory and outlined their boundaries. When the population of any of these
states reached 60,000 "free inhabitants," "such State shall be admitted, by
its delegates, into the Congress of the United States, on an equal footing
with the original States."[36] Session laws for the area that became Indiana
exist in an uninterrupted line starting with the government of the Northwest
Territory in 1788.[37]

Further organizational changes were made in 1790.[38] The governor and
judges organized a court of common pleas, which heard civil cases; a court
of quarter sessions, which tried petty crimes and set up requirements for justices of the peace; and probate judges.[39] The laws and organizational system set up for the Northwest Territory were also operative in the Indiana
Territory.[40] Finally, in 1795, English common law was adopted for the territory.[41] The first territorial legislature met at Cincinnati in 1799.[42]

Indiana Territory, 1800-1816

On March 20, 1800, the Indiana Territory was created from part of the
Northwest Territory, with Vincennes as its capital and William Henry Harrison as its governor.[43] Harrison had previously been secretary of the Northwest Territory under Governor Arthur St. Clair. The territory included what
are now the states of Indiana, Illinois, Michigan, Wisconsin, and a portion
of Minnesota.[44] During his term as governor, Harrison negotiated many
treaties with the Indians that led to the Indians ceding their lands to the
Americans.[45]

The Indiana Territory was further divided in 1805 when the Michigan
Territory was created[46] and in 1809 when the Illinois Territory was established.[47] After the Illinois country was split off from Indiana, the land basi-

cally had the boundaries that the state has today.[48] In 1813, the capital was moved from Vincennes to Corydon, which was more centrally located in the populated area of the territory.[49]

The laws governing the Indiana Territory included those laws that were in effect in 1800 when Indiana was separated from the Northwest Territory.[50] Two particular difficulties that affected all governments of the Northwest Territory were the requirement passed by the U.S. Congress that all laws in the territories were to be adopted from the laws of the existing states, and the lack of printed versions of the laws that were adopted. First, the existing states did not necessarily have laws that could be applied in frontier areas. The territories adopted the laws they needed and wrote their own if an existing law could not be found.[51] Second was the problem that Philbrick refers to as an "embarrassment in the administration of justice"— the lack of copies of the laws passed by the legislature. Neither the judges nor the people had access to copies of the laws except at "readings" in the courts, which few attended. The opening of a printing company in Vincennes in 1804 helped alleviate the problem somewhat in the Indiana Territory.[52]

The Indiana court system consisted of a general court, which met twice yearly, and circuit courts, which met once a year in each county with a judge of the general court presiding. If a prisoner was being held on a capital crime, the governor could appoint one or more judges to a special court of oyer and terminer. Below these courts were the justices of the peace. Judges were appointed by the governor and served "on good behavior."[53] In 1805, appeals from the territorial courts to the Supreme Court of the United States were granted in cases involving federal questions.[54]

In 1814, Congress empowered the House of Representatives of the Indiana Territory to divide the territory into legislative districts.[55] The Indiana Territory established its own circuit court system on August 20, 1814.[56] The territory was divided into three circuits, each presided over by a chief judge and two associate judges.[57] Each judge received a salary of $700 per year.[58] On February 24, 1815, Congress set the locations and dates where the courts should meet.[59]

Statehood, 1816

The Constitutional Convention of 1816 met at Corydon from June 10 to June 29, 1816, on which day the constitution was adopted. Except for the provision relative to amendments, the constitution was taken in its entirety from the Ohio Constitution of 1802 and the Kentucky Constitution of 1799.[60] The enabling legislation for Indiana statehood was signed by President James Madison on April 19, 1816;[61] the Ordinance of Acceptance was agreed to on June 10, 1816;[62] and Indiana entered the Union on December 11, 1816.[63]

SOURCES TO RESEARCH INDIANA PRESTATEHOOD LEGAL HISTORY

Many sources of American colonial, revolutionary, and early national history also contain some legal materials. Although many of these sources are mentioned in this chapter, the author chose to concentrate, when available, on those items that contain a significant amount of legal material.

General Secondary Sources

John D. Barnhart and Dorothy L. Riker. *Indiana to 1816: The Colonial Period.* Indianapolis: Indiana Historical Bureau, 1971.

This work, which gives a general history of the Northwest Territory and the Indiana Territory prior to the Indiana Constitution in 1816, is part of a three-volume set on the history of Indiana through 1960. This volume traces the French, Indian, and English inhabitation of the area as well as the effects of the American Revolution.

Leigh Darbee. *A Guide to Early Imprints at the Indiana Historical Society, 1619-1840.* Indianapolis: Indiana Historical Society, 2001.

Many legal publications are listed in this 944-page directory of early imprints.

Many of the documents of the U.S. government for the time period 1774-1816 can be found on the Library of Congress's Web site: "A Century of Lawmaking for a New Nation 1774-1873" at <http://memory.loc.gov/ammem/amlaw/lawhome.html>.

Other primary materials for this time period can be found at the Avalon Project of Yale Law School at <http://www.yale.edu/lawweb/avalon/avalon.htm>.

The Indiana State Archives (for official records), the Indiana Historical Society, and, to some extent, the Indiana State Library contain the major collections of unpublished materials on this period of Indiana history.

Native American

Secondary Sources

Helen Hornbeck Tanner and Erminie Wheeler Voegelin. *The Indians of Ohio and Indiana Prior to 1795*. 2 vols. New York: Garland, 1974.

Emma Helen Blair. *The Indian Tribes of the Upper Mississippi Valley and Region of the Great Lakes*. 2 vols. Cleveland: Arthur H. Clark Co., 1911.

French

Secondary Sources

Laurin A. Wollan Jr. "Law in Illinois Under France." *Ill. B. J.* 56(1968): 384.

According to Wollan, there are no comprehensive written records of the French administration of justice in the Illinois country, although there is evidence that there was systematic administration of law by the 1720s.[64]

Clarence W. Alvord. *The Illinois Country, 1673-1818*. Urbana: University of Illinois Press, 1920.

Alvord's work in this title and his compilations of historical documents of the Illinois country are classics.

Henry Putney Beers. *The French & British in the Old Northwest: A Bibliographic Guide to Archive and Records Sources*. Detroit: Wayne State University Press, 1964.

In addition to identifying the sources of both published and unpublished documents concerning the old northwest, Beers provides an excellent summary of the governance of the area. He describes the types of government that existed at various times in the Illinois country's history, and how that government was exercised.

Henry Putney Beers. *The French in North America; A Bibliographical Guide to French Archives, Reproductions, and Research Missions*. Baton Rouge: Louisiana State University Press, 1957.

This volume lists collections compiled by various U.S. institutions of materials on the French in North America. The listing for Indiana is quite short, but the listing for Illinois is quite detailed, and much of the material compiled for the Illinois country includes Indiana sites under French control.

Carl J. Ekberg. *French Roots in the Illinois Country: The Mississippi Frontier in Colonial Times.* Urbana: University of Illinois Press, 1998.

Pages 82-88, in particular, discuss Fort Vincennes, also called Port Vincennes and Port Vincent.

John Francis McDermott. "French Settlements in the Illinois Country in the Eighteenth Century." In *The French, The Indians & George Rogers Clark in the Illinois Country* 3-33. Indianapolis: Indiana Historical Society, 1977.

Primary Sources

Most of the unpublished primary sources on the French period in Indiana can be found in the French Archives in Paris, in the Public Archives of Canada, and at the Library of Congress. French Records left at Kaskaskia when the British took over can be found in either the Chicago Historical Society or the Illinois Historical Society. For further information, see the bibliography in Alvord's *The Illinois Country, 1673-1818,* and Beers's *The French & British in the Old Northwest: A Bibliographic Guide to Archive and Records Sources.*

Published primary sources about the French period in Indiana include the following titles.

Jacob P. Dunn. "Documents Relating to the French Settlement on the Wabash." In *Indiana Historical Society Publications* (Vol. 2, p. 410). Indianapolis: Indiana Historical Society, 1895.

Jacob P. Dunn. "The Mission to the Ouabache." In *Indiana Historical Society Publications* (Vol. 3, p. 253). Indianapolis: Indiana Historical Society, 1902.

Documentary material concerning Post Vincennes and its founder.

B.F. French. *Historical Collections of Louisiana.* New York: Wiley and Putnam, 1846-1853.

Frances Krauskopf, ed. "Ouiatanon Documents." In *Indiana Historical Society Publications* (Vol. 28, p. 139). Indianapolis: Indiana Historical Society, 1955.

English Control, 1763-1779

Secondary Sources

Henry P. Beers. *The French & British in the Old Northwest: A Bibliographical Guide to Archive and Manuscript Sources.* Detroit: Wayne State University Press, 1964.

Includes information about available sources of British manuscripts.

John G. Rauch and Nellie C. Armstrong. *A Bibliography of the Laws of Indiana 1788-1927 Beginning with the Northwest Territory.* Indianapolis: Indiana Historical Bureau, 1928.

In addition to listing all the various versions of the laws of Indiana, starting with the laws of the Northwest Territory, Rauch and Armstrong include an essay discussing the various entities that held control over Indiana, beginning with the Treaty of Paris in 1763.

Primary Sources

The largest collection of original sources and manuscripts for the British period in Indiana is in the Public Archives of Canada. Except for a brief period of occupation of some of the French forts, there were no resident British officials in Indiana during the British period. Jurisdiction came from the forts at Fort de Chartres, Detroit, and Fort Pitt.[65]

All of the following works by Clarence Alvord and his co-editors contain original documents concerning lawsuits, courts, and the government of the Illinois country under the French, British, and the colony of Virginia.

Clarence W. Alvord and Clarence E. Carter, eds. *The Critical Period, 1763-1765.* Illinois Historical Collections, Vol. 10. Springfield: Illinois State Historical Library, 1915.

Clarence W. Alvord and Clarence E. Carter, eds. *The New Régime, 1765-1767.* Illinois Historical Collections, Vol. 11. Springfield: Illinois State Historical Library, 1915.

Clarence W. Alvord and Clarence E. Carter, eds. *Trade and Politics, 1767-1769.* Illinois Historical Collections, Vol. 16. Springfield: Illinois State Historical Library, 1921.

Clarence W. Alvord. *Cahokia Records, 1778-1790.* Illinois Historical Collections, Vol. 2. Springfield: Illinois State Historical Library, 1907.

Clarence W. Alvord. *Kaskaskia Records, 1778-1790.* Illinois Historical Collections, Vol. 5. Springfield: Illinois State Historical Library, 1909.

Clarence E. Carter, ed. "Documents Relating to the Occupation of the Illinois Country by the British." In *Illinois State Historical Society Transactions* (pp. 202-221). Springfield: Illinois State Historical Society, 1907.

Florence G. Watts, ed. "Some Vincennes Documents of 1772." *Ind. Mag. Hist.* 34(1938): 199.

American Revolution and Territory of Virginia, 1779-1787

Secondary Sources

John D. Barnhart and Dorothy L. Riker. *Indiana to 1816: The Colonial Period,* infra note 1.

The French, the Indians, and George Rogers Clark in the Illinois Country. Indianapolis: Indiana Historical Society, 1977.

Lowell Hayes Harrison. *George Rogers Clark and the War in the West.* Lexington: University Press of Kentucky, 1976.

George M. Waller. *The American Revolution in the West.* Chicago: Nelson-Hall, 1976.

Primary Sources

Act for Establishing the County of Illinois (9 Hening [Va.] 552) (Oct. 1778).[66]

James Alton James. *George Rogers Clark Papers 1771-1784.* Collections of the Illinois State Historical Library, Vol. 8 and 19. Springfield: Trustees of the Illinois State Historical Library, 1912, 1924.

Included in Clark's papers are a few documents concerning the establishment of courts in Kaskaskia and Cahokia and of the government for Vincennes.

William R. Manning, ed. *Diplomatic Correspondence of the United States: Canadian Relations, 1784-1860,* Vol. 1. Washington, DC: Carnegie Endowment for International Peace, 1940.

Papers include U.S. correspondence with Great Britain concerning the frontier posts in the Northwest Territory.

For a discussion of the available records for the British regime in the Illinois Country, see Beers, *The French & British in the Old Northwest,* chapters 3 and 4.

The Alvord titles *Cahokia Records* and *Kaskaskia Records,* listed under the French period, also contain records for the time of the British and Virginia control of Indiana.

Journals of the Continental Congress 1774-1789. Washington, DC: Library of Congress, 1904-1937.

The journals are also available at <http://memory.loc.gov/ammem/amlaw/lwjc.html>.

Northwest Territory

Secondary Sources

Beverley Bond. *The Civilization of the Old Northwest: A Study of Political, Social, and Economic Development, 1788-1812* [particularly 149-183]. Freeport, NY: Books for Libraries Press, 1970.

This work gives a composite picture of the region between the Ohio and Mississippi Rivers and the Great Lakes. The chapter dealing with the Indiana Territory gives the reader a general history of the area from 1787 to 1812.

Merrill Jensen. *The New Nation: a History of the United States During the Confederation, 1781-1789.* New York: Knopf, 1950.

Jensen's is the classic work on the Confederation period of American history.

Peter S. Onuf. *Statehood and Union: A History of the Northwest Ordinance.* Bloomington: Indiana University Press, 1987.

John George Rauch and Nellie C. Armstrong. *Bibliography of the Laws of Indiana, 1788-1927, Beginning with the Northwest Territory.* Indiana

Historical Collections, Vol. 16. Indianapolis: Historical Bureau of the Indiana Library and Historical Department, 1928.

Malcolm J. Rohrbough. *The Trans-Appalachian Frontier: People, Societies & Institutions, 1775-1850.* New York: Oxford University Press, 1978.

Robert M. Taylor, ed. *The Northwest Ordinance, 1787.* Indianapolis: Indiana Historical Society, 1987.

William Wirt Blume. "Civil Procedure on the American Frontier: A Study of a Court of Common Pleas of the Northwest and Indiana Territories (1796-1805)." *Mich. L. Rev.* 56(1957): 161.

William Wirt Blume. "Legislation on the American Frontier: Adoption of Laws by Governor and Judges-Northwest Territory 1788-1798; Indiana Territory 1800-1804; Michigan Territory 1805-1823." *Mich. L. Rev.* 60 (1962): 317.

William Wirt Blume. "Probate and Administration on the American Frontier: A Study of the Probate Records of Wayne County-Northwest Territory 1796-1803; Indiana Territory 1803-1805; Michigan Territory 1805-1816." *Mich. L. Rev.* 58(1959): 209.

Daniel Wait Howe. "The Laws and Courts of the Northwest and Indiana Territories." In *Indiana Historical Society Publications* (Vol. 2, p. 3). Indianapolis: Indiana Historical Society, 1886.

Howe summarizes the laws of the Northwest and Indiana Territories in this article.

Primary Sources

There are no reported decisions of the judges of the Northwest Territory. There is a question whether any of the decisions were ever written out.[67] For a discussion of the organization of the courts of the Northwest Territory, see John G. Baker, "The History of the Indiana Trial Court System and Attempts at Renovation," *Ind. L Rev.* 30(1997): 233, 237-241.

Theodore Calvin Pease, ed. *The Laws of the Northwest Territory 1788-1800.* 27 Collections of the Illinois State Historical Library, Law Series, Vol. 1 (Springfield: Illinois State Historical Library, 1925).

Contains the laws passed by the government of the territory northwest of the Ohio. The "legislature" was composed of a governor and three judges appointed by Congress who were to legislate by adopting and publishing such laws as might be necessary.

The Northwest Ordinance can also be found at <http://mariettaohio.info/history/northwest/index.php>.

Northwest Territory. Journal of the Convention of the Territory of the United States Northwest of the Ohio. Chillicothe, OH: N. Willis, Printer to the Convention, 1802.

The Emerging Nation: A Documentary History of the Foreign Relations of the United States Under the Articles of Confederation, 1780-1789. Mary A. Giunta, J. Dane Hargrove, Norman A. Graebner, Peter P. Hill, Lawrence S. Kaplan, Richard B. Smith, and Mary-Jane M. Dowd, eds. Washington, DC: National Historical Publications and Records Commission, 1996.

Includes documents relating to the Northwest Territory.

Territorial Papers of the United States. Clarence E. Carter, ed. Washington, DC: U.S. Government Printing Office, 1934.

Vols. 2-3 contain 700 papers for the Territory Northwest of the River Ohio, 1787-1803, including administration, information on laws and courts, and letters of judges.

The St. Clair Papers: The Life and Public Services of Arthur St. Clair: Soldier of the Revolutionary War, President of the Continental Congress; and Governor of the North-western Territory: with His Correspondence and Other Papers. William Henry Smith, ed. Cincinnati, OH: R. Clark and Co., 1882.

St. Clair was the governor of the Northwest Territory from 1787-1802.

Indiana Territory

Secondary Sources

John D. Barnhart and Dorothy L. Riker. *Indiana to 1816: The Colonial Period,* infra note 1.

Earl D. Bragdon. The Influence of the Virginia Code on the Development of the Laws of Indiana Territory, 1800-1816. MA Thesis, Indiana University, Bloomington, 1956.

William Wirt Blume and Elizabeth Gaspar Brown. "Territorial Court and Law: Unifying Factors in the Development of American Legal Institutions, Part I: Establishment of a Standardized Judicial System." *Mich. L. Rev.* 61(1962): 39.

William Wirt Blume and Elizabeth Gaspar Brown. "Territorial Court and Law: Unifying Factors in the Development of American Legal Institutions, Part II: Influences Tending to Unify Territorial Law System." *Mich. L. Rev.* 61(1963): 467.

The two articles by Blume and Brown provide an in-depth discussion of territorial law. Much of the discussion concerns the period after 1816, but the authors include discussion of the Northwest Territory and Indiana Territory laws, both as to source of law and as to specific areas of law, such as probate.

Richard A. Brisbin Jr. "Before Bureaucracy: State Courts and the Administration of Public Services in the Northwest, 1787-1830." *Old Northwest* 10(1984): 141.

Pages 160-165 discuss Indiana.

Lee Burns. "The Revision of 1807." *Ind. Mag. Hist.* 22(1926): 10.

Discusses the 1807 major revision of the laws of the Indiana Territory.

Clarence E. Carter. "William Clarke, First Chief Justice of Indiana Territory." *Ind. Mag. Hist.* 34(1938): 1.

Daniel Wait Howe. "The Laws and Courts of the Northwest and Indiana Territories." In *Indiana Historical Society Publications* (Vol. 2, p. 3). Indianapolis: Indiana Historical Society, 1886.

Earl Finbar Murphy. "Laws of Inheritance in Indiana Before 1816." *N.Y. L. Forum* 2(1956): 249.

The article includes sections on the inheritance laws in the French and British periods, and during the Northwest Territory and Indiana Territory periods.

Francis S. Philbrick. "Laws, Courts, and Litigation of Indiana Territory (1800-09)." *Ill. L. Rev.* 24(1929): 1.

Francis S. Philbrick. "Laws, Courts, and Litigation of Indiana Territory (1800-09)." *Ill. L. Rev.* 24(1929): 193.

Philbrick's two articles, particularly pages 15-19 of the first article, and the second article, discuss the courts and litigation of the Indiana Territory.

George W. Purcell. "Collecting Taxes in the Indiana Territory, 1797-1802." *Ind. Mag. Hist.* 40(1944): 353 .

John G. Rauch and Nellie C. Armstrong. *A Bibliography of the Laws of Indiana 1788-1927.* Indianapolis: Indiana Historical Bureau, 1928.

Primary Sources—Legislation

Act of May 7, 1800, 2 *Stat.* 58 (creating the Indiana Territory).

Act to Divide the Indiana Territory into Two Separate Governments, 2 *Stat.* 309 (1805) (separating the Michigan Territory).

An Act for Dividing the Indiana Territory into Two Separate Governments, 2 *Stat.* 514 (1809) (separating the Illinois Territory).

Amended Territorial Act of March 4, 1814, 3 *Stat.* 103 (dividing the territory into legislative districts).

Francis S. Philbrick. *The Laws of Indiana Territory, 1801-1809.* In Theodore Calvin Pease, ed., Collections of the Illinois Historical Library, Vol. 21. Springfield: Illinois State Historical Library, 1931; reprinted by Indianapolis: Historical Bureau of the Indiana Library and Historical Department, 1931.

This work has an introduction that traces some of the history of Indiana prior to its statehood in 1816. The introduction also covers the history of the Indiana Territory and the Northwest Territory and how each relates to the beginnings of law in the state of Indiana. After the introduction, a record of the laws adopted by the governor and judges is given for the years between 1801 and 1809.

Louis B. Ewbank and Dorothy L. Riker, eds. *Laws of the Indiana Territory, 1809-1816.* Indiana Historical Collections, Vol. 20. Indianapolis: Indiana Historical Bureau, 1934.

In addition to the legislation adopted by the general assembly in the years 1809 to 1816, this volume contains a roster of territorial officers, delegates to Congress, circuit judges, members of the general assembly, and county officials. It also contains an essay reviewing the legislation of the period.

Laws of the Indiana Territory. Vincennes, IN: Stout and Smoot, 1807.

The laws of the Indiana Territory current as of the legislative session of 1807.

Session Laws of American States and Territories. Indiana Territory, 1801-1815. [microform] Westport, CT: Redgrave Information Resources Corporation, 198?.

Primary Sources—Journals and Papers

Executive Journal of the Indiana Territory, 1800-1816. William Wesley Woollen, Daniel Wait Howe, and Jacob Piatt Dunn, eds. Indiana Historical Society Publications, Vol. 3. Indianapolis: Indiana Historical Society, 1900; reprinted by the Family History Section of the Indiana Historical Society, 1985.

This record of the day-to-day appointments and proclamations of the territorial governor (William Henry Harrison, 1800-1813; Thomas Posey, 1813-1816) was kept by the territorial secretary, John Gibson. It covers such items as the appointments of judges, clerks, surveyors, and military officers, and proclamations dealing with county boundaries, Indian traders, and the like.

Journals of the General Assembly of the Indiana Territory, 1805-1815. Gayle Thornbrough and Dorothy Riker, eds. Indiana Historical Collections, Vol. 32. Indianapolis: Indiana Historical Bureau, 1950.

This reprint of the manuscript ten bound folio volumes of the territorial sessions of the house of representatives and the legislative council is incomplete. There are no journals for the sessions of the general assembly in 1806, 1807, and 1810. The only session of the legislative council for which the manuscript journals can be found is 1813-1814. The editors compiled any available documents that they could locate to cover principal transactions of the missing years. The volume also includes the Treasurer's Account Book for 1805-13, and a Roster and Sketches of Members of the Territorial General Assembly.

Territorial Papers of the United States. Washington, DC: U.S. Government Printing Office, 1934.

Vols. 7-8 contain the papers of the territory of Indiana, 1800-1816, collected from the Departments of State, Treasury, War, Interior, Archives, and the Post Office, and the manuscript division of the Library of Congress.

Primary Sources—Court Decisions

There are no printed sources of court decisions from the Indiana Territory. For a list of the locations when manuscript copies of Indiana territorial court decisions can be found, see the bibliographic essay in Barnhart and Riker, *Indiana to 1816,* particularly pages 483 to 487. A discussion of the organization of the Indiana territorial courts can be found in John G. Baker, "The History of the Indiana Trial Court System and Attempts at Renovation," *Ind. L. Rev.* 30(1997): 233, 241-242, and in Francis Philbrick, supra p. 22.

Indiana Territorial Order Book of the General Court, 1801-1810. Manuscript, Indiana State Library.

Primary Sources—Governors' Papers

Douglas E. Clanin and Ruth Dorrel, eds. *The Papers of William Henry Harrison, 1800-1815.* 10 microfilm reels. Indianapolis: Indiana Historical Society, 1993-1999.[68]

Harrison was the governor of the Indiana Territory from its inception in 1800 until 1812, when he became a general in the American forces during the War of 1812.

Messages and Papers of William Henry Harrison. Logan Esarey, ed. Indiana Historical Society Collections, Vol. 7 and 9. Indianapolis: Indiana Historical Society, 1922.

This earlier and less complete edition of Harrison's papers is the only one available in print. Thomas Posey was governor of the Indiana Territory from March 3, 1813, until statehood. His papers can be found in Esarey's *Messages and Papers of William Henry Harrison,* as well as in the *Territorial Papers of the United States,* Vols. 7 and 8.

Statehood

Indiana has had two constitutions. The first constitution was adopted June 29, 1816. The current constitution was adopted August 4, 1851, and became effective November 5, 1851.

Secondary Sources

Charles Kettleborough. *Constitution Making in Indiana 1780-1851*. Indianapolis: Indiana Historical Commission, 1916.

Kettleborough's work contains a discussion of the constitutional convention and the problems with the first Indiana constitution, which led to the adoption of a second constitution in 1851.

Charles Kettleborough. *Constitutional Making in Indiana—A Source Book of Constitutional Documents with Historical Introduction and Critical Notes*. 2 vols. Indianapolis: Indiana Historical Commission, 1916.

Hubert H. Hawkins. *Indiana's Road to Statehood: A Documentary Record*. Indianapolis: Indiana Sesquicentennial Commission, 1964.

William P. McLauchan. *The Indiana State Constitution: A Reference Guide*. Westport, CT: Greenwood Press, 1996.

Pages 1 to 9, in particular, discuss the Constitution of 1816 and some of the problems that led to a new constitution in 1851.

Primary Sources

Journal of the Convention of the Indiana Territory. Louisville: Butler & Wood, 1816; reprinted in *Ind. Mag. Hist.* 61(1965): 87.

Enabling Act of April 19, 1816, 3 *Stat.* 289 (enabling the people of the Indiana Territory to form a constitution and state government).

Ordinance of Acceptance, 1816. *Benjamin P. Poore, Charters and Constitutions* (Vol. 1, p. 499). Washington, DC: Government Printing Office, 1877. (In which the people of the Indiana Territory accepted the Enabling Act of April 19.)

Resolution for Admitting the State of Indiana into the Union, 1816, 3 *Stat.* 399 (which admitted Indiana to the Union on the same footing as the previous eighteen states).

Constitution of the State of Indiana: Adopted in Convention at Corydon on the 29th of June A.D. 1816 . . . Printed by Order of the House of Representatives. Washington, DC: Printed by William A. Davis, 1816.

Copies of the Indiana Constitution of 1816 can be found online at the Indiana Public Records Commission Web site at <http://www.in.gov/icpr/archives/constitution/index.html>.

Constitution of 1816. Benjamin P. Poore, *Charters and Constitutions* (Vol. 1, pp. 499-512). Washington, DC: Government Printing Office, 1877.

NOTES

1. John D. Barnhart and Dorothy L. Riker, *Indiana to 1816: The Colonial Period* 65-66 (Indianapolis: Indiana Historical Bureau and Indiana Historical Society, 1971). This book is the first of a three-volume set of books tracing most of the history of the state of Indiana. The volumes are an excellent source of general information on the history of Indiana.

2. Thomas R. Swisher, *Ohio Constitution Handbook* ix (Cleveland: Banks-Baldwin, 1990). Major treaties include the Treaty of Greenville 1795, Treaties of Fort Wayne 1803 and 1809, treaties at Vincennes in 1803, 1805, and 1809, and a treaty at Grouseland in 1809. Copies of the treaties can be found in *American State Papers, Indian Affairs,* Vol. 2 (Washington, DC: Gales and Seaton, 1832). A list of the treaties negotiated by William Henry Harrison during his time as governor of the Indiana Territory can be found at Barnhart and Riker, supra note 1, at 377. Copies of many of the treaties can be also found at <http://digital.library.okstate.edu/kappler/index.htm>.

3. James H. Madison, *The Indiana Way: A State History* (Bloomington: Indiana University Press, 1986).

4. Jacob P. Dunn, *Documents Relating to the French Settlement on the Wabash,* in *Indiana Historical Society Publications,* Vol. 2, 410 (Indianapolis: Indiana Historical Society, 1895).

5. Henry Putney Beers, *The French and British in the Old Northwest* 7 (Detroit, MI: Wayne State University Press, 1964).

6. Hubert H. Hawkins, *Indiana's Road to Statehood* 2 (Indianapolis: Indiana Sesquicentennial Commission, 1964).

7. Barnhart and Riker, supra note 1, at 71.

8. Beers, supra note 5, at 10.

9. Barnhart and Riker, supra note 1, at 75.

10. Beers, supra note 5, at 12.

11. Barnhart and Riker, supra note 1, at 127.

12. Daniel Wait Howe, *The Laws and Courts of Northwest and Indiana Territories,* in *Indiana Historical Society Publications,* Vol. 2, 3 (Indianapolis: Indiana Historical Society, 1886).

13. Connecticut, Massachusetts, New York, and Virginia all claimed an interest in the territory based on their colonial charters. Swisher, supra note 2, at ix.

14. Theodore Calvin Pease, ed., *The Laws of the Northwest Territory 1788-1800* xi, Collections of the Illinois State Historical Library, Vol. 17 (Springfield: Illinois State Historical Library, 1925).

15. Barnhart and Riker, supra note 2, at 132, 148-149.

16. Pease, supra note 14, at xi.

17. Ibid. at xii.

18. Barnhart and Riker, supra note 1, at 180.

19. Ibid.

20. Ibid. at 193-195.

21. Ibid. at 201-202.

22. Ibid. at 208.

23. Barnhart and Riker, supra note 1, at 213 citing William Waller Hening, ed., *The Statutes of Virginia,* Vol. 9, 552-555 (Richmond: Printed by and for Samuel Pleasants Junior, printer to the Commonwealth, 1809-1823).

24. Ibid. at 213.

25. John G. Rauch and Nellie C. Armstrong, *A Bibliography of the Laws of Indiana 1788-1927* xxiv, Indiana Historical Collections, Vol. 16 (Indianapolis: Indiana Historical Bureau, 1928).

26. Ibid. at xxii.

27. Swisher, supra note 2, at x.

28. *Journals of the Continental Congress* 26(1784): 275; reprinted in Charles Kettleborough, *Constitution Making in Indiana 1780-1851,* Vol. 1, 18-21 (Indianapolis: Indiana Historical Commission, 1916).

29. Barnhart and Riker, supra note 1, at 250.

30. Clarence E. Carter, ed., *Territorial Papers of the United States,* Vol. 2, 12-18 (Washington, DC: Government Printing Office, 1934).

31. Ibid. at 251.

32. Swisher, supra note 2, at 5.

33. Northwest Ordinance, *Territorial Papers,* supra note 30, at 41-42 (Sections 3 and 4/preamble).

34. Swisher, supra note 2, at 6.

35. Barnhart and Riker, supra note 1, at 273.

36. Northwest Ordinance, art. V.

37. Rauch and Armstrong, supra note 25, at xxv.

38. Barnhart and Riker, supra note 1, at 274.

39. Ibid. at 274-275.

40. Howe, supra note 12, at 14.

41. Ibid. at 11.

42. Swisher, *supra* note 2, at xi.

43. An Act to Divide the Territory of the United States Northwest of the Ohio into Two Separate Governments, 2 *Stat.* 58 (1800).

44. Hawkins, supra note 6, at 48.

45. For a list of Indian treaties covering Indiana, see supra note 2.

46. Act to Divide the Indiana Territory into Two Separate Governments, 2 *Stat.* 309 (1805).

47. Hawkins, supra note 6, at 48-49; An Act for Dividing the Indiana Territory into Two Separate Governments, 2 *Stat.* 514 (1809).

48. George Pence and Nellie C. Armstrong, *Indiana Boundaries: Territory, State and County* 9, Indiana Historical Collections, Vol. 19 (Indianapolis: Indiana Historical Bureau, 1933; reprinted 1967).

49. Madison, supra note 3, at 37.

50. Francis S. Philbrick, "Law, Courts, and Litigation of Indiana Territory (1800-09)," *Ill. L. Rev.* 24(1929): 1, 2.

51. Ibid. at 3-4.

52. Ibid. at 5.

53. Ibid. at 15-17.

54. *Annals of Congress* 8th Cong., 2d Sess. 1693 (March 3, 1805). The *Annals* are also available at <http://memory.loc.gov/ammem/amlaw/lwac.html>.

55. An Act to Establish the Mode of Laying Off the Territory of Indiana into Districts, for the Election of its Members of the Legislative Council, 3 *Stat.* 103 (1814).

56. Barnhart and Riker, supra note 1, at 417; An Act Establishing Circuit Courts, 1814 Acts Ind. Terr. ch. 2, reprinted in Louis B. Ewbank and Dorothy L. Riker, eds., *Laws of the Indiana Territory, 1809-1816* 517, Indiana Historical Collections, Vol. 20 (Indianapolis: Indiana Historical Bureau, 1934).

57. Ibid. at 518.

58. Ibid. at 519.

59. Act for the Regulation of the Court of Justice in Indiana, 3 *Stat.* 213 (February 24, 1815).

60. Kettleborough, supra note 28, at xvii, xx.

61. Enabling Act of April 19, 1816, 3 *Stat.* 289.

62. Ordinance of Acceptance, 1816, Benjamin P. Poore, *Charters and Constitutions,* Vol. 1, 499 (Washington, DC: Government Printing Office, 1877).

63. Resolution for Admitting the State of Indiana into the Union, 3 *Stat.* 399 (1816).

64. Laurin A. Wollan Jr., "Law in Illinois Under France," *Ill. B.J.* 56 (1968): 384, 386.

65. Barnhart and Riker, supra note 1, at 471.

66. Copies of this act and other enabling legislation for Indiana as well as the Indiana Constitution can be found in William F. Swindler, ed., *Sources and Documents of United States Constitutions,* Vol. 3, 341 (Dobbs Ferry, NY: Oceana, 1974).

67. Jay F. Laning, *Beginnings of Law and Order in the Northwest Territory of the United States* III (Cleveland, OH: Law Abstract Co., 1925).

68. For an interesting discussion of the compilation and production of this definitive collection of Harrison's papers, see Douglas E. Clanin, "Adventures in Historical Editing: The William Henry Harrison Papers Project," in *Indiana Territory: A Bicentennial Perspective* 149, Darrell E. Bigham, ed. (Indianapolis: Indiana Historical Society, 2001).

Chapter 16

Iowa Territory Legal Materials

David Hanson

INTRODUCTION

Iowa was recognized as a territory in June 1838 and became a state in December 1846. The nine years as a territory produced numerous primary documents, providing an insight into the governance of the Iowa Territory. In addition to covering primary documents, numerous secondary resources are also included in this chapter.

The primary documents and secondary resources are organized in five categories: Preterritorial Materials, State Constitution Materials, Judicial Branch Territory Materials, Legislative Branch Territory Materials, and Executive Branch Territory Materials. In certain citations, a page number is included in parentheses, for example, (70), to assist the researcher in finding a specific reference.

The sections Bibliography of Iowa Territory Legal Materials and Bibliography of Iowa Territory Historical Materials provide a comprehensive list of resources for researchers who are interested in learning about all different aspects of Iowa Territory legal history. All materials listed in the last two sections can be found at the Drake University Law Library, Drake University Cowles Library, State Law Library of Iowa, or State Historical Society of Iowa, which are all located in Des Moines, Iowa. For holdings of these materials in other libraries throughout the state of Iowa, one can consult the state online catalog at <http://www.silo.lib.ia.us/for_ia_libraries/SILO/locator/index.html>.

HISTORICAL BACKGROUND

The land that would become the state of Iowa became a part of the United States with the enactment of the Louisiana Purchase in 1803.[1] The first known European explorer who saw the future land of Iowa was Frenchman Louis Jolliet along with his expedition party in 1673.[2]

Long before Jolliet, at least seventeen Indian tribes occupied the land within the future territory of Iowa during the seventeenth and eighteenth centuries.[3] The government of the United States, in an effort to secure the land for a future state, signed a number of treaties with the tribes living in Iowa. Two major treaties with the Sac and Fox tribes granted the United States most of the land that would eventually become the territory of Iowa.[4]

After the Louisiana Purchase, the governmental jurisdiction control of the land was first a part of the territory of Louisiana. In 1812, the territory of Louisiana was renamed the territory of Missouri. When Missouri achieved statehood in 1821, the district of Iowa was not placed under the control of another territory until 1834, when it was made a part of the territory of Michigan. In 1836, the territory of Wisconsin took over control of the district of Iowa when Michigan appeared to be on the verge of statehood.[5]

The progress toward the creation of the Iowa Territory moved quickly when the territory of Wisconsin took control. The Wisconsin Territorial Legislature was in favor of the creation of a separate territory in part because of the great distance separating the district of Iowa from Madison, because the Mississippi River provided a natural barrier, and because a large portion of the population was not receiving judicial services. In the first sixteen months that the district of Iowa was under the control of the territory of Wisconsin, only one session of court was held west of the Mississippi River.[6]

On February 6, 1838, the U.S. House of Representatives received a bill to divide the Wisconsin Territory and establish an Iowa Territory. The bill was debated and eventually passed both the House and Senate on June 6, 1838. The bill was signed by President Martin Van Buren on June 12, 1838, to go into effect on July 4, 1838.[7]

Two constitutional conventions were held in the Iowa Territory before Iowa was admitted to the United States. In 1842, a proposition to form a constitutional convention to apply for statehood was defeated by voters in part because of the potential for heavy tax burdens. In April 1844, the question of forming a constitutional convention was once again voted on by the people and a majority voted to form a constitutional convention with seventy-three delegates. The Constitution of 1844 did not lead to statehood because the U.S. Congress imposed a smaller boundary for Iowa. The Iowa constitutional convention delegates had included a provision that any conditions attached by the U.S. Congress would have to be voted on. The constitution was rejected by a vote of 7,019 to 6,023.[8]

In January 1846, the Iowa Territorial Legislative Assembly passed an act to form a new constitutional convention to meet in May. A compromise on the boundary issue was presented by Stephen Douglas, the chairman of the U.S. House Committee on Territories.[9] The convention voted to accept the new boundaries and made only minor revisions to the 1844 constitution. The U.S. Congress passed the act for statehood with an additional minor revision to the border. A vote to accept the changes to the constitution was taken on August 3, 1846, and passed by a vote of 9,492 to 9,036. President James Polk signed the act on August 4, 1846. On September 9, 1846, Iowa Territory Governor James Clarke ratified and adopted the constitution. The U.S. Congress passed a bill admitting Iowa to statehood, which was signed by President Polk on December 28, 1846. Iowa became the twenty-ninth state of the United States.[10]

PRETERRITORIAL MATERIALS

The laws that were significant in the formation of the territory and state of Iowa are listed in this section.

Federal Laws Relating to the Creation of the Iowa Territory

Northwest Ordinance, Congress of the Confederation (July 13, 1787).

The Northwest Ordinance provided a basic pattern of government for the new territories in the United States. The act also guaranteed the fundamental rights and liberties of American citizens.

Treaty Between the United States of America and the French Republic, April 30, 1803, U.S.-Fr., 8 *Stat.* 200 (1803).

Commonly referred to as the Louisiana Purchase.

Act of March 6, 1820 (Missouri Compromise), ch. 22, 3 *Stat.* 545 (1820).

Often referred to as the Missouri Compromise, this piece of legislation was passed in response to the expansion of slavery in territory from the Louisiana Purchase and guaranteed the Iowa Territory would be admitted to the United States as a free state.

Treaty of Peace, Friendship and Cession, September 21, 1832, 7 *Stat.* 374 (1832).

This treaty provided land to the United States from the Mississippi River to approximately the Iowa River. Monetary compensation of $640,000 and some land was given to the Sac and Fox tribes.

Articles of a Treaty Made and Concluded at the Agency of the Sac and Fox
　　Indians in the Territory of Iowa, October 11, 1842, 7 *Stat.* 596 (1842).

This treaty gave all land of the Sac and Fox tribes over to the United States.
Monetary compensation of $800,000 was provided.

Organic Act

Act of June 12, 1838 (to divide the Territory of Wisconsin and to establish
　　the Territorial Government of Iowa), ch. 96, 5 *Stat.* 235 (1838).

This legislation created the Iowa Territory. The organic act defines the
boundaries of the state; details the executive, legislative, and judicial
branches of the territory; provides rules concerning the first election; lists
qualifications of voters; and provides funding for public buildings.

Enabling Act

Act of December 28, 1846 (for the admission of the state of Iowa into the
　　Union), ch. 29, 9 *Stat.* 117 (1846).

This act officially declares the admission of the state of Iowa into the United
States.

Other Documents

*The Federal and State Constitutions Colonial Charters, and Other Organic
　　Laws of the States, Territories, and Colonies Now or Heretofore Forming
　　the United States of America.* Compiled and Edited under the Act of
　　Congress of June 30, 1906 by Francis Newton Thorpe. Vol. II Florida–
　　Kansas. Washington, DC: Government Printing Office, 1909.

The federal acts relating to the admission of the state of Iowa are compiled
into one resource beginning on page 1111 of this volume.

STATE CONSTITUTION MATERIALS

　The resources associated with the creation of the state constitution are
listed in this section. Iowa held two constitutional conventions before admittance to the United States.

Federal Materials Related to the Creation of the Constitution

Act of March 3, 1845 (for the admission of the states of Iowa and Florida into the Union), ch. 48, 5 *Stat.* 742 (1845).

The initial legislation by the U.S. Congress to allow Iowa to be admitted into the Union on equal footing with the original states in all respects.

Section 2 outlines the boundaries of the state of Iowa.

Section 3 provides that the state of Iowa shall have concurrent jurisdiction on the Mississippi River and every other river bordering the state.

Section 4 directs that an election take place for the ratification or rejection of the constitution approved on November 1, 1846, by the legislative constitutional convention.

Act of March 3, 1845 (an act supplemental to the act for the admission of the states of Iowa and Florida into the Union), ch. 79, 5 *Stat.* 789 (1845).

This supplemental act provides further clarification that the laws of the United States, which are not locally inapplicable, shall have the same force and effect within the state of Iowa as elsewhere within the United States.

Territorial Materials Related to the Constitution

Constitution for the State of Iowa, Adopted in Convention, November 1, 1844. Iowa City: Jesse Williams, 1844.

This publication contains the constitution agreed upon by the convention in 1844.

Constitution for the State of Iowa, Adopted in Convention, May 18, 1846. Iowa City: Abraham Palmer, 1846.

This publication contains the constitution agreed upon by the convention in 1846.

Journal of the Convention for the Formation of the Constitution for the State of Iowa, Begun and Held at Iowa City, on the First Monday of October, Eighteen-Hundred and Forty-Four. Published by Authority. Iowa City: Jesse Williams, 1845.

This journal contains the debates during the convention of 1844. A full index and rules of the convention are in this printed volume. A memorial to the Senate and House of Representatives of the United States is also included.

Journal of the Convention for the Formation of the Constitution for the State of Iowa, Begun and Held at Iowa City, on the First Monday of May, Eighteen Hundred Forty-Six. Iowa City: Abraham Palmer, 1846.

The full journal of the debates during the convention with index and rules of the convention are in this printed volume.

Legislative Acts Related to the Formation of the Constitution

Laws of the Territory of Iowa, Enacted at the Session of the Legislature Which Commenced on the First Monday of December, A.D. 1841. Published by Authority. Iowa City: Van Antwerp and Hughes, 1842.

Chapter 84: An act to provide for the expression of the opinion of the people of the territory of Iowa, upon the subject of the formation of a state constitution and government, and to enable then to form a constitution for the state of Iowa.

Laws of Iowa, Passed at the Session of the Legislative Assembly Which Commenced on the 4th of December, 1843. Published by Authority. Burlington: James Clarke, 1844.

Chapter 9: An act to provide for the expression of the opinion of the people of the territory of Iowa upon the subject of formation of a state constitution for the state of Iowa.

Laws of Iowa, Passed at the Extra Session of the Legislative Assembly Which Commenced on the 17th Day of June, 1844. Published by Authority. Iowa City: Williams and Palmer, 1845.

Chapter 8: An act to amend an act to provide for the expression of the opinion of the people of the territory of Iowa, upon the subject of the formation of a state constitution and government, and to enable then to form a constitution for the state of Iowa.

Laws of Iowa, Passed at the Session of the Legislative Assembly Which Commenced on the 5th Day of May, 1845. Published by Authority. Iowa City: Williams and Palmer, 1845.

Chapter 13: An act to submit to the people the draft of a constitution formed by the last convention.

Laws of Iowa, Passed at the Annual Session of the Legislative Assembly Which Commenced on the 1st Day of December, 1845. Published by Authority. Iowa City: A.H. and G.D. Palmer, 1846.

Chapter 37: An act to provide for the election of delegates to a convention to form a constitution and state government.

JUDICIAL BRANCH TERRITORY MATERIALS

The laws and resources in this section provide information on the formation of the judicial branch in the Iowa Territory. Resources that report cases decided by the territorial supreme court are also listed.

Materials Related to the Creation of Territory/State

Act of June 12, 1838 (to divide the Territory of Wisconsin and to establish the Territorial Government of Iowa), ch. 96, 5 *Stat.* 235 (1838).

Section 9 creates a supreme court, district courts, and probate courts, and provides for justices of the peace. The section also outlines the composition and jurisdiction of all the courts and offices listed. The supreme court consisted of a chief justice and two associate judges and was appointed for four years. The territory of Iowa was divided into three judicial districts.

Section 10 appoints the attorney of the territory of Iowa and details the appointment process, duties, and compensation for the position.

Section 11 addresses the appointment process and oaths of the chief justice, associate justices, attorney, and marshal for the territory. Salary information for the justices is given.

Section 15 transfers all suits, process, and proceedings that are undetermined prior to the third day in July west of the Mississippi from Wisconsin Territory courts to Iowa Territory courts.

Act of March 3, 1845 (an act supplemental to the act for the admission of the States of Iowa and Florida into the Union), ch. 76, 5 *Stat.* 789 (1845).

Section 2 outlines the jurisdiction of the district courts.

Section 3 establishes the compensation for judges.

Section 4 addresses the appointment of an attorney for the United States.

Prestatehood Judicial Opinions

Reports of Cases Argued and Determined in the Supreme Court of Iowa. Edited by Eastin Morris. Iowa City: Silas Foster, 1847.

This volume contains all of the cases argued and determined in the supreme court of the territory of Iowa from the organization of the court to the January term of 1846, in which opinions have been filed. Volume is also known as Morris's Reports.

A Digest of Decisions of the Supreme Court of Iowa: From the Organization of the Territory Until the End of the January Term 1887. Edited by Emlin McClain. Chicago: Callaghan, 1887.

The work presents a complete digest of the decisions of the supreme court of the territory and state of Iowa from its organization in 1838 until 1887. The digest encompasses two volumes with an index and table of cases in Volume 2.

Legislative Acts Relating to the Judicial Branch

Statute Laws of the Territory of Iowa, Enacted at the First Session of the Legislative Assembly of Said Territory, Held at Burlington, A.D. 1838-'39. Published by Authority. Burlington: Russell and Reeves, 1839.

An act concerning the costs and fees in the supreme and district courts. (75)

An act to establish the time for the first session of the supreme court. (108)

An act to regulate criminal proceedings. (109)

An act to establish the courts of probate. (126)

An act to fix the terms of the supreme and district courts and other procedures. (128)

An act relative to the proceedings in the chancery. (130)

An act to define crimes and punishments. (142)

An act to regulate depositions and testimony. (172)

An act to appoint district prosecutors and define their duties. (178)

An act to outline the procedures and duties of grand and petit jurors. (277)

An act to appoint justices of the peace and describe their duties and procedures of the court. (281)

An act to regulate procedures in the district courts. (370)

Laws of the Territory of Iowa, Enacted at the Session of the Legislature Commencing on the First Monday of November, A.D. 1839. Published by Authority. Burlington: J.H. M'Kenny, 1840.

Chapter 2: An act in relation to the safe custody of persons arrested for crimes and misdemeanors.

Chapter 9: An act to authorize evidence by the oath of parties.

Chapter 26: An act for the limitation of suits on penal statutes and criminal prosecutions.

Chapter 33: An act to authorize the arrest and detention of fugitives from justice from other states and territories of the United States.

Chapter 45: An act to provide for the appointment of justices of the peace in townships.

Chapter 70: An act concerning habeas corpus.

Chapter 71: An act to regulate the admission of attorneys.

Chapter 88: An act to establish the date and term of the supreme court and district courts.

Resolution 21: To provide for the printing of the reports of the decisions of the supreme court.

Laws of the Territory of Iowa, Enacted at the Session of the Legislature Which Commenced on the First Monday of November, A.D. 1840. Published by Authority. Burlington: John H. M'Kenny, 1841.

Chapter 26: An act to provide that all writs of summons, issuing from any court of record in the territory, shall be served by reading and delivering an attested copy.

Chapter 27: An act to regulate the act of torts in which the plaintiff shall not recover more costs than damages.

Chapter 32: An act to define procedural practice in the district courts.

Laws of the Territory of Iowa, Enacted at the Session of the Legislature Which Commenced on the First Monday of December, A.D. 1841. Published by Authority. Iowa City: Van Antwerp and Hughes, 1842.

Chapter 25: An act to authorize evidence by the oath of parties.

Chapter 44: An act to provide for a special term of the supreme court and to change the time and place of holding annual sessions.

Chapter 47: An act to define the jurisdiction, powers, and duties of the supreme and district courts.

Chapter 63: An act to amend criminal proceedings.

Chapter 64: An act to amend costs and clerk fees in the supreme and district courts.

Chapter 73: An act to amend the act to establish the court of probate.

Chapter 101: An act to supplement the regulation of criminal proceedings.

Local Laws of the Territory of Iowa, Enacted at the Session of the Legislature Which Commenced on the First Monday of December, 1842. Published by Authority. Iowa City: Hughes and Williams, 1843.

Chapter 71: An act to provide payment to petit jurors in certain cases.

Laws of Iowa, Passed at the Session of the Legislative Assembly Which Commenced on the 4th of December, 1843. Published by Authority. Burlington: James Clarke, 1844.

Chapter 6: An act to further define the jurisdiction of the supreme court and regulating the practice.

Chapter 10: An act to establish the time of holding the district courts in several judicial districts.

Chapter 15: An act to amend the elections of justices of the peace in certain counties.

Chapter 22: An act to amend the duties and procedures of justices of the peace.

Chapter 24: An act to amend the provisions concerning grand and petit jurors.

Chapter 27: An act to amend the proceedings in relation to the chancery.

Chapter 28: An act to provide for and regulate writs of error coram nobis.

Chapter 42: An act to form a fourth judicial district.

Laws of Iowa, Passed at the Session of the Legislative Assembly Which Commenced on the 5th Day of May, 1845. Published by Authority. Iowa City: Williams and Palmer, 1845.

Chapter 3: An act to amend the regulating practice in the district courts.

Chapter 9: An act to amend the defining jurisdiction of the supreme court and regulating practice.

Chapter 14: An act to amend the time of holding district courts in various jurisdictions.

Chapter 17: An act to amend the allowing and regulating of writs of attachment.

Chapter 20: An amendatory of an act to provide for changing the venue in civil and criminal cases.

Chapter 21: An act to amend an act relative to the probate of wills, executors, administrators, guardians, trustees of minors, and probate courts, and for defining their duties.

Laws of Iowa, Passed at the Annual Session of the Legislative Assembly Which Commenced on the 1st Day of December, 1845. Published by Authority. Iowa City: A.H. and G.D. Palmer, 1846.

Chapter 3: An act to amend an act regulating criminal proceedings.

Chapter 14: An act to fix the terms of the district courts.

Chapter 19: An act to amend an act providing for the appointment of district prosecutors and defining their duties.

Chapter 26: An act to provide for the printing, publication, and preservation of the decisions of the supreme court.

LEGISLATIVE BRANCH TERRITORY MATERIALS

The laws and resources in this section provide information on the formation of the legislative branch in the Iowa Territory. Documents issued by the legislative branch are also included in this section.

Materials Related to the Creation of Territory

Act of June 12, 1838 (to divide the Territory of Wisconsin and to establish the Territorial Government of Iowa), ch. 96, 5 *Stat.* 235 (1838).

Section 4 creates and prescribes the duties and powers of the legislative branch of the Iowa Territory. The legislative branch is divided into two chambers, a council and a house of representatives. Instructions concerning the number of legislators, vacancies, voting, and elections are also defined.

Section 5 defines the qualifications of voters.

Section 6 outlines that the legislative power of the territory shall extend to all rightful subjects of legislation.

Section 7 provides that the legislative council advise and consent to all judicial officers, justices of the peace, sheriffs, and militia officers appointed by the governor.

Section 8 outlines that members of the legislature may not hold any other office during the term they were elected and one year after the expiration of their term.

Section 13 discusses the procedures, location, and budget for the first legislative assembly.

Legislative Journals

The legislative branch of the Iowa Territory consisted of a council of the legislature and a house of representatives. Each chamber published a record of daily business after the legislative session concluded.

The *Journal of the Council* includes the record of votes for all bills brought before the council. The annual message, general correspondence, and veto correspondence from the governor are also recorded in the journal. Reports from the auditor, treasurer, librarian, superintendent of public buildings, and warden are included in the appendix portion of the journal. Also included are the joint resolutions, memorials, reports from committees, standing rules of the chamber, joint rules of both houses, and a comprehensive index to the journal.

The *Journal of the House of Representatives* includes the record of votes for all bills brought before the house of representatives. The annual message, general correspondence, and veto correspondence from the governor are also recorded in the journal. Reports from the auditor, treasurer, librarian, superintendent of public buildings, and warden are included in the appendix portion of the journal. Also included are the joint resolutions, memorials, reports from committees, standing rules of the chamber, joint rules of both houses, and a comprehensive index to the journal.

Session Laws and Statute Laws

Session laws were published individually as the *Laws of the Territory of Iowa* for the second through eighth legislative sessions. Laws are arranged in chronological order by date approved and divided into chapters. Each volume contains the joint resolutions, title of acts, and an index. A compilation of the territorial laws was published by the state of Iowa in 1912.

Statute Laws of the Territory of Iowa, Enacted at the First Session of the Legislative Assembly of Said Territory, Held at Burlington, A.D. 1838- '39. Published by Authority. Burlington: Russell and Reeves, 1839.

The laws passed by the first legislative session are published as the *Statute Laws of Iowa.* The statutes are arranged alphabetically by subject.

Revised Statutes of the Territory of Iowa. Revised and Compiled by a Joint Committee of the Legislature Session 1842-1843 and Arranged by the Secretary of the Territory. Published by Authority. Iowa City: Hughes and Williams, 1843.

A comprehensive index, all joint resolutions, and titles of acts are included.

Acts and Resolutions Passed at the Several Sessions of the Territorial Legis- lature of Iowa 1840-1846. Prepared for Publication Under the Direction of W.C. Hayward, Secretary of State, Under the Provisions of Concur- rent Resolution of the Thirty-Fourth General Assembly, adopted April 12, 1911. Des Moines: Emory H. English, 1912.

This volume reprints the session laws, joint resolutions, and titles of acts from 1840 to 1846. The index includes the page numbers from the original session law volume and the compiled volume.

Legislative Acts Relating to the Legislature

Statute Laws of the Territory of Iowa, Enacted at the First Session of the Legislative Assembly of Said Territory, Held at Burlington, A.D. 1838- '39. Published by Authority. Burlington: Russell and Reeves, 1839.

An act to regulate the publication and distribution of the laws and journals of the legislative assembly. (321)

An act to divide the territory of Iowa into electoral districts and to apportion the representatives of each district. (324)

An act to fix the time for the annual meeting of the legislative assembly. (325)

An act to authorize the governor to call a special legislative assembly. (325)

An act to regulate the mode of petitioning the legislature in certain cases. (369)

Laws of the Territory of Iowa, Enacted at the Session of the Legislature Commencing on the First Monday of November, A.D. 1839. Published by Authority. Burlington: J.H. M'Kenny, 1840.

Chapter 3: An act to authorize the legislative assembly to punish for contempt and to privilege the members from arrest.

Chapter 53: An act to provide for an extra session of the legislative assembly.

Chapter 66: An act to provide for the annual organization of the council and house of representatives.

Laws of the Territory of Iowa, Enacted at the Session of the Legislature Which Commenced on the First Monday of November, A.D. 1840. Published by Authority. Burlington: John H. M'Kenny, 1841.

Chapter 51: An act to fix the time for the annual meeting of the legislative assembly.

Laws of the Territory of Iowa, Enacted at the Session of the Legislature Which Commenced on the First Monday of December, A.D. 1841. Published by Authority. Iowa City: Van Antwerp and Hughes, 1842.

Chapter 116: An act to repeal an act to regulate the mode of petitioning the legislature in certain cases, approved January 25, 1839.

Laws of Iowa, Passed at the Session of the Legislative Assembly Which Commenced on the 4th of December, 1843. Published by Authority. Burlington: James Clarke, 1844.

Chapter 26: An act to provide for an extra session of the legislative assembly.

Chapter 37: An act to amend an act to provide for the annual organization of the council and house of representatives.

Laws of Iowa, Passed at the Extra Session of the Legislative Assembly Which Commenced on the 17th Day of June, 1844. Published by Authority. Iowa City: Williams and Palmer, 1845.

Chapter 1: An act to postpone the next annual election of members of the legislature and to provide for the payment of legislative debts.

Chapter 2: An act to amend an act to divide the territory of Iowa into electoral districts and to apportion the representatives of each.

Laws of Iowa, Passed at the Session of the Legislative Assembly Which Commenced on the 5th Day of May, 1845. Published by Authority. Iowa City: Williams and Palmer, 1845.

Chapter 61: An act to postpone the next annual election of members of the house of representatives from August until April.

Laws of Iowa, Passed at the Annual Session of the Legislative Assembly Which Commenced on the 1st Day of December, 1845. Published by Authority. Iowa City: A.H. and G.D. Palmer, 1846.

Chapter 16: An act to repeal an act to postpone the election of the members of the house of representatives from August until April.

Chapter 32: An act to amend an act to divide the territory of Iowa into electoral districts and to apportion the representatives of each.

EXECUTIVE BRANCH TERRITORY MATERIALS

The laws and resources in this section provide information on the formation of the executive branch in the Iowa Territory. Resources on documents originating from the executive office are also included.

Materials Related to the Creation of Territory

Act of June 12, 1838 (to divide the Territory of Wisconsin and to establish the Territorial Government of Iowa), ch. 96, 5 *Stat.* 235 (1838).

Section 2 grants executive power and authority for the territory of Iowa in a governor. The duties, powers, and term of service of the governor are set in this section.

Section 4 discusses legislative authority and the role of the governor in that branch.

Section 7 discusses the governor's role in the appointment of judicial officers, justices of the peace, sheriffs, militia officers, and civilian officers.

Section 11 covers the appointment, duties, and salary of the governor.

Section 13 establishes that the governor set a time and place for the first legislative assembly and to establish a seat of government for the territory.

Section 18 provides funds for the governor to establish a library at the seat of government.

Section 20 grants the governor power to initially define the judicial districts, assign judges, and appoint the times for holding court until otherwise provided by law of the legislative assembly.

Addresses, Messages, and Proclamations

Legislative Journals

Both the *Journal of the Council* and *Journal of the House of Representatives* include the annual address by the governor to the council and the house of representatives. The proclamations, special messages, and veto messages to both legislative bodies are printed in the journals as well.

Special Publications

Executive Journal of Iowa 1838-1841—Governor Robert Lucas. Edited by Benjamin Shambaugh. Iowa City: State Historical Society of Iowa, 1906.

A work devoted entirely to Robert Lucas, the first Iowa Territory governor. The journal is chronological and includes appointment letters, communications to the council of the legislature, communications to the house of representatives, personal letters, and proclamations. The journal has an index and chronological calendar of contents.

Messages and Proclamations of the Governors of Iowa. Compiled and Edited by Benjamin F. Shambaugh. 7 vols. Iowa City: State Historical Society of Iowa, 1903.

This work covers all governors from 1836 until 1901. Because Iowa was formed originally from the Wisconsin Territory, the author has included the documents of Wisconsin Territory Governor Henry Dodge in this work. The chapters are arranged chronologically by governor, with a brief biographical sketch preceding the documents. The documents compiled in this work include annual messages, veto messages, special messages, and proclamations.

Legislative Acts and Resolutions Relating to the Executive Branch

Laws of the Territory of Iowa, Enacted at the Session of the Legislature Commencing on the First Monday of November, A.D. 1839. Published by Authority. Burlington: J.H. M'Kenny, 1840.

An act to authorize the governor of this territory to offer rewards for the apprehension of criminals. (182)

Laws of Iowa, Passed at the Annual Session of the Legislative Assembly Which Commenced on the 1st Day of December, 1845. Published by Authority. Iowa City: A.H. and G.D. Palmer, 1846.

Chapter 9: An act to authorize the governor to appoint commissioners to take acknowledgments of deeds, or other contracts and depositions, in other territories or states.

Chapter 23: An act to authorize the governor of Iowa Territory to employ counsel in cases growing out of the disputed boundary between the territory and the state of Missouri.

BIBLIOGRAPHY OF IOWA TERRITORY LEGAL MATERIALS

Act of June 12, 1838 (to divide the Territory of Wisconsin and to establish the Territorial Government of Iowa), ch. 96, 5 *Stat.* 235 (1838).

Act of December 28, 1846 (an act for the admission of the state of Iowa into the Union), ch. 1, 9 *Stat.* 117 (1846).

Acts and Resolutions Passed at the Several Sessions of the Territorial Legislature of Iowa 1840-1846. Prepared for Publication Under the Direction of W.C. Hayward, Secretary of State, Under the Provisions of Concurrent Resolution of the Thirty-Fourth General Assembly, adopted April 12, 1911. Des Moines: Emory H. English, 1912.

Constitution for the State of Iowa, Adopted in Convention, November 1, 1844. Iowa City: Jesse Williams, 1844.

Constitution for the State of Iowa, Adopted in Convention, May 18, 1846. Iowa City: Abraham Palmer, 1846.

A Digest of Decisions of the Supreme Court of Iowa: From the Organization of the Territory Until the End of the January Term 1887. Edited by Emlin McClain. Chicago: Callaghan, 1887.

Executive Journal of Iowa 1838-1841—Governor Robert Lucas. Edited by Benjamin Shambaugh. Iowa City: State Historical Society of Iowa, 1906.

Journal of the Convention for the Formation of the Constitution for the State of Iowa, Begun and Held at Iowa City, on the First Monday of October, Eighteen-Hundred and Forty-Four. Published by Authority. Iowa City: Jesse Williams, 1845.

Journal of the Convention for the Formation of the Constitution for the State of Iowa, Begun and Held at Iowa City, on the First Monday of May, Eighteen Hundred Forty-Six. Iowa City: Abraham Palmer, 1846.

Journal of the Council of the First Legislative Assembly of the Territory of Iowa, Begun and Held at the City of Burlington, on the Twelfth Day of November, One Thousand Eight Hundred and Thirty-Eight. Published by Authority. Dubuque: Russell and Reeves, 1839.

Journal of the Council of the Second Legislative Assembly of the Territory of Iowa, Begun and Held at the City of Burlington in the County of Des Moines, on the Fourth Day of November, One Thousand Eight Hundred and Thirty-Nine. Published by Authority. Burlington: James G. Edwards, 1840.

Journal of the Council of the Second Legislative Assembly of the Territory of Iowa at the Special Session Which Convened at the City of Burlington, July 13, 1840. Des Moines: Historical Department of Iowa, 1902.

Journal of the Council of the Third Legislative Assembly of the Territory of Iowa, Begun and Held at the City of Burlington, on the Second Day of November, One Thousand Eight Hundred and Forty. Published by Authority. Bloomington: Russell and Hughes, 1841.

Journal of the Council of the Fourth Legislative Assembly of the Territory of Iowa, Begun and Held at Iowa City, on the Sixth Day of December, One Thousand Eight Hundred and Forty-One. Published by Authority. Bloomington: Jno. B. Russell, 1842.

Journal of the Council of the Fifth Legislative Assembly of the Territory of Iowa, Begun and Held at Iowa City, on the Fifth Day of December, One Thousand Eight Hundred and Forty-Two. Published by Authority. Davenport: Alfred Sanders, 1843.

Journal of the Council of the Sixth Legislative Assembly of the Territory of Iowa, Begun and Held at Iowa City, on the Fourth Day of December, One

Thousand Eight Hundred and Forty-Three. Published by Authority. Burlington: James G. Edwards, 1844.

Journal of the Council of the Seventh Legislative Assembly of the Territory of Iowa, Begun and Held at Iowa City, on the Fifth of May, One Thousand Eight Hundred and Forty-Four. Published by Authority. Iowa City: Williams and Palmer, 1845.

Journal of the Council of the Eighth Legislative Assembly of the Territory of Iowa, Begun and Held at Iowa City, on the First Monday of December, One Thousand Eight Hundred and Forty-Five. Published by Authority. Dubuque: George Greene, 1846.

Journal of the House of Representatives of the First Legislative Assembly of the Territory of Iowa, Begun and Held at the City of Burlington, on the Twelfth Day of November, One Thousand Eight Hundred and Thirty-Eight. Published by Authority. Burlington: Clarke and M'Kenny, 1838.

Journal of the House of Representatives of the Second Legislative Assembly of the Territory of Iowa, Begun and Held at the City of Burlington in the County of Des Moines, on the Fourth Day of November, One Thousand Eight Hundred and Thirty-Nine. Published by Authority. Burlington: J. Gardiner Edwards, 1840.

Journal of the House of Representatives of the Second Legislative Assembly of the Territory of Iowa at the Special Session Which Convened at the City of Burlington, July 13, 1840. Des Moines: Historical Department of Iowa, 1902.

Journal of the House of Representatives of the Third Legislative Assembly of the Territory of Iowa, Begun and Held at the City of Burlington, on the Second Day of November, One Thousand Eight Hundred and Forty. Published by Authority. Dubuque: Wm. W. Coriell, 1841.

Journal of the House of Representatives of the Fourth Legislative Assembly of the Territory of Iowa, Begun and Held at Iowa City, on the Sixth Day of December, One Thousand Eight Hundred and Forty-One. Published by Authority. Dubuque: Wilson and Keesecker, 1842.

Journal of the House of Representatives of the Fifth Legislative Assembly of the Territory of Iowa, Begun and Held at Iowa City, on the First Monday of December, One Thousand Eight Hundred and Forty-Two. Published by Authority. Iowa City: William Crum, 1843.

Journal of the House of Representatives of the Sixth Legislative Assembly of the Territory of Iowa, Begun and Held at Iowa City, on the First Monday of December, One Thousand Eight Hundred and Forty-Three. Published by Authority. Dubuque: Wilson and Keesecker, 1844.

Journal of the House of Representatives of the Seventh Legislative Assembly of the Territory of Iowa, Begun and Held at Iowa City, on the First Monday of May, One Thousand Eight Hundred and Forty-Four. Published by Authority. Fort Madison: R. Wilson Albright, 1845.

Journal of the House of Representatives of the Eighth Legislative Assembly of the Territory of Iowa, Begun and Held at Iowa City, on the First Monday of December, One Thousand Eight Hundred and Forty-Five. Published by Authority. Keosauqua: J. and J.M. Shepherd, 1846.

Laws of the Territory of Iowa, Enacted at the Session of the Legislature Commencing on the First Monday of November, A.D. 1839. Published by Authority. Burlington: J.H. M'Kenny, 1840.

Laws of the Territory of Iowa, Enacted at the Session of the Legislature Which Commenced on the First Monday of November, A.D. 1840. Published by Authority. Burlington: John H. M'Kenny, 1841.

Laws of the Territory of Iowa, Enacted at the Session of the Legislature Which Commenced on the First Monday of December, A.D. 1841. Published by Authority. Iowa City: Van Antwerp and Hughes, 1842.

Laws of Iowa, Passed at the Session of the Legislative Assembly Which Commenced on the 4th of December, 1843. Published by Authority. Burlington: James Clarke, 1844.

Laws of Iowa, Passed at the Extra Session of the Legislative Assembly Which Commenced on the 17th Day of June, 1844. Published by Authority. Iowa City: Williams and Palmer, 1845.

Laws of Iowa, Passed at the Session of the Legislative Assembly Which Commenced on the 5th Day of May, 1845. Published by Authority. Iowa City: Williams and Palmer, 1845.

Laws of Iowa, Passed at the Annual Session of the Legislative Assembly Which Commenced on the 1st Day of December, 1845. Published by Authority. Iowa City: A.H. and G.D. Palmer, 1846.

Reports of Cases Argued and Determined in the Supreme Court of Iowa. Edited by Eastin Morris. Iowa City: Silas Foster, 1847.

Revised Statutes of the Territory of Iowa. Revised and Compiled by a Joint Committee of the Legislature Session 1842-1843 and Arranged by the Secretary of the Territory. Published by Authority. Iowa City: Hughes and Williams, 1843.

Statute Laws of the Territory of Iowa, Enacted at the First Session of the Legislative Assembly of Said Territory, Held at Burlington, A.D. 1838-'39. Published by Authority. Burlington: Russell and Reeves, 1839.

BIBLIOGRAPHY OF IOWA TERRITORY HISTORICAL MATERIALS

Acton, Richard. *To Go Free: A Treasury of Iowa's Legal History.* Ames: Iowa State University Press, 1995.

Gue, Benjamin. *History of Iowa: From the Earliest Times to the Beginning of the Twentieth Century.* New York: Century History Company, 1903.

Houlette, William. *Iowa: The Pioneer Heritage.* Des Moines, IA: Wallace-Homestead, 1970.

Sage, Leland. *A History of Iowa.* Ames: Iowa State University Press, 1974.

Shambaugh, Benjamin. *The Constitutions of Iowa.* Iowa City: State Historical Society of Iowa, 1934.

Shambaugh, Benjamin. *Fragments of the Debates of the Iowa Constitutional Conventions of 1844 and 1846: Along with Press Comments and Other Materials on the Constitutions of 1844 and 1846.* Iowa City: State Historical Society of Iowa, 1900.

Stark, Jack. *The Iowa State Constitution: A Reference Guide.* Westport, CT: Greenwood Press, 1998.

Tuttle, Charles. *An Illustrated History of the State of Iowa: Being a Complete Civil, Political, and Military History of That State from Its First Exploration Down to 1875*. Chicago, IL: R.S. Peale, 1876.

NOTES

1. Richard Action, *To Go Free: A Treasury of Iowa's Legal History* 5 (Ames: Iowa State University Press, 1995).

2. Benjamin Gue, *History of Time: From the Earliest Times to the Beginning of the Twentieth Century* 32 (New York: Century History Company, 1903).

3. Leland Sage, *A History of Iowa* 23 (Ames: Iowa State University Press, 1974).

4. Ibid., at 51.

5. Action, supra, at 5-6.

6. Sage, supra, at 59.

7. Ibid., supra, at 60.

8. Jack Stark, *The Iowa State Constitution: A Reference Guide* 2 (Westport, CT: Greenwood Press, 1998).

9. William Houlette, *Iowa: The Pioneer Heritage* 63 (Des Moines, IA: Wallace-Homestead, 1970).

10. Stark, supra, at 4.

Chapter 17

The Law in "Bleeding Kansas": A Selected Bibliography of Legal Documents from Prestatehood Kansas, 1803-1861

Robert A. Mead
Mon Yin Lung
Joseph A. Custer

INTRODUCTION

The creation of the state of Kansas was one of the most contentious processes in the political history of the United States. The issue of whether slavery would be legal in Kansas sparked competing legislative bodies, four state constitutional conventions, physical confrontations on the floor of the U.S. Senate, and guerilla warfare. The documents recording the creation of the state of Kansas and the struggle between proslavery and Free-State forces in Kansas are important primary resources for understanding the root causes of the Civil War. This chapter is structured to first provide the historical background necessary for understanding early Kansas legal history. The remaining sections provide bibliographic information regarding the primary legal documents, categorized into sections identified as preterritorial, describing materials from before Kansas was a territory, and territorial, describing materials created after Kansas became a territory in 1854. Prestatehood, as a term, encompasses both preterritorial and territorial materials and all legal documents created prior to Kansas becoming a state in 1861. The final section includes a selected bibliography of secondary resources useful for the researcher studying early Kansas legal history. Throughout the chapter, page references within bibliographic annotations will be delineated by parenthesis within the annotation. Publications printed in Kansas will include only the town in which the document was printed. In addition, citations to the *Checklist of Kansas Imprints 1854-1876* and *Kansas Imprints 1854-1876, A Supplement,* and the *Bibliography of Early*

American Law will be included within brackets following each annotation, with citations noted [CLKI], [CLKI Supp.], and [BEAL], respectively.

HISTORICAL BACKGROUND

The first recorded exploration of Kansas by Europeans was conducted by Francisco Vasquez de Coronado's party under the authority of the Spanish Crown in 1541, some sixty-six years prior to John Smith's establishment of Jamestown in Virginia. European claims of possession of Kansas shifted between France and Spain throughout the seventeenth and eighteenth centuries. European sovereignty over Kansas ended in 1803, when Napoleon sold the vast majority of Kansas to the United States as part of the Louisiana Purchase. Although the French civil code was technically the law of the upper province of Louisiana prior to the Louisiana Purchase, there were no permanent French or Spanish settlements in the area that became Kansas; hence, the prior law is of little importance to Kansas legal history. Nonetheless, the first territorial legislative assembly in Kansas justified the pro-slavery statutes of 1855, in part, upon the recognition that the "institution of domestic slavery was established and recognized"[1] in the Civil Code of French Louisiana.

After the Louisiana Purchase, Congress divided the new lands into two portions, the territory of Orleans and the district of Louisiana.[2] Initially, the district of Louisiana was governed by Indiana Territory, but in 1805 it became the territory of Louisiana and was renamed the territory of Missouri in 1812.[3] Although Kansas was technically part of Missouri from 1805 until Missouri achieved statehood in 1820, no Missouri court sat in Kansas nor did Kansas have any representation in the Missouri legislature.[4] The United States declared Kansas, along with Oklahoma, Nebraska, and the Dakotas, as Indian Territory in 1834,[5] thus Kansas was a federal enclave from 1834 to the Kansas-Nebraska Act in 1854.

The legal history of Kansas as a U.S. territory begins in earnest with the Missouri Compromise of 1820.[6] The Missouri Compromise established a system by which new slave states and new free states would be admitted to the union in equal numbers, so as to avoid disrupting the delicate balance of power in the U.S. Senate. Maine was admitted as a free state at the same time Missouri was admitted with authorization to adopt a constitution that allowed slavery.[7] Further, the Missouri Compromise prohibited new slave states north of the southern border of Missouri, thirty-six degrees, thirty minutes latitude.[8]

On May 30, 1854, Congress passed the Kansas-Nebraska Act of 1854, the organic act that created both Kansas and Nebraska as territories.[9] The

Kansas-Nebraska Act opened Indian Territory, except for Oklahoma, to settlement. It also constituted the final end of the balance established by the Missouri Compromise of 1820, in that it repealed the compromise line of thirty-six degrees, thirty minutes latitude, instead providing for popular vote on the issue of slavery in each new territory. In the name of popular sovereignty, the act notes that

> the Compromise Measures, is hereby declared inoperative and void; it being the true intent and meaning of this act not to legislate slavery into any Territory or State, nor to exclude it therefrom, but to leave the people thereof perfectly free to form and regulate their domestic institutions in their own way, subject only to the Constitution of the United States.[10]

Abolitionists, such as Charles Robinson, the first governor of the state of Kansas, viewed the Kansas-Nebraska Act as allowing slavery wherever it was approved by popular vote. Robinson notes, "Here is the removal of all Congressional barriers to the spread of slavery, not only north of thirty-six degrees and thirty minutes, but northwest of the Ohio River; between the Atlantic and Pacific oceans, and the great lakes and the Gulf of Mexico."[11] In response to the scuttling of compromise on the slavery issue, both proslavery settlers from Missouri and the South and "free-state" activists, sponsored by emigrant aid societies in New England, rushed to settle Kansas, so as to secure Kansas for their respective camps. Charles Robinson believed that in the fight against slavery, "[t]he field of battle was thus removed from the halls of Congress to the plains of Kansas."[12]

The first territorial election in Kansas took place on March 30, 1855. Proslavery delegates won a majority of seats, although there were charges by the Free-State Party that many men crossed over from Missouri for a day to vote. The first act of the council and house of representatives was to deny seats to the Free-State men who had won election, instead seating their proslavery opponents.[13] The legislature convened at Pawnee, Kansas, at the direction of Territorial Governor Andrew H. Reeder. As Pawnee was approximately 140 miles from the Missouri border, the legislature, once seated, promptly passed a law titled "An act to remove the seat of government temporarily to the Shawnee Manual Labor School, in the territory of Kansas,"[14] a mile from the Missouri border. The preface to the statutes of 1855 notes that "at Pawnee there was no place of accommodation, and members had to camp out, sleep in their wagons or tents, and cook their own provisions."[15] In addition, the delegates charged that Governor Reeder had placed the legislative assembly at Pawnee because he had land investments in the area.[16] The act moving the legislative assembly closer to Missouri was passed over Governor Reeder's veto, with the blessing of the territorial supreme court, moving the proslavery legislative assembly closer to their supporters in Missouri.

The statutes produced by the first session of the Kansas Territorial Legislative Assembly were largely based upon the statutes of Missouri. Free-State residents, and their supporters in the East, were horrified at the creation of statutes that allowed for slavery. These statutes are often referred to as the "bogus statutes" enacted by what is known to history as the "bogus Legislature."[17] In addition, the nascent Republican Party used the 1855 Kansas statutes as campaign material, republishing them, in part, under the title *The Border Ruffian Code in Kansas* in 1856.

Concurrent with the political battle for control of territorial Kansas, both sides used military force to pursue their objectives. The epithet "bleeding Kansas" was well earned. The attack and counterattack between proslavery "border ruffians" and Free-Staters was significantly violent by May 1856, when a "posse" of hundreds of border ruffians sacked Lawrence, the center of Free-State activity. In retaliation, John Brown and his sons killed five unarmed, proslavery settlers at Pottawatomie Creek by hacking them apart with broadswords in front of their families, an incident known as the Pottawatomie Creek Massacre.[18] This also contributed to the "Border War" becoming a national issue. The most bloody incident, of course, occurred after statehood, when William Quantrill attacked Lawrence on August 21, 1863, with 300 to 400 irregular cavalry. They killed around 150 civilians and burned most of Lawrence before escaping back into Missouri.

After the allegedly fraudulent elections of 1855, the Free-State Party formed its own constitutional convention in Topeka during the fall of 1855. Professor Francis Heller notes that the Free-State supporters "rejected the first legislature, from which they were systematically excluded, as 'bogus' and established a virtual countergovernment."[19] As the Topeka Constitution was drafted in a convention that included only the Free-State Party, it naturally opposed slavery. It is important to note, however, that "antislavery" did not necessarily equate to support for equal civil rights for African Americans, as the Topeka Convention attempted to solve the slavery question by prohibiting African Americans, free or slave, from living in Kansas. The Topeka Constitution was submitted to Congress, despite the fact that the territorial government had not sanctioned it, where it passed in the House of Representatives but was defeated in the Senate.

In response to the Topeka Constitution, in September 1857, the proslavery legislature drafted the Lecompton Constitution,[20] while meeting in Lecompton, Kansas. It was ratified by popular vote in Kansas in December 1857, largely because many Free-State men refused to vote. The election ballot was limited to whether Kansas should have an unlimited or limited right to slavery and did not include an option to vote against the constitution. As with the Topeka Constitution, the Lecompton Constitution was sent to Washington, where President James Buchanan argued that it justified the admission of Kansas into the Union as a slave state.[21] Congress passed a statute on May 4, 1858,[22] conditionally admitting Kansas as a slave state once the Lecompton Constitution was ratified again by a proper popular vote in Kansas. The wording of the admission was phrased that Kansas "shall be entitled to admission into the Union as a State under such constitution, thus fairly and legally made, with or without slavery, as said constitution may prescribe."[23] In 1857, the Free-State faction was able to win control of the legislature in the October election. On August 21, 1858, Kansas voters overwhelmingly rejected the Lecompton Constitution at the polls, in a vote of 11,300 against ratification and 1,788 for ratification.

The third constitutional movement in Kansas started in Mineola, Kansas, in March 1858 and was then moved to Leavenworth, Kansas, where the delegates completed the Leavenworth Constitution on April 3, 1858. It was ratified by popular vote in May 1858, despite the fact that it was relatively radical in nature, extending the right to vote to "every male citizen, regardless of race."[24] Facing opposition from the Buchanan Administration, the Leavenworth Constitution never reached Congress.

The final constitutional movement in Kansas began on January 3, 1859, with a legislative enactment during the fifth session of the Kansas Territorial Legislative Assembly that called for "the formation of a Constitution and State Government."[25] Following a popular vote authorizing a constitutional convention and another vote to select delegates, fifty-eight delegates met in Wyandotte, Kansas, in July 1859 to draft the constitution. The antislavery Wyandotte Constitution, adopted on July 29, 1859, was ratified by a nearly two-to-one margin in a popular vote on October 4, 1859.[26] It retreated from the radicalism of the Leavenworth Constitution, limiting the right to vote to "[e]very white male person of twenty-one years and upwards."[27]

In addition to setting the stage for the drafting of the definitive constitution necessary for admission as a state, the fifth session of the legislative assembly repealed all laws from the first and second and liberally revised the statutes passed during the third session of the legislative assembly, sessions in which proslavery delegates controlled the legislature. Following the conclusion of the session, the "bogus statutes" of 1855 were publicly burned in the streets of Lawrence.[28]

The congressional admission of Kansas as a state under the terms of the Wyandotte Constitution took over a year to secure. Initially, in 1860, the House of Representatives passed a bill for the admission of Kansas into the Union, but the bill failed to come to a vote in the Senate.[29] The political battles between abolitionist and southern senators on the floor of the Senate had been quite fierce. Senator Charles Sumner of Massachusetts delivered a two-day speech on May 19 and 20, 1856, titled "The Crimes Against Kansas," during which he personally insulted a number of southern senators. Congressman Preston Brooks, of South Carolina, was angry that Sumner had insulted his uncle, Senator Andrew Butler. Brooks used his cane to beat Senator Sumner, seated at his desk on the Senate floor, to unconsciousness. Brooks resigned from the House a few months following the beating. Even the atrocity of this attack failed to end the stalemate on slavery issues in the U.S. Senate.

The stalemate was finally lifted with the election of Abraham Lincoln as president. Lincoln's election prompted the secession of some of the southern states, changing the composure of the Senate. The Senate passed the act admitting Kansas as a state, in a thirty-six-to-sixteen vote on January 21, 1861.[30] The House of Representatives then passed the companion act on January 28, 1861, which was signed by President James Buchanan on January 29, 1861. The early Kansas historian William Connelley notes:

> The admission of Kansas marked the end of the first battle for freedom. This nation will never be able to pay the Kansas pioneers who stood in the breach and fought this first battle. They were fighting not only for Kansas, but for the Union. They understood well what Lincoln meant when he said the Union could not endure half slave and half free. It was plain to them that Kansas was the crucial point and the crisis in this struggle for liberty for the Union. They did not fail.[31]

PRETERRITORIAL PERIOD, 1803-1854

Materials Related to the Acquisition of Kansas from France

Treaty ceding Louisiana, April 30, 1803, in *The Federal and State Constitutions, Colonial Charters, and Other Organic Laws of the States, Territories, and Colonies Now or Heretofore Forming the United States of America,* Vol. 3, 1359-1362. Francis Newton Thorpe, ed. Washington, DC: U.S. Government Printing Office, 1909.

Convention Between the United States of America and the French Republic, April 30, 1803, in *The Federal and State Constitutions, Colonial Charters, and Other Organic Laws of the States, Territories, and Colonies Now or Heretofore Forming the United States of America,* Vol. 3,

1362-1363. Francis Newton Thorpe, ed. Washington, DC: U.S. Government Printing Office, 1909.

Act of October 31, 1803 (to enable the President of the United States to take possession of the territories ceded by France to the United States, by the treaty concluded at Paris, on the thirtieth of April last; and for the temporary government thereof), Ch. 1, 2 *Stat.* 245 (1803).

This act constituted congressional approval for the Louisiana Purchase.

Act of November 10, 1803 (An Act authorizing the creation of a stock, to the amount of eleven millions two hundred and fifty thousand dollars, for the purpose of carrying into effect the convention of the thirtieth of April, one thousand eight hundred and three, between the United States of America and the French Republic; and making provision for the payment of the same), Ch. 2, 2 *Stat.* 246 (1803).

This act appropriated the money necessary to make the Louisiana Purchase.

Act of March 26, 1804 (An Act erecting Louisiana into two territories, and providing for the temporary government thereof), Ch. 38, 2 *Stat.* 283 (1804).

This act divided the Louisiana Purchase into two territories, the territory of Louisiana, which became Missouri, and the district of Orleans, which became Louisiana.

Materials Related to the Creation of Missouri As a State

When Missouri become a territory in 1812, Kansas was technically part of Missouri, until it was defined as "Indian country" in the Indian Trade and Intercourse Act of 1834.

Act of June 4, 1812 (An Act providing for the Government of the Territory of Missouri), Ch. 95, 2 *Stat.* 743 (1812).

This act is the Organic Act for Missouri.

Act of March 6, 1820 (known as Missouri Compromise of 1820) (An Act to authorize the people of the Missouri territory to form a constitution and state government, and for the admission of such state into the Union on an equal footing with the original states, and to prohibit slavery in certain territories), Ch. 22, 13 *Stat.* 545 (1820).

In addition to being the Enabling Act for the state of Missouri, this act formed the compromise between northern and southern states on whether new states would be free or slave states and lasted until the Kansas-Nebraska Act of 1854.

Materials Related to Treaties with Tribes

A number of Native American tribes were located within Kansas, including the Kansa, or Kaw, from which the state derives its name.[32] From the Indian Trade and Intercourse Act of 1834 until the Kansas-Nebraska Act of 1854, Kansas was a federal enclave set aside for both indigenous tribes and emigrant tribes moved to Kansas from east of the Mississippi. After the Indian Removal Act of 1830, around thirty tribes from east of the Mississippi River were relocated into eastern Kansas. In 1855, Congress authorized the president to negotiate with tribes west of Missouri and Iowa for the purpose of "securing assent of said tribes to the settlement of the citizens of the United States upon lands claimed by said Indians, and for the purpose of extinguishing the title of said Indian tribes in whole or in part to said land."

Act of May 28, 1830 (to provide for an exchange of land with the Indians residing in any of the states or territories, and for their removal west of the river Mississippi), Ch. 148, 4 *Stat.* 411 (May 28, 1830).

The Indian Removal Act authorized the president to remove tribes east of the Mississippi River into lands west of the Mississippi River.

Act of June 30, 1834 (An Act to regulate trade and intercourse with the Indian tribes, and to preserve peace on the frontiers), Ch. 161, 4 *Stat.* 729 (1834).

The Indian Trade and Intercourse Act defined "Indian country" as "all that part of the United States west of the Mississippi, and not within the states of Missouri and Louisiana, or the territory of Arkansas, and also, that part of the United States east of the Mississippi river, and not within any state to which the Indian title has not been extinguished" (729). In addition, it prohibited any person from trading with the tribes in Indian Country without a license (730).

Act of July 22, 1854 (An Act to establish offices of Surveyor-General of New Mexico, Kansas, and Nebraska, to grant Donations to actual Settlers therein, and for other purposes), Ch. 103, 10 *Stat.* 308 (1854).

Section 12 of this act allows for federal preemption and public sale of lands in Kansas with extinguished Indian title. The government sold the Indian land with extinguished title to settlers.

Organic Act Creating Kansas As a Territory

Act (Kansas-Nebraska Act) of May 30, 1854 (to organize the territories of Nebraska and Kansas), Ch. 59, 10 *Stat.* 277 (1854).

The Kansas-Nebraska Act created the territories of Kansas and Nebraska. As the Organic Act for Kansas, it defines the physical boundaries of the territory and establishes the temporary government for the territory. In addition, it addresses the issue of tribal lands. The Kansas-Nebraska Act dramatically altered the national slavery debate by repealing the Missouri Compromise of 1820. The Kansas-Nebraska Act is also reprinted in *The Federal and State Constitutions, Colonial Charters, and Other Organic Laws of the States, Territories, and Colonies Now or Heretofore Forming the United States of America,* Vol. 2, 1161. Francis Newton Thorpe, ed. Washington, DC: U.S. Government Printing Office, 1909.

TERRITORIAL PERIOD, 1854-1861

Constitutional Materials

Summary Material for Kansas Constitutional History

Kansas: A Cyclopedia of State History, Embracing Events, Institutions, Industries, Counties, Cities, Towns, Prominent Persons, Etc.: With a Supplementary Volume Devoted to Selected Personal History and Reminiscence. Frank W. Blackmar, ed. Chicago: Standard Publishing Company, 1912.

Also available online at <http://skyways.lib.ks.us/genweb/archives/1912>.

Constitutional Conventions (409-415).

Constitutions (415-442).

Francis H. Heller. *The Kansas State Constitution: A Reference Guide.* Westport, CT: Greenwood Press, 1992.

Professor Heller outlines the early Kansas political environment, the struggles between the Free-Staters and the proslavery force, the attempts of both sides to put together a constitution reflecting their principles, the formation of the Wyandotte Constitution, and the fights surrounding the admission of Kansas in the U.S. Congress (1-11).

Topeka, Lecompton, and Leavenworth Constitutions

D.W. Wilder. *The Annals of Kansas,* New Ed. 1541-1885. Topeka: Kansas Publishing House, 1886.

Topeka Constitution (91-106).

Lecompton Constitution (177-191).

Leavenworth Constitution (216-231).

The Federal and State Constitutions, Colonial Charters, and Other Organic Laws of the States, Territories, and Colonies Now or Heretofore Forming the United States of America, Vol. 2. Francis Newton Thorpe, ed. Washington, DC: U.S. Government Printing Office, 1909.

Topeka Constitution (1179-1201).

Lecompton Constitution (1201-1220).

Leavenworth Constitution (1221-1241).

Wilson Shannon, John Calhoun, et al. "To the citizens of the United States and of the Territory of Kansas. At a large and respectable meeting of delegates, representing almost every portion of the Territory of Kansas, held at the city of Leavenworth on the 14th instant, the undersigned were appointed a committee to address the citizens of the United States and of the Territory of Kansas, and to lay before them a true statement of the past and present state of things in this Territory." Leavenworth, *Kansas Herald,* November 30, 1855.

This committee was organized in protest to the Free-State Party's Topeka Constitution.

Kansas (Territory). Free State Convention. 1857. Topeka. An address to the people of the United States, and of Kansas territory, by the Free state Topeka convention, held March 10, 1857. Leavenworth: *Leavenworth Times* Office, 1857.

Opposition to the adoption of the Lecompton Constitution. [BEAL 10786]

Resolutions of Legislature of Massachusetts Admission of Kansas, H.R. Misc. Doc. No. 35-124 (1858).

Resolutions of Legislature of Iowa against Admission of Kansas Under Lecompton Constitution, H.R. Misc. Doc. No. 35-44 (1858).

Resolutions of Legislature of Rhode Island Against Admission of Kansas Under Lecompton Constitution, H.R. Misc. Doc. 35-60 (1858).

Resolutions of Legislature of New York Against Admission of Kansas Under Lecompton Constitution, H.R. Misc. Doc. 35-105 (1858).

Resolutions of Legislature of Maine Against Admission of Kansas Under Lecompton Constitution, H.R. Misc. Doc. No. 35-104 (1858).

Wyandotte Constitution

Constitutional Convention, Wyandotte, 1859. *Proceedings and Debates. Embracing the Secretary's Journal of the Kansas Constitutional Convention, convened at Wyandotte, July 5, 1859, under the Act of the Territorial Legislature, entitled "An Act providing for the formation of a state government for the State of Kansas."* Approved February 11, 1859. Wyandotte: S.D. Macdonald, Printer to the Convention, 1859. [CLKI 218]

Constitutional Convention, Wyandotte, 1859. *Rules for the Government of the Constitutional Convention of the Territory of Kansas.* Wyandotte, Commercial Gazette Job Office, 1859. [CLKI 219]

Kansas Constitutional Convention: A Reprint of the Proceedings and Debates of the Convention which framed the Constitution of Kansas at Wyandotte in July, 1859; Also the Constitution Annotated to date, Historical sketches, Etc. By Authority of the State Legislature. Topeka: Kansas State Printing Plant, 1920.

This volume covers all the official records on the formation of the Wyandotte Constitution. The text of the constitution can be found on pp. 574-592. This title is a necessity for anyone researching Kansas statehood and early Kansas history.

D.W. Wilder. *The Annals of Kansas.* Topeka: T.D. Thacher, 1886.

A reprint of the original Wyandotte Constitution and amendments to November 2, 1880 (263-278).

The Federal and State Constitutions, Colonial Charters, and Other Organic Laws of the States, Territories, and Colonies Now or Heretofore Forming the United States of America, Vol. 2. Francis Newton Thorpe, ed. Washington, DC: U.S. Government Printing Office, 1909.

Wyandotte Constitution (1241-1261).

Materials Related to the Admission of Kansas As a State

Act of May 4, 1858 (for the Admission of the State of Kansas into the Union), Ch. 26, 12 *Stat.* 269 (1858).

This act of admittance was based upon the proslavery Lecompton Constitution. The admittance was conditional, depending upon whether the Lecompton Constitution would be ratified by popular election in Kansas. As discussed earlier, under Historical Background, it was defeated in a landslide vote on August 21, 1858.

The Crimes Against Kansas: The Apologies for the Crime: The True Remedy, Speech of Charles Sumner of Massachusetts, In the Senate of the United States, May 18 & 19, 1856. H.R. Rep. No. 34-182. Washington, DC: Buell and Blanchard, Printers, 1856.

Senator Charles Sumner was the leading voice in the Senate for abolition. Following this two-day speech, he was assaulted and severely beaten with a cane on the Senate floor by the nephew of a senator he had insulted during the speech.

Charles Sumner. *The barbarism of slavery. Speech of Hon. Charles Sumner, on the bill for the admission of Kansas as a free state. In the United States Senate, June 4, 1860.* Washington, DC: T. Hyatt, 1860.

William Henry Seward, The Admission of Kansas: Speech delivered in the Senate of the United States, Feb. 29, 1860. *New York Tribune,* 1860.

Act of January 29, 1861 (for the Admission of Kansas into the Union), Ch. 20, 12 *Stat.* 126 (1861).

This act successfully admitted Kansas into the Union. It was based upon the anti-slavery Wyandotte Constitution of July 29, 1859, discussed earlier in this chapter under Historical Background. The Wyandotte Constitution was ratified by popular vote in Kansas on October 4, 1859. The lag in time between ratification and admission is attributable to southern power in the

U.S. Senate. Upon secession of the first southern states, the admittance of Kansas as a state passed on a thirty-six-to-sixteen vote in the U.S. Senate.

Admission into the Union: Resolutions of Legislature of Kansas. H.R. Misc. Doc. No. 37-3 (1862).

Territorial Legislation and Legislative Materials

Territorial Statutes

The Statutes of the Territory of Kansas; Passed at the First Session of the Legislative Assembly, One Thousand Eight Hundred and Fifty-Five. To Which are Affixed The Declaration of Independence, and the Constitution of the U. States, and the Act of Congress Organizing Said Territory, and other Acts of Congress Having Immediate Relation Thereto. Shawnee M. L. School: John T. Brady, Public Printer, 1855.

An act in relation to certain citizens (Declaring Indians and anyone else declared citizens to be "for all purposes, free white citizens") (163).

An act to provide for the call of a convention to form a state constitution (171).

An act to enable persons held in slavery to sue for their freedom (381).

An act relative to fugitives from other territories or states (383).

An act to restrain intercourse with the Indians (417).

An act defining the judicial districts (443).

An act adopting the common law as the rule of action in this territory (469).

An act concerning the statutes and legislative proceedings (471).

An act to apportion the representation in the next legislative assembly (656).

An act to remove the seat of government temporarily to the Shawnee Manual Labor School, in the territory of Kansas (703).

An act to locate the seat of government (703).

An act to punish offences against slave property (715).

Laws of the Territory of Kansas, 1855, S. Exec. Doc. No. 23. Washington, DC: A.O.P. Nicholson, Senate Printer, 1886.

This is a federal reprint of the 1885 statutes.

The Border Ruffian Code in Kansas: Code of pretended laws enacted by the bogus Territorial Legislature of Kansas. Extracts . . . taken from Executive Document no. 23, submitted to Congress by the President of the United States. *New York Tribune,* 1856.

This selected partial reprint of the 1855 statutes is also available online at <http://www.hti.umich.edu/cgi/t/text/text-idx?c=moa;idno=AFK1365>, as part of the Making of America books collection.

Laws of the Territory of Kansas, passed at the second session of the General Legislative Assembly, begun and held at the city of Lecompton, on the second Monday (12th) of January, A.D. 1857. Lecompton, Kansas Territory: R.H. Bennett, Public Printer, 1857.

An act to define and establish the council and representative districts for the second legislative assembly, and for other purposes (65).

An act repealing the twelfth section of "An act to punish offences against slave property" (77).

An act to punish rebellion (80).

Acts organizing counties (90-98).

Local and private laws (103-367).

[CLKI 117]

Laws of the Territory of Kansas Passed at the Third and Fourth Sessions of the Legislative Assembly; the third session held the City of Lecompton, 1857. The Fourth Session begun at the City of Lecompton, on the First Monday of January, 1858, and held and concluded at the City of Lawrence. Lecompton, Kansas Territory: S.W. Driggs and Co., 1858.

Third Session:

An act for the prevention and punishment of election frauds (15).

An act submitting the constitution framed at Lecompton, under the act of the Legislative Assembly of Kansas Territory, titled "An Act to provide for the taking a Census and Election of Delegates to a Convention" passed February 19, A.D. 1857. An act to provide for an election on the submission of the Lecompton Constitution (17).

Concurrent resolutions reaffirming the People's Constitution, framed at Topeka on the twenty-third day of October, A.D. 1855 (20).

Fourth Session:

Code of Civil Procedure (65).

Code of Criminal Procedure (169).

An act to provide for contested elections (229).

An act providing for the investigation of election frauds (231).

An act repealing "An Act to punish offences against slave property" (345).

An act to remove and permanently locate the seat of government (345).

[CLKI 183]

General Laws of the Territory of Kansas, passed at the Fifth Session of the Legislative Assembly; Begun at the City of Lecompton, on the first Monday of Jan'y, 1859, and held and concluded at the City of Lawrence. Lawrence, Kansas Territory: Herald of Freedom Steam Press, 1859.

An act to define and establish the council and representative districts of the territory of Kansas for the next legislative assembly (48).

An act to establish a code of criminal procedure (185).

An act providing for the formation of a constitution and state government for the state of Kansas (292).

An act providing for the repeal of certain laws (544).

[CLKI 221]

General Laws Passed by the Legislative Assembly of the Territory of Kansas, at the General and Special Sessions of the year 1860: The First Session begun at the City of Lecompton, Jan'y 2 and adjourned at the City of Lawrence, Jan'y 18; The second session convened at Lecompton Jan'y 19, Adjourned to and concluded at Lawrence. Lecompton, Kansas Territory: S.A. Medary and S.W. Driggs, Printers, "Democrat" Office, 1860.

An act to restrain intercourse with Indians (127).

An act making citizens of certain Indians in Kansas Territory (128).

An act to prevent and punish armed invasions from or into this territory (131).

An act to define the judicial districts of this territory, and fix the times and places of holding the several courts therein (133).

An act to prohibit slavery in Kansas (200).

Resolutions respecting admission of Kansas into the Union (241).

[CLKI 252]

General Laws passed by the Legislative Assembly of the Territory of Kansas, for the Year 1861: commenced at the City of Lecompton January Seventh, and adjourned to and concluded at the City of Lawrence. Sam. A. Medary, Public Printer, 1861. [CLKI 287]

Private Laws

Private Laws of the Territory of Kansas, Passed at the Fourth Session of the Legislative Assembly; Begun at the City of Lecompton, on the First Monday of Jan'y, 1858, and held and concluded at the City of Lawrence. Lecompton, Kansas Territory: S.W. Driggs and Co., Printers, 1858. [CLKI 184]

Private Laws of the Territory of Kansas, Passed at the Fifth Session of the Legislative Assembly; Begun at the City of Lecompton, on the first Monday of Jan'y, 1859, and held and concluded at the City of Lawrence. Lawrence, Kansas Territory: Herald of Freedom Steam Press, 1859. [CLKI 223]

Private Laws of the Territory of Kansas, Passed at the special session of the Legislative Assembly of 1860; Begun at the City of Lecompton, January 19, 1860, and held and concluded at the City of Lawrence. Lecompton, Kansas Territory: S.A. Medary, Printer, 1860. [CLKI 254]

Private Laws passed by the Legislative Assembly of the Territory of Kansas, for the Year 1861: commenced at the City of Lecompton January Seventh, and adjourned to and concluded at the City of Lawrence. Sam. A. Medary, Public Printer, 1861. [CLKI 288]

Council and House Journals

Kansas Legislative Assembly. *Journal of the Council of the Territory of Kansas at their First Session.* Shawnee M. L. School: John T. Brady, Public Printer, 1855. [CLKI 33]

Kansas Legislative Assembly. *Journal of the Council of the Territory of Kansas at their Second Session, begun and held at the City of Lecompton, on the second Monday (12th) of January, 1857.* Lecompton: R.H. Bennett, Public Printer, 1857. [CLKI 119]

Kansas Legislative Assembly. *Council Journal (Extra Session) of the Legislative Assembly of Kansas Territory, for the year 1857.* Lawrence: Sam. A. Medary, Public Printer, 1861. [CLKI 291]

Kansas Legislative Assembly. *Council Journal of the Legislative Assembly of Kansas Territory for the year 1858: Commenced at the City of*

Lecompton January fourth, and adjourned to and concluded at the City of Lawrence. Lawrence: Sam. A. Medary, 1861. [CLKI 292]

Kansas Legislative Assembly. *Journal of the Territorial Council of Kansas, begun at Lecompton, Monday January 3d, A.D., 1859, and adjourned to and held at the City of Lawrence, January 7th, A.D. 1859.* Lawrence: J.K. Goodin, Printer, 1859. [CLKI 227]

Kansas Legislative Assembly. *Council Journal of the Legislative Assembly of Kansas Territory, begun at the city of Lecompton, Jan. 2, 1860.* Lecompton, Kansas Territory: S.A. Medary and S.W. Driggs, Public Printers, 1860. [CLKI 258]

Kansas Legislative Assembly. *Council Journal of the Legislative Assembly of Kansas Territory (Special Session), begun at the city of Lecompton, Jan. 19, 1860 and held and concluded at the City of Lawrence.* Lecompton, Kansas Territory: S.A. Medary and S.W. Driggs, Public Printers, 1860. [CLKI 259]

Kansas Legislative Assembly. *Council Journal of the Legislative Assembly of Kansas Territory, for the Year 1861: commenced at the City of Lecompton Jan'y 7th, and adjourned to and concluded at the City of Lawrence.* Lawrence: Samuel A. Medary, Public Printer, 1861. [CLKI 293]

Kansas Legislative Assembly. *Journal of the House of Representatives of the Territory of Kansas, at the First Session of the First Territorial Legislative Assembly, begun and held at the town of Pawnee, on Monday, the 2d day of July, in the year of our Lord one thousand eight hundred and fifty-five.* Shawnee M.L. School: John T. Brady, Public Printer, 1855. [CLKI 48]

Kansas Legislative Assembly. *Journal of the House of Representatives of the Territory of Kansas at their Second Session, begun and held at the City of Lecompton, on the second Monday (12th) of January, 1857.* Lecompton: R.H. Bennett, Public Printer, 1857. [CLKI 120]

Kansas Legislative Assembly. *House Journal (extra session), of the Legislative Assembly of Kansas Territory, for the Year 1857.* Lawrence: Sam. A. Medary, Public Printer, 1861. [CLKI 294]

Kansas Legislative Assembly. *House Journal of the Legislative Assembly of Kansas Territory, for the Year 1858: commenced at the City of Lecompton January Fourth, and adjourned to and concluded at the City of Lawrence.* Lawrence: Sam. A. Medary, Public Printer, 1861. [CLKI 295]

Kansas Legislative Assembly. *Journal of the Territorial House of Representatives of Kansas, begun at Lecompton, Monday January 3d, A.D., 1859, and adjourned to and held at the City of Lawrence, January 7th, A.D. 1859.* Lawrence: J.K. Goodin, Printer, 1859. [CLKI 227]

Kansas Legislative Assembly. *House Journal of the Legislative Assembly of Kansas Territory, begun at the city of Lecompton, Jan. 2, 1860.* Lecompton, Kansas Territory: S.A. Medary and S.W. Driggs, Public Printers, 1860. [CLKI 260]

Kansas Legislative Assembly. *House Journal of the Legislative Assembly of Kansas Territory, (Special Session), begun at the city of Lecompton, Jan. 19, 1860, and held and concluded at the City of Lawrence.* Lecompton, Kansas Territory: S.A. Medary and S.W. Driggs, Public Printers, 1860. [CLKI 261]

Kansas Legislative Assembly. *House Journal of the Legislative Assembly of Kansas Territory, for the Year 1861: commenced at the City of Lecompton January 7th, and adjourned to and concluded at the City of Lawrence.* Lawrence: Samuel A. Medary, Public Printer, 1861. [CLKI 296]

Legislative Documents

Legislative Assembly. *Rules and Orders for conducting business in the House of Representatives of the Territory of Kansas, and Joint Rule for the Government of the Council and House* (1855). [CLKI 32]

Legislative Assembly. *Rules for Government of the Legislative Assembly of the Territory of Kansas. Adopted at a session of the Legislature commenced January 4th, 1859.* Lawrence: Republican Book and Job Office, 1859. [CLKI 226]

Legislative Assembly. *Rules for Government of the Legislative Assembly of the Territory of Kansas. Adopted at the session of the Legislature commenced January 2, 1860.* Lawrence: Herald of Freedom Steam Printing Office, 1860. [CLKI 256]

Legislative Assembly. *Rules for Government of the Legislative Assembly of the Territory of Kansas. Adopted at the session of the Legislature commenced January 19, 1860.* Lecompton: S.A. Medary and S.W. Driggs, Printers, 1860.

Rules for the Special Session, January 19 to February 27, 1860. [CLKI 257]

Territorial Executive Branch Materials

Andrew H. Reeder. *Review of the opinion of Chief Justice Lecompte, upon the validity of the laws passed by the Kansas legislature while sitting at the Shawnee Mission.* [Lawrence]: Kansas Free State Print, 1855.

Veto Message of Andrew H. Reeder, Governor of Kansas Territory; together with a Memorial from the Legislative Assembly of the Territory of Kansas, to his Excellency, Franklin Pierce, President of the United States, July 26, 1855. Shawnee: John T. Brady, Public Printer, 1855. [CLKI 24]

Samuel A. Medary. *Gov. S. Medary's Annual and Special Messages, Delivered to the Legislative Assembly at its opening, January 3d, '59; the latter, on the occasion of the request of the House of Representatives, for information in regard to the Linn and Bourbon County difficulties.* Lecompton: Executive Office, 1859. [CLKI 220]

M. Beebe. *Governor's Annual Message.* Topeka, KS: Executive Office, 1861. [CLKI 286]

Samuel A. Medary. *Annual Message of Governor Medary.* Lecompton: Executive Officer, 1860. [CLKI 250]

Samuel A. Medary. *Veto Message of Governor Medary, on the Bill Prohibiting Slavery in Kansas.* Lawrence: The Republican, and Atchison: The Champion, 1860. [CLKI 251]

M. Beebe. *Governor's Annual Message.* Topeka, KS: Executive Office, 1861. [CLKI 286]

Territorial and Earliest State Judicial Branch Materials

Opinion of Hon. Samuel D. Lecompte, Chief Justice, Concurred in by Hon. Rush Elmore, Associate Justice, of the Supreme Court of The Territory of

Kansas, upon the right of the Legislative Assembly to locate temporarily the seat of government, and upon the validity of their acts of legislation at such place. Given in reply to a resolution of the Legislative Assembly. Shawnee M.L. School, KS: John T. Brady, Public Printer, 1855.

This is the Kansas Territorial Supreme Court's advisory opinion regarding the legality of moving the first session of the legislative assembly from Pawnee to the Shawnee Manual Labor School. [CLKI 20] [BEAL 10782]

Reports of Cases Determined in the Supreme Court of the Territory of Kansas: Together with an important case determined in the District Court of the First Judicial District of said Territory before one of the Judges of the Supreme Court and several important cases determined in the United States for the District of Kansas. James McCahon, ed. Chicago: Callaghan and Cockcroft, 1870.

In the late 1860s, James McCahon of Leavenworth, Kansas, began compiling a volume containing the incomplete list of opinions handed down by the Kansas Territorial Supreme Court. Of interest is the fact that McCahon's text covers cases decided over roughly the last two years of the Kansas territorial Supreme Court's existence. Cases decided over the prior four and one-half years of the Kansas Territorial Supreme Court's existence are not included. The reason for this is uncertain. It is suggested that Quantrill's raid and the ruins left behind may have played a part in the destruction of prior decisions.

Reports of Cases argued and determined in the Surpeme Court of the State of Kansas. Elliot V. Banks, ed. Lawrence: W.S. Rankin and Company, 1864.

Louis Carpenter, the second reporter appointed by the Kansas Supreme Court, was killed in Quantrill's Raid in 1863. Volume 1 of the state supreme court reports was being prepared by Carpenter at the time of the raid. The volume was virtually destroyed except for fragments of a few cases. Elliot V. Banks was Carpenter's successor. He finished printing Volume 1 of the *Kansas Reports* in 1864. By 1870, Banks had published the first five volumes of the *Kansas Reports*. [CLKI 405]

Reports of Cases argued and determined in the Supreme Courts of the State and Territory of Kansas. Charles Frederick William Dassler, ed. Topeka: F.P. Baker and Sons, 1881.

There are two editions of the first thirty-six volumes of the *Kansas Reports*. The second edition corrects the typographical and other errors contained in the first edition. Volume 1 of the second edition also reprints *McCahon's Reports* along with the contents of Volume 1 of the first edition of *Kansas Reports*. Dassler edited Volumes 1 through 15, 21 through 25, and 38 through 39 of the second edition.

City Charters

Charter and Ordinances of the City of Lawrence together with an Act Amending the Charter, Passed by the Legislature of 1858. By Authority of the Mayor and Board of Alderman. Lawrence: "Republican" Book and Job Office, 1858. [CLKI Supp. 38]

Charter of the City of Atchison, and Amendments thereto, with the Ordinances, from the Organization of the City Government to the Present Time; Compiled and Revised. Albert H. Horton and Richard C. Mackall, eds. Atchison: Adams and Stebbins, Printers, 1860. [CLKI Supp. 70]

BIBLIOGRAPHY OF KANSAS LEGAL HISTORY RESOURCES

Useful Bibliographies

The WPA Historical Records Survey Project No. 10. *Checklist of Kansas Imprints 1854-1876.* Topeka: WPA, 1939.

This is an outstanding bibliography of materials printed in Kansas between 1854 and 1876, including pamphlets, broadsides, and books. It was created by the Work Projects Administration during the Depression. Citations to this bibliography are noted throughout this chapter as [CLKI].

Lorene Anderson Hawley and Alan W. Farley. *Kansas Imprints 1854-1876, A Supplement.* Topeka: Kansas State Historical Society, 1958.

This booklet adds sources missed in the *Checklist of Kansas Imprints.* Citations to this bibliography are noted throughout this article as [CLKI Supp.].

Prestatehood Accounts of Kansas Political Issues

William Alanson Howard and Mordecai Oliver. *Report of the Special Committee Appointed to Investigate the Troubles in Kansas: With the views of the Minority of said Committee.* H.R. Misc. Doc. No. 200. Washington, DC: C. Wendell, 1856. [BEAL 10795]

William A. Phillips. *The conquest of Kansas by Missouri and her allies: A history of the troubles in Kansas: From the passage of the Organic Act until the close of July, 1856.* Boston: Phillips, Sampson and Company, 1856.

John H. Gihon. *Geary and Kansas: Governor Geary's administration in Kansas, with a complete history of the territory until July 1857, embracing a full account of its discovery, geography, soil, rivers, climate, products, its organization as a territory, transactions and events under Governors Reeder and Shannon, political dissensions, personal rencountres, election frauds, battles and outrages, all fully authenticated.* Philadelphia: C.C. Rhodes, 1857.

John Gihon was Governor Geary's private secretary.

William P. Tomlinson. *Kansas in Eighteen Fifty-Eight: Being chiefly a history of the recent troubles in the Territory.* New York: H. Dayton, 1859.

H.J. Strickler. *Claims of the Citizens of the Territory of Kansas.* H.R. Misc. Doc. No. 43. (Report to the 35th Cong. 2nd Sess.) (1859).

Strickler was a commissioner sent by Congress to Kansas in 1857 to make cash compensation to Kansans whose property had been destroyed in the fighting between proslavery and Free-State forces in 1856.

Sources for Kansas Political and Legal History

William E. Connelley. *A Standard History of Kansas and Kansans* (Chicago: Lewis, 1918).

William J. Cutler. *A History of the State of Kansas* (Chicago: A. T. Andreas, 1883).

Virgil W. Dean. *The Law and Lawyers in Kansas History: A Collection of Papers Presented at the 116th Annual Meeting of the Kansas State Historical Society, October 4-5, 1991* (Topeka: Kansas State Historical Society, 1991).

M.H. Hoeflich. "Legal Fees in Nineteenth-Century Kansas." *U. Kan. L. Rev.* 48(2000): 991.

Robert A. Mead and M.H. Hoeflich. "Lawyers and Law Books in Nineteenth-Century Kansas." *U. Kan. L. Rev.* 50(2002): 1015.

R. Richmond, ed. *Requisite Learning and Good Moral Character: A History of the Kansas Bench and Bar* (Topeka: Kansas Bar Association, 1982).

Charles Robinson. *The Kansas Conflict* (New York: Harper & Bros., 1892).

Paul Wilson. *Musings of a Smiling Bull: Selected Essays, Articles and Speeches* (Lawrence: University of Kansas School of Law, 2000).

NOTES

1. *The Statutes of the Territory of Kansas; Passed at the First Session of the Legislative Assembly, One Thousand Eight Hundred and Fifty-Five. To Which are Affixed The Declaration of Independence, and the Constitution of the U. States, and the Act of Congress Organizing Said Territory, and other Acts of Congress Having Immediate Relation Thereto* iv (Shawnee M. L. School: John T. Brady, Public Printer, 1855) [hereinafter 1855 Statutes].

2. Act of March 26, 1804 (An Act erecting Louisiana into two territories, and providing for the temporary government thereof), Ch. 38, 2 *Stat.* 283 (1804).

3. Paul Wilson, "How the Law Came to Kansas," in *Musings of a Smiling Bull: Selected Essays, Articles, and Speeches* 78-79 (Lawrence: University of Kansas School of Law, 2000).

4. Ibid. at 79.

5. Act (Kansas-Nebraska Act) of May 30, 1854 (to organize the territories of Nebraska and Kansas), Ch. 59, 10 *Stat.* 277 (1854).

6. Act of March 6, 1820 (An Act to authorize the people of the Missouri territory to form a constitution and state government, and for the admission of such state into the Union on an equal footing with the original states, and to prohibit slavery in certain territories), Ch. 22, 13 *Stat.* 545 (1820).

7. Ibid.

8. Ibid.

9. Act (Kansas-Nebraska Act) of May 30, 1854 (to organize the territories of Nebraska and Kansas), Ch. 59, 10 *Stat.* 277 (1854).

10. Ibid. at § 14.

11. Charles Robinson, *The Kansas Conflict* 4 (New York: Harper & Bros., 1892).

12. Ibid. at 6.

13. Wilson, supra, note 3, at 95.

14. 1855 *Statutes,* supra, note 1, at vii.

15. Ibid.

16. Wilson, supra, note 3, at 95.

17. Francis H. Heller, *The Kansas State Constitution: A Reference Guide* 1 (Westport, CT: Greenwood Press, 1992).

18. Stephen B. Oates, *To Purge This Land With Blood: A Biography of John Brown* (New York: Harper & Row, 1970).

19. Heller, supra, note 17.

20. Ibid. at 2.

21. Ibid.

22. Act of May 4, 1858 (for the Admission of the State of Kansas into the Union), Ch. 26, 12 *Stat.* 269 (1858).

23. Ibid. at 271.

24. Article II, Section 1, Leavenworth Constitution, in *The Federal and State Constitutions, Colonial Charters, and Other Organic Laws of the States, Territories, and Colonies Now or Heretofore Forming the United States of America* (Vol. 2, p. 1225), Francis Newton Thorpe, ed. (Washington, DC: U.S. Government Printing Office, 1909).

25. An Act providing for the formation of a Constitution and State government for the State of Kansas, in *General Laws of the Territory of Kansas, passed at the Fifth Session of the Legislative Assembly; Begun at the City of Lecompton, on the 1st Monday of January, 1859, and held and concluded at the City of Lawrence* 292 (Lawrence, Kansas Territory: Herald of Freedom Steam Press, 1859).

26. William E. Connelley, *A Standard History of Kansas and Kansans* (Vol. 2, p. 227) (Chicago: A.T. Andreas, 1918).

27. Article 5, section 1 Wyandotte Constitution, in *The Federal and State Constitutions, Colonial Charters, and Other Organic Laws of the States, Territories, and Colonies Now or Heretofore Forming the United States of America* (Vol. 2, p. 1251), Francis Newton Thorpe, ed. (Washington, DC: U.S. Government Printing Office, 1909).

28. Leverett Wilson Spring, *Kansas: The Prelude to the War for the Union* 262 (Boston: Houghton, Mifflin and Co., 1885).

29. Heller, supra, note 17 at 9.

30. Connelly, supra, note 26.

31. Ibid.

32. William E. Unrau, *The Kansa Indians: A History of the Wind People* (Norman: University of Oklahoma Pres, 1971).

Chapter 18

Law in the Wilderness: An Annotated Bibliography of Legal Materials of Prestatehood Kentucky, 1774-1792

Kurt X. Metzmeier

INTRODUCTION

In its rapid rise amid the spoils of Indian wars and diplomacy to its admittance as the fifteenth state of the newly constituted United States of America in 1792, the territory of Kentucky did not create a weighty library of legal materials. Nonetheless, the spirited legal tradition begun in that short period would be the foundation of one of the more democratic and independent states of the early American republic.

The first legal documents in the history of Kentucky were the treaties with Native Americans, which legally secured the land for white settlement. Other important public law documents were the agreements between Virginia and other colonies and states to mark the new territory's borders, and the resolution by which Virginia ceded any claim to the area north of the Ohio to the new United States.

The most important legal texts of Kentucky's prestatehood period were the laws enacted by the general assembly of Virginia. Responding to the petitions of its citizens on the western frontier, the legislature passed laws establishing cities, creating new counties, establishing courts, providing for education, securing land, and arranging for elections. When the people of Kentucky wanted statehood, Virginia's legislature obligingly provided for it. It is true the governors of Virginia played a role in the state, but their activities left faint lines in the documentary history of the state. More important were the counties, whose unbroken record of ordinary affairs—land transfers, wills, and marriages—often continue up to today.

I would like to acknowledge my research assistant Yuexin Li for his able assistance.

The records of Virginia's courts are another source of Kentucky's legal history. Almost exclusively devoted to litigation over land claims, they nonetheless accurately depict the main business of law in the territory—ensuring the title to land for settlers and speculators alike. This attention to land title law continued into the early years of the state of Kentucky, until a debt crisis (partially the result of land speculation) made debtor-creditor law the leading issue.

The commonwealth of Kentucky came into being after ten conventions, four acts of the Virginia legislature, and the approval of the U.S. Congress. Once born, the state of Kentucky was not without laws. The Virginia Compact and 1799 constitution laid the foundation of the commonwealth, and the common law of Virginia remained to fill out the legal firmament. The new Kentucky legislature moved quickly to explain and clarify the governmental powers set out in the constitution and took steps toward creating a uniquely Kentuckian legal tradition by providing for the publication of its laws.

PUBLIC LAW

Among the earliest legal documents in the history of Kentucky were the treaties with Native Americans that cleared title to the rich lands of their former hunting grounds. In a series of treaties, the claims of Iroquois, Seneca, Cherokee, Mingoe, and Shawnee were legally extinguished under the norms of English law. Another legal foundation of Kentucky were the royal charters of Virginia and the Carolinas, which helped set its southern boundary. Finally, the papers related to Virginia's cession of its claim to the northwestern territory to the new United States are important legal texts in the state's history, as that action set Kentucky's northern boundary.

Treaties with Native Americans

A fabled crossroads in Native America long before the first white man scaled the Appalachian Mountains, Kentucky became a territory of Virginia through an unsavory mixture of land lust, devious diplomacy, and brutal war. The title to Kentucky's rich lands can be traced back to a series of treaties that also helped carve out its current borders.

Among the frictions that contributed to the American Revolution was the conflict between the push of white settlers into the trans-Appalachian frontier and the British crown's desire to keep the "civilized tribes" as allies. Prominent in Indian policy was the Iroquois Confederacy (also known as the Six Nations for its six constituent tribes). Primarily centered in the

American northeast, the Six Nations also had ceremonial suzerainty over more southern tribes in the Ohio Valley region, including the Shawnee.

The bane of royal Indian policymakers, such as Sir William Johnson, were the disruptive, demanding, and ultimately disloyal white settlers streaming into Indian lands. The first attempt to stem this tide was the Proclamation of 1763, which forbade settlement west of the crest of the Appalachian Mountains. However, the settlers ignored this barrier and continued to move into these lands. To accommodate them, in 1763, Johnson negotiated the Treaty of Fort Stanwix, in which the Six Nations ceded land south of the Susquehanna and Ohio Rivers. Unfortunately, the Six Nations had never inhabited the southernmost portion of the ceded area and only had nominal control of the tribes who did. The southern tribes refused to accept the accord and were particularly upset that they received little of the bribes and gifts that traditionally lubricated the treaty-making practices of the time. The Cherokees effectively renounced claim to the Ohio River region in the 1768 Treaty of Hard Labor and the 1770 Lochober Treaty with the Virginia colony, both of which purported to limit white settlement to territories above the Tennessee River.

However, the Shawnee, and their allies the Mingoes, continued to hold claim to the Ohio Valley region. Spurred by land speculators and hoping to divert the revolutionary fervor that would ultimately lead to the Declaration of Independence, in 1774, Virginia Governor Lord Dunmore ordered a force into the Kentucky region to attack Mingoe and Shawnee settlements on both sides of the Ohio. After some particularly bloody skirmishes, Dunmore's army defeated the Shawnee and their allies in the battle of Point Pleasant. In the resulting 1774 Treaty of Camp Charlotte, the Shawnee ceded its claims to Kentucky to the colony of Virginia. This effectively defeated any native title to Kentucky, at least within the narrow confines of English law. Lord Dunmore's gamble won Kentucky, but it failed to stem the tide toward revolution. The War of Independence that began two years later temporarily put the gain of these treaties in peril, but the victorious American republic (including the new commonwealth of Virginia) unhesitatingly accepted these territories as part of its patrimony.

The form of colonial Indian treaties requires some explanation. Early American Indian treaty making was less a case of closed negotiations over the details of a text, than a public event of ceremonial gift giving and open oral discussions involving multiple parties. The resulting English language treaty document (if there was one) was less important than the publicly announced agreements. The following documents range from fairly modern-looking signed accords to letters from negotiators that generally described the terms of the agreement.

Proclamation of 1763

The Royal Proclamation of 7 October 1763. In *New York and New Jersey Treaties, 1754-1775* 418-19. Barbara Graymont, ed. Volume 10 of *Early American Indian Documents: Treaties and Laws, 1607-1789.* Alden T. Vaughan, ed. Washington, DC: University Publications of America, 1979.

This document is taken from University Publications of America's *Early American Indian Documents.* This excellent collection, edited by Alden T. Vaughan, Professor Emeritus of Early American Civilization, Columbia University, fills a huge gap by bringing together a vast amount of material from various disparate sources. Previous treaty collections (including the U.S. Government Printing Office's *Indian Affairs: Laws and Treaties,* edited by Charles J. Kappler) had sparse coverage of treaties prior to the formation of the United States. In addition to formal treaties, the twenty-volume UPA set includes conference reports, council minutes, commissioners' reports, deeds of land sales, and letters and personal remembrances of treaty negotiations.

Treaty of Fort Stanwix, 1768

Deed of Fort Stanwix Boundary Line, 1768. In *New York and New Jersey Treaties, 1754-1775.* 566-69. Barbara Graymont, ed. Volume 10 of *Early American Indian Documents: Treaties and Laws, 1607-1789.* Alden T. Vaughan, ed. Washington, DC: University Publications of America, 1979.

Deed of Fort Stanwix Boundary Line, 1768. In E.B. O'Callaghan, ed. *The Documentary History of the State of New York.* Albany: Weed Parsons and Co., Public Printers, 1850.

This rare New York publication is, nonetheless, a valuable resource for the official papers of Sir William Johnson, whose activities as the architect of British Indian policy took place through his role as superintendent of Indian affairs, which was loosely associated with the New York colonial government.

Treaty of Hard Labor, 1768

Treaty of Hard Labor with Cherokees. In *Virginia Treaties, 1723-1775* 326-330. W. Stitt Robinson, ed. Volume 5 of *Early American Indian Documents: Treaties and Laws, 1607-1789.* Alden T. Vaughan, ed. Washington, DC: University Publications of America, 1979.

Treaty of Lochober

Journal of Proceedings at Treaty of Lochober. In *Virginia Treaties, 1723-1775* 360-71. W. Stitt Robinson, ed. Volume 5 of *Early American Indian Documents: Treaties and Laws, 1607-1789.* Alden T. Vaughan, ed. Washington, DC: University Publications of America, 1979.

Treaty of Camp Charlotte, 1774

Governor Dunmore to Dartmouth about Dunmore's War and Informal Treaty [at Camp Charlotte]. In *Virginia Treaties, 1723-1775* 379-381. W. Stitt Robinson, ed. Volume 5 of *Early American Indian Documents: Treaties and Laws, 1607-1789.* Alden T. Vaughan, ed. Washington, DC: University Publications of America, 1979.

Reuben Gold Thwaites and Louise Phelps Kellogg. *Documentary History of Dunmore's War, 1774: Compiled from the Draper Manuscripts in the Library of the Wisconsin Historical Society and Published at the Charge of the Wisconsin Society of the Sons of the American Revolution.* Madison: Wisconsin Historical Society, 1905.

Secondary Sources on Native Treaty Making

Clarence Walworth Alvord. *The Mississippi Valley in British Politics; A Study of the Trade, Land Speculation, and Experiments in Imperialism Culminating in the American Revolution.* Cleveland: The Arthur H. Clark Co., 1917.

Andrew R.L. Cayton, Fredrika J. Teute, and Omohundro Institute of Early American History and Culture. *Contact Points: American Frontiers from the Mohawk Valley to the Mississippi, 1750-1830.* Chapel Hill: University of North Carolina Press, 1998.

Jerry E. Clark. *The Shawnee.* Lexington: University Press of Kentucky, 1993.

R. Douglas Hurt. *The Ohio Frontier: Crucible of the Old Northwest, 1720-1830—A History of the Trans-Appalachian Frontier.* Bloomington: Indiana University Press, 1996.

Walter Harrison Mohr. *Federal Indian Relations, 1774-1788.* Philadelphia: University of Pennsylvania Press, 1933.

Francis Paul Prucha. *American Indian Treaties: The History of a Political Anomaly.* Berkeley: University of California Press, 1994.

Cessions to the United States

Virginia's Cession of Northwestern Territory to the United States

In 1781, the Virginia legislature conditionally ceded to the United States all right, title, and claim to lands northwest of the Ohio River so that the

> territory so ceded should be laid out and formed into states, containing a suitable extent of territory, not less than one hundred, nor more than one hundred and fifty miles square, or as near thereto as circumstances would admit; and that the states so formed should be distinct republican states, and admitted members of the federal union, having the same rights of sovereignty, freedom and independence as the other states. (11 *Hen* 566 [1782-1784])

In order to meet certain objections from the United States, Virginia passed a revised resolution in October 1783, and Congress adopted a report accepting the cession. On March 1, 1784, Virginia executed the deed of cession to its land claims north of the Ohio River.

Resolutions and State Papers: Cession of North Western Territory. 10 *Hen.* 547-567 (1779-1781).

Cession of North Western Territory. 11 *Hen.* 566-575 (1782-1784).

Agreements with Other States

The boundary line between the royal colonies of Virginia and Carolina was set by colonial charters at a parallel of latitude thirty-six degrees and thirty minutes north, and this became the basis of the southern boundary of the commonwealth of Kentucky. In 1779, both colonies agreed to a joint commission to survey this line, headed by Dr. Thomas Walker, but containing two members from each colony. However, the commission fell into disagreement early in the survey and the two Carolinians left the party. Walker and his fellow Virginian continued. Unfortunately, they drifted north of the line after the Tennessee River, thereby starting a controversy that would continue until 1820, when a compromise was brokered by the two states.

Charter of Carolina, 1663. In *Colonial Records of North Carolina* 20-33. William L. Saunders, ed. Raleigh: P.M. Hale, Printer to the State, 1886.

Charter of Carolina, 1663. In *North Carolina Charters and Constitutions, 1578-1698* 19-29. Mattie Erma Edwards Parker, ed. Raleigh: Carolina Charter Tercentenary Commission, 1963.

William K. Boyd. *Histories of the Dividing Line Betwixt Virginia and North Carolina*. Raleigh: North Carolina Historical Commission, 1929.

LEGISLATION

The legislature was the preeminent body of government in Virginia. The Virginia General Assembly, made up of a house of delegates and a senate, not only passed laws for the public good, but also passed private legislation to redress injuries and convey benefits. The legislature licensed ferries, established educational institutions, and permitted individuals the right to construct dams and mills. The assembly also granted divorces and statutorily righted defective wills and marriage licenses.

In the frontier, where traditional governmental authority was spread thin, the legislature was even more likely to take a strong role. In response to a steady stream of petitions from settlers (see the following), the Virginia General Assembly shaped counties, established cities, attempted to ensure land title, prepared for the region's eventual statehood, and organized elections, schools, and education.

Acts of Legislature

Hening

William Waller Hening, ed. *The statutes at large; being a collection of all the laws of Virginia, from the first session of the Legislature in the year 1619*. New York: Printed for the Editor, 1819-1823.

Hening's *Statutes at Large* is the quasi-official compilation of early Virginia session laws. A reprint edition was published for the Jamestown Foundation of the Commonwealth of Virginia by the University Press of Virginia

(Charlottesville, 1969). Volumes I-IV were reproduced from the second edition (Vols. I-II, New York, 1823; Vol. III, Philadelphia, 1823; and Vol. IV, Richmond, 1820). Volumes V-XIII were reproduced from the first edition.

Petitions

The petition was an integral part of the legislative process in eighteenth-century Virginia. Citizens were encouraged to use petitions to redress grievances and to propose legislation, and the Virginia legislature felt duty bound to give their requests careful consideration. Indeed, petitions were likely the greatest single source of legislative ideas. The use of petitions as an impetus to lawmaking made good sense as Virginia expanded into frontier areas where the settlers living there could best advise the legislature on how to govern these remote areas.

The three collections of printed petitions described in the following are in many ways the "legislative history" of the acts published in Hening's *Statutes at Large*.

Robertson

James Rood Robertson. *Petitions of the Early Inhabitants of Kentucky to the General Assembly of Virginia, 1769 to 1792*. [New York]: Arno Press, 1971; Louisville: John P. Morton and Company, 1914.

This book publishes petitions from the Kentucky territory of Virginia found in that state's archives by the author in the summer of 1910. They are reprinted verbatim (in chronological order), but the names of the petitioners have been separated and arranged alphabetically in a separate section. The editor has added footnotes that explain the context of the petition and that cite to Hening's *Statutes at Large* when he can identify a law that was a direct result of the petition.

Dorman

John Frederick Dorman. *Petitions from Kentucky to the Virginia Legislature, 1776 to 1791: A Supplement to Petitions of the Early Inhabitants of Kentucky to the General Assembly of Virginia, 1769 to 1792*. Easley, SC: Southern Historical Press, 1981.

This brief publication abstracts petitions from the Kentucky region that are not included in Robertson. A name index is appended, but there is no subject index.

Virginia Legislative Petitions

Randolph W. Church, ed. *Virginia Legislative Petitions: Bibliography, Calendar, and Abstracts from Original Sources, 6 May 1776–21 June 1782.* Richmond: Virginia State Library, 1984.

This collection covers all discoverable Virginia petitions. The full texts of the petitions are not published, but the abstracts are extensively annotated as to their legislative disposition.

Subject Index of Virginia Legislation Relating to Kentucky

What follows is a subject index to all public laws of Virginia that relate to the geographic region that became the Kentucky District of Virginia. I have deliberately omitted private legislation, defined as laws enacted purely for the purpose of remedying problems or for conveying specific benefits to individuals. Happily, this type of legislation has already been indexed in Joseph J. Casey, *Personal Names in Hening's Statutes at Large of Virginia, and Shepherd's Continuation* (Bridgewater, VA: The Green Bookman, 1933).

In cases involving a published petition to the Virginia legislature that can be ascertained to be relevant to a piece of legislation, a reference is given to the collection (see Robertson and Church, cited previously), petition number, and pages where it can be found.

Borders

"Resolutions and State Papers: Cession of North Western Territory." 10 *Hen.* 547-67 (1779-1781).

Cession of North Western Territory, 11 *Hen.* 566-75 (1782-1784).

Cities in General

An Act to Establish Several Towns, 13 *Hen.* 170-73 (Oct. 1790).

An Act Giving Further Time to Purchasers of Lots in Certain Towns to Build Theron, and for Other Purposes, 13 *Hen.* 179-80 (Oct. 1790).

An Act Authorising and Directing the Court of the County of Rockingham, to Levy a Sum of Money for the Purpose Therein Mentioned, 13 *Hen.* 545 (Oct. 1792).

Specific Cities

Bardstown:

An Act for Establishing a Town in the County of Nelson, 12 *Hen.* 718-20 (Oct. 1788).

Boonsborough:

An Act for Establishing the Town of Boonsborough, in the County of Kentuckey, 10 *Hen.* 134-36 (Oct. 1779).

See Robertson, Pet. No. 9, pp. 48-52; Church, Pet. No. 1030-P, p. 309.

Charlestown:

An Act to Establish a Town on the Lands of Ignatius Mitchell, in the County of Bourbon, 12 *Hen.* 608-09 (Oct. 1787).

See Robertson, Pet. No. 41, p. 100.

Georgetown:

An Act to Establish Several Towns [Georgetown], 13 *Hen.* 170 (Oct. 1790).

Harrodsburg:

An Act Directing the Sale of Lands in the Towns of Louisville and Harrodsburg, and for Other Purposes, 12 *Hen.* 395-96 (Oct. 1786).

An Act Granting Further Time to Possessors of Lots in the Towns of Clarksburg, Morgan's Town, Harrodsburg and Louisville, for Building Thereon, 13 *Hen.* 86 (Oct. 1789).

Henderson:

An Act for Establishing a Town in the County of Lincoln, 12 *Hen.* 223-25 (Oct. 1785).

See Robertson, Pet. No. 26, pp. 82-83.

Lexington:

An Act to Establish a Town at the Court-house in the County of Fayette, 11 *Hen.* 100-01 (May 1782).

See Robertson, Pet. No. 14, pp. 60-62; Church, Pet. No. 1446-P, p. 433; No. 1483-P, p. 446; No. 1525-P, p. 462.

An Act to Amend the Act Intituled An Act for Establishing a Town on the Lands of James Wilkinson in Fayette County, and a Ferry Across Kentucky River, 12 *Hen.* 597-98 (Oct. 1787).

An Act Empowering the Trustees of the Town of Lexington, in the County of Fayette, to Sell a Part of the Public Lot in the Said Town, for the Purpose of Erecting Thereon a House of Worship, 13 *Hen.* 85-86 (Oct. 1787).

An Act Concerning Certain Regulations in the Town of Lexington and County of Fayette, 13 *Hen.* 191-92 (Oct. 1790).

See Robertson, Pet. No. 76, pp. 143-44.

An Act Empowering the Trustees of the Town of Lexington, in the County of Fayette, to Sell a Part of the Public Lot in the Said Town, for the Purpose of Erecting Thereon a House of Worship, 13 *Hen.* 85 (Oct. 1789).

Louisville:

An Act for Establishing the Town of Louisville at the Falls of the Ohio, and One Other Town in the County of Rockingham, 10 *Hen.* 293-95 (May 1780).

See Robertson, Pet. No. 11, pp. 53-55; Church, Pet. Nos. 1198-P, p. 358 and 1252-P, p. 373.

An Act for Repealing in Part the Act for Establishing the Town of Louisville, 11 *Hen.* 321-22 (Oct. 1783).

See Robertson, Pet. No. 19, pp. 72-73.

An Act to Amend and Explain an Act Intituled An Act for Repealing in Part the Act for Establishing the Town of Louisville, 11 *Hen.* 474-75 (Oct. 1784).

An Act to Establish a Town on the Lands of John Campbell, in the County of Jefferson, 12 *Hen.* 225-26 (Oct. 1785).

An Act Giving Further Time to Purchasers of Lots in the Town of Louisville to Build Thereon, 12 *Hen.* 372-73 (Oct. 1786).

An Act Directing the Sale of Lands in the Towns of Louisville and Harrodsburg, and for Other Purposes, 12 *Hen.* 395-96 (Oct. 1786).

See Robertson, Pet. No. 36, pp. 93-94.

An Act Granting Further Time to the Possessors of Lots in the Town of Clarksburg, Morgan's Town, Harrodsburg and Louisville, for Building Thereon, 13 *Hen.* 86 (Oct. 1789).

An Act for Appointing Trustees to the Town of Romney, in the County of Hampshire, and for Adding Trustees to the Town of Louisville, in the County of Jefferson, 13 *Hen.* 90-91 (Oct. 1789).

See Robertson, Pet. No. 68, pp. 133-34.

An Act to Explain and Amend the Several Acts of Assembly Concerning the Town of Louisville, in the County of Jefferson, and for Other Purposes, 13 *Hen.* 148 (Oct. 1790).

An Act Giving Further Time to the Purchasers of Lots in the Town of Warminster to Build Thereon, and for other purposes, 13 *Hen.* 299 (Oct. 1791).

Maysville:

An Act to Establish a Town in the County of Bourbon, 12 *Hen.* 633-34.

See Robertson, Pet. No. 87, pp. 155-56.

Mitford:

An Act to Establish a Town in Each of the Counties of Madison [Mitford], Albemarle and Bourbon, 13 *Hen.* 87-88 (Oct. 1789).

See Robertson, Pet. No. 62, pp. 127-28.

Paris: (Hopewell)

An Act to Establish a Town in the County of Bourbon, 12 *Hen.* 363-64 (Oct. 1787).

See Robertson, Pet. No. 34, pp. 91-92; No. 87, pp. 155-56.

An Act to Establish a Town in Each of the Counties of Madison, Albermarle and Bourbon, 13 *Hen.* 87-88 (Oct. 1789).

An Act to Amend An Act which Establishes a Town of Hopewell in the County of Bourbon, 13 *Hen.* 176-77 (Oct. 1790).

See Robertson, Pet. No. 80, pp. 147-48.

An Act to Amend an Act, Intitled An Act for Establishing a Town in the County of Bourbon, 13 *Hen.* 182-83 (Oct. 1790).

Washington:

An Act to Establish a Town in the County of Bourbon, 12 *Hen.* 361-62.

See Roberston, Pet. No. 34, pp. 91-92.

An Act to Amend an Act, Intitled An Act for Establishing a Town in the County of Bourbon, 13 *Hen.* 182-83 (Oct. 1790).

Counties

An Act for Dividing the County and Parish of Augusta, and for Adding Certain Islands, in the Fluvanna River to the Counties of Albemarle and Amherst, 8 *Hen.* 395-98 (Nov. 1769).

An Act for Dividing the County Botetourt into Two Distinct Counties, 8 *Hen.* 600-01 (Feb. 1769).

An Act for Dividing the County of Fincastle into Three Distinct Counties and the Parish of Botetourt into Four Distinct Parishes, 9 *Hen.* 257-61 (Oct. 1776).

See Robertson, Pet. No. 3, pp. 38-41; Church, Pet. No. 116-P, pp. 34-35.

An Act for Establishing Three New Counties upon the Western Waters [Jefferson, Fayette, and Lincoln], 10 *Hen.* 315-17 (May 1780).

See Robertson, Pet. No. 12, pp. 55-57; Church, Pet. No. 1253-P, p. 374.

An Act for Dividing the County of Jefferson into Two Distinct Counties, 11 *Hen.* 469-70 (Oct. 1784).

An Act for Dividing the County of Lincoln into Three Distinct Counties [Mercer and Madison], 12 *Hen.* 118-20 (Oct. 1785).

See Robertson, Pet. No. 27, pp. 84-85.

An Act for Dividing the County of Fayette, 12 *Hen.* 89-91 (Oct. 1785).
See Robertson, Pet. No. 28, pp. 85-86.

An Act for Dividing the County of Bourbon, 12 *Hen.* 658-59 (Oct. 1788).
See Robertson, Pet. No. 54, pp. 117-119.

An Act for Dividing the County of Fayette into Two Distinct Counties, 12
Hen. 663-65 (Oct. 1788).
See Robertson, Pet. No. 28, pp. 85-86; No. 52, 114-16.

Courts

An Act for the Better Support of the Supreme Court in the Kentucky District, 11 *Hen.* 397-98 (May 1784).

An Act to Amend the Act for the Better Support of the Supreme Court in the
Kentucky District, 11 *Hen.* 498-99 (Oct. 1784).

An Act for Establishing a District Court on the Western Waters, 11 *Hen.* 85-
90 (May 1782).
See Robertson, Pet. No. 15, pp. 62-66; No. 16, pp. 66-68.

An Act to Authorize and Confirm Marriages in Certain Cases, 11 *Hen.* 281-
82 (May 1783).
See Robertson, Pet. No. 17, pp. 68-69; Church, Pet. No. 1646-P, p. 493.

An Act to Amend the Act, Intituled An Act for Reforming the County
Courts, and for other Purposes, 12 *Hen.* 467-74 (Oct. 1787).

An Act to Amend an Act for Establishing a District Court on the Western
Waters, 12 *Hen.* 475-78 (Oct. 1787).

An Act Prescribing the Method of Proving Certain Wills, 12 *Hen.* 502-04
(Oct. 1787).

An Act for Further Amending an Act Intitled an Act for Establishing a District Court on the Western Waters, 12 *Hen.* 704-05 (Oct. 1788).
See Robertson, Pet. No. 39, pp. 97-98.

An Act for Further Amending the Act Establishing a Supreme Court in the
Kentuckey District, 13 *Hen.* 66-69 (Oct. 1789).

See Robertson, Pet. No. 69, pp. 134-36.

An Act Concerning the Clerks Within the District of Kentucky, 13 *Hen.* 313-14 (Oct. 1791).

See Robertson, Pet. No. 96, pp. 169-76.

Education

An Act to Cest Escheated Lands in the County of Kentucky in Trustees for a Public School, 10 *Hen.* 287-88 (May 1780).

See Robertson, Pet. No. 18, pp. 69-71.

An Act Concerning the Trustees of the Transylvania Seminary, 13 *Hen.* 147 (Oct. 1790).

See Robertson, Pet. No. 91, pp. 161-62.

An Act Authorizing Several Lotteries, and the Sale of Certain Lots in the Town of Portsmouth, 13 *Hen.* 173-75 (Oct. 1790).

See Robertson, Pet. No. 90, pp. 160-61.

An Act to Amend an Act, Intitled An Act Appropriating One Sixth Part of the Surveyor's Fees in the District of Kentuckey, to the use of the Transylvania Seminary, and for other Purposes, 13 *Hen.* 180-82 (Oct. 1790).

See Robertson, Pet. No. 18, pp. 69-71.

Elections

An Act for Confirming the Kentucky Election, 9 *Hen.* 316-17 (May 1777).

Land

An Act to Vest Certain Lands on the Ohio and Green Rivers, in Fee Simple in Richard Henderson, and Company, and Heirs, 9 *Hen.* 571-72 (Oct 1778).

See Church, Pet. No. 97-M, pp. 27-29.

An Act for Adjusting and Settling the Titles of Claimers to Unpatented Lands under the Present and Former Government, Previous to the Establishment of the Commonwealth's Land Office, 10 *Hen.* 35-50 (May 1779).

See Robertson, Pet. No. 8, pp. 45-49.

An Act for Establishing a Land Office, and Ascertaining the Terms and Manner of Granting Waste and Unappropriated Lands, 10 *Hen.* 50-65 (May 1779).

See Robertson, Pet. No. 8, pp. 45-49; Church, Pet. No. 1011-P, p. 303.

An Act for Explaining and Amending an Act Entitled An Act for Adjusting and Settling the Titles of Claimers to Unpatented Lands under the Present and Former Government, Previous to the Establishment of the Commonwealth's Land Office, 10 *Hen.* 177-80 (Oct. 1779).

See Church, Pet. No. 1167-P, p. 346.

An Act for the Relief of Certain Persons Now Residing on the Western Frontier, 10 *Hen.* 431-32 (May 1781).

An Act to Amend the Act Entitled An Act for Adjusting and Settling the Titles of Claimers to Unpatented Lands Under the Present and Former Government, Previous to the Establishment of the Commonwealth's Land Office, 10 *Hen.* 436-37 (May 1781).

See Robertson, Pet. No. 8, pp. 45-49; Church, Pet. No. 1011-P, p. 303.

An Act to Empower the Register of the Land Office to Appoint a Deputy on the Western Waters, 10 *Hen.* 445 (Nov. 1781).

An Act to Suspend the Sale of Certain Escheated Lands Late the Property of John Connolly, 11 *Hen.* 276-77 (May 1783).

An Act to Give Further Time for the Probation of Deeds and Other Instruments of Writing, and for Other Purposes, 11 *Hen.* 294-95 (May 1783).

See Robertson, Pet. No. 23, pp. 76-77.

An Act to Continue and Amend an Act Intituled An Act for the Relief of Certain Persons Now Resident on the Western Frontier, 11 *Hen.* 296 (May 1783).

An Act for the Preservation of the Entries Made for Lands in the District of Kentucky, 12 *Hen.* 509-10 (Oct. 1787).

An Act Providing Record Books for Transcribing Certain Entries for Land, Within the District of Kentuckey, 13 *Hen.* 45-46 (Oct. 1789).

An Act Authorizing the Court of Bourbon County to Admit the Recording of Deeds in Certain Cases, 13 *Hen.* 150 (Oct. 1789).

An Act Giving Further Time to the Commissioners Appointed for Surveying and Apportioning the Lands Granted to the Illinois Regiment, to Execute Deeds for the Same, 13 *Hen.* 178-79 (Oct. 1789).

See Robertson, Pet. No. 83, pp. 151-52.

An Act Giving Further Time to the Owners of Entries on the Western Waters to Survey the Same, 13 *Hen.* 120-21 (Oct. 1789).

See Robertson, Pet. No. 92, pp. 162-63.

An Act for the Relief of Persons Owning Surveys Returned to the Register's Office, on Which No Patents Can Issue in Consequence of the Erection of Kentucky into an Independent State, 13 *Hen.* 526-27 (Oct. 1792).

See Robertson, Pet. No. 93, pp. 164-65.

Marriage

An Act to Authorize and Confirm Marriages in Certain Cases, 11 *Hen.* 281-82 (May 1783).

See Robertson, Pet. No. 17, pp. 68-69; Church, Pet. No. 1646-P, p. 493.

Militia

An Act to Authorize and Direct the Commanding Officers of Certain Counties Within the District of Kentuckey, to Order Out Guards for Certain Purposes, 13 *Hen.* 202 (Oct. 1790).

Slavery

An Act Concerning the Importation of Slaves, into the District of Kentucky, 12 *Hen.* 713-14 (Oct. 1788).

See Robertson, Pet. No. 61, pp. 125-27.

Statehood

An Act Concerning the Erection of the District of Kentucky, into an Independent State, 12 *Hen.* 37-40 (Oct. 1785).

See Robertson, Pet. No. 25, pp. 79-82.

An Act Making Further Provision for the Erection of the District of Kentuckey into an Independent State, 12 *Hen.* 240-43 (Oct. 1786).

See Robertson, Pet. No. 58, pp. 121-22.

An Act Concerning the Erection of the District of Kentucky into an Independent State, 12 *Hen.* 788-91 (Oct. 1788).

See Robertson, Pet. No. 58, pp. 121-22.

An Act Concerning the Erection of the District of Kentuckey into an Independent State. 13 *Hen.* 17-21 (Oct. 1789).

See Robertson, Pet. No. 73, pp. 140-141.

Tobacco

An Act to Enable the Citizens of this Commonwealth to Discharge Certain Taxes, by the Payment of Tobacco, 12 *Hen.* 258-60 (Oct. 1786).

See Robertson, Pet. No. 43, pp. 102-03.

An Act for Establishing Several New Inspections of Tobacco, and Reviving and Establishing Others, 12 *Hen.* 580-82 (Oct. 1787).

See Robertson, Pet. No. 40, pp. 98-99.

An Act to Establishing an Inspection of Tobacco in the County of Woodford, 13 *Hen.* 272 (Oct. 1791).

See Robertson, Pet. No. 99, pp. 171-72.

Transportation

An Act for Marking and Opening a Road over the Cumberland Mountains into the County of Kentucky, 10 *Hen.* 143-44 (Oct. 1779).

An Act for Establishing Several New Ferries, and for Other Purposes [Kentucky River at Boonsborough], 10 *Hen.* 196-97 (Oct. 1779).

See Robertson, Pet. No. 10, pp. 53; No. 29, pp. 87-88.

An Act to Empower the County Courts in the District of Kentucky, to Establish Ferries Within the Same, 12 *Hen.* 500 (Oct. 1787).

An Act Removing Obstructions from the Road Leading Through the Wilderness to Kentuckey, 13 *Hen.* 184-85 (Oct. 1790).

An Act to Empower the Justices of Greenbrier and Kanhaway, to Levy a Tax on the Tithables Within Their Respective Counties, Sufficient to Repair the State Road Leading from Lewisburg, to the Falls of the Great Kanhaway, 13 *Hen.* 186-87 (Oct. 1790).

See Robertson, Pet. No. 19, pp. 72-73.

EXECUTIVE AND ADMINISTRATIVE RECORDS

In contrast to the output generated by the legislature, there are few useful legal records extant from the executive and administrative branches of government. In this early period, governors treated their papers as private property and any preservation of these documents was up to the former governors' heirs. The executive branch—as opposed to the person of the governor—generated few documents. Regulatory activities took place at the county level or by way of legislative commission. For these reasons, the best source for routine government activities, such as the registration of land, is either in the published reports of these commissions or in compilations of county court records.

State and Governors' Papers

Colonial Virginia

Governors' Papers: The only colonial governor of Virginia of any relevance to Kentucky's prestatehood period (at least that period when there was any appreciable white settlement of the area) was Lord Dunmore. Unfortunately, there are no published collections of Dunmore papers (outside of the collection relating to his war against the Shawnee described earlier), and no modern biography to serve as a guide to letters, manuscripts, and other archival resources.

State Papers: Virginia Colonial Records Project: The Virginia Colonial Records Project (VCRP) was established in the 1950s by the Virginia Historical Society, the Colonial Williamsburg Foundation, the University of Virginia Library, and Library of Virginia "to reconstitute the archive of Virginia's colonial history—a documentary record decimated by war and fire during the Old Dominion's first three centuries." The VCRP is responsible for the following resources:

Virginia Colonial Records Project Database at the Library of Virginia Web site <http://www.lva.lib.va.us/>.

A searchable online index to nearly 15,000 reports that survey and describe documents relating to colonial Virginia. Gives references to microfilm resources or, in limited cases, to online materials in the Virginia Digital Library.

Key to Survey Reports and Microfilm of the Virginia Colonial Records Project. Richmond: Library of Virginia, 1990.

The British Public Record Office: History, Description, Record Groups, Finding Aids, and Materials for American History, With Special Reference to Virginia. Richmond: Library of Virginia, 1960, 1974, 1984.

Commonwealth of Virginia

Governors' Papers: Excepting two acting governors with terms of a week or less, there were seven Virginia governors of the Commonwealth of Virginia in office during the period when Kentucky was a district of Virginia: Patrick Henry (1776-1779 and 1784-1786); Thomas Jefferson (1779-1781); Thomas Nelson Jr. (1781); Benjamin Harrison (1781-1784); Edmund Randolph (1786-1788); Beverley Randolph (1788-1791); and Henry Lee (1791-1794). Significant collections of papers of four of these governors have been published:

William W. Henry. *Patrick Henry: Life, Correspondence and Speeches.* New York: Charles Scribner's Sons, 1891.

Papers of Thomas Jefferson. Julian P. Boyd et al., eds. Princeton, NJ: Princeton University Press, 1950-.

Sixty volumes are planned; twenty-eight are complete. Where Boyd has not yet published a document, consult *Writings of Thomas Jefferson: Memorial Edition,* A.A. Lipscomb and A.E. Bergh, eds. (Washington, DC: 1903-1904).

Letters of Thomas Nelson, Jr., Governor of Virginia. Richmond: Virginia Historical Society, 1874.

Moncure D. Convay. *Omitted Chapters of History: Life and Papers of Edmund Randolph.* New York and London: G.P. Putnam's Sons, 1888; New York: Da Capo Press, 1971.

State Papers:

William P. Palmer, Sherwin McRae, Raleigh Edward Colston, and Henry W. Flournoy, eds. *Calendar of Virginia state papers and other manuscripts, 1652-1869.* Richmond: [s.n.], 1875.

The first five volumes of this eleven-volume set describe papers in the state archives that are relevant to the period when Kentucky was a territory of Virginia.

Land Records

The Virginia Compact (the legislation regulating the transition of power from Virginia to the state of Kentucky) transferred all land records to the new state. Most state records went to the new capitol, Frankfort, while Virginia county land records remained in county courthouses. Most original deeds and records have migrated to the state archives. Over the years, historians and genealogists have mined them for research purposes, publishing many excellent guides and indexes.

Samuel M. Wilson. *Kentucky Land Warrants for the French, Indian and Revolutionary Wars.* Greenville, SC: Southern Historical Press, 1994.

Willard Rouse Jillson. *Old Kentucky Entries and Deeds: A Complete Index to All of the Earliest Land Entries, Military Warrants, Deeds and Wills of the Commonwealth of Kentucky.* Louisville: The Standard Printing Company Incorporated, 1926; repr. Baltimore: Genealogical Pub. Co., 1987.

Willard Rouse Jillson. *The Kentucky Land Grants: A Systematic Index to All of the Land Grants Recorded in the State Land Office at Frankfort, Kentucky, 1782-1924.* Baltimore: Genealogical Pub. Co., 1971.

In these three works by historians Wilson and Jillson, most, if not all, of the extant Kentucky land records are thoroughly abstracted and indexed.

County Records

The custody of all county records was transferred to Kentucky under the legislation regulating the transition of power from Virginia to the new state of Kentucky, although in most cases the actual records never moved. These records included deed books, will books, minute books, and other records of the county courts. In recent years, the original copies of these records have been moved to the state archives for safe keeping, at least those that have survived the frequent courthouse fires and civil disturbances that have robbed historians of many Kentucky documents. A few collections have been published (see the following), but most can be researched only at the Kentucky Department of Libraries and Archives <http://www.kdla.ky.gov>, or at the local courthouses where they originated. A good guide to researching county records is Roseann Reinmuth Hogan, *Kentucky Ancestry: A Guide to Genealogical and Historical Research* (Salt Lake City, UT: Ancestry, 1992).

"First Census" of Kentucky, 1790. Charles B. Heinemann, ed. Greenville, SC: Southern Historical Press, 1994.

Despite the title, this work compiles prestatehood tax lists from Bourbon, Fayette, Jefferson, Lincoln, Madison, Mason, Mercer, Nelson, and Woodford County records.

REPORTS OF COURT

The decisions of courts of law are the core documents of a common law jurisdiction. However, the existence of such decisions assumes open and regularly sitting courts and an established judiciary. These were luxuries that Kentucky pioneers did not have. For much of the prestatehood era, the only courts open to litigants were hundreds of miles away to the east. As a result, the names of few Kentuckians grace the reports of Virginia appellate courts. When courts were created in Kentucky, they still had to deal with far-flung litigants, who were often detained in the defense of their community or by the necessities of a hardscrabble existence. When courts could sit, their primary work was in adjudicating the myriad land claims brought about by rightful claimants, hopeful squatters, and professional speculators.

Virginia Reports

Daniel Call, *Reports of Cases Argued and Adjudged in the Court of Appeals of Virginia.* Richmond: Robert I. Smith, 1833.

In the fourth volume of *Call's Reports,* Call went back and published omitted cases from the first court of appeals of Virginia, 1779-1795. Although only one case is readily identifiable as related to the territory that was to become Kentucky (Case of the Loyal and Greenbrier Companies, 4 *McCall* 21 [1783]), many of the land cases are relevant. There is an index.

Bushrod Washington. *Reports of cases argued and determined in the Court of Appeals of Virginia.* Philadelphia: A. Small, 1823.

The first volume of Washington's two slim volumes of reports covers the very end of the territorial period (1791-1794). No cases are readily identifiable as involving Kentucky or Kentuckians.

William Brockenbrough and Judge Holmes. *A Collection of Cases Decided by the General Court of Virginia, Chiefly Relating to the Penal Laws of the Commonwealth: Copied from the Records of said Court, with Explanatory Notes.* Richmond: J.W. Randolph, 1853.

The first cases of this collection of criminal cases cover the territorial period, although none can be identified as arising in Kentucky.

Virginia Land Commission

More legislation and litigation in the Kentucky District of Virginia concerned land than any other topic. A profusion of land claims combined with complicated land registration laws and poor surveying practices to create a situation where few land titles were secure. In 1779, the Virginia legislature attempted to settle Kentucky land titles by creating a land court within the district (10 *Hen.* 35 [1779]). Four commissioners were named and the court was in session in various locations from October 1779 to April 1780. Over 1,300 claims were settled and issued "certificates" of title. The business of the court was collected in a book known as the "certificate book," which was long held in the Fayette County Courthouse.

One reason for the confusion was the complicated Virginia land law. At least four steps were involved in the process. First, a warrant was issued granting the holder the right to stake a claim. Virginia governors had liberally granted free warrants to veterans of the French and Indian War and the independence struggle. In addition, settlers without titles could apply for preemption warrants. However, all a warrant did was give the holder the right to make an entry, which was the second step in the process. Once the holder had taken possession, step three was to survey the land. Many of these surveys were poorly done and poorly marked. The fourth step was to return the survey to the land office, where a patent of title was issued. Unfortunately, the great distances between these remote parcels of land and the land offices often delayed this final step, allowing other persons to register the land. The result was that litigation over land titles would continue long after the land commission closed its business. (See the discussion of James Hughes, *Reports of the Supreme Court for the District of Kentucky,* found in the following.)

Virginia Land Commission, Certificate Book of the Virginia Land Commission, 1779-1780. Easley, SC: Southern Historical Press, 1981.

This work, edited by lawyer-historian Samuel M. Wilson, reprints the text of the "certificate book" of the land court. Wilson's brief introduction is a good overview of the commission's work, but his published address to the annual meeting of the Kentucky State Bar Association is far more detailed and useful. Samuel M. Wilson, "The First Land Court of Kentucky," *Proc. Ky. St. Bar Assoc.* 22(1923): 226-85.

Reports of the Supreme Court for the District of Kentucky

James Hughes. *A Report on the Causes, Determined by the Late Supreme Court for the District of Kentucky, and by the Court of Appeals, in which the Titles to Land Were in Dispute.* Lexington: Printed by John Bradford, 1803.

The first volume of *Kentucky Reports,* Hughes' reports cover the activity of the Supreme Court of the District of Kentucky, 1785-1792. The volume also reports the early land cases of the court of appeals of the new state of Kentucky (1793-1801), many of which were filed prior to statehood. Hughes was a prominent land title attorney and all of the reported cases concern title litigation.

There is only the single volume; according to Martin D. Hardin's introduction to his own set of reports, Hughes lost "several hundred dollars" in the endeavor (3 Ky. [Hard.] iii [1810]). *Hughes' Reports* has a table of cases, a syllabus of cases, and an index. Several of the cases include plats of the properties being discussed.

Michael L. Cox. *Virginia Supreme Court, District of Kentucky Order Books.* Evansville, IN: Cook Publications, 1988.

This genealogical press book abstracts and indexes the order books of the Supreme Court for the District of Kentucky. This book is based on two ledger books in the Kentucky State Archives (http://www.kdla.ky.gov) that record the activity of the court over a period from 1783 to 1792. According to the archives' summary, the records "detail court actions" and entries include the "names of judges, grand jurors, trial jurors, and litigants; brief narrative accounts of cases; and court orders." The archives has two other collections related to the court: one file is a collection of rule docket and office judgments (1785-1792), and another collection is of judgment orders directed to sheriffs and other county officials.

STATEHOOD

The new state of Kentucky came into being after ten conventions and a period of fervent debate over Kentucky's place in the newly formed United States. The road to statehood began in 1784 with the first constitutional convention in Danville. That convention, similar to others that would follow, was sparsely attended due to Indian troubles and ended with a call for another convention. The first concrete step toward statehood was taken in the third convention, in 1785, which petitioned Virginia for separation. In response Virginia passed the first of four acts providing for separation. After the fourth convention asked Virginia for changes to its act of separation (which Virginia accepted), the fifth convention, in 1787, resolved to separate and petitioned the U.S. Confederation Congress for statehood. This measure was tabled during the campaign for ratification of the new U.S. Constitution. The seventh and eighth conventions renewed their call to the United States and Virginia. Virginia responded with its final separation act, the Virginia Compact. The ninth convention accepted the compact in 1791, and in 1792 the tenth convention drafted the constitution of the new state. In the third session of the first U.S. Congress, Kentucky was admitted as the fifteenth state in the union. The act set June 1, 1792, as the official day of admission.

Constitution of 1792

Text of 1792 Constitution

Text of Kentucky Constitutions of 1792, 1799 and 1850, Info. Bull. No. 41. Frankfort: Legislative Research Commission, 1965.

Journals

Journal of the First Constitutional Convention of Kentucky, Held in Danville, Kentucky, April 2 to 19, 1792. Lexington: State Bar Association of Kentucky, 1942.

Secondary Sources

Lowell H. Harrison. *Kentucky's Road to Statehood.* Lexington: University Press of Kentucky, 1992.

Lowell H. Harrison's monograph carefully examines the ten conventions that led to statehood and the first constitution, placing the controversy over

James Wilkinson's alleged conspiracy to separate Kentucky from the United States and ally it with Spain into its proper significance. For a briefer survey of the ten statehood conventions, see also George L. Willis Sr., *Kentucky Constitutions & Constitutional Conventions: A Hundred and Fifty Years of State Politics and Organic-Law Making, 1784-1933* ([Frankfort: The State Journal Company], 1930).

Patricia Watlington. *The Partisan Spirit; Kentucky Politics, 1779-1792.* New York: Atheneum, 1972.

This is an excellent political history of the prestatehood period and the issues animating the drive for separation from Virginia.

Virginia Compact

The "Virginia Compact" is the traditional name for the act regulating the creation of the state of Kentucky and the transition of governments (An Act Concerning the Erection of the District of Kentuckey into an Independent State, 13 *Hen.* 17-21 [Oct. 1789]). It was incorporated by reference in the first constitution of Kentucky and can be found in the historical documents section of both official editions of the *Kentucky Revised Statutes.*

Kentucky's Admission into the United States

An Act Declaring the Consent of Congress That a New State Be Formed within the Jurisdiction of the Commonwealth of Virginia, and Admitted into This Union by the Name of Kentucky, 1 *Stat.* 189 (Feb. 4, 1791).

THE NEW STATE

The state of Kentucky was not born without laws. The new constitution carried over the common law as it had existed within Virginia. The Virginia Compact also provided that some of the statutory laws in effect in Virginia would have a continuing effect in the state, at least until the legislature of the new state decided to repeal them.

Nonetheless, the new Kentucky legislature moved quickly in its first three sessions to establish revenue measures, provide for elections, establish courts, and to flesh out the powers and duties of the offices provided for in its constitution. In the first session of its second meeting, it took the first step toward providing for the regular publication of its own laws.

Sources of Law: Common Law

The new state of Kentucky carried on the common law tradition of Virginia. Article VIII, Section 6, of the 1792 Constitution of Kentucky declared, "All laws now in force in the State of Virginia, not inconsistent with this Constitution, which are of a general nature, and not local to the eastern part of that State, shall be in force in this State until they shall be altered or repealed by the Legislature." As the Virginia Constitutional Convention of 1776 had averred that "the common law of England, all statutes or acts parliament made in aid of the common law prior to the fourth year of the reign of King James I [1607], and not local to that kingdom ... shall be considered in full force" until changed by the Virginia legislature, that English legal tradition was also inherited by Kentucky. C. S. Morehead and Mason Brown, *Digest of The Statute Law of Kentucky,* Vol. 1, 612 (Frankfort: A.G. Hodges, 1834); *Ray v. Sweeney,* 77 Ky. 1 (1878). See also Lyman Chalkley, "The Sources, Progress and Printed Evidences of the Written Law in Kentucky," *Ky. L. J.* 12(1924): 43; *Ky. L. J.* 12(1924): 131; and *Ky. L. J.* 13 (1925): 133.

William Littell, in his *Statute Law of Kentucky,* the first statutory compilation in Kentucky, attempted to reference some of the English and Virginia statutes and legal precedents. In a appendix to the second volume of his work, he collected and reprinted the more important of these laws.

A Collection of All the Acts of Parliament and Acts of Virginia, of a General Nature, Which Remain in Force in the State of Kentucky. In William Littell, *The Statute Law of Kentucky; with Notes, Prælections, and Observations on the Public Acts; Comprehending Also, the Laws of Virginia and Acts of Parliament in Force in this Commonwealth; the Charter of Virginia, the Federal and State constitutions, and so Much of the King of England's Proclamation in 1763, as Relates to the Titles to Land in Kentucky; Together with a Table of Reference to the Cases Adjudicated in the Court of Appeals* (Vol. 2, pp. 494-584). Frankfort: Printed by and for William Hunter, 1809-1819.

Sources of Law: Establishing Acts of the Legislature

Kentucky Acts

Acts Passed at the First Session of the General Assembly, for the Commonwealth of Kentucky; Begun and Held at the Town of Lexington, on Monday, the Fourth of June in the Year of Our Lord, One Thousand Seven

Hundred and Ninety-Two. Lexington: Printed by John Bradford, Printer to the Commonwealth, 1792.

An Act Regulating the Annual Election, 1792 (June), Ky. Acts Ch. 4, pp. 5-7.

An Act for the Election of Representatives, Pursuant to the Constitution of the United States, 1792 (June), Ky. Acts Ch. 5, pp. 7-9.

An Act Establishing a Permanent Revenue, 1792 (June), Ky. Acts Ch. 6, pp. 9-15.

An Act for the Appointment of Electors to Choose a President of the United States, 1792 (June), Ky. Acts Ch. 7, pp. 15-17.

An Act for Establishing a Land Office, 1792 (June), Ky. Acts Ch. 11, p. 19.

An Act Concerning Sheriffs, 1792 (June), Ky. Acts Ch. 16, pp. 22-25.

An Act for Regulating the Militia of This Commonwealth, 1792 (June), Ky. Acts Ch. 5, pp. 7-9.

An Act Concerning the Treasury, 1792 (June), Ky. Acts Ch. 24, pp. 33-34.

An Act Concerning County Courts, Courts of Quarter-Session, and a Court of Oyer and Terminer, 1792 (June), Ky. Acts Ch. 35, pp. 40-46.

An Act Establishing the Court of Appeals, 1792 (June), Ky. Acts Ch. 36, pp. 46-51.

Acts Passed at the Second Session of the General Assembly, for the Commonwealth of Kentucky; Begun and Held at the Town of Lexington, on Monday, the Fifth of November in the Year of Our Lord, One Thousand Seven Hundred and Ninety-Two. Lexington: Printed by John Bradford, Printer to the Commonwealth, 1792.

An Act to Amend the Act Entitled An Act Concerning County Courts, Courts of Quarter-Session, and a Court of Oyer and Terminer, 1792 (Nov.), Ky. Acts Ch. 1, pp. 3-4.

An Act to Regulate and Discipline the Militia of This Commonwealth, and for Other Purposes, 1792 (Nov.), Ky. Acts Ch. 5, pp. 5-15.

An Act to Amend an Act for Establishing a Land Office, 1792 (Nov.), Ky. Acts Ch. 7, pp. 15-16.

An Act Prescribing the Duties of Constables and Regulating Their Fees, 1792 (Nov.), Ky. Acts Ch. 9, pp. 17-18.

An Act Prescribing the Duties of the Attorney General, 1792 (Nov.), Ky. Acts Ch. 11, p. 19.

An Act Prescribing the Mode of Proceeding in Cases of Impeachment, 1792 (Nov.), Ky. Acts Ch. 24, pp. 29-30.

An Act to Amend an Act Concerning Elections, 1792 (Nov.), Ky. Acts Ch. 24, pp. 32-35.

An Act Concerning [County Court] Clerks, 1792 (Nov.), Ky. Acts Ch. 50, pp. 50-51.

An Act to Provide for the Preservation, Removal and Disposal of the Records and Papers of the Late Supreme Court for the District of Kentucky, and for Other Purposes, 1792 (Nov.), Ky. Acts Ch. 51, pp. 51-52.

An Act to Explain An Act to Provide for the Preservation, Removal and Disposal of the Records and Papers of the Late Supreme Court for the District of Kentucky, and for Other Purposes, 1792 (Nov.), Ky. Acts Ch. 52, pp. 52-53.

An Act Concerning Coroners, 1792 (Nov.), Ky. Acts Ch. 55, p. 55.

Acts Passed at the First Session of the Second General Assembly, for the Commonwealth of Kentucky; Begun and Held at the Town of Frankfort, on Monday, the Fourth of November in the Year of Our Lord, One Thousand Seven Hundred and Ninety-Three, and in the Second Year of the Commonwealth. Lexington: Printed by John Bradford, Printer to the Commonwealth, 1793.

An Act to Amend An Act Concerning Coroners, 1793 (Nov.), Ky. Acts Ch. 1, pp. 3-7.

An Act to Amend An Act Establishing a Permanent Revenue, 1793 (Nov.), Ky. Acts Ch. 8, pp. 19-22.

An Act Authorizing the Treasure to Borrow Money, 1793 (Nov.), Ky. Acts Ch. 20, pp. 26-27.

An Act for the Revision of the Laws of Rhis Commonwealth, 1793 (Nov.), Ky. Acts Ch. 34, pp. 43-44.

Statute Law of Kentucky

Harry Toulmin. *A Collection of all the Public and Permanent Acts of the General Assembly of Kentucky Which Are Now in Force: Arranged and Digested According to Their Subjects: Together with Acts of Virginia Relating to Land Titles, the Recovery of Rents, and the Encouragement of Learning, Never Before Printed in this State: To Which are Prefixed a Table Explanatory of Technical Terms and a Summary of Criminal Law.* Frankfort: Printed by William Hunter, Printer to the Commonwealth, 1802.

This rare, slender volume by the then attorney-general of Kentucky was the new commonwealth's first statutory compilation. Toulmin later joined with James Blair to write the first comprehensive Kentucky law treatise, *A Review of the Criminal Law of the Commonwealth of Kentucky* (Frankfort: W. Hunter, Printer to the State, 1804-1806). The restless former Unitarian minister soon moved on to new frontiers opened by the Louisiana purchase and would go on to compile the statutes of Mississippi and Alabama. *The Statutes of the Mississippi Territory* (Natchez: Printed by Samuel Terrell, Printer to the Mississippi Territory, 1807) and *A Digest of the Laws of the State of Alabama* (Catawba, AL: Ginn and Curtis, 1823).

William Littell. *The Statute Law of Kentucky; with Notes, Prælections, and Observations on the Public Acts; Comprehending Also, the Laws of Virginia and Acts of Parliament in Force in this Commonwealth; the Charter of Virginia, the Federal and State constitutions, and so Much of the King of England's Proclamation in 1763, as Relates to the Titles to Land in Kentucky; Together with a Table of Reference to the Cases Adjudicated in the Court of Appeals.* Frankfort: Printed by and for William Hunter, 1809-1819.

Sponsored by the Kentucky legislature, this five-volume work brought together the early laws of Kentucky in a well-organized and well-indexed version. Littell's collection was not a code, but a chronological arrangement of session laws—reprinting laws that were hard to find even at that early date. Littell's work was published in large print runs and was very important to the development of Kentucky. The set also had copies of the U.S. and Kentucky Constitutions, the Virginia Compact, and many Virginia laws still in force in Kentucky.

CONCLUSION

In its unusually short period from settlement to statehood, the territory of Kentucky did not generate a large or particularly broad canon of legal materials. With the exception of those areas in which one would expect a frontier area to need laws and legislation—land, transportation, the establishment of towns—the record is thin. The state had the laws it needed, however, and the legal foundation necessary upon which to build one of the more independent-minded and democratic states of the early American republic.

Chapter 19

A Bibliographic Survey of Sources for a Study of the Law of Colonial and Territorial Louisiana

Carol D. Billings

Louisiana's legal history prior to statehood spans exactly a century, 1712 to 1812. Nothing else about it is neat and tidy. The colonial period encompasses fifty years of French rule and forty-one years of Spanish authority, culminating in a brief reversion to French ownership just in time for the Louisiana Purchase in the spring of 1803. The United States then governed the Louisiana Territory until statehood was enacted in 1812. Yet documenting the state's early legal history requires reaching back centuries earlier into French and Spanish sources that still strongly influenced the institutions and laws that governed the colony throughout the eighteenth century.

French exploration of the lower Mississippi Valley began in the late seventeenth century, and naval officer Pierre Le Moyne d'Iberville and his midshipman brother, Jean-Baptiste le Moyne de Bienville, in April 1699, left a garrison of seventy men and boys at a little fort at present-day Biloxi, Mississippi. Although appointed governor, Iberville died in 1706 without ever living there.[1] With Bienville as commander-in-chief, military rule provided the only form of government. Louis XIV's grant on September 26, 1712, to Antoine Crozat of letters patent to all of the Crown's territory "between old and new Mexico and Carolina" marked the true beginning of Louisiana colonial government. A superior council with jurisdiction in all criminal and civil matters was established.[2]

The present day bibliographer owes a great debt to historians of both general Louisiana history and legal history, in particular, who wrote from the territorial period up to the present. Anyone seeking to study the official documents that embody Louisiana law should begin by sampling the writ-

---

This chapter first appeared in *Legal Reference Services Quarterly* 23(1). Reprinted with permission of The Haworth Press, Inc.

ings of these historians to gain a general understanding of the chronology and of the institutions that generated the law. A comprehensive survey of scholarly publications predating 1983 on the colonial and territorial periods is provided by *A Guide to the History of Louisiana,* edited by Light Townsend Cummins and Glen Jeansonne (Westport, CT: Greenwood Press, 1982). Not only well-known American monographs, but also journal articles, dissertations, and works in French and Spanish are evaluated. This more limited bibliographic essay will cite only selections that concentrate on legal and political history.

In the years since Cummins and Jeansonne's guide was published, a new wave of Louisiana legal historians has produced works that illuminate the colonial and territorial periods from fresh perspectives. Several of their publications will be cited in this essay. Determined to commemorate appropriately the forthcoming anniversary of one of the landmark events in American history, the Center for Louisiana Studies at the University of Louisiana at Lafayette (formerly known as the University of Southwestern Louisiana) in the early 1990s set out to publish *The Louisiana Purchase Bicentennial Series in Louisiana History,* 19 vols. (Lafayette: University of Southwestern Louisiana, 1995-2002). As the general editor Glenn R. Conrad explained in the introduction, the set would provide a sampling of the scholarship of the last half of the twentieth century, especially that embracing new methodologies allowing broader interpretations of Louisiana's history. The first three volumes comprise 125 articles by contemporary historians examining early Louisiana's social, religious, political, and economic life prior to 1830. Many illuminate her law and legal institutions. Conrad himself edited Volume I, *The French Experience in Louisiana* (1995); Gilbert C. Din edited Volume II, *The Spanish Presence in Louisiana, 1763-1803* (1996); and Volume III, *The Louisiana Purchase and Its Aftermath, 1800-1830,* was edited by Dolores Egger Labbe. Of greatest interest to scholars and students of legal history, however, is Volume XIII, *An Uncommon Experience: Law and Judicial Institutions in Louisiana, 1803-2003* (1997). Edited by Judith Kelleher Schafer and Warren M. Billings, the collection of forty-four essays brings together both classics from the past and examples of the work of proponents of "the new Louisiana legal history."

Louisiana's first historian, Francois-Xavier Martin, was also one of her foremost jurists. In *The History of Louisiana, from the Earliest Period,* 2 vols. (New Orleans: Lyman and Beardslee, 1827-1829), he chronicled the years up to 1815. The 1882 edition (New Orleans: J. A. Gresham), containing both volumes, includes a memoir of the author by Judge W. W. Howe. Charles Étienne Arthur Gayarré recounted the French, Spanish, and early American periods in a succession of volumes published completely in 1866 as his *History of Louisiana,* 4 vols. (New York: Redfield). The next comprehensive treatment, beginning with sixteenth-century explorations, was Alcée Fortier's *A History of Louisiana* (New York: Goupil and Company of Paris, Manzi, Joyant and Company successors, 1904). Early in the twentieth century, lawyer and legal scholar Henry Plauché Dart began his prolific labor of love as interpreter of Louisiana's legal past. His "The Legal Institutions of Louisiana," covering French colonial rule, appeared in 1918 in *Southern Law Quarterly* 3: 247, and was reprinted in *Louisiana Historical Quarterly* 2: 72 in 1919. Lawrence V. Wroth and Gertrude L. Annan compiled a list of "Acts of French Royal Administration Concerning Canada, Guiana, the West Indies and Louisiana, Prior to 1791" in *Bulletin of the New York Public Library* 34: 21-55, 87-126, and 155-193 (1930), also published that year as a monograph. Each entry indicates where the text of the act may be located in another source.

As a member of the editorial committee appointed by Louisiana's Governor Leche in 1936 to prepare historical notes and other aids to accompany the reprint of the *Projet of the Civil Code of 1825* and the *Projet of the Code of Practice of 1825,* John H. Tucker contributed "Source Books of Louisiana Law," one of the most useful guides to Louisiana's early legal literature. Having first been published serially between 1932 and 1935 in the *Tulane Law Review* 6: 280, 7: 82, 8: 396, and 9: 244, the articles were then reprinted in *Louisiana Legal Archives* (New Orleans: Thos. J. Moran's Sons, 1937). Tucker's copious footnotes cite and elucidate both primary sources and historical writings. Louisiana's most famous law librarian, Kate Wallach of Louisiana State University, in 1955 published *Bibliographical History of Louisiana, Civil Law Sources, Roman, French and Spanish* (Baton Rouge: Louisiana State Law Institute), a comprehensive survey of the European sources that influenced the state's law.

Volumes 1, 2, and 5 of the original French edition of Marcel Giraud's *Histoire de la Louisiane Française,* which were published in English translation between 1974 and 1993 (Baton Rouge: Louisiana State University Press), contain an impressive list of French sources, mainly in the Archives Nationales in Paris and other French depositories. Documents in the British Public Record Office and various American libraries and archives are included. Several compilations of primary documents facilitate the work of the modern researcher. The U.S. Government Printing Office's seven-volume compilation by Francis Newton Thorpe, *The Federal and State Constitutions, Colonial Charters, and Other Organic Laws of the States, Territories, and Colonies Now or Heretofore Forming the United States of America* (Washington, DC, 1909) and its predecessor by Ben Perley Poore, published in 1877, are convenient sources of primary documents. *Constitutions of the State of Louisiana, and Select Federal Laws,* edited and annotated by Benjamin W. Dart (Indianapolis: Bobbs-Merrill, 1932), carries early federal legislation relating to Louisiana on pages 409-442.

The Louisiana Historical Society made accessible many manuscripts from the French colonial period in their original language. Volume 4, pages 4-144 of the Louisiana Historical Society Publications, hereafter cited as LHS (New Orleans, 1904), contains a reprint of *A Collection of French Manuscripts: Mississippi Valley 1679-1769.* Foremost among the documents printed there is the charter granted by Louis XIV to Crozat on September 14, 1712 (pp. 13-20). It proclaimed that the law and customs observed in Louisiana would be those of the Prévosté et Vicomté de Paris. Henry Dart's *The Legal Institutions of Louisiana* on page 250 provides a translated passage from the document establishing Louisiana's first court, the superior council, on December 18, 1712. The edict amending the law in 1716 to enlarge the council and make it more permanent also appears (pp. 256-258).

The superior council had jurisdiction in all civil and criminal causes, operating in the same fashion as councils in other French colonies. James D. Hardy Jr.'s "The Superior Council in Colonial Louisiana," in John Francis McDermott, ed., *Frenchmen and French Ways in the Mississippi Valley* 87-103 (Urbana: University of Illinois Press, 1969), accurately describes the council, as does Henry P. Dart's article "Legal Institutions of Louisiana," *Louisiana Historical Quarterly* 2: (January 1919) 72.

In 1717 financier John Law obtained Crozat's charter for the Western Company, a proprietary venture aimed to enlarge the population and promote economic expansion. The "Lettres Patentes en forme d'édit . . ." may be found in LHS, page 48, and Wroth lists other sources at pages 601-604. Inferior courts were added to assist the superior council, which was given responsibility for hearing appeals and for certain administrative duties.[3] When the Western Company's efforts proved unprofitable, in 1731, it relinquished its title to the colony to the Crown. Reorganizing the form of government in 1732, the Crown set up a superior council with thirteen members. Benignly neglected, this judicial system—relying on the Coutumes de Paris and royal edicts—lasted until the end of French rule in 1768.[4]

Before moving on to the period of Spanish dominance, it is necessary to give some attention to the French legal documents that provided the foundation for colonial Louisiana government for more than fifty years. In her *Bibliographical History of Louisiana Civil Law Sources,* pages 17-32, Kate Wallach succinctly reviewed the major ones. For locating them, she frequently refers the reader to Armand-Gaston Camus, *Profession d'Avocat, Bibliothèque Choisie des Livres de Droit,* 5 éd. augmentee par M. Dupin, t. 2 (Paris: Alex-Gobelet, 1832).

Les Coutumes de Paris, originating around the eleventh century from Germanic sources, says Wallach, was a compilation of local customs done in 1510 as ordered by Charles VII. A new edition in 1580 comprised "372 articles covering feudal law, property, possession, mortgages, servitudes, dower, marital community, guardianship, gifts, wills, and successions."[5] For a convenient edition of the 1580 revision, Wallach recommends turning to Charles Giraud, *Précis de l'Ancien Droit Coutumier Français,* 2 éd. 137-197 (Paris: Cotillon, 1875).

Ordonnance Civile pour la Reformation de la Justice, sometimes referred to as *Code Louis* or *Code Civil,* promulgated in 1667, according to Wallach has had some influence on Louisiana procedure. Likewise, a commercial ordinance of 1673, the *Code Savary* or *Code Marchand* and the *Code de la Marine* of 1681 have been cited in American cases. She recommends George Wilfred Stumberg's *Guide to the Law and Legal Literature of France* (Washington, DC: Library of Congress, 1931) as an authoritative critical and descriptive bibliography covering these sources. Of special significance is *Le Code Noir,* introduced in Louisiana in 1724 for the purpose of regulating Negro slavery. A 1765 edition in French is printed in *Recueils de Réglemens, Edits, Declarations et Arrêts Concernant le Commerce, l'Administration de la Justice, et la Police des Colonies Françaises de l'Amerique et les Engagés* (Paris: Chez les Libraires Associés). For a later version in English one may turn to pages 151-213 of *Acts Passed at the First Session of the First Legislature of the Territory of Orleans* (New Orleans: Printed by Bradford & Anderson, 1806). For other royal ordinances, Wallach suggests as most complete Athanase Jean Léger Jourdan and François André Isambert's *Recueil Général des Anciennes Lois Françaises depuis l'an 420 jusqu'à la Revolution de 1789* (Paris: Berlin-Le-Prieur, 1821-1833), 29 vols. Wroth, pages 7-11, also lists collections of ordinances affecting the French colonies.

Two important writers of French legal doctrine during Louisiana's colonial period, whom Wallach mentions, have had a lasting effect upon the state's civil law tradition. At one time required reading for Louisiana bar admission, Jean Domat's *Les Lois Civiles dans leur Ordre Naturel,* published between 1689 and 1697, is considered the first treatise on French civil law. William Strahan's English translation, *The Civil Law in Its Natural Order,* was published in 1722 (London: J. Bettenham). The principal sources used by the redactors of the French *Code Civil* were the treatises of Robert Joseph Pothier, which began appearing in the middle of the eighteenth century. Of the various editions of Pothier's collected works, Wallach recommended as best for research *Oeuvres de Pothier* by Bugnet (Paris: Cosse et Marchal, 1845-1848, in 10 vols.). The notes lead to corresponding *Code Civil* articles. *A Treatise on the Law of Obligations,* from which whole passages were borrowed for the *Louisiana Civil Code*, appears in several English translations, such as that by William David Evans (Philadelphia: R. H. Small, 1826, in 2 vols.). Another type of legal publication from the eighteenth century that had strong influence in both France and colonial Louisiana was the encyclopedia or *repertoire*, the precursor of the modern *Corpus Juris* and *American Jurisprudence*. A good example is *Répertoire Universel et Raisonné de Jurisprudence* begun by Guyot in 1777 and continued in various editions.

Serious scholars of colonial Louisiana legal institutions will of course want to delve into extant manuscript collections. The Louisiana State Museum Historical Center in the New Orleans French Quarter houses the records of the French Superior Council, 1714 to 1769. Most of the case law involves creditors' attempts to collect debts, but many successions are included as well. These afford access to estate inventories, records of commercial transactions, family legal matters, and slave petitions for manumission. The Historical Center also prizes a number of the premier French documents, such as the letters patent to Crozat and the Company of the West, the proclamation creating the superior council, and the 1724 *Code Noir*. A monumental undertaking of the Center for Louisiana Studies at the University of Louisiana at Lafayette has been the continuing project, begun in the early 1970s, to microfilm French archival materials relating to the French experience in the Mississippi Valley. With the cooperation of the Archives Nationales, the Library of Congress, and several universities, microfilm containing more than 1 million frames has been deposited at the University of Louisiana at Lafayette, resulting in a new historiography for French Louisiana.

With plenty of fish bigger than Louisiana to fry, "France stumbled through a series of imperial wars and continental entanglements throughout the eighteenth century."[6] To compensate the Spanish Bourbons for their support during the Seven Years' War, France ceded Louisiana to Spain in a secret treaty in 1762. The text of the treaty may be found in Alejandro del Cantillo, *Tratados, Convenios y Declaraciones de Paz y Comercio* (Madrid: Alegria y Charlain, 1843), and in A. de Clercq, *Recueil des Traités de la France, 1713-1906* (Paris: Amjot, Pedone, 1864-1917, 23 vols.). It was not until 1766, however, that Spain got its imperial bureaucracy in sufficient order to take possession of its new colony. Carlos III unwisely appointed as governor the scholarly, but administratively and militarily inexperienced, Antonio de Ulloa. The local French elite resented Ulloa's autocratic attempts to assimilate the colony into the Spanish empire.[7] While campaigning to have the royal authorities dissolve the superior council and give sole judicial power to him, Ulloa advocated a revised municipal code that affected many aspects of the colonists' daily lives. New regulations restricting river traffic and commercial activity threatened the livelihoods of influential inhabitants. A financial crisis brought on by Ulloa's inept monetary policies helped to turn growing dissatisfaction into rebellion. The superior council, which Ulloa had not managed to eliminate, acted on the colonists' grievances and issued an expulsion order. Amid victory celebrations, Ulloa left on his frigate for Havana.[8]

Carlos III's response was to repress the rebellion with brutal force. Irish soldier of fortune Alejandro O'Reilly, who had aided the Spanish during the Seven Years' War, arrived in July 1769 to take command. Without delay he had the rebellion's leaders arrested and tried. Five were executed by firing squad, and five received six- to ten-year prison sentences, earning the new governor the sobriquet "Bloody O'Reilly."

O'Reilly was a talented, decisive administrator who established undisputed control for Spain. "From a legal and judicial standpoint, O'Reilly's administrative reforms composed the core of the systems that provided Louisiana with stable conflict resolution until Pierre Clément de Laussat reclaimed the colony for France in 1803."[9] His proclamation of November 25, 1769, abolished the superior council and installed the cabildo, its Spanish counterpart. He took on the task of creating a system of laws in keeping with Spanish interests. Two lawyers, Don Felix Del Rey and Manuel José de Urrutia, were charged by the governor with redacting into what became known as the Code O'Reilly, a mingling of the laws of the Indies and Castile with selected French customs. Major sources were *Recopilación de las Indias,* the *Siete Partidas,* and the French *Code Noir* of 1724. Among the English translations are Gustavus Schmidt's in *Louisiana Law Journal,* 1(1) (1841) and that in *American State Papers,* Vol. 1 Misc., Documents, Legislative and Executive of the Congress of the United States 362-376 (Washington, DC: Gales and Seaton, 1834), which includes references to Spanish laws. Benjamin Franklin French's *Historical Collections of Louisiana,* part 5, 269-288 (Wiley and Putnam, 1846-1853), provides another English translation, and Gayarré's *Histoire de la Louisiana* (appendix to Vol. 2) includes one in French. Kate Wallach cautions that "O'Reilly's Code is not an orderly arrangement of the body of Spanish law, but merely a digest of the most important Spanish laws applicable to Louisiana."[10] She notes that although Gustavus Schmidt, the attorney-historian who founded Louisiana's first law school in 1844 (the forerunner of Tulane), argued that Spanish law was never legitimately in force in Louisiana, the Supreme Court has always pronounced it valid, as do scholars writing today.

A number of Spanish laws were enacted especially for Louisiana. Many dealt with practical matters, such as land and livestock, but a far larger combination of laws was declared applicable in Louisiana and Spain's other colonies. John Thomas Vance described the important compilations in *The*

Background of Hispanic American Law (New York: Central Book Company, 1942). *Recopilacion de Leyes de Las Reinos de Indias* (Madrid: Julian de Paredes, 1681), a nine-book compendium of over 6,000 earlier royal enactments relating to colonial administration, was promulgated in 1680. Vance stated (p. 164) that "according to the Spanish and Hispanic-American historians [the *Recopilacion*] despite its defects deserves to rank higher than anything done in the English and French colonies, because of its humanitarian spirit and the protection afforded to the native subjects of the Spanish crown."

So important an element in Louisiana's Spanish legal foundations was *Las Siete Partidas,* compiled between 1256 and 1265 during the reign of Alfonso XI (or el Sabio), that the legislature on March 3, 1819, "authorized and encouraged the translation of such parts . . . as are considered to have the force of law in this state" (Louisiana Acts, 1819, pp. 44-46). The translation by Louis Moreau Lislet and Henry Carleton, which did not include the portions dealing with the Catholic Church or criminal matters, was published in 1820 (New Orleans: James M'Karaher). Strongly influenced by Roman and canon law, *Las Partidas* consists of seven parts: the Catholic faith; royalty and nobility; justice; betrothals and marriages; loans, sales, contracts, etc.; wills and inheritance; and crimes and offenses.

The governing cabildo that O'Reilly installed was an institution of mixed government, possessing both administrative and judicial authority. The governor and other cabildo officials could each hear cases individually. The judicial system was divided by class: elite citizens—military, clergy, and civil officials—were considered *fueros,* and ordinary people were termed *alcaldes ordinarias.* The governor's court and other high-level tribunals handled matters involving *fueros,* while the *alcaldes ordinarias* courts had original jurisdiction in a whole range of civil and criminal cases, as well as appellate jurisdiction in civil matters involving less-privileged colonists. In 1771, the Crown followed O'Reilly's recommendation to establish a superior court of appeals in Havana. Military and treasury officials reviewed death penalty and some other criminal cases as well as those involving substantial sums of money. In the eleven districts throughout the colony that O'Reilly placed under military commanders, an inferior court system functioned similar to the justices of the peace in Britain's North American colonies.[11]

Scholars interested in research in original manuscript records of Spanish colonial government have two significant depositories available in New Orleans. The Louisiana State Museum Historical Center, whose French colonial documents were mentioned earlier, houses records of the Spanish judiciary. The New Orleans City Archives owe their origin to Governor O'Reilly's establishment of the office of Escribano of the Cabildo. Charged with preserving all the papers concerning the cabildo and its proceedings, this clerk turned over the archives that he had collected to the French Prefect Laussat, who then transferred them to the Americans in 1803. They now form an important part of the Louisiana Division of the New Orleans Public Library at its main building.

O'Reilly's government functioned well as "Cabildo officials dispensed Spanish justice with prudence and good will."[12] French colonists gradually accepted the new regime peacefully, but continental diplomatic events soon upset the progress toward a stabilization of colonial society. By the terms of the Treaty of San Ildefonso, adopted on October 1, 1800, Spain returned Louisiana to France. The Web site of the Avalon Project at Yale Law School (http://www.yale.edu/lawweb/avalon/ildefens.htm) provides an English translation of the treaty. Having persuaded Napoleon to appoint him governor of the newly acquired French colony, Prefect Pierre Clément de Laussat arrived in Louisiana only to find that the emperor had negotiated its sale to the United States. The transfers from Spain to France to the United States were intended to take place on the same day. However, a delay in the arrival of American Governor W. C. C. Claiborne and General James Wilkinson for the official ceremony caused Laussat to oversee Louisiana for only three weeks. That gave him just enough time inexplicably to complicate the legal arrangements—either by incompetence or design. Laussat dissolved the cabildo but had no time to resurrect a French legal system, leaving the colonists with no means to handle disputes or administrative business. Naturally the *ancienne population* were anxious about possibly being dispossessed of their land and about what laws and government would control their lives.

The Treaty of Paris, the agreement authorizing the Louisiana Purchase, was signed on April 30, 1803, by Robert R. Livingston, James Monroe, and François Barbé Marbois. Ratifications were exchanged on October 21. The formal ceremony of transfer when Laussat passed to the Americans the keys to the city of New Orleans took place at the city hall, the present-day cabildo, on December 20, 1803.[13] As one of the most important documents in American history, the purchase agreement has been widely published. Two sources from the Government Printing Office commonly held by large law libraries are Thorpe, *The Federal and State Constitutions . . . ,* Vol. III, pages 1359-1362, and the similarly named 1877 compilation by Ben Perley Poore, at pages 687-690. Both publications print next to the treaty (Thorpe, p. 1364, and Poore, p. 690) the Act of the 8th Congress, 1st Session, approved on October 31, 1803,[14] enabling the president to take possession of Louisiana. Dart's *Constitutions of the State of Louisiana . . .* also includes the treaty at pages 409-411.

With the occupants of the new American territory anxious about what laws governed them, President Jefferson and Congress moved quickly to bring order. By the Breckinridge Act of March 26, 1804,[15] found in Thorpe, Vol. 3, pages 1364-1371, and Benjamin Dart, pages 414-421, Congress divided the purchase into the Orleans Territory, consisting of most of present-day Louisiana, and the district—later territory—of Louisiana, over which the governor of the Indiana Territory would hold power. The act also specified the forms of government for the two territories. In Orleans executive power was vested in the governor, legislative power in the governor and a thirteen-man legislative council appointed by the president, and judicial power in a superior court and in such inferior courts and justices of the peace as the legislature might establish. Federal laws were declared to apply in the territory, but laws in force not inconsistent with them would remain effective. A single-judge federal district court with the same powers as its counterpart in Kentucky would sit quarterly in New Orleans. Free white male property owners resident for a year were qualified to serve as grand or petit jurors. The district of Louisiana for the most part was to operate as an appendage of the Indiana Territory.

President Jefferson and Governor Claiborne, desiring to introduce a common law system of justice, nevertheless wisely realized that the civilian traditions of the Creole population must be respected to avoid discord. The court system that they installed represented a mingling of the two systems. A nine-man court of pleas like those in other states was created to handle the large volume of minor civil cases. For major civil actions and certain civil and criminal appeals, a short-lived governor's court was assigned jurisdiction. Claiborne laid the foundations for a county court system to render judgment in original civil and criminal matters. The new judicial system proved, however, to be inadequate because a sufficient number of competent judges could not be found, and the governor was too busy to handle the appellate caseload assigned the governor's court.

Volume IX of *The Territorial Papers of the United States,* compiled and edited by Clarence Edwin Carter (Washington, DC: Government Printing Office, 1940), is devoted to official documents of the territory of Orleans in the federal archives. Excluding documents published previously, such as territorial laws and court decisions, the volume nevertheless provides insight into the administration of the territory by way of correspondence among a veritable "who's who" of Louisiana and federal officials.

Because of the uncertainty about what laws were in force in the new territory, the residents were naturally concerned about the validity of their land titles. A quarter of a century later, in the administration of John Quincy Adams, Joseph M. White was employed to compile a list of all the French and Spanish ordinances affecting land titles in what had been their colonies. His resulting work was a document of the 20th Congress, 2nd Session, appearing in *American State Papers Relating to Public Lands,* Vol. 5, 218-315

(Washington, DC: Duff Green, 1834). Additional White translations were published in *American State Papers Relating to Public Lands,* Vol. 6, 928-937, containing Document 1189 of the lst Session of the 23rd Congress, and Vol. 7, 564-580, containing Document 1290 of the 2nd Session (Washington, DC: Gales and Seaton, 1860). In 1839, an enlarged two-volume edition of White's works containing other valuable material on the law of Spain appeared as *A New Collection of Laws, Charters and Local Ordinances of the Governments of Great Britain, France and Spain Relating to the Concessions of Land in their Respective Colonies* (Philadelphia: T. and J. W. Johnson).

From the outset the federal Breckinridge Act of March 26, 1804, establishing the territorial government disappointed the inhabitants because the governor, with the legislative council's approval, could repeal or modify local laws still in force. Especially troublesome to the *ancienne population* was the provision placing an embargo on the importation of slaves into the territory—contrary to the treaty of cession guaranteeing "the free enjoyment of their property."[16]

In protest, in the spring of 1804, a group of Creoles and natives, including Edward Livingston, presented a memorial to Congress complaining about Claiborne's management and petitioning for statehood.[17] In response they received permission to organize a territorial government under the provisions of the Northwest Ordinance of 1787,[18] which afforded them the same rights enjoyed by citizens of the Mississippi Territory. The ordinance mandated a common law system, but allowed localities to retain "laws in force."[19]

The legislative council had survived in New Orleans for only two sessions beginning on December 3, 1804, and June 20, 1805. The acts for each were printed in French and English on opposite pages by James M. Bradford in New Orleans. Notable among the actions of the first session was its adoption on April 10, 1805, of An Act Regulating the Practice of the Superior Court in Civil Cases[20] and another creating inferior courts and providing rules of practice for them.[21] A few weeks later, the legislative council, on May 4, 1805, passed An Act for the Punishment of Crimes and Misdemeanors.[22] Drafted by James Workman, the act embodied many enlightened ideas to guarantee the rights of the accused. Unfortunately, it left many questions unresolved. To achieve clarification, Governor Claiborne called upon Lewis Kerr to produce a commentary. The result was *An Exposition of the Criminal Laws of the Territory of Orleans: The Practice of the Courts of Criminal Jurisdiction, the Duties of Their Officers, with a Collection of Forms for the Use of Magistrates and Others* (New Orleans: Printed by Bradford and Anderson, 1806; reprinted Holmes Beach, FL: Wm. W. Gaunt, 1986). An article in *Louisiana History* 32(1) (1991): 63, "Origins of

Criminal Law in Louisiana," by Warren M. Billings provides a detailed explanation of the significance of Kerr's contribution as well as future developments in the criminal law.

Under the Northwest Ordinance of 1787, a new government was established with a general assembly consisting of an elected twenty-five-man house of representatives and a reduced five-man legislative council appointed by the president. The new legislature created a superior court with original and appellate jurisdiction. "Since Laussàt's suspension of the Cabildo in 1803 had cast doubt on what the existing laws were, the legislature set out immediately to define them."[23] Rulings by the earliest superior court judges, John Prevost and George Mathews, proclaimed that Louisiana private law derived from Roman, French, and Spanish civil traditions. Nevertheless, the need remained for a definite body of laws in force.[24] Thus, the legislature appointed James Brown and Louis Moreau Lislet as jurisconsults to digest the civil laws. The result of their labors, *A Digest of the Civil Laws Now in force in the Territory of Orleans . . .* (New Orleans: Printed by Bradford and Anderson, 1808), has been analyzed by a number of contemporary legal scholars. Richard Holcombe Kilbourne Jr.'s *A History of the Louisiana Civil Code: The Formative Years, 1803-1839* xiv (Baton Rouge: Paul M. Hebert Law Center, Louisiana State University, 1987) unequivocally proclaims in the introduction that "[the Digest's] ancient sources were the laws and jurisprudence of Spain, which continued in effect after the cession of Louisiana to the United States." In *Jefferson's Louisiana: Politics and the Clash of Legal Traditions* 160 (Cambridge, MA: Harvard University Press, 1975), George Dargo agreed that "the ancient Spanish law was the fundamental law in Louisiana both before and after the *Digest of 1808*." Dargo provides an excellent summary of the pre-1975 arguments between scholars propounding either the dominance of French or Spanish influences on Louisiana law.[25] In what *Tulane Law Review* 46 (1972) dubbed the "Tournament of Scholars," Tulane's Professor Rodolfo Batiza, defending the French origins,[26] and LSU's Professor Robert A. Pascal, upholding the Spanish,[27] engaged in a lively exchange of articles. Professor Batiza returned in Vol. 56 (1982) with a final word in support of his position.[28]

The new expanded legislature sat for the first time on January 25, 1806. In addition to the second session of that legislature a year later, two more legislatures, each sitting for two sessions, would enact laws for the territory prior to the attainment of statehood.

Sessions of the Legislature of the Territory of Orleans:

- 1st Legislature, 1st Session
  Acts Passed at the First Session of the First Legislature of the Territory of Orleans begun and held in the City of New Orleans on the twenty-

fifth day of January, 1806 (New Orleans: Bradford and Anderson, 1806)
- 1st Legislature, 2nd Session
  Beginning January 12, 1807 (New Orleans: Bradford and Anderson, 1807)
- 2nd Legislature, 1st Session
  Beginning January 18, 1808 (New Orleans: Bradford and Anderson, 1808)
- 2nd Legislature, 2nd Session
  Beginning January 13, 1809 (New Orleans: Louisiana Courier, 1809)
- 3rd Legislature, 1st Session
  Beginning January 9, 1810 (New Orleans: Thierry and Dacqueny, 1810)
- 3rd Legislature, 2nd Session
  Beginning January 23, 1811 (New Orleans: Thierry, 1811)
- Index to the Acts of the Legislature of the Territory of Orleans, from the 1st Session of the 1st Legislature to the 2nd Session of the 3rd Legislature, inclusive (New Orleans: J. Mitchell, 1812)

Win-Shin S. Chiang, in *Louisiana Legal Research* 127-145 (Austin: Butterworth, 1985), provides a list of all of Louisiana's legislative acts with detailed publication information.

In 1810, the superior court held[29] that the English and French texts were of equal validity, to be construed as two laws on the same subject. After adoption of the Constitution of 1812, the supreme court ruled that in instances of conflict between the texts, the English version would control.[30] Two early compilations or digests of laws in force in the territorial period were published by Martin in 1816 and Moreau Lislet in 1828.[31] Both supply the full text of the extant acts arranged in subject order.

Although the superior court came into existence on November 5, 1804, no printed reports of decisions predate 1811. When François-Xavier Martin was appointed to the court in 1810, he immediately determined to remedy the dearth of records by creating them himself. The first volume of Louisiana superior court decisions, now known as 1 Martin (Old Series), covered decisions from the fall term of 1809 through the spring term of 1811. Eleven more Martin volumes carried into the terms of the new state of Louisiana's supreme court, which originated in 1813:

Vol. 1 (New Orleans: John Dacqueny, 1811)
Vol. 2 (New Orleans: Roche Brothers, 1813)
Vol. 3 (New Orleans: Roche Brothers, 1816)

Vol. 4 (New Orleans: Benjamin Hanna, 1819)
Vol. 5 (New Orleans: Benjamin Hanna, 1819)
Vol. 6 (New Orleans: J. C. De St. Romes, 1819)
Vol. 7 (New Orleans: Benjamin Hanna, 1820
Vol. 8 (New Orleans: Roche Brothers, 1820)
Vol. 9 (New Orleans: Benjamin Levy, 1822)
Vol. 10 (New Orleans: Benjamin Levy, 1822)
Vol. 11 (New Orleans: Benjamin Levy, 1822)
Vol. 12 (New Orleans: Benjamin Levy, 1823)

One particular decision of the territorial superior court predating Martin's Reports must be mentioned because of the extended controversy that emanated from it. On May 23, 1807, the court rendered its judgment for the plaintiff in the case of *John Gravier v. The Mayor, Aldermen, and Inhabitants of the City of New Orleans.* The case involved the ownership of the "batture," the alluvial ground deposited between the Mississippi River at its low water mark and the levee. By custom the land was considered "commons" for the use of the public and for anchorage and wharfage. After the superior court validated John Gravier's private ownership of a tract of batture land, Edward Livington acquired one-third of the property and began erecting improvements on it. Governor Claiborne and city officials, asserting the public's right to the land, initiated its transfer to the federal government, leaving the matter to President Jefferson to settle. A complex series of legal and political maneuvers, involving the likes of not only Jefferson but also President Madison, Treasury Secretary Albert Gallatin, and Chief Justice John Marshall, kept the controversy alive until 1823. The story, which is recounted in detail by George Dargo and William B. Hatcher,[32] is a dramatic example of the clash between different legal traditions.

The delegation of prominent Creoles who had petitioned Washington for statehood in 1804 had received only half a loaf for their efforts: the passage of legislation creating an improved territorial government under the provisions of the Northwest Ordinance of 1787. In 1809, however, they persuaded the territorial legislature to petition Congress for statehood once again. The enabling legislation, An Act to enable the people of the Territory of Louisiana to form a constitution and state government, and for the admission of such state into the Union . . . may be found in either the Acts of the 11th Congress, 3rd Session, 1811,[33] or in Thorpe, Vol. III, 1376. It was signed by President Madison on February 20, 1811. Governor Claiborne, who had earlier urged Louisianians to wait until they were better prepared for self-government, became an ardent lobbyist for the cause of statehood. He extended the 1811 session of the legislature in hopes that good news from Washington would allow it to proceed without delay. Word came in mid-April, and Claiborne achieved passage of the call for a constitutional convention to open on November 4, 1812, in New Orleans. The act specified that forty-five delegates, apportioned among the twelve counties, were to be elected September 7th, 8th, and 9th. Any white, male, taxpaying American citizen resident in the territory for at least a year could vote and be a candidate.

Twenty-six of the forty-three elected delegates who attended the convention, held at Tremolet's coffeehouse, were of French origin. A handful of other Europeans and an assortment of Americans from various states rounded out the assemblage. Allan B. Magruder and James Brown, who had been a member of the first Kentucky constitutional convention, probably prepared the first draft of the constitution. They drew upon their knowledge of the Kentucky Constitutions of 1792 and 1799, the federal Constitution, and those of other states. "Unlike the Philadelphia meeting, no one at the Louisiana convention performed the part of James Madison as the chronicler of its deliberations. There was no need. Their proceedings were open to the press, as secrecy was not invoked, but none of the editors who covered the debates saw fit to report them fully." There are no verbatim transcripts of debates. The journal, which was intended to be merely a summary of proceedings, contains committee assignments, the order of business, resolutions, and the results of votes on motions. The original manuscript of the journal was lost, and even the scarce transcripts are rare items. One prepared by Harold King in 1939 is a typescript volume in the Louisiana Division of the New Orleans Public Library.[34]

The constitution document having been agreed upon by the delegates on January 22, 1812, scribes were called in to engross it into English and French. After the delegates signed the engrossed documents on January 28, the convention adjourned. The title page of the original 1812 edition bears the name of "Jo. Bar. Baird, Printer to the Convention." Congressional approval followed quickly on April 8,[35] and on April 30, 1812, Louisiana became the eighteenth state in the Union. The text of the first constitution has been published widely. The one which appears in *West's Louisiana Statutes Annotated,* Vol. 3, 27 (St. Paul: West, 1977) is very likely the most commonly found in law libraries.

What then stands the Constitution of 1812 apart? It is unique among the state's ten constitutions. Its framers looked to the future by looking back to the past and conceived their instrument as a succinct statement of organizing principles, and no more.... [T]he nine subsequent constitutions have been lengthy, complex statements of fundamental law, the very intricacy of which bespoke a public fear of constitutional elasticity. By virtue of being first, however, the Constitution of 1812 set the foundations for institutions that exist to this day. It started traditions of self government that are acknowledged still. It contributed to the blending of Anglo-American precepts of law and constitutionalism with continental European practices into customs that give the state its distinctive legal coloration. It was the seed from which all things constitutional grew in Louisiana.[36]

NOTES

1. Henry Plauché Dart, "The Legal Institutions of Louisiana," *Southern Law Q.* 3(1918): 247, 247.

2. Mark F. Fernandez, *From Chaos to Continuity: The Evolution of Louisiana's Judicial System, 1712-1862* 1 (Baton Rouge: Louisiana State University Press, 2001).

3. Ibid. at 2.

4. Ibid. at 4.

5. Kate Wallach, *Bibliographical History of Louisiana Civil Law Resources, Roman, French, and Spanish,* 20-21 (Baton Rouge: Louisiana State Law Institute, 1955).

6. Fernandez at 3.

7. Ibid. at 5.

8. Ibid. at 6-11.

9. Ibid. at 12.

10. Wallach at 70.

11. Fernandez at 13-15.

12. Ibid. at 15.

13. Ibid. at 16.

14. *Laws of the United States of America from the 4th of March, 1789, to the 4th of March, 1815.* Vol. 3, Ch. 354, 562 (Philadelphia: John Bioren and W. John Duane; Washington, DC: R.C. Weightman, 1815, 5 vols.); or Ch. 1, 2 *Stat.* 245.

15. Ibid. at vol. 3, Ch. 391, 603-610; or Ch. 38, 2 *Stat.* 283.

16. George Dargo, *Jefferson's Louisiana: Politics and the Clash of Legal Traditions* 30 (Cambridge, MA: Harvard University Press, 1975).

17. Fernandez at 24.

18. Act of March 2, 1805, 2 *Stat.* 331, 8th Congress, 1st Session, Ch. 437.

19. Fernandez at 24.

20. Act of 1805, Ch. 26, 210.

21. Act of 1805, Ch. 25, 144.

22. Act of 1805, Ch. 50, 416-454.

23. Dargo at 132.

24. Fernandez at 31.

25. Dargo at 160-164.

26. Rudolfo Batiza, "The Louisiana Civil Code of 1808: Its Actual Sources and Present Relevance," *Tulane* 46(1971): 4; "Sources of the Civil Code of 1808, Facts and Speculation: A Rejoinder," *Tulane* 46(1972): 628.

27. Robert A. Pascal, "Sources of the Digest of 1808: A Reply to Professor Batiza," *Tulane* 46(1972): 603.

28. "Origins of Modern Codification of the Civil Law: The French Experience and Its Implications for Louisiana Law," *Tulane* 56(1982).

29. *Hudson v. Grieve,* 1 Mart. (o.s.) 143 (1810).

30. *Breedlove & al. v. Turner,* 9 Mart. (o.s.) 353, 364.

31. *General Digest of the Acts of the Legislatures of the Late Territory of Orleans and of the State of Louisiana . . . ,* by Francois-Xavier Martin, parallel English and French text on opposite pages (New Orleans: Printed by Peter K. Wagner, 1816, and Nouvelle-Orleans: De l'Imprimerie de Roche freres, 1816); *A General Digest of the Acts of the Legislature of Louisiana: Passed from the year 1804, to 1827, inclusive, and in force at this last period . . . ,* by L. Moreau Lislet (New Orleans: Printed by B. Levy, 1828).

32. Dargo at 74-101; William B. Hatcher, *Edward Livingston: Jeffersonian Republican and Jacksonian Democrat,* Chapter 8 (Baton Rouge: Louisiana State University, 1940).

33. Ch. 21, 2 *Stat.* 641.

34. Warren M. Billings, "From This Seed: The Constitution of 1812," in *In Search of Fundamental Law: Louisiana's Constitutions 1812-1974,* edited by Warren M. Billings and Edward F. Haas (Lafayette: The Center for Louisiana Studies, University of Southwestern Louisiana, 1993).

35. Ch. 50, 2 *Stat.* 701. On April 14 Congress passed An Act to Enlarge the limits of the State of Louisiana, thereby creating its present-day boundaries. 12th Congress, 1st Session, Ch. 380, 409.

36. Billings at 20.

Chapter 20

Maine Prestatehood Legal Materials

Isa Lang
Maureen Quinlan

INTRODUCTION

Although Maine was settled in the seventeenth century, it was not one of the original American colonies. The population was too small, diffuse, and unsettled, and the geographical area was too large for any form of centralized government. However, Maine's geography and localized government made it ripe pickings for its sophisticated neighbor, Massachusetts. Thus, in 1691, Maine became a district of the Commonwealth of Massachusetts. The first part of this chapter focuses on Maine's legal history before 1691; the second part discusses the laws and legal structure of the district of Maine.

PART I: LEGAL DOCUMENTS IN THEIR HISTORICAL CONTEXT, 1607-1691

Introduction

The first four volumes of the six-volume set *Province and Court Records of Maine,* compiled by the Maine Historical Society and published in 1928, reprint the major historical documents and all existing records from the established courts in prestatehood Maine from 1607-1691. The court records are the only primary source of prestatehood Maine law from this period; the courts *were* the government. Nonetheless, this period was historically tumultuous and legally colorful. In this section I (Isa Lang) have attempted to place Maine's early legal documents in their historical context, citing helpful secondary sources in footnotes and hoping to make some sense out of the confusing events of nearly a century.

"Pre-Judicial" Maine: 1607-1636

The early history of European settlement in Maine has a "Wild West" aspect about it, for it is one of individuals in small groups, rather than organized colonies of settlers. Unlike the Pilgrims in Massachusetts, Maine's earliest settlers were not bound by religious observance, fervor, or organization. Undoubtedly, the members of the first known expedition to Maine from England (1607-1608) endured great privations during the winter of 1608. Although most of them kept their health, harvested grapes, and trapped abundant animals, they did not have the heart to remain in their settlement on the Maine coast and returned to England that summer. In contrast, the early Massachusetts settlers, including the Pilgrims and the expedition under John Winthrop, suffered great personal devastation but remained there because of their strong commitments to their faith.[1]

The lack of a common ideal or goal delayed further settlement of Maine, to the disappointment of its English promoter, Sir Ferdinando Gorges.[2] Captain John Smith, of "Pocahontas" fame, led one financially successful expedition in 1614, followed by another (with too few volunteers) that was overtaken on the high seas by French privateers. While detained by the French, he wrote a book (complete with map) touting the riches of New England, as he called the region (heretofore part of a vast area known as northern Virginia).[3] Upon his return, he marketed the region (and the book) with presentations in London and a tour through the larger towns in the west of England.[4] Although he was unsuccessful in raising the manpower for a third expedition, his dissemination of knowledge familiarized the populace with and encouraged their subsequent interest in Maine.

The first legal document pertaining to Maine land was the Charter of the Council of Plymouth, granted by King James in 1620 to about forty "noblemen" and covering an immense territory, including Massachusetts and Maine.[5] Gorges, the mastermind behind the charter, was known for his tolerance. Although he did not share the religious beliefs of the Pilgrims, who were not members of the Council of Plymouth, he helped them obtain a patent to their colony in Massachusetts (Plymouth Colony).[6] Religious tolerance has been a marked feature of Maine history and has influenced its legal tradition.[7]

Patents granted under the Charter of the Council of Plymouth resulted in small and scattered settlements along the Maine coast. The largest of these, at Agamenticus (now York), Winter Harbor, and Richmond's Island, had sketchy governments called combinations or voluntary associations. Documentary fragments provide evidence of the existence of a court in York, in which civil cases were tried and verdicts rendered by juries.[8] The earliest formal court in Maine held its first session in Saco in March 1636, after

Gorges, having received a patent to the lands between the Piscataqua (present border with New Hampshire) and Kennebec Rivers, sent his nephew William to take possession of and govern his "Province of New Somersetshire."[9]

Maine's First Legal Body: 1636-1637

Although William Gorges' government of New Somersetshire had little authority behind it[10] and was of short duration, it is notable for holding the first continuing court sessions in Maine. This court, staffed by seven commissioners, began its first session in late March 1636, in Saco. The commissioners heard a wide variety of both civil and criminal cases, some with a jury.

The records of this court are amusing and colorful. The majority of criminal prosecutions were for drunkenness. The courts also imposed fines for an "uprore . . . in shouting divers peeces in the night";[11] for "abusing the Court";[12] and on a young man for "Incontency with Ane his father's servant . . . the said Ane 20s hee to keepe the Child."[13] Civil suits ran the gamut of first-year law school courses from torts to contracts to real property. The absence of any lawyers from this court rendered the pleadings comprehensible and the verdicts simple.

More interesting (and troublesome, perhaps) was this court's legislation. Presumably, the seven commissioners had authority to draft and enact laws (how well they enforced them is another question). One sensible enactment, fining sellers of " strong liquor or wyne" for the continuing drunkenness of their patrons after they leave,[14] was a precursor of "dram shop" laws. A more disturbing enactment ordered white men to "apprehend, execut or kill" any Indian who harmed people, cattle, or property and who would not make satisfaction.[15] Since the penalty for disobeying this law was a discretionary fine, one wonders how often or severely it was imposed.

Records for this court exist for less than a year and a half, at which point William Gorges returned to England. His uncle, Ferdinando, had suspended the government of New Somersetshire in anticipation of greater power.[16] During William's tenure in New Somersetshire, Ferdinando had his thumb in the air, testing the political winds. King Charles I was suspicious of the republican tendencies of many of the patent holders under the Charter of the Council of Plymouth.[17] Revoking that charter, he granted loyal Gorges a new patent for the province of Maine, extending north from the Piscataqua (present border with New Hampshire) to the Kennebec Rivers and west 120 miles from the seacoast (the old geographical borders of New Somersetshire).[18]

Government Under the Gorges Patent: 1639-1652

Politics was not the only basis for the province of Maine patent. Previous charters were territorial grants without any powers of government. Moreover, the patent holders were supposed to pay rents to the Plymouth Council to be apportioned among the council members, but, once the patent holders built up their estates in the New World, they asserted their independence from rent.[19]

Gorges realized that the settlers would be ungovernable unless the terms of his patent were changed.[20] He worked for two years to obtain a patent granting him powers to form a government (such a patent, making the holder Lord Palatine, had been granted to Sir George Calvert in 1623 for "Avalon," now Maryland).[21] Although the patent was extreme politically, it was sensible legally, for Gorges was now able to establish systems for maintaining law and order in the province of Maine. To this end, he sent his young cousin, Thomas Gorges, to Maine as his deputy governor and head of a new council. Thomas Gorges was the first active lawyer in Maine.[22]

The king's patent to Gorges granted him the power to govern his province through local bodies.[23] He divided the province into eight "bailiwicks" (counties) and further divided those into parishes, or boroughs. As a result, the province of Maine was home to the first municipal corporation in the New World, the borough of Agamenticus (present-day York), chartered in 1641.[24] Commissioners (equivalent to justices of the peace or magistrates) were appointed in each governmental subdivision to hear cases; their jurisdiction was limited to forty shillings, with appeals allowed to higher courts.[25]

Ferdinando Gorges' commissions to his councillors demonstrate his knowledge about and desire for orderly disposition of cases. The commissions (there were two, one repeating the other) dictated that there should be a regular place and time for a court, that the court should adjudicate both civil and criminal matters (enumerated in detail), that it should administer oaths, and that it should mete out appropriate punishment justly.[26] He understood the legal ignorance of both judges and litigants, for he spelled out "short forms" of civil and criminal complaints.[27] Clear recitals of the facts and reasoned judgments in the reported cases demonstrate the efficiency of his recommendations.

Beginning in 1640, a general court was held in Saco each year. Three inferior courts held quarter sessions at Agamenticus and three at Saco, to meet the needs of people who lived far away and were able to travel only at certain times.[28] The general court was busy in 1640; a virtual suspension of the judiciary from 1637-1640 could have created a backlog. Its judgments touched on every conceivable legal problem of the time, with opinions on real property disputes taking up the most space and consideration.[29] In addition to adjudicating the secular legal problems of the day, the court touched on religious matters by ordering baptisms[30] and by disciplining Sabbath breakers.[31] It got involved in politics once, when a grand jury indicted George Puddington of Agamenticus for claiming that his combination was stronger than the power of the king. Notably, the court dismissed the indictment with a finding of *ignoramus* (we do not know if the bill is true).[32]

The records of the court from 1641-1644 are missing, for a curious reason. Apparently, court records were considered documents with monetary value. Basill Parker, a member of the court, pledged the records to various tavern keepers in southern Maine as security for tavern expenses (either his own or for entertaining others). When Massachusetts sought these records in the early 1650s by a published order, they were sold privately in defiance of the order.[33] They have not come to light.

Throughout the 1640s, disruptions in England resulting in the Civil War reverberated in the province of Maine. Sir Ferdinando Gorges focused on serving the king (he died in 1647 in the king's service) and ignored provincial affairs. Meanwhile, George Cleeve, "the first settler of Portland, and all his life an agitator,"[34] traveled to England and convinced his fellow Republican Sir Alexander Rigby to purchase an invalid patent for some land in the southeastern portion of the province of Maine. Subsequently, Rigby sent Cleeve back to Maine to hold rival courts in Casco and Scarborough. Cleeve was familiar with legal process; he had been a prominent party in legal actions, as well as an arbitrator of cases in which he was not involved.[35]

Statements by the councillors of the Gorges court in 1645 attested to the Gorges court's ignorance of Rigby's and Cleeves' maneuvers and vowed protection of anyone adversely affected by the Cleeves court's adjudications.[36] The Gorges court's efforts to function as a court under a succession of deputy governors, all of whom had been original councillors under the Charter of the Council of Plymouth, ensured its continuation until 1652.[37]

Growing Judicial Dominance by Massachusetts: 1652-1677

The judicial history of Maine during the periods of rule by Massachusetts centers on two provinces in the southern part of the present-day state, the provinces of Maine and Lygonia. The rest of Maine was either territory claimed by the French or sparsely settled and minimally governed lands in the east-central part of the state (Pemaquid Province). Court records embody the legal history of York County and the southern half of Cumberland

County, the two southernmost counties in the state. In light of Gorges' distraction by the English Civil War and subsequent death, the efforts of the residents of the two provinces to continue some form of government were commendable. Nonetheless, the supremacy of the Puritans in England during this period was making its mark in Massachusetts and Maine. In 1651, Massachusetts decided to focus on the northern boundaries of her territory.[38]

Throughout the 1650s, Massachusetts gradually asserted dominance over the provinces of Maine and Lygonia, obtaining the final submission from their citizens to the "government of Massachusetts Bay" in July 1658.[39] Massachusetts continued to hold courts in Maine throughout the 1660s and 1670s, with a four-year hiatus from 1665-1668, resulting from the political battle between Massachusetts and the descendants of Sir Ferdinando Gorges over rightful title to Maine. During this period, justices of the peace appointed by King Charles II held court sessions in York and Casco (eastern and western divisions). Throughout this protracted tug-of-war, "commissioners and judges held their terms, sometimes guarded by soldiers, and sometimes driven by them from their seats."[40] Understandably, not all of their judgments were executed, but it is to their credit that total anarchy did not prevail.

Massachusetts courts, with commissioners holding annual sessions at York, may be described as "busybody" courts, assessing criminal charges on individuals for sleeping in church;[41] setting up a charitable fund for a needy person;[42] requiring the town of York to build a jail;[43] and threatening to impose fines on towns who neglected to build roads and ferries (at the town's expense) when asked (by Massachusetts).[44] The court records from this period also indicate that after Massachusetts recognized the annexation of part of the Isles of Shoals to Kittery in 1654,[45] it ordered the constable of the annexed land to court the next year for failing to collect taxes from its inhabitants.[46] Despite the somewhat tyrannical attitude of Massachusetts, the colony should be given credit for its attempts to oversee improvements in Maine's transportation system[47] and to initiate a rudimentary census of landholders.[48] Moreover, the colony's order for buying law books for the towns in York County in 1659 demonstrated its genuine interest in the fair administration of justice.[49]

The court of associates (sessions held from 1658-1679) was strictly for Massachusetts' annexed territories in New Hampshire and Maine. Associates were allowed to hold court with limited jurisdiction and without a jury,[50] while the county court, with broader jurisdiction, was strictly governed by the Massachusetts general court (its legislative body) and commissioners. The court of associates heard complaints for assault and for defamation, awarded damages in petty civil suits, and functioned as a probate court for small estates. Curiously, records of this court indicate infrequent meetings; in some years, records exist for only one session. Nonetheless, many people depended upon it, for each session was jam-packed with litigation.

Looking back at this period in Maine's history, it seems almost inevitable that Massachusetts would "grow into" Maine. The tiny ocean frontage of Massachusetts was unacceptable to that colony of merchants and traders. A Massachusetts government for Maine was palatable to many Maine residents for two overriding reasons: its courts offered a "just and unpurchasable trial of civil lawsuits,"[51] and its laws provided for boundaries for each town, within which every person could own land.[52] The descendants of Ferdinando Gorges, for all their efforts to maintain a stable government in Maine, could not duplicate the organization and protection afforded by Massachusetts and finally sold their patent to the colony in March 1677, after the king had denied any claims of Massachusetts to Maine lands.

Judicial Systems in the Province of Maine: 1677-1691

Throughout the 1670s, the province of Maine was devastated by wars with the Indians. Massachusetts helped finance Maine's "defense" of its settlements, paying out £8,000 in military expenses on Maine's behalf.[53] Moreover, most of the vocal opponents to Massachusetts' rule had disappeared from the scene by 1677. Massachusetts seemed firmly entrenched in the territory.

In 1680, Thomas Danforth was appointed president of the province of Maine by the Massachusetts general court and held a representative assembly at York. By this time, Massachusetts had already decided that the province's legal system should follow the guidelines of the Gorges Charter rather than parallel the Massachusetts system. Therefore, all cases could be appealed to the assembly from the superior courts; no capital sentences could be meted out without the approval of the assembly; either party to litigation could object to a judge; and all prior laws, indictments, and precedents would remain in force.[54] Other privileges accorded by the Gorges Charter included legislation by electorate, raising militia, building forts, incorporation of towns, and admiralty jurisdiction.[55]

Nonetheless, the Gorges Charter was broad and had room in it for some features of the Massachusetts government and legal system. For example, Maine's general assembly was like Massachusetts' general court; Maine's councillors (President Danforth's deputies) performed functions similar to Massachusetts' assistants; and Maine's court of sessions handled smaller cases, as did Massachusetts' county courts. The general assembly was Maine's legislative body, although its enactments were subject to veto by the Massachusetts general court. This legislative body did not enact a code of laws; rather, it oversaw legislation by case law and precedent, observing laws and holdings that were already in place.[56] The general assembly also functioned as the court of appeals from both the court of pleas (an intermediate-level court, handling larger cases than the court of sessions) and the court of sessions.

During this period, the defense of Maine against both the French and the Indians was supposedly financed by quitrents owed by the towns to their proprietor (Massachusetts). Massachusetts instituted a system of taxation based on landholding and family size. It was universally acknowledged that the quitrents were difficult to collect, partly because of a general scarcity of money (for example, dried wheat and peas were acceptable tax payments).[57] Partly because of the quitrent system, the most serious legal problem in the province of Maine was the verification of land titles.[58] Grants from Ferdinando Gorges were clear, but grants made by Maine towns during the periods of government by Massachusetts had no legal basis after the king upheld the validity of the Gorges patent against any claims by Massachusetts. Finally, in 1680, the general assembly upheld the Massachusetts Law of Possessions, securing the titles of landholders who had received grants from Massachusetts in the 1650s.[59] As well as confirming the validity of many land titles, this act by the general assembly made it easier to collect the quitrents that were necessary for Maine's defense.

The political picture changed drastically in 1686, when the king formed a new territory called the Dominion of New England, extending from Maine to New Jersey, under Governor Edmund Andros. Andros changed both the legislative and judicial systems in place under Massachusetts' rule; the legislative bodies in both Maine and Massachusetts disappeared. While the county courts (combining the former courts of pleas and sessions) in Maine continued to function, appeals in large cases (over £350) were made to the king and in smaller cases to the governor and council.[60] The major legal development during these years was the formalization of procedure, with rules laid out for "appeals, writs, registration of deeds, affidavits, marriages by minister [now legalized] and by justices, registration of births and burials, and the drawing of juries."[61]

By 1689, the residents of Massachusetts, in particular, were extremely dissatisfied with the royal government under Sir Edmund Andros. Many residents had been sent up to Maine in the winter of 1688-1689 to fight the Indians and to guard forts constructed by Andros, commanded by British rather than native officers.[62] Moreover, King James II was burdened by his own wars in Europe, culminating in the invasion of England by William of

Orange. In April 1689, in a bloodless coup in Boston, Governor Andros was replaced by a council of twenty-two citizens under the aged Governor Bradstreet. Massachusetts was self-governing, and, once again, Governor Danforth took the reins in Maine.

Word of the coup slowly trickled back to England through explanatory letters from prominent Massachusetts residents. While the military situation in Maine deteriorated rapidly, King William concluded that he wanted a strong government in Massachusetts to defend against encroaching French interests to the north. Thus, he encouraged the development of a new charter for the Bay Colony, under which Massachusetts would govern Maine, the Plymouth Colony, the islands off Cape Cod, and Nova Scotia. This charter was granted in 1691, ending independent government in Maine until 1820.

PART II: THE DISTRICT OF MAINE, 1691-1820

During the years 1691-1820, Maine was a district of the commonwealth of Massachusetts. The influence of the commonwealth of Massachusetts is felt to this day.[63] In this section I (Maureen Quinlan) will look at the 1691 Charter of Massachusetts Bay that created the union; the courts; sources for cases during the period of control by Massachusetts; events that led to separation; and then, finally, the resolution of northern boundary lines and Massachusetts ownership of land in Maine. During this period primary sources become more readily available through the *Acts and Resolves Passed by the General Court of Massachusetts.*

1691

The year 1691 marked the complete absorption of Maine by the commonwealth. The commonwealth of Massachusetts was granted a royal charter that gave it control of Maine, Nova Scotia, Acadia, and the territory in between. Massachusetts had been claiming portions of Maine for some time, and this royal charter put the issue to rest, giving it the territory it desired. It authorized the Massachusetts Bay Colony to establish a system of government and hold court in Maine.[64]

1691-1820

Criminal problems dealt with included excessive drinking, stealing of timber off others' land, and mistreatment of slaves.[65] Prosecutions for premarital relations were also common criminal cases brought before the court between 1692-1711. Often the parties were married later and a fine was paid in "lieu of the strap."[66]

There were also family feuds. One continued for fifty years. The original lawsuit was by Winn to be reimbursed for the costs of caring for Littlefield's children after Littlefield had been captured by Indians. By the time this lawsuit was brought in 1714, Littlefield had been killed during another raid. Littlefield's widow won the original case, but the families were in court for years.[67]

On a positive note, "Maine . . . remained untouched by the Salem and Boston witchcraft scare of 1692 and 1693; the few scattered cases of investigations of witchcraft in the region recorded before then are neither serious or significant."[68] The few cases involving accusations of witchcraft can be found in the *Maine Province and Court Records*.[69]

A thorough understanding of the court structure during this period can be obtained in the article "The Maine Connection: Massachusetts Justice Downeast, 1620-1820," published in *The History of the Law in Massachusetts: The Supreme Judicial Court 1692-1992*. The superior court was formed by 1692 to hear civil cases, criminal cases, and civil appeals from the inferior court of common pleas, and it had original jurisdiction in capital cases. By 1699, the court structure had changed again. A court of general session of the peace was established for "petty criminal jurisdiction" and an inferior court of common pleas "was established with general common law civil jurisdiction." At the same time, the superior court kept its jurisdiction in criminal and Crown matters and heard only appeals in civil cases. The parties in civil cases were entitled to a trial de novo before the superior court. Appeals to the superior court were mostly heard in Boston until 1720. In 1720, a court was established in York to hear appeals once a year. By 1760, the court sat annually in both York and Falmouth (Portland). The court of general sessions of the peace "acted primarily as a county administrative body but also exercised some criminal jurisdiction."[70]

As the circuits extended and business increased, it was found impossible for the full court to travel into each county and dispose of all the cases. So cases accumulated and delays increased. This is a theme that emerges in numerous sources. It was difficult to travel to Maine, and, once there, it was difficult to travel within Maine. Roads were poor and travel was tedious.[71] Although Massachusetts passed numerous laws to make travel easier in the district of Maine and to run the district efficiently,[72] this effort seemed to make little difference in the travel conditions in the district. Judges were appointed, but many had to travel up from Massachusetts.[73] Three different groups of attorneys practiced in Maine during this period: men who were admitted to practice in the courts of Maine, although most resided in New Hampshire; attorneys who traveled up from Boston to practice for "persons of large interests"; and "men who appeared as advocates without being admitted."[74]

The commonwealth of Massachusetts entered into treaties with the tribes of the district of Maine. In 1843, Maine republished the treaties that pertained to Maine and were entered into between Massachusetts and the tribes. Treaties between the state of Maine and the tribes were also republished.[75]

The passing of property was an important concern to settlers in the district. Cases, in this area, can be found in the *Maine Province and Court Records.* A compilation of wills gives an idea of the type and extent of property people had acquired during their lives. *The Probate Records of Lincoln County, Maine, 1760-1800,* includes numerous wills filed in Lincoln County during this period.[76]

Federal Courts

For about a year, a federal circuit court, which was established under the Judiciary Act of 1801, sat in Maine. This act was abolished in 1802, when the Judiciary Act of 1802 was passed. The act of 1802 excluded the district of Maine, and Maine no longer had a sitting federal court.[77]

In 1818, Senator Prentiss Mellon submitted a request to the U.S. Senate that a circuit court be established in Maine.[78] (Prentiss Mellon became the first chief justice of the Maine Supreme Court after the separation.) After separation in 1820, Maine became part of the first circuit, and it was required that two sessions be held each year.[79]

1820 Separation

The reasons for separation from Massachusetts are varied and include geography, religion, politics, taxes, and representation.

Various sources discuss the difficulties in the administrative and practical applications of law in an area this size.[80] The size of Maine and its distance from Massachusetts impeded the ability to govern the district and lent support to the decision to separate. Geographic separation from Massachusetts and within the district meant that Maine was often left without a formal system of government. Travel was a problem, as the roads were poor. As a consequence, it was difficult traveling to and from Massachusetts as well as having judges from Massachusetts travel to and around Maine.[81] In addition, some citizens in Maine wanted increased access to representation and the right to have input into the passage of laws.

Taxation was another area of contention, since a farmer in Maine paid the same taxes on an acre of land as a Massachusetts farmer, although Maine land was worth less.[82] Politics also played a part in the move toward separaton. Maine was granted statehood under the Missouri Compromise,[83] and one of the reasons some had advocated for separation was a desire to be another antislavery state.[84] The separation movement started in 1785.[85] At the convention of 1819, the topic of religion was discussed, calling for removing "all religious tests, as qualifications for office," and "placing all religious denominations on the footing of most perfect equality."[86]

The prestatehood legal history of Maine ends with separation from Massachusetts. It should be noted that at the time of statehood large parts of the state were still unsettled, with ownership claimed by both the United States and Canada. The matter of separation from Massachusetts did not concern these people as the northern boundary issue would years later.[87]

Between 1785 and 1807, numerous conventions to vote on the issue of separation were held.[88] In 1791, Daniel Davis published an address that brought attention back to the issue of separation and prompted another unsuccessful convention.[89]

Between 1812 and 1816, petitions circulated asking Massachusetts to again allow a vote on separation.[90] In 1819, the commonwealth of Massachusetts again gave the district of Maine the right to vote to separate.[91] The 1819 convention was held, and Maine voted to form its own state. The constitution for Maine was written at the convention, and a state system of government was decided upon. At the convention, Maine again expressed its liberal leanings. A group calling themselves the "Catholics of Maine" presented a petition requesting they be allowed to fully participate in government, as they were not allowed to participate in Massachusetts. This petition prompted a speech by Judge Thacher, hoping "all religious distinctions would now be done away."[92]

A year later Massachusetts passed the law that enabled Maine to form its own state and be admitted into the Union.[93] The act included all the details of how separation would work[94] and provided for a smooth transition to a new government.[95] Maine, in many ways, simply picked up the status quo established by Massachusetts and adopted its courts and legislative system. Massachusetts kept half of all the lands it currently owned in Maine. Arms received from the United States were divided in proportion to the size of each state's militia. Maine agreed "not to pass laws with regard to taxes, actions, remedies at law, bars or limitations which made distinctions between" Maine citizens and noncitizens.[96]

Final Settlement of the Northern Boundary and Massachusetts Holdings in Maine

"The schemes for the formation of a new State did not all embrace the whole territory of the District of Maine."[97] What is thought of as the state of Maine today is not the same geographic area that covered the province of Maine. The charter of 1691 included the province of Maine, and also the provinces of Sagadahoc and Nova Scotia. Some of these areas were conceded to England at the end of the Revolutionary War.[98]

However, territory on the Maine border continued to be disputed between the United States and Great Britain (what is now Canada) until 1843, and flare-ups between the citizens of Maine and British citizens would occasionally occur. In one case, U.S. citizens simply moved into the disputed territory of Madawaska and declared loyalty to the United States.[99] Since these areas were generally unpopulated or sparsely populated, the British government was in no hurry to settle the dispute. The area did not have towns or government, and to the British, it was of little value. Those living in the territories were mainly lumberjacks logging the wood, many of whom did not know, and may not have cared, who governed the land.[100]

The land at the northern part of Maine did concern the commonwealth of Massachusetts. Massachusetts owned half the land under the separation agreement with Maine and valued it at $2 million. It estimated that the disputed land was larger then the entire commonwealth.[101] The land issue was settled under the Webster-Ashburton Treaty, which established a permanent boundary line.[102]

1854 Settlement of Land Holdings with Massachusetts

When Maine separated from Massachusetts, Massachusetts continued to own land in Maine. In 1854, Massachusetts sold its remaining land holdings to the state of Maine. There was ongoing communication to resolve concerns and to reach a settlement regarding this land. In particular, Maine was expressing concerns regarding Massachusetts' land holdings.[103] Maine was concerned that Massachusetts was not applying 10 percent of receipt from sales to the construction and repairing of roads, as had been agreed upon.[104] Maine was also interested in increasing the size of its population. Maine wanted land sold to farmers and as such wanted to control the sale of land owned by Massachusetts.[105] This was done with the understanding that the sale would not end any of the other obligations under the separation agreement. Maine was obligated to honor previous land sales entered into by the commonwealth.[106] Maine now had control of all the land within the state's borders.

CONCLUSION

This chapter gives an overview of the legal history that shaped the state of Maine. An understanding of this history allows the reader to know what shaped the state's laws and where those laws were derived.

NOTES

1. George Folsom, *A Discourse Delivered Before the Maine Historical Society at Its Annual Meeting, September 6th, 1846* 31 (Portland: Maine Historical Society, 1847).

2. Gorges "was recognized wherever he went as the personification of England's lust for extended dominions." Charles Thornton Libby, Preface, in *Province and Court Records of Maine,* vol. 1, vii, xlviii-xlix (Portland: Maine Historical Society, 1991) (originally published 1928).

3. Folsom, supra n. 1, at 34-35.

4. Ibid. at 39.

5. Avalon Project at the Yale Law School, The Charter of New England: 1620, <http://www.yale.edu/lawweb/avalon/states/mass01.htm> (last updated on May 20, 2005).

6. Folsom, supra n. 1, at 41-42.

7. For example, the earliest compilation of Maine statutes allowed witnesses who were not Christians to take their own form of binding oath. 1821 Me. Laws 263.

8. William Willis, *A History of the Law, the Courts, and the Lawyers of Maine from Its First Colonization to the Early Part of the Present Century* 12 (Portland, ME: Bailey and Noyes, 1863).

9. Ibid.

10. Libby, supra n. 2, at l.

11. "Province of New Somersetshire," in *Province and Court Records of Maine,* Vol. 1, supra n. 2, at 1.

12. Ibid. at 6.

13. Ibid. at 1.

14. Ibid. at 3.

15. Ibid. at 3-4.

16. Court records for this period begin on March 25, 1636, and end on June 28, 1637. "Province of New Somersetshire," supra n. 11, at 1-8.

17. James Sullivan, *The History of the District of Maine* 72 (Bowie, MD: Heritage Books, 1994) (originally published 1795). See also n. 19, infra.

18. "The King's Patent to Gorges," in *Province and Court Records of Maine,* Vol. 1, supra n. 2, at 9, 10, 11.

19. Libby, supra n. 2, at xxix-xxx.

20. In his first commission to his councillors, Gorges expressed his desire for the "peacable goverment" of the province. "First Commission from Sir Ferdinando Gorges," in *Province and Court Records of Maine,* Vol. 1, supra n. 2, at 30, 32.

21. Libby, supra n. 2, at xxx-xxxiv.

22. Willis, supra n. 8, at 14.

23. Gorges had authority to "devide all or anie parte of the Territories . . . into Provinces Counties Citties Townes Hundredes and Parishes or such other portions of lande as hee . . . shall think fitt. . . . "The King's Patent to Gorges," supra n. 18, at 22.

24. Henry Wade Rogers, "Municipal Corporations," in *Two Centuries Growth of American Law: 1701-1901* 209-210 (New York: Charles Scribner's Sons, 1901). In his journal, Massachusetts Governor John Winthrop sneered at the borough of Agamenticus, calling it a poor village with a tailor as mayor.

25. Willis, supra n. 8, at 20-21.

26. ". . . I doe ordeyne that the court shall proceed to a diligent hearing of the complainte and *to be well assured of the truth of those contempts he stands accused of* [author's italics] . . ." before sentencing a defendant. "First Commission from Sir Ferdinando Gorges," supra n. 20, at 35.

27. Ibid. at 34.

28. *Province and Court Records of Maine,* Vol. 1, supra note 2, at 76.

29. The uncharted wilderness of Maine led to the granting of inaccurate deeds in England. Boundary disputes needed resolution as the wilderness was settled more thickly.

30. *Province and Court Records of Maine,* Vol. 1, supra note 2, at 77.

31. Ibid. at 87.

32. Ibid. at 75 n. 26. The settlers on both the Maine and New Hampshire sides of the Piscataqua River joined in political combinations to govern themselves. On the eve of the English Civil War, Mr. Puddington's statement may not have been far from the truth. This may account for the court's excusing him.

33. Ibid. at 82.

34. Willis, supra n. 8, at 22.

35. Henry Burrage, *The Beginnings of Colonial Maine: 1602-1658.* 293 (Portland, ME: Marks Printing House, 1914).

36. *Province and Court Records of Maine,* Vol. 1, supra note 2, at 88-89.

37. Ibid. at 133-134.

38. Burrage, supra n. 35, at 365.

39. Willis, supra n. 8, at 23.

40. Ibid. at 24.

41. *Province and Court Records of Maine,* vol. 2 (Charles Thornton Libby, ed., Maine Historical Society 1947) at 30.

42. Ibid. at 16-17.

43. Ibid. at 78.

44. Ibid. at 66, 68-69.

45. Ibid. at 29.

46. Ibid. at 38-39.

47. Ibid. at 68-69. There are a number of references to building roads and ferries throughout the county court records.

48. Ibid. at 68. "It is hence forth ordered that every Towne within this County annually shall . . . send in a list . . . of every particular mans estate. . . ."

49. Ibid. at 78. "It is therefore ordered that the Treasurer of this County shall . . . pay . . . for fivety law bookes, which in aequall proportion the said Treasurer is to distribute unto the severall Towns of this County."

50. Charles Thornton Libby, "Preface," *in Province and Court Records of Maine,* supra n. 41, at vii, x. "Even the *name* of 'Associates' Court' was hardly known in Boston. . . . [T]he thought of local control made them fidget."

51. Ibid. at xxxii.

52. Ibid. at xxxiii.

53. Willis, supra note 8, at 25.

54. Ibid. at 27.

55. Robert E. Moody, "Introduction," in *Province and Court Records of Maine,* Vol. 3 (Robert E. Moody, ed., Portland: Maine Historical Society, 1947), vii, xvii.

56. Ibid. at xviii.

57. Ibid. at xl-xlii. The author explains that ". . . in payments to be made in money, no money passed. . . . [T]he producers were robbed of a great part of their earnings by lack of a circulating medium."

58. Moody, supra n. 55, at xxx-xxxi.

59. Ibid.

60. Ibid. at xlv-xlvi.

61. Ibid. at xliv.

62. Benjamin W. Labaree, *Colonial Massachusetts: A History* 115 (Millwood, NY: KTO Press, 1979). ". . . Andros proved to be an unusual Indian fighter—provoking hostilities to begin with . . . and suspending the lucrative Indian trade."

63. L. Kinvin Wroth, "The History of the Law in Massachusetts: The Supreme Judicial Court 1692-1992," in *The Maine Connection: Massachusetts Justice Downeast, 1620-1820* 171, 171-172, Russell K. Osgood, ed. (Boston: Supreme Judicial Court Historical Society, 1992).

64. Ibid. at 172-173; The Charter of the Providence of the Massachusetts-Bay 1692-1714 *Mass Acts* 1; The Avalon Project at Yale Law School, *The Charter of Massachusetts Bay of 1691,* <http://www.yale.edu/lawweb/avalon/states/mass07.htm> (last updated May 20, 2005).

65. Charles E. Clark, *The Eastern Frontier: The Settlement of Northern New England, 1610-1763* 342 (New York: Alfred A. Knopf, 1970).

66. Clark, supra n. 65, at 74-75.

67. *Maine Province and Court Records,* vol. V, 21-31, Neal W. Allen Jr., ed. (Portland: Maine Historical Society, 1975).

68. Clark, supra n. 65, at 81.

69. Robert E. Moody, Introduction, *Maine Province and Court Records,* vol. VI, xxx-xxxi, Neal W. Allen Jr., ed. (Portland: Maine Historical Society, 1975).

70. Wroth, supra n. 63, at 176-177, 178, 181.

71. Henry Burt Montague, "Some Legal Incidents in the Separation of Maine from Massachusetts," *Maine Law Review* 3(1909-1910): 126-127, 135.

72. Resolve for the Appointment of an Agent to Superintend the Public Lands in the District of Maine 1802-1803 *Mass. Acts* 438; Resolve for the Appointment of an Agent to Superintend the Public Lands in the District of Maine 1802-1803 *Mass Acts* 884 (authorizing the building of roads and collection of tolls to maintain the roads); An Act to Establish the Kennebeck and Penobscott Turnpike Corporation 1802-1803 *Mass. Acts* 61; An Act to Establish a Corporation by the Name of the Maine Turnpike Association 1802-1803 *Mass. Acts* 307.

73. Montague, supra n. 71, at 126-128.

74. Neal W. Allen, "Law and Authority to the Eastward: Maine Courts, Magistrates, and Lawyers, 1690-1730," in *Law in Colonial Massachusetts 1630-1800* 273, 283-284, Daniel R. Coquillette, ed. (Boston: The Colonial Society of Massachusetts, 1984).

75. Treaty made by the commonwealth of Massachusetts with the Penobscot tribe of Indians, June 29, 1818. 1842-1843 Me. Laws 253; Resolve on the report of Alexander Campbell and others, committee in behalf of this commonwealth, to negotiate and settle any misunderstandings or difference with Passamaquoddy Indians and those of other tribes connected with them. Feb. 10, 1795. 1842-1842 Me. Laws 263. (For discussion of treaties, see Francis J. O'Toole and Thomas N. Tureen, "State Power and the Passamaquoddy Tribe: A Gross National Hypocrisy?" *Maine Law Review* 23[1971]: 1.)

76. *The Probate Auxiliary; Or a Director and Assistant to Probate Courts, Executors, Administrators and Guardians. Being the Law of the Commonwealth of Massachusetts, especting the Estate of Testators, Intestates and Wards. Carefully Collected. Together With a Comprehensive Alphabetical Index to the Same. To Which Are Added a Variety of Forms, for the Use of Probate Courts, and of Such Persons, As May Have Business to Transact Therein,* Samuel Freeman, ed. (Portland: MA: printed by Benjamin Titcomb, 1793).

77. Federal Judicial Center, History of the Federal Judiciary, Courts of the Federal Judiciary, <http://www.fjc.gov/history/home.nsf/page/uscc_01_leg> (last updated May 20, 2005); An Act to provide for the more convenient organization of the courts of the United States, 2 *Stat.* 89; An Act to repeal certain acts respecting the organization of the Courts of the United States; and for other purposes, 2 *Stat.* 132; An Act to amend the Judicial System of the United States, 2 *Stat.* 156.

78. Sen. Res., 15th Cong., That the committee on the judiciary be instructed to inquire as to the expediency of establishing, by law, a circuit court of the United States, to be holden at Portland, within and for the district of Maine (November 24, 1818) (microformed on Early American Imprints, S46280, American Antiquarian Society).

79. Federal Judicial Center, supra n. 77; An Act establishing a circuit court within and for the district of Maine, 3 *Stat.* 554.

80. Montague, supra n. 71, at 126-129, Wroth, supra n. 63, at 190-194.

81. Montague, supra n. 71, at 126-128.

82. Daniel Davis, Address, *An Address to the Inhabitants of the District of Maine, upon the Subject of Their Separation from the Present Government of Massachusetts. By One of their Follow Citizens* 50-52 (Portland: Printed by Thomas B. Wait, 1791).

83. P. Emory Aldrich, Address, *Massachusetts and Maine, Their Union and Separation* 60 (Proceedings of the American Antiquarian Society Boston, Worcester, MA: April 24, 1878); An Act for the admission of the state of Maine into the Union, 3 *Stat.* 544.

84. Maine Historical Society, *Maine's Beginnings,* <http://www.mainehistory. org/pdf/Maines_beginnins.pdf> (last updated 2000).

85. Aldrich, supra n. 83, at 44.

86. Montague, supra n. 71, at 130.

87. Howard Jones, *The Webster-Ashburton Treaty: A Study in Anglo-American Relations, 1783-1843* 36, 47 (Chapel Hill: University of North Carolina Press, 1977).

88. Aldrich, supra n. 83, at 52; for example, Resolve on Memorial of the Senators and Representative of the District of Maine, 1790-1791 *Mass. Acts* 510; Resolve for the Taking the Question on the Separation of the District of Maine from This Commonwealth, 1796-1797 *Mass. Acts* 311.

89. Aldrich, supra n. 83, at 50-52.

90. Aldrich, supra n. 83, at 52-54.

91. Laws of the Commonwealth of Massachusetts passed by the General Court. An Act Relating to the Separation of the District of Maine from Massachusetts Proper, and forming the same into a Separate and Independent State, June 19, 1819, 1819 *Mass. Acts* 248.

92. *The Debates, Resolutions, and Other Proceedings of the Convention of Delegates, Assembled at Portland on the 11th, and Continued Until, the 29th Day of October, 1919, for the Purpose of Forming a Constitution for the State of Maine to Which is Prefixed the Constitution,* Jeremiah Perley, ed. (Portland: A. Shirley Printer, 1820).

Republished as *The Debates and Journal of the Constitutional Convention of the State of Maine 1819-'20. And Amendments Subsequently Made to the Constitution* (Augusta: Maine Farmer's Almanac Press 1894). This is a reprint of the *Debates, Resolutions, and Other Proceedings . . .* but it includes indexes, biographical information on the delegates and the amendments passed to the Constitution since 1820.

93. An Act in addition to an Act, Entitled "An Act relating to the Separation of the District of Maine from Massachusetts Proper, and forming the same into a Separate and Independent State," 1820 *Mass. Acts* 425.

94. Montague, supra n. 71, at 131-133.

95. Wroth, supra n. 63, at 204; Aldrich, supra n. 83, at 60.

96. Montague, supra n. 71, at 131-132.

97. Aldrich, supra. n. 83, at 44.

98. Ibid.

99. Jones, supra n. 87, at 12.

100. Jones, supra n. 87, at 36.

101. Reports and Resolves in Relation to the Northeastern Boundary. 1838 *Mass. Acts* 2. This Resolve gives support to Maine in its effort to obtain the land Maine believes it is entitled to under the treaty of 1783.

102. Jones, supra n. 87, at 5; To settle and define the boundaries between the territories of the United States and the possessions of Her Britannic Majesty in North

America; for the final suppression of the African slave trade; and for the giving up criminal, fugitive from justice in certain cases, 8 *Stat.* 572; The Avalon Project at Yale Law School, *The Webster-Ashburton Treaty,* August 9, 1842, <http://www.yale.edu/lawweb/avalon/diplomacy/britian/br-1842.htm> (last updated May 20, 2005).

103. *Public Laws*, Me. H. Doc. 2, 32nd Leg., Reg. Sess. of 1853 (December 18, 1852). This is a compilation of documents relating to correspondence between the governors of Maine and Massachusetts to resolve the ownership of lands sitting in Maine.

104. *Public Laws,* Me. H. Doc. 1, 32nd Leg., Reg. Sess. of 1853 (April 16, 1852).

105. Ibid.

106. *Deed of Conveyance,* Me. H. Doc. 2, 33rd Leg., Reg. Sess. of 1854 (March 10, 1854).

Chapter 21

Maryland Prestatehood Legal Materials

Michael S. Miller
Ruth A. Hodgson
Dee Van Nest

INTRODUCTION

This partially annotated, selective bibliography has been prepared to provide the researcher of prestatehood Maryland with a detailed guide to primary and secondary sources documenting governmental formation and legal history prior to 1788. Incorporating both primary and secondary print and electronic sources, the guide is divided into six sections: historical background, state constitution, judicial branch, legislative branch, executive branch, and, finally, miscellaneous legal sources. Most categories are preceded by a brief overview followed by a selective annotated bibliography of sources on that topic.

HISTORICAL BACKGROUND

Roughly 156 years separates the birth of the establishment of colonial Maryland as a proprietary form of government in 1632 from the date it transitioned into the seventh state under the new federal Constitution in 1788. Over that course of a century and a half "Mariland," which was named in honor of the wife of King Charles I, Henrietta Maria, and was the third colony settled by the English in America, after Virginia and Massachusetts, grew from a band of 200 adventuresome settlers to over 200,000 inhabitants.

The proprietary charter of 1632 granted Lord Baltimore, Cecilius Calvert, and his successors, what was up to that time, considerable freedom in government making in a wilderness situated between the later disputed boundaries of Pennsylvania and Virginia. Leonard Calvert, younger brother of Cecilius, served as the province's first governor (1634-1644); three gentlemen appointed by Lord Baltimore served as his council of advisors. A secretary kept the colony's records and coordinated the distribution of land. Together these people comprised the "executive" branch of the neophyte government. The judicial branch was comprised of the governor himself and his council, who met as the provincial court and settled land disputes, debt collection problems, family law quarrels, and inheritance claims. On February 26, 1635, only eleven months after the first Maryland settlers landed on St. Clement's Island in the Potomac River, the freemen of the new colony of Lord Baltimore gathered at St. Mary's City for the first general assembly. They were there acting under the 1632 charter, giving the proprietary authority to enact laws, "with the Advice, Assent and Approbation of the free-men, or their Delegates or Deputies, shall be called together for the framing of laws, when, and as often as Need shall require."[1]

A few benchmark events and personalities have placed Maryland's early legal history in the textbooks. In 1638 Calvert extended to the provincial legislature the authority to initiate legislation; in 1648 Margaret Brent, who became Governor Leonard Calvert's estate executor, was given the authority to act as his attorney by the assembly and was subsequently denied the right to vote in that body. In 1649 while under royal authority and in an effort to attract Virginia Puritans to settle in Maryland, the legislature passed the Act Concerning Religion (the Toleration Act). Although limited to Christians and repealed in 1692, this was the first such legislation in the English-speaking world.

Maryland continued to be ruled as a royal colony at the beginning of the eighteenth century, governed directly by the king and Parliament. Although the Lords Baltimore had retained their ownership of the land, the colony's own "Glorious Revolution" of 1689 had wrested from them the right to appoint officials and approve laws. In 1692, the same year the Church of England was made the province's official church, the first royal governor arrived in Maryland. The change in regimes also resulted in the move of the provincial capital in 1694 from St. Mary's City to Annapolis. In 1715 Benedict Leonard Calvert, who had converted to the Protestant faith, became the fourth Lord Baltimore and successfully petitioned to have Maryland restored to the Calvert family as a proprietary colony, which lasted until the advent of the American Revolution in 1776. For the remainder of this colonial period, settlers whose interests were opposed to those of the proprietor no longer engaged in outright rebellion but utilized the general assembly to advance their views. Disputes centered around claims that the colonists enjoyed all the protections of English law; fees paid to proprietary colonial officials; and the printing of money instead of the continued use of tobacco as a currency. The upheaval of 1689 and the restoration of 1715 reaffirmed that Maryland was a government of institutions—a constitution (charter), governor, council, assembly, county courts, and militia.

Although Marylanders' battles with authority up to this time focused on the proprietor, rather than the king and Parliament, the Stamp Act of 1765, then the Townsend Duties of 1767, and finally the Tea Act of 1773 roused almost universal opposition among the colonies. Maryland was accustomed to being taxed by the proprietor and by its own assembly, but for the first time in its brief history it faced taxes from England itself. A century of antiproprietary feeling now welled up against the king.

In June 1774, as the governor was in England, members of the assembly issued a call for the establishment of a Maryland Provincial Convention consisting of deputies elected from each county. This convention and its executive arm, the council of safety, gradually assumed governmental power of the province. Maryland's revolution—the break with the proprietor and king—had occurred, and this extralegal body, the provincial convention, governed from 1774 until 1777. The last proprietary governor, Robert Eden, left to return to England in 1776, and in July that same year, Maryland's delegates to the Continental Congress, Charles Carroll, Samuel Chase, William Paca, and Thomas Stone, signed the Declaration of Independence for the province.

Maryland's own constitutional convention that met from August to November 1776 was the ninth provincial convention. It hammered out one of the least revolutionary documents of this revolutionary period, the state constitution, which included a declaration of rights articulating a new social and political contract between the citizens and their governors. Maryland's "bill of rights," though preceded by similar declarations from Virginia, Pennsylvania, and Delaware, was the most forceful and elaborate at that time and became a model for many state constitutions that would follow, including some of the provisions that surfaced in the federal Constitution.

Maryland's first constitutional governor was Thomas Johnson (1777-1779); the first session of the new state general assembly convened on February 5, 1777. On March 1, 1781, Maryland was the last state to ratify, and thereby make effective, the Articles of Confederation setting forth a system of government of the United States. The first working session of the court of appeals under the new state constitution was held in Annapolis on October 3, 1780. It was not until May 12, 1783, that the first oral argument was heard before this court. The first full published opinion of this court appears in the case *Ward v. Reeder*, 2 Harris and McHenry 145 (1789). On January 14, 1784, the Treaty of Paris ending the Revolutionary War was ratified by Congress assembled at Annapolis. On September 17, 1787, the new federal Constitution was signed by Marylanders Daniel Carroll, James McHenry, and Daniel of St. Thomas Jennifer at Philadelphia, and on April 28, 1788, a Maryland convention ratified the U.S. Constitution, making it the seventh state to do so.

Bibliography of Sources Used in Historical Introduction

Callcott, George H. *Maryland Political Behavior: Four Centuries of Political Culture.* Baltimore: Maryland Historical Society; Annapolis: Maryland State Archives, 1986.

Chapelle, Suzanne Ellery Greene. *Maryland: A History of Its People.* Baltimore: Johns Hopkins University Press, 1986.

Gambrall, Theodore C. *History of Early Maryland.* New York: Thomas Whittaker, 1893.
Also available online: <http://www.ls.net/~newriver/md/hemd.htm>.

Lewis, H.H. Walker. *The Maryland Constitution—1776.* Baltimore: Author, 1976.

Ridgway, Whitman H. *Maryland History and Culture Bibliography: Interpretive Essays.* "Politics and Law." Available online: <http://mdhc.neutralgood.org/essays.php?essay=22>.

Russo, Jean. *Maryland History and Culture Bibliography: Interpretive Essays,* "From Revolution to Revolution: Eighteenth Century Maryland." Available online: <http://mdhc.neutralgood.org/essays.php?essay=30>.

MARYLAND CONSTITUTION

An overview of Maryland's "constitutional" history prior to 1788 focuses on two primary documents: the Charter of 1632 granted by King Charles I of England to Cecilius Calvert, the Second Baron Baltimore, and the 1776 Constitution. The first, a grant of land north of the Potomac River, passed ownership of over 10 million acres of land to the Calverts, as proprietors to sell off and rule as they wished. This charter was a reactionary contract passing along to the proprietor powers that had historically rested with the king. One great exception in this written document, the likes of which England had never had, was that the people were extended rights to own land given or sold to them by the Calverts. In addition, the charter granted them the right, as Englishmen, to be consulted in any law-making process. It was this "constitution" which provided the initial legal basis for a form of representative government in Maryland.

The Continental Congress and the majority of the American colonists had opted for independence from England in the early months of 1776. Although the Declaration of Independence was not approved until July 4, 1776, the Congress, on May 10, had advised the colonies to adopt new forms of government. By the spring of 1777, ten colonies had adopted "constitutions" that replaced the former royal or proprietary establishments.

A look at state constitutional development in the United States shows that constitution making is forever an evolving process, as illustrated by frequent wholesale revisions and countless amendments. Maryland has had four constitutions since declaring its independence in 1776. They bear the dates 1776, 1851, 1864, and 1867. The last three were drafted by actual "constitutional conventions." That of 1776, the Provincial Convention, however, cannot be classified with the others since that body was actually the de facto governing body of the province from 1774 to 1776. The ninth assemblage of this convention, on August 17, 1776, elected a special committee to prepare a declaration and charter of rights and a form of government. On November 3, the convention adopted a comprehensive declaration of rights, and on November 8, the constitution. Popular ratification was neither sought nor considered necessary; therefore, both took effect immediately. This very conservative constitution was one of the least revolutionary documents of this period, with its frame of government designed to continue the status quo minus the king and proprietary. It established a government consisting of a bicameral legislature; a governor and five-member council elected by the assembly; and an independent judiciary, appointed for life by the governor. Local institutions were not granted constitutional autonomy and were subjected to strong oversight by the state. The county sheriff was the only popularly elected local official.

Bibliography of Sources Used in Constitution Overview

"Constitution Making in Maryland." In *Report of the Constitutional Convention Commission 1967*. Annapolis: State of Maryland for the Constitutional Convention Commission, 1967.

Lewis, H.H. Walker. *The Maryland Constitution—1776*. Baltimore: Author, 1976.

Tomlinson, Edward A. "The Establishment of State Government in Maryland: the Constitution of 1776." *Maryland Bar Journal* 9(1976): 4.

Maryland Constitution—Primary Sources

The Charter of Maryland, June 20, 1632. Reprint with Introduction by Edward C. Papenfuse, State Archivist. Annapolis: Maryland Hall of Records Commission, 1982.

Available online: <http://aomol.net/000001/000549/html/index.html>; <http://aomol.net/megafile/msa/speccol/sc2900/sc2908/html/charter.html>.

The Charter of Maryland, Together with the Debates and Proceedings of the Upper and Lower Houses of Assembly, in the Years 1722, 1723 and 1724. Relating to the Government and Judicature of That Province. Collected from the Journals, and published by order of the lower-house. Philadelphia: Printed and sold by Andrew Bradford, 1725.

Constitution of Maryland: At a Convention of the Delegates Chosen by the Several Counties and Districts . . . of the Province of Maryland, at the City of Annapolis on Wednesday, the 14th of August and Continued by Adjournments to the, 11th of November, 1776 [with Chancellor Bland's notes] (1776).

Constitutional Records 1632-1851. Unit 1 (1632 to June 1776); Unit 2 (Convention, August 14, 1776 to November 11, 1776).

Also available online: <aomol.net/megafile/msa/speccol/sc4800/sc4872/003145/html/index.html>.

The Decisive Blow Is Struck: A Facsimile Edition of the Proceedings of the Constitutional Convention of 1776 and the First Maryland Constitution. Introduction by Edward C. Papenfuse and Gregory A. Stiverson. Annapolis: Hall of Records Commission, 1977.

Photo reprint from the 1787 edition of *Laws of Maryland* compiled by A.C. Hanson.

Declaration of Rights and Constitution of Maryland, as adopted by the Ninth Convention, August-November 1776.

Also available online at <http://aomol.net/megafile/msa/speccol/sc2900/sc2908/000001/000203/html/index.html>. Text taken from Hanson's *Laws of Maryland,* 1787.

A Declaration of the Lord Baltemore's Plantation in Mary-land; Wherein Is Set Forth How Englishmen May Become Angels, the King's Dominions

Be Extended and the Adventurers Attain Land and Gear; Together with Other Advantages of That Sweet Land. Annapolis: Maryland Hall of Records Commission, 1983. Also available online at <http://aomol.net/ megafile/msa/speccol/sc2900/sc2908/000001/000550/html/index.html>.

A facsimile of the original tract of 1633, made, by permission, from the only known copy in the possession of his Eminence the Cardinal Archbishop of Westminster. Introduction by Lawrence C. Wroth.

Proceedings of the Conventions of the Province of Maryland, Held at the City of Annapolis, in 1774, 1775, & 1776. Baltimore: James Lucas and K. Deader; Annapolis: Jonas Green, 1836.

The conventions dealt largely with issues relating to the governing hostilities with Great Britain. The ninth (and final) convention, which met from August to November 1776, framed the first state constitution. Also available online: http://aomol.net/megafile/msa/speccol/sc2900/sc2908/000001/ 000078/html/index.html>.

Maryland Constitution—Secondary Sources

Anderson, Thornton. "Maryland's Property Qualifications for Office: A Reinterpretation of the Constitutional Convention of 1776." *Maryland Historical Magazine* 73(1978): 327.

Browne, Cynthia E. *State Constitutional Conventions from Independence to the Completion of the Present Union, 1776-1959; Maryland, a Bibliography.* Westport, CT: Greenwood Press, 1972.

Burghardt, Walter J. *The Charter of Maryland: 1632, 1965, 1983.* Annapolis: Maryland Hall of Records, 1983.

Chapman, James W., Jr. "Maryland Laid the Cornerstone of Our Federal Union." *Transactions of the Maryland State Bar Association* 36(1931): 4.

"Constitution Making in Maryland." In *Report of the Constitutional Convention Commission—1967.* Annapolis: State of Maryland, 1967.

Pages 25-37 of this document, generated by an effort to rewrite Maryland's constitution in 1967-1968, provide good historical background on the evolution of the 1776 constitution.

Crowl, Philip Axtell. "Maryland During and After the Revolution: A Political and Economic Study." *The Johns Hopkins University Studies in Historical and Political Science,* vol. 61, pp. 1-185. Baltimore: The Johns Hopkins University Press, 1943.

Delaplaine, Edward S. "Thomas Johnson, Maryland and the Constitution." *Transactions of the Maryland State Bar Association* 30(1925): 75.

Thomas Johnson, as a member of the colonial legislature and later the first governor under Maryland's first state constitution of 1776 was the major force behind having the state legislature assent to becoming the thirteenth state under the Articles of Confederation in 1781. He later was instrumental in leading the Maryland convention on April 26, 1788, to ratify the new federal Constitution.

Devecmon, William C. "A History of Our State Constitution Conventions." *Transactions of the Maryland State Bar Association* 14(1909): 3.

Concentrates on the state's first convention that led up to the constitution of 1776.

Friedman, Dan. "The History, Development, and Interpretations of the Maryland Declaration of Rights." *Temple Law Review* 71(1998): 637. Also available online at <http://aomol.net/megafile/msa/speccol/sc2900/sc2908/html/convention1776.html>.

Haw, James Alfred. *Politics in Revolutionary Maryland, 1753-1788.* Ann Arbor, MI: University Microfilm International, 1986.

PhD dissertation—University of Virginia.

High, James. "A Facet of Sovereignty: The Proprietary Governor and the Maryland Charter." *Maryland Historical Magazine* 55(June 1960): 67.

Hoffer, Peter Charles. "Their 'Trustees and Servants': Eighteenth-Century Maryland Lawyers and the Constitutional Implications of Equity Precepts." *Maryland Historical Magazine* 82(Summer 1987): 142.

Hoffman, Ronald. *A Spirit of Dissension: Economics, Politics and the Revolution in Maryland.* Baltimore: Johns Hopkins University Press, 1973.

Jordan, David W. *Foundations of Representative Government in Maryland, 1632-1715.* Cambridge, MA: Cambridge University Press, 1987.

Klingelhofer, Herbert E. "The Cautious Revolution: Maryland and the Movement Toward Independence, 1774-1776." *Maryland Historical Magazine* 60(September 1965): 261.

Lewis, H.H. Walker. *The Maryland Constitution, 1776.* Baltimore: H.H. Walker Lewis, 1976.

————. "The Tax Article of the Maryland Declaration of Rights." *University of Maryland Law Review* 13(1953): 83.

McClintock, Gertrude Mary Smith. *Maryland Ratifying Convention of 1788.* MA thesis—American University, 1930.

McMahon, John V.L. *An Historical View of the Government of Maryland, from Its Colonization to the Present Day.* Baltimore: F. Lucas, 1831.

Marbury, William L. "How Maryland Became a Sovereign State." *Maryland Historical Magazine* 21(1926): 325.

Obrecht, Everett D. "The Influence of Luther Martin in the Making of the Constitutions of the United States." *Maryland Historical Magazine* 27(1932): 173, 280.
A fascinating look at one of Maryland's most famous legal minds, who was an antifederalist during the years leading up to Maryland's ratification of the U.S. Constitution on April 26, 1788.

Onuf, Peter S., ed. *Maryland and the Empire, 1773: The Antilon-First Citizen Letter.* Baltimore: Johns Hopkins University Press, 1974.
Daniel Dulany's "Antilon" letter and Carroll's "First citizen" replies first appeared in the *Maryland Gazette,* January-July 1773. Centers on the Maryland colonial interpretation of the Petition of Right.

Papenfuse, Edward C., ed. *Archives of Maryland: New Series, I. An Historical List of Public Officials of Maryland. Governors, Legislators, and Other Principal Officers of Government, 1632 to 1990.* Annapolis: Maryland State Archives, 1990.
Also available online: <http://www.mdarchives.state.md.us/msa/speccol/sc2600/sc2685/html/histlist.html>.

Papenfuse, Edward C. and Robert C. Murphy. "But for the Sake of a Comma: The Constitution, the Bill of Rights, and Changing Perceptions of Peaceable Assembly and Representative Government in Maryland, 1765-1802."

Also available online: <http://www.geocities.com/collegepark/union/3405/ecp-6-494/comma.html>.

Papenfuse, Edward C. and M. Mercer Neale. "Writing It All Down: The Art of Constitution Making for the State and the Nation, 1776-1833." *The Archives of Maryland Documents for the Classroom.*

Also available online: <http://www.mdarchives.state.md.us/msa/stagser/s1259/121/3918/html/0000.html>.

Rainbolt, John C. "A Note on the Maryland Declaration of Rights and Constitution of 1776." *Maryland Historical Magazine* 66(Winter 1971): 420.

Rees, Charles A. "The First American Bill of Rights: Was It Maryland's 1639 Act for the Liberties of the People?" *University of Baltimore Law Review* 31(Fall 2001): 41.

Riley, Elihu S. *Correspondence of "First Citizen"—Charles Carroll of Carrollton, and "Antilon"—Daniel Dulany, Jr., 1773; With a History of Governor Eden's Administration in Maryland, 1769-1776.* Baltimore: King Brothers, 1902.

Rohr, Charles James. *The Governor of Maryland: A Constitutional Study.* Baltimore: Johns Hopkins University Press, 1932.

Schweitzer, Mary McKinney. "A New Look at Economic Causes of the Constitution: Monetary and Trade Policy in Maryland, Pennsylvania, and Virginia." *Social Science Journal* 26(1989): 15.

Silver, John Archer. "The Provisional Government of Maryland (1774-1777)." *Johns Hopkins University Studies in Historical and Political Science,* 13th Series, October 1894. Baltimore: The Johns Hopkins Press, 1895.

Skaggs, David Curtis. *Roots of Maryland Democracy 1753-1776.* Westport, CT: Greenwood Press, 1973.

―――"Origins of the Maryland Party System: The Constitutional Convention of 1776." *Maryland Historical Magazine* 75(June 1980): 95.

Stiverson, Gregory A. "To Maintain Inviolate Our Liberties: Maryland and the Bill of Rights." *The Bill of Rights and the States; The Colonial and Revolutionary Origins of American Liberties.* Madison, WI: Madison House, 1992.

Tomlinson, Edward A. "The Establishment of State Government in Maryland: The Constitution of 1776." *Maryland Bar Journal* 9(June 1976): 4.

JUDICIAL BRANCH

Maryland's initial charter clearly outlined the judicial powers of the lord proprietor, giving him the sole authority to establish courts, appoint judges, and do what was necessary to establish justice in the colony. Cecilius Calvert, the colony's first proprietor, named his brother Leonard Calvert "Lieutenant-General, Chief Justice, Chancellor and Chief Magistrate of Maryland." In 1638 this court, called the county court, was composed of the governor as chief justice and members of the upper house sitting as associate justices. This same group of men also comprised a court of appeals. Maryland was sparsely populated and the courts heard only a small number of cases. By 1642 the name of the court was changed to the provincial court. Members of this court were not required to have any special legal training. Surprisingly, there were appeals from the provincial court to the same group of men who sat on the court of appeals. This puzzling aspect of the governor and members of the legislative assembly acting as the court of last resort was actually based on the English model of Parliament, which historically was the court of final appeal.

Maryland's early local justice, firmly based in English tradition, was meted out by the manor and leet or peoples' courts. A jury composed of residents of the manor could decide cases; impose fines and punishments; enact by-laws regulating the residents; and elect constables, bailiffs, and even ale tasters. The role of the manor and leet courts was gradually taken over by the county courts. Sometime between 1658 and 1661 the county courts were officially organized. Four or more justices were appointed to the county bench, and court could not be held unless at least four were present. Clerks were appointed for the counties and given the power to call a grand jury inquest. The courts had jurisdiction in criminal cases. They were limited in civil cases to matters that "did not exceed three thousand pounds of tobacco."

After the royal government was established in 1689 the appellate courts were decentralized, and the court of appeals and provincial court became separate entities. An increase in population and settlements throughout the colony also brought an increase in the variety of courts. Another court, the court of chancery, formerly part of the provincial court, was established as an independent court in 1661. This court had jurisdiction in cases that could not be decided using statutory or common law. The admiralty court, which had also been part of the provincial court, was headed at times by the justice-appointed vice admiral. This court functioned on and off during the colonial period, on both the eastern and western shores, deciding maritime-related cases.

The prerogative or orphans' court, which had functioned in Maryland by being part of the duties of Philip Calvert, son of the first proprietor, did not become officially established until 1671 in St. Mary's County. The protection of orphans and their estates from creditors was the primary duty of the court. The court also had control over the succession of land and could control the administration of the estate by requiring bonds for performance. Many of the documents from the early prerogative courts still remain housed at the Maryland State Archives and give clues to the existence and work of this court.

In 1776 the provincial court was renamed the general court; judgments from the court of chancery and court of admiralty were appealed to the general court until it was abolished in 1806. Thereafter, the court of appeals became the only Maryland appellate court. The 1776 constitution brought about several additional changes in the judicial branch. Some of the changes addressed the final separation of the "legislative, executive and judicial powers of government"; gave the governor the sole power to appoint judges; created the office of the register of wills; and empowered the orphans' courts to handle all matters regarding probate and orphan care. In 1777 the justices of the peace were handling cases when the issues involved did not exceed five pounds; parties had a right to appeal to the county courts. County courts had jurisdiction over amounts up to twenty pounds; this amount was later increased to 100 pounds. These changes led to the creation of a court system close to the twenty-first-century judiciary. Maryland courts have long rested on a strong foundation created by the early colonial settlers.

Bibliography of Sources Used in Judicial Branch Overview

Bond, Carroll T. *The Court of Appeals of Maryland.* Baltimore: Barton-Gillet Company, 1928. Also available online at <http://aomol.net/megafile/msa/speccol/sc2900/sc2908/000001/000368/index.html>.

Bozmon, John Leeds. *History of Maryland, I.* Baltimore: J. Lucas and E. K. Deaver, 1837.

Carr, Lois Green, Aubrey C. Land, and Edward C. Papenfuse, eds. *Law, Society, and Politics in Early Maryland: Proceedings of the First Conference on Maryland History, June 14-15, 1974.* Baltimore: Johns Hopkins University Press, 1977.

Johnson, John A.B. "Old Maryland Manors with the Records of a Court Leet and Court Baron." *Johns Hopkins University Studies in Historical and Political Science* [1st Series] VII. Baltimore: Johns Hopkins, 1883.

McSherry, James. "The Former Chief Judges of the Court of Appeals of Maryland." *Maryland State Bar Transactions, Report of the Ninth Annual Meeting* (1904).

Meister, Douglas C. *The Development of the Maryland Reports.* S.l.: Author, 1994.

Mereness, Newton D. *Maryland As a Proprietary Province.* London: Macmillan, 1901.

Wichers, Marilyn G. *Administration of Justice in Colonial Maryland, 1632-1689.* Ann Arbor, MI: University Microfilms International, 1983.

Judicial Branch—Primary Sources

Archives of Maryland. 72 vols. Baltimore: Published by authority of the state under the direction of the Maryland Historical Society, 1883-1972.
Also available and searchable online: <http://aomol.net>.

Crowl, Philip A. and Joseph H. Smith. *Court Records of Prince Georges County, Maryland, 1696-1699.* Washington, DC: American Historical Association, 1964.

Harris, Thomas and John McHenry. *Maryland Reports Being a Series of the Most Important Law Cases Argued and Determined in the Provincial Court and Court of Appeals of the Then Province of Maryland, from the Year 1700 Down to the American Revolution,* 1 *Harris and McHenry* (1658-1774). New York: I. Riley, 1809.

Harris, Thomas and John McHenry. *Maryland Reports Being a Series of the Most Important Law Cases Argued and Determined in the General Court and Court of Appeals of the State of Maryland, from May, 1780, to May, 1790, 2 Harris and McHenry* (1780-1790). New York: C. Wiley, 1812.

Thomas Harris Jr., clerk of the court of appeals, and John McHenry, attorney at law, published five volumes of early Maryland cases beginning with Volume 1 (1658-1774); Volume 2 (1780-1790); and continuing post-Revolution through Volume 5 (1804-1835). The first volume, published in 1809, was written by using a collection of private papers from practicing attorneys and state records that Harris and McHenry had assembled. This volume included cases from both the provincial court and the court of appeals. The writings were greatly enhanced by Harris and McHenry's addition of annotations consisting of early English reports, notes from practicing attorneys, and numerous references to prominent legal treatises.

Kilty, William. *A Report of All Such English Statutes As Existed at the Time of the First Emigration of the People of Maryland, and Which by Experience Have Been Found Applicable to Their Local and Other Circumstances; and of Such Others As Have Since Been Made in England or Great-Britain, and Have Been Introduced, Used and Practised, by the Courts of Law or Equity; Also All Such Parts of the Same As May Be Proper to Be Introduced and Incorporated into the Body of the Statute Law of the State. Made According to the Directions of the Legislature, by William Kilty . . . To Which Are Prefixed, an Introduction and Lists of the Statutes Which Had Not Been Found Applicable to the Circumstances of the People: With Full and Complete Indexes.* Published under the directions of the governor and council, pursuant to a resolution of the general assembly. Annapolis: Printed by Jehu Chandler, 1811.

Kilty (1757-1821) served as chancellor of Massachusetts, 1806-1821, and wrote on Maryland law. Also available online at <http://aomol.net/mega file/msa/speccol/sc2900/sc2908/000001/000143/html/index.html>.

Merritt, Elizabeth. *Proceedings of the Provincial Court of Maryland, 1670-1675.* Baltimore: Maryland Historical Society, 1952.

Judicial Branch—Secondary Sources

Bond, Carroll T. *The Court of Appeals of Maryland: A History.* Baltimore: The Barton-Gillet Co., 1928. Also available online at <http://aomol. net/megafile/msa/speccol/sc2900/sc2908/000001/000368/html/index.html>.

Carr, Lois Green, Aubrey C. Land, and Edward C. Papenfuse, eds. *Law, Society, and Politics in Early Maryland: Proceedings of the First Conference on Maryland History, June 14-15, 1974.* Baltimore: Johns Hopkins University Press, 1977.

DePauw, Linda Grant. "Land of the Unfree: Legal Limitations on Liberty in Pre-Revolutionary America." *Maryland Historical Magazine* 68(Winter 1973): 355.

Didier, Eugene L. "The Courts of Appeals of Maryland." *The Green Bag* 6(1894): 225.

Ellefson, C. Ashley. *The County Courts and the Provincial Court in Maryland.* Ann Arbor, MI: University Microfilms International, 1986.

PhD dissertation—University of Maryland, 1963.

Hammond, Hall. "Commemoration of the Two Hundredth Anniversary of the Maryland Court of Appeals: A Short History." *Maryland Law Review* 38(1978): 229.

This article was based on Chief Judge Carroll Bond's book *The Court of Appeals of Maryland.*

Hartogensis, B.H. "Maryland Statutory Modifications of the Common Law of Real Property." *Maryland Law Review* 1(1936): 238.

Hartsook, Elisabeth S. and Gust Skordas. *Land Office and Prerogative Court Records of Colonial Maryland.* Annapolis: Hall of Records Commission, 1946.

Henderson, Jacob. *The Rev. Mr. Jacob Henderson's Fifth Letter to Daniel Dulany, Esq; in Relation to the Case and Petition of the Clergy of Maryland.* Philadelphia, PA: Published by the author, 1732.

In this letter, signed and dated, "Finished the 15th of May, 1731" (p. 36), Henderson refutes the arguments of Dulany's previous letter, received on February 24, and sets out to prove, "before the Law, Under the Law, and under the Gospel," that "divine Wisdom . . . had expressly provided a Support [for the sustinance of the clergy of Maryland] . . . viz. Tythes of the tenth Part of the Fruits of the Earth." He also counters Dulany's charge that he is dishonest and a "pretender to Inspiration."

Dulany (1685-1753), a Maryland lawyer, served in the state general assembly and governor's council.

Hoffer, Peter Charles. "Their 'Trustees and Servants': Eighteenth-Century Maryland Lawyers and the Constitutional Implications of Equity Precepts." *Maryland Historical Magazine* 82(Summer 1987): 142.

Invernizzi, Frederick W. and Henry R. Lord. *The Historical Development of the Maryland Courts, 1974.* n. p.

Jacobsohn, Gary J. "The Right to Disagree: Judges, Juries, and the Administration of Criminal Justice in Maryland." *Washington University Law Quarterly* 1976(Fall 1976): 571.

Johnson, John A.B. "Old Maryland Manors, with the Records of a Court Leet and a Court Baron." *Johns Hopkins University Studies in Historical and Political Science* [1st Series] VII. Baltimore: Johns Hopkins University, 1883.

Land, Aubrey C. "Lord Baltimore and the Maryland County Courts." *Maryland Law Review* 20(1960): 133.

Lankford, Wilmer O., transcriber. *Court Records of Somerset County, Maryland, 1694.* Princess Anne, MD: Manokin Press, 1992.

A Letter from Daniel Dulany, Esq.; To the Reverend Mr. Jacob Henderson. In answer to Mr. Henderson's printed letter, dated September 23, 1731. To which is prefix'd the case and petition of the clergy of Maryland, as published in London, by Mr. Henderson, 1729. Annapolis: W. Parks, 1732.

In this letter, Dulany aggressively refutes Henderson's January 4 letter, quoting extensively from it.

Marbury, William L. "The High Court of Chancery and the Chancellors of Maryland." *Transactions of the Maryland State Bar Association* 10 (1905): 113.

McGuinn, Henry Jared. *The Courts and the Changing Status of Negroes in Maryland.* Richmond, VA: Published by the author, 1940.

Comment, "More Light on an Old Court: The Kent County Court, 1647-1655." *Northwestern University Law Review* 68(March-April 1973): 110.

Newbold, David Marion. *Notes on the Introduction of Equity Jurisdiction into Maryland, 1634-1720.* Baltimore: M. Curlander, 1906.

Papenfuse, Edward C., ed. *Archives of Maryland: New Series, I. A Historical List of Public Officials of Maryland. Governors, Legislators, and Other Principal Officers of Government, 1632 to 1990.* Annapolis: Maryland State Archives, 1990.
Also available online: <http://www.mdarchives.state.md.us/msa/speccol/sc2600/sc2685/html/histlist.html>.

Phelps, Charles E. "Some Characteristics of the Provincial Judiciary, with Modern Footnotes." *Maryland State Bar Association Report* 2(July 28-29, 1897): 93.

Report of the Committee on Legal Biography. "The Courts and Bench of Colonial Maryland." *Maryland Bar Association Report* 3(1898): 77-92.

Rice, James D. "The Criminal Trial Before and After the Lawyers: Authority, Law and Culture in Maryland Jury Trials, 1681-1837." *American Journal of Legal History* 40(October 1996): 455.

Sawyer, Jeffrey K. "'Benefit of Clergy' in Maryland and Virginia." *American Journal of Legal History* 34(January 1990): 49.

Sioussat, St. George Leakin. "The English Statutes in Maryland." *Johns Hopkins University Studies in Historical and Political Science,* Series XXI, nos. 11-12. Baltimore: Johns Hopkins Press, 1903.

Smith, Joseph H. *The Foundations of Law in Maryland: 1634-1715.* Barre, MA: Barre Publishers, 1965.

Steiner, Bernard C. "Maryland's First Courts." *American Historical Association Annual Report* 1(1901): 211. Washington, DC: Government Printing Office, 1902.

Surrency, Erwin C. "Report on Court Procedures in the Colonies, 1700." *American Journal of Legal History* 9(1967): 167.

Tolley, Michael C. and David R. Owen. *Courts of Admiralty in Colonial America: The Maryland Experience, 1634-1776.* Durham, NC: Carolina Academic Press, 1995.

Van Ness, James S. *The Maryland Courts in the American Revolution: A Case Study.* Ann Arbor, MI: University Microfilms International, 1986.

PhD dissertation—University of Maryland, 1968.

Weichers, Marilyn Geiger. *The Administration of Justice in Colonial Maryland, 1632-1688.* Ann Arbor, MI: University Microfilms International, c1983, 1979.

Yackel, Peter Garrett, ed. "Criminal Justice and Loyalists in Maryland: *Maryland v. Caspar Frietschie,* 1781." *Maryland Historical Magazine* 73(1978): 46.

———. The Original Jurisdiction of the Superior Courts of Judicature of Colonial Maryland, New York, and Massachusetts.

PhD dissertation—Ohio State University, 1973.

"Treason" in Maryland's courts was governed both substantively and procedurally by the English common law of treason, though, subsequent to the Declaration of Independence, legislative assemblies passed statutes addressing the substantive issues of this crime.

LEGISLATIVE BRANCH

The origin of the general assembly can be found in the 1632 Charter of Maryland granted by Charles I, king of Great Britain and Ireland, to Cecilius Calvert, second Lord Baltimore. This document gave the authority to Lord Baltimore to make laws "with the advice, assent and approbation of the Free Men of the same Province, or of the greater part of them, or of their delegates, or of the greater part of them, whom we will shall be called together for the framing of laws, when, as often as need shall require."

The first Maryland General Assembly, a lawmaking assembly of freemen, met in 1634-1635 at St. Mary's City; the second session met in 1637. In 1638 the assembly's adoption of English law provided an important element of continuity. The lines of legislative power were established with the general assembly to initiate legislation, and with the governor having the power of the veto, with no right of overriding available to the assembly. The Act for Religion of 1649 was enacted to address the proprietor's policy of religious toleration; it was the first law of this type in the American colonies.

There were unicameral assemblies until 1650, when the general assembly was divided into upper and lower houses. The upper house consisted of the governor's council. Freemen formed the lower house with elected delegates from each hundred.[2] In 1652 parliamentary commissioners temporarily replaced the proprietary regime, until Lord Baltimore reestablished proprietary authority in 1657.

The Maryland Revolution of 1689 allowed the Protestant associators to overthrow the proprietary officers and form an interim government. In 1692 William and Mary declared Maryland a royal colony and governed it as such, replacing the proprietary province. The crown made few changes, except for the establishment of the Church of England and the creation of parishes. In 1694 the Maryland capital was moved from St. Mary's City to Annapolis. The colony was again returned to proprietary control in 1715, although it had little resemblance to the one of twenty-five years earlier. The lower house had gained political independence under royal control and played a stronger role in relation to the upper house.

The last colonial general assembly was suspended in 1774, and the first provincial convention, an extralegal body, met and sent delegates to the first continental congress. The provincial convention governed the colony from 1774 until 1777. In 1776, after the Declaration of Independence was signed, Maryland held its constitutional convention. The constitution of 1776 established the senate and house of delegates, and enabled the senate to sever all ties with the governor's council. The first general assembly elected under the state constitution of 1776 met in Annapolis in 1777. There was a smooth transition to the new government. During the Revolutionary War years, the general assembly operated much as it had during the provincial period. The post-Revolutionary era was controlled more closely by the constitution of 1776.

Bibliography of Sources Used in Legislative Branch Overview

Carr, Lois G. "Maryland's Seventeenth Century." *Maryland History and Culture: Bibliography, Interpretative Essays.*

Available online: <http://mdhc.neutralgood.org/essays.php?essay=29>.

Everstine, Carl N. *The General Assembly of Maryland, 1634-1776.* Charlottesville, VA: The Michie Company, 1980.

————.The General Assembly of Maryland, 1776-1850. Charlottesville, VA: The Michie Company, 1982.

Maryland Manual On-Line: A Guide to Maryland Government. Annapolis: The Maryland State Archives.

Updated daily online: <http://www.mdarchives.state.md.us/msa/mdmanual/html/mmtoc.html>.

Ridgway, Whitman H. "Politics and Law." *Maryland History and Culture: Bibliography, Interpretative Essays.*

Available online: <http://mdhc.neutralgood.org/essays.php?essay=22>.

Russo, Jean. "From Revolution to Revolution: Eighteenth-Century Maryland." *Maryland History and Culture: Bibliography, Interpretative Essays.*

Available online: <http://mdhc.neutralgood.org/essays.php?essay=30>.

Walsh, Lorena S. "Major Themes and Issues in Seventeenth Century Maryland History: A Historiographical Approach." *Maryland History and Culture: Bibliography, Interpretative Essays.*

Available online: <http://mdhc.neutralgood.org/essays.php?essay=hist>.

Legislative Branch—Primary Sources

"An Act for the Liberties of the People, General Assembly of Maryland, 1639." *Archives of Maryland: Proceedings and Acts of the General Assembly of Maryland,* Vol. 1. Baltimore: Maryland Historical Society, 1883.

Also available online: <http://press-pubs.uchicago.edu/founders/documents/v1ch14sl.html>.

Constitutional law scholar Bernard Schwartz, documenting the history of the Bill of Rights of the U.S. Constitution beginning with the English Magna Carta (1215), claimed that the "first American Bill of Rights," enacted by a colonial assembly, was Maryland's Act for the Liberties of the People in 1639. The settlers' rights as Englishmen were typically protected under a colonial charter granted by the king, but those rights were only generally stated. Maryland's 1639 act, passed by the settlers' own assembly, gave more specific content to these rights.

"An Act Ordeining Certain Laws for the Government of this Province, 1638." *Archives of Maryland: Proceedings and Acts of the General Assembly of Maryland,* Vol. 1. Baltimore: Maryland Historical Society, 1883.

Available online: <http://www.aomol.net/megafile/msa/speccol/sc2900/sc2908/000001/0000001/html/index/html>.

The 1639 Maryland Act for the Liberties of the People never passed in the Maryland General Assembly. An earlier 1638 Maryland Act for the Liberties of the People also does not qualify because, although it passed the general assembly, it was vetoed by the proprietor. However, the "first American Bill of Rights" may be the 1639 Maryland Omnibus Act Ordeining Certain Laws for the Government of this Province, which passed the general assembly and was approved by the proprietor.

Acts of Assembly of the Province of Maryland: Made and Passed at a Session of Assembly, Begun and Held at the City of Annapolis.

Archives of Maryland. Baltimore: Published by authority of the state under the direction of the Maryland Historical Society, 1883-1972.

Available and searchable online: <http://aomol.net>.

Bacon, Thomas. *Laws of Maryland, at Large, with Proper Indexes: Now First Collected into One Compleat Body, and Published from the original acts and records, remaining in the secretary's-office of the said province: together with notes and other matters, relative to the constitution thereof, extracted from the provincial records: to which is prefixed, the charter, with an English translation.* Annapolis: Jonas Greene, 1765.

Also available online at <http://aomol.net/megafile/msa/speccol/sc2900/sc2908/000001/000075/html/index.html>.

Bisset, James. *Abridgment and Collection of the Acts of Assembly of the Province of Maryland, at Present in Force. With a Small Choice Collection of Precedents in Law and Conveyancing. Calculated for the use of the gentlemen of the Province.* Philadelphia, PA: William Bradford, 1759.

Also available online at <http://aomol.net/megafile/msa/speccol/sc4800/ sc4872/011781/html/index.html>.

A Compleat Collection of the Laws of Maryland: With an Index, and marginal notes, directing to the several laws and the chief matters contained in them. Collected and printed by authority. Annapolis: William Parks, 1727.

Also available online at <http://aomol.net/megafile/msa/speccol/sc4800/ sc4872/011781/html/index.html>.

A Digest of the Laws of Maryland: being an abridgment, alphabetically arranged, of all the public acts of assembly now in force and of general use from the first settlement of the state, to the end of November session, 1797, with references to the acts at large. Includes appendix of public acts of assembly passed November session, 1799. Baltimore, MD: Printed for the Editor, 1799.

Also available online at <http://aomol.net/megafile/msa/speccol/sc4800/ sc4872/003150/html/index.html>.

A Digest of the Laws of Maryland. Being a Complete System (alphabetically arranged) of all the public acts of Assembly, now in force and of general use. From the first settlement of the state, to the end of November session 1803, inclusive. To which is added, the acts of Congress for the District of Columbia, from the assumption of jurisdiction to the end of the session, which terminated in April 1804, inclusive. Also, a variety of precedents, (adapted to the several acts) for the use of justices of the peace, &c. And also a table explanatory of sundry technical law terms. Washington, DC: Printed for the editor by J.C. O'Reilly, 1804.

Dorsey, Clement. *General Public Statutory Law and Public Local Law of the State of Maryland: From the Year 1692 to 1839 Inclusive, with Annotations Thereto, and a Copious Index.* Baltimore: J.D. Troy, 1840.

Also available online at <http://aomol.net/megafile/msa/speccol/sc2900/ sc2908/000001/000141/html/index.htm>.

A Journal of the Votes and Proceedings of the Lower House of Assembly of the Province of Maryland, at Their Session Begun, May 1, 1739. Annapolis: Jonas Green, 1739.

Also available online at <http://aomol.net/megafile/msa/speccol/sc2900/sc2908/000001/000203/html/index.html>.

Laws of Maryland, made and passed at a sessions of assembly; begun and held at the city of Annapolis from 1765 to 1784. Annapolis: Frederick Green, 1784.

Laws of Maryland, Made Since 1763 Consisting of Acts of Assembly Under the Proprietary Government, Resolves of Conventions. Annapolis: Frederick Green, 1787.

Also available online at <http://aomol.net/megafile/msa/speccol/sc2900/sc2908/000001/000203/html/index.htm>.

The Laws of Maryland, to which are prefixed the original charter, with an English translation. Annapolis: Frederick Green, 1799-1800.

Also available online at <http://aomol.net/megafile/msa/speccol/sc4800/sc4872/003150/html/index.html>.

The Laws of Maryland; with the charter, the Bill of rights, the Constitution of the State, and its alterations, the Declaration of Independence, and the Constitution of the United States, and its amendments; with a general index. Revised by Virgil Maxcey. Baltimore: P.H. Nicklin and Co., 1811.

Kilty, William. *A Report of All Such English Statutes as existed at the time of the first emigration of the people of Maryland, and which by experience have been found applicable to their local and other circumstances; and of such others as have since been made in England or Great-Britain, and have been introduced, used and practised, by the courts of law or equity; and incorporated into the body of the statute law of the state. Made according to the directions of the legislature, by William Kilty . . . To which are prefixed, an introduction and lists of the statutes which had not been found applicable to the circumstances of the people: with full and complete indexes.* Published under the directions of the governor and council, pursuant to a resolution of the General Assembly. Annapolis: Jehu Chandler, 1811.

Also available online at <http://aomol.net/megafile/msa/speccol/sc2900/sc2908/000001/000143/html/index.html>.

Votes and Proceedings of the Lower House of Assembly of the Province of Maryland, at a session of assembly, begun and held at the City of Annapolis . . .

Votes and Proceedings of the Lower House of Assembly of the Province of Maryland at a Convention begun and held, December 22, 1747: at an assembly held at the City of Annapolis, on Tuesday the twenty-second day of December, in the year 1747. Annapolis, MD: Jonas Green, 1747. Published in *Archives of Maryland* 44 and also available online at <http://aomol.net/megafile/msa/speccol/sc2900/sc2908/000001/000044/html/index.html>.

Legislative Branch—Secondary Sources

Alexander, Julian J. *A Collection of the British Statutes in Force in Maryland, According to the Report Thereof Made to the General Assembly by the Late Chancellor Kilty: With Notes and Reverences to the Acts of Assembly and the Code, and to Principal English and Maryland Cases.* Baltimore: Cushing and Bailey, 1870. The second edition (1912) is available online at <http://aomol.net/megafile/msa/speccol/sc2900/sc2908/000001/000194/html/index.htm>.

Carr, Lois Green, Aubrey C. Land, and Edward C. Papenfuse, eds. *Law, Society, and Politics in Early Maryland: Proceedings of the First Conference on Maryland History, June 14-15, 1974.* Baltimore: Johns Hopkins University Press, 1977.

Dodd, Walter F. "Maryland Compiled Laws of 1700." *Maryland Historical Magazine* 5(1910): 185.

Everstine, Carl N. "The Establishment of Legislative Power in Maryland." *Maryland Law Review* 12(Spring 1951): 99.

———. *The General Assembly of Maryland, 1634-1776.* Charlottesville, VA: The Michie Co., 1980.

———. "Maryland's Tolerance Act: An Appraisal." *Maryland Historical Magazine* 79(Summer 1984): 99.

Falb, Susan R. *Advice and Ascent: The Development of the Maryland Assembly, 1635-1689.* Ann Arbor, MI: University Microfilms International, 1986.
PhD dissertation—Georgetown University, 1976.

————. "Proxy Voting in Early Maryland Assemblies." *Maryland Historical Magazine* 73(September 1978): 217.

Hanley, Thomas O'Brien. "Church and State in the Maryland Ordinance of 1639." *Church History* 26(December 1957): 325.

Hartogensis, B.H. "Maryland Statutory Modifications of the Common Law of Real Property." *Maryland Law Review* 1(1936-1937): 238.

Johnson, Bradley T. "The Foundation of Maryland and the Origin of the Act Concerning Religion of April 21, 1649." Prepared for and partly read before the Maryland Historical Society. Peabody Publication Fund, No. 18. Baltimore: J. Murphy and Co., 1883.

Johnson, Gerald W. *The Maryland Act of Religious Toleration: An Interpretation.* Annapolis: Maryland Department of Information, 1957.

Three-hundredth anniversary of an act concerning religion, passed April 21, 1649, by the Maryland General Assembly. Reprint of the 1949 edition published for the state of Maryland by the committee for the three-hundredth anniversary of the Maryland Act of Religious Toleration. Additional information about the Act of Religious Toleration is available online at <http://www.mdarchives.state.md.us/msa/speccol/sc2200/sc2221/000025/html/toleration.html>.

Jordan, David W. "Elections and Voting in Early Colonial Maryland." *Maryland Historical Magazine* 77(Fall 1982): 238.

————. "The Miracle of This Age: Maryland's Experiment in Religious Toleration, 1649-1689." *Historian* 47(May 1985): 338.

Kinnaman, John Allen. *The Internal Revenues of Colonial Maryland.* Ann Arbor, MI: University Microfilms International, 1980.

PhD dissertation—Indiana University, 1955.

————. "The Public Levy in Colonial Maryland to 1689." *Maryland Historical Magazine* 53(September 1958): 253.

Michener, John H. "The History of Legislative Apportionment in Maryland." *Maryland Law Review* 25(Winter 1965): 1.

O'Brien, Edward Joseph. *Child Welfare Legislation in Maryland, 1634-1936.* Washington, DC: Catholic University of America, 1937.
PhD dissertation—Catholic University.

Papenfuse, Edward C., ed. *Archives of Maryland: New Series, I. A Historical List of Public Officials of Maryland. Governors, Legislators, and Other Principal Officers of Government, 1632 to 1990.* Annapolis: Maryland State Archives, 1990.
Available online: <http://www.mdarchives.state.md.us/msa/speccol/sc2600/sc2685/html/histlist.html>.

Papenfuse, Edward C., Alan F. Day, David W. Jordan, and Gregory A. Stiverson. *A Biographical Dictionary of the Maryland Legislature, 1635-1789.* Baltimore: Johns Hopkins University Press, 1979-1985.

Rees, Charles A. "The First American Bill of Rights: Was It Maryland's 1639 Act for the Liberties of the People?" *University of Baltimore Law Review* 31(Fall 2001): 41.

Riley, Elihu S. *A History of the General Assembly of Maryland, 1635-1904.* Port Washington, NY: Kennikat Press, 1972.

Russell, William Thomas. *Maryland: The Land of Sanctuary. A History of Religious Toleration in Maryland from the First Settlement until the American Revolution.* Baltimore: Forst, 1907.

Schweitzer, Mary McKinney. "Economic Regulation and the Colonial Economy: The Maryland Tobacco Inspection Act." *Journal of Economic History* 40(September 1980): 551.

Sioussat, St. George Leakin. "The English Statutes in Maryland." *Johns Hopkins University Studies in Historical and Political Science,* Series XXI, nos. 11-12. Baltimore: Johns Hopkins Press, 1903.

Thompson, Tommy R. "Debtors, Creditors and the General Assembly in Colonial Maryland." *Maryland Historical Magazine* 72(Spring 1977): 59.

Van Ness, James S. "On Untieing the Knot: The Maryland Legislature and Divorce Petitions." *Maryland Historical Magazine* 67(Summer 1972) 171.

Vivian, Jean H. "The Poll Tax Controversy in Maryland, 1770-76: A Case of Taxation *with* Representation." *Maryland Historical Magazine* 71 (Summer 1976): 151.

EXECUTIVE BRANCH

Primary Source

The Proceedings of the Committee Appointed to Examine into the Importation of Goods by the Brigantine Good Intent, Capt. Errington, from London, in February 1770. Annapolis: Anne Catharine Green, 1770.

The report of a committee appointed by an association of traders formed to enforce a self-imposed nonimportation agreement.

Secondary Sources

Calendar of Maryland State Papers. Annapolis: Maryland Hall of Records Commission, 1943-1958.

A Collection of the Governor's Several Speeches, and the Addresses of Each House: Together with Several Messages and Answers Thereto, Which Passed Between Each House: At a Convention of an Assembly, Begun the First of May, 1739. To which is added, the copy of an order of Council, made on occasion of some members being stiled, and acting after the prorogation of the assembly, as a committee of the House of Delegates. Annapolis: Jonas Green, 1739. The correspondence of Governor Sharpe was published in *Archives of Maryland* 6, 9, and 14, which are available online at <http://aomol.net/000001/0000064/html/index.html>, <http://aomol.net/000001/000009/html/index.html>, <http://aomol.net/000001/000014/html/index.html>.

This collection of documents and speeches concerns Governor Samuel Ogle's prorogation of the general assembly after animosity between the two houses over the financial affairs of the government became too acrimonious. Some members of the lower house continued to function as a legislative body after the dissolution of the assembly, prompting further action from Ogle.

Edgar, Matilda R. *A Colonial Governor in Maryland: Horatio Sharpe and His Times, 1753-1773.* New York: Longmans, Green, and Co., 1912.

Gleissner, Richard Anthony. *The Establishment of Royal Government in Maryland: A Study of Crown Policy and Provincial Politics, 1660-1700.* Ann Arbor, MI: University Microfilms International, 1977.

PhD dissertation—University of Maryland.

Jordan, David William. *The Royal Period of Colonial Maryland, 1689-1715.* Ann Arbor, MI: University Microfilms International, 1986.

PhD dissertation—Princeton University, 1966.

Owings, Donnell MacClure. *His Lordship's Patronage: Offices of Profit in Colonial Maryland.* Baltimore: Maryland Historical Society, 1953.

Papenfuse, Edward C., ed. *Archives of Maryland: New Series, I. An Historical List of Public Officials of Maryland. Governors, Legislators, and Other Principal Officers of Government, 1632 to 1990.* Annapolis: Maryland State Archives, 1990.

Available online: <http://www.mdarchives.state.md.us/msa/speccol/sc2600/sc2685/html/histlist.html>.

Rockefeller, Russell John. *Their Magistrates and Officers: Executive Government in Eighteenth Century Maryland.* Ann Arbor, MI: University Microfilms International, 1999.

PhD dissertation—University of Maryland, 1998.

Rohr, Charles James. *The Governor of Maryland, Constitutional Study.* Baltimore: Johns Hopkins University Press, 1932.

Rollo, Vera F. *Henry Harford: Last Proprietor of Maryland.* Annapolis: Maryland Bicentennial Commission, Harford County Committee, 1976.

Steiner, Bernard C. "The Chief Executive Officers of Maryland During the Provincial Period." *Maryland Historical Magazine* 7(September 1912): 321.

Lists of all chief executive officers from 1631-1776.

———. "Life and Administration of Sir Robert Eden." *Johns Hopkins University Studies in Historical and Political Science,* Series XVI, Nos. 7-9. Baltimore: The Johns Hopkins Press, 1898.

MISCELLANEOUS MARYLAND LEGAL MATERIALS

Acton, Jonathan W. "The Maryland Sheriff v. Modern and Efficient Administration of Justice." *University of Baltimore Law Review* 2(Spring 1973): 282.

Allen, Rev. Ethan. *Maryland Toleration: or, Sketches of the Early History of Maryland, to the Year 1650.* Baltimore: J. S. Waters, 1855.
Available online: <http://www.hti.umich.edu/cgi/t/text/text-idx?c=moa;idno =AAV9639>.

Alpert, Jonathan L. "The Origin of Slavery in the United States—The Maryland Precedent." *American Journal of Legal History* 14(July 1970): 189.

American Archives: Consisting of a Collection of Authentick Records, State Papers, Debates, and Letters and Other Notices of Public Affairs, the Whole Forming a Documentary History of the Origin and Progress of the North American Colonies; of the Causes and Accomplishment of the American Revolution; and of the Constitution of Government for the United States, to the Final Ratification Thereof. In six series . . . Peter Force, comp. Washington, DC: Prepared and published under authority of an act of Congress, 1837-1853.

Anderson, Thornton. "Eighteenth Century Suffrage: The Case of Maryland." *Maryland Historical Magazine* 76(Summer 1981): 141.

Andrews, Matthew Page. "Separation of Church and State in Maryland." *The Catholic Historical Review* 21(July 1935): 163.

Baer, Elizabeth, comp. *Seventeenth Century Maryland: A Bibliography.* Baltimore: John Work Garrett Library, 1949.

Barker, Charles Albro. *The Background of the Revolution in Maryland.* New Haven, CT: Yale University Press, 1940.

———. "Property Rights in the Provincial System of Maryland: Proprietary Policy." *Journal of Social History* 2(February, May 1936): 43-68, 211-232.

Behrens, Kathryn L. *Paper Money in Maryland 1727-1789.* Baltimore: Johns Hopkins Press, 1923.

PhD dissertation—Johns Hopkins University.

Bibbins, Ruthella Bernard Mory. *The Beginnings of Maryland in England and America.* Baltimore: Norman Remington Co., 1934.

Bond, Beverly W., Jr. "The Quit Rent in Maryland." *Maryland Historical Magazine* 5(December 1910): 350.

Bozman, John Leeds. *History of Maryland: Its First Settlement, in 1633, to the Restoration, in 1660.* Baltimore: James Lucas and E.K. Deaver, 1837.

Brugger, Robert J. *Maryland: A Middle Temperament, 1634-1980.* Baltimore: Johns Hopkins University Press, 1988.

Byrns, Ruth Katherine. "Religious Tolerance in Colonial Maryland." *The Catholic World* 138(March 1934): 694.

Callcott, George H. *Maryland Political Behavior: Four Centuries of Political Culture.* Baltimore: Maryland Historical Society; Annapolis: Maryland State Archives, 1986.

The Calvert Papers MS 174 in the Maryland Historical Society (microform). Baltimore: Maryland Historical Society, 1973.

Collection of Calvert family manuscripts (1516-1805) that includes family papers; documents relating to the Avalon, Virginia, and Maryland colonies; land, financial, and government records; papers dealing with the Maryland-Pennsylvania boundary dispute; correspondence; and miscellaneous documents. Originals in the Maryland Historical Society.

Carr, Lois Green. *County Government in Maryland 1689-1709.* PhD dissertation—Harvard, 1968, reprinted in 2 vols. New York: Garland Publishing, 1987.

Carr, Lois Green and David William Jordan. *Maryland's Revolution of Government, 1689-1692.* Ithaca, NY: Cornell University Press, 1974.

Carr, Lois Green, Russell R. Menard, and Louis Peddicord. *Maryland . . . At the Beginning.* Annapolis: Maryland Department of Economic and Community Development, 1984.

Cohen, Morris L. *Bibliography of Early American Law.* Buffalo, NY: William S. Hein, 1998.

Corrigan, R. "Maryland, Cradle of Religious Liberty." *Mid-America* 16 (April 1934): 213.

The Counties of Maryland and Baltimore City: Their Origin, Growth, and Development, 1634-1967. Baltimore: Maryland State Planning Department, 1968.

Cox, R.J. "Public Records in Colonial Maryland." *American Archivist* 37(1974): 263.

Crowl, Philip Axtell. *Maryland During and After the Revolution: A Political and Economic Study.* Baltimore: The Johns Hopkins University Press, 1943.

Davis, George Lynn-Lachan. *The Day-Star of American Freedom: or, The Birth and Early Growth of Toleration, in the Province of Maryland.* New York: Scribner, 1855.

Day, Alan F. "Lawyers in Colonial Maryland, 1660-1715." *American Journal of Legal History* 17(April 1973): 145.

———. *A Social Study of Lawyers in Maryland 1660-1775.* New York: Garland Publishing, 1989.

DeCourcy, W. Thomas. "Three Foundational Services of Maryland to the American System of Government." *Maryland Historical Magazine* 23 (1928): 1.

Delaplaine, Edward S. *Maryland in Law and History.* New York: Vantage Press, 1964.

DeMichele, Michael David. *The Glorious Revolution in Maryland: A Study of the Provincial Revolution of 1689.* Ann Arbor, MI: University Microfilms International, 1986.
PhD dissertation—Pennsylvania State University, 1967.

Donnelly, Ralph H. "The Colonial Land Patent System in Maryland." *Surveying and Mapping* 40(March 1980): 51.

Douglass, John E. "Between Pettifoggers and Professionals: Pleaders and Practitioners and the Beginnings of the Legal Profession in Colonial Maryland 1634-1731." *American Journal of Legal History* 39(July 1995): 359.

Dulany, Daniel. "The Right of the Inhabitants of Maryland to the Benefit of the English Laws." *Johns Hopkins University Studies in Historical and Political Science,* Series 21, nos. 11-12. Baltimore: Johns Hopkins Press, 1903.

Daniel Dulany (1721-1797), a Maryland lawyer, statesman, and member of the Maryland assembly, opposed the American Revolution.

Fogarty, Gerald P. "Property and Religious Liberty in Colonial Maryland Catholic Thought." *Catholic History Review* 72(October 1986): 573.

Gadsby, Elizabeth. "The Harford County (MD) Declaration of Independence." *American Monthly Magazine* 31(October 1907): 605.

Giddens, Paul H. "Land Policies and Administration in Colonial Maryland, 1753-1769." *Maryland Historical Magazine* 28(June 1933): 142.

————. "Maryland and the Stamp Act Controversy." *Maryland Historical Magazine* 27(1932): 79.

Parliament's passage of the stamp tax in 1765 generated a groundswell of opposition in Maryland. This article highlights the activities of the provincial assembly and other leaders in Maryland leading up to the later repeal of that act.

Gould, Clarence Pembroke. *The Land System in Maryland, 1770-1765.* Baltimore: The Johns Hopkins Press, 1913.

Griffin, Martin I.J. "Religious Liberty for Protestants and Toleration for Catholics in Maryland—Liberty for All in Pennsylvania." *American Catholic History Research,* New series 5(January 1909): 13.

Henderson, Jacob. *The Case of the Clergy of Maryland.* Annapolis: William Parks, 1730?.

Jacob Henderson (1686?-1751), a Maryland clergyman, was sent to London to protest against the Maryland General Assembly's Tobacco Act of October 3, 1728, which, among other provisions, reduced the local clergy's share of the tobacco tax by 25 percent. Most of the clergy's income was paid in tobacco.

Includes a petition to the Crown to intervene on behalf of the clergy.

Ingle, Edward. "Parish Institutions of Maryland, with Illustrations from Parish Records." *Johns Hopkins University Studies in Historical and Political Science,* VI, pp. 1-48. Baltimore: The Johns Hopkins University Press, 1883.

Ives, J. Moss. *The Ark and the Dove: The Beginning of Civil and Religious Liberties in America.* New York: Longmans, Green, 1936.

Jordan, David William. *The Royal Period of Colonial Maryland, 1689-1715.* Ann Arbor, MI: University Microfilms International, 1986.

PhD dissertation—Princeton University, 1966.

————. "The Miracle of This Age: Maryland's Experiment in Religious Toleration, 1649-1689." *Historian* 47(May 1985): 338.

Karraker, Cyrus H. "Deodands in Colonial Virginia and Maryland." *Academy of Human Rights* 37(July 1932): 712.

————. *The Seventeenth Century Sheriff: A Comparative Study of the Sheriff in England and the Chesapeake Colonies, 1607-1689.* Chapel Hill: Univeristy of North Carolina Press, 1930.

Kimmel, Ross M. "Free Blacks in Seventeenth-Century Maryland." *Maryland Historical Magazine* 71(Spring 1976): 19.

Kinnaman, John Allen. *The Internal Revenues of Colonial Maryland.* Ann Arbor, MI: University Microfilms International, 1980.

PhD dissertation—Indiana University, 1955.

Krugler, John D. "With Promise of Liberty in Religion: The Catholic Lords Baltimore and Toleration in Seventeenth-Century Maryland, 1634-1692." *Maryland Historical Magazine* 79(Spring 1984): 21.

———. "Lord Baltimore, Roman Catholics, and Toleration: Religious Policy in Maryland During the Early Catholic Years, 1634-1649." *Catholic History Review* 65(January 1979): 49.

Lasson, Kenneth L. "Religious Freedom and the Church-State Relationship in Maryland." *Catholic Lawyer* 14(Winter 1968): 4.

The Lord Baltemore's Case, Concerning the Province of Maryland, Adjoyning to Virginia in America. With full and clear Answers to all material Objections, touching his rights, jurisdiction, and proceedings there. And certaine reasons of state, why the Parliament should not impeach the same. Unto which is also annexed, a true copy of a commission from the late King's Eldest son, to Mr. William Davenant, to dispossess the Lord Baltemore of the said Province, because of his adherance to this Common-Wealth. London: 1653. [*Note:* This document is reprinted in full in *Narratives of Early Maryland, 1633-1684,* edited by Clayton Coleman Hall (New York: Barnes & Noble, Inc., 1967, reprint), pp. 167-180.]

After the commissioners sent by Parliament to reduce Virginia also removed Lord Baltimore's governor of Maryland, Lord Baltimore (and others) petitioned Parliament to recognize his patent and to restore his government of Maryland. The competing claims to Maryland of the commissioners controlling Virginia and Lord Baltimore were heard by the Committee of the Navy, which in turn referred the matter to a subcommittee. This pamphlet includes a summary of the objections to Lord Baltimore's patent and government and his answers to them, which were presented in writing to the committee, as well as a list of six reasons for maintaining Lord Baltimore's government and a copy of the commission from Charles II to William Davenant instructing Davenant to take over as governor of Maryland. The Lord Baltimore of this case is Cecil Calvert, the second Lord Baltimore, who directed the colonization of Maryland from 1632 to his death in 1675.

Luckett, Margie H., ed. *Margaret Brent.* Baltimore: King Brothers, 1931.

Main, Gloria Lund. *Personal Wealth in Colonial America: Explorations in the Use of Probate Records from Maryland and Massachusetts, 1650-1720.* Ann Arbor, MI: University Microfilms International, 1986.

PhD thesis—Columbia University, 1972.

Marbury, William L. "How Maryland Became a Sovereign State." *Maryland Historical Magazine* 21(December 1926): 325.

McCormac, Eugene Irving. "White Servitude in Maryland, 1634-1820." *Johns Hopkins University Studies in Historical and Political Science,* Series 22, nos. 3-4. Baltimore: Johns Hopkins Press, 1904.

McIlwaine, Henry R. *The Struggle of Protestant Dissenters for Religious Toleration in Virginia.* PhD dissertation—Johns Hopkins University, 1893.

McKinley, Edward N. "Religious Freedom in the Maryland Colony." *American Church Monthly* 30(July-August 1931): 50-57, 140-147.

McMahon, John V.L. *A Historical View of the Government of Maryland: From Its Colonization to the Present Day.* Baltimore: Frederick Lucas Jr., 1831.

Mereness, Newton D. *Maryland As a Proprietary Province.* New York: Macmillan, 1901.

Meyers, Debra. "The Civic Lives of White Women in Seventeenth-Century Maryland." *Maryland Historical Magazine* 94(Fall 1999): 309.

Middleton, Arthur Pierce. "Toleration and the Established Church in Maryland." *Historical Magazine of the Protestant Episcopal Church* 53 (March 1984): 13.

Newman, Harry Wright. *The Flowering of the Maryland Palatinate: An Intimate and Objective History of the Province of Maryland to the Overthrow of Proprietary Rule in 1654: With Accounts of Lord Baltimore's Settlement at Avalon.* Washington, DC: Published by the author, 1961.

Nolan, Dennis R. "The Effect of the Revolution on the Bar: The Maryland Experience." *Virginia Law Review* 62(1976): 969.

Norton, Mary Beth. "Gender and Defamation in Seventeenth-Century Maryland." *William & Mary Quarterly,* 3d Series, 44(1987): 38.

O'Brien, Thomas. *Their Rights and Liberties: The Beginnings of Religious and Political Freedom in Maryland.* Westminster, MD: Newman Press, 1959.

Parke, Francis Neal. "Witchcraft in Maryland." *Maryland Historical Magazine* 31(December 1936): 271.

Petrie, George. "Church and State in Early Maryland." *Johns Hopkins University Studies in Historical and Political Science,* Tenth Series, IV, pp. 193-238. Baltimore: The Johns Hopkins Press, 1892.

A Relation of the Successefull Beginnings of the Lord Baltemore's Plantation in Mary-land. Annapolis: Maryland State Archives, Hall of Records Commission, 1984.

Ridgway, Whitman H. "Interpretative Essays—Politics and Law." *Maryland History and Culture Bibliography.*
Available online: <http://mdhc.neutralgood.org/essays.php?essay=22>.

Riley, Elihu S. "Development of the Legal Profession, 1669-1715." *Maryland Bar Association Report* 4(1899): 87.

————. *Maryland—The Pioneer of Religious Liberty: The Only Catholic Colony of the Thirteen and the First to Establish Civil and Religious Freedom.* Annapolis: The Daily Record, 1917.

Russell, William T. *Maryland: The Land of Sanctuary: A History of Religious Toleration in Maryland from the First Settlement Until the American Revolution.* Baltimore: J.H. Furst, 1907.

Scharf, J. Thomas. *History of Maryland, from Earliest Period to the Present Day.* Baltimore: John B. Piet, 1879.

Scott, Kenneth. "Counterfeiting in Colonial Maryland." *Maryland Historical Magazine* 51(June 1956): 81.

Semmes, Raphael. *Crime and Punishment in Early Maryland.* Baltimore: Johns Hopkins University Press, 1996.
Originally published in a hardcover edition by The Johns Hopkins Press, 1938.

Silver, John Archer. "The Provisional Government of Maryland (1774-1777)." *Johns Hopkins University Studies,* Thirteenth Series, X, pp. 481-537. Baltimore: The Johns Hopkins Press, 1895.

Smith, Joseph. "The Foundations of Law in Maryland: 1634-1715." In George Billias, ed., *Selected Essays: Law and Authority in Colonial America.* Barre, MA: Barre, 1965.

Sparks, Francis Edgar. "Causes of the Maryland Revolution of 1689." *Johns Hopkins University Studies in Historical and Political Science,* Thirteenth Series, XI-XII, pp. 477-579. Baltimore: The Johns Hopkins Press, 1896.

Steiner, Bernard C. "The Adoption of English Law in Maryland." *Yale Law Journal* 8(May 1899): 353.

―――. *Beginnings of Maryland, 1631-1639.* Baltimore: The Johns Hopkins University Press, 1903.

―――. *Maryland under the Commonwealth: A Chronicle of Years 1649-1658.* Baltimore: The Johns Hopkins University Press, 1911.

―――. "The Royal Province of Maryland in 1692." *Maryland Historical Magazine* 15(1920): 125.

Stiverson, Gregory A. *Poverty in a Land of Plenty: Tenancy in Eighteenth-Century Maryland.* Baltimore: Johns Hopkins University Press, 1977.

Strong, Leonard. *Babylon's Fall in Maryland; A Fair Warning to Lord Baltamore. Or, a Relation of an Assault Made by Divers Papists, and Popish Officers of the Lord Baltamore's Against the Protestants in Maryland, to Whom God Gave a Great Victory Against a Greater Force of Souldiers and Armed Men, Who Came to Destroy Them.* London: Published by the author, 1655.

Thom, DeCourcy W. "Three Foundational Services of Maryland to the American System of Government." *Maryland Historical Magazine* 23 (March 1928): 1.

Tolley, Michael Carlton. "Maryland and Its Anglo-Legal Inheritance." *The Journal of Legal History* 11(1990): 353.

Vallette, Elie. *The Deputy Commissary's Guide Within the Province of Maryland: Together with Plain and Sufficient Directions for Testators to Form, and Executors to Perform Their Wills and Testaments: For Administrators to Compleat Their Administrations, and for Every Person Any Way Concerned in Deceased Person's Estates, to Proceed with Safety to Themselves and Others.* Annapolis: Ann Catherine Grenn, 1774.
Vallette was register of the Prerogative Office of Maryland Province.

Walsh, Lorena S. "Major Themes and Issues in Seventeenth Century Maryland History: A Historiographical Approach." *Maryland History and Culture Bibliography.*

Available online: <http://mdhc.neutralgood.org/essays.php?essay=hist>.

Werline, Albert W. *Problems of Church and State in Maryland during the Seventeenth and Eighteenth Centuries.* South Lancaster, MA: College Press, 1948.

Wilhelm, Lewis W. "Local Institutions of Maryland." *Johns Hopkins University Studies in Historical and Political Science,* Third Series, V-VI-VII, pp. 311-433. Baltimore: Johns Hopkins University Press, 1885.

Wright, James M. "The Free Negro in Maryland, 1634-1860." *Columbia University Studies* 97(3): 222. New York: Columbia University, 1921.

NOTES

1. The Charter of Maryland, June 20, 1632, Annapolis, Maryland Hall of Records Commission, 1982.

2. Hundred is an old English term, which may have originally indicated a hundred taxable units within royal estates. Hundreds were used in Maryland during the colonial period and for some years after to designate divisions within a county. They were established by county officials for taxation and other purposes. Tax records sometimes show two or more hundreds grouped together, which as time went on became a numbered election district.

Chapter 22

Colonial Massachusetts Legal Resources

Robert J. Brink
Stephen C. O'Neill

INTRODUCTION

Massachusetts boasts one of the longest colonial histories of any state in the nation. Thousands of Pilgrims, Puritans, Quakers, French Huguenots, Africans, and Native Americans (to name only some of the larger groups) lived in the Plymouth and Massachusetts Colonies in the century and a half between the years of 1620 and 1776.[1] These fairly literate English-speaking immigrants kept an overwhelming array of legal records, documenting every aspect of their lives. Historians, genealogists, archivists, and general researchers are often confronted with such an overwhelming mass of published and unpublished materials that just navigating the guides to these sources becomes a project itself.

This chapter presents a bibliographic essay designed to provide a brief overview of the sources for the legal records of colonial Massachusetts. Records included here are legislative acts, deeds, probate records, court papers, trial transcripts and files, town records, and the ever popular miscellaneous category—which in this case contains those items both rare and unique to colonial Massachusetts. Original colonial court records are under the jurisdiction of the Massachusetts Supreme Judicial Court's Division of Archives and Records Preservation, which is discussed in the chapter. Consideration is also given to previous bibliographical sources and useful historical texts that can provide researchers with both context and direction. A list of some of the more useful institutions is provided with explanations and summaries of their holdings. Institutions both private and public are represented here in an attempt to clarify the diverse nature of holdings found throughout the commonwealth. Internet archives and resources are noted where they contain Massachusetts materials. The goal of this essay is to present readers with not only what kinds of records may be found but also where to find them. Since there is no way to separate the history from the records, and the records described can be understood only if the history is known, this chapter attempts to combine the two, as briefly and simply as possible.

PRIMARY RECORDS AND SOURCES

Published Records

Plymouth Colony, 1620-1692

The Plymouth Colony, often referred to as the Old Colony, was founded in late December 1620, when the *Mayflower* Pilgrims landed at Plymouth on the interior side of Cape Cod Bay. The Pilgrims were radical English Protestants, called Separatists or sometimes Brownists, who believed that each congregation should govern its own affairs. The colony they founded existed as a separate entity until 1692, when it was annexed to the Province of Massachusetts Bay.[2] The Plymouth Colony was never very wealthy or populous and was always overshadowed by Massachusetts. The area of the Old Colony covered what is today the three counties of Plymouth, Bristol, and Barnstable in southeastern Massachusetts.

Governor William Bradford's thoughtful history, *Of Plymouth Plantation,* is not only an American literary classic but also a prime source for the colony's legal information in the period from 1620 to 1646. Legal information for the same period and the years after Bradford are found in the comprehensive *Records of the Colony of New Plymouth in New England,* edited by David Pulsifer and published in the nineteenth century. Trials generally occurred before Plymouth's general court, made up of the governor and his assistants, and information about the cases can be found in the *Records.* Relations among Plymouth's inhabitants, which included Quakers and a large population of Native Americans, were relatively stable until the outbreak of King Philip's War in 1675-1676. The war's devastation was quickly followed by the Dominion of New England and the end of Plymouth as a separate colony in 1692.

The earliest original records of the Plymouth Colony are housed at the Massachusetts State Archives. The original Bradford manuscript is housed at the Massachusetts State Library at the State House in Boston.

Records of the Colony of New Plymouth in New England. Printed by order of the legislature of the Commonwealth of Massachusetts. Edited by David Pulsifer. Boston, MA: From the press of William White, Printer to the Commonwealth, 1861.

These twelve volumes are not only the legislative history of the Plymouth Colony but also the records of the commissioners for the New England Confederation (1643-1678/1679), which was made up of representatives from the colonies of Massachusetts, Plymouth, Connecticut, and New Haven.

Plymouth Court Records, 1686-1859. Edited by David Thomas Konig; with an introductory essay by William E. Nelson. Wilmington, DE: M. Glazier, in association with the Pilgrim Society, 1978-1981.

This sixteen-volume collection of court record abstracts covers both the court of general sessions and the court of common pleas. The volumes are useful but are not indexed, nor are they complete transcriptions of the records. What the *Records* do reveal are the day-to-day workings on the county level of local courts.

William Bradford. *Of Plymouth Plantation*. Edited and with an introduction by Samuel Eliot Morison. New York: Knopf, 1952.

There are several editions of Bradford's history, but the Morison edition is the most common and accessible one. Bradford was one of the *Mayflower* Pilgrims and served as the colony's governor for over thirty years.

Massachusetts Colony, 1628-1684

The Massachusetts Colony began with the various fishing stations and outposts of Massachusetts Bay in the mid-1620s. An advance group of Puritan settlers under John Endecott (the family later spelled it Endicott) landed at Salem (Naumkeag) in 1628, which signified changes to come. The first of several fleets of Puritans arrived in the summer of 1630 under the leadership of John Winthrop with the first charter of 1629. This was the start of the "Great Migration" that would bring an estimated 30,000 to 40,000 English settlers to New England during the 1630s. The Puritans wanted to "purify" the Anglican Church of all its Catholic trappings but faced hostility from the English Church hierarchy. Unlike their neighbors in Plymouth, the Puritans fully intended to remain within the Church of England. Their purpose in establishing New England was to create a model of a "Godly" commonwealth, to be an example, in Winthrop's words, of a "city upon a hill," with the eyes of all people turned toward them.

Massachusetts Colony was divided into four counties in the 1640s: Suffolk, Middlesex, Essex, and the interior Hampshire. Worcester County was added in 1731. County courts and justices of the peace were established in keeping with English practice. Massachusetts Colony as a whole maintained close ties with England, while beginning to establish its own independent nature in commercial trading. The Civil War in England virtually ended the large-scale emigration to New England. When the war ended with the beheading of King Charles I in 1649, Massachusetts assumed an almost neutral stance, between the victorious Parliamentarians (whose excesses New Englanders did not agree with) and the deposed Royalists. This later enabled the colony to survive when the monarchy was restored in 1660. During the war years in England, Massachusetts fishermen and merchants found ready markets in the West Indies, Spain, and Portugal. Boston grew on the profits of trade wherever there was opportunity. The monarchy's attempt to impose navigation and trade restrictions on its colonies resulted in strained tensions and the growth of widespread smuggling. Flagrant trade violations and rigid interpretation of franchise ultimately contributed to the revocation of the first charter and the end of Puritan-controlled government.

John Winthrop. *The Journal of John Winthrop, 1630-1649.* Edited by Richard S. Dunn and Laetitia Yeandle. Cambridge, MA: Belknap Press of Harvard University Press, 1996.

This is the history journal kept by the first governor of the Massachusetts Colony. John Winthrop was an attorney by profession, and many of the legal and political happenings of the early colony are found in his narrative.

Records of the Governor and Company of the Massachusetts Bay in New England. Edited by Nathaniel B. Shurtleff. Boston, MA: W. White, Printer to the Commonwealth, 1853-1854.

These volumes are the legislative acts of the Massachusetts General Court, the formal name of the legislature. Vol. 1. 1628-1641; Vol. 2. 1642-1649; Vol. 3. 1644-1657; Vol. 4, pt. 1. 1650-1660; Vol. 4, pt. 2. 1661-1674; Vol. 5. 1674-1686.

Records of the Court of Assistants of the Colony of the Massachusetts Bay, 1630-1692. Printed under the supervision of John Noble. Boston: Published by the County of Suffolk, 1901-1928.

The court of assistants was made up of the governor and magistrates sitting as the court of original jurisdiction on cases civil and criminal after the creation of the counties. This court heard appeals from the inferior county courts and final appeal was to the general court consisting of the governor, magistrates, and deputies. Vol. 1. 1673-1692, from the original book of records [designated as the "Second booke of reccords begunne the 3d of

March 1673"]; Vol. 2, pt. 1. 1630-1641, from the first volume of the colony records, in the Massachusetts state archives, and pt. 2. 1641-1644, from a contemporaneous copy now in the Boston Public Library; Vol. 3, restored fragments of records from 1642 to 1673.

The Laws and Liberties of Massachusetts, 1641-1691. A facsimile edition, containing also the council orders and executive proclamations. Compiled with an introduction by John D. Cushing. Wilmington, DE: Scholarly Resources, 1976.

This three-volume work presents facsimiles of the periodic compilations of Massachusetts laws from the seventeenth century. The laws were listed alphabetically and covered everything from capital crimes to the restrictions and responsibilities of local officials.

Colonial Justice in Western Massachusetts, 1639-1792: The Pynchon Court Record, an original judges' diary of the administration of justice in the Springfield courts in the Massachusetts Bay Colony. Edited with a legal and historical introduction by Joseph H. Smith. Cambridge, MA: Harvard University Press, 1961.

The Pynchons were the first family of Springfield, Massachusetts, an interior town along the Connecticut River. This volume is the published edition of a manuscript kept by William Pynchon (and his son and son-in-law) as a record of legal matters that occurred below the level of the county courts, in the Pynchons' capacity as the local presiding magistrates.

Note-book kept by Thomas Lechford, Esq., Lawyer: In Boston, Massachusetts Bay, from June 27, 1638, to July 29, 1641. Cambridge, MA: J. Wilson and Son, 1885.

Lechford was the earliest professionally practicing attorney in Massachusetts, and his notebook documents the difficult time he was given by the local magistrates. Massachusetts Puritans held a strong dislike for attorneys even into the eighteenth century.

Suffolk Deeds: liber I-XIV [1629-1697]. Boston: 1880-1906. 14 v. Published by order of the Boston Board of Aldermen, acting as County Commissioners for the County of Suffolk.

Editors: vol. 1-4, W. B. Trask; vol. 5-8, F. E. Bradish; vol. 9-12, C. A. Drew; vol. 13- A. Grace Small. Indexes for vol. 1-12 prepared under supervision of J. T. Hassan; those for vol. 13- under supervision of A. Grace Small. [F72.S9 S9]

This is a fourteen-volume compilation of seventeenth-century deeds, recording land transfers from the original documents. Suffolk County, although today limited to the city of Boston, originally contained the towns of the present Norfolk County.

William T. Davis. *History of the Judiciary of Massachusetts: Including the Plymouth and Massachusetts Colonies, the Province of the Massachusetts Bay, and the Commonwealth.* Boston: Boston Book Company, 1900; New York: Da Capo Press, 1974.

Davis's two-volume history contains the history of Suffolk County (i.e., Boston) in volume one and the other counties in volume two. This work contains information regarding the courts, as well as biographical information about judges and attorneys, and lists of all colonial legal offices on the county and colony levels.

Emory Washburn. *Sketches of the Judicial History of Massachusetts: From 1630 to the Revolution in 1775.* Boston: C. C. Little and J. Brown, 1840; New York: Da Capo Press, 1974.

The *Judicial History* provides the early legal history of Massachusetts, containing much information describing the functioning of the colonial courts.

Records and Files of the Quarterly Courts of Essex County, Massachusetts. Edited by George Francis Dow. Salem, MA: Essex Institute, 1911-1921.

These courts were held at Salem, 1636-1641, and at Salem and Ipswich, 1641-1692. The records of sessions at the latter town are wanting before 1646. Another transcript of the earlier part of this material was printed in the *Essex Antiquarian,* vol. 3-13, 1899-1909.

vol. 1. 1636-1656; vol. 2. 1652-1662; vol. 3. 1662-1667; vol. 4. 1667-1671; vol. 5. 1672-1674; vol. 6. 1675-1678; vol. 7. 1678-1680; vol. 8. 1680-1683.

These are the records of the inferior Essex County courts as transcribed from the original documents. Essex County is north of Boston and includes Salem and most of the areas involved in the witchcraft hysteria of 1692.

The Probate Records of Essex County, Massachusetts. Edited by George Francis Dow. Salem, MA: The Essex Institute, 1916-1920.

This three-volume work covering the years 1635-1664 is a compilation of original probate records, transcribed and published. They not only provide a vast wealth of material about colonial lives but also reveal the administration of early probate matters and the settling of estates in colonial Massachusetts.

John J. Whittlesey. *Law of the Seashore, Tidewaters and Great Ponds in Massachusetts and Maine: Under the Colony Ordinance of 1641-47.* Boston: J. Whittlesey, 1932; Cambridge, MA: Murray Print. Co.

This slim volume is a survey of the influence of colonial laws on later cases surrounding wetlands in Massachusetts.

Records of the Suffolk County Court 1671-1680 I (Sessions of October 31, 1671, to January, 26, 1674/1765). *Records of the Suffolk County Court 1671-1680 II* (Sessions of April, 27, 1675, to January 1679-1680). Collections of the Colonial Society of Massachusetts. Boston: Colonial Society of Massachusetts, 1933.

These two volumes are the edited compilations of the court records for the local Suffolk County court during the decade that included King Philip's War (1675-1676).

Dominion of New England and Its Aftermath, 1684-1692

In 1684, the Massachusetts Charter was revoked. Two years later, a royal governor arrived in Boston to take control of the newly formed Dominion of New England. Sir Edmund Andros was appointed by King James II to combine the colonies of New Hampshire, Massachusetts, Plymouth, Rhode Island, Connecticut, and New York. Andros was not only an Anglican in a land of Puritans but also arrogant and autocratic by all accounts, appointing his cronies to government positions and generally angering the populace. In 1688, when news of the Glorious Revolution in England (replacing James II with William and Mary) reached Massachusetts, the leading Puritans arrested Andros and his followers and sent them back to England. The uncertainty that resulted from resuming the original charter and a disastrous military expedition against the French in Quebec in 1690 left the colony bankrupt and the populace in an anxious and troubled state.

This was the setting of the Salem witchcraft hysteria of 1692, arguably the most famous trials in colonial history. The hysteria began in late winter in the rural Salem Village section of the town. Hundreds of people were accused and jailed. A series of trials resulted in nineteen executions and one death by pressing by the end of the year. Two good introductory surveys of the witchcraft hysteria, among the many published, are Peter Charles Hoffer, *The Salem Witchcraft Trials: A Legal History* (Lawrence, KS: University Press of Kansas, 1997), and Paul Boyer and Stephen Nissenbaum, *Salem Possessed: The Social Origins of Witchcraft* (Cambridge, MA: Harvard University Press, 1974), the groundbreaking study of the hysteria that looked closely at the divisions and arguments among the neighboring families of Salem Village.

The Glorious Revolution in Massachusetts: Selected Documents, 1689-1692. Edited by Robert Earle Moody and Richard Clive Simmons. Boston: Colonial Society of Massachusetts; [Charlottesville, VA]: Distributed by the University Press of Virginia, 1988.

These documents follow the political upheaval Massachusetts was plunged into by the arrest and imprisonment of Governor Sir Edmund Andros. They chart the course of the Puritan leaders in Massachusetts' attempt to restore the old charter.

The Diary of Samuel Sewall, 1674-1729. Edited from the manuscript at the Massachusetts Historical Society by M. Halsey Thomas. New York: Farrar, Straus and Giroux, 1973.

Sewall was a judge at the Salem witchcraft trials (the only one who later repented) and an original justice of the superior court of judicature. His diary contains many references to cases, courts, judges, and attorneys, all through his perspective as the last Puritan justice of the colonial high court.

The Salem Witchcraft Papers: Verbatim Transcripts of the Legal Documents of the Salem Witchcraft Outbreak of 1692. Compiled and transcribed in 1938 by the Works Progress Administration, under the supervision of Archie N. Frost; edited and with an introduction and index by Paul Boyer and Stephen Nissenbaum. New York: Da Capo Press, 1977.

This is the most complete compilation of the court records of the Salem witchcraft trials, including warrants, statements, witness testimonies, and depositions. Most of the original documents are held either by the Philips Library of the Peabody-Essex Museum or by the Supreme Judicial Court's Division of Archives and Records Preservation, whose earliest records are housed at the Massachusetts State Archives.

The Province of Massachusetts Bay, 1692-1776

A new charter, granted by William and Mary, arrived in Massachusetts in 1692. The charter restored the practice of electing representatives (which then elected the council) that had been done away with by Governor Andros but retained a royally appointed governor. The charter also formally annexed the territory of Maine and the Plymouth Colony into the Province of Massachusetts Bay. This charter also allowed for other religious groups besides the Puritans to have a say in the government, and it specifically created the high court of the province, which was officially titled the Massachusetts Superior Court of Judicature, Court of Assize and General Gaol Delivery. This charter was the basis of Massachusetts government through the decades of turmoil that led up to the American Revolution. It was finally replaced by the Massachusetts Constitution of 1780 (which is still in effect).[3]

The Province of Massachusetts Bay began this period (1692-1776) as the second most populous colony, after Virginia, and with Boston as the largest English port outside the British Isles. The formation of "court" and "country" parties soon developed during the early decades of the 1700s, giving rise to serious opposition to all Crown prerogative in the province, including the civil law vice admiralty court. The rise of the Patriot cause can be seen through the legal history of this period in such notable trials as the Writs of Assistance in 1761 and the Boston Massacre trials of 1770. The courts were often the scene for resistance to the royal governors, played out by the attorneys and judges on both the Patriot and Tory sides.

There are two in-depth studies of particular trials. The first is Maurice Henry Smith's *The Writs of Assistance Case* (Berkeley: University of California Press, 1978), which examines the case that marked the start of radical Patriot opposition to Crown measures designed to regulate shipping and stop smuggling. The case also made James Otis and Governor Thomas Hutchinson lasting enemies, with Otis becoming the acknowledged leader, along with Samuel Adams, of the Patriot faction for the next decade, and Hutchinson becoming the leader of the Tories. The other in-depth study is Hiller B. Zobel's *The Boston Massacre* (New York: W. W. Norton, 1970) which is the fullest treatment of the massacre and the trials of the British officer and soldiers that followed.

The Acts and Resolves, Public and Private, of the Province of the Massachusetts Bay: to which are prefixed the charters of the province: with historical and explanatory notes, and an appendix. Boston: Wright and Potter, Printers to the State, 1869-1922.

These are the legislative materials of the Massachusetts General Court both public and private. All matter of regulations, laws, and cases, including much information regarding Maine, can be found here. The volumes are well indexed and edited. Vol. 1. 1692-1714; vol. 2. 1715-1741(1742); vol. 3. 1742-1757; vol. 4. 1757-1768; vol. 5. 1769-1780; vol. 6. 1692-1780; vol. 7. 1692-1702(1703); vol. 8. 1703-1707; vol. 9. 1708-1720; vol. 10. 1720-1725(1726); vol. 11. 1726-1734; vol. 12. 1734-1740(1741); vol. 13. 1741-1747; vol. 14. 1747-1752(1753); vol. 15. 1753-1756(1757); vol. 16. 1757-

1760(1761); vol. 17. 1761-1764(1765); vol. 18. 1765-1774; vol. 19. 1775-1776(1777); vol. 20. 1777-1778(1779); vol. 21. 1779-1780.

The Journals of the House of Representatives. Republished in facsimile by the Massachusetts Historical Society. 55 volumes.

These facsimile reproductions of the house journals contain a record of the legislative work done in the Massachusetts house. These documents record the deliberations, committee meetings and appointments, and day-to-day transacting of house business from 1715 until 1779 when the new constitution was adopted.

Massachusetts, Colony to Commonwealth: Documents on the Formation of Its Constitution, 1775-1780. Robert J. Taylor, editor. Published for the Institute of Early American History and Culture at Williamsburg, Virginia. Chapel Hill, NC: The University of North Carolina Press, 1961.

This volume is a collection of documents leading up to the adoption of the 1780 Massachusetts Constitution, covering the years from the outbreak of the Revolution.

The Diaries of Benjamin Lynde and of Benjamin Lynde, Jr.: with an appendix. Boston: [s.n.], 1880. Cambridge: Riverside Press, Printed by H. O. Houghton and Co.

Both the elder and younger Lynde were justices of the superior court of judicature. The elder Lynde was the first trained barrister (called to the bar at the Middle Temple) to serve as a justice in Massachusetts. Their laconic diaries reveal only contextual matters for their careers as jurists.

Thomas Hutchinson. *The History of the Colony and Province of Massachusetts-Bay.* Edited from the author's own copies of volumes I and II and his manuscript of volume III, with a memoir and additional notes, by Lawrence Shaw Mayo. Cambridge, MA: Harvard University Press, 1936.

Hutchinson was the last civilian royal governor of Massachusetts and also the chief justice of the superior court from 1761 to 1769. His *History* provides insight into the Tory view of the legal matters that led up to the outbreak of the American Revolution.

Josiah Quincy Jr. *Reports of Cases Argued and Adjudged in the Superior Court of Judicature of the Province of Massachusetts Bay, Between 1761 and 1772.* Printed from his original manuscript in the possession of his son, Josiah Quincy, and edited by his great grandson, Samuel M. Quincy; with an appendix on the Writs of Assistance. Boston: Little, Brown, 1865.

Quincy was a leader among the radical Patriots and a skilled attorney. His *Reports* were written and compiled over the turbulent decade that saw much of the open hostility toward the Tories play out in the courts. The *Reports* remained unpublished until 1865, when an edition was published that contained useful notes, appendixes, and extra information.

The Trial of the British Soldiers, of the 29th regiment of foot, for the murder of Crispus Attucks, Samuel Gray, Samuel Maverick, James Caldwell, and Patrick Carr, on Monday evening, March 5, 1770, before the Honorable Benjamin Lynde, John Cushing, Peter Oliver, and Edmund Trowbridge, Esquires, justices of the Superior Court of Judicature, Court of Assize, and General Gaol Delivery, held at Boston, by adjournment, November 27, 1770. Boston, MA: Published by William Emmons, 1824.

This is the published transcript of the trial of *Rex v. Wemms, et al.,* in which eight British soldiers were accused of firing into a threatening mob. They were successfully defended by Patriot attorneys John Adams and Josiah Quincy. A transcript of the trial of the British officer was never published.

Diary and Autobiography of John Adams. Edited by Lyman Henry Butterfield. Cambridge, MA: Belknap Press, 1961.

Four well-edited volumes chronicle the life of John Adams as an attorney, a Patriot leader, and as one of the Revolution's founding fathers.

Legal Papers of John Adams. Edited by L. Kinvin Wroth and Hiller B. Zobel. Cambridge, MA: Belknap Press, 1965.

These three volumes detail the legal practice of John Adams in the years from 1758, the year of his admission to the bar, to 1774, when he devoted himself to leading the Revolution. Volume three is exclusively devoted to the cases of the Boston Massacre, the trial of the British officer, and the trial of the eight soldiers and contains the most complete collection of papers concerning these trials. Adams was one of the successful defense attorneys in both cases.

Unpublished Manuscript Records

Thousands of individual Massachusetts court records from the seventeenth and eighteenth centuries are unpublished. Generally, use of the original records is restricted by the institution holding them depending on the purpose and needs of the researcher. Microfilm copies of some of these records are available, but these are in only a handful of institutions and only for on-site use. Many of the court records are still in the offices of the county courthouse clerks, county commissioners, probate and registry offices, and the local town clerks' offices. The following titles are only some of the sources available, but most of these titles were prepared in the late 1970s and early 1980s when the court records were in the process of being inventoried and moved from the various repositories to the Judicial Archives at the Massachusetts State Archives. Much information in these guides is, therefore, out of date and will need to be supplemented by current guides available at the Massachusetts State Archives or through the Massachusetts Supreme Judicial Court's Division of Archives and Records Preservation.

The Records of the Massachusetts Superior Court and Its Predecessors: An Inventory and Guide. Michael S. Hindus; inventory prepared by Mary J. Bularzik, Mary Eleanor Murphy, Michael S. Hindus. Boston, MA: Archives Division, Office of the Secretary of the Commonwealth, 1978.

Michael Hindus. "A Guide to the Court Records of Early Massachusetts." In *Law in Colonial Massachusetts.* Boston: Publications of the Colonial Society of Massachusetts, 1984.

A Research Guide to the Massachusetts Courts and Their Records. Catherine S. Menand. Boston: Massachusetts Supreme Judicial Court, Archives and Records Preservation, 1987.

Guide to the Records of the Secretary of State in the Massachusetts Archives. Boston: Massachusetts Archives at Columbia Point, 1987.

These guides were produced in an effort to begin an inventory of the thousands of colonial court documents. The court structure changed during the years from 1620 to 1776 and was not always strictly followed, which often leads to confusion on the part of researchers. For more information on the structure of the courts in colonial Massachusetts, see especially Catherine Menand, "A 'Magistracy Fit and Necessary': A Guide to the Massachusetts Court System," in *Law in Colonial Massachusetts 1630-1800* (Boston: The Colonial Society of Massachusetts, 1984), edited by Daniel R. Coquillette, which gives the dates of courts as well as easy-to-understand hierarchical diagrams for the appellate and trial court structure of the colony. See also Alan J. Dimond, *A Short History of the Massachusetts Courts* (Boston, MA: National Center for State Courts, Northeastern

Regional Office, 1975), for a brief synopsis of the entire colonial court system and its subsequent evolution. Researchers interested in accessing the manuscript records of the early Massachusetts courts should contact the Massachusetts Supreme Judicial Court's Division of Archives and Records Preservation, 1600 New Court House, Boston, MA 02108.

SECONDARY AND BIBLIOGRAPHICAL SOURCES

There are several good bibliographies already in existence for researchers of colonial records in Massachusetts. *A Guide to the History of Massachusetts* (Westport, CT: Greenwood Press, 1988), edited by Martin Kaufman, John W. Ifkovic, and Joseph Carvalho III, contains three excellent bibliographic essays on the history of Massachusetts. These are mostly general history works, but they do contain references to important legal history sources. The first essay is "From the Old World to the New, 1620-1689," by Francis Bremer, which looks at the primary and secondary historical sources for the theocratic Massachusetts and Plymouth Colonies before the creation of the Dominion of New England. The second essay, "Between Puritanism and Revolution: The Historiography of Royal Massachusetts, 1689-1765," by William Pencak, surveys similar sources for Massachusetts history under the second charter, when the province's legal mechanisms were brought more in line with traditional English legal procedures. The third essay is "Samuel Adams' Bumpy Ride: Recent Views of the American Revolution in Massachusetts," by Bruce C. Daniels, which looks at developments in historiography from the 1950s to the 1980s, a period marked by the emergence of social history interpretations and reevaluations.

A second major bibliographical source is *Law in Colonial Massachusetts 1630-1800.* This is Volume 62 of the Publications of the Colonial Society of Massachusetts and is a compilation of essays based on a Colonial Society Conference in 1981. There are three sections: part one is eleven essays based on conference papers; part two contains four articles on the use of sources, primarily court records; and the third part identifies four major repositories for the study of colonial legal history in Massachusetts. The four institutions are the American Antiquarian Society, the Essex Institute (now the Peabody-Essex Museum), Harvard Law School, and the Massachusetts Historical Society.

A third source for bibliographical information is *The History of the Law in Massachusetts: The Supreme Judicial Court 1692-1992* (Boston: Supreme Judicial Court Historical Society, 1992), edited by Russell K. Osgood. This volume of essays was produced in celebration of the three-hundredth anniversary of the Massachusetts Supreme Judicial Court (known as the Massachusetts Superior Court of Judicature before the Revolution). In addition to several essays on the practice of law and the administration of justice in colonial Massachusetts, there is also an extensive bibliographical listing by author and subject.

The following titles, cited as specific studies in colonial Massachusetts legal history, will also provide further bibliographical information.

David Grayson Allen. *In English Ways: The Movement of Societies and Transferal of English Local Law and Custom to Massachusetts in the Seventeenth Century.* Chapel Hill, NC: University of North Carolina Press, 1981.

David Thomas Konig. *Law and Society in Puritan Massachusetts: Essex County, 1629-1692.* Chapel Hill, NC: University of North Carolina Press, 1979.

George Lee Haskins. *Law and Authority in Early Massachusetts: A Study in Tradition and Design.* New York: Macmillan, 1960.

William E. Nelson. *Americanization of the Common Law: The Impact of Legal Change on Massachusetts Society, 1760-1830.* Cambridge, MA: Harvard University Press, 1975.

Ronald P. Dufour. *Modernization in Colonial Massachusetts, 1630-1763.* New York: Garland Pub., 1987.

Yasuhide Kawashima. *Puritan Justice and the Indian: White Man's Law in Massachusetts, 1630-1763.* Middletown, CT: Wesleyan University Press, 1986.

Barbara Aronstein Black. "The Judicial Power and the General Court in Early Massachusetts." PhD dissertation, Yale University, 1975.

John M. Murrin. "Magistrates, Sinners, and a Precarious Liberty: Trial by Jury in Seventeenth-Century New England." *Saints and Revolutionaries: Essays on Early American History.* Edited by David D. Hall, John M. Murrin, and Thad W. Tate. New York: Norton, 1984.

Edwin Powers. *Crime and Punishment in Early Massachusetts 1620-1692: A Documentary History.* Boston: Beacon Press, 1966.

John Phillip Reid. *In a Rebellious Spirit: The Argument of Facts, the Liberty Riot, and the Coming of the American Revolution.* University Park, PA: Pennsylvania State University Press, 1979.

John Phillip Reid. *In a Defiant Stance: The Conditions of Law in Massachusetts Bay, the Irish Comparison, and the Coming of the American Revolution.* University Park, PA: Pennsylvania State University Press, 1977.

William E. Nelson. *Dispute and Conflict Resolution in Plymouth County, Massachusetts, 1725-1825.* Chapel Hill, NC: University of North Carolina Press, 1981.

James Ronda. "Red and White at the Bench: Indians and the Law in Plymouth Colony, 1620-1691." *Essex Institute Historical Collections,* 110 (1974): 200-215.

C. Dallett Hemphill. "Women in Court: Sex-Role Differentiation in Salem, Massachusetts, 1636 to 1683." *William & Mary Quarterly,* 39 (1982): 164-175.

George D. Langdon. *Pilgrim Colony; A History of New Plymouth, 1620-1691.* New Haven, CT: Yale University Press, 1966.

John Demos. *A Little Commonwealth.* New York: Oxford University Press, 1970.

INSTITUTIONS, SUMMARIES OF COLLECTIONS, AND FINDING AIDS

Massachusetts contains some of the oldest historical and cultural societies and libraries in the nation. The collections of these institutions reflect their various missions, but all contain legal resources of invaluable worth to researchers. Manuscript legal materials are held by many institutions, and only a few of them have been published. These may come in the form of minute books, diaries, record books, or individual papers. They can often be found in "family papers" collections, such as those of the Adams, Winthrop, or Saltonstall family collections at the Massachusetts Historical Society. Because of the unique nature of items and collections, it is best to check first with the reference staff at each institution.

Massachusetts Historical Society, Boston

The Massachusetts Historical Society, founded in 1792, is the oldest historical society in the nation. The holdings represent over two centuries of thoughtful collecting, scholarship, editing, and publishing. Colonial legal materials are well represented in the society's collection. The society holds millions of manuscripts, published works, photographs, artifacts, and other ephemera. Legal resources can be found among any of these types of holdings.

Representative of the legislative materials in the collections are the earliest compilations of Massachusetts laws, dating to 1641, successive editions of the general laws for the colony, broadsides (one-page, printed announcements) of important legislative measures, published acts of the province, and printed abridgements of the laws of Massachusetts. Executive materials are represented by printed copies of letters, acts, and committee and council minutes. There are also manuscript volumes of executive materials from several of the colonial and provincial royal governors. Items relating to the colonial courts and legal profession are particularly well represented, many only in manuscript form. Highlights of these collections include John Adams's handwritten notes from the Boston Massacre trials, depositions and examinations of accused witches in Salem, and the commonplace books of many Revolutionary-era attorneys. Also found in the collection are printed transcripts of trials for piracy, murder, and libel; broadsides and newspaper accounts of executions; and some of the earliest attempts at court reporting.

Updated guides to the collections are available in print as well as in the online catalog available on the society's Web site (http://www.masshist. org/). For more information, see John D. Cushing, "Sources for the Study of Law in Colonial Massachusetts at the Massachusetts Historical Society," in *Law in Colonial Massachusetts 1630-1800,* edited by Daniel R. Coquillette (Boston: The Colonial Society of Massachusetts, 1984), 569-585; and *A Guide to the History of Massachusetts,* edited by Martin Kaufman, John W. Ifkovic, and Joseph Carvalho III (Westport, CT: Greenwood Press, 1988), 241-243.

The Massachusetts State Archives, Boston

The Massachusetts State Archives is located at Columbia Point in South Boston. The archives is the primary repository for the commonwealth's colonial records of the executive and legislative branches, including the original first and second charters of Massachusetts. Of particular importance and value is the Massachusetts Archives Collection, a 328-volume compilation, also known as the Felt Collection, of records and materials dating from 1629 to 1799.

A complete description of the collections is available on the Archives Web site (http://www.state.ma.us/sec/arc/arcidx.htm). For more information, see *A Guide to the History of Massachusetts,* edited by Martin Kaufman, John W. Ifkovic, and Joseph Carvalho III (Westport, CT: Greenwood Press, 1988), 246-248.

Division of Archives and Records Preservation, Massachusetts Supreme Judicial Court

The Judicial Archives are currently housed at the Massachusetts State Archives by a special agreement allowing the judicial branch records to be stored in an executive branch facility and are administered by the Massachusetts Supreme Judicial Court's Division of Archives and Records Preservation. The Judicial Archives contain the pre-1860 records of the predecessor courts of the superior court (court of general sessions of the peace and inferior court of common pleas) for nine or more counties. Other records in the Judicial Archives include those of the supreme judicial court and superior court of judicature; predominantly pre-1900 probate records of several counties; a limited number of county court records (consolidation is ongoing); records of some justices of the peace; many naturalization records; and records of a small number of special courts, including divorce records.

Another collection, known as the "Suffolk Files," contains the earliest file papers of the Massachusetts Supreme Judicial Court and its predecessors, the court of assistants, and the superior court of judicature, and records of the county courts, court of common pleas and general sessions of the peace. The records contain cases from Massachusetts as well as parts of Maine and New Hampshire. The records were arranged and indexed over a twenty-five-year period beginning in 1883. There are extensive indexes of every person, place, and subject, as well as date and calendar indexes available for cross-referencing and searching the files.

Some collections of court records may still remain in original courthouses. Detailed inventories, finding aids, and guides are available at the archives and from the reference staff of the Massachusetts Supreme Judicial Court's Division of Archives and Records Preservation. The staff can provide reference assistance as well as consultation on special inquiries when using the Judicial Archives. For contact information about the Judicial Archives, see the Massachusetts Supreme Judicial Court Web site (http://www.mass.gov/courtsandjudges/courts/supremejudicialcourt/) or the description of the Division of Archives and Records Preservation materials at the Web site for the Massachusetts State Archives.

Harvard Law School Library, Cambridge

Easily one of the finest university law libraries in the country and recently renovated, the Harvard Law School Library holds a stunning collection of rare and manuscript legal materials. Similar to the Massachusetts Historical Society, the Library of Harvard Law School is particularly strong in early Massachusetts printed statutes, including several unique copies of the early printed laws. Case law is represented by the original manuscripts of several important works, in the form of office books, notebooks, and notes on cases. There are a number of individually printed trials from the eighteenth century in the collection. There are also treatises printed in Boston, Worcester, or Maine and dating up until the early nineteenth century. From the law library, scholars can be directed to other vast resources and archives of the university, which is especially beneficial, since the majority of seventeenth- and eighteenth-century judges and attorneys in Massachusetts were graduates of Harvard College.

For more information, see Edith G. Henderson, "Sources for the Study of Law in Colonial Massachusetts at the Harvard Law School, Cambridge, Massachusetts," in *Law in Colonial Massachusetts 1630-1800,* edited by Daniel R. Coquillette (Boston: The Colonial Society of Massachusetts, 1984), 569-585; and *A Guide to the History of Massachusetts,* edited by Martin Kaufman, John W. Ifkovic, and Joseph Carvalho III (Westport, CT: Greenwood Press, 1988), 231-234; see also the law library's Web site. <http://www.law.harvard.edu/library/>.

Peabody-Essex Museum, Phillips Library, Salem

The James Duncan Phillips Library is the research library of the Peabody-Essex Museum in Salem, Massachusetts. It is also one of the prime repositories for the study of the Salem witchcraft trials. Many of the original documents either are held by the museum or are on loan from the Massachusetts Supreme Judicial Court. Previously, the Phillips Library was the library for the Essex Institute, an independent historical institution founded in 1821, until it merged with the Peabody Museum. This explains why some of the sources cited here refer to the Essex Institute.

The collections of the Phillips Library are particularly strong for legal materials relating to Salem and the other towns of Essex County. Manuscript materials are represented in the four categories of court records, justice of the peace records, notary public records, and individual lawyers' and judges' records. Many items refer directly to the participants in the Salem witchcraft trials of 1692. But since Salem was second only to Boston in population, shipping, and cultural importance during the colonial period, most of the materials involve other, far less famous matters.

For more information, see Caroline Preston, "Sources for the Study of Law in Colonial Massachusetts at the Essex Institute, Salem, Massachusetts," in *Law in Colonial Massachusetts 1630-1800,* edited by Daniel R. Coquillette (Boston: The Colonial Society of Massachusetts, 1984), 555-558; and *A Guide to the History of Massachusetts,* edited by Martin Kaufman, John W. Ifkovic, and Joseph Carvalho III (Westport, CT: Greenwood Press, 1988), 223-225; see also the museum's Web site (http://www.pem.org/homepage/); and the James Duncan Phillips Library (formerly the Essex Institute Library) at <http://www.pem.org/museum/library.php>.

Social Law Library, Boston

The Social Law Library was founded in 1803, just two decades after the end of the Revolutionary War. It was created by attorneys in Boston as a membership library to replace the law libraries of the many Tories, who were forced to flee the colony during the war. The collection as originally purchased was comprised of the most useful and important English works for practicing attorneys. Over the years the collection has added many antiquarian volumes of treatises and reports that were frequently cited and studied by colonial judges and attorneys. The Social Law Library today has many editions of those texts, such as Dalton's *Country Justice,* Fitz-Herbert's *Natura Brevium, Lex Mercatoria,* Dugdale's *Originales Judicales,* and Bracton's *De Legibus,* that formed the basic working libraries of colonial practitioners.

For more information, see the library's Web site <http://www.socialaw.com>.

Boston Public Library, Boston

This is the nation's oldest public library and one of the finest research libraries in the country. The collections of printed and manuscript material are a rich source for any researcher of colonial Massachusetts. Most of the printed materials mentioned in this chapter can be found at the Boston Public Library. The newspaper holdings and microfilm archives are extensive, boasting copies of materials found in only one or two other institutions.

Subject divisions and collection abstracts are available on the library's Web site (http://www.bpl.org).

Two collections of note are the Mellen Chamberlain Autograph Collection and the Elijah Adlow Collection. The Adlow Collection contains approximately 10,000 legal documents relating to the history of Suffolk County. The Chamberlain Collection contains approximately 20,000 documents relating to American and European history and literature. These two collections complement the more than 12,000 pre-Revolutionary documents of Boston and Massachusetts, which contain the records of Boston and neighboring towns. These collections are filled with the original records of the courts, the Salem witchcraft trials, the Boston Massacre trials, and many of the great figures of the Revolution, including John Adams, John Hancock, and Samuel Adams.

For more information, see *A Guide to the History of Massachusetts,* edited by Martin Kaufman, John W. Ifkovic, and Joseph Carvalho III (Westport, CT: Greenwood Press, 1988), 213-214.

The Boston Athenaeum

The Boston Athenaeum is a private independent library founded in 1807. The library's collection includes great resources for Massachusetts and New England local history, general colonial subjects, and rare printed materials. Several notable manuscript and special collections contain valuable resources for legal history, including eighteenth- and nineteenth-century tracts, early newspapers, and early government documents. The Athenaeum also boasts a nationally known collection of artwork, prints, photographs, and other visual materials. The facility was recently reopened after major restoration, making items once again available to scholars and researchers.

For more information, see the library's Web site (http://www.boston athenaeum.org/).

American Antiquarian Society, Worcester

Worcester's American Antiquarian Society is perhaps the finest single repository for pre-1860 printed American materials. The society's collection is more national in scope than some of the others listed in this chapter, but Massachusetts materials are well represented among the holdings. The collections include manuscript sources in the forms of lawyers' notebooks, records of justices of the peace, family legal documents (such as wills and deeds), and town records for Worcester and the Worcester County area. In all of these areas can be found documents relating to the entire legal practice of colonial Massachusetts, the workings of the local courts, matters civil and criminal, transactions involving probate, land transference, and local lawsuits.

For more information see Kathleen A. Major, "Sources for the Study of Law in Colonial Massachusetts at the American Antiquarian Society, Worcester, Massachusetts," in *Law in Colonial Massachusetts 1630-1800,* edited by Daniel R. Coquillette (Boston: The Colonial Society of Massachusetts, 1984), 551-553; and *A Guide to the History of Massachusetts,* edited by Martin Kaufman, John W. Ifkovic, and Joseph Carvalho III (Westport, CT: Greenwood Press, 1988) 202; see also the society's Web site (http://www.americanantiquarian.org/).

ONLINE RESOURCES

With the availability of texts that have been digitized and are now accessible over the Internet, it has become easier and even more enjoyable to do original research. Not every document is available, of course, and most records probably never will be available via the Internet, but, for now, researchers of colonial Massachusetts legal history are fortunate in that many records and formative documents have online versions. The most popular subjects, of course, are the Salem witchcraft trials, the charters, and the wills and probate inventories that prove so useful to material culture scholars. Online resources are also available as contacts for researching Massachusetts county resources, such as the registry of deeds and the probate records. The following resources are some of the most useful among many sites.

The Avalon Project, Yale University

This Web site (http://www.yale.edu/lawweb/avalon/purpose.htm) is produced by the Yale Law School. It contains a judicious selection of primary source documents from American history, many of which are from colonial Massachusetts. Each document is fully cited to its source, making further research easy.

Salem Witch Trials, Documentary Archive and Transcription Project

This well-designed site (http://etext.virginia.edu/salem/witchcraft/home.html) is an online version of all the papers associated with the Salem witchcraft trials of 1692 and is maintained by the University of Virginia. Included on the site are transcriptions and images of the original court records. These are all indexed and searchable. There is also a listing of archival collections and images of the original records found there.

Plymouth Colony Archive Project at the University of Virginia

This site (http://etext.virginia.edu/users/deetz/) was the work of the late archaeologist James Deetz, who was one of the first to use court and probate records to augment the archaeological study of Plymouth's early colonists. There is a section on court records, laws, and seventeenth-century texts.

Massachusetts Registry of Deeds

Although designed primarily for genealogical research, this site (http://www.mass-doc.com/land_registry_dir.htm) provides an informational link to the county offices of the Massachusetts Registry of Deeds. It also contains useful information for searching probate records and the vital records of towns and cities. Many of the county commissioners' offices still hold original records and deeds going back to the seventeenth century and are only available for onsite research. This site and similar sites provide information about where to find these materials.

OTHER RESOURCES AND CONCLUSION

Researchers into colonial Massachusetts in general should also be aware of the vast amount of material located in a handful of other unique publications. The New England Historic Genealogical Society (http://www.newenglandancestors.org/) has published the vital records of almost every Massachusetts town up to 1850, including births, deaths, and marriages.

Much information on the imperial governance of Massachusetts and other British colonies can be found in the *Calendar of State Papers, Colonial Series, America and West Indies,* v. 15-24, edited by Cecil Headlam (London: His Majesty's Stationery Office, 1905-1936), produced from the vast holdings of the United Kingdom's Public Record Office. Records found in the *Calendar* include such documents as official reports and letters between Massachusetts governors, the lords of trade, and the Crown.

Specific reports on violations of imperial laws by Massachusetts can be found in *Edward Randolph,* Prince Society Publications, v. 24-30 (Boston: Printed for the [Prince] Society, 1899-1909), which includes his letters and official papers from all the colonies and specifically with other documents relating chiefly to the vacating of the first charter of the colony of Massachusetts Bay in 1684. Randolph was justly hated by New Englanders, especially in Massachusetts, for his complaining about their independent attitude and their own court structure. Among the publications of the Prince Society are the papers of Governor Sir Edmund Andros, the royally appointed governor of the short-lived Dominion of New England.

A final treasure trove of bibliographical information is found in the six-volume *Bibliography of American Law* by Morris L. Cohen of Yale Law School (Buffalo, NY: William S. Hein and Co., Inc., 1998). This is a general work but contains many references to original publications of Massachusetts laws, monographs, and trials of the colonial period.

This provides the legal scholar with enough information and direction to conduct research on colonial Massachusetts, its laws, its courts, and its early governance. As always, reference staff members at the institutions listed herein, and many others around Massachusetts, are always willing to help scholars navigate the often confusing and difficult areas of colonial legal research.

NOTES

1. The territory of Maine was a part of Massachusetts off and on through the seventeenth century. It was officially combined with Massachusetts under the charter of 1692. Maine was finally granted statehood in 1820. This chapter does not look at any Maine records specifically, although there is of course some overlap. Many of the Massachusetts materials will contain information on activities, legislation, or court documents concerning Maine.

2. For clarification, the Plymouth Colony refers to the independent colony that existed from 1620 until 1692, without a royal charter. The Massachusetts Colony refers to the Puritan-dominated colony during the period from 1629 until 1692 and was governed under the charter of 1629. The Dominion of New England refers to the brief period from 1686 until 1688 when the New England colonies and New York were all combined under one administration. Following 1688, and the arrest of the royal governor, the colonies returned to their previous governments. The Province of Massachusetts Bay, the official title, combined Massachusetts, Plymouth, and Maine under the second charter of 1692. This was the colony as it existed until the American Revolution.

3. The charter remained the effective government after the outbreak of hostilities in April 1775. The only difference was that the provincial congress (the legislature) assumed all the executive duties. These duties were then assumed by the council, which remained in control for five years until the adoption of the constitution (drafted by John Adams) in 1780.

Chapter 23

Michigan Legal Materials: Seventeenth Century to 1837

Janice Selberg

Michigan had its full share of lawyers, many of whom were well trained in their profession, and would be a credit to it anywhere. Others were untrained, unlettered, and unkempt, and in their vulgarity and insolence would be tolerated nowhere but in the woods. They tried small cases for smaller pay on still smaller knowledge, and were never so well satisfied as when they gained a suit by a trick.

Thomas M. Cooley
Michigan, A History of Governments (1886)

INTRODUCTION

Strictly speaking, Michigan's prestatehood legal history spans only fifty-three years, with the Ordinance of 1784.[1] However, this chapter would not be complete without a discussion of the disparate groups that occupied the region before Michigan became a state and, in turn, administered justice and settled disputes according to their own legal and religious traditions.

At least nine Native American tribes are known to have inhabited Michigan into the seventeenth century.[2] For several thousand years these communities existed, from the Hopewell in earliest times, to the estimated 100,000[3] Huron, Odawa, Ojibway, Potawatomi, Menominee, Sac (Sauk), Fox, Winnabago, and Miami populating the region when the French began to explore the Great Lakes. Although each tribe had distinct cultural and linguistic differences,[4] in general they shared three beliefs, which may be said to be the basis of a legal code: (1) spirits were more powerful than humans; (2) nature (the land and its animals and plants) belongs to everyone; (3) no one had the right to control another person's life.[5] Formal tribal courts were almost certainly not in existence in the same form as today.

FRENCH RULE, 1608-1763

As every Michigan fourth-grader learns, the French were the first Europeans to discover the area now known as Michigan, at approximately the same time the Pilgrims landed in New England.[6] Samuel de Champlain, founder of the city of Quebec, sent an assistant, Etienne Brulé, to venture further into Huron territory. He became the first European to reach the St. Mary's River, and thus the first in Michigan.[7] This was followed in the 1660s by the Jesuit missionaries' establishment of posts in New France, including those by Fr. Marquette[8] and others.

The fur trade dominated the interest of most of the French kings at this time. Although the original idea was to find a northern route by water to China, the French discovery of apparently limitless fur-bearing animals in the wilderness made New France a bonanza for the French nobility. Fur was an extremely lucrative business, and Kings Louis XIII and XIV granted monopolies to their governors, who in turn chose the ones favored to hunt and trap the animals for shipping back to France and to the European market.[9] Although Louis XIV's minister Jean-Baptiste Colbert insisted that all furs be brought to the St. Lawrence for trading, this law was widely ignored, even by the soldiers and governors sent to enforce it.[10] As fur became scarce in the known regions of New France, trappers pushed further south and west. Their Native American associates also saw no reason to obey a law they saw as senseless, particularly since the British often paid more than the French for the furs. The price of beaver pelts began to drop and the fur monopoly began to lose money.[11] Eventually, by 1696, King Louis ordered all traders and the soldiers sent to enforce the monopoly back to lower Canada. Only the missionaries were allowed to stay legally.[12]

Antoine de La Mothe Cadillac, commander at Michilimackinac, convinced Louis XIV to allow true colonization in the region and, in 1701, founded La Ville d'Etroit.[13] Detroit's Fort Pontchartrain was governed by the military for the next sixty years. Cadillac and the subsequent commandants adjudicated disputes for the community in military courts.[14] Reports of these courts were found and compiled in the late 1880s. There was no printing press in all of New France[15] in the early and middle seventeenth century.

BRITISH RULE, 1763-1796

The situation changed in 1760, when the British won the last battle of the French and Indian War. Michigan was surrendered to the British despite having no battles within its current borders. The few French settlements within the borders of Michigan were left alone, provided that the residents swore allegiance to the British crown.[16] Indeed, into the 1820s, most Michigan residents were of either Native American or French descent.[17]

When the Seven Years' War in Europe ended in 1763, the Treaty of Paris[18] officially granted the French possessions east of the Mississippi to Great Britain, and those west of the Mississippi, including New Orleans, to Spain.[19] There followed in Michigan several distinct periods of British rule.[20] The first, which was actually a régime militaire, was put into place to enforce the British conquest until the treaty was officially signed.[21] Military courts were established by the British in Montreal, Quebec, and Three Rivers, but there is no record of the formation of the same in Detroit or Michilimackinac.[22] The terms of capitulation of Quebec provided that the French and native-born Canadians would be governed by the "custom of Paris, and the Laws and usages established for this country, and they shall not be subject to any other imposts than those which were established under the French Dominion."[23]

One case is recorded in English from this period, a criminal case tried by court-martial, which is reprinted in *Michigan Pioneer and Historical Collections.*[24] It concerns the homicide of a merchant by his two "Indian Slaves," a man and a woman. The man escaped to the Illinois country and apparently was never recaptured. The woman was convicted and hanged.[25]

The second period, which is said to have extended from 1763-1774, consisted of a period whereby the government in Great Britain pondered how to treat the region, what form of government to establish, and "in what mode least burdensome and most palatable to the Colonies can they contribute to the Support of the Additional Expense."[26] The British ministers at that time took a similar approach to the French; that is, settlement was not encouraged. The Royal Proclamation of October 7, 1763, created the new government of Quebec and restricted the Great Lakes region to the Native Americans:

> And we do hereby strictly forbid, on pain of Our Displeasure, all our loving subjects from making any Purchases or Settlements whatever, or taking Possession of any of the Lands above reserved, without our especial leave and Licence for the Purpose first obtained.

> And we do further strictly enjoin and require all Persons whatever who have willfully or inadvertently seated themselves upon any Lands within the Countries above described, or upon any Lands which, not having been ceded to or to be purchased by Us, are still reserved to the said Indians as aforesaid, forthwith to remove themselves from such Settlements.[27]

The proclamation further provided that, while in the "Government of Quebec," the "Royal Protection for the Enjoyment of the Benefit of the Laws of Our Realm of England" was extended, this apparently did not apply to the region reserved to the Native Americans, nor did the proclamation make any formal provision for law in that region.[28]

Records mentioning the appointment of judges in Detroit are assumed to be military officers, who also would "Decide on all actions of Debt, Bond, Bills, Contracts, and Trespasses above the value of 5 pounds New York Currency."[29]

The third period of British rule, 1774-1788, included the implementation of civil government. Parliament passed the Quebec Act in 1774,[30] which extended the boundaries of the province of Quebec west to the Mississippi River and south to the Ohio River. French civil law would be applied, but criminal matters would be controlled by British law, which was not codified but well established in common law.[31] Four lieutenant governors would be appointed for the region, including one in Detroit. Religious liberty was awarded to Roman Catholics, which is thought to have had a later effect on the French-Canadian loyalty to the British during the Revolutionary War.[32] No elected assemblies were provided for, and the raising of taxes to pay for the maintenance of the region angered the colonies. In addition, colonies such as Virginia, with a population pushing further west, resented the restrictions on settlement in the Great Lakes, even though they were widely ignored.[33]

The Quebec Act, the only law mentioned by name in the Declaration of Independence, also provided a nonmilitary court system for the first time in Michigan. The implementation of inferior courts was delayed by the revolution[34] in the western region, although the province was divided into two districts, Quebec and Montreal, with Detroit in the Montreal District. The Montreal District had two sessions of the court of king's bench with criminal jurisdiction each year, as well as a court of quarter sessions four times each year. There was a weekly sitting of the court of common pleas.[35] Obviously, this arrangement was not suitable for those living in and around the village of Detroit.

During this time, the merchants at Detroit entered into a general arbitration bond to work out their differences through arbitration. Merchants signing onto the bond agreed to submit their disputes to a panel of arbitrators (the merchants sitting in rotation).[36] The awards were often effectively enforced by economic peer pressure on the one refusing to pay, but sometimes an action had to be filed in the court of common pleas in Montreal. This could take years, depending upon the weather and possible error in the writ (which is reported to have happened three times in five, including for the reason of improper service by an "Ignorant Person").[37]

With as many as forty of these suits filed every year by Detroiters, pressure was brought to bear on the Quebec government by Montreal merchants, presumably seeing their common pleas courts clogged with Detroit claims,[38] to further divide the district into upper and lower sections in 1788. The new district of Hesse was formed and included all of present-day Michigan.

Criminal matters in this period were supposed to be tried in Montreal and Quebec in the court of king's bench. The procedure was that the justice of the peace in Detroit would commit the accused for trial and send him under guard to Montreal for trial. After it was pointed out that the great distance, especially for witnesses, might prevent the delivery to Montreal while the court was in session, an ordinance[39] was passed providing for alternate trial at Quebec.

The lieutenant governor in Detroit in 1775 was Colonel Henry Hamilton. He allowed the commissioned justice of the peace, Philippe Dejean, to conduct felony trials, clearly exceeding his jurisdiction.[40] Dejean impaneled juries and often tried several cases at once, with the same jury sitting.[41] He sentenced them, sometimes to hanging, and the sentences were carried out. By 1778, these irregularities came to the attention of Montreal and then London, and a presentment was prepared to deliver both Hamilton and Dejean for trial on a felony charge for acts "contrary to good Government and the safety of His Majesty's Liege subjects."[42] However, both of these men had set off earlier from Detroit to capture Vincennes and were captured by the Revolutionary Army and imprisoned in Virginia. The attorney general of the province then dropped the matter.[43]

The fourth period of British rule, 1788-1792, was marked by the appointment of judiciary for the district of Hesse. The process was the same as for the other new districts, but in Detroit there was much objection to the result. The three men originally chosen for the "Court of Common Pleas in and for the District of Hesse" were three well-known and well-respected residents: Jacques Duperon Baby, a French Canadian merchant and fur trader; Alexander McKee, an Indian Department official; and William Robertson, a businessman. The positions were to be unsalaried, payment for the judges coming from fines and court fees.

Objections, not to the men themselves, but to the obvious conflicts of interest the cases before them would present, were immediate and loud. A memorial[44] was written by the villagers (though it is surmised that the true author was Robertson). The memorial to Lord Dorchester in Quebec stated, in part, that the "Professions of Judge and Merchant combined in the same person are wholly incompatible,"[45] and that the men currently appointed "must be deficient in that Knowledge of Law necessary to so important a station."[46]

After all three appointees resigned in agreement with the memorial writers, William Dummer Powell, originally of Boston, was appointed.[47] He was a member of the bar, was fluent in French, and was familiar with both English common law and French civil law. A "liberal" salary was arranged, and the first (and only) justice of the Court of Common Pleas for the District of Hesse began work in July 1789.[48] He presided over the court for five years, until the Judicature Acts of the Province of Upper Canada[49] abolished it. The system comprised eight commissioned justices of the peace: Alexander Grant, Guillaume La Motte, St. Martin Adhemar, William Macomb, Joncaire de Chabert, Alexander Maisonville, William Caldwell, and Mathew Elliott.[50] There was in addition a sheriff, a coroner, and a clerk of the court. Powell also presided over serious felony cases in the court of oyer and terminal and general gaol delivery,[51] and in the prerogative court, a probate and estate court.[52]

The records of Powell's court were preserved in the archives in the Ottawa, Ontario, Canada Archives, as well as at Osgoode Hall, Toronto. They have been reprinted in Riddell's *Michigan Under British Rule: Law and Law Courts, 1760-1796,*[53] as well as in some volumes of *Michigan Pioneer and Historical Collections.*[54]

Pursuant to the Canada Act of 1791[55] the province of Upper Canada was formed from part of the province of Quebec. The district of Hesse, to which Michigan belonged, was a division of the new province. The more important change related to this act, however, was the declaration that the province of Upper Canada, being mainly populated with citizens of British extraction, would now have English common law applied in all cases, rather than, in many cases prior to this, French civil law.[56]

There appears to have been only one legally qualified attorney in the years that Powell presided over the district of Hesse. Although others could be appointed to act as attorney for a litigant, this seems to have been unusual.[57] The attorney mentioned most often in the records was Walter Roe, who spent most of his time at sea as a young man, finally arriving in Montreal. He was persuaded to join a law office and later admitted to practice.[58] Riddell states that Roe "appeared on one side or the other in practically every case of importance and his name appears as witness to many of the conveyances of the period, no doubt drawn by himself."[59] He appears on the record beginning with the first month of operation of the Court of Common Pleas of the District of Hesse, until it was abolished five years later.

In 1794, William Dummer Powell was appointed to the new Court of King's Bench for Upper Canada as a puisne justice.[60]

When the Revolutionary War ended in 1781 with an American victory, the signing of the Treaty of Paris of 1783 provided for the British to evacuate their Western posts, including present-day Michigan, "with all convenient speed."[61] It took thirteen years. Meanwhile, the British continued to govern the region and keep troops at both Detroit and Mackinac and to urge the Native Americans to resist the advance of settlers, who were pouring into what was known as the Old Northwest.[62]

The British realized that the state's enforcement powers in the Articles of Confederation (1781)[63] were weak. Until the Battle of Fallen Timbers was won by General "Mad" Anthony Wayne against the Native Americans in present-day northern Ohio in 1794, it looked as though the British were content to keep possession of most of the land ceded by the Treaty of Paris. After that battle, the British, who had armed and encouraged the Native Americans and then abandoned them, fearing another war with the United States, left the Northwest to north and east of a boundary line through the middle of Lakes Ontario, Erie, Huron, and Superior, and the rivers connecting these lakes.[64]

THE NORTHWEST TERRITORIES, 1787-1805

The Ordinance of 1784[65] provided for as many as ten states, and that the future states would be received on the same basis as the original thirteen.[66] Drafted by Thomas Jefferson, it had several flaws, but the Northwest Ordinance remedied these.[67] This 1787 ordinance had several vital specifications:[68]

1. The Northwest Territory would be divided into no fewer than three, and no more than five, territories.
2. Congress would appoint a governor, a secretary, and three judges to administer each territory.
3. When more than 5,000 free adult males lived in a territory, elections would be held to form a legislative council and to select a nonvoting representative to Congress.
4. When a territory reached a free adult male population of 60,000, it could petition Congress to write a constitution and apply for statehood.
5. Slavery was forbidden in the territory.
6. "Schools and the means of education" were encouraged.
7. Indian land and property could not be taken without consent, unless through "just and lawful war authorized by Congress."
8. Religious toleration and liberty were guaranteed.

The three judges forming a court for the territory would also join with the governor in adopting in the district such laws of the original States, civil and criminal, as may be necessary and best suited to the circumstances of the district, and report them to Congress from time to time: which laws shall be in force in the district until the organization of the General Assembly therein.[69]

The Northwest Ordinance thereby provided a general power to legislate.[70] Until statehood in 1837, Michigan's legislative agencies consisted of the following:

> Northwest Territory, 1787-1798: governor and judges
> Northwest Territory, 1799-1801: governor, council, and representatives
> Indiana Territory, 1802-1804: governor and judges[71]
> Michigan Territory, 1805-1823: governor and judges
> Michigan Territory, 1823-1836: governor and council[72]

The judicial system of the Northwest Territory, pursuant to the Ordinance of 1787, was organized as follows in present-day Michigan:[73]

> Northwest Territory, 1787-1802: supreme-general-superior court—three judges, any two to form a court, one to hold court in the absence of others; probate court; magistrate court
> Indiana Territory, 1802-1804: same as Northwest Territory
> Michigan Territory, 1805-1823: same as Northwest Territory
> Michigan Territory, 1823-1836: additional judge

The appointment of judges was made either by Congress or, beginning in 1789, by the President, with the advice and consent of the Senate. The tenure duration was either "During Good Behavior" (Northwest Territory, Indiana Territory, and Michigan Territory until 1824) or four years, beginning in Michigan Territory in 1824.[74]

Since the legislative and judicial powers were in the same hands, this made for interesting court sessions. According to one account:

> The laws were comparatively few in number, easily understood, and gave general satisfaction. If any law was found to work badly, the governor, or one of the judges, notified the others, the "legislature" assembled, and the law was repealed or amended. On one occasion, I recollect, two Indians were arrested on a charge of murder . . . and brought to Detroit for trial. When the Supreme Court assembled, it was found that the law relative to grand jurors was defective. The

court adjourned, the legislature assembled, the law was amended, and the prisoners were tried, convicted and executed.[75]

MICHIGAN TERRITORY, 1805-1836

In the period of time during which Michigan was a territory apart, the law was shaped by an eccentric and colorful character, Judge Augustus Woodward, a classmate and close friend of Thomas Jefferson.[76] He was "extremely aggressive, very sensitive, and quite domineering in his attitudes."[77] He was also "not overly clean . . . and suffered from no inferiority complex."[78] This political appointee to the post as Chief Judge of the new territory of Michigan began his work in 1805, just after the town of Detroit burned to the ground. Court was held in one of the two remaining homes.[79] Woodward was also the influence and draftsman behind the Michigan Territory's first printed code, known as the Woodward Code.[80]

Woodward had difficulty with his fellow judges and legislators. While he was away for four months in 1808-1809, Governor Hull, with the support of James Witherell, a new judge, passed no fewer than forty-five acts in Woodward's absence (this group of acts was named the Witherell Code), many of which governed legal procedure. Woodward promptly "impeached" (his language) them all upon his return and declared them unconstitutional.[81] This led to a situation in which there were two competing sets of codes, until eight months later when the Witherell Code was repealed, with the governor and judges agreeing in future that all acts be signed by at least three of the four legislators.[82]

Woodward was a founder of the University of Michigan and the architect of the postfire plan for rebuilding Detroit. After nineteen years on the bench, he saw the Michigan judicial system "changed, largely to be rid of him."[83] In 1824, the tenure for judges was changed in the territory from "Good Behavior" to four years. Woodward was not reappointed in Michigan but was given an appointment as a federal judge in Florida. He died in Tallahassee three years later.[84]

The War of 1812 halted the progress of Michigan Territory for over two years. Detroit was surrendered to the British by Governor and Commander Hull, who was court-martialed and acquitted after the war. Part of his defense against the charges of treason and cowardice was that the secretary of war never informed him that the United States was at war with the British, although he deduced the situation correctly after the British began to attack the fort.[85]

The territory of Michigan grew slowly during the early nineteenth century. The war, some financial irregularities with the charter of banks,[86] and some unfortunate incidents with swamps and biting insects in the region[87] contributed to this. By the late 1820s, however, land promotions back east, and some more favorable publicity in the newspapers, led to a rush to settle the territory.[88] The Northwest Ordinance required 60,000 free adult male residents in the territory before an application for statehood could be considered. The federal census of 1830 indicated a territorial population of about 30,000, but after a state census taken in 1834, the conclusion was reached by the territorial legislature that a state constitutional convention should be called.[89]

The convention delegates were a reasonable cross section of the population; half were farmers, and the rest were small merchants, lumbermen, and professionals, such as lawyers, surveyors, teachers, and doctors. They began work in May 1835 and composed a simple, direct document that is still noted for its elegance.[90] Due, probably, to the problems with, and concerns about, conflicts of interests of the early territorial days, the 1835 constitution made the three branches of state government "distinct"[91] and stipulated that one should never exercise the powers of another. Many provisions of the 1835 constitution were taken from Connecticut, New York, and other eastern states, since most of the delegates were from that region.[92]

The constitutional convention also set off the events known as the Toledo War. It was to some extent the inaccurate surveying and mapping at the time of the Northwest Ordinance that caused the controversy. Ohio, which had been the first state admitted out of the Northwest Territories in 1803, had set its border according to the description of a line in the Ohio Constitution of 1802. This description had been written to correct a border inaccuracy, and to keep the Maumee River entirely within Ohio; Congress had accepted the Ohio Constitution without either approval or disapproval of this particular provision, which contradicted the Northwest Ordinance.[93]

This was Michigan's best argument to regain the "Toledo Strip," since the Northwest Ordinance was considered a compact, the provisions of which could not be violated by the United States. Nonetheless, the entire situation had a comic opera quality to it, with Michiganians ceremoniously burning the Ohio flag, and secret Ohio court sessions late at night on the strip to establish rights to the area. Congress proposed a compromise in 1836, which called for Michigan to be admitted as a state if it agreed to give up the 500-square-mile Toledo Strip in exchange for what is now known as the Upper Peninsula.[94] It had been noted for some time that the last of the five states to be admitted under the Northwest Ordinance (Wisconsin, 1848) would be too large.[95]

At first, this congressional proposal was rejected by the Michigan Territorial Convention, but it was eventually recognized that there was truly nothing to gain by refusing the offer. A new assembly known as the "Frost-

Bitten" Convention was held in Ann Arbor and voted to accept the compromise. Michigan became a state on January 26, 1837.[96]

SOURCES OF MICHIGAN PRESTATEHOOD LAW

The following pages list the available sources of law for the period indicated. Although there is not one single place in the state where all the materials can be located, these five libraries were listed most often as owning the sources cited. Those researching the prestatehood law of Michigan would obtain most of what is available by visiting these. In some cases, the libraries require permission for use. Please contact the directors for information.

> Bentley Historical Library, University of Michigan, Ann Arbor
> University of Michigan Law Library, Ann Arbor
> Library of Michigan, Lansing
> Burton Historical Collection, Detroit Public Library
> National Library of Canada, Ottawa, Ontario

The Library of Congress's American Memory Project provides one of the best collections of Michigan legal history (http://memory.loc.gov). The complete text of several of the volumes of *Michigan Pioneer and Historical Collections* has been added to the project. Another source for the *MPHC* material is Ancestry.com (http://www.ancestry.com).

Sources of Law Under French Rule, 1608-1763

French Customary Law

Charles Giraud. *Précis de l'Ancien Droit Coutumier Francais,* 2 ed., 137-197. Paris: Cotillon, 1875.

Reports

Jugements et deliberations du Conseil soverain de la Nouvell France [1663-1709], 6 vols. Quebec: J. Dussault, 1885-1889.

Pierre George Roy. *Inventaire des jugements et deliberations du Conseil superieur de la Nouvelle-France de 1717 a 1760,* 7 vols. Quebec: l'Eclaireur, 1932-1935.

Joseph-Francois Perrault. *Extraits ou precedents, tires des Registres de la juges, aux gens du roi, aux avocats, procureurs, et praticiens de la province du Bas-Canada* [1726-1756]. Quebec: T. Cary, 1824.

Revised Reports, Province of Quebec [includes supreme court and privy council cases decided 1726-1891], 28 vols. Montreal: C.O. Beauchemin, 1891-1903.

Joseph-Francois Perrault. *Extraits ou precedents, des arrest tires des registres du Conseil superieur de Quebec* [1727-1759]. Quebec: T. Cary, 1824.

Sources of Law Under British Rule, 1760-1796

Danby Pickering. *The Statutes at Large from the Magna Carta, to the End of the Eleventh Parliament of Great Britain* [continued to 1806], 46 vols. Cambridge: J. Bentham, 1762-1807.

Revised Reports, Province of Quebec [includes supreme court and privy council cases decided 1726-1891], 28 vols. Montreal: C.O. Beauchemin, 1891-1903.

Michigan Pioneer and Historical Collections [includes reports of cases from the Court of Common Pleas for the District of Hesse], 40 vols. Lansing: Michigan Historical Commission, 1876-1929.

William Renwick Riddell, *Michigan Under British Rule: Law and Law Courts 1760-1796* [reprint of reports of cases from the Court of Common Pleas for the District of Hesse, as well as other courts]. Lansing: Michigan Historical Commission, 1926.

Donald Fyson, with the assistance of Evelyn Kolish and Virginia Schweitzer. *The Court Structure of Quebec and Lower Canada, 1764-1860.* Montreal: Montreal History Group, 1997. See <http://www.fl.ulaval.ca/hst/profs/dfyson/courtstr/> [contains excellent table of courts active in this period].

Sources of Law Under the Northwest Territory, 1787-1805

Clarence Edwin Carter. *Territorial Papers of the United States,* 28 vols. Washington, DC: Government Printing Office, 1934. [Northwest Territory, vols. 2-3; Indiana Territory, vols. 7-8; Michigan Territory, vols. 10-12.]

Theodore Calvin Pease. *The Laws of the Northwest Territory, 1788-1800.* Springfield: Illinois State Historical Library, 1925.

Northwest Territory. *Laws Passed in the Territory of the United States North-West of the River Ohio.* Philadelphia: F. Childs and J. Swaine, 1788-1801. [Microfiche. Buffalo, NY: W.S. Hein and Co., 1986.]

C.C. Williams. *Laws of the Northwest Territory, Notes and References.* Cambridge, MA: Harvard Law School, 1932. [Thesis, Harvard Law School.]

Corporation of the Town of Detroit. Act of Incorporation and Journal of the Board of Trustees 1802-1803. Detroit: Detroit Public Library, 1922.

William Wirt Blume. "Civil Procedure on the American Frontier: A Study of the Records of a Court of Common Pleas of the Northwest and Indiana Territories 1796-1805." *Michigan Law Review* 56(1957): 161.

William Wirt Blume. "Legislation on the American Frontier: Adoption of Laws by Governor and Judges—Northwest Territory 1788-1798; Indiana Territory 1800-1804; Michigan Territory 1805-1823." *Michigan Law Review* 60(1962): 317-372.

William H. Harrington. *Requirements for Admission to the Bar of the State of Michigan and the Preceding Territorial Governments* (1942). [Held by Bentley Historical Library.]

William Lee Jenks. "Territorial Legislation by Governor and Judges." *Mississippi Valley Historical Review* 5(1918): 36-50.

Sources of Law Under the Michigan Territory, 1805-1836

Laws of the Territory of Michigan, with marginal notes and index; to which are prefixed, the Ordinance and several acts of Congress relating to this territory. Detroit: Sheldon and Reed, 1820.

Laws of the Territory of Michigan. Lansing: W.S. George and Co., printers to the state, 1871-1884 [known as the "Reprint of Territorial Laws"].

The Cass Code, or Digest of Laws of the Territory of Michigan, in force in 1816. Detroit: T. Mettez, 1816.

Michigan Legislative Council. *Journal of the Proceedings of the Legislative Council of the Territory of Michigan, Begun and Held in the City of Detroit.* Detroit: S. M'Knight, 1824-1835.

Michigan Supreme Court Records, 1796-1857 [archival material consisting of case files, court journals, calendars, and judgment record books, at Bentley Historical Library].

Michigan Supreme Court. *Reports of Cases Argued and Determined in the Supreme Court of the Territory of Michigan* [1807-1821].

Michigan Supreme Court. *Transactions of the Supreme Court of the Territory of Michigan, 1805-1836,* 6 vols. Ann Arbor: The University of Michigan Press, 1935.

Michigan Supreme Court. *A Digest of the Rules of the Supreme Court of the Territory of Michigan.* Detroit: Sheldon and Reed, 1821.

Olive Clarissa Lathrop. "Some Unreported Opinions of a Territorial Judge, 1805-1823." *Law Library Journal* 21(1928): 66-77.

William Wirt Blume. "Criminal Procedure on the American Frontier: A Study of the Statutes and Court Records of Michigan Territory, 1805-1825." *Michigan Law Review* 57(1958): 195-256.

William Wirt Blume. "Chancery Practice on the American Frontier: A Study of the Records of the Supreme Court of Michigan Territory, 1805-1836." *Michigan Law Review* 59(1960): 49-96.

Miscellaneous Sources

United States Congress. *Memorials, Claims, etc., During Michigan's Territorial Period.* [1 box; held at Bentley Historical Library.]

United States Congress. *Document Relating to the bill to enable the people of the eastern division of the Michigan Territory to form a constitution and state government.* Washington[, DC]: 1834. 23rd Cong. 1st Sess. 1833-34. Senate.

Michigan Citizens. *Michigan—Southern Boundary. Memorial of Citizens of Michigan, In Relation to the Southern Boundary of the Territory.* Washington[, DC]: Blair and Reeves, printers, 1836. House Document, 24th Cong. 1st Sess., no. 221.

United States President. *Message from the President of the United States, with reports from the secretaries of state and war, relative to the boundary line between Ohio and Territory of Michigan.* Washington[, DC]: Gales and Seaton, printers, 1836.

NOTES

1. Susan P. Fino, *The Michigan State Constitution: A Reference Guide* (Westport, CT: Greenwood Press, 1996) at 4 (hereafter Fino).
2. Willis F. Dunbar and George S. May, *Michigan, A History of the Wolverine State* (Grand Rapids, MI: W. B. Ferdman's Pub Co., 1995) at 13 (hereafter Dunbar and May).
3. Dunbar and May at 12.
4. Ibid. at 13.
5. Roger L. Rosentreter, ed., *Introducing Michigan's Past* (Lansing: Michigan History Magazine, 2001) at 6.
6. Dunbar and May at 17.
7. Bruce Catton, *Michigan, A Bicentennial History* (New York: Norton, 1976) at 8 (hereafter Catton).
8. Ibid. at 11.
9. Dunbar and May at 28.
10. Catton at 8.
11. Ibid. at 19.
12. Ibid. at 20.
13. Ibid. at 24.
14. Thomas M. Cooley, *Michigan, A History of Governments* (Boston: Houghton Mifflin, 1886) at 39 (hereafter Cooley).
15. Ibid.

16. Catton at 33.

17. Dunbar and May at 63.

18. <http://www.yale.edu/lawweb/avalon/paris763.htm>.

19. Dunbar and May at 63.

20. William Renwick Riddell, *Michigan Under British Rule: Law and Law Courts 1760-1796* (Lansing: Michigan Historical Commission, 1926) generally (hereafter Riddell).

21. Riddell at 14.

22. Ibid. at 29.

23. Ibid. at 28.

24. *Michigan Pioneer and Historical Collections* (Lansing, MI: Wynkoop Hallenbeck Crawford Co., State Printers, 1874-1906) in vol. 19 at 151, 160-161.

25. Ibid. at 161.

26. Riddell at 16.

27. Ibid. at 19.

28. Ibid.

29. Ibid. at 32.

30. 14 George III c. 83.

31. Dunbar and May at 77.

32. Ibid.

33. Ibid. at 78.

34. Ibid.

35. Riddell at 44.

36. 11 *Michigan Pioneer and Historical Collections*, 631, 632.

37. Riddell at 46.

38. Ibid.

39. 27 George III, c. 1: Ordinances, Pt. 2 p. 179.

40. Riddell at 49.

41. 3 *Michigan Pioneer and Historical Collections*, 17.

42. Riddell at 50.

43. Ibid. at 51.

44. 11 *Michigan Pioneer and Historical Collections*, 627, 630.

45. Riddell at 55.

46. Ibid.

47. Riddell at 58.

48. Ibid.

49. 34 George III, c. 2.

50. Riddell at 60.

51. Ibid.

52. Ibid. at 364-370.

53. Riddell, supra note 20.

54. *Michigan Pioneer and Historical Collections*, 40 vols. (1876-1929). Some volumes available in digital format at the Library of Congress's American Memory Web site (http://lcweb2.loc.gov/ammen/umhtml/umhome.html).

55. 31 George III, c. 31.

56. It is interesting to note, in reading the reports of the cases reprinted in the sources listed supra, that a great many of the names of plaintiffs, defendants, and members of the jury are French.

57. William Renwick Riddell, *The First Judge at Detroit and his Court* (Lansing, MI: Michigan State Bar Association, 1915) at 31.

58. Ibid.

59. Ibid. at 32.

60. Ibid. at 16.

61. Paris Peace Treaty of 1783, Art. 7 (http://www.yale.edu/lawweb/avalon/diplomacy/britian/paris.htm).

62. Dunbar and May at 90.

63. <http://www.yale.edu/lawweb/avalon/artconf.htm>.

64. Dunbar and May at 86.

65. 26 *Journals of the Continental Congress* 259 (Hunt. ed. 1928). Digital copy at Library of Congress's American Memory Web site (http://memory.loc.gov/ammen/amlaw/lwjc.html).

66. Fino at 4.

67. 1 *Stat.* 51.

68. Fino at 4-5.

69. Ibid. at Art. 5.

70. William Wirt Blume and Elizabeth Gaspar Brown, "Territorial Courts and Law," *Michigan Law Review* 61(1963): 39, 43 (hereafter Blume).

71. After Ohio achieved statehood in 1803, the Northwest Territories were re-aligned and present-day Michigan became part of the Indiana Territory for a brief time.

72. Blume at 43.

73. Ibid. at 46.

74. Ibid. at 47.

75. B.F.H. Witherell, "The Territorial and State Judges," *Michigan Reports* 4 (1857): 9, 10.

76. Dunbar and May at 112.

77. Ibid. at 113.

78. Olive C. Lathrop, "Unreported Opinions of a Territorial Judge," *Law Library Journal* 21(1928): 66 (hereafter Lathrop).

79. Ibid.

80. Alec R. Gilpin, *The Territory of Michigan, 1805-1837* (East Lansing: Michigan State University Press, 1970) at 24 (hereafter Gilpin).

81. Lathrop at 69-70.

82. Gilpin at 32.

83. Moore, "A.B. Woodward," 4 *Michigan Pioneer and Historical Collections* 127.

84. Lathrop at 77.

85. Timothy Frederick Sherer, *The Rule of the Governor and Judges in Michigan Territory 1805-1823* (PhD thesis, Michigan State University Department of History, East Lansing, 1976) at 169.

86. Gilpin at 25-26.

87. Catton at 72.
88. Dunbar and May at 204.
89. Fino at 5.
90. Ibid. at 7-8.
91. Constitution of the State of Michigan, 1835, Art. III, Sec. 1.
92. Fino at 5.
93. Dunbar and May at 213.
94. Cooley at 222.
95. Dunbar and May at 216.
96. Ibid. at 218-219.

Chapter 24

Minnesota Legal Materials
from Wilderness to Statehood

Anna M. Cherry

COMPETING CLAIMS TO THE LAND

The land that is now the state of Minnesota emerged with the retreat of
the last glacial icepack approximately 11,000 years ago[1] to become a diverse land of lakes and rivers, forests and prairie. The first human inhabitants are known today primarily by the mounds they left behind.[2] A pattern
of diverse and shifting claims and a tendency to be left behind have also
marked Minnesota's journey from wilderness to statehood.

The first inhabitants known to history were the Dakota (or Sioux) people.[3] They were probably not represented when a council of chiefs of the indigenous nations met at Sault de Ste. Marie on June 14, 1671, to hear the
French proclaim, with great ceremony, their sovereignty over "Lakes Huron
and Superior . . . and all other Countries, rivers, lakes and tributaries, contig-
uous and adjacent thereunto, as well discovered as to be discovered . . .
bounded on the one side by the Northern and Western Seas and on the other
side by the South Sea."[4] This claim would have included all of Minnesota as
well as most of North America.[5]

Ten years later, the explorer La Salle began a journey down the Mississippi River. On April 9, 1682, on an island at the mouth of that river, he
erected a wooden column bearing the French coat of arms and claimed the
entire valley of the Mississippi and all of its tributaries for France. He named
this land Louisiana.[6] Although the British may not have been aware of it at
the time, their discovery of Hudson Bay and the claim to all waters flowing
into it would have included the Red River Valley of northwestern Minnesota.[7] As a practical matter, however, the Dakota people who lived in the
Minnesota country during this time remained largely undisturbed.

That situation would not last. As European settlement pushed westward,
so did displaced indigenous peoples. The Ojibwa (or Chippewa) came from
the St. Lawrence River Valley, bringing with them steel knives and muskets

unknown to the Dakota.[8] By the end of the eighteenth century, the Dakota had completely abandoned the lands east of the Mississippi and north of St. Anthony Falls.[9]

Meanwhile, although Britain and France both included the Minnesota country within their land claims, neither had established permanent settlements there. Itinerant fur traders were the only European presence in 1755 when the French and Indian War broke out.[10]

In this North American branch of the larger Seven Years' War in Europe, Minnesota was only a small part of the New World land claims at stake. As a precaution against defeat, France made a secret treaty with her ally Spain, ceding all lands *west* of the Mississippi.[11] It turned out to be a wise precaution. In the Treaty of Paris—which ended that war on February 10, 1763—France ceded to England all of her North American holdings *east* of the Mississippi, except for the island of New Orleans.[12]

This settled any disputes as to sovereignty in the lands that would later become the Northwest Territory. The British Parliament subsequently passed the Quebec Act of 1774, consolidating the part of Minnesota east of the Mississippi River into the province of Quebec and giving it its first written constitution.[13] Nevertheless, fur trading remained the primary European intrusion into the area. In 1787, the British monopolized this activity with the organization of the Northwest Company.[14]

During the period of the American Revolution, Minnesota was divided roughly into two parts, with the lands east of the Mississippi in the British domain and the lands to the west owned by Spain. For convenience, let us call these Minnesota East and Minnesota West. The Peace Treaty of September 3, 1783, ended British rule of the territory including Minnesota East,[15] but that was not the end of competing claims. Virginia had already sent an army into the western lands.[16]

Virginia's claim was based not only on its colonial charter of 1609 (which included the land extending "from the Sea Coast . . . up into the Land throughout from Sea to Sea, West and Northwest,"[17] but also on a deed from the Iroquois in 1744 that recognized the British claim to lands in the colony of Virginia.[18] As early as 1738, the colonial legislature of Virginia had created a county that extended from the Blue Ridge west and northwest to the "utmost limits of Virginia."[19] Fortunately, this disputed claim was resolved amicably when Virginia deeded the new territory to the United States in 1784.[20] When the Continental Congress passed the Ordinance of July 13, 1787, creating the Northwest Territory,[21] Minnesota East finally acquired an organized government.[22]

As a practical matter, however, not much had changed in the Minnesota country. The British did not withdraw their garrisons south of the Canadian border until 1794 with the conclusion of Jay's Treaty.[23] Even after the forts were transferred to American hands, the largest economic presence in Minnesota remained the British-owned Northwest Company and the largest nonnative presence was its fur traders.[24]

Meanwhile, in France, Napoleon was making plans for empire. Since, in those days, no self-respecting empire could be without colonies in the New World, he reacquired Louisiana from Spain by secret treaty in 1800.[25] Within a year, however, the secret was out.[26] Feeling threatened by the change, the United States sent emissaries to France with authority to negotiate the purchase of strategic portions of the territory. By the time they arrived, however, Napoleon had rethought his colonial plans and offered the surprised delegates the chance to buy the entire parcel. The offer was accepted.[27] By treaty of April 30, 1803, the United States acquired all of Louisiana, including Minnesota West.[28]

At this point, it would seem that—claims of indigenous peoples notwithstanding—the United States held clear title to all of the Minnesota country, but there were still two problems. The first was a matter of geographical ignorance—no one knew the true source of the Mississippi River. The language of the treaty of 1783, reflecting this confusion, described a boundary line between the United States and Canada that was physically impossible to draw.[29] The second problem was the Northwest Company, which still operated in Minnesota under the British flag, without serious competition from other commercial enterprises or settlers. When the War of 1812 broke out, the British government gave commissions to agents of the Northwest Company, who then recruited their Indian trading partners to fight for England. Thus, Minnesota remained in British hands throughout the war.[30]

The Treaty of Ghent ended the War of 1812 but did not settle the question of Minnesota's northwest boundary.[31] An agreement was eventually reached in a convention signed in London on October 20, 1818, which set the boundary along the forty-ninth parallel.[32] At last, the territory that was to become the state of Minnesota was all firmly settled under the jurisdiction of the United States.[33]

THE SHIFTING BOUNDARIES OF TERRITORY

Having all of the Minnesota country under the U.S. flag did not change the fact that it was still a land of forests and fur traders populated mostly by its indigenous inhabitants. In 1805, the U.S. Army sent an expedition under the command of First Lieutenant Zebulon Pike to explore the upper Mississippi. During the course of this expedition, Pike negotiated the first treaty between the Dakota and the U.S. government exchanging land for consideration.[34] Nevertheless, there was no significant, permanent military presence in the region until September 10, 1820, when the cornerstone of Fort Snelling was laid at the junction of the Mississippi and Minnesota Rivers.[35]

Sparsely settled and remote, the Minnesota country was easy to overlook. The Northwest Ordinance provided for the Northwest Territory to be eventually divided into not fewer than three nor more than five states.[36] As these states were carved out, Minnesota East was shuffled from one territory to another. It was first organized into the Indiana Territory in 1800,[37] then Illinois in 1809,[38] and Michigan in 1818.[39]

On the opposite side of the Mississippi, the northern half of the Louisiana Purchase became the district of Louisiana when the territory was divided in 1804.[40] Until its own government was organized in 1805,[41] the same officers of the Indiana Territory who governed Minnesota East governed this district.[42] In 1812, the district of Louisiana was organized into the territory of Missouri.[43] When the state of Missouri was carved out in 1820, the only provision made for the lands to the north was the prohibition of slavery.[44] When the state of Missouri was admitted to the Union a year later, there was again no provision made for a territorial government for the remaining lands, including the Minnesota country.[45] Apparently, the Dakota people who lived there did not mind. It was not until 1834 that Congress got around to attaching this territory to Michigan,[46] again bringing the eastern and western parts of Minnesota together under one government, if only temporarily.[47]

They remained together when the territory of Wisconsin was formed in 1836,[48] but were split apart again along the Mississippi River when that territory was divided to create the territory of Iowa in 1838.[49] When Iowa became a state, Minnesota West was again left without a government.[50]

Meanwhile, Wisconsin was attempting to form itself into a state that would include the entire remainder of the old Northwest Territory, all the way to the Mississippi.[51] There was now, however, a significant number of nonnative settlers in the St. Croix Valley of Minnesota East, and they had plans for a state of their own.[52] After much politicking and lobbying, Wisconsin was admitted to the Union,[53] its western boundary set where it stands today, and the Minnesota country was left without a government yet again.[54]

THE WINDING PATH TO STATEHOOD

Minnesota now consisted of the last remnants of the Northwest Territory, most recently part of Wisconsin, and the oddments to the north and west that were most recently part of Iowa, all without any organized government.[55] Feeling rightly neglected by Washington, the people of the region took matters into their own hands.[56] On August 4, 1848, the call went out for a convention to be held in Stillwater on August 26 for the purpose of organizing a territory.[57] Sixty-one delegates from all parts of the territory attended, and the convention elected Henry Hastings Sibley to make the journey to Washington with the mission of petitioning the government for the creation of the Minnesota Territory.[58]

Another wrinkle was added a few weeks later when James Catlin, the secretary of Wisconsin Territory at the time of its statehood, proposed using the fiction that the Wisconsin Territory still existed in the lands left over when that state was admitted to the Union and was, therefore, entitled to send a bona fide delegate to Congress. It was apparently thought that a delegate to Congress would have more clout than an emissary from an unorganized territory. A general election was set, Sibley was duly elected delegate, and he thereafter left for Washington.[59]

Sibley still had to convince the House Committee on Elections to seat him. Not only was his election as a territorial delegate questionable, but he also resided in Mendota, a town situated west of the Mississippi River and, therefore, not a part of the late Wisconsin Territory.[60] It did not matter. A combination of Sibley's charm and training in the law—along with Catlin's correct assumption that no one would inquire too deeply into the legality of the election—carried the day and Sibley was seated as a territorial delegate.[61] This official position gave him an advantage in pursuing his real purpose—the creation of a territory of Minnesota.[62]

It was not an easy job. The Senate, controlled by Democrats, had no problem passing the bill, but the Whig majority in the House added an amendment to delay the effective date until March 10, 1849, after the newly elected Whig President was scheduled to be sworn in.[63] This would deny outgoing President Polk the opportunity to appoint the first territorial officers, and it did not sit well with the Democrats.[64] With only three days left in the session, the bill seemed to be dead in the water, despite all of Sibley's efforts. Then, at the last moment, a group of Democratic senators suggested that Sibley inform the Whig leaders in the House that they would vote against the bill to create the new Department of the Interior (with many more potential appointive offices) unless the House dropped the amendment.[65] The strategy worked. The House dropped its amendment, so the bill passed and was signed. It went into effect on March 3, 1849, the last day of the session.[66] Ironically, with the Senate out of session, no appointments could be ratified. Therefore, it was incoming Whig President Zachary Taylor[67] who appointed as the first governor of the territory of Minnesota Alexander Ramsey of Pennsylvania, a leading Whig from a state that had voted for Taylor.[68]

The organic act provided for the laws of the territory of Wisconsin to continue in effect in the new territory of Minnesota until superceded.[69] Since most of the population still lived east of the Mississippi, this caused little, if any, confusion.[70] The population grew at a rapid pace starting in 1854, as the railroads extended closer to the territory, making a move toward statehood inevitable.[71] Part of the push in that direction also came from Washington, where Congress was growing weary of paying the expenses of its territories.[72] First, however, the final boundary question had to be settled.

The northern, eastern, and southern boundary lines were set by the organic act, but the territory extended west to the Missouri and White Earth rivers, encompassing a large chunk of what are now North Dakota and South Dakota, and making it too large to be admitted as a single state.[73] The highly political question of whether to divide the territory north to south or east to west pitted the newly established farming communities on the southern prairies against the political power centers of St. Paul, Stillwater, and St. Anthony in the east-central part of the territory.[74]

The north-south dividing line finally prevailed when the enabling act was passed by Congress in 1857,[75] but the ideological and geographical divide between political factions would make itself felt again in the process of forming a constitution.[76]

The election of delegates to the constitutional convention resulted in a nearly even split between Republicans (mostly newcomers) and Democrats (of the old political power structure), with the Republicans holding a slight advantage and contested credentials on both sides.[77] Both sides also wanted control of the convention. The enabling act had specified the date the convention was to convene (the second Monday in July 1857, which was, coincidentally, also the seventieth anniversary of the Northwest Ordinance), but not the time for the opening session.[78] The question remained ambiguous even as the delegates began to gather in St. Paul.[79] Fearing Democratic treachery, the Republicans began gathering at the capitol at midnight. When the room where the convention was to take place opened, they moved in.[80] All through the morning, their numbers increased. At fifteen minutes before noon, the Democrats marched in en masse. Designated representatives from both parties attempted to call the convention to order simultaneously. The Democrats then immediately moved to adjourn until the next day, voted, and marched out again en masse.[81] It was the only time the convention came even close to meeting as a whole.[82]

When the Democrats walked out, the Republicans stayed and got down to business on their own.[83] When the Democrats returned the next day, they demanded possession of the room. Upon being informed by the Republicans that the constitutional convention was already in session there, the

Democrats convened their delegation in the council chamber in the west wing of the capitol.[84] The convention had divided permanently into separate caucuses, each claiming to be the only legitimate convention and each blaming the other for the split.[85]

It was not a situation that could continue. As July sweltered into August, movements were being made toward compromise.[86] There was no chance of reuniting the two factions, but through carefully worded resolutions and backdoor meetings, a conference committee was finally appointed and met for the first time on August 18.[87] Since both caucuses had been working from essentially the same templates—constitutions adopted by other recently admitted states—there were few actual controversies.[88] The two largest were also the most political—suffrage and districting—but, in the end, compromise was reached even on these.[89] On August 28, the conference report was adopted by both conventions, essentially substituting the conference committee's work for all the prior work of both conventions.[90]

Eager to adjourn after seven long weeks, both conventions passed resolutions authorizing copies to be enrolled for signature the next morning. It would have been no small task for the conference committee, working by lamplight, to handwrite one enrolled copy, but many on both sides, including the president of the Democratic wing, refused to sign the same document as members of the other faction. The committee members found themselves working through the night.[91] Eight distinct handwritings have been identified in each document, and 299 differences in punctuation have been found between the two, along with small differences in wording.[92] It was the Democratic copy that was submitted to the president to be laid before the Senate, but when the Committee on Territories reported back to the full Senate, it was the Republican version that was attached to the report.[93] Thus, Minnesota, which had seen four flags and nine different territorial governments, started its existence as a state with two constitutions. Fortunately, the net effect of the differences between documents turned out to be trivial and no question was ever raised about the validity of the constitution adopted by the people of Minnesota.[94]

There was even a question raised at the time about the date of Minnesota's admission to the Union.[95] The enabling act provided that the people within what are the present boundaries of the state were "authorized to form for themselves a constitution and State government, by the name of the State of Minnesota, and to come into the Union on an equal footing with the original States, according to the Federal Constitution."[96] The question was whether this language provided for Minnesota to become a state upon the adoption of a constitution by the people without further act of Congress.[97] Congress did act, however,[98] and most authorities accept May 11, 1858, as the date of Minnesota's admission to the Union.

MINNESOTA PRESTATEHOOD DOCUMENTS

Minnesota East of the Mississippi, British Claims, and the Northwest Territory

The Quebec Act of 1774, 14 George III, c. 83 (U.K.).

Definitive Treaty of Peace Between the United States of America and His Britannic Majesty (September 3, 1783), 8 *Stat.* 80, also reprinted in volume 1 of *Minnesota Statutes Annotated* (1976) at 29.

Virginia Act of Cession, December 20, 1783. *The Federal and State Constitutions Colonial Charters, and Other Organic Laws of the States, Territories, and Colonies Now or Heretofore Forming the United States of America* vol. 2, 955 (compiled and edited under the Act of Congress of June 30, 1906, by Francis Newton Thorpe, Government Printing Office 1909), also reprinted in volume 1 of *Minnesota Statutes Annotated* (1976) at 35.

Deed of Cession from Virginia, March 1, 1784. *The Federal and State Constitutions Colonial Charters, and Other Organic Laws of the States, Territories, and Colonies Now or Heretofore Forming the United States of America* vol. 2, 957 (compiled and edited under the Act of Congress of June 30, 1906, by Francis Newton Thorpe, Government Printing Office 1909).

An Ordinance for the government of the territory of the United States northwest of the river Ohio, (by the Congress of the Confederation, July 13, 1787) *U.S. Rev. Stats.,* 2d ed. 13 (1878). Continued and amended by An Act to provide for the Government of the Territory Northwest of the river Ohio, 1 *Stat.* 50 (1789) (which includes the act of July 13, 1787, in a footnote). Both acts are also reprinted in volume 1 of *Minnesota Statutes Annotated* (1976) at 39-47.

Virginia Act of Ratification, 1788 (ratifying the Northwest Ordinance of 1787 against anything to the contrary that may have been in the Deed of Cession of 1784). *The Federal and State Constitutions Colonial Charters, and Other Organic Laws of the States, Territories, and Colonies Now or Heretofore Forming the United States of America* vol. 2, 963 (compiled and edited under the Act of Congress of June 30, 1906, by Francis Newton Thorpe, Government Printing Office 1909).

Treaty of Amity, Commerce and Navigation, between His Britannic Majesty and the United States of America, by their President, with the Advice and Consent of their Senate (Nov. 19, 1794), 8 *Stat.* 116 (Jay's Treaty).

An Act to divide the territory of the United States northwest of the Ohio, into two separate governments, ch. 41, 2 *Stat.* 58 (1800), also reprinted in volume 1 of *Minnesota Statutes Annotated* (1976) at 48 (creating the Indiana Territory).

An Act for dividing the Indiana Territory into two separate governments, ch. 13, 2 *Stat.* 514 (1809) (creating the territory of Illinois).

Treaty of Peace and Amity Between His Britannic Majesty and the United States of America (Dec. 24, 1814), 8 *Stat.* 218 (Treaty of Ghent).

Convention with Great Britain on Fisheries, Boundary and Restoration of Slaves (Oct. 20, 1818), 8 *Stat.* 248.

An Act to enable the people of the Illinois territory to form a constitution and state government, and for the admission of such state into the Union on an equal footing with the original states, ch. 67, 3 *Stat.* 428 (1818). (Surplus lands became part of the Michigan Territory, sec. 7 at 431.)

Minnesota West of the Mississippi and the Louisiana Territory

Definitive act of cession of Louisiana by the King of France to the King of Spain (at Fontainebleau, Nov. 3, 1762), translated in 13, part 2, Register of Debates appendix 226 (1837).

Definitive Treaty of Peace between France, Great Britain and Spain, signed at Paris, Feb. 10, 1763, 42 *Consolidated Treaty Series* 279, also available at <http://www.yale.edu/lawweb/avalon/paris763.htm>.

Preliminary and Secret Treaty Between France and Spain, signed at San Ildefonso, Oct. 1, 1800, 55 *Consolidated Treaty Series* 375.

Treaty between the United States of America and the French Republic for the Cession of Louisiana (April 30, 1803), 8 *Stat.* 200; Payment Conventions (April 30, 1803), 8 *Stat.* 206, 208.

An Act to enable the President of the United States to take possession of the territories ceded by France to the United States, by the treaty concluded at Paris, on the thirtieth of April last; and for the temporary government thereof, ch. 1, 2 *Stat.* 245 (1803).

An Act erecting Louisiana into two territories, and providing for the temporary government thereof, ch. 38, 2 *Stat.* 283 (1804).

An Act further providing for the government of the district of Louisiana, ch. 31, 2 *Stat.* 331 (1805).

An Act providing for the government of the territory of Missouri, ch. 95, 2 *Stat.* 743 (1812).

An Act to authorize the people of the Missouri territory to form a constitution and state government, and for the admission of such state into the Union on an equal footing with the original states, and to prohibit slavery in certain territories, ch. 22, 3 *Stat.* 545 (1820) (the Missouri Compromise).

An Act to attach the territory of the United States west of the Mississippi river, and north of the State of Missouri, to the territory of Michigan, ch. 98, 4 *Stat.* 701 (1834).

Minnesota Becomes Its Own Territory

An Act establishing the Territorial Government of Wisconsin, ch. 54, 5 *Stat.* 10 (1836).

An Act to divide the Territory of Wisconsin and to establish the Territorial Government of Iowa, ch. 96, 5 *Stat.* 235 (1838).

An Act for the Admission of the State of Iowa into the Union, ch. 1, 9 *Stat.* 117 (1846).

An Act for the Admission of the State of Wisconsin into the Union, ch. 50, 9 *Stat.* 233 (1848).

An Act to establish the Territorial Government of Minnesota, ch. 121, 9 *Stat.* 403 (1849), also reprinted in volume 1 of *Minnesota Statutes Annotated* (1976) at 51.

An Act to authorize the People of the Territory of Minnesota to form a Constitution and State Government, preparatory to their Admission in the Union on an equal Footing with the original States, ch. 60, 11 *Stat.* 166 (1857), also reprinted in volume 1 of *Minnesota Statutes Annotated* (1976) at 61.

An Act for the Admission of the State of Minnesota into the Union, ch. 31, 11 *Stat.* 285 (1858), also reprinted in volume 1 of *Minnesota Statutes Annotated* (1976) at 67.

Territorial Legislature

Journal of the House of the Territory of Minnesota (The Assembly 1850-1857) (9 vol., includes first through eighth sessions, 1849-1857, plus the extra session, April-May 1857).

Journal of the Council of the Territory of Minnesota (The Assembly 1850-1857) (9 vol., includes first through eighth sessions, 1849-1857, plus the extra session, April-May 1857).

Acts, Joint Resolutions and Memorials passed by the First Legislative Assembly of the Territory of Minnesota at its First Session, begun and held at St. Paul, on the third day of September, one Thousand Eight Hundred and Forty-nine. St. Paul: Printed by James M. Goodhue and Nathaniel M'Lean, 1850.

Session Laws of the Territory of Minnesota (by authority of the Legislature 1851-1857) (8 vols.).

See Tables 24.1 and 24.2 for details on session laws and statutory compilations.

Reports of Court Decisions

Reports of Cases Argued and Determined in the Supreme Court of the Territory of Minnesota from the Organization of the Territory until its Admission into the Union in 1858. St. Paul: Earle. S. Goodrich, state printer, Pioneer and Democrat Office, 1858 (Volume 1 of *Minnesota Reports*).

Volume one of *Minnesota Reports* is supposed to include "all cases decided by the Supreme Court of Minnesota, from the organization of the Territory [1849] until its admission into the Union in 1858." Unfortunately, records were lost or destroyed by a fire at the Capitol in July 1857. The first cases reported date from the Court's second term in 1851 which was the first term to have an official Reporter appointed. Cases from this term and those terms reported by the second Reporter survived the fire intact. The extent of the loss of later case files cannot be determined.

. . . Minnesota never had nominative reporters per se. The first two preparers of reports did have their reports published as part of the *Collated Statutes of the Territory of Minnesota,* 1853 (*see* Appendix 4) under the titles of Hollingshead's Reports and Atwater's Reports. These reports were reprinted along with all subsequent cases starting with volume 1 of *Minnesota Reports*. Then, in 1877, because an insufficient number of the first twenty original volumes of *Minnesota Reports* were printed, James Gilfillan, a former Chief Justice of the Minnesota Supreme Court, republished them as Gilfillan's Reports (*Gil.*). These are not exact reprints of the original reports; Justice Gilfillan deleted some material and added other information. Differences exist in the addition of briefs, in headnotes, punctuation, paragraphing, and page numbering, but Justice Gilfillan did give the citation to the original volume at the beginning of each case. Pages, however, are not starred except in volume one.[99]

The Constitution

See Table 24.3 for details on constitutional documents.

S. Rpt. no. 21, 35th Cong., 1st Sess. (Jan. 26, 1858). (Committee on Territories report on the proposed constitution of the State of Minnesota.)

The original handwritten Democratic and Republican constitutions are reproduced in volume 1 of *Minnesota Statutes Annotated* (1976) at 159.

Selected Historical Sources

William Watts Folwell. *A History of Minnesota.* St. Paul: Minnesota Historical Society, 1921.

William Anderson. *A History of the Constitution of Minnesota.* Minneapolis, MN: University of Minnesota, 1921.

Robert J. Sheran and Timothy J. Baland. "The Law, Courts, and Lawyers in the Frontier Days of Minnesota: An Informal Legal History of the Years 1835 to 1865." *Wm. Mitchell L. Rev.* 2(1976): 1.

TABLE 24.1. Checklist of Session Laws[a]

Date	Session	Legislation	Pages
1849 (September)	1st Legislative Assembly	Acts	xxxvii, 107, 2, 106-213[b]
1851 (January)	2d Session	Session Laws	53
1852 (January)	3d Session	Session Laws	78
1853 (January)	4th Session	Session Laws	89
1854 (January)	5th Session	Session Laws	184
1855 (January)	6th Session	Session Laws	200
1856 (January)	7th Session	Session Laws	376
1857 (January)	8th Session	Session Laws	304
1857 (April)	Extra Session	Session Laws	361

Source: Data from Appendix 3 of Arlette M. Soderberg and Barbara L. Golden, *Minnesota Legal Research Guide* (Buffalo, NY: William S. Hein and Co., 1985). Reprinted with permission.

[a]Pagination varies in other copies. This publication gives the collation in the copies examined. Laws 1849 through 1859 are available on microfilm from Photoduplication Service, Library of Congress.

[b]This includes "Republication of Important General Laws of Wisconsin Now in Force in the Territory of Minnesota by provision of the Organic Act" at 106-160. It also contains the U.S. Constitution and acts of Congress regarding the Northwest Territory.

TABLE 24.2. Statutory Compilations

Title	Publication Data	Description
Republication of Important General Laws of Wisconsin Now in Force in the Territory of Minnesota by Provision of the Organic Act.	St. Paul: James M. Goodhue, 1850, pp. 106-160.	This was printed as chapter numbers xlv through lxiii of the first volume of the session laws of the Territory of Minnesota in 1849. The index to these Wisconsin laws begins on page 203. These laws comprise the laws of Wisconsin which were in force in the territory of Minnesota and which were later incorporated into *Revised Statutes* 1851.
The Revised Statutes of the Territory of Minnesota, Passed at the Second Session of the Legislative Assembly Commencing January 1, 1851.....	St. Paul: James M. Goodhue, 1851, xvi, 734 p.	The outline and the arrangement of *Revised Statutes* 1851 follow the outline and arrangement of the 1849 *Revised Statutes of the State of Wisconsin*; the numbering system, however, is different. Some of the sections appear to be verbatim copy; others have been revised extensively. The volume represents only a compilation of the Wisconsin laws applicable in Minnesota. Other laws from *Laws of Minnesota* 1849 are appended but not incorporated in the compilation.
Amendments to the Revised Statutes, of the Territory of Minnesota, Passed at the Third Session of the Legislative Assembly, Commencing January 6, 1852.	St. Paul: Owens and Moore, Printer, Minnesotian Office, 1852, 45 p.	This publication is arranged in the same order as *Revised Statutes* 1851, and it must be used in connection with it.

594

Collated Statutes of the Territory of Minnesota and Decisions of Supreme Court.

Collated Pursuant to a Resolution of March 5, 1853. St. Paul: Joseph R. Brown, 1853; 198, 96 p.

This in an official listing, not in chronological order or in any other apparent logical arrangement, of both the general laws and the private acts that were in force July 1, 1853, and that had not been included in *Revised Statutes* 1851. A joint resolution of the Legislature authorized these acts to be "collated, properly noted and indexed." (Authorizing the Secretary of the Territory to collate, and cause to be printed, certain acts, and for other purposes. J. Res. 3, 1853 Minn. [Territorial] Laws 64.)

Also included in the volume are William Hollinshead's reports of cases argued and determined in the Supreme Court of the Minnesota Territory in July term, 1851, and Isaac Atwater's reports, July term, 1852.

Code Pleadings and Practice in Civil Actions in the Courts of this State, reported to the Legislature of Minnesota by Aaron Goodrich, one of the Commissioners appointed to review the laws.

St. Paul: Earle S. Goodrich, state printer, Pioneer and Democrat office, 1858. 280 p.

There had been much disagreement in Minnesota about whether to retain the old common law or to adopt a new statutory code of practice and pleadings such as the *Code of Procedure of the State of New York*, also known as the "Field Code," which New York adopted in 1848. The Minnesota legislature chose to adopt a code. According to the Minnesota *Code's* introduction, a joint resolution was passed by the Minnesota legislature in March 1858, directing that commissioners Aaron Goodrich, Moses Sherburne, and William Hollinshead prepare a system of pleadings and practice to be followed in the state courts, using the "Field Code" as a guide, "having reference to the brevity and legal intent of the pleadings; and that they cause the result of their labors to be printed and laid before the Legislature at the earliest day practicable." The dissents of Goodrich from many of the Minnesota *Code's* provisions are reported in the introduction. A "Report of the Select Committee on the Code of Procedure," which urged the adoption of the proposed code, is published in the *Journal* of the house of representatives for March 19, 1858, at page 558. This code somewhat conforms to the Field Code.

TABLE 24.2 *(continued)*

Title	Publication Data	Description
Public Statutes of the State of Minnesota (1849-1858).	Compiled by Moses Sherburne and William Hollinshead, Commissioners. Published by state authority. St. Paul: The Pioneer Printing Co., 1858. 14, ix-lxxi, 73-1071 p.	The object of this official compilation was to republish the general laws contained in *Revised Statutes* 1851 and incorporate the laws contained in *Laws of Minnesota* for the years 1849 through 1858. An attempt was made to include only the laws in force and to omit those repealed. Chapter 7 and 37 of *Laws of Minnesota* 1858 provided that commissioners were to prepare this compilation and that Justices of the Supreme Court were to examine and approve it. Chapter 3, section 31, of *Public Statutes* (1849-1858) provided that when so approved and published, the compilation "shall be received in all places whatsoever as the laws of the state. . . ." The statutes were not enacted by the legislature.[a]
An Analytical Index to the General and Special Laws of the Territory and State of Minnesota from 1849 to 1875.	By John C. Shaw and John B. West. St. Paul: John B. West, 1876. 121, [3], 63 p.	This is an index of session laws only, with general and special laws indexed separately. Special laws, especially those related to roads, taxes, and titles to real estate, are fully indexed.
Index Digest to All the Laws of the State of Minnesota General and Special Including the Joint Resolutions and Memorials to Congress.	By John F. Kelly. St. Paul: The Kelly Law Book Co., 1894. 417 p.	The indexes of the session laws were incomplete and hard to use, so an index of this sort had much value. It included laws, passed from the first territorial session in 1849 through the session of 1893, arranged to show all the law in force as well as the amended, repealed, superseded, and obsolete laws. Tables were included to show the changes made in revisions and compilations so that any general laws could be traced to its origin.

Source: Table data from Appendix 4 of Arlette M. Soderberg and Barbara L. Golden, *Minnesota Legal Research Guide* (Buffalo, NY: William S. Hein and Co., 1985). Reprinted with permission.

[a]Another feature of this set is the "Special Index to Introduction," indexing, among other documents, the U.S. Constitution, the Minnesota Constitution, the organic act, and the Northwest Ordinance.

TABLE 24.3. Constitutional Documents

Title	Publication Data	Comments
Debates and Proceedings of the Constitutional Convention for the Territory of Minnesota, to Form a State Constitution Preparatory to its Admission into the Union as a State.	T. F. Andrews, Official Reporter to the Convention. St. Paul: George W. Moore, Printer, Minnesotian Office, 7, xviii, [9]-624 p.	Constitutional Convention, 1857, Republican debates and proceedings. Also available in microform.
The Debates and Proceedings of the Minnesota Constitutional Convention, Including the Organic Act of the Territory, with the Enabling Act of Congress, the Act of the Territorial Legislature Relative to the Convention, and the Vote of the People on the Constitution.	Reported Officially by Francis H. Smith. St. Paul: Earle S. Goodrich, Territorial Printer. Pioneer and Democrat Office. 1857. xix, 1, 685 p.	Constitutional Convention, 1857, Democratic debates and proceedings. Also available in microform.
Journal of the Constitutional Convention, of the Territory of Minnesota, Begun and Held in the City of St. Paul: Capital of Said Territory, on Monday, the Thirteenth Day of July, One Thousand Eight Hundred and Fifty-Seven.	St. Paul: Earle S. Goodrich, State Printer, Pioneer and Democrat Office. 1857. 209 p.	Also available in microform.
Message of the President of the United States, Communicating a Copy of the Constitution of Minnesota. January 11, 1858.	Referred to the Committee on Territories. Senate Executive Document No. 14, 35th Cong., 1st Sess. Washington, DC: Government Printing Office, 1858. 24 p.	

Source: Table data from Appendix 1 of Arlette M. Soderberg and Barbara L. Golden, *Minnesota Legal Research Guide* (Buffalo, NY: William S. Hein and Co., 1985). Reprinted with permission.

NOTES

1. *Minnesota Guidebook to State Agency Services 2001-2003* 446, Robin PanLener, ed. (Minnesota's Bookstore 2001), also available under "Glaciers, Ecosystems, Earthquakes" at <http://www.yellowpages.state.mn.us>.

2. Ibid. at 447-448, also available under "Mississippian Tradition, Mound Builders" at <http://www.yellowpages.state.mn.us>.

3. Ibid. at 448, also available under "Indian Culture, Dakota, Ojibwa" at <http://www.yellowpages.state.mn.us>.

4. William Watts Folwell. *A History of Minnesota,* vol. 1, 17 (St. Paul: Minnesota Historical Society, 1921).

5. Ibid.

6. Folwell, supra n. 4 at 33.

7. William Anderson, *A History of the Constitution of Minnesota* 5-6 (Minneapolis: University of Minnesota, 1921).

8. Folwell, supra n. 4 at 80.

9. Ibid. at 81.

10. Ibid. at 50-51.

11. Definitive act of cession of Louisiana by the King of France to the King of Spain (at Fontainebleau, Nov. 3, 1762), translated in, 13, part 2, Register of Debates appendix 226 (1837).

12. Definitive Treaty of Peace between France, Great Britain and Spain, signed at Paris, Feb. 10, 1763, art. VII, 42 Consolidated Treaty Series 279, also available at <http://www.yale.edu/lawweb/avalon/paris763.htm>; Folwell, supra n. 4 at 51-52.

13. The Quebec Act of 1774, 14 George III, c. 83 (U.K.); Folwell, supra n. 4 at 65.

14. Folwell, supra n. 4 at 66-67.

15. Definitive Treaty of Peace Between the United States of America and his Britannic Majesty (September 3, 1783), 8 *Stat.* 80.

16. Folwell, supra n. 4 at 69.

17. Ibid.; Second Charter of Virginia. *The Federal and State Constitutions Colonial Charters, and Other Organic Laws of the States, Territories, and Colonies Now or Heretofore Forming the United States of America* vol. 7, 3790, 3795, compiled and edited under the Act of Congress of June 30, 1906, by Francis Newton Thorpe (Washington, DC: Government Printing Office, 1909).

18. Folwell, supra n. 4 at 69.

19. Ibid.

20. Deed of Cession from Virginia, March 1, 1784. *The Federal and State Constitutions Colonial Charters, and Other Organic Laws of the States, Territories, and Colonies Now or Heretofore Forming the United States of America* vol. 2, 957, compiled and edited under the Act of Congress of June 30, 1906, by Francis Newton Thorpe (Washington, DC: Government Printing Office, 1909).

21. An Ordinance for the government of the territory of the United States northwest of the river Ohio, (by the Congress of the Confederation, July 13, 1787) *U.S. Rev. Stats.,* 2d ed. 13 (1878).

22. Folwell, supra n. 4 at 70.

23. Treaty of Amity, Commerce and Navigation, Between His Britannic Majesty; and the United States of America, by their President, with the Advice and Consent of Their Senate (Nov. 19, 1794), 8 *Stat.* 116.

24. Folwell, supra n. 4 at 70-72.

25. Preliminary and Secret Treaty Between France and Spain, signed at San Ildefonso, Oct. 1, 1800, 55 Consolidated Treaty Series 375; Folwell, supra n. 4 at 76-77.

26. Folwell, supra n. 4 at 77.

27. Folwell, supra n. 4 at 77-78; Anderson, supra n. 7 at 8.

28. Treaty Between the United States of America and the French Republic for the Cession of Louisiana (April 30, 1803), 8 *Stat.* 200; Payment Conventions (April 30, 1803), 8 *Stat.* 206, 208.

29. Anderson, supra n. 7 at 6-8.

30. Folwell, supra n. 4 at 100-101.

31. Treaty of Peace and Amity Between His Britannic Majesty and the United States of America (Dec. 24, 1814), 8 *Stat.* 218; Anderson supra n. 7 at 8.

32. Convention with Great Britain on Fisheries, Boundary and Restoration of Slaves, Art. 2 (Oct. 20, 1818), 8 *Stat.* 248, 249.

33. Anderson, supra n. 7 at 8-9.

34. Folwell, supra n. 4 at 90-94. A full discussion of Indian treaties is beyond the scope of this text.

35. Folwell, supra n. 4 at 139.

36. Anderson, supra n. 7 at 10; An Ordinance for the government of the territory of the United States northwest of the river Ohio, art. V (by the Congress of the Confederation, July 13, 1787) *U.S. Rev. Stats.,* 2d ed. 13, 16 (1878).

37. An Act to divide the territory of the United States northwest of the Ohio, into two separate governments, ch. 41, 2 *Stat.* 58 (1800).

38. An Act for dividing the Indiana Territory into two separate governments, ch. 13, 2 *Stat.* 514 (1809).

39. An Act to enable the people of the Illinois territory to form a constitution and state government, and for the admission of such state into the Union on an equal footing with the original states, ch. 67, sec. 7, 3 *Stat.* 428, 431 (1818).

40. An Act erecting Louisiana into two territories, and providing for the temporary government thereof, ch. 38, 2 *Stat.* 283 (1804).

41. An Act further providing for the government of the district of Louisiana, ch. 31, 2 *Stat.* 331 (1805).

42. Anderson, supra n. 7 at 12.

43. An Act providing for the government of the territory of Missouri, ch. 95, 2 *Stat.* 743 (1812).

44. An Act to authorize the people of the Missouri territory to form a constitution and state government, and for the admission of such state into the Union on an equal footing with the original states, and to prohibit slavery in certain territories, ch. 22, § 8, 3 *Stat.* 545, 548 (1820).

45. Resolution providing for the admission of the state of Missouri, into the Union, on a certain condition, res. I, 3 *Stat.* 645 (1821).

46. An Act to attach the territory of the United States west of the Mississippi river, and north of the State of Missouri, to the territory of Michigan, ch. 98, 4 *Stat.* 701 (1834).

47. Anderson, supra n. 7 at 13-14.

48. An Act establishing the Territorial Government of Wisconsin, ch. 54, 5 *Stat.* 10 (1836).

49. An Act to divide the Territory of Wisconsin and to establish the Territorial Government of Iowa, ch. 96, 5 *Stat.* 235 (1838).

50. An Act for the Admission of the State of Iowa into the Union, ch. 1, 9 *Stat.* 117 (1846); Anderson, supra n. 7 at 17.

51. Anderson, supra n. 7 at 17.

52. Ibid. at 17-19.

53. Ibid. at 17-20; An Act for the Admission of the State of Wisconsin into the Union, ch. 50, 9 *Stat.* 233 (1848).

54. Anderson, supra n. 7 at 21.

55. Ibid.

56. Ibid. at 21-22.

57. Ibid. at 22.

58. Ibid.

59. Ibid. at 24-25; Robert J. Sheran and Timothy J. Baland, "The Law, Courts, and Lawyers in the Frontiers Days of Minnesota: An Informal Legal History of the Years 1835 to 1865," *Wm. Mitchell L. Rev.* 2(1976): 1, 17.

60. Anderson, supra n. 7 at 25.

61. Ibid. at 25-26; Folwell, supra n. 4 at 242.

62. Folwell, supra n. 4 at 243.

63. Anderson, supra n. 7 at 29; Folwell, supra n. 4 at 245.

64. Anderson, supra n. 7 at 30; Folwell, supra n. 4 at 245-246.

65. Anderson, supra n. 7 at 30; Folwell, supra n. 4 at 246.

66. Ibid.

67. Which, coincidentally, is also the name of the author's dog.

68. Folwell, supra n. 4 at 248.

69. An Act to establish the Territorial Government of Minnesota, ch. 121, § 12, 9 *Stat.* 403, 412 (1849).

70. Anderson, supra n. 7 at 35.

71. Ibid. at 43-44.

72. Ibid. at 43.

73. Ibid. at 44.

74. Ibid. at 44-47.

75. An Act to authorize the People of the Territory of Minnesota to form a Constitution and State Government, preparatory to their Admission in the Union on an equal Footing with the original States, ch. 60, § 1, 11 *Stat.* 166, 166 (1857).

76. Anderson, supra n. 7 at 71-72.

77. Ibid. at 73-75.

78. An Act to authorize the People of the Territory of Minnesota to form a Constitution and State Government, preparatory to their Admission in the Union on an equal Footing with the original States, ch. 60, § 3, 11 *Stat.* 166, 166 (1857).

79. Anderson, supra n. 7 at 78.

80. Ibid. at 79.

81. Ibid. at 80-81.

82. Ibid. at 82.

83. Ibid. at 81.

84. Ibid. at 85.

85. Ibid. at 85-86.

86. Ibid. at 93; Folwell, supra n. 4 at 414-415.

87. Anderson, supra n. 7 at 92-98; Folwell, supra n. 4 at 414-417.

88. Folwell, supra n. 4 at 418; Sheran and Baland, supra n. 59 at 35-37.

89. Folwell, supra n. 4 at 418-419.

90. Anderson, supra n. 7 at 109.

91. Ibid.

92. Ibid., at 109-110. The original handwritten Democratic and Republican constitutions are reproduced in volume 1 of *Minnesota Statutes Annotated* (1976) at
159.

93. Folwell, supra n. 4 at 421, n. 43.

94. Anderson, supra n. 7 at 110.

95. Ibid. at 63.

96. An Act to authorize the People of the Territory of Minnesota to form a Constitution and State Government, preparatory to their Admission in the Union on an
equal Footing with the original States, ch. 60, § 1, 11 *Stat.* 166, 166 (1857).

97. Anderson, supra n. 7 at 63.

98. An Act for the Admission of the State of Minnesota into the Union, ch. 31, 11
Stat. 285 (1858).

99. Arlette M. Soderberg and Barbara L. Golden, *Minnesota Legal Research
Guide* (Buffalo, NY: William S. Hein and Co., 1985) 99-100.

Chapter 25

Mississippi, 1699-1817

Kris Gilliland

INTRODUCTION

In April 1699 Pierre LeMoyne, Sieur d'Iberville, and 200 French colonists sailed into Biloxi Bay and, near present-day Ocean Springs, Mississippi, established the first permanent European settlement in the lower Mississippi River Valley.[1] The region was already home to numerous Native
Americans, including the Choctaw, Chickasaw, and Natchez.[2] For the next
century, they remained the sole inhabitants of almost all the lands that, in
1817, would form the state of Mississippi.[3]

Until the late 1700s, the only notable European settlements in Mississippi north of the coast were within the Natchez District, framed on the west
and north by the Mississippi and Yazoo rivers. With conditions ideal for lucrative cotton farming, Natchez would eventually become one of the wealthi-
est communities in the antebellum United States. In the intervening years,
although far removed from the colonial seats of government and sometimes
nearly deserted, it would play a strategic role in the French, Spanish, British, and American efforts to control the "Old Southwest" frontier.[4]

This chapter's objective is to provide a brief historical overview of the
four prestatehood regimes in Mississippi and the foundations of statehood,
with a selected bibliography of related legal materials, including published
collections of primary documents in English and finding aids.[5] Although
few scholarly works address Mississippi distinct from Louisiana and the
other states that share its provenance,[6] a growing body of literature addresses the legal history of the Mississippi River Valley and the colonial
southeast generally.[7] Atlases of the early southeast are an addtional reference tool that can be helpful to researchers.[8]

General Histories of Mississippi

Claiborne, John F. H. *Mississippi, As a Province, Territory, and State,* Volume 1. Jackson: Power and Barksdale, 1880. Reprinted 1964, Louisiana
State University Press.

The classic work on Mississippi history authored by the nephew of W.C.C. Claiborne, territorial governor of Mississippi. Volume 2 was not published.

McLemore, Richard Aubrey, ed. *A History of Mississippi.* 2 vols. Jackson: University and College Press of Mississippi, 1973.

The most thorough and scholarly history of the state to date.

Skates, John R. *Mississippi, A Bicentennial History.* New York: Norton, 1979.

Wells, Mary Ann. *Native Land: Mississippi 1540-1798.* Jackson: University Press of Mississippi, 1994.

FRENCH LOUISIANE, 1682-1762

In 1682 Rober Cavelier, Sieur de LaSalle, claimed for France the vast and largely uncharted territory that lay between the English colonies east of the Appalachian Mountains and the Spanish possessions west of the Red River.[9] Named in honor of its king, "Louisiane" became a proprietary colony in 1712, when its charter was given to Antoine Crozat, a prominent Parisian financier.[10] In 1719 John Law's Company of the West succeeded Crozat as holder of the royal letters patent.[11] By 1722, when the colony's capital was moved to New Orleans, a handful of French posts dotted the map, including Fort Rosalie (Natchez), about 200 miles north of New Orleans.[12]

In 1712 purely military rule in the colony came to an end. As provided in Crozat's charter, the fundamental law of the colony was the Coutume de Paris (the customary law of Paris and the Ile-de-France) and the royal edicts.[13] Authority for its administration was vested, as in other French colonies, in a "superior council." The New Orleans Superior Council was comprised of the governor, military commander, procureur-general (attorney general), and other company and military officials.[14] To assist the council, inferior courts were added in 1717, and, in the late 1720s, Louisiana was divided into nine judicial districts.[15]

By 1762 France was ready to rid itself of the struggling colony.[16] In the secret Cession of Fountainebleu, it gave New Orleans and its territories west of the Mississippi River to its ally Spain.[17] The next year, following its defeat in the Seven Years' War, France ceded the lands east of the river, including the Biloxi and Natchez districts, to Great Britain.[18]

Sources of Law

After the cessions to Spain and Great Britain, most official records related to Louisiane were sent to archives in France and are found today in repositories such as the Archives des Colonies in the Archives Nationales in
Paris.[19] (The original superior council documents, however, were left in
New Orleans and are now housed at the Louisiana State Museum.) In the
early 1900s several libraries and other organizations in the United States set
out to copy, translate, and index these records. The contributions of librarians and scholars in Louisiana and the Mississippi Department of Archives
and History are particularly impressive.

In 1906 Mississippi Department of Archives and History Director Dunbar Rowland visited the Ministry of the Marine in Paris, the site of the largest collection of Mississippi-related materials. He selected thousands of
documents for transcription and translation, including correspondence,
military and census reports, and legal materials. Published as *Mississippi
Provincial Archives: French Dominion, 1683-1762,* the collection is especially rich with materials related to Indian affairs, industry and commerce,
religion, and education.

Organic Laws

Royal Letters Patent of September 14, 1712 [Crozat's Charter]. Translated
in *Publications of the Louisiana Historical Society* 4 (1908): 13.

Royal Letters Patent of December 18, 1712 Establishing a Superior Council
in Louisiana During Three Years, trans. H. Dart. "The Legal Institutions
of Louisiana." *Louisiana Historical Quarterly* 2 (1919): 76-78.

Royal Letters Patent of August of August 17, 1717 [Company of the West's
Charter]. Translated in *Publications of the Louisiana Historical Society*
4 (1908): 43.

Modern Compilations

French, B.F. *Historical Collections of Louisiana and Florida, Including
Translations of Original Manuscripts Related to Their Discovery and
Settlement.* 1869. Reprint, New York: AMS Press, 1976. Available on-
line at <http://www.lib.lsu.edu/special/bffrench/>.

Louisiana Historical Quarterly

Includes indexes and translations of many colonial Louisiana laws, including French and Spanish judicial records produced by the superior council and its Spanish successor, the cabildo.

Publications of the Louisiana Historical Society 4 (1908): 3-120.

Includes translations of many colonial Louisiana laws, including the 1724 Code Noir, or slave code.

Rowland, Dunbar, comp. and ed. *Mississippi Provincial Archives, French Dominion, 1678-1763*. 5 vols. Jackson: Department of Archives and History, 1927-1932.

Vol. I: 1678-1700; Vol. II: 1701-1729; Vol. III: 1729-1740; Vol. IV: 1741-1748; Vol. V: 1749-1763. Rev. and ed. by Patricia K. Galloway. Baton Rouge: Louisiana State University Press, 1984.

Finding Aids

Beers, Henry Putney. *French and Spanish Records of Louisiana: A Bibliographical Guide to Archive and Manuscript Sources*. Baton Rouge: Louisiana State University Press, 1989.

Brasseaux, Carl A. and Glenn R. Conrad. *A Bibliography of Scholarly Literature on Colonial Louisiana and New France*. Lafayette, LA: Center for Louisiana Studies, University of Southwestern Louisiana, 1992.

Cummins, Light Townsend and Glen Jeansonne, eds. *A Guide to the History of Louisiana*. Westport, CT: Greenwood Press, 1982.

Surrey, Nancy M. Miller. *Calendar of Manuscripts in Paris Archives and Libraries Relating to the History of the Mississippi Valley to 1803*. 2 vols. Washington, DC: Carnegie Institution of Washington, 1926-1928.

Tucker, John H. "Source Books of Louisiana Law." In *Louisiana Legal Archives*. 3 vols. New Orleans: Thos. J. Moran's Sons, 1937.

Thorough review of sources of colonial Louisiana law. Originally published in four parts in the *Tulane Law Review* between 1932 and 1935.

BRITISH WEST FLORIDA, 1763-1783

After the Seven Years' War, Great Britain divided its North American holdings into three provinces: Canada, East Florida, and West Florida. West Florida, separated from East Florida by the Perdido River, was bound on the north by the thirty-first parallel.[20] By royal proclamation, the lands above this line were closed to white settlement.[21] An exception was soon made, however, when colonial officials realized that the Natchez District lay above the thirty-first parallel.[22]

By 1765 civil government was installed in Pensacola, the new provincial capital, with the arrival of the first governor, George Johnstone.[23] The Proclamation of 1763, the governor's commission, and his instructions provided the constitutional foundations of West Florida's government.[24] A court of pleas was created and given criminal and civil jurisdiction, and justices of the peace were appointed to handle lesser crimes.[25]

Representational government was provided by a general assembly. In late 1766 the first assembly enacted fifteen laws, including regulations for taverns, indentured servants, and slaves.[26] Over the next five years, six more assemblies were called, but the governor, assisted by his council, held "mastery of life and death" over the assembly through his absolute veto power.[27] A quick succession of unpopular and incompetent governors led to political stalemate; after 1771 no new bills were enacted.[28] In any event, "it appears that the laws and ordinances passed by the provincial assembly did not extend in most cases to the outlying regions of the province."[29]

Natchez, sparsely populated and separated from Pensacola by 400 miles of wilderness, was one of these regions. However, after the Declaration of Independence, its fortunes again began to rise, as it became "an asylum for distressed friends of England."[30] Loyalists from Virginia, the Carolinas, and Georgia flocked to the Natchez District, and by 1778, it boasted a population of over 3,000 white settlers, enough to justify representation in the assembly and the establishment of its own court.[31]

However, with British military attention focused elsewhere, West Florida was vulnerable to invasion from the west. Bernardo de Galvez, governor of Spanish Luisiana, seized the opportunity, and, in September 1799, British troops surrendered Natchez to the Spanish.[32] At the end of the Revolutionary War, the Floridas were formally awarded to Spain under the terms of the Treaty of Paris (1783).[33]

Sources of Law and Finding Aids

In 1906, the Mississippi Department of Archives and History's Dunbar Rowland visited the British Public Records Office in London and arranged for the copying of thousands of documents related to Mississippi. Similar to the French collection discussed previously, *Mississippi Provincial Archives: English Dominion* includes correspondence, military and census reports, and other documents related to the district's political and social culture.

Organic Acts

Proclamation of October 7, 1763, Creating the Government of West Florida.

Reprinted in *Louisiana Historical Quarterly* 13 (1930): 611-613. Available online at <http://www.yale.edu/lawweb/avalon/proc1763.htm>.

Governor George Johnstone's Instructions. Reprinted in *Louisiana Histori-cal Quarterly* 21 (1938): 1025.

Modern Compilations and Finding Aids

Fabel, Robin F.A. "British Florida, 1763-1784." In *A Guide to the History of Florida,* edited by Paul S. George (pp. 37-48). Westport, CT: Greenwood Press, 1989.

Grant, W. L. and James Monro, eds. *Acts of the Privy Council of England, Colonial Series, 1613-1783.* 6 vols. London: H. M. Stationery Office, 1908-1912.

Rea, Robert R., Jr. and Milo B. Howard Jr., comps. and eds. *The Minutes, Journals, and Acts of the General Assembly of British West Florida.* University, AL: University of Alabama Press, 1979.

Also includes a very helpful bibliographic essay describing archival and secondary sources.

Rowland, Dunbar, comp. and ed. *Mississippi Provincial Archives: English Dominion, 1763-1781.* 2 vols. Nashville: Brandon Printing Company, 1911.

SPANISH LUISIANA, 1783-1798

In Spanish Luisiana, laws issued in 1769 and 1770 by the colony's then-governor Alexander O'Reilly provided for the province's governance in New Orleans and the remoter districts, respectively. Abrogating all preexisting French law except the 1724 Code Noir, or slave code, the "O'Reilly

Code" was derived from the Spanish colonial law deemed most relevant to Luisiana, the *Recopilacion de Leyes de los Reinos de las Indias,* the *Neueva Recopilacion de Castilla,* and the *Siete Partidas.*[34]

In a unique concession to the province's predominantly French and Anglo-American population, the restrictions on trade, slavery, and religion found elsewhere in New Spain were relaxed by cedula or royal edict in 1782.[35] In Natchez, traditional Spanish colonial law was further modified by "frontier and . . . English common law traditions."[36] In addition, English was permitted in cases in Natchez that involved Anglo-American residents.[37]

For military and administrative purposes, the province was divided into districts. Within these districts, the local military commandant functioned as "legislator, judge, notary, custodian of deeds and records, mayor, and chief of police."[38] Criminal cases and civil cases involving amounts larger than twenty-five dollars could be appealed to the governor-general of Louisiana in New Orleans, then to the capital-general in Cuba, the Audencia of Santo Domingo, and, finally, the Council of the Indies in Spain.[39]

By 1789 the Natchez District had grown sufficiently large to justify its own (and only) Spanish colonial governor, Manuel Gayoso de Lemos.[40] Gayoso was popular with Natchez residents but faced considerable threat from the east: the new United States claimed Natchez as its possession under the terms of the Treaty of Paris (1783) and maintained that the thirty-first parallel served as the border between it and Spanish Luisiana. Spain held, however, that Great Britain had raised the northern boundary of British West Florida to 32°28' in 1764.[41] In 1795, with the threat of war with both Great Britain and the United States looming, the Spanish conceded the "Mississippi Question" and agreed to leave Natchez.[42]

Sources of Law

Like the French, Spanish colonial officials produced millions of documents. Most are now stored in the Spain's Archivo General de Indias (AGI), Archivo Historico Nacional, and the Archivo General de Simancas. In 1906, at Dunbar Rowland's request, Dr. W. R. Shepherd of Columbia University arranged for the transcription and translation of several thousand documents in the AGI collection known as the Papales Procedentes de Cuba. In the end, funds were unavailable for their publication, and the handwritten documents were bound in nine volumes now housed at Mississippi Department of Archives and History. Also available at MDAH is a microfilm copy of the Natchez Chancery Court records from the Spanish period.[43] Charles A. Week's recent article in the *Journal of Mississippi His-*

tory provides an excellent survey of the "Spanish Provincial Transcripts," the Natchez Chancery Court records, and other related collections.

Organic Laws

Ordinances of the Ayuntamiento of New Orleans and Instructions for Adjudicating Civil and Criminal Cases in Louisiana of November 25, 1769 and Instructions of February 8, 1770. Translated in *Digest of the Laws of Louisiana, American State Papers: Documents, Legislative, and Executive of the Congress of the United States: Miscellaneous Affairs*. Edited by Walter Lowrie and Matthew St. Clair Clark. Washington, DC, 1834. Also available *in Annals of Congress* 8: 1526-1570. Washington, DC, 1803.

Modern Compilations

Kinnaird, Lawrence, ed. and trans. *Spain in the Mississippi Valley, 1765-1794.* 4 vols. Annual Report of the American Historical Association for the Year 1945. Washington, DC: American Historical Association, 1946-1949.

White, Joseph M. *A New Collection of Laws, Charters and Local Ordinances of the Governments of Great Britain, France and Spain Relating to the Concessions of Land in their Respective Colinies, Together with the Laws of Mexico and Texas on the Same Subject, to which is Prefixed Judge Johnson's Translation of Azo and Manuel's Institutes of the Civil Law of Spain.* 2 vols. Philadelphia: T. and J.W. Johnson, 1839. Reprint, Holmes Beach, FL: Gaunt, 2002.

Finding Aids

Beers, Henry Putney. *French and Spanish Records of Louisiana: A Bibliographical Guide to Archive and Manuscript Sources.* Baton Rouge: Louisiana State University Press, 1989.

Codinach, Estella Guadalupe Jimenez. *The Hispanic World 1492-1898: A Guide to the Photoreproduced Manuscripts from Spain in the Collections of the United States, Guam, and Puerto Rico.* Washington, DC: U.S. Government Printing Office, 1994.

Coker, William S. "Research in the Spanish Borderlands: Mississippi, 1779-1798." *Latin American Research Review* 8 (Summer 1972): 40-54.

Hill, Roscoe R. *Descriptive Catalogue of the Documents Relating to the History of the United States in the Papeles Procedentes de Cuba Deposited in the Archivo General de Indias at Seville.* Washington, DC: Carnegie Institution of Washington, 1916. Reprint, New York: Kraus Reprint Co., 1965.

Holmes, Jack D.L. *A Guide to Spanish Louisiana: 1762-1806.* New Orleans: [A.F. Laborde], 1970.

McBee, May Wilson. *The Natchez County Records, 1767-1805: Abstracts of Early Records.* Ann Arbor, MI: Edward Brothers, 1953. Reprinted, Baltimore: Genealogical Publishing Co., 1979.

McMurtrie, Douglas C. *Early Printing in New Orleans, 1764-1810.* New Orleans: Searcy and Pfaff, 1929. Supplemented by McMurtrie, Douglas C. *Louisiana Imprints, 1768-1810.* Hattiesburg: The Book Farm, 1942.

Sanchez, Joseph P. *A Selected Bibliography of the Florida-Louisiana Frontier with References to the Caribbean, 1492-1812.* Albuquerque, NM: U.S. Dept. of the Interior, National Park Service, Spanish Colonial Research Center, 1991.

Tucker, John H. "Source Books of Louisiana Law." In *Louisiana Legal Archives.* 3 vols. New Orleans: Thos. J. Moran's Sons, 1937.

Vance, John T. *The Background of Hispanic-American Law: Legal Sources and Judicial Literature of Spain.* Washington, DC: The Catholic University of America, 1937. Reprint, Wesport, CT: Hyperion Press, 1979.

Wallach, Kate. *Research in Louisiana Law.* Baton Rouge: Louisiana State University Press, 1958.

Weeks, Charles A. "Voices from Mississippi's Past: Spanish Provincial Records in the Mississippi Department of Archives and History." *Journal of Mississippi History* 61 (1999): 149-179.

BOURBON COUNTY, GEORGIA, 1785-1796

From its earliest days, the Natchez District had drawn the interest of land speculators, beginning in 1718 with the "Mississippi Bubble" created by French colonial governor John Law. After the Revolutionary War, the fever struck again, Georgia, South Carolina, and North Carolina each laying claim to all lands lying south of Tennessee and north of the thirty-first parallel, and between the Chattahoochee River (the modern boundary between Georgia and Alabama) and the Mississippi River.[44] Although the Carolinas eventually relinquished their claims, Georgia incorporated the vast area—most of modern Mississippi and Alabama—as "Bourbon County" in 1785.[45]

Three years later, under pressure from the federal government, Georgia repealed the Bourbon County Act.[46] However, in 1795, corrupt legislators and other state officials sold over 30 million acres in and around the Natchez District for a fraction of their value. [47] Outraged Georgians voted in a new legislature that immediately repudiated all Yazoo land grants.

By then, many Yazoo investors had already sold their interests to third parties, and the result was "a wild tangle of doubtful, overlapping, and contradictory claims without parallel in the entire history of the public domain."[48] The Yazoo Land Fraud became a national scandal involving prominent businessmen throughout the country, as well as members of Congress and the president's Cabinet, a Supreme Court justice, and other federal and state judges, taking decades to resolve.[49]

Sources of Law and Related Documents

Burnett, Edmund C., ed. "Papers Relating to Bourbon County, Georgia, 1785-1786." Parts 1 and 2. *American Historical Review* 15 (1909): 66-111; 15 (1910): 297-353.

Cushing, John D., comp. *The First Laws of the State of Georgia.* 2 vols. Wilmington, DE: Michael Glazier, 1981.

Facsimile reprint of Watkins, Robert and George Watkins, comps. *A Digest of the Laws of the State of Georgia, from its First Establishment as a British Province Down to the year 1798, Inclusive, and the Principal Acts of 1799.* Philadelphia: Printed by R. Aitken, 1800.

THE U.S. TERRITORY OF MISSISSIPPI, 1798-1817

In 1798 the United States created the Mississippi Territory, with Natchez as its capital.[50] The Mississippi Territory's enabling act expressly incorporated the governmental provisions of the Ordinance of 1787, the instrument that had established the Northwest Territory.[51] In one critical distinction, slavery was permitted to continue in the new territory.[52]

The Northwest Ordinance set forth three stages of territorial government.[53] In the first, legislative powers were vested in a governor and three judges. The governor and a majority of the judges were given the authority to "adopt and publish in the district such laws of the original States, criminal and civil, as may be necessary, and best suited to the circumstances of the district," subject to the veto of Congress. When the territory's population included 5,000 white males, the governors and judges were to share authority with an elected legislature and a council appointed by the president from members of the lower house. The final stage—statehood—became possible when the territory's population reached 60,000.

Territorial judges, "any two of whom shall form a Court," were to "have a common law jurisdiction."[54] The Mississippi Territory's enabling act also provided that territorial citizens were to have "all and singular the rights, privileges and advantages [of the Northwest Territory] including judicial proceedings according to the course of common law."[55] While the Mississippi territorial court held that Spanish law governed in cases arising before 1798 and referred occasionally to Spanish doctrinal works, the civilian tradition's influence soon faded.[56]

In February 1799, Winthrop Sargent, Mississippi Territory's first governor, and two of the three territorial judges issued the territory's first legislation. "Sargent's Code" organized a militia and a system of inferior civil and criminal courts[57] and set forth a severe penal code. The new laws also regulated Indian affairs, slavery, taxation, marriage and divorce, liquor sales and consumption, and road and bridge construction.[58]

The next year territorial residents unhappy with Governor Sargent's autocratic rule successfully petitioned Congress for "second stage," or representational, government.[59] The enactments of the general assembly were unofficially codified in 1807 by Territorial Judge Harry Toulmin.[60] Toulmin's *Digest,* which also included English statutes that had not been adopted by the assembly, was subsequently adopted into positive law.

In 1807 the first calls for statehood were also heard.[61] Administration of the large territory was made difficult by the distance between the territory's few sizable communities. Initially, the territory had occupied roughly the lower one-third of today's Mississippi and Alabama. However, by the end of the next decade, with the settlement of Georgia's claims and the annexation of the Spanish lands to the south,[62] it had grown to almost 100,000 square miles.[63]

Sources of Law

For research on the territorial period, the single best collection of primary sources is Clarence Erwin Carter's great achievement, *The Territorial Papers of the United States.* The fifth and sixth volumes of the set cover the "Territory of Mississippi" and include documents "drawn principally from the archives of the Department of State, Treasury, War, Interior, and Post Office, the Manuscripts Division of the Library of Congress, and the Senate and House files in Washington, DC." These papers include annotated reprints of federal legislation and governmental documents (e.g., correspondence, petitions, and memorials) with an emphasis on "political and land aspects." The text of territorial legislation is not included, but useful finding lists and other bibliographic aids for these materials are provided. Original copies of territorial imprints are exceedingly rare,[64] but most primary legal materials have been reproduced in microform as part of the *Early American Imprints, 2d Series.*

Organic Laws

An Ordinance for the Government of the Territory of the United States Northwest of the River Ohio [1787], 1 *Stat.* 51 n.(a) (1789).

An Act for an Amicable Settlement of Limits with the State of Georgia, and Authorizing the Establishment of a Government in the Mississippi Territory, 1 *Stat.* 549 (1798).

An Act Supplemental to the Act Entitled "An Act for an Amicable Settlement of the Limits with the State of Georgia, and Authorizing the Establishment of a Government in the Mississippi Territory," 2 *Stat.* 69 (1800) [Second-stage territorial government].

An Act for the Appointment of an Additional Judge for the Mississippi Territory, and for Other Purposes, 2 *Stat.* 301 (1804).

An Act Extending the Right of Suffrage in the Mississippi Territory, and for Other Purposes, 2 *Stat.* 455 (1808).

An Act for the Appointment of an Additional Judge, and Extending the Right of Suffrage to the Citizens of Madison County, in the Mississippi Territory, 2 *Stat.* 563 (1810).

Resolution Relative to the Occupation of the Floridas by the United States of America, 3 *Stat.* 471 (1811).

An Act to Enable the President of the United States, under Certain Contingencies, to Take Possession of the Country Lying East of the River Perdido, and South of the State of Georgia and the Mississippi Territory, and for Other Purposes, 3 *Stat.* 471 (1811).

An Act to Enlarge the Boundaries of the Mississippi Territory, 2 *Stat.* 734 (1812).

An Act Further to Extend the Right of Suffrage, and to Increase the Number of Members of the Legislative Council in the Mississippi Territory, 3 *Stat.* 143 (1814).

Modern Compilations

American State Papers, Miscellaneous Affairs [1789-1823]. Edited by Walter Lowrie and Matthew St. Clair Clark. 2 vols. Washington, DC: Gales and Seaton, 1834.

Available electronically at <http://memory.loc.gov/ammem/amlaw/lwsp.html>.

American State Papers, Public Lands [1789-1837]. Edited by Walter Lowrie and Matthew St. Clair Clark. 8 vols. Washington, DC: Gales and Seaton, 1832-1861.

Available electronically at <http://memory.loc.gov/ammem/amlaw/lwsp.html>.

Carter, Clarence Erwin, comp. and ed. *The Territory of Mississippi.* Vol. V-VI of *The Territorial Papers of the United States.* Washington, DC: Government Printing Office, 1937-1938.

Rowland, Dunbar, comp. and ed. *Mississippi Territorial Archives, 1798-1803,* Vol. 1 [Executive Journals of Governor Winthrop Sargent and Governor William Charles Cole Claiborne]. Nashville: Brandon Printing Co., 1904.

―――. *Official Letter Books of W.C.C. Claiborne, 1801-1816.* 6 vols. Jackson: Department of Archives and History, 1917. Reprinted, New York: AMS Press, Inc., 1972.

Statutory Codes and Digests

Code of Mississippi, Being an Analytical Compilation of the Public and General Statutes of the Territory and State, with Tabular Reference to the Local and Private Acts, from 1798-1848. Compiled by A. Hutchinson. Jackson: Price and Fall, State Printers, 1848.

Sargent's Code: A Collection of the Original Laws of the Mississippi Territory Enacted 1799-1800 by Governor Winthrop Sargent and the Territorial Judges, prepared by the Historical Records Survey, Division of Professional and Service Projects, Works Progress Administration, 1939. Reprinted in *American Journal of Legal History* 11 (1972): 157-189, 282-346.

The Statutes of the Mississippi Territory, Revised and Digested by the Authority of the General Assembly. Compiled by Harry S. Toulmin. *Early American Imprints, Second Series,* No. 13102. Natchez: Printed by Samuel Terrell, Printer to the Mississippi Territory, 1807.

Statutes of the Mississippi Territory; the Constitution of the United States, with the several amendments thereto; the ordinance for the government of the Territory of the United States, North-West of the River Ohio; the Articles of Agreement and Cession, between the United States and the State of Georgia; and such Acts of Congress as relate to the Mississippi Territory. Digested by the authority of the General Assembly. 2 vols. Natchez: Printed by Peter Isler, Printer to the Territory, 1816.

Known as "Turner's Code." Contains a significant number of omissions and errors, including inclusion of previously repealed acts.

Session Laws

Laws of the Missisippi Territory; Published at a Session of the Legislature began in the Town of Natchez, in the County of Adams, and Territory aforesaid, upon the 22d Day of January, Anno Domini 1799, and in the 23d Year of the Independance of the United States of America: and continued by Adjournments to the 25th day of May, in the same Year. By authority. Early American Imprints, Second Series, No. 35828. Natchez: Printed by A. Marschalk, 1799.[65]

Laws of the Mississippi Territory, September 21-October 5, 1799. Reprinted in *Heartman's Historical Series,* No. 74. Beauvoir Community: The Book Farm, 1948.

Laws of the Mississippi Territory, May 27, 1800. Reprinted *in Heartman's Historical Series,* No. 75. Beauvoir Community: Book Farm, 1948.

Laws of the Mississippi Territory; Published at a Session of the Legislature Begun in the Town of Natchez in October, 1800. Natchez: Printed by Benjamin M. Stokes[?], 1800.

Laws of the Mississippi Territory, Passed at a Session of the Legislature Begun and Held on October 24, 1801, and Continued by Adjournments to February 1, 1802. Natchez: Printed by James Ferrall, 1802.

Acts Passed by the First General Assembly of the Mississippi Territory at their First and Second Sessions. Natchez: Printed by Andrew Marschalk, 1802. Reprinted partially in *Fragments of the Mississippi Session laws Passed at the First Session of the Second General Assembly of Mississippi Territory, December 1802 to March 1803: Reproduced Photographically, from Three Leaves Recently Discovered in the Department of Archives and History, Jackson, Mississippi.* Compiled by Douglas C. McMurtrie. Chicago: [s.n.], 1939.

Acts Passed at the Third Session of the First General Assembly of the Missisippi Territory; Began and Held at the Town of Washington, on Monday, the Third Day of May, in the Year of our Lord, One Thousand Eight Hundred and Two; and of the American Independence, the Twenty-sixth. Published by Authority. Natchez: Printed by Andrew Marschalk, 1802. Reprinted in *The Mississippi Territorial Session Laws of May, 1802.* Compiled by Douglas C. McMurtrie. Chicago: John Calhoun Club, 1938.

Acts of the First Session, Second General Assembly, Feb. 10-Mar. 10, 1803. Available in *Early American Imprints, Second Series,* No. 4665.

Acts Passed by the Second General Assembly of the Mississippi Territory During Their First [i.e., second] *Session; Began and Held in the Town of Washington, on the First Monday in October, in the Year of Our Lord, One Thousand Eight Hundred and Three and of the Independence of the United States of America, the Twenty-eight. Published by Authority.* Available in *Early American Imprints, Second Series,* No. 6794. Natchez: Printed by Andrew Marschalk, 1804.

Acts Passed by the Third General Assembly of the Mississippi Territory, During Their First Session, Began and Held in the Town of Washington, on the First Monday in December, in the Year of Our Lord One Thousand Eight Hundred and Four and of the Independence of the United States of

America the Twenty-ninth. Published by Authority. Natchez: Printed by T. and S. Terrell, Printers to the Mississippi Territory, 1805.

Acts Passed by the Third General Assembly of the Mississippi Territory, During Their Extra Session, Began and Held in the Town of Washington, on the First Monday in July, in the Year of Our Lord One Thousand Eight Hundred and Five, and of the Independence of the United States of America the Twenty-ninth. Published by Authority. Natchez: Printed by T. and S. Terrell, Printers to the Mississippi Territory, 1805.

Acts Passed by the Third General Assembly of the Mississippi Territory, during Their Third Session, Began and Held in the Town of Washington, on the First Monday in December, in the Year of Our Lord, One Thousand Eight Hundred and Five, and of the Independence of the United States of America the Thirtieth. Published by Authority. Available in *Early American Imprints, Second Series,* No. 10882. Natchez: Printed by T. and S. Terrell, Printers to the Mississippi Territory, 1806.

Acts Passed by the Fourth General Assembly of the Mississippi Territory, During Their Second Session, Began and Held in the Town of Washington, on the First Monday in December, in the year of Our Lord, One Thousand Eight Hundred and Seven, and of the Independence of the United States of America the Thirty-second. Published by Authority. Available in *Early American Imprints, Second Series,* No. 15622. Natchez: Printed by Andrew Marchaik, 1808.

Acts Passed at the First Session of the Fifth General Assembly of the Mississippi Territory, Begun and Held at the Town of Washington, on the [blank] *day of February, 1809.* Available in *Early American Imprints, Second Series,* No. 20753. Natchez: Printed by John Shaw, Printer to the Mississippi Territory, 1810.

Acts Passed at the First Session of the Sixth General Assembly of the Mississippi Territory, Begun and Held at the town of Washington, on Monday the 6th day of November, Anno Dominni 1809. Available in *Early American Imprints, Second Series,* No. 20754. Natchez: Printed by John Shaw, Printer to the Mississippi Territory, 1810.

Acts Passed at the Second Session of the Sixth General Assembly of the Mississippi Territory, Begun and Held at the Town of Washington, on the Fifth day of November, One Thousand, Eight Hundred and Ten. Available in *Early American Imprints, Second Series,* No. 23403. Natchez: Printed by William O. Winston, Printer to the Mississippi Territory, 1811.

Acts Passed at the First Session of the Seventh General Assembly of the Mississippi Territory, Begun and Held at the Town of Washington, on the Fourth Day of November, One Thousand Eight Hundred and Eleven. Available in *Early American Imprints, Second Series,* No. 26094. Natchez: Printed by P. Isler, Printer to the Mississippi Territory, 1812.

Acts Passed at the Second Session of the Seventh General Assembly of the Mississippi Territory, Begun and Held at the Town of Washington, on the Second Day of November, One Thousand Eight Hundred and Twelve. Available in *Early American Imprints, Second Series,* No. 26095. Natchez: Printed by P. Isler, Printer to the Mississippi Territory, 1812.

Acts Passed at the First Session of the Eighth General Assembly of the Mississippi Territory, Begun and Held at the Town of Washington, on the Seventh Day of November, One Thousand Eight Hundred and Thirteen. Published by Authority. Available in *Early American Imprints, Second Series,* No. 32143. Natchez: Printed by P. Isler and J. M'Curdy, 1814.

Acts Passed at the Second Session of the Eighth General Assembly of the Mississippi Territory, Begun and Held at the Town of Washington, on the Seventh Day of November, One Thousand Eight Hundred and Fourteen. Published by Authority. Available in *Early American Imprints, Second Series,* No. 32144. Natchez: Printed by P. Isler and J. M'Curdy, 1814.

Acts Passed at the First Session of the Ninth General Assembly of the Mississippi Territory, Begun and Held at the Town of Washington, the Sixth Day of November, One Thousand Eight Hundred and Fifteen. Published by authority. Available in *Early American Imprints, Second Series,* No. 35290. Natchez: Printed by Peter Isler, 1815.

Acts Passed by the Second Session of the Ninth General Assembly of the Mississippi Territory, Begun and Held at the Town of Washington, Monday, the Fourth Day of November, One Thousand Eight Hundred and Sixteen and of American Independence the Forty-first. Published by authority. Available in *Early American Imprints, Second Series,* No. 38264. Natchez: Printed by P. Isler, 1816.

Legislative Journals

Journals of General Assembly of the Mississippi Territory. Journal of the House of Representatives, Second General Assembly, Second Session, October 3-November 19, 1803. Reprinted in William D. McCain, ed., *Heartman's Historical Series,* No. 54 and No. 55. Beauvoir Community: The Book Farm, 1940.

Journal of the House of Representatives of the Mississippi Territory, at the First Session of the Seventh General Assembly, Began and Held at the town of Washington, on Monday the Fourth of Novemeer, One Thousand Eight Hundred and Eleven. Available in *Early American Imprints, Second Series,* No. 26097. Natchez: Printed by P. Isler, Printer to the Mississippi Territory, 1812.

Journal of the House of Representatives, of the Mississippi Territory, at the Second Session of the Seventh General Assembly, Begun and held at the town of Washington, on Monday the second Day of November, in the year of Our Lord One Thousand Eight Hundred and Twelve, and in the Thirty Seventh Year of the Independence of the United States. Natchez: Printed by P. Isler, Printer to the Mississippi Territory, 1812.

Journal of the House of Representatives of the Mississippi Territory, at the Second Session of the Eighth General Assembly, in the Thirty-ninth year of the American Independence. Published by Authority. Available in *Early American Imprints, Second Series,* No. 32145. Natchez: Printed by P. Isler and J. M'Curdy, 1814.

Journal of the Legislative Council, of the Second General Assembly of the Mississippi Territory at their second Session begun, and held, on Monday, the third day of October, eighteen hundred and three, and of the independence of the United States of America, the twentyeighth; held under the Act of Congress, entitled an Act Supplementary to An Act for an Amicable Settlement of Limits with the State of Georgia, and Authorising theestablishment of a Government in the Mississippi Territory. Published by Authority. Natchez: Printed by Andrew Marschalk, 1804.

A Journal of the Legislative Council, at the Third Session of the Third General Assembly of the Mississippi Territory; Begun and Held at the Town of Washington, on Monday the First Day of December, in the Year of Our Lord, One Thousand Eight Hundred and Five, and of the Independence of the United States the Thirtieth. Published by Authority. Available in *Early American Imprints, Second Series,* No. 10883. Natchez: Printed by Timothy and Samuel Terrell, Printers to the Mississippi Territory, 1806.

A Journal of the Legislative Council, at the First Session of the Fourth General Assembly of the Mississippi Territory; Began and Held at the Town of Washington, on Monday the First Day of December, in the Year of Our Lord, One Thousand Eight Hundred and Six, and of the Independence of the United States the Thirty-first. Published by Authority. Available in *Early American Imprints, Second Series,* No. 13100. Natchez: Printed by Samuel Terrell, Printer to the Mississippi Territory, 1807.

Resolutions of the General Assembly of the Mississippi Territory of the United States and, a Memorial from the said General Assembly, Annexed thereto, Addressed to the President, Senate, and House of Representatives of the United States. Available in *Early American Imprints, Second Series,* No. 5479. Washington City: Printed by William Duane and Son, 1803.

Court Documents

Judicial Notebooks of Judge Thomas Rodney, Mississippi Territory. Edited by William B. Hamilton. In *Anglo-American Law on the Frontier: Thomas Rodney and His Territorial Cases* (1953): 159-473.

Covers cases in the Mississippi Territory Supreme Court and the inferior courts from 1804 through 1809.

Rules of Practice Established by the Supreme Court of the Mississippi Territory; at Their November Term, 1805. Available in *Early American Imprints, Second Series,* No. 10885. Natchez: Printed by Andrew Marschalk, 1806.

Newspapers[66]

Green's Impartial Observer (Natchez) (1800-1801)
Intelligencer (Natchez) (1801)
Mississippi Gazette (Natchez, 1800-1801, 1811-1812)
Mississippi Herald (Natchez) (1802-1803): Merged with the *Natchez Gazette* in 1806, forming the *Mississippi Herald Natchez Gazette,* which, in 1808, again became the *Natchez Gazette* (1808-1818).

Mississippi Messenger (Natchez) (1804-1808)
Mississippi Republican (Natchez) (1810-1824)
Mississippian (Natchez) (1808-1810)
Washington Republican (1813-1815): Consolidated with the *Natchez Intelligencer* to form the *Washington Republican and Natchez Intelligencer* (1815-1817)
Weekly Chronicle (1808-1811)

Finding Aids

Henderson, Thomas W. and Ronald E. Tomlin. *Guide to Official Records in the Mississippi Department of Archives and History.* Jackson: Mississippi Department of Archives and History, 1975.

McMurtrie, Douglas C. *A Bibliography of Mississippi Imprints 1798-1830.* Beauvoir Community: The Book Farm, 1945.

Lacks subsequently discovered titles but is still the most comprehensive source of information on materials published within prestatehood Mississippi.

Rowland, Dunbar. *Courts, Judges and Lawyers of Mississippi, 1798-1935.* Jackson: Mississippi Department of Archives and History, 1935.

THE STATE OF MISSISSIPPI, 1817

On March 1, 1817, after heated debates in Washington and elsewhere over whether Mississippi Territory should be admitted to the Union as a single slaveholding state or divided into two, President Madison signed legislation authorizing citizens in the western half of the territory to elect a convention to decide whether they wanted statehood and to draft a constitution.[67] In July forty-seven delegates from fourteen counties convened in the territorial capital.[68]

On the first vote, thirty-six delegates voted in favor of statehood; a second vote two weeks later found the delegates evenly divided.[69] However, by August 15, a new constitution had been drafted, debated, signed by forty-five delegates, and sent to President Monroe.[70] On December 10, by congressional resolution, Mississippi was admitted as the twentieth state of the Union.[71]

Sources of Law and Finding Aids

An Act to Enable the People of the Western Part of Mississippi Territory to Form a Constitution and State Government, and for the Admission of such State into the Union on an Equal Footing with the Original States, 3 *Stat.* 348 (1817).

Resolution for the Admission of the State of Mississippi into the Union, 3 *Stat.* 472 (1817).

Constitution and Form of Government for the State of Mississippi. Natchez: Printed by P. Isler, Public Printer, 1817. Reprinted in *Sources and Documents of United States Constitutions.* Edited by William Swindler. Vol. 5. Dobbs Ferry, NY: Oceana Pub., 1973-1979.

Winkle, John W. *The Mississippi State Constitution: A Reference Guide.* Westport, CT: Greenwood Press, 1993.

Winter, William F. "Journal of the Convention of the Western Part of the Mississippi Territory, Begun and Held at the Town of Washington, on the Seventh Day of July, 1817." *Journal of Mississippi History* 29 (1967).

Also includes a reproduction of an 1831 "reprint" by B.F. Stockton of Port-Gibson, Mississippi, of the proceedings and the constitution, with references to manuscript notes in the Territorial Legislative Records in the Mississippi Department of Archives and History.

NOTES

1. Over a century and a half earlier, Spanish explorers, including the Pineda expedition along the coast in 1519 and the Hernando de Soto expedition in 1540-1541, were the first Europeans to sight the future Mississippi. See Martha M. Bigelow, "Conquistadors, Voyageurs and Mississippi," in Richard A. McLemore, ed., *A History of Mississippi,* Vol. 1, 90-102 (Jackson: University and College Press of Mississippi, 1973). For an in-depth discussion of Spanish and French exploration of the region generally, see Robert E. Weddle, *Spanish Sea: The Gulf of Mexico in North American Discovery, 1500-1685* (College Station: Texas A&M University Press, 1985) and its sequels, *The French Thorn: Rival Explorers in the Spanish Sea* (College Station: Texas A&M University Press, 1991), and *Changing Tides: Twilight and Dawn in the Spanish Sea, 1763-1803* (College Station: Texas A&M University Press, 1995). For a succinct survey of the most important works on "first contact" in the South, see Paul Hoffman, "Spanish and French Exploration and Colonization,"

in John E. Boles, ed., *A Companion to the American South* 24-38 (Malden, MA: Blackwell Publishers, 2002).

2. The classic work about the indigenous people of the region is John R. Swanton, *The Indians of the Southeastern United States* (Washington, DC: Smithsonian Institution, 1946). Notable recent works include James R. Atkinson, *Splendid Land, Splendid People: The Chickasaw Indians to Removal* (Jackson: University of Mississippi Press, 2004); Daniel H. Usner Jr., *American Indians in the Lower Mississippi Valley: Social and Economic Histories* (Lincoln: University of Nebraska, 1998; and James Taylor Carson, *Searching for the Bright Path: The Mississippi Choctaws from Prehistory to Removal* (Lincoln: University of Nebraska Press, 1999).

3. Native American title to Mississippi lands was first extinguished in treaties with the French, British, and Spanish during the eighteenth century; major cessions began only with Andrew Jackson's forced-removal policy in the 1830s. For English translations of these agreements, see Vine Deloria Jr. and Raymond J. DeMallie, eds., *Documents of American Indian Diplomacy: Treaties, Agreements, and Conventions, 1775-1979* (Norman: University of Oklahoma Press, 1999). The Deloria and DeMallie set also contains helpful substantive discussions and finding lists.

4. As one noted historian remarked, there "almost every thread of frontier history was gathered up." Arthur P. Whitaker, *The Mississippi Question, 1795-1803: A Study in Trade, Politics and Diplomacy* 58 (1934; reprint, Gloucester, MA: P. Smith, 1962). In Natchez, "Britain, France, and Spain expended their final efforts to thwart the growth of the United States." John D.W. Guice, "Windows on the Old Southwest," in Katherine J. Adams and Lewis L. Gould, eds., *Inside the Natchez Trace Collection: New Sources for Southern History* 9 (Baton Rouge: Louisiana State University Press, 1999).

5. Descriptions of the extensive unpublished archives related to prestatehood Mississippi held by libraries throughout the United States are not included in this chapter, but an excellent place to begin their exploration is the Mississippi Department of Archives and History (P.O. Box 571, Jackson, Mississippi 39205, 1-601-576-6850; http://www.mdah.state.ms.us). See also Philip Hamer, *A Guide to Archives and Manuscripts in the United States* (New Haven, CT: Yale University Press, 1961); the Louisiana State University Libraries, Special Collections, "Louisiana and the Lower Mississippi Valley" at <http://www.lib.lsu.edu/special/frames/llmvc.html>; and the New Orleans Public Library's City Archives at <http://nutrias.org/~nopl/spec/speclist.htm>.

6. See, e.g., Daniel C. Vogt, "Poor Relief in Frontier Mississippi, 1798-1832," *J. Miss. Hist.* 51 (1989): 181; William S. Coker, "Spanish Regulation of the Natchez Indigo Industry, 1793-94: The South's First Antipollution Laws?" *Tech. and Culture* 13(1972): 55; Clayton D. James, "Municipal Government in Territorial Natchez," *J. Miss. Hist.* 27(1965): 148; David J. Libby, *Slavery and Frontier Mississippi 1720-1835* (Jackson: University Press of Mississippi, 2003).

7. The "Spanish borderlands" school of history, for example, is particularly well developed, as seen in the useful bibliographic notes in the John Francis Bannon's *The Spanish Borderlands, 1531-1821* 257-288 (Albuquerque: University of New Mexico Press, 1997). Other examples include Morris S. Arnold, *Unequal*

Laws unto a Savage Race: European Legal Traditions in Arkansas, 1686-1836 (Fayetteville: University of Arkansas Press, 1985); Stuart Banner, *Legal Systems in Conflict: Property and Sovereignty in Missouri, 1750-1860* (Norman: Univeristy of Oklahoma Press, 2000); David J. Bodenhamer and James W. Ely Jr., eds., *Ambivalent Legacy: A Legal History of the South* (Jackson: University Press of Mississippi, 1984); Mark P. Fernandez, "Louisiana Legal History: Past, Present, and Future, in A Law Unto Itself?" in Warren M. Billings and Mark P. Fernandez, eds., *Essays in the New Louisiana History* (Baton Rouge: Louisiana State University Press, 2001); George Lee Flint Jr. and Marie Juliet Alfaro, "Secured Transactions History: The Impact of English Smuggling on Chattel Mortgage Acts in the Spanish Borderlands," *Valparaiso L. Rev.* 37(2003): 703; Gilbert C. Din, *Spaniards, Planters, and Slaves: The Spanish Regulation of Slavery in Louisiana, 1762-1803* (College Station: Texas A&M University Press, 1999).

8. A handy source of maps is Charles R. Goins and Michael L. Caldwell, *Historical Atlas of Louisiana* (Norman: University of Oklahoma Press, 1995).

9. A frequently cited modern history of French Louisiana is Marcel Giraud, *Histoire de la Louisiane Francaise* (Paris: Presses Universitaires de France, 1953-1974). Volumes 1, 2, and 5 are now available in English translation from the Louisiana State University Press.

10. Walter G. Howell, "The French Period 1699-1763," in McLemore, supra note 1, at 122.

11. Law is famous, in part, for fueling the first of several large-scale land-speculation fevers in early Mississippi. See Peter M. Garber, *Famous First Bubbles: The Fundamentals of Early Manias* (Cambridge, MA: MIT Press, 2000).

12. Historians often refer to Natchez by its official names under the successive prestatehood regimes: Fort Rosalie (French), Fort Panmure (British and Spanish), and Fort Sargent (United States). For more information about Natchez's earliest years, see Jack D. Elliott Jr., "The Fort at Natchez and the Colonial Origins of Mississippi," *J. Miss. Hist.* 52(1990): 159; Clayton D. James, *Antebellum Natchez* (Baton Rouge: Louisiana State University Press, 1968); and Noah Polk, ed., *Natchez Before 1830* (Jackson: University Press of Mississippi, 1989).

13. See James D. Hardy Jr., "The Superior Council in Colonial Louisiana," in John F. McDermott, ed., *Frenchmen and French Ways in the Mississippi Valley* 99 (Urbana: University of Illinois Press, 1969), citing *Collection of Regulations, Edicts and Decrees Concerning the Commerce, Administration and Justice and the Policing of the French Colonies in America* (Paris: [n.p.], 1765) (translated and reprinted by O. Blanchard in 1940).

14. For more discussion of the superior council, see Mark F. Fernandez, *From Chaos to Continuity: The Evolution of Louisiana's Judicial System, 1712-1862* (Baton Rouge: Louisiana State University Press, 2001); John A. Micelle, "From Law Court to Local Government: Metamorphosis of the Superior Council of French Louisiana," *La. Hist.* 9(1968): 85-107; Hans W. Baade, "Marriage Contracts in French and Spanish Louisiana: A Study in 'Notarial' Jurisprudence," *Tul. L. Rev.* 53(1978): 1, 6-12.

15. See Fernandez, supra note 14, at 2-3.

16. In 1729, Natchez, one of the colony's most promising districts, was attacked in an uprising by the local Natchez Indians, described by early histories as the "Natchez Massacre." Angered by French demands and encroachment on their villages and sacred sites, the Natchez killed or took captive nearly all of the settlers. In the ensuing French and Indian wars, the Natchez were decimated. See Mary Ann Wells, *Native Land: Mississippi 1540-1798* 119-131 (Jackson: University Press of Mississippi, 1994). Soon after, the Company of the West returned the colony to the Crown.

17. Particular Convention of Offensive and Defensive Alliance Between France and Spain, Feb. 4, 1762, Fr.-Sp., 42 C.T.S. 33.

18. Definitive Treaty of Peace between France, Great Britain and Spain, Feb. 10, 1763, Fr.-Gr.Br.-Sp., 42 C.T.S. 279.

19. See Henry P. Beers, *French and Spanish Records of Louisiana: A Bibliographical Guide to Archive and Manuscript Sources* (Baton Rouge: Louisiana State University Press, 1989).

20. For more information about the province generally, see Cecil Johnson, *British West Florida, 1763-1783* (New Haven, CT: Yale University Press, 1943). Also see Robert V. Haynes, "Mississippi Under British Rule—British West Florida," *Mississippi History Now: An Online Publication of the Mississippi Historical Society,* available at <http://mshistory.k12.ms.us> (last visited January 12, 2004).

21. Proclamation of October 7, 1763, reprinted in Frances N. Thorpe, ed., *The Federal and State Constitutions, Colonial Charters, and Other Organic Laws of the States, Territories, and Colonies Now or Heretofore Forming the United States of America,* Vol. 5, 2743 (Washington, DC: U.S. Government Printing Office, 1909).

22. See James, supra note 12, at 13 (citing W. L. Grant and James Monro, eds., Acts of the Privy Council of England, Colonial Series, 1613-1783, Vol. 4, 668 [6 vol., London: H. M. Stationery Office, 1908-1912]). See generally Robert V. Haynes, *The Natchez District and the American Revolution* (Jackson: University Press of Mississippi, 1976).

23. For a general description of the governmental structure of British colonies in America, see William Holdsworth, *A History of English Law,* Vol. 9, 43-63 (Boston, MA: Little, Brown and Company, 1938).

24. See Robert R. Rea Jr. and Milo B. Howard Jr., eds., *The Minutes, Journals and Acts of the General Assembly of British West Florida,* Vol. 1, x (University: University of Alabama Press, 1979). Rea and Howard's preface to the set provides a detailed description of the organization and activities of the British West Florida government.

25. Byrle A. Kynerd, "British West Florida," in McLemore, supra note 1, at 138.

26. Ibid. at 142.

27. Rea and Howard, supra note 24, at xi.

28. See generally Rea and Howard, supra note 24.

29. Clarence E. Carter, "Some Aspects of British Administration in West Florida," *Miss. Valley Hist. Rev.* 1(1915): 365, 371.

30. Kynerd, supra note 25, at 153.

31. Ibid. at 154.

32. See generally William S. Coker and Robert R. Rea, eds., *Anglo-Spanish Confrontation on the Gulf Coast During the American Revolution* (Pensacola, FL: Gulf Coast History and Humanities Conference, 1982).

33. Treaty of Paris, U.S.-Gr.Br., Sept. 3, 1783, 8 *Stat.* 80.

34. For more information about Spanish colonial law, see Rodolfo Batiza, "The Influence of Spanish Law in Louisiana," *Tul. L. Rev.* 23(1958): 29; Oscar M. Trelles II, "Spanish Law and Its Influence in the Americas," in Roy M. Mersky, Stanley Ferguson, and Daniel Martin, eds., *Collecting and Managing Rare Law Books* 165-225 (Dobbs Ferry, NY: Glanville Publishers, 1981) (describing the Spanish law in force in colonial Louisiana, including Las Siete Partidas, Leyes de Toro, Fuero de Real, Fuero Juzgo, and the royal cedulas, or edicts). The *Encyclopedia of the North American Colonies* (New York: C. Scribner and Sons, 1993) also includes good introductions to various law-related topics, such as the legal profession and civil law, in the "Spanish Borderlands."

35. For an overview of the general system of government in New Spain, see Clarence H. Haring, *The Spanish Empire in America* 342-343 (New York: Oxford University Press, 1947).

36. See Jack D.L. Holmes, "A Spanish Province," in McLemore, supra note 1, at 158-173.

37. William S. Coker, "Research in the Spanish Borderlands: Mississippi, 1779-1798," *Latin Am. Res. Rev.* 8(1972): 40, 51.

38. Beers, supra note 19, at 184.

39. Ibid. at 34.

40. See Jack D.L. Holmes, *Gayoso: The Life of a Spanish Governor in the Mississippi Valley 1789-1799* (Baton Rouge: Louisiana State University Press, 1965). A lively, well-documented account of the colorful personalities and events in Natchez's most tumultuous prestatehood years, it also includes a chapter devoted to law and law enforcement.

41. More significantly, Spain held that free navigation of the Mississippi River had not been Great Britain's right to cede, as the United States now demanded. See generally Whitaker, supra note 4.

42. See Treaty of Friendship, Limits, and Navigation, Oct. 27, 1795, U.S.-Sp., 8 *Stat.* 138 (commonly referred to as the Treaty of San Lorenzo, or Pinckney's Treaty). See generally Samuel F. Bemis, *Pinckney's Treaty: America's Advantage from Europe's Distress, 1783-1800* (New Haven, CT: Yale University Press, 1960).

43. On March 4, 1803, the Mississippi Territory General Assembly authorized the translation, indexing, and binding of the records that remained in Natchez. A century later, Dunbar Rowland found the Spanish-era Natchez Chancery Court records in the Adams County Chancery Court's offices, including orders from the Crown, the governor, and the district commandant; records of civil and criminal lawsuits; bills of sale of personal property, including slaves, wills, and inventories of estates; and laws and regulations issued by the governor and the district commandants.

44. They based their claims on Charles II's 1662 charter establishing the colony of Carolina. See Thorpe, supra note 23, at 2745. (An electronic text of the charter is available at <http://www.yale.edu/lawweb/avalon/states/nc01.htm>, last visited

May 11, 2005.) For the first century after the charter, Carolina's "western extent was purely academic, since it passed through territory held by the French who did not recognize the line." Jack D. Elliott Jr., "Fort of Natchez and the Colonial Origins of Mississippi," *J. Miss. Hist.* 52(1990): 159, 184.

45. See 1785 Ga. Laws, No. 296, reprinted in John Cushing, comp., *The First Laws of the State of Georgia,* Vol. 1, 305-306. The Bourbon County Act is also reprinted in Edmund C. Burnett, ed., "Papers Relating to Bourbon County, Georgia, 1785-1786, I," *Am. Hist. Rev.* 15(1909): 66, 70.

46. See 1788 Ga. Laws, No. 386, reprinted in Cushing, supra note 45, at 370-371.

47. See generally C. Peter Magrath, *Yazoo, Law and Politics in the New Republic: The Case of Fletcher v. Peck* (Providence, RI: Brown University Press, 1966). Also see Lindsay G. Robertson, "A 'Mere Feigned Case': Rethinking the *Fletcher v. Peck* Conspiracy and Early Republican Legal Culture," *Utah L. Rev.* 249 (2000).

48. R.S. Cotterill, "The National Land System in the South: 1803-1812," *Miss. Valley Hist. Rev.* 16(1930): 495, 496. A short summary of the land claims situation in Natchez can also be found in William B. Hamilton's *Anglo-American Law on the Frontier: Thomas Rodney and His Territorial Cases* 66-71 (Durham, NC: Duke University Press, 1953).

49. In 1802, Georgia finally agreed to "cede" all lands west of the Chattahoochee River to the United States for $1,250,000 (see Act of March 27, 1804, 2 *Stat.* 305 [1804]). Investors objected and took their claims to court. Finally, in 1810, the matter reached the U.S. Supreme Court. In the landmark case of *Fletcher v. Peck,* the court agreed with the investors that the land grant was a kind of contract that Georgia could not unilaterally rescind and struck down the 1796 act repudiating the Yazoo land grants as unconstitutional (see 6 Cranch 87[1810] [holding a statute unconstitutional for the first time]). Congress eventually agreed to pay the speculators from the proceeds of the sale of lands in the Mississippi Territory. See Act of March 31, 1814, 3 *Stat.* 116 (1814); Act of Jan 23, 1815, 3 *Stat.* 192 (1815); and Act of Apr. 24, 1816, 3 *Stat.* 300 (1816).

50. See An Act for an Amicable Settlement of Limits with the State of Georgia, and Authorizing the Establishment of a Government in the Mississippi Territory, 1 *Stat.* 549 (1798) (also providing for the creation of a commission to negotiate with Georgia for cession of the lands west of the Chattahoochee River). For a good general history and maps of the the Mississippi Territory, see Thomas D. Clark and John D.W. Guice. *The Old Southwest, 1795-1830: Frontiers in Conflict* (Norman: University of Oklahoma Press, 1996).

51. 1 *Stat.* 51 n.(a) (1789). For further discussion of the Northwest Ordinance's provisions, see Peter S. Onuf, *Statehood and Union: A History of the Northwest Ordinance* (Bloomington: Indiana University Press, 1987). See, generally, Gary Lawson and Guy Seidman, *The Constitution of the Empire: Territorial Expansion and American Legal History* (New Haven: Yale University Press, 2004).

52. See Mike P. Mills, "Slave Law in Mississippi from 1817-1861: Constitutions, Codes and Cases," *Miss. L. J.* 71(2001): 153, 162-163.

53. The text of the Northwest Ordinance is available online at <http://memory.loc.gov/ammem/amlaw/lwsl.html>.

54. For further discussion of the territorial court system and its issues, see William Wirt Blume and Elizabeth Gaspar Brown, "Territorial Courts and Law: Unifying Factors in the Development of American Legal Institutions, I," *Mich. L. Rev.* 61(1962): 39; William Wirt Blume and Elizabeth Gaspar Brown, "Territorial Courts and Law: Unifying Factors in the Development of American Legal Institutions, II," *Mich. L. Rev.* 61(1963): 467.

55. See Hamilton, supra note 49, at 117-132. Hamilton's history is a particularly rich source of information about the foundation of Mississippi's legal traditions and the territorial court system in general. Describing the reception of English common law and English statutes as well as the lingering influence of Spanish and French law in the Mississippi Territory, this text is unique among works on Mississippi legal history for its scope, detail, and scholarly synthesis of primary sources. For an excellent discussion of the Mississippi territorial court system and its evolution, see also Michael H. Hoffheimer, "Mississippi Courts: 1790-1868," *Miss. L. J.* 65(1995): 99.

56. See Hamilton, supra note 49, at 132-136.

57. The court apparently had no law books, at least in the earliest days, and critics charged that the judges made laws, rather than adopting them from the original states as Congress had required in the Northwest Ordinance. See William Jenks, "Territorial Legislation by Governor and Judges," *Miss. Valley Hist. Rev.* 4(1918): 36, 41.

58. See John Wunder, "American Law and Order Comes to the Mississippi Territory: The Making of Sargent's Code, 1798-1800," *J. Miss. Law* 38(1976): 131, 136-151. See also William N. Ethridge Jr., "An Introduction to Sargent's Code of the Mississippi Territory (1799-1800)," *Am. J. Leg. His.* 148 (1967). For a discussion of the section providing poor relief in particular, see William P. Quigley, "The Quicksands of the Poor Law: Poor Relief Legislation in a Growing Nation, 1790-1820," *N. Ill. U. L. Rev.* 18(1997): 1, 29-31.

59. See An Act Supplemental to the Act Entitled "An Act for an Amicable Settlement of the Limits with the State of Georgia, and Authorizing the Establishment of a Government in the Mississippi Territory," 2 *Stat.* 69 (1800). The same year W.C.C. Claiborne replaced Sargent as territorial governor. For a list of territorial governors and judges, see Dunbar Rowland, *History of Mississippi: The Heart of the South,* Vol. 2 (Chicago, IL: S.J. Clarke Publishing Company, 1925).

60. Judge Toulmin was also author of the first secondary source of law printed in the territory, a justice of the peace manual titled *The Magistrates' Assistant* (Natchez: Printed by Samuel Terrell, 1807).

61. See Robert V. Haynes, "The Road to Statehood," in McLemore, supra note 1, at 217-250.

62. In 1813 Spain formally ceded West Florida, which the United States had already claimed by presidential proclamation. See Treaty of Amity, Settlement, and Limits, Between the United States of America and his Catholic Majesty [Adams-Onis Treaty], Feb. 22, 1819, U.S.-Sp., 8 *Stat.* 252. Mississippi's coastal area, between the Pearl and Perdido Rivers, was then added to the territory. See An Act to Enlarge the Boundaries of the Mississippi Territory, 2 *Stat.* 734 (1812). For further discussion of the U.S.-Spanish conflict, see Isaac Joslin Cox, *The West Flordia Controversy, 1798-1813* (Baltimore, MD: Johns Hopkins Press, 1918). A briefer ac-

count is available in David P. Currie, "Rumors of Wars: Presidential and Congressional War Powers, 1809-1829," *U. Chi. L. Rev.* 67(2000): 1.

63. See the University of Alabama Libraries, "Historical Maps of Mississippi" at <http://alabamamaps.ua.edu/historicalmaps/mississippi>.

64. The WPA Historical Records Survey in the 1930s also preserved, translated, and indexed huge numbers of colonial documents throughout the southeast, including "Sargent's Code" and the "Despatches of the Spanish Governors of Louisiana." See Burl Noggle, *Working with History: The Historical Records Survey in Louisiana and the Nation, 1936-1942* (Baton Rouge: Louisiana State University Press, 1981).

65. The titles of these acts can be found in Clarence E. Carter, comp. and ed., *Territorial Papers of the United States,* Vol. 5, 94-95 (Washington, DC: U.S. Government Printing Office, 1937-1938).

66. For additional bibliographic detail, see Douglas C. McMurtrie, *A Bibliography of Mississippi Imprints 1798-1830* 141-155 (Beauvoir Community, MS: The Book Farm, 1945).

67. Three days later Congress established the eastern half of the former Mississippi Territory as the Territory of Alabama. See Act of March 3, 1817, 3. *Stat.* 371.

68. In 1802 the capital had been moved from Natchez to Washington, a converted plantation six miles east, "when the Jeffersonian republicans who had taken control of the government found the aristocratic character of Natchez unfavorable and unfriendly." Richard M. McLemore, "The Birth of Mississippi," *J. Miss. His.* 20 (1967): 255, 262 .

69. Ibid. at 265. For other analyses of the constitution's drafting and debate, see Winbourne M. Drake, "Mississippi's First Constitutional Convention," *J. Miss. Hist.* 18(1956): 79; David G. Sansing, "Mississippi's Four Constitutions," *Miss. L. J.* 56 (1982).

70. See Winbourne M. Drake, "The Framing of Mississippi's First Constitution," *J. Miss. Hist.* 29(1967): 301, 310.

71. Ibid.

Chapter 26

Missouri Prestatehood Legal Materials

Margaret McDermott

INTRODUCTION

Under both the French and the Spanish, Upper Louisiana formed part of the province of Louisiana. Encompassing a great deal of land, the province of Louisiana was divided into two districts. New Orleans was the seat of government of Lower Louisiana, and St. Louis was the home of the lieutenant governor who controlled Upper Louisiana.[1] In the early part of the nineteenth century, due to both timing and location, the history of Missouri was to become closely tied to the question of slavery. These two distinct periods produced a variety of historical records and legal materials.

The early records of St. Louis and other settlements in Upper Louisiana were transferred to the authority of the United States in 1805 after the Louisiana Purchase. They eventually became part of the Papeles de Cuba in the Archivo General de Indias at Seville.[2] The Missouri Historical Society in St. Louis obtained transcripts from the Papeles de Cuba, which had been prepared by the Archivo General de Indias.[3] The society also has copies of dispatches of the Spanish governors of Louisiana between 1768 and 1791. The Western Historical Manuscripts Collection at the University of Missouri in Columbia also contains microform reproductions of both the French and Spanish archives. Historian Louis Houck eventually published a compilation of documents containing English translations of selected texts. His two-volume work is referenced later in this chapter under Resources.

For anyone doing research involving the legal materials of Missouri from 1804 to statehood in 1821, the two most helpful secondary sources will be the works by Floyd Shoemaker[4] and Louis Houck.[5] This chapter also contains references to two microform collections that will prove useful to researchers in identifying primary legal materials. *Early State Records,*[6] a project by the Library of Congress, contains legislative records, statutory law, constitutional records, and court records for the Missouri Territory. It also identifies the libraries and archives containing the actual manuscripts and documents. The other microform collection that will be helpful is Shaw and Shoemaker's *Early American Imprints, Second Series.*[7] This chapter's Resources section identifies the major library and archival collections in Missouri where prestatehood legal materials may be found.

HISTORY

Treaties

A treaty between the United States of America and the French Republic (April 30, 1803), 8 *Stat.* 200.

Known as the "Treaty of Cession," it gave the land involved in the Louisiana Purchase to the United States. Article III stated:

> The inhabitants of the ceded territory shall be incorporated in the Union of the United States, and admitted as soon as possible, according to the principles of the federal constitution, to the enjoyment of all the rights, advantages, and immunities of citizens of the United States; and in the meantime they shall be maintained and protected in the free enjoyment of their liberty, property, and the religion which they profess.

A Convention between the United States of America and the French Republic (April 30, 1803), 8 *Stat.* 206.

This convention established the amount (60 million francs) to be paid by the United States to France for the territory and set out how payments should be made.

Organic Acts

An Act to enable the President of the United States to take possession of the territories ceded by France to the United States by the treaty concluded at Paris, on the thirtieth of April last; and for the temporary government thereof, ch. 1, 2 *Stat.* 245 (1803).

This act empowered the president of the United States to take possession of Louisiana and placed under his direction all military, civil, and judicial powers that had been exercised by the officials of the existing government.

An Act erecting Louisiana into two territories, and providing for the temporary government thereof, ch. 38, 2 *Stat.* 283 (1804).

All land south of the thirty-third degree of north latitude was to be called the "Territory of Orleans" and all land north, the "District of Louisiana." The Louisiana District was placed under the government of Indiana Territory, which consisted of a governor, secretary, and three judges.

An Act further providing for the government of the District of Louisiana, ch. 31, 2 *Stat.* 331 (1805).

The "District of Louisiana" was changed to the "Territory of Louisiana." This territory was separated from the government of the Indiana Territory, and a new government of Louisiana Territory was established. Missouri became a territory of the lowest grade. The executive power was placed in the hands of the governor who was appointed by the president. The legislative power was held by the governor and the three territorial judges, and the judicial power was vested in the three territorial judges.

An Act Providing for the government of the Territory of Missouri, ch. 95, 2 *Stat.* 743 (1812).

Changed the name of the "Territory of Louisiana" to the "Territory of Missouri." Raised Missouri to the second grade of territories and gave the inhabitants control of the lower house of the legislature through the election of a delegate to Congress. The legislative power was vested in a bicameral body called the "General Assembly." The judiciary was composed of a superior court, inferior courts, and courts of justice of the peace.

An Act for the Appointment of an Additional judge for the Missouri Territory and for other purposes, ch. 8, 3 *Stat.* 95 (1814).

An Act to alter certain parts of the act providing for the government of the territory of Missouri, ch. 155, 3 *Stat.* 328 (1816).

Missouri became a territory of the highest grade.

An Act further to regulate the Territories of the United States, and their electing delegates to Congress, ch. 42, 3 *Stat.* 363 (1817).

The citizens of the Missouri Territory were permitted to elect a delegate to Congress.

Enabling Act and Other Relevant Legislation

An Act to authorize the people of the Missouri Territory to form a constitution and state government, and for the admission of such state into the

Union on an equal footing with the original states, and to prohibit slavery in certain territories, ch. 22, 3 *Stat.* 545 (1820).

Provided for the election of representatives to a constitutional convention. Section eight contained what is referred to as the "First Missouri Compromise," in which slavery was forever prohibited in the territory north of thirty-six minutes north latitude except in Missouri. There was a proviso that fugitives may be reclaimed.

Resolution Providing for the admission of Missouri into the Union, on a certain condition, Resolution 1, 3 *Stat.* 645 (1821).

The fundamental condition involved the third article of the constitution that had recently been adopted. The article said that it should be the duty of the general assembly to pass such laws as might be necessary "to prevent free Negroes and Mulattoes from coming to and settling in the state under any pretext whatsoever." The "fundamental condition" established by Congress for statehood was that this should never be construed to authorize passage of any law by which any citizen "shall be excluded from the enjoyment of any of the privileges and immunities to which such citizen is entitled under the constitution of the United States." Missouri was allowed to come into the Union with the constitution she had adopted, provided the condition was met. This has been referred to as the "Second Missouri Compromise."

A Solemn Public Act, declaring the assent of this State to the fundamental condition contained in a resolution passed by the Congress of the United States, providing for the admission of the State of Missouri into the Union on certain conditions (Approved June 26, 1821). *Laws of a public and general nature of the District of Louisiana, of the Territory of Louisiana, of the Territory of Missouri and of the State of Missouri, up to the year 1824,* vol. 1, p. 758, Chapter 311. Jefferson City, MO: W. Lusk and Son, 1842.

Missouri agreed to the fundamental condition that the third article of the constitution shall never be construed to authorize the passage of any law, and that no law shall be passed in conformity thereto, by which any citizen of either of the United States shall be excluded from the enjoyment of any of the privileges and immunities to which citizens are entitled under the constitution of the United States.

Presidential Proclamation (Aug. 10, 1821), *Annals of the Congress of the United States,* 16th Congress, 2nd Session, 1784. Washington, DC: Gales and Seaton, 1855.

MISSOURI CONSTITUTION

Journal of the Missouri State Convention, 1820. St. Louis: I.N. Henry and Co., 1820.

Covers the constitutional convention held in St. Louis (June 12, 1820 to June 19, 1820). Available in the microfilm collection of *Early State Records*.

Constitution of the State of Missouri, 1820. St. Louis: I.N. Henry and Co., 1820.

Available in the microfilm collection of *Early State Records*.

JOURNALS AND LEGISLATIVE PROCEEDINGS

Journal of the Proceedings of the Legislature of the Territory of Louisiana commencing June 3, 1806 to October 9, 1811.

Manuscripts are available at the St. Louis Mercantile Library at the University of Missouri–St. Louis and at the Missouri Historical Society Library in St. Louis, Missouri. The journal is also available in the microfilm collection of *Early State Records*.

Journal of the Legislative Council and *Journal of the House of Representatives.* St. Louis: The Assembly, 1806-1810.

Title varies. At times referred to as *Journal of the Proceedings of the Legislature.* Available in the microfilm collection of *Early State Records*.

Missouri Gazette. St. Louis: Joseph Charless, 1812-1818.

Published under the title *Missouri Gazette* and *Missouri Gazette & Illinois Advertiser.* This newspaper published the *Journal of the Legislative Council* and the *Journal of the House of Representatives.* Relevant time periods are available in the *Early State Records* microfilm collection. Selected issues are available at the Missouri Historical Society Library in St. Louis, Missouri.

TERRITORIAL SESSION LAWS

Laws for the Government of the District of Louisiana passed by the Governor and Judges of the Indiana Territory at their first Session begun on October 1, 1804. Vincennes, Indiana Territory: E. Stout, 1804.

Available in the microfilm collection of *Early State Records*. See the Resources section for a description of this collection. A paper copy is held by the Missouri State Library in Jefferson City, Missouri.

Laws for the Government of the District of Louisiana, 1804 (Facsimile Reprint). Washington, DC: Statute Law Book Co., 1905.

Facsimile reprint available at the Missouri Historical Society Library in St. Louis, Missouri.

Laws of the Territory of Louisiana passed by the Governor and Judges assembled in Legislature, in the month of October, 1810. St. Louis: Joseph Charless, 1810.

Supplement and partial revision of the first laws of the Louisiana Territory printed in 1808. Available in the microfilm collection of *Early State Records* and Shaw and Shoemaker's *Early American Imprints, Second Series,* No. 20593 (micro-opaque).

Acts passed by the General Assembly of the Territory of Missouri in July and August, 1813. St. Louis: Joseph Charless, 1813.

Available in the microfilm collection of *Early State Records* and Shaw and Shoemaker's *Early American Imprints, Second Series,* No. 29180 (micro-opaque).

Acts passed by the General Assembly of the Territory of Missouri in December and January 1813 and 1814. St. Louis: Joseph Charless, 1814.

Available in the microfilm collection of *Early State Records* and Shaw and Shoemaker's *Early American Imprints, Second Series,* No. 32148 (micro-opaque).

Acts passed by the General Assembly of the Territory of Missouri in December and January 1814 and 1815. St. Louis: Joseph Charless, 1815.

Available in the microfilm collection of *Early State Records* and Shaw and Shoemaker's *Early American Imprints, Second Series,* No. 35293 (micro-opaque).

Acts passed by the General Assembly of the Territory of Missouri in December and January 1815 and 1816. St. Louis: Joseph Charless, 1816.

Available in the microfilm collection of *Early State Records* and Shaw and Shoemaker's *Early American Imprints, Second Series,* No. 38271 (micro-opaque).

Acts passed by the General Assembly of the Territory of Missouri in December and January 1816 and 1817. St. Louis: Joseph Charless, 1817.

Available in the microfilm collection of *Early State Records.*

Acts passed by the General Assembly of the Territory of Missouri in October, November and December 1818. St. Louis: Joseph Charless, 1819.

Available in the microfilm collection of *Early State Records* and Shaw and Shoemaker's *Early American Imprints, Second Series,* No. 48716 (microopaque).

Acts of the First General Assembly of the State of Missouri; passed at the First Session which was begun and held at the town of St. Louis on Monday, the 18th of September, 1820. St. Louis: Isaac N. Henry and Co., 1820.

Available in the microfilm collection of *Early State Records.*

TERRITORIAL CODES AND DIGESTS

Laws of the Territory of Louisiana: Comprising all those which are now actually in force within the same. St. Louis: Joseph Charless, 1808.

Joseph Charless subsequently published the acts of each session of the territorial legislature. Refer to the section Territorial Session Laws. Contains the Treaty of Cession and the organic laws. Available in the microfilm collection of *Early State Records.*

Henry S. Geyer. *A Digest of Missouri Territory, to which have been added a variety of Forms Useful to Magistrates.* St. Louis: Joseph Charless, 1818.

An early guide to Missouri laws. Arranged by broad subject such as arson, alimony, bigamy, lunatics, and slaves. Complete with a subject index and table of contents. Separate index to a collection of forms, including a form allowing a free black to carry a gun. Reprints Treaty of Cession, the organic laws, Spanish regulations for the allotment of lands, and laws of the United States for adjusting title to lands. Available in the microfilm collection of *Early State Records* and Shaw and Shoemaker's *Early American Imprints, Second Series,* No. 44874. Paper copies are available at the Missouri Historical Society Library in St. Louis, Missouri, and the St. Louis University Law Library.

Laws of a Public and General Nature of the District of Louisiana of the Territory of Louisiana, the Territory of Missouri, and of the State of Missouri, up to the Year 1824, vol. 1. Jefferson City, MO: W. Lusk and Son, 1842.

Volume I of this two-volume set contains laws of the territory of Missouri from 1813 to December 24, 1818. The set continues with Volume II, which contains laws of the state from 1824 to 1836. Both volumes contain an index by broad subject (conveyances, bail, courts, etc.). Also contains the Treaty of Cession and the organic laws. Paper copies are available at the Missouri Historical Society Library in St. Louis, Missouri, and the St. Louis University Law Library.

Index to the Statute Laws of Missouri from the inauguration of the territorial government to the close of 1868. James S. Garland, comp. St. Louis: St. Louis Book and News Co., 1869.

Paper copy available at the Missouri Historical Society Library in St. Louis, Missouri.

COURT RECORDS

Records of the Superior Court of the Territory of Missouri from May, 1811 to November, 1826.

Manuscripts of handwritten court records are available at the Missouri Supreme Court Archives in Jefferson City, Missouri. The manuscripts are also available in the microfilm collection of *Early State Records.*

RESOURCES

Bibliography of Sources Documenting Missouri's Prestatehood Period

Mrs. Arthui Acton. *Early History of Missouri.* St. Louis: Prepared by the Missouri Historical Records Survey, Division of Community Service Programs, Works Projects Administration, 1941.

Stuart Banner. *Legal Systems in Conflict: Property and Sovereignty in Missouri, 1750-1860.* Norman: University of Oklahoma Press, 2000.

Explains the transition from the civil law tradition of France and Spain to the Anglo-American common law tradition. Numerous bibliographic references.

Henry Putney Beers. *French and Spanish Records of Louisiana: A Bibliographical Guide to Archive and Manuscript Sources.* Baton Rouge: Louisiana State University Press, 1989.

William E. Foley. *A History of Missouri: 1673 to 1820,* Vol. 1. William E. Parrish, general ed. 2d printing. Columbia: University of Missouri Press, 1986.

A Guide to the Microfilm Collection of Early State Records. William Sumner Jenkins, comp. Washington, DC: Library of Congress, 1950.

A guide to 2,400 reels of microfilm of primary source material for the states. The classes of material in the *Early State Records* collection include legislative, statutory, constitutional, executive, and court records. For Missouri this set includes copies of materials held by the major archives and libraries in the state.

James Griffith Harris. *The Background and Development of Early Missouri Trial Courts.* University of Missouri–Columbia, 1949.

Louis Houck. *A History of Missouri from the Earliest Explorations and Settlements until the Admission of the State into the Union.* Chicago, IL: R.R. Donnelley and Sons Company, 1908.

Louis Houck. *The Spanish Regime in Missouri; a collection of papers and documents relating to upper Louisiana principally within the present limits of Missouri during the dominion of Spain, from the Archives of the Indies at Seville, etc., translated from the original Spanish into English, and including also some papers concerning the supposed grant to Col. George Morgan at the mouth of the Ohio, found in the Congressional library.* Chicago: R.R. Donnelley and Sons Company, 1909.

Laurance Hyde. *Historical Review of the Judicial System of Missouri.* Kansas City, MO: Vernon Law Company, 1952.

Article reprinted from Volume 27 of *Vernon's Annotated Missouri Statutes* published in 1952.

John D. Lawson. *A Centennial of Missouri Legal Literature.* Columbia, MO: The State Historical Society of Missouri, 1921.

Reprinted from the *Missouri Historical Review,* 15(4)(July 1921).

David D. March. *The History of Missouri.* New York: Lewis Historical Pub. Co., 1967.

Thomas A. Pearson and Anne Watts. *Legal Information.* St. Louis: St. Louis Public Library, 1996.

Consists of photocopies of various legal documents and court decisions. Volume I covers the eighteenth and nineteenth centuries and Volume II covers the twentieth century.

Perry Scott Rader. *Civil Government of the United States and the State of Missouri,* Rev. Ed. Jefferson City, MO: Hugh Stephens Company, 1912.

Perry Scott Rader. *The History of Missouri from the earliest times to the present,* Rev. Ed. Jefferson City, MO: Hugh Stephens Printing Company, 1922.

Elihu Hotchkiss Shepard. *The Early History of St. Louis and Missouri from its first exploration by white men in 1673 to 1843.* St. Louis: Southwestern Book and Publishing Company, 1870.

Floyd Calvin Shoemaker. *Missouri's Struggle for Statehood: 1804-1821.* New York: Russell and Russell, 1969.

Reprints the memorials and resolutions of 1818 and 1820 requesting statehood. Also includes the constitution of 1820 and the Missouri Solemn Public Act of 1821.

Walter Barlow Stevens. *The Travail of Missouri for Statehood.* St. Louis: State Historical Society of Missouri, 1920.

Reprinted from the *Missouri Historical Review,* 15(1) (October 1920).

Monas Nathan Squires. *The Early Governments and Governors of Missouri under the United States, 1804-1820.* Columbia: State Historical Society of Missouri, 1930.

Eugene Morrow Violette. *History of Missouri,* Rep. Ed. Cape Girardeau, MO: Ramfre Press, 1957.

*Libraries and Archives for Research
Involving Missouri Legal Materials*

Missouri Historical Society Library and Research Center
225 South Skinker Blvd.
St. Louis, MO 63112-0040
314-746-4500
http://www.mohistory.org/LRC.html

Missouri State Archives
Office of the Secretary of State
P.O. Box 1747, 600 W. Main St.
Jefferson City, MO 65102-0778
573-751-3280
http://www.sos.state.mo.us/archives

Missouri State Library
P.O. Box 387, 600 W. Main St.
Jefferson City, MO 65102-0387
573-751-3615
http://www.sos.state.mo.us

Missouri Supreme Court Library
207 W. High St., Second Floor
Jefferson City, MO 65101
314-751-2636

St. Louis Mercantile Library at the University of Missouri–St. Louis
8001 Natural Bridge Road
St. Louis, MO 63121
314-516-7243
http://www.umsl.edu/mercantile

St. Louis Public Library
1301 Olive St.
St. Louis, MO 63103
314-241-2288
http://www.slpl.lib.mo.us/

State Historical Society of Missouri Reference Library
1020 Lowry St.
Columbia, MO 65201-7298
573-882-7083
http://www.umsystem.edu/shs/reference/htm

Western Historical Manuscript Collection–Columbia
University of Missouri/State Historical Society of Missouri
23 Ellis Library
Columbia, Missouri 65201-5149
573-882-6028
http://www.umsystem.edu/whmc/

NOTES

1. Floyd Calvin Shoemaker, *Missouri's Struggle for Statehood: 1804-1821* 10 (New York: Russell and Russell, 1969).

2. Henry Putney Beers, *French and Spanish Records of Louisiana: A Bibliographical Guide to Archive and Manuscript Sources* 239 (Baton Rouge: Louisiana State University Press, 1989).

3. Ibid. at 240-241.

4. Shoemaker, supra n. 1.

5. Louis Houck, *A History of Missouri from the Earliest Explorations and Settlements until the Admission of the State into the Union* (Chicago: R.R. Donnelley and Sons, 1908).

6. *Early State Records* (Washington, DC: U.S. Library of Congress, 1983).

7. *Early American Imprints, Second Series* (Chester, VT: Readex, 1998).

Chapter 27

Early Justice Under the Big Sky: Prestatehood Legal Resources of Montana

Lisa Mecklenberg Jackson

INTRODUCTION

The state of Montana is uniquely beautiful and uniquely rough-and-tumble. One has only to think of modern-day militia and freemen to realize Montana's past must be filled with equally colorful characters with their own ideas of homegrown justice. A look at prestatehood Montana confirms that pattern. Even before becoming a state in 1889, Montana had its own special kind of justice. It is the purpose of this chapter to explore that early brand of justice in Montana.

Before the white settlers arrived, two groups of Indian tribes lived in the region that is now Montana. The Arapaho, Assiniboine, Blackfeet, Cheyenne, Crow, and Gros Ventre (also called the Atsina) tribes lived in the plains. The mountains in the west were the home of the Bannock, Salish, Kalispell, Kootenai, and Shoshone tribes. Other nearby tribes, such as the Sioux, Mandan, and Nez Perce, hunted in the Montana region.

French trappers may have visited the Montana area as early as the 1740s. The American explorers Meriwether Lewis and William Clark led their expedition across Montana to the Pacific Coast in 1805. They returned in 1806, stopping once again to explore Montana. After 1807, fur traders began more aggressive trapping in the newly charted areas of Montana. In 1841, Jesuit missionaries established St. Mary's Mission, the first attempt at a permanent settlement, near what is now Stevensville, Montana. In 1847, the American Fur Company built Fort Benton on the Missouri River. The city that formed there is Montana's oldest continuously populated town.

The United States acquired most of what is now Montana as part of the Louisiana Purchase. The northwestern part was gained by treaty with Britain in 1846. At various times, parts of Montana were in the territories of Louisiana, Missouri, Nebraska, Dakota, Oregon, Washington, and Idaho.

In 1862, prospectors found gold in Grasshopper Creek in southwestern Montana. Other gold strikes followed, and wild mining camps grew around the gold fields. These included Bannack, Diamond City, Virginia City, and others.

The mining camps had almost no effective law enforcement. Accordingly, the citizens took the law into their own hands. One famous incident involved the two biggest gold camps—Bannack and Virginia City. The settlers learned that their sheriff, Henry Plummer, was actually an outlaw leader. The men of Bannack and Virginia City formed a vigilante committee to rid themselves of the outlaws. These vigilantes hanged twenty-one men, including Plummer, in January 1864. The vigilantes adopted as their symbol the numbers 3-7-77. Two possible explanations have been given for their symbol: the numbers may have referred to dimensions of a grave—3 feet wide, 7 feet deep, and 77 inches long—or the symbol may have been associated with a Masonic ritual, as many of the vigilantes were members of the Masons, a fraternal organization. Many outlaws were hanged or driven from Montana by similar vigilante groups.

Many of the early prospectors came to Montana from the South, including some from Confederate Army units that broke up early in the Civil War (1861-1865). One of the major gold fields was called Confederate Gulch because three Southerners found the first gold there.

During the boom years, gold dust was the principal currency in the Montana territory. For example, missionaries did not pass collection plates at services. Instead, they passed a tin cup for gold dust. Chinese launderers even found gold in their wash water when they had finished washing the miners' clothing.

Sidney Edgerton, an Idaho official, saw the need for better government of the wild mining camps. At the time, Montana was part of Idaho Territory. Edgerton traveled to Washington, DC, to lobby for territorial status. Montana became a territory on May 26, 1864, via an organic act, and Edgerton served as its first governor. On November 8, 1889, Montana was formally admitted as the nation's forty-first state.

PRIMARY LAW

Organic Act

In drafting the 1864 Organic Act[1] establishing the Montana Territory, Congress followed a system of government that had become the standard for most western territories. Lawmaking power was placed in the hands of the territory's citizens through a popular election of a bicameral legislature.

The upper house of the legislature was a seven-member "council," and the lower house a thirteen-member "assembly." The organic act also authorized the citizenry to elect one nonvoting "delegate" to the U.S. House of Representatives, who would speak for their interests.[2]

Organic Act of Montana [An Act to provide a temporary Government for the Territory of Montana], ch. 95, 13 *Stat.* 85 (May 26, 1864).

Enabling Act

The Enabling Act authorized the territories of Montana, Dakota, and Washington to become the states of Montana, North Dakota, South Dakota, and Washington upon the adoption and ratification of state constitutions.[3]

Enabling Act of Montana, ch. 180, 25 *Stat.* 676 (Feb. 22, 1889).

Constitution

For a territory to be admitted into the Union as a state, the people of the territory had to first adopt and ratify a constitution. After several unsuccessful attempts at constitution making, on July 4, 1889, seventy-five delegates convened in Helena to draft a constitution. Nearly 90 percent of an earlier constitution-drafting attempt in 1884 was readopted.[4] The 1889 constitution was enacted more as a tool to achieve statehood than to provide a well-organized and carefully planned structure of governance for the new state. Not surprising, the delegates were driven by self-interest and concerns about government abuse of power. Typical of state constitutions of its time, it minimized the powers of the executive branch and maximized the powers of the legislature.[5]

Constitution of the State of Montana as adopted by the Constitutional Convention of the Territory of Montana [reprint of 1884 ed.]. Helena, MT: Montana Constitutional Convention Commission, 1971.

COURT REPORTS AND OTHER JUDICIAL MATERIALS

The land west of the Rockies in what is now Montana was once a part of Oregon, later a part of Washington, and still later a part of the territory of Idaho. It was, however, so far removed from the centers of population and the seats of government of those territories that the country in what is now Montana was left ungoverned, without any legislative, executive, or judicial authority, leaving the early inhabitants unrestrained by any laws other than their own sense of right.[6] However, this is not to say that no legal system existed. There were courts in Montana before there was in reality any formal or established government. These courts were called miners' courts,[7] and they formed the basis of Montana's present-day court system.

The first legally organized court ever held in the territory of Montana was convened in the dining room of the Planters' House at Virginia City on the first Monday in December 1864. As Montana had most recently been part of the territory of Idaho, the territorial district court decided to use the statutes of Idaho as applicable; otherwise the rule of common law would govern. On this day, the chief justice empanelled a grand jury, which was the first grand jury ever in the territory of what is now known as Montana.[8] The district court met for about six months. One of the greatest problems that arose from this session is that there were no libraries and no precedent for many of the complex questions submitted and decided by the court. Hence, it was determined that a code was needed.

The supreme court of the territory of Montana convened for the first time on May 17, 1865, in Virginia City, at the time the territorial seat of government.[9] Hezekiah L. Hosmer presided as chief justice, and Lorenzo P. Williston and Lyman E. Munson served as associate justices. Prior to December 1868, the court would either enter brief or formal orders, confirming or reversing the judgments of the district courts. Accordingly, the first volume of case reports by the supreme court of the territory of Montana contains only the written opinions of the judges from the beginning of the December term (1868) to the end of the January term (1873).[10]

Henry R. Blake, Reporter. *Montana Reports [Reports of cases argued and determined in the Supreme Court of Montana Territory].* Virginia City, MT: George F. Cope, Publisher, 1873 [Vol. 1 (Dec. 1868-Jan. 1873) through Vol. 9 (July 1889-April 1890)].

Horace R. Buck. *A Digest of the first eight volumes of the Montana Reports: containing all cases decided by the Supreme Court of the Territory of Montana.* New Haven, CT: Tuttle, Morehouse and Taylor, 1890.

Thomas A. Mapes. *The Montana Digest: A brief digest of all the decisions of the Supreme Court of the Territory and State of Montana reported in volumes 1 to 32, inclusive, of the Montana Reports.* Helena, MT: State Publishing Co., 1907.

STATUTES AND CODES

In December 1864, the first Montana territorial legislative assembly convened at Bannack and enacted a code, which they called the Bannack Statutes. This code, though somewhat crude, did prescribe rules for court procedure and supplied many provisions of substantive law. Via the organic act, the justices of the supreme court had the power to split the territory into judicial districts. However, no record of any apportionment can be found earlier than June 12, 1867.[11]

The second and third legislative assemblies of the territory of Montana convened and completed their work before the end of 1866, but Congress afterward abrogated all laws passed by these assemblies.[12] In 1867 the fourth legislative assembly convened and enacted what has commonly been called the California Practice Act.[13]

By an act of the legislature of the territory, passed in 1869, the judges of the supreme court were appointed to a commission to codify and arrange the statutes. The result of the work is the Codified Statutes, Seventh Session, 1871-1872. After the codification of these laws by Judges Warren, Knowles, and Symes, the statutes were again revised in 1879 and in 1887. In 1889 an act of the territorial legislature was passed authorizing the creation of a code commission to prepare and submit to the legislature four codes: a civil code, a penal code, a code of civil procedure, and a political code. The codes were finally adopted by the state legislature in 1895.[14] The State Bar of Montana, organized in Helena on January 8, 1885, deserves much of the credit for that adoption, having "agitated for the codification of the laws" after the report of the code commission and until the admission of the codes in 1895.[15]

Bannack Statutes

The first legislative assembly of the Montana Territory, convened at Bannack in 1864, created the first statutes for the territory, known as the Bannack Statutes. The Bannack Statutes were not printed until 1866, and those of the session of 1867 were not printed until the summer of 1868. The territory also borrowed heavily from the "Field Code," which was the proposed Civil Code of New York. In 1872 the Field Code was copied and adopted in California. Montana's Civil Code, adopted in 1895, was copied from the Field Code and the Civil Code of California.

Acts, Resolutions, and Memorials of the Territory of Montana passed at the First Legislative Assembly [convened at Bannack, December 12, 1864]. Virginia City, MT: D.W. Tilton and Co., 1866.

Contains the Declaration of Independence, the Constitution of the United States, the Organic Act, and the Homestead Act of the United States.

Revised Statutes of the Territory of Montana

Published in 1880 by the Helena "Independent," this one-volume work reflected the laws in force as of February 21, 1879, which was the end of the eleventh regular legislative session. It is divided into five divisions: Code of Civil Procedure, Probate Practice Act, Criminal Practice Act, Criminal Laws, and General Laws.

The Revised Statutes of the Territory of Montana [Embracing the laws of a general and permanent nature, in force at the expiration of the eleventh regular session of the Legislative Assembly, on the 21st day of February, A.D. 1879]. Helena, MT: Helena "Independent," 1880.

Codified, arranged, and published by Harry R. Comly.

The Revised Statutes of Montana

The next updating occurred in 1881, with laws in force as of February 23, 1881, the end of the twelfth legislative session. The Revised Statutes also include legislation enacted by the Extraordinary Session of the eleventh regular session: July 1 to 22, 1879. This too is a one-volume work.

The Revised Statutes of Montana [Enacted at the regular session of the twelfth Legislative Assembly of Montana, embracing the laws of a general and permanent nature, in force at the expiration of the eleventh regular session of the Legislative Assembly, on the 21st day of February, A.D. 1879]. Springfield, IL: H.W. Rokker, 1881.

Compiled Statutes of Montana

In 1888 the Journal Publishing Company of Helena published the laws in force at the completion of the fifteenth regular session, which ended March 20, 1867.

Compiled Statutes of Montana Enacted at the Regular Session of the Fifteenth Legislative Assembly of Montana [Embracing the Laws of a General and Permanent Nature, in Force at the Expiration of the Fifteenth Regular Session of the Legislative Assembly]. Helena, MT: Journal Publishing Co., 1888.

Includes the Declaration of Independence, the Constitution of the United States and Amendments thereto, Provisions of the Revised Statutes of the United States Common to all Territories, and those Particularly Relating to Montana, and Sessions Laws of the United States Relating to Montana Enacted Subsequent to the Revision.

The Complete Codes and Statutes of Montana

This compilation is popularly known as the "Sanders Edition," so named after its editor, Wilbur F. Sanders, a prominent figure at the time. It reflected the laws in force as of July 1, 1895. A new format was instituted in this compilation. Instead of five divisions, there are four: Political Code, Civil Code, Code of Civil Procedure, and a Penal Code. It was published in Butte in 1895 as a one-volume work.

The Code and Statutes of Montana in Force July 1, 1895 [Including the Political Code, Civil Code, Code of Civil Procedure, and Penal Code]. Butte, MT: InterMountain Publishing Co., 1895.

Includes the Magna Carta, the Declaration of Independence, the U.S. Constitution, the Organic Act, the Enabling Act, and the Montana Constitution.

SESSION LAWS

Acts, Resolutions, and Memorials of the Territory of Montana, passed by the Legislative Assembly [1st session (1864) through 16th session (1889)]. Virginia City, MT: D.W. Tilton and Co., 1866-1889.

BILLS

The Territorial Legislative Assembly, 1864-1889

Congress created the Montana Territory in May 1864, and members of the first legislative assembly were elected October 24, 1864.[16] All but a few hundred of the 6,500 male voters were situated in the mining camps of

Beaverhead, Jefferson, and Madison Counties. Seven members were elected to an "upper chamber" called the council and thirteen to the house of representatives.[17] They convened December 12, 1864, in Bannack (now a ghost town), located in the mountains just a few miles from the Idaho border. They met until February 9, 1865. That was the first of sixteen regular and several special sessions of the territorial legislature.[18] The next seven sessions, 1866-1874, were held in Virginia City. In 1876 the ninth session met in Helena.

Congress regulated the size, organization, and functions of the territorial legislatures, and the regulations were frequently changed. Poor communication, confusion about intent, and special local circumstances caused additional irregularities in the organization and function of the Montana territorial legislature.

Representation in both chambers was apportioned rather closely to county population by assignment of more than one representative and council member to counties with larger populations. Further equalization was achieved by "floterial" position seats held by members elected in districts that comprised a populous county plus one or more neighboring counties of lesser population.[19]

Sessions of the territorial legislature were limited by Congress to forty calendar days.

House Bills 1-146, 1864-1865, available sporadically at the Montana Historical Society, Helena, Montana.

House Joint Resolutions 1-3, 1864-1865, available at the Montana Historical Society, Helena, Montana.

Council Bills 1-129, 1864-1865, available sporadically at the Montana Historical Society, Helena, Montana.

Council Joint Resolutions 9, 11, and several unnumbered, 1864-1865, available at the Montana Historical Society, Helena, Montana.

House Bills 1-66, 1866, available sporadically at the Montana Historical Society, Helena, Montana.

House Joint Resolutions 1-21, 1866, available at the Montana Historical Society, Helena, Montana.

Council Bills 1-75, 1866, available sporadically at the Montana Historical Society, Helena, Montana.

Council Resolutions, various, 1866, available at the Montana Historical Society, Helena, Montana.

Council Joint Resolutions 1-19, 1866, available at the Montana Historical Society, Helena, Montana.

Later bills and resolutions are also available at the Montana Historical Society.

HOUSE AND COUNCIL (SENATE) JOURNALS

The Montana journals (1864-1889) provide a listing of members and a daily account of legislative action, such as the introduction of bills, their readings, and roll call votes. Both House and Council Journals were published biannually through the sixteenth session.

House Journal of the First Legislative Assembly of Montana Territory [begun at Bannack, the Capital of said Territory on the 12th day of December 1864, and concluded on the 9th day of February 1865]. Virginia City, MT: D.W. Tilton and Co., 1866.

Council Journal of the First Legislative Assembly of Montana Territory [convened at Bannack, December 12, 1864]. Virginia City, MT: D.W. Tilton and Co., 1866.

House Journal of the Sixteenth Session of the Legislative Assembly of the Territory of Montana [convened at Helena, on the 17th day of January, 1889, and concluded on the 14th day of March, A.D. 1889]. Helena, MT: Journal Publishing Co., 1889.

Council Journal of the Sixteenth Session of the Legislative Assembly of the Territory of Montana [convened at Helena, on the 17th day of January, 1889, and concluded on the 14th day of March, A.D. 1889]. Helena, MT: Journal Publishing Co., 1889.

MISCELLANEOUS LEGISLATIVE MATERIALS

Montana Territorial Legislative Assembly, 5th: 1868-1869, available at the Montana Historical Society, Helena, Montana.

Consists of a report of the Select Committee on House Bill 46 (re: sale of liquor to soldiers) and petitions (re: fishing rights, county seats, county boundaries, and Sunday law).

Montana Territorial Legislative Assembly, 6th: 1869-1870, available at the Montana Historical Society, Helena, Montana.

Consists of correspondence with the governor, a report to the council by the territorial treasurer, a report of a special state convention committee, notes from executive sessions on appointments, and a petition (re: Chinese businesses).

Montana Territorial Legislative Assembly, 7th: 1871-1873, available at the Montana Historical Society, Helena, Montana.

Consists of correspondence of the general assembly, house, and council with Governor Benjamin Potts and Secretary James Callaway, reports of the code commissioner to the legislature, and committee reports.

Montana Territorial Legislative Assembly, 8th: 1873-1874, available at the Montana Historical Society, Helena, Montana.

Consists of report by a select committee on the contested election between J.P. Barnes and A.H. Beattie, a council bill (re: the spending of county revenue), and petitions (re: alien mine ownership, Sunday closing laws, aid to railroads, fire protection, and county officials' fees).

Montana Territorial Legislative Assembly, 9th: 1876, available at the Montana Historical Society, Helena, Montana.

Consists of correspondence with Governor Benjamin Potts and others, committee reports, and petitions (re: county seats and boundaries, Sunday closing laws, aid to railroads, etc.).

Montana Territorial Legislative Assembly, 10th: 1877, available at the Montana Historical Society, Helena, Montana.

Consists of correspondence, committee reports, and petitions (re: county formation and boundaries, Sunday closing of saloons, aid to railroads, etc.).

Montana Territorial Legislative Assembly, 11th: 1879, available at the Montana Historical Society, Helena, Montana.

Consists of correspondence with Governor Benjamin Potts and others, members' financial accounts, a report of the territorial law library, a report on the financial condition of Missoula County, committee reports, and petitions (re: railroad taxation, Sunday closings, equalization of taxation among counties, establishment of Deer Lodge County branch offices at Butte, etc.).

Montana Territorial Legislative Assembly, 12th: 1881, available at the Montana Historical Society, Helena, Montana.

Consists of correspondence with Governor Benjamin Potts (re: pardons, standardized school texts) and with T.C. Power (re: steamboats on Missouri River above the Great Falls); reports of county expenses of the state law library, state auditor, and code commission; a committee report on HB 6 (re: Silver Bow County); and petitions (re: formation of Dawson County and Silver Bow County, prison labor, and cattle skinning).

Montana Territorial Legislative Assembly, 13th: 1883, available at the Montana Historical Society, Helena, Montana.

Consists of correspondence with Governor Benjamin Potts and petitions (re: Sunday closing law, Butte city boundaries, barbed wire, Dawson County boundaries, creation of Park County, removal of the Custer County commissioner, county seats and boundaries, fishing on the North Boulder River, incorporation of Bozeman, and ban on liquor sales in houses of prostitution).

Montana Territorial Legislative Assembly, 14th: 1885, available at the Montana Historical Society, Helena, Montana.

Consists of the annual message of the governor, general correspondence, members' financial accounts, reports to the legislature by the orphan's asylum, the penitentiary, and the World's Fair Commission, and petitions (re: gambling, county boundaries, liquor education, licensing of salesmen and photographers, Sunday closings, school textbook selection, and rules of council).

Montana Territorial Legislative Assembly, 15th: 1887, available at the Montana Historical Society, Helena, Montana.

Consists of incoming correspondence, members' financial accounts, committee reports, petitions (re: protection of women, Sunday closure of saloons, variety theaters, opium, local liquor option, gambling, private rooms in saloons, county boundaries, bounties of ground squirrels, game and fish detectives, and the building of a new penitentiary).

Montana Territorial Legislative Assembly, 16th: 1889, available at the Montana Historical Society, Helena, Montana.

Consists of correspondence (including the governor's annual message), members' financial accounts, reports to the legislature by the auditor and treasurer, a subject file on a Missoula County contested election, and petitions (re: Northern Pacific Railroad land claims, county reorganization, codification, liquor license fees, school bonds, building of a reform school, Sunday closure of saloons, and compensation of sheriffs).

EXECUTIVE BRANCH MATERIALS

Montana's territorial governors included Sidney Edgerton (1864-1866), Republican; Thomas Meagher (acting governor 1865-1866 while Governor Edgerton was in Washington on territorial business), Union Democrat; Green Clay Smith (1866-1869), Republican; James Monroe Ashley (1869-1870), Republican; Benjamin F. Potts (1870-1883), Republican; John Schuyler Crosby (1883-1884), Democrat; B. Platt Carpenter (1884-1885), Republican; Samuel Thomas Hauser (1885-1887), Democrat; Preston Hopkins Leslie (1887-1889), Democrat; Benjamin F. White (1889-statehood), Republican.

Executive Office (letter press books), 1868-1889, available at the Montana Historical Society, Helena, Montana.

Account books, 1883-1891, available at the Montana Historical Society, Helena, Montana.

Consists of territorial governor with national government, registry of appropriate bills by the legislature, and accounts against Montana Territory approved by the governor.

Territorial governor and secretary expenses, 1867-1879, available at the Montana Historical Society, Helena, Montana.

Appointments, 1866-1873, available at the Montana Historical Society, Helena, Montana.

Consists of appointments of state auditor, treasurer, clerks of district court, and notaries.

Appointments (territorial governor), 1881-1887, available at the Montana Historical Society, Helena, Montana.

Governor's (territorial) messages to the legislature, 1873, available at the Montana Historical Society, Helena, Montana.

Register of bills received by the territorial governor's office, 1883-1887, available at the Montana Historical Society, Helena, Montana.

Reports

Attorney general to Governor Leslie, no date, available at the Montana Historical Society, Helena, Montana.

Governor Crosby to U.S. Secretary of Interior, 1884, available at the Montana Historical Society, Helena, Montana.

OTHER PRESTATEHOOD LEGAL MATERIALS

Books

Elbert F. Allen. *Sources of the Montana Constitution*. Helena, MT: Montana Constitutional Convention Commission, 1971.

Merrill G. Burlingame and K. Ross Toole. *A History of Montana* (3 volumes). New York: Lewis Historical Pub. Co., 1957.

Lew L. Callaway. *Montana Frontier Lawyer: A Memoir: From Law School to Chief Justice Amid Pioneers and Prospectors, Cowboys and Indians, Rustlers, and Outlaws, 1891-1951*. Helena, MT: Skyhouse Publishers, 1991.

Jabez F. Cowdery. *Supplement to a Treatise on the Law and Practice in Justices' Courts: As construed by the courts of the states of California, Colorado, Nevada, Oregon, Idaho, Montana, Utah, and Washington, and the Territory of Arizona, in civil and criminal cases.* San Francisco, CA: Bancroft-Whitney Co., 1900.

Larry M. Elison and Fritz Snyder. *The Montana State Constitution: A Reference Guide*. Westport, CT: Greenwood Press, 2000.

Encyclopedia of Montana. Santa Barbara, CA: Somerset Publishers, Inc., 2000.

Stephen Jordan, updated by Meredith Hoffman. *A Guide to Montana Legal Research.* Helena, MT: State Law Library of Montana, 2002.

Neil J. Lynch. *Montana's Legislature Through the Years: An Historical Analysis of the Legislature from Territorial Days to the Present.* Butte, MT: Lynch, 1977.

Michael P. Malone, Richard B. Roeder, and William L. Lang. *Montana: A History of Two Centuries.* Seattle, WA: University of Washington Press, 1991.

Andrea Merrill and Judy Jacobson. *Montana Almanac.* Helena, MT: Falcon Press, 1997.

The Montana Constitution Revision Commission. *Montana Constitutional Revision.* Bozeman, MT: Artcraft Printers, 1969.

Robert George Raymer. *Montana, the Land and the People.* Chicago: Lewis Publishing Co., 1930.

Helen Fitzgerald Sanders. *A History of Montana.* Chicago: Lewis Publishing Co., 1913.

Lucile Speer. *We, the People . . . An Introduction to the Montana Constitutional Convention.* Bozeman, MT: Cooperative Extension Service, Montana State University, 1971.

Ellis Waldron. *Montana Legislators 1864-1979: Profiles and Biographical Directory.* Missoula, MT: Bureau of Government Research, University of Montana, 1980.

Journal Articles

Judith K. Cole. "A wide field for usefulness: Women's civil status and the evolution of women's suffrage on the Montana frontier, 1864-1914." *American Journal of Legal History,* 34(3) (1990): 262-294.

Diana S. Dowling. "Creation of the Montana Code Annotated." *Montana Law Review,* 40(1) (1978): 1-30.

Andrew P. Morriss. "'This state will soon have plenty of laws'—Lessons from one hundred years of codification in Montana." *Montana Law Review,* 56(2) (1995): 359-450.

Thesis

James Edith. "Claims' law and miners' courts of the Montana gold camps, 1862-1870." Chicago, University of Chicago, 1949.

Various

Oaths of Council and House Employees, 1864-1865, available at the Montana Historical Society, Helena, Montana.

Petitions, 1864-1865, available at the Montana Historical Society, Helena, Montana.

Vouchers and Warrants, 1864-1865, available at the Montana Historical Society, Helena, Montana.

By the time Montana became a state in 1889, its legal scene was already full of colorful characters, political intrigue, and rogue justice.[20] Thus, it should be no surprise that today scores of militia and freemen still call Montana home. Such groups can trace their beginnings to the trappings of early justice under the Big Sky.

NOTES

1. Chapter 95, 13 *Stat.* 85. In addition to setting the geographic boundaries of the new territory, the organic act created the executive, legislative, and judicial branches of government.

2. Michael P. Malone, Richard B. Roeder, and William L. Lang, *A History of Two Centuries* 97 (Seattle: University of Washington Press, 1991). Despite the shadow of congressional annulment and limited restrictions on the power to tax and spend, the territorial legislature levied taxes; organized and regulated local governments; adopted civil and criminal codes; established lower courts and an educational system; provided for roads and other public services; and passed mining, water, and range laws. Larry M. Elison and Fritz Snyder, *The Montana State Constitution*, 1 (2000).

3. *Encyclopedia of Montana*, 41 (2000). Consequently, a constitutional convention was held in Helena from July 4, 1889, to August 17, 1889. At the October 1889 general election, voters ratified the constitution by a vote of 26,950 to 2,274. On November 8, 1889, Montana was formally admitted as the forty-first state.

4. Montana's 1889 constitution was the culmination of three formal instruments drafted during the process of achieving statehood. Two previous attempts to gain statehood were made through citizen initiatives in 1866 and 1884. *We, the People . . .*

An Introduction to the Montana Constitutional Convention, 15 (Bozeman, MT: Cooperative Extension Service, 1971).

Convention of 1866: Montana's first convention was called by Acting Governor Thomas Frances Meagher after only two years of territorial status. In the first of many irregularities, this convention did not meet at the capital in Virginia City, but in Helena. At the end of the sixth day, the fifty-five-member convention adjourned—no public money was available to keep it going. The only copy of the 1866 constitution was lost, never printed or presented to the voters for ratification. However, historian Margery H. Brown believes the 1866 convention made some positive contributions to constitution building in Montana:

"Although there were no immediate results of the 1866 convention, it did launch concern for statehood at a very early point in the territory's development. Montana remained more persistent than any of its neighboring territories in seeking enabling legislation from Congress to call a new convention, and the Montana legislature acted on its own initiative in assembling the convention of 1884." (Ibid.)

Convention of 1884: Dissatisfied with the treatment of territories by Congress, a second constitutional convention was called in Helena on January 2, 1884. This time, forty-five delegates deliberated for twenty-seven days. The completed draft was signed on February 9, 1884, and was ratified by voters in the November 1884 general election by a vote of 15,506 to 4,266; however, Montana's bid for statehood was the victim of political disputes in Congress, which wanted no changes in the party balance in the Senate or electoral college. However, this convention was essential, as an estimated 90 percent of the text of the constitutional articles framed in 1884 were incorporated in the 1889 constitution and remain the substance of Montana's fundamental law to this day. Ibid.

5. Larry M. Elison and Fritz Snyder, *The Montana State Constitution,* 4 (2000). Many of the changes were in the details. For example, legislative sessions were increased from forty to sixty days; there were to be sixteen members of the senate, one senator from each county, and fifty-five members of the house of representatives. Executive terms were extended from two to four years, and county courts were eliminated, with their probate responsibilities assigned to district courts. Eight instead of four judicial districts were established, with the legislature authorized to increase that number.

6. Ibid.

7. Helen Fitzgerald Sanders, *A History of Montana,* 579 (Chicago, New York: Lewis Pub. Co., 1913).

8. Ibid. at 582.

9. Ibid. at 587. The first question that was brought to the supreme court was whether Robert Hill, who had been appointed by Governor Edgerton to the office of county recorder, or R.M. Hagerman, the appointee of the miners to the same office, was entitled to that office until an election should be held under legislative enactment. The court decided in favor of Hagerman by a majority decision, with the chief justice and Associate Justice Williston concurring in the majority opinion, while Judge Munson dissented. Thus, the first decision of the territory of Montana was by a divided court.

10. Ibid. at 591. By an act of the legislature passed January 4, 1872, the publication of the opinions of the judges of the supreme court were provided for, and all the opinions since have been written, filed, and published.

11. Ibid. at 583.

12. Under the organic act, it was the duty of the first legislative assembly to provide for the apportionment of the territory into districts for the election of members of the council and lower house of the second session of the legislature. The first legislature failed to do this but did provide for the election of the members of the second legislature. This oversight of the first legislature was brought into question by a court case in which the supreme court of the territory held that the second and third legislative sessions were illegal. Afterward Congress approved the opinion of the court and annulled all the acts of the second and third legislative assemblies.

13. Sanders, supra, note 7 at 586.

14. In February 1892, the code commission completed its labors and submitted the result to the legislative assembly in January 1893, with the recommendation that the four codes be enacted into law. However, the legislature adjourned without taking action on the codes.

15. Sanders, supra, note 7 at 601. Had the Montana Bar Association accomplished nothing else in all the years of its existence from its inception until the current time, it would still be entitled to the lasting gratitude of the people of Montana for bringing about the codification of the common law.

16. Ellis Waldron, *Montana Legislators 1864-1979: Profiles and Biographical Directory* 1 (Missoula: University of Montana, Bureau of Government Research, 1980).

17. Ibid. The chambers increased in size from seven council members and thirteen representatives to thirteen councilors and twenty-six representatives, but stabilized at twelve council members and twenty-four representatives during the 1880s.

18. Ibid.

19. Ibid.

20. Chronology of Montana's Territorial Days:

1852	Francois Finlay finds gold on what is now Gold Creek, between Garrison and Drummond.
1863	May 28: Edgar-Fairweather party discovers gold in Alder Gulch, near present site of Virginia City.
	Idaho Territory is organized, including Montana.
1864	May 26: Montana Territory is created; Bannack is the first capital.
	July 14: Gold is discovered in Last Chance Gulch, present site of Helena.
	December 12: First territorial legislature meets at Bannack.
1865	February 5: Original nine counties of Montana are established.
	February 7: Virginia City becomes territorial capital.
1866	First constitutional convention meets at Helena.
1875	Seat of government is moved from Virginia City to Helena.
1884	January 14 to February 9: Second constitutional convention meets in Helena.

November 4: Constitution is ratified; Congress is asked to admit Montana as a state.

1889   July 4: Third constitutional convention meets at Helena.

October 1: New constitution is ratified.

November 8: President Harrison's proclamation announces admission of Montana as forty-first state in the Union.

November 23: First state legislature convenes at Helena.

Order a copy of this book with this form or online at:
http://www.haworthpress.com/store/product.asp?sku=5382

PRESTATEHOOD LEGAL MATERIALS
A Fifty-State Research Guide, Including New York City and the District of Columbia
(two-volume set)

_____in hardbound at $149.95 (ISBN: 0-7890-2056-4)

Or order online and use special offer code HEC25 in the shopping cart.

COST OF BOOKS_____

☐ **BILL ME LATER:** (Bill-me option is good on US/Canada/Mexico orders only; not good to jobbers, wholesalers, or subscription agencies.)

POSTAGE & HANDLING_____
(US: $4.00 for first book & $1.50 for each additional book)
(Outside US: $5.00 for first book & $2.00 for each additional book)

☐ Check here if billing address is different from shipping address and attach purchase order and billing address information.

Signature_____

SUBTOTAL_____

☐ **PAYMENT ENCLOSED: $_____**

IN CANADA: ADD 7% GST_____

☐ **PLEASE CHARGE TO MY CREDIT CARD.**

STATE TAX_____
(NJ, NY, OH, MN, CA, IL, IN, PA, & SD residents, add appropriate local sales tax)

☐ Visa ☐ MasterCard ☐ AmEx ☐ Discover
☐ Diner's Club ☐ Eurocard ☐ JCB

Account # _____

FINAL TOTAL_____
(If paying in Canadian funds, convert using the current exchange rate, UNESCO coupons welcome)

Exp. Date_____

Signature_____

Prices in US dollars and subject to change without notice.

NAME_____

INSTITUTION_____

ADDRESS_____

CITY_____

STATE/ZIP_____

COUNTRY_____ COUNTY (NY residents only)_____

TEL_____ FAX_____

E-MAIL_____

May we use your e-mail address for confirmations and other types of information? ☐ Yes ☐ No
We appreciate receiving your e-mail address and fax number. Haworth would like to e-mail or fax special discount offers to you, as a preferred customer. **We will never share, rent, or exchange your e-mail address or fax number.** We regard such actions as an invasion of your privacy.

Order From Your Local Bookstore or Directly From
The Haworth Press, Inc.
10 Alice Street, Binghamton, New York 13904-1580 • USA
TELEPHONE: 1-800-HAWORTH (1-800-429-6784) / Outside US/Canada: (607) 722-5857
FAX: 1-800-895-0582 / Outside US/Canada: (607) 771-0012
E-mail to: orders@haworthpress.com

For orders outside US and Canada, you may wish to order through your local
sales representative, distributor, or bookseller.
For information, see http://haworthpress.com/distributors

(Discounts are available for individual orders in US and Canada only, not booksellers/distributors.)

PLEASE PHOTOCOPY THIS FORM FOR YOUR PERSONAL USE.
http://www.HaworthPress.com

BOF06